S0-ARM-895

Contemporary Cultures and Societies of LATIN AMERICA

SECOND EDITION

Contemporary Cultures and Societies of LATIN AMERICA

A Reader in the Social Anthropology of Middle and South America

Edited
WITH INTRODUCTIONS AND NOTES
by

DWIGHT B. HEATH
BROWN UNIVERSITY

Prospect Heights, Illinois

For information about this book, write or call:
Waveland Press, Inc.
P.O. Box 400
Prospect Heights, Illinois 60070
(312) 634-0081

Copyright © 1974, 1965 by Dwight B. Heath
1988 reissued with changes by Waveland Press, Inc.

ISBN 0-88133-359-X

All rights reserved. No part of this book may be reproduced, stored in a retrieval system, or transmitted in any form or by any means without permission in writing from the publisher.

Printed in the United States of America

To
the basement of
Peabody Museum at Harvard
(the crossroads)

Preface to the Waveland Press Reissue

Much has happened, both in Latin America as a region and in the social sciences as a field of study, since this book was first published. Nevertheless, a number of specialists in the field suggested to the original publisher and to this new publisher that it would be helpful to have the book reissued. The reasons why these papers are still important explain much about the value of anthropological perspectives on the one hand, and about the nature of Latin American cultures and societies on the other. However gratifying it may be, it is also a little surprising that a timely successor to this volume has not appeared in the interim, but anyone who has attempted any such effort must appreciate the enormous investment of time, thought, and effort that would entail.

The rationale for the book and its contents is briefly articulated in my "Preface to the Second Edition" (pp. xv-xviii). Apparently, I was successful in my aim to select "papers that contain substantive and theoretic relevance and that show a variety of approaches to both current concerns and long-term processes" (p. xvi). In a sense, what has kept this book from becoming outdated is a combination of substantive data, set in explicit relation to concepts and theory, and a sustained attempt on the part of all contributing authors to understand long-term processes rather than simply to interpret current events. Despite recent developments in much of Latin America, and a variety of fresh insights that we have from the social sciences, these articles have continuing relevance both individually and collectively.

The importance of transdisciplinary perspectives has, if anything, come to be more acutely appreciated in recent years. It was unusual in 1974 that I included contributions by sociologists, economists, a geographer, an historian, and a political scientist as well as anthropologists. Similarly, there may be other books now in which the authors reflect Brazilian, Colombian, English, French, and Mexican as well as U.S. concerns and academic traditions, but there were none then.

An ironic fact is that, in spite of all that has happened in Latin America – and in inter-American relations – during the decade and a half since this book was compiled, there has been so little change of the real kind that matters in the lives of most of the people who live there. This is not to say that a social anthropologist views everything in the glacial time-frame of cultural evolution, but that cultural processes show remarkable continuity. Patterns of belief and behavior that shape the lives of individuals, and the related institutions that shape the lives of communities and larger aggregations affect and are affected by similar forces over time.

Over the years, all of the contemporary societies and cultures of Latin America have undergone change; it is a constant in the human experience. Perhaps more dramatic is the fact that Latin America has been very much in the news, although the datelines and topics have been constantly changing.

In a few countries the same political regimes remain in power, some that were democratic have come under the control of military oligarchs, and some that had been dominated by the military now have the trappings of participatory democracy, but the overall mix is not very different. Although the conditions of life for individuals may have changed drastically in one place or another, the institutional and other patterned relationships, are much as they had been described earlier. Wars, both internecine and international, have brought enormous human suffering but, just as they have done little to change boundaries, they have also done little to change patterns of ethnic status or access to power. The numbers may be different now, but galloping inflation has many of the same causes and consequences, and today's so-called debt-crisis is a predictable continuation of processes that were well underway then. Neither Castro's attempt to export revolution nor Uncle Sam's resolution to maintain ideological and economic dominance throughout the hemisphere has succeeded, with both nations exerting less influence throughout Latin America than before, but with little lessening of the rhetorical posturing on either side. Their relative standing is very similar to what it had been, even though the United States has shifted from being the world's major creditor-nation to being the world's major debtor-nation, losing much of the political and economic dominance it had so long wielded throughout the Americas.

So the reason why this collection of papers has withstood the flood of headlines and remains valid and helpful for understanding Latin America today and for years to come is not that current events are unimportant. No one believes that a shift from participatory democracy to military dictatorship (or vice versa) is inconsequential, whatever one's political and moral philosophy may be. Rather, the key concern in terms of social science lies not so much in tracing the details of all such happenings as it does in trying to understand how such things happen and why they come about in a particular place at a particular time – as well as why they don't happen elsewhere or at other times. That is why pattern analysis is important, based on one's understanding of the decision-processes of individuals, and of the ways those relate to institutions and broader social systems. From one perspective, it can be said that social scientists, starting from the idiosyncratic large-scale events that are reported in the headlines, try to dig down and lay bare the underlying structures of belief and behavior – in effect, to reveal the skeleton, musculature, and functioning of the body politic. But this is possible only because of a very different perspective that is also brought to such analysis. Almost as if from the other end of the telescope, some social scientists prefer a view from the grass-roots in order to reach another equally important kind of understanding. Only on the basis of close and sustained analysis of a vast array of quotidian minutiae – the nitty-gritty details of everyday behavior in which people enact and express their values and concerns – can we realistically delineate the complex range of phenomena that comprise a society or a culture. The underlying structures of belief and behavior can best be ascertained by a sort of triangulation from different viewpoints, macroscopic and microscopic. This book is deliberately transdisciplinary for that reason, and many of the individual chapters combine perspectives from different levels of systemic integration.

RECENT DEVELOPMENTS IN CULTURES AND SOCIAL SYSTEMS

This book originally appeared at the same time as the first volume of Wallerstein's thoughtful analysis of "the modern world-system." His book (Wallerstein 1974) has had an enormous impact on the ways in which laypersons as well as scholars in many disciplines think and talk about economic and political relationships, and many authors in ensuing years have claimed to use a systemic approach or even systems theory, with only vague allusions to Wallerstein's global formulation, and without any regular or rigorous attempt to follow the full implications of his grandly synthetic idea. Wolf's paper in this book on "group relations in a complex society" (pp. 68-82) uses Mexico as a case-study, but by focusing on "crucial junctures or synapses of relationships which connect the local system to the larger whole," it helps to make the functioning of the world-system more comprehensible, and provides a method for showing how specific individuals can be important actors within it. Wolf went on later to apply this approach imaginatively, and many believe effectively, to an ambitious reappraisal of a major era of colonialism, tracing relations between "Europe and the people without history" (Wolf 1983). Many others have demonstrated the value of his method by applying it to a wide range of more limited issues, both contemporary and historical, in Latin America and around the world.

In much the same way, Cardoso and Faletto (1978) significantly reoriented the ways in which people think and feel about unequal relations of political and economic access and exchange, both within countries and on an international scale. Their contribution is important not only because the dependency model so clearly challenged the modernization model (and, in the view of many, discredited it), but also because it was a fresh and powerful idea that came from Latin America rather than having been formulated in western Europe or North America. It does not at all diminish their major contribution to point out that Stavenhagen, also a Latin American, in his corrective to "seven fallacies about Latin America" (pp. 22-35), clearly spelled out the core ideas of internal colonialism, and underpaid producers on the periphery (but integral to) the multinational industrial profiteering complex. His deceptively simple presentation, without the strident rhetoric that has come to mark some of the literature on dependency, should highlight rather than obscure the insights that are presented here.

Similarly, although few scholars in the social sciences today would invest much time and effort in elaborating "a typology of Latin American subcultures" as did Wagley and Harris (pp. 35-58), the themes of cultural pluralism and ethnic diversity, with special attention to the needs and demands of minority populations, are widely recognized as having not only theoretic interest for academics, but also immediate and practical significance for policy-makers and administrators. In an understated way, the scale of "social differentiation in Latin American communities" devised by Young and Fujimoto (pp. 58-68) still has much to say about differential access to goods and information at lower levels within the world-system. Adams' analysis of "brokers and career mobility systems" (pp. 82-93) applied Wolf's insights to Guatemala, with special emphasis on the distribution of power. Casagrande's comparison of various Ecuadorian Indian communities' "strategies for survivel" (pp. 93-107) is a vivid reminder that local variation can be important even when ethnicity and dependence are similar, a view that contrasts dramatically with the fatalistic resignation that is too often mistakenly attributed to poor people throughout the Third World.

NEW COMMENTS ON AGRICULTURE AND ECONOMY

Although sub-Saharan Africa has become a focus of attention with respect to the causes and consequences of large-scale hunger, no one who cares about Latin America should imagine that the structural impediments to economic equity have been surmounted there. In many Latin American countries, internal migration has proceeded so rapidly that the population is now more urban than rural, and increasing emphasis on export crops provides foreign exchange, but at a cost in that foodstuffs must increasingly be imported. The so-called opening of new frontiers throughout the Amazonian Basin has afforded some hardy homesteaders an opportunity to become small-scale landowners, but it has also displaced many of the tribal populations that had long lived in symbiosis with that special habitat. Destruction of the forest, whether for lumbering or for ranching, offers short-term gains for a few, but only at enormous ecological cost that is already being felt around the world.

Although the numbers in the tables would be different today, most of what Mitchell and Schatan said about "the outlook for agricultural development in Latin America" (pp. 128-135), is equally applicable now. The same can be said of Gonzalez's caveats about "the effects of population growth" (pp. 210-228). Miller's description of the process of "proletarianization of Indian peasants in Peru" (pp. 135-142) depicts a kind of cultural reorientation that many individuals throughout the world are experiencing in recent years, and can also be viewed as an illustration of progressive integration within the modern world-system. The distinction that Erasmus made between "agrarian reform vs. land reform" (pp. 143-157) is still a vital issue in many Latin American countries, where one or both remains to be implemented. The fact that everyone is affected by economic forces over which they have no immediate control is dramatically illustrated in very different ways in Vogt's description of "ceremonial life in a modern Maya community" (pp. 158-163), Nisbet's analysis of "the informal credit market of rural Chile" (pp. 163-178), and in the large-scale integration of markets in northeastern Brazil as described by Forman and Riegelhaupt (pp. 179-201). Although Dobyns' summary of "experimental intervention in Vicos" (pp. 201-210) is more upbeat than some, it offers a succinct introduction to that famous effort at directed cultural change on the community level.

NEW COMMENTS ON SOCIAL GROUPINGS AND AUTHORITY

The structure and organization of societies and their constituent parts is a vast subject that has gained popularity in recent years as people other than academics have come to recognize the dynamism and power of ethnicity, patronage, and myriad other formal and informal networks which people use and on which they rely, not only in terms of self-identity but also in terms of access to goods and power. The fundamental importance of kinship cannot be overlooked either; the meanings of relationships may be very different even when the terminology is superficially similar (see Hunt, pp. 254-270), and godparenthood often has less to do with religion than with economics and politics (Ingham, pp. 395-404). The "confusion between race and class" (pp. 307-316) such as Patch described in Peru is widespread (although with different labels being used) throughout much of Latin America, with Blacks more openly showing pride in their heritage than used to be the case in many regions (cf. Whitten, pp. 327-340), although van den Berghe implies that Guatemalan Indians are increasingly "passing" across what used to be a caste-like ethnic boundary (pp. 316-327). In spite of such new opportunities for economic and social mobility, there are many places where members of a traditional oligarchy still enjoy marked advantages (Leeds, pp. 285-307; Stone, pp. 404-421). Politicization is helping provide a voice for many who had been effectively kept on the fringes of public discourse and decisions until recent years (Goldrich, pp. 365-387; Mangin, pp. 340-365), and a village priest who may never have heard of liberation theology can nevertheless play crucial roles as a culture broker in the village where he works (Hicks pp. 387-395).

NEW COMMENTS ON WORLD VIEWS

Worldwide cultural homogenization that some predicted as a dire consequence of the proliferation of mass media and industrialization did not materialize, and still seems remote. Whether readers "understand" them or not, contemporary Latin American novelists and poets are reaching an increasingly broad international audience and impressing them with different ways of viewing things. The quest for national identity has not yet been resolved by many throughout Latin America, while others take fierce pride in their new estimation of ethnic or other roots. Despite a shortage of clergy, and some striking dissension among them, the Catholic Church continues to be a cardinal focus of both devotion and social action in many parts of Latin America, even while Protestantism (and presumably agnosticism) are making inroads among individuals and families.

The stereotypical differences that used to be cited between Anglo-Americans and Latin Americans may be diminishing, but the direction of change is not what many had foreseen. The Anglo-Saxon tradition of frankness and honesty, whatever the emotional cost to anyone, seems to be bending instead of the Latin traditions becoming more rigid. By and large, North Americans today seem to be far less compulsive about punctuality than was the case a decade or so ago, and the so-called electronic age appears not to have forced Latins uniformly to be clock-watchers. Insofar as the broad concept of ethos has heuristic value, it can well be said that Anglo patterns are, in many respects, approximating Latin patterns – just the opposite of what had been predicted in the middle of this century.

The stark contrast between evolution and revolution that was a focus of attention when this book was first published has been tempered, as people have come to realize that revolution is also a process rather than an event, and that the waves of history often result in striking contrasts occurring even in the absence of violence or identifiable intent. Even without mentioning The Shining Path movement, Whyte's account of rural Peruvian "peasants as activists" (pp. 526-541) clearly helps us to set the current situation into a meaningful context. Similarly, Father Torres' "message to the students" (pp. 525-526) presaged clerical activism beyond what is now popularly labeled theology of liberation, just as Fernandes was ahead of his time in pointing out and criticizing the pervasive racial prejudice (pp. 521-524) that many Brazilians denied existed in their country. Lewis' discussion of the culture of poverty (pp. 469-479) was similarly controversial, partly because some politicians rephrased it as justifying a government's "benign neglect" of the poor, and partly because others took it as a veiled indictment of unbridled capitalistic free enterprise.

By focusing on a small aspect of culture, the use of alcoholic beverages, the Madsens were able to show how views of the world and social relationships differ among ethnic populations even within a small Mexican village (pp. 438-451). Similarly, Aron-Schaar paid attention to the minutiae of what many outsiders would call bribery and corruption in a Bolivian provincial capital (pp. 495-501) but she did so in a way that should help us better to understand how drug traffickers can be effectively immune to the law, and why party affiliation has little to do with the actions of so many government officials who take turns in public office often without significantly changing budgets or policies. Willems' account of "religious mass-movements in Brazil" (pp. 452-468) reflects both cultural and ideological pluralism, and shows how they relate to strong currents of social change. Increasingly rapid urbanization is a characteristic of most Latin American countries, although cities have long held special power and attraction. Morse discusses both historical reality and imagery in this connection, using Buenos Aires as one of his illustrative case-studies (pp. 480-494); Strickon's account of the images and realities of class and ethnic relations of an Argentine landowning family (pp. 501-520) nicely complements that view.

COMMENTS ON THE WAVELAND PRESS REISSUE

In a sense, all of the papers throughout this book can be viewed as, in one way or another, throwing light on each of the key books that have been cited as having significantly influenced our understanding of contemporary cultures and societies of Latin America since this volume was first compiled. Without ever mentioning "the modern world-system" (Wallerstein 1974), it is evident that most of the authors who contributed here were striving valiantly to show how specific human actions, viewed in the course of daily living, affect and are affected by relationships at unnumerable other levels, eventually connecting with the world community.

The vast majority of all those relationships clearly fit the model of dependency (Cardoso and Faletto, 1978), whether as internal colonialism within a country, or as a metropole-periphery contrast internationally, although they were not cast in such terms by these authors. Contemporary cultures and societies of Latin America can only be understood as a combined resultant of such relationships and as a precipitate of history. For all these reasons, this book is at least as relevant today as when it first appeared.

The contents and organization of the book remain unchanged. The sections on "Research Aids and Bibliographies," "Journals," and "Monograph Series" (pp. 542-547) will be helpful to interested readers who may want to locate more recent sources on any relevant place or topic. Without reiterating the acknowledgements that were made in my Preface to the Second Edition (pp. xvii-xviii), I am glad to add my appreciation to Random House, which assigned the copyright to me a few years ago, and to Tom Curtin of Waveland Press and a number of unknown colleagues who expressed interest in having the book reissued at this time. As always, A.M. Cooper has been enormously helpful in terms of both ideas and actions.

In continuing recognition that a volume such as this represents essentially a collective effort, I am again assigning royalties to further research, this time through the Tozzer Library of Harvard University.

Providence, Rhode Island — Dwight B. Heath

Cardoso, Fernando Henrique, and Enzo Faletto
1978 *Dependency and Development in Latin America* (expanded and emended edition). University of California Press, Berkeley. [original in Spanish, 1971].

Wallerstein, Immanuel
1974 *The Modern World-System I: Capitalist Agriculture and the Origins of the European World-Economy in the Sixteenth Century.* Academic Press, New York.

Wolf, Eric R.
1983 *Europe and the People without History.* University of California Press, Berkeley.

Preface to the Second Edition

In view of the substantial revision that has been made, this is in a very real sense a different book, rather than an updated version of the original edition that appeared in 1965, prepared in collaboration with Richard N. Adams. The attempt at broad areal and topical coverage remains, but some shifts in emphasis deserve explanation.

It is obvious that I am able to take advantage of a whole new corpus of information that was not available when the first edition was prepared. In that book, a series of "classic" articles were included, both because of their intrinsic importance and in an attempt to show how the concerns and approaches of Latin American studies had changed over the years. Without for a moment belittling the historical significance, theoretical validity, and other values of much of the work done before 1965, including those papers that were omitted from this revision, I feel that so many exciting developments have taken place in recent years that it is appropriate to focus on the abundant and varied material written since the book originally appeared; nearly 90 percent of the articles included here are that recent.

In the Introduction to each section, I will refer to a few specific sources, but more often to important authors whose works should be read. The list of "Recommended Readings" at the end of each Introduction, together with the general and areal bibliography at the end of the book, should be consulted for a wide range of outstanding sources that can only be partially represented in a volume such as this. At the very least, this book should serve to introduce the reader to a variety of data and approaches, provide some insight into selected local situations and some national and regional concerns, and guide him or her to other relevant source material.

Obviously, no single volume can satisfy the diversity of interests that characterize students of Latin America—anthropologists, sociologists, political scientists, geographers, economists, historians, administrators, technicians, missionaries, and others—although each should profit from the work of colleagues in related fields. The present volume is addressed primarily to those whose concerns are the understanding of human groups and of patterns of thought and behavior—this broad view was shared by anthropologists, who pioneered in the study of society and culture in Latin America and who have recently been joined by other social scientists in a variety of disciplines. The breadth of anthropological concerns is reflected in the diversity of academic disciplines represented among the contributors: sociology (van den Berghe, Fernandes, Fujimoto, Stavenhagen, Stone, Torres, Whyte, Young), economics (Mitchell, Nisbet, Schatan), geography (Gonzalez), history (Morse), and political science (Goldrich), as well as anthropology.

The scope of these papers amply demonstrates the close interrelationship among several academic disciplines, and illustrates the truism that a scholar's primary professional identification is not an adequate index of his interests and perspective. Similarly, it is noteworthy that the contributors were trained in Brazil, Colombia, England, France, and Mexico, as well as the United States, and include Europeans and Latin Americans as well as North Americans.

It is altogether fair for the reader to ask, "What were the criteria for inclusion in this volume?" The literature is immense and diverse, and there are obviously more excellent papers than I could include in this compilation. The basis for selection involved a complex combination of factors, including overall area distribution, range of subject matter, accessibility of the original, and so forth, all in relation to a realistic limitation on the length of the book.

On the basis of my experience in preparing the first edition, I was not surprised that it was difficult to maintain a general regional balance in the selection of papers, offering treatment of each major topic in each of the areas of Middle America, the Andes, Brazil, northern and southern South America. The Caribbean has been deleted from this revision for a variety of reasons. Apart from the complex question of how "Latin" that part of America is, it is increasingly the case that, with noteworthy exceptions, most students tend to treat the mainland and the islands as distinct areas of interest. Furthermore, Michael M. Horowitz has recently edited an excellent volume, entitled *Peoples and Cultures of the Caribbean* (Garden City, N.Y.: The Natural History Press, 1971), that should serve as a complement to this book. David Lowenthal and Lambros Comitas have also prepared a series of anthologies on "West Indian Perspectives" soon to be published by Doubleday and Company, New York.

With respect to topical coverage, I have selected papers that combine substantive and theoretic relevance and that show a variety of approaches to both current concerns and long-term processes. The special relevance of each article included here is briefly indicated in a note preceding it, and in the Introductions.

The traditional emphasis of anthropology on tribal, rural, and generally less developed populations and aspects of culture has been expanded in recent years, to include townsmen, peasants, and many aspects of modern complex society. One of my major concerns in organizing this book has been to reflect that broad view, without abandoning the substantive bias that is still one of the special strengths of anthropology. So it is that, although "revolution" is a subject of increasing interest to students, I have no specific paper on "revolution." Rather, I have included a series of papers, such as those by Erasmus, Gonzalez,

Torres, and Whyte that concern certain aspects of social and political relations that relate to the problems and prospects for violent change.

In an age characterized by a widespread preoccupation with "relevance," I have refrained, insofar as possible, from giving in to a strong temptation to pay more attention to matters of current political importance, but have chosen instead to emphasize matters of more general and enduring concern to social scientists. Therefore, specific events are treated as more illustrative of processes than as historically critical in themselves. That is not to say the editor or the authors are unaware of or unconcerned about crucial problems; a number of the papers, such as those by Dobyns, Fernandes, Lewis, Mangin, and Nisbet, offer significant insights for understanding contemporary social problems.

Although this volume contains little material about those tribal peoples who tend to remain politically and economically isolated from participation in national systems, I have retained an emphasis on rural and proletarian portions of the population. This emphasis is appropriate not only in that it reflects a traditional anthropological bias, but also because the focus of life in most of Latin America is, in fact, still rural. For this reason, the papers on economics focus on the nonindustrial sector, and a number of authors deal with the ways in which small communities articulate with regional and national systems.

When the first edition of this book appeared in 1965, it was virtually alone in focusing on nonelite components of Latin American society and culture. Since then, a number of other collections of papers have become available, many of which are excellent (e.g., Horowitz, 1970; Stavenhagen, 1970; Field, 1970), but there is still no other that combines the unifying anthropological perspective and the breadth of approach of that volume; this revision is intended to update those very strengths.

Of the 34 articles, 5 were prepared expressly for this book (Aron-Schaar, Casagrande, Dobyns, Stone, Whitten); Fernandes's chapter appears here for the first time in translation; and both Lewis and Gonzalez took advantage of this opportunity to revise and update their papers. Only a few of the articles have been abridged, usually omitting only small portions, without otherwise altering the author's phraseology or meaning (Willems, Mangin, Mitchell and Schatan). An equal number have been strengthened by the correction, with authors' approval, of minor errors that occurred in the original publications (Mangin, Nisbet, Wagley and Harris).

The Introductions to the various sections are purposely brief, intended only to set the papers in historical and intellectual context. Each introductory essay is followed by a brief bibliography that lists both references cited and other selected readings on the subject. Each paper is prefaced by a brief note by the editor, indicating both the importance of that paper and the ways in which it relates to other works, as well as identifying the author. At the end of the volume is a general bibliography.

The editor is indebted to a number of people for varied contributions at all stages of the preparation of the book. Clyde Kluckhohn first sparked my enthusiasm for anthropology, and George P. Murdock and Richard Schaedel supported my decision to work in Latin America at a time when encouragement was scarce. Eric Wolf, Floyd Lounsbury, William Davenport, Edward Bruner, and George Foster helped me to relate specific local findings to broader problems, and J. Louis Giddings, Sidney Goldstein, Philip Leis, and other friends and colleagues at Brown University provided the context in which I have been able to effectively continue and expand my work on a variety of contemporary cultures and societies of Latin America.

Although Richard N. Adams did not actively collaborate in this revision, his breadth and depth of concern for Latin America and its people, and for anthropology and its practitioners, has had a significant influence. Suggestions by Frederic Hicks, Emilio Willems, and Eric Wolf were helpful in selecting and organizing the papers, and Nancy Tiedemann of Random House saw the manuscript through press. I am also grateful to the authors and publishers who kindly gave permission for me to reprint the papers.

In recognition that a volume such as this represents essentially a collective effort, I have assigned royalties to further research, through Harvard University.

Providence, Rhode Island — Dwight B. Heath

Field, Arthur J. (ed.)
1970 *City and Country in the Third World: Issues in the Modernization of Latin America.* Schenkman, Cambridge, Mass.
Horowitz, Irving L. (ed.)
1970 *Masses in Latin America.* Oxford University Press, New York.
Stavenhagen, Rodolfo (ed.)
1970 *Agrarian Problems and Peasant Movements in Latin America.* Doubleday, Garden City, N.Y.

Preface to the First Edition

The recent resurgence of Latin American studies programs reflects the increasing importance, to governments and individuals, of understanding the peoples and societies of that area. This book attempts to combine outstanding descriptions of fundamental aspects of Latin American life with the insights of social scientists concerning the dynamics of important processes.

It is unlikely that anyone could in a single volume satisfy the diversity of interests that characterize students of Latin America—anthropologists, sociologists, political scientists, geographers, historians, missionaries, government administrators and technicians, and others. And although the student in each of these fields has a distinctive focus, each also finds himself heavily dependent on the work of colleagues in related fields. The present volume is not designed to be all things to all these men. Although its scope is broad, in subject matter as well as area, it has a specifically social anthropological emphasis. Anthropologists pioneered in the study of society and culture in Latin America. Their focus, dictated by earlier interests in the discipline, has been on the rural and more primitive or underdeveloped aspects of society. In recent years, Latin America has been increasingly studied by economists, sociologists, and political scientists. In this volume, therefore, explicit recognition is given to contributions from these fields, as illustrated by the work of Hill, Mosk, Germani, Goldrich, and others.

The substantive bias of anthropology has led to a relative weakness in the literature with respect to many aspects of modern society. We have made some attempt in this book to correct this weakness, but to do so from the point of view of anthropological interests. So it is that although "the city" is an object of increasing interest to students, we have no specific papers on "cities." Rather, we have included a series of papers, such as those by Lewis, Mangin, Leeds, Strickon, and Germani, that concern certain aspects of social relations that are manifested in the city. Similarly, we have included papers that concern traits found in city and country alike, such as those by Simmons, Gillin, Wagley (on race), De Azevedo, Wolf, and Beals, as well as the general descriptions in the first section.

We have refrained, insofar as possible, from giving in to a strong temptation to pay more attention to matters of current political importance, but have, instead, chosen to emphasize matters of more general and enduring concern to social scientists. Therefore, specific events are treated more as illustrative of processes than as historically critical in themselves. This is not to say that social scientists have been unaware of or unconcerned about crucial problems; a number of the papers in this book deal with topics that are important to political understanding, notably those by Germani, Goldrich, Wolf, Wagley, Gillin, Kunkel, and Leeds.

Although we have little to say about tribal peoples who tend to remain politically and economically isolated from participation in their nations, emphasis on the rural side of life remains. This is appropriate not only in that it reflects a traditional anthropological bias, but also because the focus of life in Latin America is, in fact, still primarily rural. Only four major countries have populations that are over 50 percent urban: Argentina, Chile, Cuba, and Venezuela. Therefore, important papers on land and agriculture are included, since these subjects are still more representative of Latin American economic life than is the occupational complex of the nonagrarian sector. In short, a number of general processes are illustrated, with specific examples from throughout Latin America.

At the outset, it was hoped that some kind of regional balance could be maintained in the selection of papers. Our thinking was in terms of Middle America, the Andes, southern South America, Brazil, and the Caribbean (including the Guianas). If the twenty-odd papers that explicitly deal with specific areas are set against the relative populations of these regions, we find that Middle America and the Andes are over-represented, whereas Brazil, the Caribbean, and southern South America have been somewhat slighted. This ratio, however, reflects the amount of work done in these areas, as well as the editors' competence and confidence in the material.

Although on some topics we could find no suitable papers, there are obviously more good papers than we could use in this compilation. The basis for selection involved a complex combination of factors, including overall area distribution of the articles, overlap in subject matter between papers, accessibility of the original, and so forth, all in relation to a realistic limitation on the length of the book. Arbitrarily, some papers of considerable importance have been omitted simply because they are readily available in other form—notably in the Bobbs-Merrill Reprint Series in the Social Sciences, or in Olen E. Leonard and Charles P. Loomis, eds., *Readings in Latin American Social Organization and Institutions* (East Lansing, Michigan State College Press, 1953). These collections should be consulted for further outstanding reading on the subjects dealt with here. Of the 28 articles, two were prepared expressly for this volume (Goldrich, Leeds), and four appear here for the first time in translation (De Azevedo; Hill, Silva, and Hill; Germani; Vázquez). The last two translations are the only articles that have been slightly abridged; all others are reprinted with only minor editorial revision.

The Introductions are purposely brief, intended only to set the papers in historical and intellectual context. Each introductory essay is followed by a list of References Cited and a bibliography of Further Readings that serves as a guide to other selected readings on the subject. At the end of the volume is a general bibliography.

The editors are indebted to a number of people for their suggestions, both as to specific items and emphasis. Charles Wagley, Elman Service, and Anthony Leeds are primary among these; responsibility for the final product is entirely ours, however. Editing the book was a joint effort. As is evident, each of the editors prepared certain of the introductory sections and topical bibliographies. . . .

We are also grateful to the authors who kindly gave permission for us to reprint their papers—especially to those whose papers had to be omitted in later stages, owing to space problems—and to the publishers who kindly gave reprint permissions.

Believing that a volume such as this represents essentially a collective effort, we have chosen to forego any profits, and all royalties will be turned back to further research in Latin America, through Human Relations Research, Ltd. and the Institute of Latin American Studies, University of Texas.

[1965]

DWIGHT B. HEATH
Providence, Rhode Island

RICHARD N. ADAMS
Austin, Texas

Contents

APPROACHES TO CULTURES AND SOCIAL SYSTEMS

LAND, AGRICULTURE, AND ECONOMICS

SOCIAL GROUPINGS AND AUTHORITY

VIEWS OF THE WORLD

Approaches to Cultures and Social Systems

It is a truism that a collection of papers on a subject as broad as "contemporary societies and cultures of Latin America" will tell much about attitudes and viewpoints of outsiders as well as about the peoples of the area. In this book I have tried to show not only what anthropologists have been able to tell the world about Latin America, but also the ways in which Latin American studies have contributed to the advance of anthropological insights around the world. In so doing, it seems useful to review briefly a number of different approaches that have been used over the years in attempts to understand the peoples of Latin America. In this section, I have selected papers that should serve two important purposes: first, to provide the beginning student with some general descriptions that illustrate the variety and complexity of the subject matter itself, and second, to indicate approaches through which social scientists go beyond description to analyze and interpret the data—that is, to understand how the parts relate to each other and how they work.

This is not the place to undertake to write a critical history of approaches to cultures and social systems, even with reference to only Latin America. But it is important to show how thinking about different approaches has developed, and I have done so in terms of nine broad rubrics which reflect changing areas of interest and theoretic perspectives: precursors to social science, *indigenismo*, early cultural anthropology, other social disciplines, applied anthropology, psychological anthropology, structural studies, classification, and systemic analysis.

PRECURSORS TO SOCIAL SCIENCE

There is an abundant and varied body of information on the cultures and societies of Latin America that dates from long before anyone thought in terms of "social science," or even of "Latin America." In a sense, men and women in groups have left records of their ways of life ever since they crossed southward over what is now the Rio Grande, at least 10,000 years ago. By this, I do not mean written records, but rather the fragmentary records that skilled archeologists can discern in tools, artifacts, and other remains, many of which were unintentionally left behind in the routine of daily living. From more recent millennia, carved and painted representations of native life still survive to give a vivid picture of patterns of dress, gesture, and other aspects of behavior that would otherwise be unknown. The oral tradition of most peoples—that which is often patronizingly dismissed as folklore or mythology—combines accounts of events and social processes in ways that are increasingly being substantiated, sometimes as consistent metaphor and sometimes even as "historical fact." In a few limited areas, notably northern Mesoamerica, forms of writing were developed even before Europeans discovered what they arrogantly called "the New World."

For the past four hundred years, people have been writing accounts of different cultures and societies throughout Middle and South America, for a variety of reasons. Not all of these are credible as literally accurate reports, and it is not always easy to interpret the different meanings and purposes of authors who are as remote from us in terms of their world view as they are in terms of time and space. In light of the hardship of their immediate tasks, and of survival itself at times, a number of explorers and conquistadors wrote remarkably detailed accounts of what they encountered, and the ways of life of native peoples were among their principal subjects. Narratives of occasional white men who survived shipwrecks, lived among Indians for several years, and then returned to write about their experiences constitute a special genre from the early decades of Euro-Indian contact.

Missionaries played an important role in compiling early linguistic and ethnographic information; it matters little whether they were motivated by disinterested scholarship or were pragmatically collecting information that would be useful in their work. Many named groups ("tribes") are known only through brief word-lists or ethnographic sketches submitted by churchmen to their superiors.

A few scholars worked closely and meticulously with key informants in the first decades of contact, especially in attempting to understand the details of native religions and to reconstruct the pre-Columbian histories of local peoples. And it was not long before some of the natives themselves had been schooled in the European manner and wrote their own accounts of life before the conquest.

It is obvious that accounts from such varied sources differ not only in emphasis and interpretation but sometimes even in detail. Comparison and assessment of any source must include an evaluation of the purpose and the audience as well as of the author and the intellectual milieu of the time. This is similarly true of the wealth of official documents that began to accumulate as soon as European flags were planted. The archival resources include a bewildering range of material, from laws and decrees (which allow cautious inferences about what people were really doing, as well as defining what they ought to do), to detailed house-by-house social and economic censuses, questionnaires, tax records, and so forth. Throughout the colonial period, bureaucratic administrations amassed documentary riches that only a few scholars have begun to tap.

It would be a mistake to imagine that these sources were wholly descriptive and not analytic. Although some of the interpretations are probably no longer shared by anyone, it is clear that several of the authors systematically mustered their evidence to support specific conclusions. The controversy over whether the Indians should be enslaved was obviously no less important economically than it was theologically. And in an age in which the Scriptures were considered to be divinely inspired, it was more than an academic tour de force for one author to "prove" that the upper Amazon River was the site of the Garden of Eden.

Some authors have interpreted the Wars of Independence—not a unitary revolution, but a fifteen-year series of scattered outbreaks in response to a variety of local grievances—as a result of the Enlightenment, and point to the liberal rhetoric of the early republican period in support of their view. Regardless of whether we accept that idea, it is clear that new kinds of interests are reflected in the richly detailed descriptions of the lands and peoples of the area that were written in the nineteenth century by men whom some would call "encyclopedic scientists" and others might call "gentlemen travelers." In their attention to the minutiae of workaday life, as well as the flora, fauna, and topology, a number of these men offered meticulous characterizations of what they encountered in areas that even today remain relatively inaccessible, and in the cities through which they passed.

Such a wealth of material written before the twentieth century, even though it is not couched in anthropological terms or analyzed in terms of conceptual schemes of the other social sciences, nevertheless lends itself to reexamination through new perspectives, and such fruitful work is being undertaken in a number of fields. By strictly coordinating chronology of the native as well as Spanish accounts of the conquest of the Aztecs, Robert Padden has provided new insights into that familiar story. In Peru and Bolivia, John Murra's meticulous study of early Spanish administrative records promises to bridge the gap between contemporary ethnography and archeological remains. Careful annotation by editors has given life to some old documents, more revealing in their newly published form than in the original manuscripts written centuries ago (e.g., Hanke and Mendoza's edition of Arzans's history of Potosí, Tozzer's edition of Landa's description of Yucatan, etc.).

In general, however, it was not until the 1920s that sociology became anything more than social philosophy, and anthropology went beyond the acquisition of artifacts for display, or of quaint and curious customs for description to small groups interested in exotica.

INDIGENISMO

It was the ideological current of *indigenismo* that prompted a few Latin American intellectuals to look at "the masses" as human beings rather than a silent undifferentiated labor force. It is doubly unfortunate that many Latin Americans have come to view social research by foreigners as a threatening force for academic imperialism. To be sure, the sad case of "Project Camelot," an abortive experiment in large-scale social science research planned by the U.S. Department of Defense in 1965, provided some brief basis for suspicion (cf. Horowitz, 1967), but most scholars from outside have shared their findings with Latins, and many have served their host countries more than they have their own. One should also remember that, at least during the early years of social anthropology in Mexico and Peru, sometimes the native scholars had a greater impact on their northern colleagues than the reverse.

One of the ways in which nationalism was expressed during the Mexican Revolution, which preceded the Russian Revolution—as every Mexican fervently knows but many foreigners are unaware—was in an idealization of the pre-Columbian indigenous societies. To be sure, this does not mean that the intellectuals embraced the Indians. It is one thing to reject the bloody history of Spanish conquistadors as violent intruders in a remote, idyllic "golden age" of prehistory, and quite another thing to go beyond expressions of sympathy for contemporary Indians whose dress, diet, language, and religion are totally alien. Nevertheless, a few men made a start in that direction and, although many of their contributions show little concern with methodology or with recent standards of contextual reporting, they introduced a new kind of awareness and also influenced a generation of students who shaped social anthropology.

To be sure, much of the indigenist quasi-sociological literature was based more on empathy than on understanding, just as the novels of social protest eloquently and forcefully denounced the miserable living conditions of peasants and miners, although they did not accurately describe or even reflect them.

This is not to say that all of the *indigenistas* were armchair scholars or critics. Manuel Gamio played an active role in the Mexican Revolution, and also did field work, following the precepts of his teacher, Franz Boas. Hildebrando Castro Pozo similarly based his writings on a familiarity with Indian communities that virtually none of his fellow Peruvians shared at the time. Moisés Sáenz, José Carlos Mariátegui, and others not only championed the Indians in idealistic terms, but also argued strongly that they should be brought into the national political and economic systems. In Bolivia, a pioneering effort in regional rural education, combining extension work with adults and appropriate schooling for children, was initiated as early as 1931. In short, a number of early *indigenistas* contributed substantially to the scholarly literature, but even those who did not do so managed to have an impact on anthropology inasmuch as few other people were interested in contemporary Indians then. This impact was strengthened when World War II ushered in a nationalistic fervor throughout much of the world, including Latin America. That broader concern seems to have incorporated *indigenismo* where it did not displace it, and more direct forms of social action now include applied anthropology, revolution, or a variety of intermediate alternatives.

EARLY CULTURAL ANTHROPOLOGY

During the first two decades of this century, anthropological research in Latin America generally was limited to either archeological excavation or attempts to identify the historical derivation of various individual traits encountered in Afro-American enclaves (as in the early works of Gonzalo Aguirre Beltrán and Melville Herskovits) or in "hispanicized Indian" communities (as did Elsie Clews Parsons and a few of her contemporaries). It was not until the 1930s that North American scholars went south of the border to conduct research based on the kind of close and sustained contact with native peoples that is now the hallmark of cultural anthropology in the Americas. Interdisciplinary research, which many consider a recent innovation, has rarely reached the level of mutual relevance and excitement that characterized the early work of the Carnegie Institution of Washington. Robert Redfield was the principal cultural anthropologist with the group, and his formulations about "the folk society," as being qualitatively different from the urban type, dominated theoretic discussions and provided a benchmark, even for those who vehemently disagreed with his interpretations. Although the ideas can easily be traced back to European sociology, the impact both of those ideas and of the man himself was enormous. Not only was he an eloquent and indefatigable writer, but he was also an effective teacher whose students greatly enlarged the scope and scale of the discipline and of field studies in Latin America. Sol Tax started a large-scale study of highland Guatemala that still draws students and colleagues to deal with various problems in a group of diverse but constantly interacting communities. Oscar Lewis's early work in Mexico is sometimes interpreted as a series of contradictions of Redfield, not only in his restudy of Tepoztlán but also in his work on the adjustment of migrants in Mexico City. Sidney Mintz was reacting to the "folk-urban continuum" when he focused attention on the rural proletariat as a major component of most Latin American populations. Gonzalo Aguirre Beltrán, Antonio Goubaud, Calixta Guiteras-Holmes, and Alfonso Villa Rojas are among the Latin American anthropologists whose work was directly influenced by Redfield. Whatever the imprecision and inconsistency of Redfield's formulations, his impact was important both in making Latin America a major focus of attention for North American scholars and in making anthropology a dominant discipline among those studying in Latin America.

Another man whose imprint is great on both Latin American studies and anthropology as a discipline is Julian H. Steward. In coordinating the monumental *Handbook of South American Indians* (1946–1950), he not only brought together contributions from specialists around the world, but he also attempted to digest the mass of data and to reconstruct culture-history on the basis of an historical materialist developmental scheme, the basis of his "multi-linear evolution." He also got the Institute of Social Anthropology under way, one of the earliest experiments in the international exchange of scholars, which served as an important training ground and educational platform for Donald Brand, George Foster, Isabel Kelly and F. W. McBryde (in Mexico); Kalervo Oberg and Donald Pierson (in Brazil); John Gillin, George Kubler, John Rowe, Ozzie Simmons, and Harry Tschopik (in Peru); Allan Holmberg (in Bolivia); and Charles Erasmus (in Colombia and Ecuador); among the Latin American scholars who benefited similarly were Gabriel Esobar, José Matos Mar, Jorge Muelle, and Oscar Núñez del Prado. As a professor at Columbia University, Steward further influenced the direction of early work by Robert Manners, Sidney Mintz, Elman Service, and Eric Wolf, and introduced "levels of sociocultural integration" as an analytic tool on the basis of a large-scale study in Puerto Rico.

One of the most persistent approaches to societies and cultures throughout Latin America has been that of the "community study," intensive, almost ethnographically comprehensive, study of individual towns, *municipios*, and other administrative political entities. There is no doubt that many research workers uncritically accepted municipal boundaries as convenient, ready-made means of delimiting their areas of study, politically and historically documented, and presumably meaningful enough to the local people to warrant their treatment as units of analysis. Although it did not necessarily coincide with folk-models, such analysis of "the community" was sometimes justified as being sufficiently typical to constitute a sort of representative sample of a given national society. In other instances, it was spoken of as a sort of microcosm, in which the dynamics of broader regional and national systems could be analyzed on a scale where they were more easily comprehensible. So many and varied were such studies in the 1940s and 1950s that few observers questioned the validity or relevance of treating political units as if they were socially significant units, and few investigators seriously tried to show how local activities and institutions affected and were affected by more encompassing systems.

Not only have different communities been studied in different ways, but in a few instances the same community has been the subject of very different kinds of studies. For example, Elsie Parsons's study of Mitla, Oaxaca, Mexico (1936) was concerned with limited historical reconstruction, attempting to differentiate those elements of contemporary religion that were survivals of indigenous patterns from those that had been introduced since the conquest by the Spaniards. When Charles Leslie (1960) restudied the same community he was primarily concerned with the views of local people concerning themselves and their relations to the rest of the world. Over the span of several years and in a number of Mexican communities, Robert Redfield increasingly sharpened his concern with "the folk society" (1934, 1941, 1947) and its contrasting type; in a pioneering replicative study of Tepoztlán (Morelos, Mexico), Oscar Lewis (1951) offered a more comprehensive holistic approach, but most readers have emphasized the two authors' contrasting descriptions of the "social character" of the Tepoztecos. In one of the Yucatecan communities studied by Redfield, Victor Goldkind (1966) has described very different kinds of power and social stratification. Although many "community studies" can be criticized as simplistic in applying traditional ethnographic techniques and concepts to inappropriate units, they served an important role in the early legitimation of anthropological studies of complex plural societies.

Perhaps more than in other areas of the world, a few regions of Latin America have been the subject of long-term research by a number of students using a variety of approaches. For example, various Maya-speaking groups in the highlands of Chiapas, Mexico, have been studied over the years by Evon Vogt, Benjamin Colby, Frank Cancian, and others; the Quechua-speakers of the Callejón de Huaylas in central Peru have been analyzed, from various perspectives, by William Stein, Paul Doughty, Mario Vázquez, and others; insights on the Quiché-speakers of Guatemala's western highlands have been offered by Sol Tax, Richard Adams, Manning Nash, Robert Hinshaw, F. W. McBryde, and others; George Foster's work on the Tarascans of Mexico is complemented by that of Zantwijk, Belshaw, and others. It is evident that this sort of collaborative and cumulative research offers both advantages and disadvantages when compared with the traditional, and still predominant, pattern, whereby a single investigator attempts to comprehend a smaller system in a year or so of study, and perhaps to assess change in the course of a restudy some years later.

OTHER SOCIAL DISCIPLINES

Traditionally, anthropologists have been the only scholars to live in close and sustained contact with nonliterate ("primitive" or "tribal") peoples, although a few economists, political scientists, and others have undertaken field work by participant-observation and other techniques in recent years. With respect to the "contemporary" (peasant, proletarian, "mass") peoples, there was never any such disciplinary monopoly, and it is sometimes difficult to distinguish among the approaches of individuals whose professional affiliations label them as "rural sociologist," "agricultural economist," "cultural geographer," "historian," or "anthropologist." Most scholars view this with satisfaction, but it can be confusing to a beginning student who tends to conceive of academic disciplines as more clearly delimited, with a stricter division of labor.

Among the earliest studies of Latin American towns, regions, and countries by North Americans were a series done by rural sociologists, under the auspices of the U.S. Department of Agriculture, during World War II. The outcomes of this project have been many, varied, and lasting, including much of the work by George Hill in Venezuela, Olen Leonard in Bolivia and Ecuador, T. Lynn Smith in Brazil and Colombia, Carl Taylor in Argentina, and Nathan Whetten in Guatemala and Mexico. Not only did many of them write landmark monographs, but some of them also played a crucial role in the stimulation of work by others, including such Latin American scholars as Antonio Arce, Manuel Alers-Montalvo, Orlando Fals-Borda, and others; the Institute of Agricultural Sciences at Turrialba, Costa Rica, continues to encourage such work among young Latin Americans.

A number of other areas of social concern have attracted considerable attention. Only a few of the many scholars who have contributed to our understanding of contemporary cultures and societies of Latin America can be mentioned here, not as a guide to the literature, but only to indicate the range of relevant writing that is available. With respect to demography, outstanding researchers are Kingsley Davis and J. Mayone Stycos. In social history, Gilberto Freyre's and Richard Morse's Brazilian works are well known; excellent studies on many other countries are also available. For economic development, Celso Furtado, Victor Alba, Victor Urquidi, and Rodolfo Stavenhagen are some of the more influential Latin writers. Political science, as practised by Gino Germani, Kalman Silvert, and others, offers useful insights, as does the sociology of interethnic relations (Alejandro Lipschutz, Manuel Diegues, Magnus Mörner, and others). It is important to emphasize that these investigators have, in most instances, not merely added to our understanding of specific local situations but have also had important influence in terms of national decision-making and in terms of their respective fields of study on an international basis.

APPLIED ANTHROPOLOGY

In Latin America, the line between "pure" and "applied" anthropology has been less hotly defended than in many other areas. In part, this is the heritage of the *indigenista* approach, which remains a vital current in both academic and administrative concerns in many of those countries that have large Indian populations. It is also in part a vestige of the "Good Neighbor Policy" and sporadic ventures in foreign aid and development, both bi-national and multinational. For example, CREFAL (Latin American Regional Center for Basic Education) in Pátzcuaro, Mexico, has long emphasized transcultural sensitivity in its preparation of educators, extension agents, and others from throughout Latin America. The Organization of American States sponsored "Project 208" in Bolivia and Mexico during the mid-1960s in order to expose lower-echelon white-collar workers to Indian communities.

George Foster succeeded Steward as director of the Institute of Social Anthropology, which was dissolved soon after World War II. Many of those anthropologists then joined the Institute of Inter-American Affairs, an early United States agency for technical aid, which provided a variety of field experience with an emphasis on action programs in health, agriculture, and grass-roots economic development in a number of Latin American countries. The Inter-American Indian Institute, also started in the 1940s, laid the groundwork for similar action programs in support of native peoples in several countries; outstanding Latins active in I.I.I. include Alfonso Caso and Juan Comas in Mexico and Luis Valcarcel in Peru. The Mexican Indian Institute was especially strong, profiting from the services of a number of well-trained Mexican anthropologists, including Fernando Cámara, Gonzalo Aguirre, Julio de la Fuente, Ricardo Pozas, and Alfonso Villa. Other international agencies that have sponsored work by social scientists in Latin America include Pan American Union, Inter-American Committee on Agricultural Development, Inter-American Development Bank, and United Nations.

North American anthropologists have often served as consultants to other agencies of their own government, such as Peace Corps and Agency for International Development (and its predecessors, often generically called "Point Four"). Social scientists working in their own countries have also played important roles in the development of such vast government programs as rural education in Mexico, Indian affairs in Brazil, and agrarian reform in Peru.

A unique and already famous experiment in applied anthropology, "the Vicos project," is briefly described by Henry Dobyns in this volume. Nowhere else have anthropologists come so close to having a laboratory situation, and the Cornell staff, as surrogate hacendados, did manipulate many variables in that situation which afforded unusual controls. The death of Allan Holmberg, who conceived and oversaw the program for many years, has unfortunately delayed publication of a critical analysis of its successes and shortcomings, but insights are afforded by the writings of others who worked with what is officially called "the Cornell-Peru Project": William Mangin, Mario Vázquez, Paul Doughty, Harold Lasswell, and others.

Latin America again became a focus of attention in the arena of world affairs in the 1960s, when the Cuban Revolution was quickly followed by the Alliance for Progress. Most of the same scholars continued to work there, but a number of other people became suddenly aware of how little they knew about that major world area. Rodolfo Stavenhagen's article reprinted in this section is aimed at dispelling some of the more widespread misconceptions that still persist.

Clearly there is no sharp division of labor between "applied anthropology" and "academic anthropology" with respect to Latin America. On the contrary, the same people have often achieved distinction in both kinds of work, and the publications that emerge often differ only slightly in terms of emphasis. While many consider this to be a good thing, there are still some who consider scientific objectivity to be incompatible with an ethic of social service, others who favor no change at all, and still others who scorn any effort short of violent revolution.

PSYCHOLOGICAL ANTHROPOLOGY

In the 1950s a new concern for the integration of the psychological, sociological, and anthropological approaches to behavior, which had been going separate ways for several years, brought a variety of attempts at interdisciplinary collaboration and analysis. As had been the case with *indigenismo,* the rhetoric often outpaced the action, but a few fruitful links were forged between psychoanalytic approaches to motivation, applications of learning-theory to human socialization, and an appreciation of cultural factors as influencing individual behavior.

Some pioneering work in this connection was the collaboration of John Gillin and others in the analysis of inter-ethnic relations in a single community in Guatemala, where Melvin Tumin dealt with the same problem from a more traditional sociological approach. Gillin gradually elaborated his views on Latin American value orientations in general, and laid the groundwork for more detailed studies of the Spanish-speaking *ladinos* (elsewhere called *criollos* or *mestizos*) who had previously been ignored by most anthropologists, despite their political and economic dominance in most of the towns and cities. The work of Allan Holmberg among the Siriono (1950) was significant in challenging some psychoanalytic premises about the priority of sexual concerns, and Jules Henry challenged some assumptions about the universality of the family on the basis of his Kaingang study (1941). Harry Tschopik's approach to Aymara magic (1951) was one of the earliest efforts in Latin America to use psychological concepts in the analysis of cultural events; this approach has been done increasingly, by Gerardo and Alicia Reichel-Domatoff, Erich Fromm, Michael Maccoby, and others.

STRUCTURAL STUDIES

Anthropology has had two contrasting styles called "structuralism," and they have had not only different derivations and concerns, but also very different impacts within and beyond the discipline. The "British structuralist" approach that took kinship and other status relationships as basic and focal in societal analysis was little applied in the New World except in the Caribbean area (e.g., the work of M. G. and Raymond Smith), and it had few adherents outside of anthropology, although its concern with cultural pluralism is shared by the other social sciences. In contrast, the *structuralisme* made famous by Claude Lévi-Strauss has become a primary stimulus to reevaluation by intellectuals of many bents. Instead of relationships, it takes symbols as basic and focal, and is in large part based on fragmentary studies from the Amazon Basin of South America. A more rigorous and systematic approach to symbols and structures has been taken by a group under the direction of David Maybury-Lewis in Brazil, and by members of the Harvard-Chiapas Project in Mexico, headed by Evon Vogt.

CLASSIFICATION

Once a corpus of descriptive literature on various tribal and peasant peoples throughout an area becomes available, attempts at classification become important, if only as heuristic devices. Attempts to delineate gross culture-areas had already been made by Duncan Strong, George Murdock, Julian Steward, Clark Wissler, and others, but it was not until the mid-1950s, when intensive studies were available for virtually every region within the vast area of Latin America, that efforts were made to compare forms and functions of social and cultural systems as wholes. Redfield's early "folk-urban" dichotomy and the structuralists' work on pluralism around the Caribbean had already stimulated some controversy. A special Latin American issue of the *American Anthropologist* (vol. 57, no. 3, 1955) brought together a variety of other approaches: Elman Service emphasized different kinds of pre-Columbian social organization as the basis for different kinds of Indian-white relations after the conquest; Kalervo Oberg suggested an evolutionary sequence for the culture history of the lowlands; Eric Wolf wrote about types of Latin American peasantry in terms of social structure; and Charles Wagley and Marvin Harris (in an article reprinted here) offered a typology of many of the kinds of subcultures that are found throughout the area. During the next year, Richard Adams undertook to classify the entire population of Central America in terms of "cultural components," combining cultural and social relational criteria.

As in any scientific endeavor, attempts at classification in cultural anthropology are not to be treated with a misplaced sense of concreteness; they are, at best, convenient aids in thinking and talking about the real variety of social and cultural systems that occur and that are not yet sufficiently understood in terms of their own internal dynamics.

Not all attempts at classification are merely descriptive, however. Another concern is analytic, attempting to spell out specific indices on the basis of which various members of a category can be compared with each other, and their relationship "measured" along some unitary dimension. Considerable controversy persists even today among social scientists about the feasibility, or, for that matter, the possibility of doing this with relation to communities, even though few laymen have any doubt about the objective reality of clear-cut and measurable differences among communities with respect to social or cultural complexity. Included in this section is a paper by Frank Young and Isao Fujimoto in which they have attempted to construct and test just such a scale, using much more than common sense. Other applications of the scaling approach, strikingly different in detail but conceptually related, have been made by John Kunkel with respect to economic development, Gino Germani in relation to social stratification and political participation, Ruth Young in analyzing plantations, John Poggie and others with respect to urbanization, and so forth. Despite pointed criticism by some who consider it a revival of evolutionistic thinking, others share enthusiasm for such scaling as a promising start toward more meaningful quantification in areas where objective indices have been relatively neglected.

Since the first edition of this book was published in 1965, controversy over the defining characteristics of peasants, the nature of the community, and other classificatory problems has tended to be phrased in markedly different terms, following the lead of Eric Wolf, whose landmark paper on complex societies is reprinted in this section.

SYSTEMIC ANALYSIS

Social scientists who have focused on statistics, formal governmental structures, and other high-level data are clearly aware that their descriptions and analyses sometimes do violence to the complexity and inconsistency of workaday behavior of individuals in various communities, but they provide an indispensable guide to some parts of the stuff of social action. Similarly, anthropologists have long recognized that their understanding of how particular people work out their lives in particular places is a resultant of many factors, including many over which members of the local community have no control and, for that matter, of which they may not even be aware.

The prototypical "primitive isolated society" probably occurs nowhere in the world today and has always been rare. At the same time that some anthropologists were beginning deliberately to deal with cities, factories, and complex social systems that had previously been ignored by their colleagues, others were recognizing that even the hamlets, haciendas, and tribes with which they dealt were immensely affected by more encompassing institutions such as the Roman Catholic Church, the national government, the world market, and so forth.

Eric Wolf's paper is important—not only in Latin American studies, but in social science as a whole—in pointing out one way of dealing with local and national systems together, and a number of the more recent papers in this book attest the effectiveness of his approach.

The concern with identifying "culture brokers" and understanding how they work is imaginatively expanded by Richard Adams in another article reprinted in this section. He integrates brokerage with the concept of career mobility systems spelled out by Anthony Leeds (also in this book), and with his own sophisticated elucidation of power and power domains.

Each of these authors is, in a sense, attempting to use ecological perspectives in understanding changes in structure. Joseph Casagrande, in writing about "strategies of survival" of several Ecuadorean communities, seems to be doing much the same thing in a less formalistic manner in the final paper in this section.

The fact that these papers generally include a higher proportion of methodological statements than do others in the book should not obscure the fact that approaches to contemporary cultures and social systems are the primary concern of many of the contributing authors. For example, Nathan Whitten's paper below is an excellent companion piece to Casagrande's, using the same approach in another part of Ecuador, but emphasizing differences in time rather than space; Samuel Stone has taken a traditional genealogical emphasis but used it in a wholly new way that integrates history, economics, sociology, and political science; and most other authors combine data and theory in unique ways.

Recommended Readings on
APPROACHES TO CULTURES AND SOCIAL SYSTEMS*

Adams, Richard N.

1956 *Encuesta sobre la cultura de los ladinos en Guatemala.* Seminario de Integración Social Guatemalteca Publicación 2, Guatemala.

1956 Cultural components of Central America. *American Anthropologist* 58:881–907.

1967 *The Second Sowing: Power and Secondary Development in Latin America.* Chandler, Chicago.

Aguirre Beltrán, Gonzalo

1957 *El proceso de aculturación.* Colección de Problemas Científicos y Filosóficos, México.

1967 *Regiones de refugio: el desarrollo de la comunidad y el proceso dominical en mestizo América.* Instituto Indigenista Interamericano Ediciones Especiales 46, México.

Alba, Victor

1965 *Alliance Without Allies: The Mythology of Progress in Latin America.* Frederick A. Praeger, New York.

Alegría, Ciro

1941 *Broad and Alien Is the World.* Farrar and Rinehart, New York.

Alers Montalvo, Manuel

1957 Cultural change in a Costa Rican village. *Human Organization* 15, 4:2–7.

Arce, Antonio M.

1965 *Desarrollo social y reforma agraria.* Instituto Interamericano de Ciencias Agrícolas, San José, Costa Rica.

Bastide, Roger

1972 *African Civilizations in the New World.* Harper & Row, New York.

Beals, Ralph L.

1961 Community typologies in Latin America. *Anthropological Linguistics* 3:8–16.

Belshaw, Michael

1967 *Land and People of Huecorio: A Village Economy.* Columbia University Press, New York.

Billig, Otto, John Gillin, and William Davidson

1947–1948 Aspects of personality and culture in a Guatemalan community: Ethnological and Rorschach approaches. *Journal of Personality* 16, 1:153–178; 16, 2:328–368.

Brand, Donald

1951 *Quiroga: A Mexican Municipio.* Smithsonian Institution, Institute of Social Anthropology Publication 11, Washington.

Cámara B., Fernando

1967 Contemporary Mexican Indian cultures: The problem of integration. In Betty Bell (ed.), *Indian Mexico: Past and Present.* University of California, Latin American Center, Los Angeles.

* This is by no means a comprehensive bibliography on the topics discussed in the Introduction, but is rather a guide to key books and articles that illustrate the approaches and provide a valuable starting point from which any student can further pursue his special interests.

Cancian, Frank
1965 *Economics and Prestige in a Maya Community: The Religious Cargo System in Zinacantan.* Stanford University Press, Stanford, Cal.

Caso, Alfonso
1958 *Indigenismo.* Colección Culturas Indígenas, México.

Castro Aranda, Hugo
1966 Bibliografía fundamental para la sociología en México. *Ciencias Políticas y Sociales* (México) 12:209–319.

Castro Pozo, Hildebrando
1924 *Nuestra comunidad indígena.* El Lucero, Lima.

Cline, Howard F.
1952 Mexican community studies. *Hispanic American Historical Review* 32:212–242.

Colby, Benjamin N., and Pierre van den Berghe
1961 Ethnic relations in southeastern Mexico. *American Anthropologist* 63:772–792.
1969 *Ixil Country: A Plural Society in Highland Guatemala.* University of California Press, Berkeley.

Comas, Juan
1953 *Ensayos sobre el indigenismo.* Interamerican Indian Institute, Mexico.

Davis, Kingsley
1972 *Population Studies in Latin America.* Columbia University Press, New York.

Deutschmann, Paul J., Haber Ellingsworth, and John T. McNelly
1968 *Communication and Social Change in Latin America: Introducing New Technology.* Frederick A. Praeger, New York.

Diegues Junior, Manuel
1952 *Etnias e Culturas no Brasil.* Ministerio de Educação e Saude Os Cadernos de Cultura, Rio de Janeiro.

Diegues Junior, Manuel, and Bryce Wood (eds.)
1967 *Social Science in Latin America.* Columbia University Press, New York.

Dobyns, Henry F., and Paul Doughty (eds.)
1971 *Peasants, Power, and Applied Social Change: Vicos as a Model.* Sage Publications, Beverly Hills, Cal.

Doughty, Paul L.
1968 *Huaylas: An Andean District in Search of Progress.* Cornell University Press, Ithaca, N.Y.

Erasmus, Charles J.
1961 *Man Takes Control: Cultural Development and American Aid.* University of Minnesota Press, Minneapolis.
1965 The occurrence and disappearance of reciprocal labor in Latin America. In Heath and Adams, 1965.

Escobar, Gabriel
1967 *Organización social y cultural del sur del Perú.* Instituto Indigenista Interamericano, Serie Antropología Social 7, México.

Fals-Borda, Orlando
1955 *Peasant Society in the Colombian Andes: A Sociological Study of Saucío.* University of Florida Press, Gainesville.

Fernandes, Florestan
1965 *A integração do negro á sociedade de clases* (2 vols.). São Paulo (partially translated as: *The Negro in Brazilian Society,* Columbia University Press, New York, 1969).

Foster, George M.
1948 *Empire's Children: The People of Tzintzuntzan*. Smithsonian Institution, Institute of Social Anthropology Publication 6, Washington.
1967 *Tzintzuntzan: Mexican Peasants in a Changing World.* Little, Brown, Boston.
1972 *Traditional Societies and Technological Change* (2nd ed.). Harper & Row, New York.

Freyre, Gilberto
1956 *The Masters and the Slaves: A Study in the Development of Brazilian Civilization* (rev. Eng. ed.). Alfred A. Knopf, New York.
1966 *The Mansions and the Shanties: The Making of Modern Brazil.* Alfred A. Knopf, New York.

Fromm, Erich, and Michael Maccoby
1970 *Social Character in a Mexican Village: A Sociopsychoanalytic Study.* Prentice-Hall, Englewood Cliffs, N.J.

Fuente, Julio de la
1949 *Yalalag: Una villa zapoteca serrana.* Museo Nacional de Antropología Serie Científica 1, México.

Furtado, Celso
1970 *Economic Development in Latin America: A Survey from Colonial Times to the Cuban Revolution.* Cambridge University Press, Cambridge, England.

Gamio, Manuel
1922 *La población del Valle de Teotihuacán.* Dirección de Talleres Gráficos, México.

Germani, Gino
1961 El proceso de transición a una democracia de masa en la Argentina. *Política* 16:10–27 (reprinted in English in Heath and Adams, 1965).
[1969] *Sociología de la modernización: Estudios teóricos, metodológicos y aplicados a América Latina.* Paidos, Buenos Aires.

Gillin, John P.
1947 *Moche: A Peruvian Coastal Community.* Smithsonian Institution, Institute of Social Anthropology Publication 3, Washington.
1951 *The Culture of Security in San Carlos.* Tulane University, Middle American Research Institute Publication 16, New Orleans.
1955 Ethos components in modern Latin American culture. *American Anthropologist* 53:488–500 (reprinted in Heath and Adams, 1965).

Goldkind, Victor
1966 Class conflict and cacique in Chan Kom. *Southwestern Journal of Anthropology* 22:325–345.
1970 Anthropologists, informants, and achievement of power in Chan Kom. *Sociologus* (n.s.) 20:17–41.

Goubaud, Antonio
1952 Indian adjustments to modern national cultures. In Sol Tax (ed.), *Acculturation in the Americas.* University of Chicago Press, Chicago.

Guiteras-Holmes, Calixta
1961 *Perils of the Soul: The World View of a Tzotzil Indian.* Free Press, Glencoe, Ill.

Hanke, Lewis, and Gunnar Mendoza (eds.)
1965 *Bartolome Arzans de Orsua y Vela's "Historia de la Villa Imperial de Potosí"* (3 vols.). Brown University Press, Providence, R.I.

Havens, A. Eugene, and William L. Flinn (eds.)
1970 *Internal Colonialism and Structural Change in Colombia.* Frederick A. Praeger, New York.

Heath, Dwight B., and Richard N. Adams (eds.)
1965 *Contemporary Cultures and Societies of Latin America* (1st ed.). Random House, New York.

Henry, Jules
1941 *Jungle People: A Kaingang Tribe of the Highlands of Brazil.* J. J. Augustin, New York.

Herskovits, Melville J.
1941 *The Myth of the Negro Past.* Harper & Row, New York.
1945 Problem, method, and theory in Afro-American studies. *Afroamerica* 1:5–24.

Hill, George W., José A. Silva M., and Ruth Oliver de Hill
1960 *La vida rural en Venezuela.* Ministerio de Agricultura y Cría, Caracas.

Holmberg, Allan R.
1950 *Nomads of the Long Bow: The Siriono of Eastern Bolivia.* Smithsonian Institution, Institute of Social Anthropology Publication 10, Washington.

Holmberg, Allan R. (ed.)
1966 *Vicos: Método y práctica de antropología aplicada.* Editorial Estudios Andinos, Lima.

Horowitz, Irving L.
1967 *The Rise and Fall of Project Camelot: Studies in the Relationship Between Social Sciences and Practical Politics.* M.I.T. Press, Cambridge, Mass.

Horowitz, Irving L. (ed.)
1970 *Masses in Latin America.* Oxford University Press, New York.

Icaza, Jorge
1964 *Huasipungo: The Villagers.* Southern Illinois University Press, Carbondale.

Kelly, Isabel, and Angel Palerm
1952 *The Tajin Totonac, Part I: History, Subsistence, Shelter and Technology.* Smithsonian Institution, Institute of Social Anthropology Publication 13, Washington.

Kubler, George
1952 *The Indian Caste of Peru, 1795–1940: A Population Study Based upon Tax Records and Census Reports.* Smithsonian Institution, Institute of Social Anthropology Publication 14, Washington.

Leonard, Olen E.
1952 *Bolivia: Land, People, and Institutions.* Scarecrow, Washington.

Leonard, Olen E., and Charles P. Loomis (eds.)
1953 *Readings in Latin American Social Organization and Institutions.* Michigan State College Press, East Lansing.

Leslie, Charles M.
1960 *Now We Are Civilized: A Study of the World View of the Zapotec Indians of Mitla, Oaxaca.* Wayne University Press, Detroit.

Lévi-Strauss, Claude
1963 *Structural Anthropology.* Basic Books, New York.
1964 *Tristes Tropiques: An Anthropological Study of Primitive Societies in Brazil.* Atheneum, New York.

Lewis, Oscar
1951 *Life in a Mexican Village: Tepoztlán Restudied.* University of Illinois Press, Urbana.
1952 Urbanization without breakdown: A case study. *The Scientific Monthly* 75:31–41 (reprinted in Heath and Adams, 1965).
1959 *Five Families: Mexican Case Studies in the Culture of Poverty.* Basic Books, New York.
1961 *The Children of Sánchez.* Random House, New York.
1964 *Pedro Martínez: A Mexican Peasant and His Family.* Random House, New York.
1969 *A Death in the Sánchez Family.* Random House, New York.

Lipset, Seymour M., and Aldo Solari (eds.)
1967 *Elites in Latin America.* Oxford University Press, New York.

Lipschutz, Alejandro
1967 *El problema racial en la conquista de América y el mestizaje* (2a ed.). Andrés Bello, Santiago.

Loomis, Charles P., et al.
1953 *Turrialba: Social Systems and Social Change.* Free Press, Glencoe, Ill.

McBryde, F. Webster
1947 *Cultural and Historical Geography of Southwest Guatemala.* Smithsonian Institution, Institute of Social Anthropology Publication 4, Washington.

Mangin, William
1967 *Las comunidades alteñas en América Latina.* Instituto Indigenista Interamericano Serie Antropología Social 5, México.

Mariátegui, José Carlos
1971 *Seven Interpretive Essays on Peruvian Reality.* University of Texas Press, Austin.

Matos Mar, José
1966 *Estudio de las barriadas limeñas.* Universidad Nacional Mayor de San Marcos, Lima.

Mayberry-Lewis, David
1967 *Akwẽ-Shavante Society.* Clarendon Press, Oxford.

Miner, Horace
1952 The folk-urban continuum. *American Sociological Review* 17:529–537.

Mintz, Sidney W.
1953 The folk-urban continuum and the rural proletarian community. *American Journal of Sociology* 59:136–143.

Mörner, Magnus
1967 *Race Mixture in the History of Latin America.* Little, Brown, Boston.

Mörner, Magnus (ed.)
1969 *Race and Class in Latin America.* Columbia University Press, New York.

Morse, Richard M.
1958 *From Community to Metropolis: A Biography of São Paulo, Brazil.* University of Florida Press, Gainesville.

Murdock, George P.
1951 *Outline of South American Cultures.* Human Relations Area Files, New Haven, Conn.

Murra, John V.
1970 Current research and prospects in Andean ethnohistory. *Latin American Research Review* 5, 1:3–36.

Nelson, Lowry

1967 Rural sociology: Some inter-American aspects. *Journal of Inter-American Studies* 9:323–339.

Núñez del Prado, Oscar

1955 Aspects of Andean native life. *Kroeber Anthropological Society Papers* 12:1–21 (reprinted in Heath and Adams, 1965).

Oberg, Kalervo

1949 *The Terena and Caduveo of Southern Mato Grosso, Brazil.* Smithsonian Institution, Institute of Social Anthropology Publication 9, Washington.

1955 Types of social structure among the lowland tribes of South and Central America. *American Anthropologist* 57:472–488.

Padden, Robert

1967 *The Hummingbird and the Hawk.* Ohio State University Press, Columbus, Ohio.

Parsons, Elsie C.

1936 *Mitla: Town of Souls.* University of Chicago Press, Chicago.

Pierson, Donald

1951 *Cruz das Almas: A Brazilian Village.* Smithsonian Institution, Institute of Social Anthropology Publication 12, Washington.

Poggie, John J., Jr., and Frank C. Miller

1969 Contact, change and industrialization in a network of Mexican villages. *Human Organization* 28:190–198.

Pozas, Ricardo

1962 *Juan, the Chamula.* University of California Press, Berkeley.

Ray, Talton F.

1969 *Politics of the Barrios of Venezuela.* University of California Press, Berkeley.

Redfield, Robert

1930 *Tepoztlán: A Mexican Village.* University of Chicago Press, Chicago.

1934 Culture change in Yucatan. *American Anthropologist* 36:57–69 (reprinted in Heath and Adams, 1965).

1941 *The Folk Culture of Yucatan.* University of Chicago Press, Chicago.

1947 The folk society. *American Journal of Sociology* 52:293–308.

1955 *The Little Community.* University of Chicago Press, Chicago.

1956 *Peasant Society and Culture.* University of Chicago Press, Chicago.

Redfield, Robert, and Alfonso Villa-Rojas

1934 *Chan Kom: A Maya Village.* Carnegie Institution of Washington Publication 448, Washington.

Reichel-Dolmatoff, Gerardo, and Alicia Reichel-Dolmatoff

1961 *The People of Aritama: The Cultural Personality of a Colombian Mestizo Village.* University of Chicago Press, Chicago.

Rubel, Arthur J.

1966 The role of social science research in recent health programs in Latin America. *Latin American Research Review* 2, 1:37–56.

Sáenz, Moisés

1933 *Sobre el indio peruano y su incorporación al medio nacional.* Secretario de Educación Pública, México.

Schaedel, Richard P.

1964 Anthropology and AID overseas missions: Its practical and theoretical potential. *Human Organization* 23:190–192.

1967 *La demografía y los recursos humanos del sur del Perú.* Instituto Indigenista Interamericano Serie Antropología Social 8, México.

Service, Elman R.

1955 Indian–European relations in colonial Latin America. *American Anthropologist* 57:411–425.

Silvert, Kalman H.

1965 (Jul) American academic ethics and social research abroad: The lesson of Project Camelot. *American Universities Field Staff Reports,* West Coast South American Series, vol. XII, no. 3 (General), New York.

1966 *The Conflict Society: Reaction and Revolution in Latin America* (rev. ed.). American Universities Field Staff, New York.

Simmons, Ozzie G.

1955 The criollo outlook in the mestizo culture of coastal Peru. *American Anthropologist* 57:107–117 (reprinted in Heath and Adams, 1965).

Smith, M[ichael] G.

1965 *The Plural Society in the British West Indies.* University of California Press, Berkeley.

Smith, T. Lynn

1963 *Brazil: People and Institutions* (3d ed.). Louisiana State University Press, Baton Rouge.

1967 *Colombia: Social Structure and the Process of Development.* University of Florida Press, Gainesville.

1970 *Studies of Latin American Societies.* Doubleday, Garden City, N.Y.

Solari, Aldo E.

1971 *Sociología rural latinoamericana.* Paidos, Buenos Aires.

Sommers, Joseph

1964 The Indian-oriented novel in Latin-America: New spirit, new forms, new scope. *Journal of Inter-American Studies* 6:249–266.

Stavenhagen, Rodolfo

1969 *Las clases sociales en las sociedades agrarias.* Siglo XX, México.

Stein, William W.

1961 *Hualcan: Life in the Highlands of Peru.* Cornell University Press, Ithaca, N.Y.

Steward, Julian H.

1955 *The Theory of Culture Change.* University of Illinois Press, Urbana.

Steward, Julian H. (ed.)

1946–1950 *Handbook of South American Indians* (6 vols.). Bureau of American Ethnology Bulletin 143, Washington.

1956 *The People of Puerto Rico.* University of Illinois Press, Urbana.

Stout, David B.

1938 Culture types and culture areas in South America. *Michigan Academy of Sciences, Arts, and Letters Papers* 23:73–86.

Stycos, J. Mayone

1968 *Human Fertility in Latin America: Sociological Perspectives.* Cornell University Press, Ithaca, N.Y.

Tax, Sol

1937 The municipios of the midwestern highlands of Guatemala. *American Anthropologist* 39:423–444.

1953 *Penny Capitalism: A Guatemalan Indian Economy.* Smithsonian Institution, Institute of Social Anthropology Publication 16, Washington.

Tax, Sol (ed.)
1952 *Heritage of Conquest: The Ethnology of Middle America*. Free Press, Glencoe, Ill.

Taylor, Carl C.
1948 *Rural Life in Argentina*. Louisiana State University Press, Baton Rouge.

Tozzer, Alfred M. (ed.)
1941 *Landa's "Relación de las cosas de Yucatan."* Papers of the Peabody Museum of Archaeology and Ethnology 17, Cambridge, Mass.

Tschopik, Harry
1947 *Highland Communities of Central Peru*. Smithsonian Institution, Institute of Social Anthropology Publication 5, Washington.
1951 *The Aymara of Chucuito, Peru; I: Magic*. Anthropological Papers of the American Museum of Natural History 44, 2, New York.

Tumin, Melvin M.
1952 *Caste in a Peasant Society*. Princeton University Press, Princeton, N.J.

Urquidi, Victor L.
1964 *The Challenge of Development in Latin America*. Frederick A. Praeger, New York.

Valcarcel, Luis Eduardo, et al.
1964 *Estudios sobre la cultura actual del Perú*. Universidad Nacional de San Marcos, Lima.

Vázquez V., Mario C.
1957 Cambios en estratificación social en una hacienda andina. *Perú Indígena* 6:4–5, 67–87 (reprinted in English in Heath and Adams, 1965).

Veliz, Claudio (ed.)
1965 *Obstacles to Change in Latin America*. Oxford University Press, New York.

Villa Rojas, Alfonso
1962 Distribución y estado cultural de los grupos Mayances del México actual. *Estudios de Cultura Maya* 2:45–77.

Vogt, Evon Z.
1970 *Zinacantan: A Maya Community in the Highlands of Chiapas*. Harvard University Press, Cambridge, Mass.

Vries, Egbert de (ed.)
1966 *Social Research and Rural Life in Central America, Mexico and the Caribbean Region*. UNESCO, New York.

Wagley, Charles
1948 Regionalism and cultural unity in Brazil. *Social Forces* 26:457–464 (reprinted in Heath and Adams, 1965).
1968 *The Latin American Tradition: Essays on the Unity and the Diversity of Latin American Culture*. Columbia University Press, New York.

Wagley, Charles (ed.)
1964 *Social Science Research on Latin America*. Columbia University Press, New York.

Wagley, Charles, and Marvin Harris
1955 A typology of Latin American subcultures. *American Anthropologist* 57:428–451 (reprinted herein).
1958 *Minorities in the New World: Six Case Studies*. Columbia University Press, New York.

West, Robert C.
1948 *Cultural Geography of the Modern Tarascan Area*. Smithsonian Institution, Institute of Social Anthropology Publication 7, Washington.

Whetten, Nathan L.
1948 *Rural Mexico.* University of Chicago Press, Chicago.
1961 *Guatemala: Land and People.* Yale University Press, New Haven.

Whiteford, Andrew H.
1960 *Two Cities of Latin America.* Logan Museum of Anthropology, Beloit, Wis.

Whitten, Norman E., Jr.
1965 *Class, Kinship, and Power in an Ecuadorian Town: The Negroes of San Lorenzo.* Stanford University Press, Stanford, Cal.

Wissler, Clark
1938 *The American Indian: An Introduction to the Anthropology of the New World* (3d ed.). Oxford University Press, New York.

Wolf, Eric R.
1955 Types of Latin American peasantry: A preliminary discussion. *American Anthropologist* 57:452–471.
1956 Aspects of group relations in a complex society: Mexico. *American Anthropologist* 58:1065–1078 (reprinted in Heath and Adams, 1965; also herein).
1957 Closed corporate peasant communities in Mesoamerica and central Java. *Southwestern Journal of Anthropology* 13:1–18.

Wolf, Eric R., and Edward C. Hansen
1972 *The Human Condition in Latin America.* Oxford University Press, New York.

Young, Frank W., and Ruth C. Young
1960 Social integration and change in twenty-four Mexican villages. *Economic Development and Cultural Change* 8:366–377.

Zantwijk, R. A. M. van
1967 *Servants of the Saints: The Social and Cultural Identity of a Tarascan Community in Mexico.* Royal van Gorcum, Hague.

Seven Fallacies about Latin America

RODOLFO STAVENHAGEN

Interest in Latin American studies has been notably episodic, but a number of misconceptions have endured, not only in terms of popular stereotypes but even in much of the descriptive and analytic literature of social science. In this paper, written during an efflorescence of such interest, a Mexican scholar succinctly corrects a few of the "many doubtful, mistaken, and ambiguous theses . . . [which] form a major part of the conceptual framework of Latin American studies." Readers who have not previously encountered the concept of internal colonialism, *questioned the primacy of "the middle class" as a force for progressive development, or have uncritically accepted any of these "seven fallacies" should find this paper a useful framework in which to evaluate much that has been written about Latin America.*

Rodolfo Stavenhagen, a Mexican social scientist trained in Mexico, France, and the United States, is Professor of Sociology at El Colegio de México. He has done applied anthropology for a number of national and international agencies; his books include Las clases sociales en las sociedades agrarias (1969), Agrarian Problems and Peasant Movements in Latin America (1970), Sociología y subdesarrollo (1972), *and, as coauthor,* La estructura agraria y el desarrollo agrícola en México (3 vols., 1970).

NOTE TO AMERICAN READERS

The purpose of this article is to review critically and refute a number of ideas on social development and underdevelopment that are current in Latin America. If the general tone of the article is outspoken and polemical, it is because the "theses" and "antitheses" it develops are directly pertinent to the great political and ideological issues that Latin America is facing today.

In the massive literature dealing with social and economic development and underdevelopment produced in recent years, many doubtful, mistaken, and ambiguous theses have appeared. Many of these are accepted as the working truth, and form a major part of the conceptual framework of Latin American intellectuals, politicians, students, researchers, and professors. Neither facts nor recent research, which contradict these theses, have been able to weaken them. Constant repetition in innumerable books and articles, particularly foreign ones, have given these concepts a growing life of their own, turning some of them, despite evidence to the contrary, into dogmas.

In this article I will deal with the sociological theses, since the debate about similar mistaken economic theses has been quite widespread.

Reprinted from James Petras and Maurice Zeitlin (eds.), *Latin America: Reform or Revolution?* (Greenwich, Conn.: Fawcett, 1968), 14–31, by permission of the author. Copyright © 1968 by Fawcett Publications, Inc. An earlier version appeared in *New University Thought* in 1966; when invited to revise it if he chose, the author indicated that ". . . this is the version I would like to see included in your book . . . I think it's a 'period piece' . . . and should probably stand as it is."

The first thesis: The Latin American countries are dual societies. In essence this thesis affirms that two different, and to a certain extent independent—though necessarily connected—societies exist in the Latin American countries: one is an archaic, traditional, agrarian, and stagnant or retrogressive society; the other is a modern, urban, industrialized, dynamic, progressive, developing society. The "archaic society" is characterized by personal and family (kinship) relations; by traditional institutions (ritual coparenthood, certain types of collective labor, certain forms of personalistic political domination, and patron-client relationships); by rigid stratification of ascribed social statuses (i.e., where the individual's status in the social structure is determined by birth, with little likelihood of change during his lifetime); and by norms and values that exalt—or at least accept—the *status quo* and the inherited traditional forms of social life, which are said to constitute an obstacle to economically "rational" thought. The "modern society," on the other hand, supposedly consists of the type of social relations that sociologists call secondary, determined by interpersonal actions that are motivated by rational and utilitarian ends; by functionally-oriented institutions; and by comparatively flexible social stratifications, in which status is attained through personal effort, and is expressed by quantitative indices (like income or level of education) and social function (like occupation). In the so-called "modern society," the norms and values of the people tend to be oriented toward change, progress, innovation, and economic rationality (e.g., maximum benefits at minimum costs).

According to this thesis, each of the two societies facing each other in the Latin American countries has its own characteristic dynamics. The first, the "archaic society," has its origins in the colonial epoch (or perhaps earlier) and preserves many ancient cultural and social elements. It changes little, or does so very slowly. At any rate, changes are not internally generated, but are imposed upon it by the modern society. The other society, the "modern" one, is oriented toward change; it generates within itself its own transformations and is the focal point of economic development, whereas the "archaic" society constitutes an obstacle to such development.

The dual society thesis is expressed on a more sophisticated level by positing an alleged duality between feudalism and capitalism in the Latin American countries. In fact, it is claimed that in a large part of Latin America a feudal type of society and economic structure exists, which constitutes the base for retrogressive and conservative social and economic groups (i.e., the land-owning aristocracy, the oligarchy, local political strongmen, etc.). On the other hand, the theory affirms, there exist nuclei of a capitalist economy, in which we find the entrepreneurial, progressive, urbanized middle class. Implicit in this description is the idea that "feudalism" is an obstacle to development in Latin American countries and must be eliminated to give way for a progressive capitalism, which will be developed by the entrepreneurial capitalists for the benefit of the country as a whole.

There is no doubt that in all the Latin American countries great social and economic differences exist—between rural and urban areas, between the Indian and non-Indian populations, between the mass of peasants and the urban and rural elites, and between the very backward and the relatively developed regions.

Nevertheless, these differences do not justify the use of the concept of dual society for two principal reasons. First, the relations between the "archaic" or "feudal" regions and groups and the "modern" or "capitalistic" ones represent the functioning of a single unified society of which the two poles are integral parts; the second, these two poles originate in the course of a single historical process.

Let us take the first point. What is important is not the mere existence of two "societies" or a "dual society"—two contrasting poles at the ends of a socioeconomic continuum—but rather the relationships that exist between these two "worlds" and that bind them into a functional whole. To the extent that the localized development of certain areas in Latin America is based on the use of cheap labor (is this not what principally attracts foreign capital to our countries?), the backward regions—those that provide the cheap labor—fulfill a specific function in the national society and not merely zones in which, for one reason or another, development has not taken place. Moreover, the archaic zones are generally exporters of raw materials to the urban centers of the country and abroad. As we shall see later, the developed areas of the underdeveloped countries operate like a pumping mechanism, drawing from their backward, underdeveloped *hinterland* the very elements that make for their own development. This situation is not new to the underdeveloped countries. It is the result of a long historical process that began with the expansion of mercantilist and colonialist Europe.

Let us turn now to the second point, the single historical process that gave rise to the two poles of Latin American society. The conquest of Latin America was accomplished principally in the context of commercial goals. Essentially, it was accomplished by a series of joint (private and state) mercantile enterprises. In some regions veritable feudal areas were created by means of *encomiendas* and *mercedes* (respectively, grants of Indian labor and land, by which the Spanish Crown rewarded the conquerors). The conquered indigenous populations were subjected to the most brutal oppression and exploitation on the part of the Spaniards. In the same way the slavery of the African Negroes on the Caribbean and Brazilian sugar plantations which satisfied the needs of a mercantilist economy oriented toward the consumer markets of Europe was not characterized by a closed, self-sufficient economy (as was the case in classical European feudalism), but rather satisfied the needs of the export mining industry and of agriculture that supplied these mining centers or the European markets.

During the whole colonial epoch the driving force of the Latin American economy was the mercantilist-capitalist system. The Spanish and Portuguese colonies were large producers of raw materials that supplied various European markets, directly or indirectly, and thus contributed to the later industrial development of Western Europe. The "feudal" economy, if it ever really existed, was subsidiary to the dynamic centers—the mines and export agriculture—which, in turn, responded to the needs of the colonial metropolis.

The one constant factor of the colonial economy was the search for and control of cheap labor for the colonial enterprises. First the colonists tried enslaving the indigenous populations; then the slavery of Africans was introduced. Later they assured themselves of servile Indian labor through a series of arrangements that varied from the encomienda to the forced distribution of Indian workers. The "feudal" living and working conditions of the majority of the Indian peasant population reduced to a minimum the costs of production in mining and in colonial agriculture. Thus, the "feudalism" in labor relations may be considered a function of the development of the colonial economy in its entirety, which in turn formed an integral part of the world mercantilist system.

The colonial economy was subjected to strong cyclical variations. In Brazil one after another of the major industries grew and then declined. This was true for the primitive extraction of wood, sugar production in the great slave plantations of the Northeast, mining in the central part of the country, the extraction of rubber in the Amazon, and finally, during this century, coffee production in the South and Southeast of Brazil. Each one of these cycles brought an epoch of growth and prosperity to the area in which it occurred. Each corresponded at that moment to a foreign demand. And each one left, in the end, a stagnant, underdeveloped, backward economy and an archaic social structure. In a large part of Brazil, then, *underdevelopment followed upon and did not precede development*. The underdevelopment of these areas is largely the result of a previous period of development that was of short duration and followed by the development of new activities in other parts of the country.

This pattern also can be observed in the rest of Latin America, principally in the mining zones that flourished in one epoch and whose economies decayed thereafter. The economic cycles of colonial Latin America were determined, in large part, by the economic cycles of the Western World. In Middle America, Indian communities that are now closed, isolated, and self-sufficient were not always like that. On the one hand, the colonists displaced the Indian populations who were removed into inhospitable and isolated zones, in which their living standards were reduced to a miserable subsistence level; on the other hand, during the periods of economic depression, those communities that had previously been relatively integrated into the global economy cut themselves off from the world and were depressed through necessity to a subsistence level. We see, then, that in historical terms development and underdevelopment are connected in Latin America, and that frequently the development of one zone implies the underdevelopment of others. We also see that the "feudal" conditions largely respond to the needs of the colonial metropolis and the colonial elite, whom it is hardly possible to define as feudal.

The kinds of relationships that were established between a colonial metropolis and its colonies were repeated within the colonial countries themselves, in the relationships that developed between a few "poles of growth" and the rest of the country. As Spain was to her colonies, so the centers of colonial power in New Spain (and in the rest of Latin America) stood to the outlying, backward areas that surrounded them.

Indeed, the backward, underdeveloped regions of our countries have always played the role of *internal colonies* in relation to the developing urban centers or the productive agricultural areas. And to avoid the mistaken idea that there are two (or more) independent social and economic systems at work in the Latin American countries, we propose to describe the situation in terms of *internal colonialism* rather than in terms of "dual societies." This will become clearer as we discuss the next thesis.

The second thesis: Progress in Latin America will come about by the spread of industrial products into the backward, archaic, and traditional areas. The diffusionist thesis is found on many levels. Some speak of an urban—or Western—culture that will spread gradually over the world, and that will little by little absorb all the backward and primitive peoples. Others speak of the effects of modernization as if it were a spot of oil that spreads slowly outward from a central focus. Others affirm that all stimuli for change in the rural areas come of necessity from the urban zones. The fact that transistor radios, bicycles, toothpaste, and Coca-Cola can be found in the most remote parts of the world is cited to support these arguments.

This thesis implies three others, which are not always stated as clearly: (1) the development of the modern sector, which is essentially expansionist, brings with it *ipso facto* the development of the traditional and archaic sector; (2) the "transition" from traditionalism to modernism is a current, permanent, and inescapable process that will eventually involve all traditional societies; and (3) the centers of modernism themselves are nothing but the result of the diffusion of "modernist" traits (technology, know-how, the spirit of capitalism, and, of course, capital) that come from the already developed countries. The thesis can be considered mistaken for the following reasons:

(1) While it is certain that a large number of consumer goods has been distributed to the underdeveloped areas in recent years, this does not automatically imply the development of these areas, if by development we mean an increase in per capita output of goods and services and in the general social welfare. Often this diffusion of products is nothing but the diffusion of the culture of poverty into the backward, rural areas, for it involves no basic institutional changes.

(2) The spread of manufactured industrial goods into the backward zones often displaces flourishing local industries or manufacturers, and therefore destroys the productive base for a significant part of the population, provoking what is known as rural proletarianization, rural exodus, and economic stagnation in these areas.

(3) The same process of diffusion has contributed to the development of a class of merchants, usurers, middlemen, monopolists, and moneylenders in the backward rural areas, in whose hands is concentrated a growing part of the regional income, and who, far from constituting an element of progress, represent an obstacle to the productive use of capital and to development in general.

(4) The "diffusion" is often nothing more than the extension into the rural areas of monopolies and monopsonies, with negative consequences for a balanced and a harmonious development.

(5) The process of diffusion of *capital* has taken place *from* the backward to the modern areas. Constant decapitalization of the underdeveloped areas in Latin America accompanies the migration of the best-trained part of the population out of the backward zones: young people with a bit of education who are looking for better opportunities in other areas. It is not the presence or absence of factory-made goods but this unfavorable outward flow from the backward zones that determines the level of development or underdevelopment of these areas.

(6) This process of "diffusion," to which are attributed so many beneficial

results, has been going on in Latin America for more than 400 years—and aside from certain dynamic focal points of growth, the continent is still as underdeveloped as ever.

In reality, the correct thesis would be: the progress of the modern, urban, and industrial areas of Latin America has taken place at the expense of backward, archaic, and traditional zones. In other words, the channeling of capital, raw materials, abundant foods, and manual labor coming from the backward zones permits the rapid development of these poles or focal points of growth, and condemns the supplying zones to an increasing stagnation and underdevelopment. The trade relations between the urban and the backward areas is unfavorable to the latter in the same way that the trade relations between underdeveloped and developed countries on a world scale are unfavorable to the underdeveloped countries.

The third thesis: The existence of backward, traditional, and archaic rural areas is an obstacle to the formation of an internal market and to the development of a progressive and national capitalism. It is claimed that progressive national capitalism—located in the modern industrial and urban centers—is interested in agrarian reform, the development of the Indian communities, the raising of minimum wages paid to agricultural workers, and other programs of a similar sort. This thesis is mistaken for the following reasons:

(1) With rare exceptions, no progressive or national capitalism exists in Latin America, nor do the international conditions exist that would allow its development. By a "progressive" and "national" capitalism, we mean one which is committed in word and in deed to the independent economic development of the country—i.e., of the masses of the population. This would mean the formulation and acceptance by the capitalist class of economic policies furthering: (a) diversified agriculture for the internal market; (b) transformation of the country's principal raw materials for use in the country itself; (c) increasing industrialization; (d) a high rate of reinvestment in the country's agriculture; (e) increasing state participation in large economic enterprises; (f) strict control of foreign investments and their subordination to national needs; (g) strict control over exports of capital and profits; (h) preference for nationally owned enterprises over foreign-owned companies; (i) strict limitation of unnecessary imports; (j) strict limitation of the manufacture of nonessential consumer goods; and other such objectives.

These policies are not being pursued in most Latin American countries, and the countries that have tried at one time or another to implement them have suffered tremendous external political and economic pressures. The recent history of Brazil is a case in point. After the U.S.-supported military coup in that country in 1964, the previous economic policies that had furthered a progressive and national capitalism were thrown overboard in favor of the increasing control of the economy by U.S. corporations. The same thing has happened in Argentina, Chile, Bolivia, and other countries. With the exception of Mexico (and at one time, of Brazil), the "national bourgeoisie" in Latin American countries does not have enough power or influence anywhere to make its interests really felt.

(2) Up to this time—and for the foreseeable future—a significant internal market exists among the urban population, a market that is growing continuously and one that is not yet fully supplied. On the other hand, in these same urban areas there is an industrial sector that works at less than full capacity for reasons that have little to do with the internal market, but rather with profits; and for a long time there will be no need for these industries to do more than supply the growing urban zones. That is to say that metropolitan areas like Lima, Callao, São Paulo, Santiago, and Mexico City can grow economically for the indefinite future without necessarily effecting any basic changes in the structure of the backward rural areas, the internal colonies.

The question of the internal market is essentially a question of income distribution. Economists and sociologists speak constantly about the need of incorporating the "backward" subsistence peasants into the money economy in order to strengthen the internal market and further economic development. Yet nowhere in Latin America is the gap between rich and poor greater than in the cities, where the desperately poor "marginal" urban population of the shantytowns is growing rapidly. If the internal market were indeed the driving force of Latin America's bourgeoisie, Mexico's capitalists would not be seeking, as they are, investment opportunities in Central America, or Brazil's in Paraguay and Bolivia; they would not be exporting millions of dollars a year to the security of American and European banks; they would, instead, favor more equitable tax policies, lower profit margins and higher turnovers, lower prices for their products, and higher levels of production. Generally, however, they favor none of these things.

The fourth thesis: The national bourgeoisie has an interest in breaking the power and the dominion of the landed oligarchy. It has often been said that there is a profound conflict of interests between the new elite (or the new upper class) represented by modern commercial and industrial entrepreneurs and the old elite (or the traditional upper class), which derives its prominence from the ownership of the land. Although the latifundist aristocracy was eliminated by revolutionary means in some Latin American countries (however, always by the people, never by the bourgeoisie), there does not seem to be a conflict of interests between the bourgeoisie and the oligarchy in the other countries. On the contrary, the agricultural, financial, and industrial interests are often found in the same economic groups, in the same companies, and even in the same families.

For example, much of the capital coming from the archaic latifundia of Northeast Brazil is invested by their owners in lucrative enterprises in São Paulo. And in Peru the grand families of Lima, associated with progressive foreign capital, are also the owners of the major "feudal" latifundias in the Andes. There is no structural reason why the national bourgeoisie and the latifundista oligarchy should not understand one another; on the contrary, they complement each other very well. And in those cases where there is a possibility of a conflict of interests (as with some legislation that would benefit one group and be prejudicial to the other, for example), there is no lack of bourgeois or military government that will give ample compensation to the group whose interest is prejudiced.

The sorry spectacle of some recent "agrarian reforms" is a case in point. Stung by the Cuban experience and pressured by the U.S., many conservative Latin American governments, at the 1961 Punta del Este economic conference, subscribed to the proposition that it would be safer to bear some sort of land reform than to court peasant revolution. Much publicity has been given to the Colombian and Venezuelan "reforms," and land reform laws or projects in Brazil, Chile, Ecuador, Peru, and other countries have been widely hailed. Where these projects have not been talked to death in parliament (as in Chile), or simply evaded by legal chicanery or specially erected institutional stumbling blocks (as in Brazil, Ecuador, and Peru), the experts agree that what is being done (as in Colombia and Venezuela) is too little, too late, too costly, too badly planned and executed, and these "reforms" are simply insufficient to even keep up with the natural growth of the peasant population, let alone redistribute the land or break the rural power structure. And none of these governments are controlled by the "landed aristocracy" to such an extent that it could be said of them that the local "bourgeoisie" is excluded. Quite the contrary.

The disappearance of the latifundista oligarchy has been exclusively the result of popular movements, not of the bourgeoisie. The bourgeoisie finds a very good ally in the land-owning oligarchy in maintaining internal colonialism, which in the last analysis benefits both of these social classes equally.

The fifth thesis: Latin American development is the work and creation of a nationalist, progressive, enterprising, and dynamic middle class, and the social and economic policy objectives of the Latin American governments should be to stimulate "social mobility" and the development of that class. There is probably no other thesis about Latin America more widespread than this one. It is supported by researchers, journalists, and politicians; it is the theme of seminars and conferences, the subject of voluminous books, and one of the implicit but basic assumptions of the Alliance for Progress; it has been transformed into a virtual dogma. But this thesis is false, for the following reasons:

(1) In the first place, the concept "middle class" itself contains ambiguities and equivocations. If it deals, as is often the case, with middle-income groups situated between the two extremes of a given economic scale, then it is not a social class but a statistical aggregate. Generally, however, this concept refers to people who have a certain type of occupation, particularly in the tertiary sector of the economy—in commerce or services—and mostly in the urban areas. In this case, it refers to white collar workers, the bureaucracy, businessmen, and certain professions. At times this concept also refers to certain social groups that have no place in the traditional structural model of Latin America, in which there supposedly exists only a landed aristocracy and peons without land. All other groups, from the small land owners to the urban population as a whole, are then lumped together under the catch-all term of "middle class." As long as there is no clear definition of this term, information concerning the virtues and potentialities of this "middle class" is only a subjective opinion of those who state it.

(2) Very often the term "middle class" is a euphemism for "ruling class." When one speaks of the entrepreneurs, the financiers, and the industrialists in

relation to the development of the Latin American countries, reference is made to a class that has the power in the society, that occupies the apex of the social, economic, and political pyramid, and that makes, as such, the overall decisions that affect these countries. In other words, the class in question is in no sense "middle."

When liberal authors (such as John Johnson and Robert J. Alexander, for example) extol the virtues of this "new" class in Latin American politics, it is obviously less embarrassing to use the neutral term "middle class" than to accurately define the nature of this group at the top of the power structure as a new ruling class or power elite.

(3) This thesis of the middle class usually suggests the idea of a potentially majoritarian mass of the population, primarily recruited from the lower strata of society, which will sooner or later totally occupy the social universe. At that time, it is implied, the upper classes will no longer have any economic, nor the lower class any numerical, importance. There could be nothing more utopian or mistaken. The growth of the tertiary economic sector is no guarantee of development, nor will the growth of the middle social sectors (a statistical fiction) guarantee the disappearance of the economic and social inequalities of society. No matter how accelerated the growth of these middle strata may be in Latin America as a whole, the growth of the lower income groups in both the countryside and the city on the one hand, and that of the minuscule upper income strata on the other, is still greater.

(4) The sectors that compose the middle class in its restricted sense—small- and medium-sized farm owners, small businessmen, public employees, small entrepreneurs, artisans, different types of professionals, etc. (i.e., those who work on their own or who receive a salary for nonmanual labor)—usually do not have the characteristics that are attributed to them. Instead they are economically and socially dependent upon the upper strata; they are tied politically to the ruling class; they are conservative in their tastes and opinions, defenders of the *status quo*; and they search only for individual privileges. Far from being nationalists, they like everything foreign—from imported clothing to the *Reader's Digest*. They constitute a true reflection of the ruling class, deriving sizeable benefits from the internal colonial situation. This group constitutes the most important support for military dictatorships in Latin America.

(5) The concept "middle class" is also understood at times in terms of the consumption habits of a certain part of the population. In this way, for example, the fact that the peasants buy bottled beer instead of Chicha or Pulque, or that the urban population buys furniture or electrical appliances on credit, is considered by some as an indisputable sign that we have taken great steps in the march toward a "middle-class" civilization. Everyone in Latin America, these authors tell us, has "the aspirations of the middle class." It is only a question of time as to when these aspirations will be realized. This assertion is incorrect for the following reasons:

A social class is not defined by the articles it consumes, nor does the level of aspirations reveal the structure of social institutions and the quality of inter-group relations. The diffusion of manufactured articles is directly related to the overall level of technology as well as to effective demand. The majority of the population—particularly in the urban areas—can enjoy this type of consumption, to some extent, but it requires no basic change in the class structure or in the inequalities of income, social status, political power, or labor relations.

The creation of "aspirations" or "necessities" of a certain type is increasingly the result of an all-powerful advertising industry that has infiltrated all social milieus. Levels of aspiration are rising everywhere, but so is the level of unfulfilled aspirations; and this, as any psychologist would confirm, leads to rising levels of frustration and feelings of deprivation. Thus, the aspirations of the middle class could well be transformed into revolutionary consciousness.

Furthermore, economic studies have demonstrated that in Latin America the proportion of wages in the national income—on which most of the population is dependent—tends to diminish, while the profits and capital returns of a minority tend to increase. This tendency, which has been accelerated in recent years by the process of inflation (especially in countries like Argentina, Brazil, Chile, Bolivia, and Colombia) does not fit with the idea of the slow, harmonious growth of the middle class.

(6) The strengthening of the middle class, as a goal of social policy, is not essentially intended to further economic development in a country, but rather to create a political force capable of supporting the existing ruling class, and of serving as a buffer in the class struggles that endanger the stability of the existing social and economic structure. The ideologues of the middle class have lamented that this class was not sufficiently strong in Cuba to oppose the socialist revolution. On the other hand, they give credit to the "middle class" for the fact that the Mexican and Bolivian revolutions have become "stabilized" and "institutionalized."

The so-called middle classes are closely tied to the existing economic and political structure, and lack an internal dynamic which could transform them into promoters of an independent economic development. Their relative numerical importance is one thing, and their condition and capacity to make decisions as a class that could affect economic structures and processes is altogether another thing. It is noteworthy that the authors who are most attached to the idea of the growth of the middle class give little or no importance to the fact that the lower strata still constitute the largest part of the Latin American population.

(7) Finally, the thesis of the middle class tends to obscure the fact that there are tensions, oppositions, and conflicts between ethnic groups as well as between classes in Latin America; that the social and economic development of the Latin American countries depend, in the last analysis, upon an adequate solution to these conflicts; and that the growth of the "middle sectors" (as one North American author calls them), though very impressive in certain regions, does not contribute to the solution of these problems. At times, such growth may even postpone a solution and sharpen the conflicts.

The sixth thesis: National integration in Latin America is the product of miscegenation. This thesis is frequent in the countries that have major ethnic problems—those that have a large proportion of Indians in the population, and Brazil, with its Negro population. It is argued that the Spanish and Portuguese colonization of America brought two main racial groups, two civilizations, into confrontation, and that the process of national integration represents both a biological and a cultural mixture. In the Indo-American countries it is thought that *ladinoziation* (acculturation of Indians) constitutes a universalizing process in which the major differences between the dominant white minority and the Indian peasant masses will disappear. It is said that out of the traditional bipolar social structure a new, intermediate biological and cultural element is appearing—the *Ladino,* or *Cholo,* or *Mestizo,* or *Mulato,* as the case may be—who bears the "essence of nationality" and who possesses all the virtues necessary for progress in Latin American countries.

The fallacy in this thesis is that biological and cultural mixing (a common process in many parts of Latin America) does not constitute, in itself, a change in the existing social structure.

National integration, as an objective process, and the birth of a national consciousness, as a subjective process, depend on structural factors (i.e., on the nature of the relations between men and between social groups) and not on the biological or cultural attributes of certain individuals. National integration (in the sense of full participation of all citizens in the same cultural values, and the relative equality of social and economic opportunities) will be achieved in the Indian areas, not with the development of a new biocultural category, but with the disappearance of internal colonialism. In the internal colonies of our countries, the Mestizos (or racially mixed population) are, in fact, representatives of the local and regional ruling class who help to maintain the Indian population in a state of oppression. They have not the slightest interest in true national integration. On the other hand, in the increasingly important urban centers, the immigrant rural population, often of Indian stock, is rapidly "integrated" from the national point of view; but this is due more to the positions it occupies in the class structure than to the process of miscegenation.

Furthermore, the thesis of miscegenation very often hides a racist prejudice (which may be unconscious); in the countries where a majority of the population has Indian traits, biological miscegenation signifies "whitening," and in that sense citing the virtues of miscegenation really hides anti-Indian biases. The same prejudice is found in the cultural version of this theory—indeed, it means the disappearance of Indian culture. Thus, making miscegenation the prerequisite for national integration condemns the Indians of America, a group that numbers in the tens of millions, to a slow agony.

The seventh thesis: Progress in Latin America will only take place by means of an alliance between the workers and the peasants, as a result of the identity of interests of these two classes. We cannot leave this discussion of Latin America without referring to a thesis that is quite prevalent among the orthodox left. Indeed, on the basis of theories developed by Lenin and Mao Tsetung, it is said that the success of the democratic revolution in Latin America depends on the ability of the working and peasant classes to forge a common front against the reactionary bourgeoisie and against imperialism.

While this may be correct as a revolutionary ideal or as the desired goal for political organization and action, it must be pointed out that if the analysis of the last six points is correct, particularly if the concept "internal colonialism" is valid, then the existing social structures and their present tendencies in Latin America do not "naturally" favor such an ideal alliance, though I will not offhand deny its possibility. Recent historical experience does not show a single instance of such an alliance having in fact taken place. The Mexican peasant revolution took place when there was hardly an urban working class to speak of. The Bolivian revolution, while greatly beneficial to the peasants, was mainly the work of the tin miners and an intellectual elite. The Cuban revolutionaries finally achieved the support of the organized urban working class only toward the end of the armed uprising when Batista's downfall was assured. The working class of São Paulo (Brazil's largest concentration of industrial workers) has consistently elected the country's most conservative—albeit "populist"—governors and was certainly unable to join forces with the relatively well organized rural workers in the Northeast to save Goulart's democratic regime from military overthrow. In Argentina the organized urban workers (either peronistas or antiperonistas) have not been able or willing to establish an alliance with the peasants and rural workers. In other countries the experience is similar.

In the future, as most of Latin America will become increasingly underdeveloped and will be increasingly controlled by the U.S., through military or pseudodemocratic regimes, the situation may change. Many governments will continue to attempt to carry out some sort of land reform and certainly the political forces of the left will continue to press for it everywhere. In regard to these land reforms (be they the first steps of a democratic revolution or the delaying action of an increasingly frightened bourgeoisie) it is pertinent to emphasize the following points:

(1) One of the indisputable steps in all democratic revolutions is agrarian reform. But the acquisition of land by the peasantry through a noncollectivist agrarian reform transforms them into proprietors whose class interests are those of other landed proprietors.

(2) The objective interests of the peasants and the workers are not identical in the matter of agrarian reform. An agrarian reform usually implies an initial diminution of food deliveries to the cities, the effects of which are first felt by the working class. It also means the channeling of public investments into the rural sectors, with a consequent disfavoring of the urban sector—which, as we have seen, is about the only sector that really benefits from economic development in a situation of internal colonialism.

(3) The struggle of the urban working class (which is politically more powerful than the peasantry) for higher wages, more and better public social services, price controls, etc., finds no seconding in the peasant sector because benefits obtained by the working class in this way are usually obtained at the cost of agriculture—i.e., the peasants.

In Latin America almost half of the economically active population works in agriculture, yet the agricultural sector receives little more than 20 percent of the total income, and its share in the total income has been declining much faster than its share in the total population. Capital formation is much more important in the nonagricultural sector and public and private investment (in public services, education, health, social security, etc.) principally benefits the urban populations.

In other words, the urban working class of our countries is also a beneficiary of internal colonialism. That is one of the reasons why a truly revolutionary labor movement does not exist in Latin America.

(4) In nineteenth-century England the expulsion of peasants from the land and their migration to the industrial sweatshops signified a diminution of their standard of living; in Czarist Russia, rural-urban mobility was strictly limited and the worker-peasant alliance was made in the field of battle; and in People's China the same alliance was forged in the fight against the Japanese invaders. In sharp contrast to all of these examples, rural emigration is not only possible for the discontented of the countryside in Latin America, but in most cases it represents an improvement in economic and social conditions (even in the favelas, the barriadas, the ranchos, or the colonias proletarias—the shantytowns—of the Latin American cities), as compared with conditions in the countryside. One can theorize that the revolutionary consciousness of the peasants increases in *inverse* proportion to the possibility of their individual upward social mobility, and that this relationship would hold even more strongly if the latter also implies geographic mobility.

(5) We may also suppose that the more severe the internal colonialism in Latin America (i.e., the greater the difference between the metropolis and its internal colonies), the further the possibilities of a true political alliance between workers and peasants will be reduced. The example of recent events in Brazil and Bolivia should illustrate this point.

The preceding picture of Latin America might seem overly pessimistic. If so, it is only because the picture given us by those "experts" who perpetuate these seven fallacies is uncritically optimistic and leads easily to an underestimation of the tremendous tasks that Latin America faces today. Perhaps the greatest single obstacle to economic and social development in Latin America (not localized growth) is the existence of internal colonialism, an organic, structural relationship between a developing pole of growth or metropolis, and its backward, underdeveloped, and underdeveloping internal colony. Quite often not even the best-intentioned policy makers are aware of this relationship, which exists on the economic, political, social, and cultural levels. Whereas several measures of a partial and limited nature can no doubt be taken by progressive governments to remedy this situation, the only way out in the long run seems to be the social and political mobilization of the "colonized" peasantry, which will have to fight its own battles, except for the usual support it can hope to receive from radical segments of the intelligentsia, the students, and the working class. It is noteworthy that not even the governments that have formally acknowledged the need for land reform are willing to tolerate independent peasant organizations.

The myth of the middle class is another false panacea. This does not mean that the diploma-holding sons of the middle-income strata have no role to play in their country's development. Some of them will probably lead the coming peasant revolutions themselves. Others will of course continue to run the petroleum industry, the sugar mills, the hospitals, the universities, and the chain stores. It is rather a question of in whose interest and for whose benefit these organizations will be managed. And in this sense, the "middle class" has hardly ever been able to see further than to their own pocketbooks. The thousands of

Latin American technicians and professional people who emigrate yearly to the U.S. and better-paying jobs are a case in point.

In Latin America today there is growing awareness among all sectors of the population of what the real obstacles are to the socioeconomic growth and to democratic political development. Thoughtful people are less and less concerned with single factors such as "lack of resources," "traditionalism of the peasantry," "overpopulation," and "cultural and racial heterogeneity," which are still current among some scholars. They are increasingly conscious of the internal structure and dynamics of the total society and, of course, of the relation of dependence this society has with respect to the industrial metropolis, i.e., the phenomenon of imperialism and neocolonialism. Such awareness can only lead to deeper and more refined analysis of the Latin American situation and to newer and more correct courses of action.

A Typology of Latin American Subcultures

CHARLES WAGLEY AND MARVIN HARRIS

Although it was written in 1956, this "typology of Latin American subcultures" remains an exceptionally vivid and succinct introduction to the range of variation that students should know exists in the area—and, for that matter, within many of the individual nations. Unlike most of the other contributors to this book, Wagley and Harris emphasize cultural rather than social characteristics. One must recognize that these types do not correspond in detail with specific communities with which he or she is familiar; ". . . their content differs according to the environment, history, and distinctive local traditions of the nation or subregion in which they are found." Nevertheless, such a typology provides a useful frame of reference for organizing and comparing data, as illustrated in the authors' discussion of the immensely varied Brazilian and Mexican cases.

Charles Wagley is Graduate Research Professor of Anthropology and Latin American Studies at the University of Florida. The scope of his interests is only partially reflected in his books: Economics of a Guatemalan Village (1941), The Social and Religious Life of a Guatemalan Village (1949), Amazon Town (1953), Race and Class in Rural Brazil (*rev. ed.,* 1963), Brazil: Crisis and Change (1964), The Latin American Tradition (1968), An Introduction to Brazil (*rev. ed.,* 1971), *and others. With Marvin Harris he wrote* Minorities in the New World (1958).

Marvin Harris is Professor of Anthropology at Columbia University. In recent years, his progressively broadened concern for conceptualization can be traced through: Town and Country in Brazil (1956), Portugal's African "Wards" (1958), Patterns of Race in the Americas (1964), The Nature of Cultural Things (1964), The Rise of Anthropological Theory (1968), *and* Culture, Man, and Nature (1971).

From *American Anthropologist* LVII (1955), 428–451. By permission of the authors and publisher.

I

One of the most perplexing problems in the study of complex national or regional cultures such as those of Latin America is the diversity of pattern and institution which they contain. There are a series of institutions, values, and modes of behavior which constitute throughout Latin America a "cultural common denominator" and which distinguish Latin American culture from other major culture spheres of the Western world (cf. Gillin 1947b and Wagley 1948). But the "common denominator" of modern Latin America does not consist simply of those institutions, values, and behavior patterns held in common by most of the Latin American population. Regular cultural differences within the complex and heterogeneous national societies must also be considered. A conceptual framework based on these differences is much needed to provide a context for the extant data and to guide future research. This is especially true with respect to the numerous anthropological community studies, whose contribution to our knowledge of a national culture is often lessened by an inadequate definition of just what variety of the national culture is being considered —or, in other words, what segment of the diverse population they treat. The purpose of the present article is to suggest a taxonomic system of subcultures which we hope will have operational utility throughout Latin America.

This attempt to provide a classificatory system for ordering cultural data on Latin America is obviously not unique. As we shall discuss in more detail below, Redfield (1941), by implication at least, distinguished four types of communities for Yucatan, although only the folk and urban types were emphasized. Steward (1953) and his associates in the Puerto Rican project isolated a series of significant Puerto Rican subcultures for study.[1] And recently, there has been published a series of articles, dealing mainly with Latin America, aimed at refining and extending Redfields' folk-urban concepts. Most of these discussions of Redfield's classification and most attempts to develop a sociocultural taxonomic system have dealt with varieties of whole local communities treated as whole societies. This is to be expected from a discipline whose traditional research methods involved prolonged, sedentary, and intimate contact with a restricted locale and the analysis of local sociocultural wholes. But it is apparent that many of the communities studied in Latin America by anthropologists have an internal heterogeneity of culture pattern depending upon class differences, differences between rural and urban residents of the same community, and other factors, too numerous to list. It is therefore often difficult to classify the culture of a whole local community as "folk culture" or as "urban culture"—or as "Indian," "mestizo," or "Creole." The present taxonomy of subcultures attempts to distinguish between culture and society and to take into account not only the differences among communities but also internal cultural heterogeneity within communities.

We distinguish nine significant Latin American subculture types. They are called "subcultures" because they are variations of a larger cultural tradition and represent the way of life of significant segments of the Latin American population. They are called "types" because their content differs according to the environment, history, and distinctive local traditions of the nation or subregion in which they are found. Thus, the subculture types we have called

"Peasant" differ in content in the western countries of Central and South America, with their strong American Indian tradition, from the same type as found in the West Indies and lowland Brazil, which have felt strong African influences. Yet it seems to us that Peasant subcultures throughout Latin America share certain basic features which make it possible to include them in the same typological category.

At least in a preliminary fashion, the following subculture types would seem to be useful for ordering the universe of Latin American cultural materials: (1) *Tribal Indian*, comprising the cultures of the few remaining aboriginal peoples; (2) *Modern Indian*, resulting from the fusion of aboriginal and, in the main, sixteenth- and seventeenth-century Iberian institutions and culture patterns; (3) *Peasant*, carried by the relatively isolated horticultural peoples of Latin America (and frequently by the lower classes of small isolated towns), who are called variously *mestizos, cholos, ladinos, caboclos*, or other local terms; (4) *Engenho Plantation*, the subculture of the workers on family-owned estates; (5) *Usina Plantation*, the way of life on the large modern corporation-owned agricultural establishments; (6) *Town*, the way of life of the middle- and upper-class inhabitants of the numerous settlements serving as administrative, market, and religious centers throughout Latin America; (7) *Metropolitan Upper Class*, characteristic of the highest socioeconomic strata in the large cities and of the owners of plantations; (8) *Metropolitan Middle Class*, characteristic of an emerging group of big-city professional and white-collar workers and owners of medium-size business; and (9) *Urban Proletariat*, characteristic of a mass of unskilled and semiskilled industrial and menial workers in the larger cities.

Undoubtedly there are many other important Latin American subcultural types, and it is hoped that the present taxonomy will be refined and extended—or that it will stimulate others to formulate a more useful system.

II

(1) TRIBAL INDIAN TYPES

In 1500, when the Europeans came to that part of the New World which is now Latin America, the natives of the lowlands (except for certain parts of the circum-Caribbean) lacked true tribal or political organization. There were innumerable "tribes" made up of villages or bands united only by a common language, common custom, and the consciousness of forming "a people" as against all outsiders. The power of chiefs seldom extended beyond one or more villages or bands; and the "tribes," sometimes even the villages or bands of the same tribe, were generally at war with one another. The population was sparse in aboriginal times, and disease, slavery, and European warfare against these highly divided groups rapidly led to the decimation and extinction of the native peoples in many localities. Nowadays, only an insignificant few of these tribal groups persist in localities such as the Chaco, the headwaters of the Amazon tributaries, and on isolated reservations and mission stations. Such tribesmen constitute an insignificant segment of the modern Latin American population, and as long as they retain their aboriginal cultures and their identity as tribesmen they are, in reality, carriers of distinct cultures within the geographic boundaries of Latin America and not subcultures of modern Latin America.

However, the process of acculturation now taking place among these tribal groups does pertain to the study of Latin American culture, and, as Foster recently pointed out in his discussion of the folk culture concept, it is important to distinguish between tribal cultures and the mixed rural cultures of Latin America (1953:162).

(2) MODERN INDIAN TYPES

The Indians of the highland regions of Latin America must be included in any study of modern Latin American culture. Although their way of life differs strikingly from that of the nationals of the countries in which they live, they share many patterns and institutions, mainly of European origin, with the other inhabitants, and numerically they are an important segment of the population. Unlike the lowlands, the highland region was inhabited by a dense aboriginal population organized into native states. After the initial shock of armed conquest and disease, these peoples were brought under the control of the Spanish colonials. Through mechanisms such as the *encomienda, repartimiento, mita,* and other forms of forced labor, they were made to work for their conquerors and were integrated into colonial society. Missionaries taught them Catholicism and, in many cases, they were concentrated into Spanish-type villages and a European form of community organization was forced upon them. They borrowed freely from the European culture of the sixteenth and seventeenth centuries—a culture which in many respects contained as many "folk" features as their own. By at least the beginning of the eighteenth century, a new culture had taken form among these peoples out of the fusion of aboriginal and colonial Spanish patterns. This culture persists today, unchanged in its main outlines, and constitutes an important variant of national patterns in many highland countries.

Modern Indians generally speak an aboriginal language, although they may also be bilingual. Some of them work in mines, on coffee *fincas,* or on large haciendas, but most characteristically they are horticulturalists planting native American crops, although many European plants have also been adopted. Despite the tendency to individualize landholdings which began in the nineteenth century, among many Modern Indian groups the community is still the landholding unit. Community cohesion generally persists at a high level despite the encroaching power of the national states. Indian *alcaldes, regidores,* and other officials are often maintained alongside the national bureaucracy. While the Modern Indian is nominally Catholic, it is characteristic that a large segment of aboriginal belief has been fused with Catholic ideology. In addition, Catholic saints are endowed with local characteristics and powers. The Indians of each community generally think of themselves as ethnic units separate from other Indian groups and from the nationals of the country in which they reside; they are the people of Santiago Chimaltenango, of Chamula or of Chucuito, rather than Guatemalans or Peruvians. Frequently they wear a distinctive costume which identifies them as Indians of a particular *pueblo,* and it is characteristic for the Indians of each community to be endogamous.

Numerous examples of this subcultural type have been studied in Latin America by anthropologists. The Indians of Santiago Chimaltenango (Wagley 1942, 1950), of Chichicastenango (Bunzel 1952), of Panajachel (Tax 1953), of Quintana Roo, Yucatan (Villa 1945), of Kauri (Mishkin 1946) and of Chucuito in Peru (Tschopik 1951), to mention but a few, are carriers of Modern Indian-type subcultures. Yet, as noted above, few of these communities contain only carriers of the Modern Indian subculture type. In most of these communities, there are also a few non-Indians, carriers of a Peasant-type subculture, who form an integral part of community life. Any full community study must treat not only the two subcultures of these communities but also the "castelike" relationship between them. As Gillin has written, "Each group [Ladino and Indian] has culture patterns more or less exclusive to itself, but the two castes are part of a reciprocal pattern which characterizes the community as a whole" (1951:11). Too often our community studies have treated Modern Indian subcultures as if they were isolated tribal groups.

(3) PEASANT TYPES

Throughout Latin America, the people who inhabit rural farms and the numerous small and isolated agricultural villages have a way of life which is analogous in many respects to that of peasants in other parts of the world. Latin American peasants may be physically American Indians, Negroes or Europeans, or mixtures of these racial stocks. They are the people who are called *mestizos* (Mexico and other countries), *ladinos* (Guatemala), *cholos* (Peru), or *caboclos, tabareus, caipiras,* and *matutos* (Brazil). In some respects, their way of life is similar to that of the Modern Indian. They are generally horticulturalists using essentially the same "slash-and-burn" techniques of farming as the Modern Indians, and they frequently depend primarily upon native plants such as maize, manioc, and potatoes. As stated earlier, Peasant-type subcultures are strongly flavored with aboriginal traits in some areas, as for example in the Amazon Valley, where native shamanism is an integral part of peasant religion. In other areas, such as the West Indies and the Guianas, African traits persist in varying degrees among the Peasant subcultures just as American Indian traits do elsewhere. But everywhere Peasant-type subcultures are characterized by a predominance of archaic European patterns, which survive alongside the American Indian or African patterns and which are slowly giving way to new national patterns and institutions. Unlike the Modern Indians, Peasants generally consider themselves to be nationals of the country in which they reside. Although they tend to be regional in their loyalties and to have but a vague idea of what it means to be a member of a nation, national patterns and institutions play a larger role in Peasant than in Modern Indian subcultures. Peasant subculture economies are closely tied in with regional and national economies. There is fairly extensive participation in commercial transactions through the medium of markets, to which Peasant farmers regularly go to sell their surplus for cash. Peasants maintain accounts at stores and trading posts from which they receive goods of nation-wide circulation such as kerosene, steel tools, cloth, thread, and sewing machines.

Peasants characteristically speak the national language (i.e., Spanish or Portuguese), although sometimes an aboriginal tongue (e.g., the Tarascan of the Michoacan mestizos), or, as in Haiti, a *créole*, is spoken. Peasants participate to some extent in political life, voting if there are elections and if they have the franchise. Catholicism in Peasant subcultures tends to be more orthodox than that of the Modern Indian. Peasants share national fashions, values, and aspirations, although in all of these they are generally "behind the times" since they tend to be isolated from the centers of diffusion. Thus young men may play soccer if it is the national sport, as it is in Brazil. Peasants often celebrate national holidays and perhaps know something of their national heroes. Literacy is valued as an aid in social and economic improvement. Nowadays, Peasants tend to dress after the style of the city as soon as such styles are known and when people can afford them. Because such people are generally poor, illiterate, and isolated, they have little in the way of modern technological facilities such as electric lights, motor-driven vehicles, and modern housing.

Again, it is not difficult to cite examples of this type of Latin American subculture which have been studied by anthropologists. Both Modern Indian and Peasant-type subcultures tend to be carried by relatively small and simply organized social units which thus lend themselves to investigation by the traditional field techniques of ethnology. The rural agriculturalists living in the environs of Moche in Peru (Gillin 1947a), those of the community of Tzintzuntzan in Mexico (Foster 1948), those of Cruz das Almas in southern Brazil (Pierson 1951), those of Itá in the Brazilian Amazon (Wagley 1953), and those of Marbial Valley in Haiti (Métraux 1951) are carriers of subcultures which correspond to the Peasant type. The Small Farmer subculture of Puerto Rico would also seem to correspond to this category (Steward 1953; Manners 1950).

But it must be emphasized that most of the communities mentioned above also contain people who are not peasants, not even rural, but townsmen with urban aspirations and urban patterns of behavior. The subculture of these people will be considered below as the Town type. Due to the tendency to regard "folk culture" as a way of life characteristic of a type of community, the folk subcultures (or in our terms, Peasant subcultures) of such communities have often been emphasized to the exclusion of the nonfolk elements. The restudy of Redfield's Tepoztlán by Lewis (1951) is an example of how the concept of a homogeneous folk community needs to be qualified in view of the internal heterogeneity of cultural patterns found in rural communities.

The fact probably is that the carriers of Peasant-type subcultures live everywhere in communities which also contain carriers of Town-type subcultures—whose ties with national life are the intermediate bonds by which the peasant is also tied into national life. Indeed, many peasants are actually town dwellers who have their domiciles in town and their farms in the nearby area. Although settlements inhabited exclusively by people who have a homogeneous Peasant subculture are extremely common, it is a distortion to view them as isolated communities, or even as total communities. Since the Peasant subculture is distinguished from the Modern Indian precisely on the grounds of greater identification with and participation in national patterns and institutions, it is clear that a group of peasants can only be *part* of a community, and that the terms "folk society" and "folk culture" are misleading when applied to a community which actually and necessarily contains more than one subculture. It may perhaps help to clarify the matter if the communities in which peasant households, hamlets, and villages occur are thought of as larger Town-Peasant communities, implying that Town and Peasant subcultures must be considered together if a proper understanding of either is to be attained. This symbiotic relationship between Peasant subcultures and Town subcultures (i.e., "folk and nonfolk") has been recently emphasized by Foster (1953:169 ff.).

(4) ENGENHO PLANTATION AND (5) USINA PLANTATION TYPES

The Europeans who settled in the Caribbean and in the lowland parts of northern South America did not find the riches in gold and silver nor the large aboriginal labor force which their contemporaries encountered in the highlands. But by the middle of the sixteenth century sugar cane had become an important commercial crop in Brazil and in parts of the West Indies. For a time, the great wealth which sugar brought to this lowland region was comparable to that derived from minerals in the highlands. From the Old World the planters brought a commercialized version of large-scale agricultural enterprise, which had its roots in sixteenth-century Europe and even earlier in the ancient Mediterranean world. In the New World this agricultural system was modified by the massive use of slave labor, by the exigencies of sugar as a commercial crop, and by the physical and social environment of the New World colonies. The result was the New World plantation—the *hacienda,* the *finca,* the *estancia,* the *fazenda,* or whatever it happens to be called in the various countries.

Such plantations came to form veritable communities, or neighborhoods of large communities, with their own variety of Latin American culture. Although large-scale agricultural establishments differ from one part of Latin America to another and in accordance with the crop to which they are dedicated (i.e., sugar, coffee, bananas, cotton, cacao, henequen, etc.), there are numerous social and cultural similarities among them. Furthermore, some fundamental changes in the way of life on Latin American plantations have followed essentially the same developmental process throughout the whole area, despite differences in the commercial crops.

The general characteristics of the *Engenho* Plantation subculture type may best be illustrated by reference to plantations dedicated to sugar cane, which was for centuries Latin America's most important commercial crop. Although there were local differences, sugar-cane plantations during the period of slavery seem to have followed a similar pattern throughout the area. The center of the plantation, and of the community or neighborhood which it formed, was the mansion in which the owner, his large family, and the many domestic servants lived. A chapel, which was either attached to the mansion or situated near it, served as the church for the owners and for the slave workers. Behind the mansion were the slave quarters—a street of huts. Nearby there were sheds used to store tools and equipment and to house the oxen and other animals. A storehouse, where the food and other supplies for the field hands were kept and periodically distributed, was also a common feature. Then, nearby, there was the *engenho* (Spanish *ingenio*), which was a small sugar factory containing a mill driven by hand, by animal traction, or by water power. Such plantations were generally situated on waterways which furnished easy transportation to market centers. Characteristically, the plantation settlement pattern was a concentrated one resembling that of a small village.

The number of people on such plantations was generally not large during the slave period. On the average, no more than 200 to 300 people lived on a relatively large sugar plantation, and within this small "village-like" society social relations tended to be intimate and highly personal. The members of the owner's family were tied together into a large, extended patriarchal group. Between these aristocrats and the slaves there was a stable set of relations often accompanied by personal intimacy and intense loyalty. It was, in other words, a "caste" society made up of Negro slaves and European owners in which each "caste" was conscious of the rights and obligations of the other. Leadership was provided automatically by the dominant European group, and economics, religion, and almost all aspects of life were directed and controlled by the aristocratic owner or his administrators.

The abolition of slavery, the vagaries of the international market, and finally the industrialization of sugar refining brought about important changes in the old colonial sugar plantations. However, many plantations may still be found throughout Latin America which strongly resemble the old *engenho* despite the substitution of wage labor for slavery, and other innovations. Such plantations are still owned, and often administered, by descendants of the same aristocratic slave-owning families of the nineteenth century. The workers, some of whom may actually be descendants of former slaves, show much the same dependency and loyalty toward their employers as the slaves are said to have shown for their masters. Each of these *engenho*-type plantations, with its cluster of houses and sheds and its small chapel, forms, as in the past, a small concentrated village or neighborhood (Smith 1946:396ff.). Economic life is still focused upon monoculture, and little land or time is left for the workers to grow their own gardens. Today, the sugar factory itself is no longer a part of the *engenho*-type plantations. The *engenho*-type plantations have become, instead, suppliers of sugar cane to large mechanized sugar mills, or *usinas*, which do the processing and marketing. But in many respects the way of life on these old-style plantations has changed remarkably little since the nineteenth century.

Here again, the community unit consists of the carriers of two distinct subcultures, that of the workers and that of the owners. Although it would be tempting to make the *engenho* plantation community unit and the *Engenho* Plantation subculture coincide, the fact is that the plantation owner is generally also an urban Latin American cosmopolitan who is found in the upper strata of the principal large cities. Since early colonial times he has had both a "town house" and his place in the country, and has alternated his residence, sometimes seasonally, between one and the other. His employees, formerly his slaves or peons, including domestic servants in town as well as the workers in the country, are treated by him with characteristic patriarchal, intimate, and usually benevolent concern. To this treatment the *engenho* plantation worker responds with loyalty and attitudes of dependence. It is this dependence and allegiance to the *patrão* (boss), together with the distinctive land tenure, occupational and communal arrangements peculiar to the monoculture regime, which distinguish *Engenho* Plantation subcultures from Peasant subcultures.[2]

Throughout Latin America, a transition from the *engenho* plantation to the modern industrialized agricultural enterprise has occurred or is now taking place. We have called the newer form the *usina* plantation, from the term used for the modern industrialized sugar mill.[3] Speaking again in terms of sugar plantations, as steam-driven mills were introduced capital came to play a more important role than land. The central-power-driven *usina* could process and distribute far more efficiently than the smaller installations, and so the small plantations came more and more to depend upon the *usina* to process the cane. Gradually, great corporations have bought out the smaller properties and welded them together into large agricultural factories. There is a transitional phase, however, in which each *engenho* plantation is administered as a separate unit by employees of the corporation. During this phase much of the old way of life continues. This period of transition is one which is particularly vulnerable to social tension and economic instability. The workers have lost the security provided by the traditional *patrão*, and the new system of social welfare and social security of the national government has not as yet been extended to cover them.

Then, as industrialization progresses, it becomes more efficient to fuse these smaller properties into one large centralized commercial farm. Where this process has been completed, as in Cuba, Puerto Rico, and Brazil, the result is a type of Plantation subculture which differs profoundly from that of the old-style *engenho* plantation. The traditional pattern of intimacy and mutual dependence between the workers and their employers is replaced by a more strictly economic relationship between the workers and the administrators and officials of the corporation. The local group becomes larger as the number of workers increases and the social unit is more heterogeneous as new specialized occupations appear. The workers, without the old emotional ties to their fellows and to their employers, are more mobile than before, often leaving the plantations to seek higher wages elsewhere. The *usina* plantation is more closely integrated with national institutions and culture patterns. Labor unions are sometimes active among the workers, and social welfare legislation is enforced more often than in the *engenho* plantation. There may be electric lights, modern housing, schools, medical clinics, public health facilities, and excellent communications with the metropolitan centers. The workers on such establishments seem to have a way of life more similar to that of the growing urban-industrial proletariat of Latin America than to that of the workers on the *engenho* plantations. Mintz has recently characterized the workers on these large commercial plantations as the "Rural Proletariat" (1953a:139 ff).

The discussion of these two types of Plantation subculture has been based on plantations involved in sugar production. Large-scale agricultural estates that grow other kinds of commercial crops for export are of course also found in Latin America. Such crops as cacao, coffee, maté tea, henequen, and cotton are also produced on large-scale, monoculture plantations. It is probable that the regime of exploitation of each different crop determines distinctive sociocultural conditions. Thus when more data become available it may be convenient to formulate a series of additional subtypes for *Engenho* and *Usina* Plantation subcultures based on crop specialties. Livestock ranches, for example, with their small number of workers, their exclusion of female laborers, and their saturation with a kind of horse complex, clearly merit treatment as a subtype.

From another point of view, the widespread occurrence of sharecropping suggests an additional sector of refinements for our categories. Sharecropping of a commercial crop as a substitute for wages can probably be subsumed under the category of *Engenho* Plantation subcultures. Relationships between the owner and his workers approach the highly personal ones characteristic of *engenho* plantations, with the employer offering assistance in a crisis and in many instances being the sole purchaser of his tenants' produce. The individual sharecropping regime, however, may act to reduce the community cohesion characteristic of nucleated wage laborers on the other *engenho*-type plantations.

For the purpose of this paper, it seems sufficient to set forth the hypothesis that at least two broad types, the *Engenho* Plantation and the *Usina* Plantation subcultures, may be found throughout Latin America. No matter what crop the plantation produces, there has been a transition from the old traditional enterprise to the modern industrialized establishment analogous to that which has taken place in sugar production. Everywhere this transition has involved a shift from a more personal and stable set of relations between the classes to a mobile, impersonal one based on economic values and urban standards. It has involved a change from a small and relatively homogeneous society to a larger and more variegated one; and it has led to a more important role for national institutions and patterns on all levels of plantation life.

It is surprising that so few examples of the Plantation subcultures of either type have been studied by anthropologists, especially in view of the obvious numerical importance of plantation workers in the Latin American population and in view of the importance of plantation production in the national economies of the Latin American nations. A study of an *Engenho* Plantation subculture has been carried out by Hutchinson as part of a community study in the Recôncavo region of Bahia in Brazil (1954).[4] A study of a government-owned sugar plantation was made by Elena Padilla Seda in Puerto Rico (1951), and on the same island Mintz studied a large sugar plantation owned and operated by a commercial corporation (1951). Loomis and Powell have studied a Costa Rica *finca* producing sugar and coffee, and have given us a comparison of a hacienda and a peasant community in rural Costa Rica (1951). A study of a community in Brazil in which there are cacao-producing plantations has been carried out by Anthony Leeds. If the present classification of Latin American subculture types serves no other purpose, it indicates that a large segment of the Latin American population—and an important variant of the culture of the area—has been relatively neglected in our field investigations.

(6) TOWN TYPES

Towns where periodic fairs are held and which serve as the administrative and religious centers for rural districts are old in Latin America. They have their roots both in the European and in the aboriginal traditions. With the improvement of transportation (especially with the use of trucks), many of these towns have become regional markets similar to the market towns that serve the rural United States. As these market centers enlarge their range of trading, the rural population no longer produces only for local consumption but comes to plant by more modern methods cash crops that are sold on the national market. The towns thus become more closely integrated with national economic and political life. Their populations increase, and new concepts and patterns are introduced from the cities. Life in these larger towns is more like that of the great urban centers by which they are more directly influenced, than like that of the surrounding countryside.

Yet in Latin America today there are still innumerable small towns serving only an immediate rural area and preserving many traditional patterns. Such towns cannot be understood without reference to the whole community of which they are the centers. For it is characteristic of Town subcultures that their "city folk" look down upon the "country people" as "hicks," and that behavior patterns, values, standards of dress, speech and etiquette differ for the upper-class townspeople as opposed to both the lower-class townspeople and to the inhabitants of the rural countryside.

As we have already indicated, such towns are part of communities which include two strongly contrasting subcultures. The contrast between the two corresponds to a marked schism in socioeconomic class status between a non-farming, landlord, business-owning, bureaucratic, "white-collar" group and a farming, manual-laboring group. Within the town itself, there are a small number of people who are craft specialists, like shoemakers, blacksmiths, and carpenters, who are permanent residents of the town, and who do not engage in agricultural activities. From the point of view of the local upper class these people may be "hicks" just as much as the town-dwelling and country-dwelling farmers. Although these artisans themselves often regard the rural people with condescension, the fact is that they are generally more closely related (by kinship, by marriage, by social and cultural values, by economics, and by social intercourse) with the rural farmers than with the town upper class. The stigma of poverty, of illiteracy, and of manual labor is on both groups. Thus in isolated areas, town-dwelling farmers, town-dwelling artisans and laborers, and domestic servants can generally be classed as carriers of a Peasant subculture. But such people represent a gradient of contact between isolated semi-subsistence farmers and the upper-class townspeople who are carriers of Town subculture.

The life of the upper-class townsman differs radically from that of the carriers of the Peasant subcultures. The small-town upper-class "urbanite" manifests in many respects an archaic version of the ideals and patterns of the big-city cosmopolitans and the plantation gentry of bygone days. Although upper-class townspeople are often more familiar with the geography of the nearest large city than with the geography of the rural areas of the community they live in, and although they seek to emulate cosmopolitanism with respect to dress, manners, and outlook, they are often thwarted in these ambitions by the incompleteness and inaccuracy of their notions of the contemporary standards of sophistication. Thus, in most Latin American small towns, culture patterns persist which are today considered "old-fashioned" in the metropolitan cities. Courting, for example, is closely chaperoned, and it is a common sight to see a young man quietly conversing with his fiancée from the street while she looks down at him safely from the window of the house. And in the plaza there is often the *paseo*, during which the young men circulate in one direction as the young ladies go in the other.

Except in regions where there are large plantations owned by a rural gentry, upper-class townsmen control most of the political and economic power in the community. Their political life is intense, and there is great competition for the support of lower-class peasant electors. Upper-class social life frequently revolves around clubs which sponsor dances and other forms of entertainment from which the peasants are excluded. Upper-class Catholicism is more orthodox in Town subcultures than in Modern Indian and Peasant subcultures. More emphasis is placed upon church-going and on formal sacraments as against household saints and unorthodox cults. Where deviations from Catholic tradition occur, they are apt to take the form of Protestantism or spiritualism. Upper-class townsmen have radios, receive mail, magazines, newspapers, and send their children to be educated in big-city high schools and colleges. They own fashionable clothing and often have servants to cook, wash, carry water, and take care of their house for them.

The existence of Town subcultures in isolated communities furnishes the key to the problem of the relationship of Peasant subcultures to lines of national political and economic integration. Local standards are set and maintained by this sociocultural segment, and it is through the upper class of the town that changes emanating from national legislation and metropolitan influences must filter before reaching the peasant stratum (cf. Foster 1953:169 ff.).

Many studies of local variations of Town subcultures have been made in Latin America by anthropologists as part of the study of communities which also include Peasant or even Modern Indian subcultures. But frequently, in such studies, it is difficult to know which data pertain to the Town subculture as distinguished from the subculture of the community's rural population. The town of Cunha in São Paulo, Brazil (Willems 1947), and the town of Moche in Peru (Gillin 1947a)—as against the rural peasants of both communities—seem to have subcultures of this type. Two community studies recently carried out in Brazil, namely, Monte Serrat in the arid northeast (Zimmerman 1952) and Minas Velhas in the central mountain region (Harris 1953), both distinguish between the Town and Peasant subcultures. In general, however, anthropologists have tended to emphasize the Latin American Peasants or Modern Indians. A large portion of the population in countries such as Argentina, Uruguay, Paraguay, Brazil, Chile, and Colombia live in small towns. Not until we know more about the way of life distinctive of these small urban centers will our knowledge of Latin American culture be anything more than relatively superficial. It is not, in our opinion, the so-called mestizo or Creole patterns (i.e., in our terms, Peasant subcultures) which, as Gillin maintains (1947b), are the emergent culture patterns of Latin America. Rather, the predominant trend in contemporary Latin America would seem to be toward Town subcultures which are closely identified with the urbanized and industrialized world.

(7) METROPOLITAN UPPER-CLASS,
(8) METROPOLITAN MIDDLE-CLASS, AND
(9) URBAN PROLETARIAT TYPES

Little research has been carried out, either by sociologists or by anthropologists, on the modern Latin American city. As far as anthropology is concerned, such cities pose a difficult problem in research methodology, since the traditional field methods are best applied to relatively small populations and relatively homogeneous societies The problem of class differences in the Latin American urban centers presents one of the most pressing and difficult challenges to students of

Latin American culture. There is a critical lack of information about socioeconomic stratification as well as about the basic subcultural differences which attend the various levels. Accordingly in this paper we can do little more than speculate about the subcultures to be found in the great metropolitan centers of Latin America.

It is quite clear to all who have visited Latin America that while the metropolitan centers share much with cities throughout the Western world, they have their own peculiar characteristics. Caplow has pointed out two distinctive features of Latin American cities (1952:255):

> . . . those traits which are common to metropolitan cultures everywhere in the modern world are most concentrated in groups of high status, whence they are diffused rather raggedly down through the social system of each community; second, that there is more cultural variation within the Latin American city than within cities of the United States or Europe.

These two differences between the cities of Latin America and those of the United States and Europe explain why the population of the Latin American city often seems, in a sense, to be smaller than the census data indicate. For the number of people who participate effectively in city life (i.e., buy newspapers, attend the cinema, have electric lights and telephone service, and so forth) is exceedingly small as compared with the actual population. The largest proportion of the population lives, in one sense, outside the stream of city life, differing little in many respects from inhabitants of rural areas; as a matter of fact, a large number of these Latin American city dwellers have but recently migrated from the rural zones.

The people of the metropolitan upper class attempt to maintain, as far as possible, the traditional patterns and ideals of an aristocratic landed gentry. It is this group which participates in and generally dominates local and national politics. Its members are absentee landlords, high-level government employees and officials, owners of industry and large commercial enterprises, and many well-to-do doctors, lawyers, and other professionals. No matter whether such people are the actual descendants of the landed gentry of the nineteenth century or descendants of immigrants or others who have recently achieved wealth and position, they tend to adopt many of the ideal patterns of nineteenth-century agrarian society. There is an emphasis among them upon widely extended kinship ties which is strongly reminiscent of nineteenth-century aristocratic society. They have a disdain for manual labor and admiration for courtly manners, and a love of luxury. But, at the same time, it is this group in Latin America that permits its daughters to have "dates" and allows them to enter the professions, thus breaking the old traditional patterns of highly chaperoned courtship and the confinement of women to purely domestic realms. At least the better educated and the wealthier members of this group are in close touch with Europe and the United States. Until the last two decades, it was France to which they looked for innovations, and French tended to be their second language. Recently, however, the United States has come to supplant France in this respect, and English has become the preferred foreign language. Hence the metropolitan upper class tends both to preserve old traditional forms and to be the innovator, accepting new forms from abroad, diffusing them down to the lower class of the city, outward to the people of the towns, and ultimately to the peasants and to the workers on plantations. To a large extent, therefore, many of the ideal patterns common to the other Latin American subcultures derive from Metropolitan Upper-Class patterns.

Studies specifically pertaining to the subculture of the Metropolitan Upper Class have not been carried out by anthropologists except for one by Raymond Scheele, which was part of the Puerto Rican project directed by Steward (1950:139–40; 1953:102; 1956). To date most of our information comes from data acquired by anthropologists and others during their casual relations with Latin Americans of this group, and from what Latin Americans write about themselves. It is suggested that the ethnographic method should be used in the study of representative local segments of the Latin American upper class. Until this is done, much of what we say about this important segment of Latin American culture will remain entirely hypothetical.

Even less of a concrete nature is known about the Metropolitan Middle-Class and Urban Proletariat subcultures. The middle class in the large cities of Latin America is made up of a rapidly increasing group of first-generation professionals and of white-collar workers in business and government. Most observers tend to agree that this middle class maintains standards of material consumption and prestige closely patterned after those of the metropolitan upper class. Its members place a high value on freedom from manual labor and in matters of housing, clothing, and etiquette consciously strive to reduce the gap between themselves and their wealthier models. The presence in the cities of a vast substratum of marginal wage earners, constantly replenished by rural emigration, permits the metropolitan middle class to employ domestic servants and to avoid the stigma of menial labor. But there is intense competition for white-collar positions, and salaries are often insufficient to maintain leisure-class standards in other respects. One result noted by many observers has been the multiplication of the number of jobs held by each middle-class wage earner. Some high-school teachers in Rio de Janeiro, for example, teach in as many as five or six different schools and have to rush from one place to the next with split-second precision in order to arrive at their classes on time. Caught between low incomes and high standards of consumption modeled after those of the upper class, the middle class is forced to devote a large part of its income to items of high display value such as fashionable apartments, stylish clothing, and greatly overpriced automobiles. Thus, in contrast to the middle classes of other world areas, the Latin American metropolitan middle class appears not to have developed an emphasis on savings nor as yet to have distinctive "middle-class ideology."

Although the urban proletariat is numerically the dominant segment of the metropolitan centers, it is the least well-known of all. The phenomenal growth of Latin American urban centers in the last generation, mainly as a result of migration from rural zones, indicates that a large percentage of the urban proletariat may actually be carriers of Peasant, Plantation, or Town subcultures. A recent study by Lewis of migrants from Tepoztlán to Mexico City (1952) indicates that their ideological culture remains basically unchanged despite the urban setting. Only empirical research will answer the question whether there is a type of Latin American subculture distinctive of the urban proletariat and different from the subcultures of small towns and rural areas.

III

Whether or not the present typology of subcultures will be of any value in controlling variations and differences in the complexity of Latin American culture, and whether it will provide a useful frame of reference for research, depends on its operational utility in concrete situations. Its final usefulness over such a large area as Latin America as a whole will, of course, depend upon considerably more research and upon whether or not the available data can be ordered meaningfully within this framework. But an illustration of the use of this typology in a specific research project may indicate its possible value in the study of complex modern cultures. The research in question was carried out in the state of Bahia in Brazil in 1950–51 and comprised the study of three communities, each in a different ecological zone of the state. The communities studied were: Vila Recôncavo, in the sugar-planting area near the coast; Minas Velhas, an old mining center in the central mountain zone; and Monte Serrat, a community in the arid semi-desert of the northeast.[5] An analysis of the subcultures present in these communities and in the state of Bahia seemed to be most meaningful in describing this sociocultural diversity.

Not all subculture types outlined in this paper will, of course, be present in any particular area of Latin America. In the state of Bahia, the indigenous population was quickly exterminated or assimilated. Thus, the subculture types called Tribal Indian and Modern Indian are not present. But throughout the state there are numerous rural agriculturalists, many of whom are descendants of Indians, whose subculture is of the type identified above as Peasant. Throughout the state there are also small towns which are essentially trading and administrative centers with Town subcultures. The coast of Bahia, especially around the Bay of Todos os Santos, where it is known as the Recôncavo, was one of the earliest sites of sugar plantations in Latin America. Here are found both the old-style *engenho*-type and the new *usina*-type sugar plantations. And finally, in the city of Salvador, the capital and largest metropolitan center of the state, there is a culturally conservative urban upper class preserving many old Brazilian traditions, as well as a large metropolitan proletariat.

Each of the communities in which field research was carried out contains at least two subcultures. The old mining town of Minas Velhas is a trading, manufacturing, and administrative center for a larger community encompassing a number of satellite villages inhabited by simple peasant farmers. Monte Serrat contains these same two subcultures: a religious, administrative, and trading town which is visited periodically by the surrounding scattered peasant population. The third community, Vila Recôncavo, contains a town which is inhabited by traders, government employees, a group of fishermen, a few artisans, manual laborers, and a variety of marginal wage earners. It also contains in the rural zone a series of *engenho*-type plantations, a small *usina* which still administers its various plantations as separate units (in transition between the *engenho*-type and *usina*-type plantations), and a number of metropolitan upper-class families, owners of plantations and of the *usina*, who participate in community life. The other Metropolitan subcultures (Middle Class and Urban Proletariat) are found in the city of Salvador but were not studied by this research project.[6] Thus, of the major subculture types found within the state of Bahia, four are represented in the communities of research.

Despite differences deriving from the degree of isolation, from different environments and different local historical circumstances, there are many crucial similarities in the Town subcultures of Monte Serrat, Minas Velhas, and Vila Recôncavo, on the one hand, and in the Peasant subcultures of these same communities, on the other hand. Likewise, there are crucial differences between these subcultures of each community as well as between these subcultures and the Plantation and Metropolitan Upper-Class subcultures of Vila Recôncavo. The broad sociocultural differences between subcultures of different type in the Bahia area conform to the criteria upon which this taxonomy of Latin American subcultures had been based and have therefore been described above. But a specific illustration may help to clarify how such a typology can be used to explore additional categories of patterned behavior.

During the period of field work general elections were held throughout Brazil. There was considerable regularity in the communities being studied in regard to political behavior during the campaigns and during the election.

(*a*) *Peasant subcultures:* There was little or no interest in the elections among the peasant segment of population in both Minas Velhas and Monte Serrat. On election day in Monte Serrat, political parties sent trucks out to the rural zones to bring peasants to town to vote. The day was treated as an outing by peasants who came to town with their families dressed in their best clothes. They were served free meals by the political party which claimed their vote and whose truck had transported them to town. They voted according to the dictates of an influential townsman, motivated by personal loyalty and economic bonds (i.e., debts) rather than by strong political feelings or beliefs. Similar behavior was reported also for the peasants in Minas Velhas as well as for other communities with Peasant type subcultures in which more casual observations were made during the political campaign and the elections.

(*b*) *Town subcultures:* The political campaign in both Minas Velhas and Monte Serrat (communities with Peasant and Town subcultures) was intense among the townspeople, yet their interest was focused upon local and state rather than national issues. In both Minas Velhas and Monte Serrat, the townspeople were split by allegiances to opposing political parties. In Monte Serrat each of the principal bars was frequented by men belonging to but one political party and anyone known to have any sympathy for the opposing party would not dare enter the bar of the other. Two public address systems blared forth each day competing with each other in sheer volume and in political promises and accusations. Practically all conversation revolved around the coming elections. In both Minas Velhas and Monte Serrat almost everyone had something at stake; municipal, state, and federal employees were anxious for their jobs, and commercial men and artisans stood to gain favors from being on the winning side. Even the parish priests were intensely active in the campaign and their sermons were not free of political propaganda. During the campaign, normal social life (i.e., visiting among families, dances, and the like) was almost entirely suspended. Election day was a tense and active occasion for the townspeople, most of whom were busy attempting to influence the peasant voter until he actually walked into the polls. Short visits during this period to other Bahian communities made it clear that this intense political activity was typical of Town subculture political behavior.

In the third community which contained a Town subculture, namely Vila Recôncavo, the political behavior of the town dwellers was deviant from that described above as typical for Town subcultures. In Vila Recôncavo, the political scene was dominated by metropolitan upper-class families. The local candidate for mayor was a member of one of these families rather than of the town upper class as in the two communities described above. Because of the powerful personal and economic hold which this landed gentry exerted in local affairs, the townspeople were not able to organize an effective opposition and the candidate ran virtually unopposed. The townspeople (i.e., commercial men, bureaucrats, artisans, etc.) put on a weak imitation of the political campaign which took place in Minas Velhas and Monte Serrat, but it was a foregone conclusion that the party of the metropolitan upper class (i.e., landed gentry) would win. Thus, in regions or areas, such as the Recôncavo of Bahia State, where the town is overshadowed by the surrounding plantations and the communities dominated by a landed gentry, the criteria of intense political activity for Town-type subcultures will be regularly absent.

(*c*) *Engenho Plantation subcultures:* As stated above, the community of Vila Recôncavo contained family-owned, *engenho*-type sugar plantations. During the political campaigns of 1950 little was heard about politics from the workers on these plantations. When the question was asked as to how they might vote, they were apt to answer, "I don't know, I haven't found out how the *patrão* will vote," or, "With the *patrão*, Senhor." For them, election day was a day without work when those who were literate (i.e., able to sign their names) went to town to vote as did the plantation owners. Such behavior seemed to be typical of workers on *engenho* plantations throughout the state of Bahia.

(*d*) *Usina Plantation subcultures:* Although as stated above there was not a large *usina* plantation in any of the communities studied intensively in the Bahia area, we were able to observe political behavior in nearby highly industrialized sugar plantations. Simply from the messages painted on walls in red and black paint at night urging the election of one candidate or another (especially of left-wing groups) and from the numerous political posters, it was obvious that political activity was intense among the *usina* workers. Far from voting with the administrators, these workers on large industrialized plantations supported the opposing political party. Labor unions exerted considerable influence and in general the workers were much interested in politics. Furthermore, since much of their political education came from national organizations such as labor unions and Vargas' Brazilian Labor Party (Partido Trabalhista Brasileiro), their interest focused more on national elections than local and state elections.

(*e*) *Metropolitan Upper-Class subcultures:* Representatives of the upper class were present in only one of the communities studied, Vila Recôncavo. For this group, political activity on a high level is characteristic and traditional. Most individuals in this class had friends or relatives to whom success or failure at the polls was of the utmost importance. Cousins of important families in Vila Recôncavo were candidates for federal deputy, while one of the candidates for governor was a lifelong friend of most of the members of the same families. In Salvador large, united families from this group were pitted against each other for political control of the state and city. But, as stated above, in Vila Recôncavo, since the metropolitan upper-class families have intermarried, they presented in a sense a united front. Thus, the outcome of the election in Vila Recôncavo was easily predicted.

(*f*) *Metropolitan Middle-Class* and (*g*) *Urban Proletariat subcultures:* Little can be said regarding the political behavior of these groups during the 1950 campaigns and elections. It was obvious that political reactions of both groups were emotional and intense but large-scale quantitative techniques would be necessary to study the political behavior of this large mass of people.[7]

A great number of subcultural differences and similarities which are valid for the area studied might also be pointed out. Material culture, technology, concepts of the cause and cure of disease, work patterns, occupational specialization, settlement patterns, housing, etiquette, speech habits, social ranking, and many other items are variable within the communities but constant within the subcultures of the area. Even the use made of tobacco is regular according to subculture type rather than community: peasant women smoke pipes, town women do not smoke, while metropolitan upper-class women smoke cigarettes. Thus a typology of subcultures is an indispensable tool for relating the community to its larger sociocultural context. Such a typology not only lends order to research materials and directs attention to the need for additional comparative data, but it also provides a basis for predicting with reasonable accuracy the reactions of certain segments of the population to new social stimuli. It is therefore of utility for both theoretical and applied purposes.

IV

Through a comparison of four Yucatan communities—Tusik, a "tribal" village of Quintana Roo; Chan Kom, a "peasant" community; Dzitas, a town on the railroad; and the city of Merida—Redfield concluded in his *The Folk Culture of Yucatan* (1941:339):

> . . . the peasant village as compared with the tribal village, the town as compared with the peasant village, or the city as compared with the town is less isolated, is more heterogeneous; is characterized by a more complex division of labor; has a more completely developed money economy; has professional specialists who are more secular and less sacred; has kinship and godparental institutions that are less well organized and less effective in social control; is correspondingly more dependent on impersonally acting institutions of control, is less religious, with respect to both beliefs and practices of Catholic origin as well as those of Indian origin; exhibits less tendency to regard sickness as resulting from a breach of moral or merely customary rule; allows a greater freedom of action and choice to the individual; and . . . shows a greater emphasis upon black magic as an ascribed cause of sickness.

Except as these differences relate to the regional culture of Yucatan they are also implied in the present taxonomy of subcultures, and it should be noted that six of the subculture types discussed above are carried by the local societies or by segments of the societies studied by Redfield in Yucatan. Thus, Merida would presumably contain subcultures of all three Metropolitan types. Dzitas seems to have both a Town and a Peasant type of subculture. Chan Kom, in our terms, would be a community with a Peasant subculture and [Tusik]* would be representative of our Modern Indian subculture. Although neglected by Redfield, Plantation subculture types are also present in the henequen-producing areas of Yucatan (Mintz 1953b:138). Tribal Indian subcultures, as defined above, are no longer present in the peninsula. Thus the present classification is clearly related to Redfield's folk-urban gradient. A fundamental difference exists, however. If the present taxonomy were to be used as the basis of a study of the urban-folk continuum in Latin America, the lines in the gradient would have to consist not of whole communities but of segments of whole communities. In this way one of the most serious defects in the use of the "folk culture" concept can be circumvented, for, as Lewis has shown for Tepoztlán (1951) the homogeneity of a rural community with respect to its folk characteristics is easily overemphasized when it is the whole local society which is the subject of characterization.

Redfield was primarily interested in culture change, especially the effects of modern urbanization upon "folk culture" and the resulting "disorganization of the culture, secularization, and individualization," to use his well-known terms. The primary purpose of the present taxonomy is not to analyze the direction and effects of culture change but to establish categories which may help to orient many additional problems. Many of the subculture types we have been describing are more or less stable features of the Latin American scene. Although individual settlements or large segments of their populations may change rapidly from carriers of one subculture type to another (e.g., "Indians" become "mestizos") and while new subculture types have appeared, most of these subculture types have been part of the cultural scene of Latin America since the sixteenth century. They have changed in culture content and in their relative importance to the wider cultural scene, but they have constantly maintained their distinctiveness as variations of Latin American culture and their essential relationship to one another.

Soon after 1500, when the distinctive culture of Latin America began to take form, at least Modern Indian, Peasant, Town, *Engenho* Plantation, and Metropolitan Upper-Class types were already present in the New World. The European conquerors brought with them a strong tradition of urbanism. In their European homelands there were cities, towns, and peasant villages. Large agrarian estates, similar in some ways to the New World plantations, were also present. Furthermore, as is well known, the native civilizations of America also had their cities, their market centers, and their villages and hamlets. The Europeans transplanted to the New World a culture which was already characterized by a number of subcultures analogous to those described for modern Latin America, but in the New World they were modified in content and in the form of interaction between them.

The Spanish and Portuguese (also the other nationals who controlled more limited areas of Latin America) who were given land grants, *encomiendas*, or other economic rights in the New World soon established a colonial aristocracy

* [Editor's note: In the original, the word "Dzitas" appeared here, although it was apparent from context that "Tusik" was intended; Wagley concurs in my interpretation.]

with its traditions derived from the feudal aristocratic patterns of their homeland. In the region of native American civilization, these colonial aristocrats supplanted the native ruling class, and in lowland Latin America they came to dominate the segmented tribal groups and became the owners of African slaves. Although only small numbers of European peasants came to the New World to work the land as they had done in Europe, a few did come, transposing their way of life almost intact. Before long, however, a distinctive Latin American Peasant subculture took form as the various tribal groups of the lowland region came under the influence of missionaries and colonial governments, lost their identity as autochthonous peoples and borrowed or had forced upon them European culture patterns. Under the impact of Spanish rule, the Indians of the highland regions acquired numerous Spanish culture patterns which fused with aboriginal patterns to form the subculture type called herein Modern Indian. The content of each of these subculture types differed, of course, from that of today, but those of 1600 were the historical antecedents of the contemporary types.

The transition of populations from one subculture type to another still goes on. The Tenetehara, a Tupí-speaking tribe of northern Brazil, for example, still have a culture which is essentially aboriginal and distinct from the culture of the Brazilian nation within the borders of which they happen to live. But the Tenetehara are slowly adopting Brazilian culture patterns; they are being brought into the orbit of the Brazilian commercial system through the sale of palm nuts and the increasing necessity to purchase imported and manufactured supplies (Wagley and Galvão 1949). The Tenetehara might now be classed as a Modern Indian subculture and, as the process of acculturation continues, they will lose their identity as "distinct people" and their culture will be transformed into that of a Peasant subculture of modern Brazil. Likewise, in Ecuador, Guatemala, Mexico, Peru, and other countries where there are large numbers of people living by Modern Indian subculture patterns, there is a noted trend for such Indians to adopt Peasant patterns (i.e., mestizo, Ladino, or *cholo* patterns) and to lose their identity as Indians. In many localities of Latin America both Indians and peasants are still being drawn upon as plantation workers, especially as communal forms of land tenure break down and as commercial agricultural enterprises expand their holdings. In other localities, many isolated areas inhabited by peasants are being connected with national markets by roads and other means of communication, and towns are taking form where a small local market place once existed. Under similar impulses, small towns are growing in size and in complexity to become veritable cities. And, as noted earlier, there is a continuing trend for family-owned *engenho*-type plantations to be welded into large industrialized *usina*-type plantations.

All Latin American subcultures are certainly changing under urban and industrial influences, and yet the differences between some of them may remain great for many years to come. The content of Peasant and Metropolitan subcultures in Europe has in both cases changed profoundly during the last five hundred years, but the differences between city folk and peasants in almost any European nation are still striking. In the future, certain subcultures may diminish in importance or entirely disappear as the people who carry them adopt other culture patterns. Tribal Indian subculture types will probably disappear well within the next hundred years, and *Engenho* Plantation types are becoming extinct with at least equal rapidity. Modern Indian types, on the other hand, especially where enlightened policies of government assistance prevail, are likely to endure for much longer. Barring wide political upheaval, Peasant, Town, *Usina* Plantation, and Metropolitan Upper-Class subculture types also appear to have long futures ahead of them, while the Metropolitan Middle-Class and Urban Proletariat types are just now beginning to emerge.

The changes in content which all these subculture types are undergoing are adequately embraced by the folk-urban transition suggested by Redfield. But any such picture of progressive urbanization must take into account the possibility that as the subculture types change toward greater urbanization, most of them do not merge in content, but remain as distinctly defined as ever within the national context. This is true because throughout all the stages of the urbanization of a nation, the city subcultures are not static but rather continue to be the innovators of most of the new features. Furthermore, although the rural-urban concept provides us with excellent hypotheses for the general direction of diffusion of new cultural items on a national scale, it does not prepare us for the problem of fundamental structural changes such as the emergence of new subcultures or the realignment of power. To describe the structure of a complex nation and the changes it is undergoing we need a taxonomy of parts such as that which has been tentatively developed in this paper. The emergence of new and the extinction of old sociocultural segments is an aspect of cultural change which the student of complex national cultures cannot afford to neglect.

NOTES

1. Our proposed taxonomy of Latin American subculture types and our general approach to the concept of national subcultures owe much to Julian Steward and his associates in the Puerto Rican project. The relationship between several of our subculture types and those distinguished in Puerto Rico will be indicated below.

2. Our *Engenho* Plantation type seems to correspond to the Coffee Hacienda subculture of Puerto Rico (cf. Steward 1953:98–100; Wolf 1951).

3. In tracing the development of a Puerto Rican sugar plantation, Mintz has distinguished three historical periods or types of sugar-cane plantations: the "slave-and-*agregado*," the "family-type hacienda," and the "corporate land-and-factory combine" (1953b). The first corresponds to our *engenho* plantation during slavery, the second to our *engenho* plantation after slavery, and the third to our *usina* plantation.

4. Hutchinson's study and the other studies carried out in Bahia State in Brazil which are cited below were part of the State of Bahia—Columbia University Research Program during which four community studies were carried out. Some of the data which made possible the distinction between the *engenho* plantation and the *usina* plantation were provided by Dr. Hutchinson.

5. A fourth community study was carried out later in southern Bahia State by Anthony Leeds, but sufficient data are not yet available to be used here. [Portions of this study have subsequently been published in various professional journals.]

6. A study of a working-class district is now being carried out by Thales de Azevedo of the University of Bahia, as a follow-up on our research. [This study has subsequently

been published as *Social Change in Brazil*, Latin American Monograph Series 22 (Gainesville, Fla.: University of Florida Press, 1963).]

7. This observation is based upon questionnaires devoted to family size and cohesiveness answered by upper-class urban residents in Salvador. It is confirmed by the data on the Metropolitan Upper-Class families of Vila Recôncavo.

REFERENCES CITED

Bunzel, Ruth

1952 *Chichicastenango: A Guatemalan Village*, Seattle, University of Washington Press.

Caplow, Theodore

1952 "The Modern Latin American City," in *Acculturation in the Americas*, Sol Tax, ed., pp. 255–260, Proceedings of the XXIX International Congress of Americanists, Chicago, University of Chicago Press.

Foster, George M.

1948 *Empire's Children: The People of Tzintzuntzan*, Smithsonian Institution, Institute of Social Anthropology Publication 6, Washington, D.C.

1953 "What Is Folk Culture?" *American Anthropologist* 55:159–173, Menasha.

Gillin, John

1947a *Moche: A Peruvian Coastal Community*, Smithsonian Institution, Institute of Social Anthropology Publication 3, Washington, D.C.

1947b "Modern Latin American Culture," *Social Forces* 25:3:243–248, Baltimore.

1951 *The Culture of Security in San Carlos: A Study of a Guatemalan Community of Indians and Ladinos*, New Orleans, Tulane University, Middle American Research Institute Publication 16.

Harris, Marvin

1953 *Minas Velhas: A Study of Urbanism in the Mountains of Eastern Brazil*, Ph.D. dissertation, Columbia University, New York. Ann Arbor, Mich., University Microfilm.

Hutchinson, Harry

1954 *Vila Recôncavo: A Brazilian Sugar-Cane Plantation Community*, Ph.D. dissertation, Columbia University, New York. Ann Arbor, Mich., University Microfilm.

La Farge, Oliver

1940 "Maya Ethnology: The Sequence of Cultures," in *The Maya and Their Neighbors*, pp. 281–291, New York, Appleton-Century Co.

Lewis, Oscar

1951 *Life in a Mexican Village: Tepoztlán Restudied*, Urbana, University of Illinois Press.

1952 "Urbanization without Breakdown: A Case Study," *The Scientific Monthly* 75:31–41.

Loomis, Charles P., and Reed M. Powell

1951 "Class Status in Rural Costa Rica: A Peasant Community Compared with a Hacienda Community," in *Materiales para el Estudio de la Clase Media en la América Latina*, Vol. 5, Washington, D.C., Pan American Union.

Manners, Robert

1950 *Culture and Agriculture in an Eastern Highland Community of Puerto Rico*, Ph.D. dissertation, Columbia University, New York. Ann Arbor, Mich., University Microfilm.

Métraux, Alfred

1951 *Making a Living in the Marbial Valley (Haiti)*, Paris, UNESCO.

Mintz, Sidney W.

1951 *Cañamelar: The Contemporary Culture of a Rural Puerto Rican Proletariat*, Ph.D. dissertation, Columbia University, New York. Ann Arbor, Mich., University Microfilm.

1953a "The Folk-Urban Continuum and the Rural Proletarian Community," *American Journal of Sociology* 59:2:136–143.

1953b "The Culture History of a Puerto Rican Sugar Cane Plantation, 1876–1949," *Hispanic American Historical Review* 33:2:224–251, Duke University Press.

Mishkin, Bernard

1946 "The Contemporary Quechua," in *Handbook of South American Indians*, Julian Steward, ed., Vol. II, 411–470, Smithsonian Institution, Bureau of American Ethnology Bulletin 143, Washington, D.C.

Padilla Seda, Elena

1951 *Nocora: An Agrarian Reform Sugar Community in Puerto Rico*, Ph.D. dissertation, Columbia University, New York. Ann Arbor, Mich., University Microfilm.

Pierson, Donald

1951 *Cruz das Almas: A Brazilian Village*, Smithsonian Institution, Institute of Social Anthropology Publication 12, Washington, D.C.

Redfield, Robert

1941 *The Folk Culture of Yucatan*, Chicago, University of Chicago Press.

Smith, T. Lynn

1946 *Brazil: People and Institutions*, Baton Rouge, Louisiana State University Press.

Steward, Julian

1950 *Area Research: Theory and Practice*, Social Science Research Council Bulletin 63, New York.

1953 "Culture Patterns of Puerto Rico," *Annals of the American Academy of Political and Social Science*, January, pp. 95–102, Philadelphia.

1956 *The People of Puerto Rico*, University of Illinois Press, Urbana.

Tax, Sol

1953 *Penny Capitalism: A Guatemalan Indian Economy*, Smithsonian Institution, Institute of Social Anthropology Publication 16, Washington, D.C.

Tschopik, Harry

1951 *The Aymara of Chucuito, Peru: I, Magic*, American Museum of Natural History Anthropological Paper, Vol. 44, Pt. 2, New York.

Villa Rojas, Alfonso

1945 *The Maya of East Central Quintana Roo*, Carnegie Institution of Washington Publication 559, Washington, D.C.

Wagley, Charles

1942 *The Economics of a Guatemalan Village*, American Anthropological Association Memoir 58, Menasha.

1948 "Regionalism and Cultural Unity in Brazil," *Social Forces* 26:457–464, Baltimore.

1950 *Social and Religious Life of a Guatemalan Village*, American Anthropological Association Memoir 71, Menasha.
1953 *Amazon Town: A Study of Man in the Tropics*, New York, Macmillan.

Wagley, Charles, and Eduardo Galvão
1949 *The Tenetehara Indians of Brazil*, New York, Columbia University Press.

Willems, Emilio
1947 *Cunha: tradição e transição em uma cultura rural do Brasil*, São Paulo, Secretaria da Agricultura do Estado de São Paulo.

Wolf, Eric
1951 *Culture Change and Culture Stability in a Puerto Rican Coffee Community*, Ph.D. dissertation, Columbia University, New York. Cambridge, Eagle Enterprises.

Zimmerman, Ben
1952 "Race Relations in the Arid Sertão," in *Race and Class in Rural Brazil*, Charles Wagley, ed., pp. 82–115, Paris, UNESCO.

Social Differentiation in Latin American Communities

FRANK W. YOUNG AND ISAO FUJIMOTO

One of the major problems in attempting to deal with such a large and diverse area as Latin America is that of comparison among individual communities that show unique local variations on common traits and themes. A typology based on cultural patterns, such as that of Wagley and Harris, is useful for description, but many kinds of analysis, and especially the testing of certain hypotheses, require some direct and uniform indices.

On the basis of a review of specific institutions as reported in more than fifty individual community studies, Young and Fujimoto have constructed a cumulative scale of social differentiation. The broad implications of such a scale, as it relates to theories of economic growth, cultural evolution, or other comparative concerns, reflect a cumulative potential of micro-level field research that is rarely realized.

Frank W. Young is Associate Professor of Rural Sociology and of Anthropology at Cornell University. He has supplemented field work on community structure and development in Mexico, Puerto Rico, and Nova Scotia with documentary studies of ritual, research methods, and cross-cultural regularities.

Isao Fujimoto is Professor of Behavioral Sciences at the University of California, Davis. His field work on applications of the differentiation concept in the Philippines is augmented by other research on agricultural development, Asian-Americans, and inter-ethnic relations.

From *Economic Development and Cultural Change* XIII (1965), 344–352. Copyright © 1965 by The University of Chicago. Reprinted by permission of the authors and publisher.

From the time that Redfield proposed his folk-urban typology to the more recent attempt[1] to characterize communities or their parts as Indian, peasant, town, and metropolitan, such classifications have implied a common denominator for the obvious cultural diversity of Latin American communities. Such generalization faces formidable difficulties, in addition to the general doubt that it is possible. It is clear that each community contains numerous subcultures. How can a classification that uses the community as a unit of analysis take them into account? A second problem is empirical. What kind of a sample of Latin American communities is possible? How can one demonstrate its representativeness?

Recent work on cumulative scales of social differentiation suggests a solution to these problems in terms of a scale based on data coded from available community studies. If all such studies are used in the sample, the claim can be made that there are no other cases to consider and that the results hold up to that point. Also, if the items used for the scale are institutions like the presence of a school, a doctor, etc., then the measure can be defended as applying to the whole community regardless of subcommunity variation. Finally, the choice of a formal concept like differentiation makes generalization possible. No matter what the particular patterns of a community, they can be analyzed in terms of the complexity dimension. It is along these lines that a cumulative scale of social differentiation for the 54 available community studies is proposed.

THE SAMPLE

A search through bibliographies, dissertation abstracts, book reviews in the major journals, and the *Handbook of Latin American Studies* turned up about 100 community descriptions. This list was quickly narrowed to about 70 when we excluded incomplete or inadequate accounts as judged by a length of less than 50 pages or an overly specialized treatment. Another reason for excluding accounts was that they dealt with only a part, usually the Indian sector, of the whole unit. Thus, Tax's study of Panajachel[2] could not be coded for this reason. At this point, we defined the universe as all autonomous communities that had not attained city status. The upper bound is admittedly vague and affected only a few cases. In general, the upper population limit is about 10,000 and the lower about 75. The criterion of autonomy required the rejection of studies of plantations and of subcommunities. An example of the latter is Fals-Borda's study of Saucío,[3] an outlying neighborhood, that could not be classified in terms of the community-level categories used in the study.

The resulting sample includes 54 communities.[4] It is probable that a more intensive search would unearth as many as 20 more usable cases, and eventually the sample will be so extended, but the present report covers most of the well-known studies. It will come as no surprise to learn that they are not randomly distributed as to countries. At least one community is located in each of 12 countries, as shown in Table 1, but Mexico and Guatemala are clearly over-represented when compared to the others. Communities from these two countries comprise 58 percent of the sample, and it might be more correct to say that this is the universe of Central American countries. But to repeat, that is all the data there are. Within Mexico, the communities are clustered according to

TABLE 1. Distribution of Community Sample by Country

Country	Proportion of sample
Brazil	11
Colombia	2
Costa Rica	4
Cuba	2
Ecuador	4
El Salvador	2
Guatemala	19
Mexico	39
Paraguay	2
Peru	11
Uruguay	2
Venezuela	2
	100
Total cases	(54)

well-known subregions. Several are located in Yucatan as a result of Redfield's studies; another cluster appears in Michoacan, where the Institute of Social Anthropology worked under the direction of Julian Steward; and the fact that the states of Oaxaca and Chiapas still have Indians accounts for two other clusters. The high concentration in Guatemala probably reflects a similar quest for relatively "untouched" Indian groups. Indeed, no less than 57 percent of the sample were estimated to have over half of the population still speaking a native language.

A CUMULATIVE SCALE OF DIFFERENTIATION

A number of studies[5] suggest the possibility that communities may be ordered on a single dimension of complexity or differentiation, but the immediate stimulus for this research was a field study of some 24 Mexican villages.[6] It was demonstrated there that the institutions of a community could be so ordered and that the resulting dimension is a powerful predictor of contact with urban centers and of general social change. Inasmuch as the kind of data required was simply the presence or absence of various institutions, it seemed feasible to use the secondary information of community studies. The feasibility of using data which, although crude, have the virtue of extensiveness, has been shown in the many studies that have made use of the Human Relations Area Files and in a more recent study by Kunkel[7] that specifically demonstrated the utility of 15 localities in Mexico.

The resulting scale is shown in Table 2. It consists of 14 steps, although the first is simply a threshhold item. The coefficient of scalability is .82, as measured by Menzel's[8] method that corrects for extreme marginals either for items or communities. Inasmuch as such extreme marginals are quite common, and in fact are usually desirable in object scales, it is important to use a measure of

TABLE 2. Scale of Differentiation for Latin American Communities

Step #	Item content	Proportion of sample	Scale error for items
1	Community is autonomous and has a name that is publicly recognized.	100	0
2	There is an elementary school.	93	0
3	Village has a public square or plaza.	85	1
4	Village has at least one government organization such as a branch of agriculture, health, welfare, police, telegraph, post office, etc.	83	2
5	There is a bar or cantina.	78	5
6	There is a bakery.	72	5
7	There is a barber shop.	59	4
8	There is a butcher shop or butchering place where meat can be bought regularly.	44	2
9	A priest resides in the village.	41	6
10	There is a hotel, inn, or place known to provide accommodation.	37	2
11	There is a pool hall or place where similar commercial recreation is available.	24	3
12	There is a doctor resident in the community.	15	3
13	There is a theater where movies are regularly shown.	13	1
14	There is a gas station.	9	0
	Coefficient of scalability = .82		

scalability that is not inflated by this tendency, as is the case for the coefficient of reproducibility.

Although a number of the items are commercial institutions (and these can be shown to form an equivalent, but more easily coded scale), the range is wide enough to justify the claim that the scale measures the over-all differentiation of the community. That is, if the diverse institutions of the community are considered in terms of whether they reflect greater or less differentiation, they form one dimension. It has long been doubted that the institutional categories so widely used in common speech and introductory sociology texts represent fundamental scientific categories, and this scale is evidence that the doubt has substance.

Of the 25 items that were coded, 11 did not fit the scale and were dropped. It is probable, however, that "grocery store," "restaurant," "secondary school," "church," "non-church organization," and "government official" were so vague that they could not be coded reliably. Three other items, "one or more telephones," "newspaper comes at least once a week," and "mass said at least once a year," involve quantifications that may or may not reflect the social realities of the community; in general, such quantitative items do not fit this type of scale. "Access to shipping service" and "passenger service" involve factors outside the community structure. Had we coded the actual use of such service, it might have scaled. We conclude, then, that the rejected items were technically deficient and do not require the rejection of the hypothesis underlying the differentiation scale.

This scale is only an index of the concept of differentiation, and therefore it should be possible to find other sets of items either of general differentiation, or of the differentiation of particular sectors, such as religious, political, or economic. This conclusion follows from the well-known fact of interchangeable indices and from the abstract nature of differentiation. This concept may be defined as the degree to which diverse areas of social meaning are publicly discriminated. That is, to the degree that separate sectors of the structure of meanings maintained by the community are institutionalized and made visible by symbol or artifact, there is social differentiation. This formulation is structural in the sense that it applies to the unit as a whole. Consequently, group-level indices must be sought; statistical aggregations of individuals or of families are either misleading or totally erroneous as indices.

A further implication of this scale is that it is incorrect to attempt to theorize about the concrete sequence. Interpretations along the lines of the need for a doctor to care for the wounds from fighting in a newly built pool hall are irrelevant, because all the items are simple indicators of differentiation. The real issue is what are the preconditions of high and low differentiation, but that question is beyond the scope of the present research.

Table 3 gives the scalogram for the 54 communities. Aside from its intrinsic interest in showing the rank of well-known communities, it permits the visualization of a number of other problems of this type of research. For instance, item

TABLE 3. Scalogram for General Differentiation Scale[a]

	Items (see Table 2 for content)													
Community	1	2	3	4	5	6	7	8	9	10	11	12	13	14
Bejucal	1	1	1	1	1	1	1	1	1	1	1	1	1	1
Turrialba	1	1	1	1	1	1	1	1	1	1	1	1	1	1
Quiroga	1	1	1	1	1	1	1	1	1	1	1	1	1	1
Bramon	1	1	0	1	1	1	1	1	0	1	1	1	1	1
Villa Reconcavo	1	1	1	1	1	1	1	1	0	0	1	1	1	0
Dzitas	1	1	1	1	1	1	1	1	0	1	1	1	1	0
Sayula	1	1	1	1	1	0	1	1	0	0	1	1	1	0
Chacaltianguis	1	1	1	1	1	1	1	1	1	1	1	1	1	0
Cunha	1	1	1	1	1	1	1	1	1	1	1	1	0	0
Cheran	1	1	1	1	1	1	1	1	1	1	1	2	0	0
Tepoztlan	1	1	1	1	1	1	1	1	1	1	1	2	0	0
Minas Velhas	1	1	1	1	1	1	0	1	1	1	1	2	0	0
Tobati	1	1	1	1	0	1	1	1	1	1	0	2	0	0
Huaylas	1	1	1	1	1	1	0	1	1	1	0	0	0	0
Mitla	1	1	1	1	1	1	1	1	1	1	0	0	0	0
Moche	1	1	1	1	1	1	1	1	1	0	0	2	1	0
Cantel	1	1	1	1	1	1	1	1	1	0	0	1	0	–
San Lorenzo de Quinti	1	1	1	1	1	1	1	1	1	0	0	2	0	0
El Palmar	1	1	1	1	1	1	–	1	1	–	0	2	0	0
Yalalag	1	1	1	1	1	1	1	1	1	0	0	2	0	0
Panchimalco	1	1	1	1	1	0	1	1	1	0	0	2	0	0
San Miquel Acatan	1	1	1	1	1	1	1	1	1	0	0	0	0	0

TABLE 3. (*Cont.*)

Community	Items (see Table 2 for content)													
	1	2	3	4	5	6	7	8	9	10	11	12	13	14
San Carlos	1	1	1	1	1	1	1	1	0	0	1	2	0	0
Oxchuc	1	1	1	1	1	0	1	1	0	0	–	0	0	0
Aguacatan	1	1	1	1	1	1	1	1	0	0	0	2	0	0
San Pedro La Laguna	1	1	1	1	1	1	1	1	0	0	0	0	0	0
Cruz das Almas	1	1	1	1	1	1	0	1	0	0	0	0	0	0
Muquiyauyo	1	1	1	1	0	1	1	1	0	0	0	2	0	0
Teotitlan del Valle	1	1	1	1	1	1	1	1	0	0	0	2	0	0
Atzompa	1	1	1	–	1	0	1	1	0	0	0	0	0	0
Ita	1	1	1	1	1	1	1	0	0	0	0	1	0	0
Potam	1	1	1	1	0	1	1	0	0	0	1	1	0	0
Tzintzuntzan	1	1	1	1	1	1	0	0	1	0	0	2	0	0
San Juan Sur	1	1	1	1	1	1	0	0	0	0	0	0	0	0
Cancuc	1	1	1	1	1	0	0	1	0	0	0	0	0	0
Aritama	1	1	1	1	1	0	0	0	1	0	1	0	0	0
San Antonio Palopo	1	1	1	1	1	0	0	1	0	0	0	0	0	0
Chamula	1	1	1	1	1	0	0	0	0	0	0	0	0	0
Chinaulta	1	1	–	1	1	0	0	0	0	0	0	2	0	0
Sta. Catarina Palopo	1	1	1	1	1	0	0	0	0	0	0	2	0	0
Peguche	1	1	1	0	1	0	0	0	0	0	0	2	0	0
Recuayhuanca	1	1	1	1	0	0	0	0	0	0	0	0	0	0
Amatenango del Valle	1	1	1	1	0	0	0	0	0	0	0	2	0	0
Santiago Chimaltenango	1	1	1	1	0	0	0	0	0	0	0	0	0	0
Chan Kom	1	1	1	1	0	0	1	0	0	0	0	2	0	0
Todos Santos Cuchumatan	1	1	1	1	0	0	0	0	0	0	0	0	0	0
Hualcan	1	1	1	0	0	0	0	0	0	0	0	0	0	0
Canas (del Tacuarembo)	1	1	0	0	1	0	0	0	0	0	0	2	0	0
Santa Cruz Etla	1	1	0	0	0	1	0	0	0	0	0	0	0	0
Soteapan	1	–	0	0	1	0	0	–	0	0	0	0	0	0
El Nacimiento	1	0	–	0	0	0	0	0	0	0	0	2	0	0
Punyaro	1	0	0	1	0	0	0	0	0	0	0	2	0	0
Buzios Island	1	0	0	0	0	0	0	0	0	0	0	2	0	0
Tusik	1	0	0	0	0	0	0	0	0	0	0	0	0	0

[a] Code: 1—present within community; 2—not present in community, but service is readily accessible and regularly used; 0—absent.

12, the presence of a doctor in the community, has in addition to the digits for present and absent, some "2's." These indicate a situation in between that of present or absent in the community, namely, not present in the community but readily accessible and actively used. We introduced this category in this case in order to explore a problem that frequently arose. A small community might not have a local service, but the service may be readily available. The consolidated school is the obvious example. Should an elementary school be considered absent even though a school bus takes children to central school? In the case of the doctor in these Latin American communities it appears that ready access to a doctor is equivalent, from the point of view of the optimal scale patterning, to absence. However, this one test does not settle the issue; it might very well be that a doctor in another town is tantamount to absence in countries where transportation is poor, but equivalent to institutional presence in places where the idea of modern medicine is taken for granted and transportation is easy. The problem requires larger samples with more cases of modern communities for its adequate solution.

Another point about this particular item, presence of a doctor, is that it discriminates only one place, Cunha. Normally, such slight discrimination power would lead to its exclusion, but it was retained here in the thought that larger samples may find it a useful discrimination item.

The scalogram has dashes where data were lacking, and these were disregarded in the calculation of the coefficient of scalability. A more delicate problem is the interpretation of an "error." In general, we evaluated errors in terms of probability. Thus, the presence of a barber shop in Chan Kom is most probably an error, in the sense that chance factors account for the barber shop being out of sequence. When an item may be interpreted as erroneous or correct with equal probability, as in the case of Peguche, we took the zero to be an error, because in these accounts it is more difficult to be sure about the absence of an institution than about the presence.

A number of variables are correlated with the scale and serve to validate it. Population size correlates .44, using Kendall's measure of rank correlation. The number of grades in the school bears a relationship of .62 and the number of stores, .60. The estimated proportion of adults in non-agricultural work correlates .41 with differentiation. The proportion of Indians in the community correlates −.24 and is significant at the 5 percent level, although this measure was not expected to correlate and is only tenuously interpretable as differentiation.

DIFFERENTIATION AND THE ECONOMIC THEORY OF GROWTH

If differentiation is a general dimension that applies equally to all institutional sectors, any relationship between the differentiation within two given sectors should be tautological. Thus, assertions about economic factors leading to social change, or religious factors leading to economic change, may be true only because they reflect the same underlying variable. An illustration of what is probably a tautology of this type is contained in the previously mentioned study by John Kunkel. His hypothesis is that "as small agricultural, economically autonomous villages begin to participate in the economic system of the nation, their social organization becomes consistent with that of the nation."[9] He defines economic participation in terms of what is almost a cumulative scale of the following five attributes: staple foods are imported; external wage labor is present; sufficient land is not available; there is internal wage labor and the use of cash; and a cash crop is exported. Congruency of the local social organization with that of the nation is measured by a ratio based on 12 items. A few of these will be sufficient to indicate their nature: there is no definite hierarchy of political offices, or there is one through which all villagers are expected to pass in their lifetimes; political officials are paid, or they are not; there is no compulsory communal labor, or there is; land may be sold to anyone, or the sale of land is restricted to fellow-villagers only; the extended family is relatively unimportant, or it is important; etc.

When we attempted to code these items for all 54 communities, we encountered the usual difficulties of replication. Consequently, we rephrased the items slightly in order to make them more precise. For instance, compulsory communal labor was specified as being supported by sanctions, in contrast to occasional cooperative efforts with no sanctions. However, it was still impossible to code reliably some attributes that called for judgments of what was "significant" or items that were ambiguous when applied to the larger sample. Therefore, we dropped four of the social characteristics: the importance of the extended family, the stability of marriages, the importance of ritual kinship, the economic level of those chosen in ritual kinship. Thus, the ratios were computed for five economic items and eight social attributes, with appropriate adjustments to the base when data were lacking. The resulting correlation of economic participation and social congruence with the nation is .33, which confirms Kunkel's finding.

However, the very statement of Kunkel's hypothesis, as well as the similarity in the content of the economic and social items, suggests that the relationship is essentially tautological and that the two measures are tapping an underlying dimension of general differentiation. Of course, a correlation of .33 is low if two variables are essentially one, but given the problems of measurement, such a result is not too surprising. If Kunkel's relationship is tautological, it should be dissolved by controlling on general differentiation. The outcome would be analogous to dissolving a correlation between income and social participation by controlling on a more general measure of status, such as style of life. The more general measure subsumes the first two, and this fact shows up as a reduction of the original correlation. In the present case, Kendall's method of partial rank correlation may be applied, with the result that the original relationship between Kunkel's economic participation and social congruence reduces from .33 to .25 when the effect of differentiation is partialled out. However, such an amount is too small to support the hypothesis. Similarly, there is only a small reduction (from the original .76 to .67) when 14 of the original 15 Mexican cases in Kunkel's sample are used. Thus, in both the original and the general sample, Kunkel's variable of economic participation predicts social congruence of the small community with national customs independently of the effect of general differentiation.

However, it may be that Kunkel's two variables are still aspects of one dimension, but that the dimension is not differentiation. Inspection of the items suggests that they could also be interpreted as reflecting the "closed, corporate" community structure that Wolf has described.[10] The hierarchy of religious offices, the restrictions on selling land, and the strong influence of other traditional ways suggest that economic and social autonomy are both aspects of a strongly traditional, rigid social structure. On this hypothesis, we partialled out the influence of the proportion of the community who still spoke an Indian language, with the result that the correlation between economic and social participation dropped from the original .33 to .30, an insignificant amount. This is so despite a correlation of −.38 between Kunkel's social variable and

Indianism. It may be that the proportion who speaks an Indian language is not a sensitive indicator of closed corporate structure, or perhaps that Kunkel's measures are actually very direct measures of rigidity, but only more analysis with new data will decide those possibilities.

A more positive outcome is that differentiation is a strong and independent predictor of Kunkel's measure of social congruence. The relationship is .50, as compared to .33 obtained with the economic participation measure. Moreover, when economic participation is partialled out, the original relationship holds at .46. Finally, differentiation even predicts economic participation to the extent of a .25 correlation, which, if the sample is assumed to be random, is significant at the .05 level.

Despite our lack of success in subsuming Kunkel's economic and social factors by differentiation, we believe the approach may still apply in other cases. For instance, the many studies of national growth using indicators such as urbanism, industrialization, mass media use, voting, telephones per capita, etc., seem to be open to this interpretation. In short, the trouble with many neo-Marxian interpretations of development may be that they are too true, that economic factors predict social forms, because fundamentally they reflect the same structural dimension.

THE PROCESS OF SOCIAL DIFFERENTIATION

As previously stated, the explanation of change in differentiation is outside the scope of this research. It is probable that such change is a function of the interrelations of communities, and these with the national structure, and the data for the relevant variables is not contained in community studies. But within the purview of the investigation, there is a challenging question: does the scale indicate that communities actually develop in this cumulative manner?

The question is sharpened by remembering that if any considerable number of these 54 communities had taken a different sequence in the course of their development, then it is probable that such an alternative sequence would have shown up on the scalogram as scale error. Of course, a community might have progressed up the scale and then retrogressed to the particular scale step for which it was coded without showing scale error, or, indeed, it might have moved up and down several times; but this does not reduce the force of the generalization that there is one sequence of growth through which all these communities had to have passed at least once.

What alternatives are there? A community might have developed all its institutional levels, as they are reflected in the scale, simultaneously. The creation of "new towns" is increasingly frequent in the modern world, but certainly none of these communities is such a new place. And even if it were, the fact that all the scale items were created simultaneously so that the community fits the cumulative pattern is all the more remarkable. Another possibility is that one institution, say, a movie theater, developed, and its presence created pressure for supporting institutions, which were then quickly created. The scale evidence does not negate such a phenomenon if it was not too frequent. But if many villages were rushing ahead and then, so to speak, bringing up their institutional rears later, these gaps should show up as scale error. It is possible, for instance, that the barber shop in Chan Kom is such a case, and that the intervening institutions, a bar and a bakery, developed very quickly afterwards. But too many such cases would have made it impossible to have found a scale.

Still another possibility is that there are waves of social change and that at any one time the institutions form a cumulative sequence, interpretable, however, only as a measure of complexity and not of actual change over time. This view reminds us that the actual items of the scale are simply indicators of levels of complexity and are not necessarily the actual components of change. Therefore, at best the scale suggests a rather abstract sequence of differentiation levels through which communities pass over time, but once the variable is seen in this light, it is equally easy to see it more conservatively, as simply a measure of complexity at any one time. It is true that this conservative view of the meaning of the scale implies a more radical interpretation of social change: evidently it is possible to reshuffle the concrete indicators of differentiation without changing the fact that communities may always be ranked on such a dimension. That is, major jumps in development may completely reorganize the concrete indicators of differentiation without altering their underlying cumulative patterning.

Whether or not scales of differentiation reflect evolution, revolution, or both, there is clearly a need for field studies of the process of differentiation. The fact that the institutions used in the scale are quite visible and easily remembered makes it possible to construct scales at earlier points in time, so that before-and-after comparisons are feasible. Even more important, the advent of each institution could be pinpointed in time and the sequence of growth examined. As a counterpoint to comparative studies based on available data, a field study of a single community could be a more valuable and pertinent probe.

NOTES

This research was financed by Cornell University's Latin American Studies Program and the International Agricultural Development Program. Stephen Denner and John Rowley ably assisted in coding the data.

1. See Charles Wagley and Marvin Harris, "A Typology of Latin American Subcultures," *American Anthropologist*, LVII (June 1955), 428–51, for the recent typology, as well as comments on Redfield's work.

2. Sol Tax, *Penny Capitalism: A Guatemalan Indian Economy*, Institute of Social Anthropology Publication 16 (Washington, D.C.: Smithsonian Institution, 1953).

3. Orlando Fals-Borda, *Peasant Society in the Colombian Andes: A Sociological Study of Saucio* (Gainesville: University of Florida Press, 1955).

4. A complete bibliography is available on request.

5. Perhaps the earliest of this genre is Edward Hassinger's "The Relationship of Retail-Service Patterns to Trade-Center Population Change," *Rural Sociology*, XXII (September 1957), 235–40. The work of L. C. Freeman and R. F. Winch, "Societal Complexity: An Empirical Test of a Typology of Societies," *American Journal of Sociology*, LXII (March 1957), 461–66, demonstrated the cross-cultural feasibility of the approach.

6. Frank W. Young and Ruth C. Young, "Social Integration and Change in Twenty-four Mexican Villages," *Economic Development and Culture Change,* VIII (July 1960), 366–77.
7. John H. Kunkel, "Economic Autonomy and Social Change in Mexican Villages," *Economic Development and Cultural Change,* X (October 1961), 51–63.
8. Herbert Menzel, "A New Coefficient for Scalogram Analysis," *Public Opinion Quarterly,* XVII (September 1953), 268–80.
9. Kunkel, *op. cit.,* p. 55.
10. Eric R. Wolf, "Types of Latin American Peasantry: A Preliminary Discussion," *American Anthropologist,* LVII (June 1955), 452–71.

Aspects of Group Relations in a Complex Society: Mexico

ERIC R. WOLF

In a sense, this paper represents an intellectual cornerstone of this book, because Wolf here provides a way of dealing with local institutions and small communities in relation to larger systems in complex nation-states. Although he illustrates his approach in terms of a brief analysis of the social history of Mexico, his spotlighting of "brokers" as key individuals or groups who ". . . stand guard over the crucial junctures or synapses of relationships which connect the local system to the larger whole" has set the direction of much of the anthropological work that has been done since this paper was written.

Eric R. Wolf is Distinguished Professor of Anthropology at Herbert H. Lehman College of the City University of New York. He has done field work in Europe as well as Latin America, and many of his writings are broadly comparative. His major books are Sons of the Shaking Earth (1959), Anthropology (1964), Peasants (1966), Peasant Wars of the Twentieth Century (1969), *and, jointly,* The Human Condition in Latin America (1972).

I

Starting from simple beginnings in the twenties, anthropologists have grown increasingly sophisticated about the relationship of nation and community. First, they studied the community in its own terms, taking but little account of its larger matrix. Later, they began to describe "outside factors" which affected the life of the local group under study. Recently they have come to recognize that nations or "systems of the higher level do not consist merely of more numerous and diversified parts," and that it is therefore "methodologically

---

From *American Anthropologist* LVIII (1956), 1065–1078. By permission of the author and publisher.

incorrect to treat each part as though it were an independent whole in itself" (Steward 1950:107). Communities are "modified and acquire new characteristics because of their functional dependence upon a new and larger system" (*ibid.* 111). The present paper is concerned with a continuation of this anthropological discussion in terms of Mexican material.[1]

The dependence of communities on a larger system has affected them in two ways. On the one hand, whole communities have come to play specialized parts within the larger whole. On the other, special functions pertaining to the whole have become the tasks of special groups within communities. These groups Steward calls horizontal sociocultural segments. I shall simply call them nation-oriented groups. They are usually found in more than one community and follow ways of life different from those of their community-oriented fellow villagers. They are often the agents of the great national institutions which reach down into the community, and form "the bones, nerves and sinews running through the total society, binding it together, and affecting it at every point" (*ibid.* 115). Communities which form parts of a complex society can thus be viewed no longer as self-contained and integrated systems in their own right. It is more appropriate to view them as the local termini of a web of group relations which extend through intermediate levels from the level of the community to that of the nation. In the community itself, these relationships may be wholly tangential to each other.

Forced to understand the community in terms of forces impinging on it from the outside, we have also found it necessary to gain a better understanding of national-level institutions. Yet to date most anthropologists have hesitated to commit themselves to such a study, even when they have become half convinced that such a step would be desirable. National institutions seem so complex that even a small measure of competence in their operations seems to require full-time specialization. We have therefore left their description and analysis to specialists in other disciplines. Yet the specialists in law, politics, or economics have themselves discovered that anthropologists can be of almost as much use to them as they can be to the anthropologist. For they have become increasingly aware that the legal, political or other systems to which they devote their attention are not closed systems either, but possess social and cultural dimensions which cannot be understood in purely institutional terms. They have discovered that they must pay attention to shifting group relationships and interests if their studies are to reflect this other dimension of institutional "reality." This is hardly surprising if we consider that institutions are ultimately but cultural patterns for group relationships. Their complex forms allow groups to relate themselves to each other in the multiple processes of conflict and accommodation which must characterize any complex society. They furnish the forms through which some nation-oriented groups may manipulate other nation-oriented or community-oriented groups. The complex apparatus of such institutions is indeed a subject for specialists, but anthropologists may properly attempt to assess some of their functions.

If the communities of a complex system such as Mexico represent but the local termini of group relationships which go beyond the community level, we cannot hope to construct a model of how the larger society operates by simply adding more community studies. Mexico—or any complex system—is more than the arithmetic sum of its constituent communities. It is also more than the sum of its national-level institutions, or the sum of all the communities and national-level institutions taken together. From the point of view of this paper, it is rather the web of group relationships which connect localities and national-level institutions. The focus of study is not communities or institutions, but groups of people.

In dealing with the group relationships of a complex society, we cannot neglect to underline the fact that the exercise of power by some people over others enters into all of them, on all levels of integration. Certain economic and political relationships are crucial to the functioning of any complex society. No matter what other functions such a society may contain or elaborate, it must both produce surpluses and exercise power to transfer a part of these surpluses from the producing communities to people other than the producers. No matter what combination of cultural forms such a society may utilize, it must also wield power to limit the autonomy of its constituent communities and to interfere in their affairs. This means that all interpersonal and intergroup relationships of such a society must at some point conform to the dictates of economic or political power. Let it be said again, however, that these dictates of power are but aspects of group relationships, mediated in this case through the forms of an economic or political apparatus.

Finally, we must be aware that a web of group relationships implies a historical dimension. Group relationships involve conflict and accommodation, integration and disintegration, processes which take place over time. And just as Mexico in its synchronic aspect is a web of group relationships with termini in both communities and national-level institutions, so it is also more in its diachronic aspect than a sum of the histories of these termini. Local histories are important, as are the histories of national-level institutions, but they are not enough. They are but local or institutional manifestations of group relations in continuous change.

In this paper, then, we shall deal with the relations of community-oriented and nation-oriented groups which characterize Mexico as a whole. We shall emphasize the economic and political aspects of these relationships, and we shall stress their historical dimension, their present as a rearrangement of their past, and their past as a determinant of their present.

II

From the beginning of Spanish rule in Mexico, we confront a society riven by group conflicts for economic and political control. The Spanish Crown sought to limit the economic and political autonomy of the military entrepreneurs who had conquered the country in its name. It hoped to convert the conquistadores into town dwellers, not directly involved in the process of production on the community level but dependent rather on carefully graded handouts by the Crown. They were to have no roots in local communities, but to depend directly on a group of officials operating at the level of the nation. The strategic cultural form selected for this purpose was the *encomienda,* in which the recipient received rights to a specified amount of Indian tribute and services, but was not permitted to organize his own labor force nor to settle in Indian towns. Both control of Indian labor and the allocation of tribute payments were to remain in the hands of royal bureaucrats (Simpson 1950: esp. 123, 144; Zavala 1940).

To this end, the Crown encouraged the organization of the Indian population into compact communities with self-rule over their own affairs, subject to supervision and interference at the hands of royal officials (Zavala and Miranda 1954:75–79). Many of the cultural forms of this community organization are pre-Hispanic in origin, but they were generally repatterned and charged with new functions. We must remember that the Indian sector of society underwent a serious reduction in social complexity during the sixteenth and seventeenth centuries. The Indians lost some of their best lands and water supply, as well as the larger part of their population. As a result of this social cataclysm, as well as of government policy, the repatterned Indian community emerged as something qualitatively new: a corporate organization of a local group inhabited by peasants (Wolf 1955a:456–461). Each community was granted a legal charter and communal lands (Zavala and Miranda 1954:70); equipped with a communal treasury (*ibid.* 87–88; Chávez Orozco 1943:23–24) and administrative center (Zavala and Miranda 1954:80–82); and connected with one of the newly established churches. It was charged with the autonomous enforcement of social control, and with the payment of dues (*ibid.* 82).

Thus equipped to function in terms of their own resources, these communities became in the centuries after the Conquest veritable redoubts of cultural homeostasis. Communal jurisdiction over land, obligations to expend surplus funds in religious ceremonies, negative attitudes toward personal display of wealth and self-assertion, strong defenses against deviant behavior, all served to emphasize social and cultural homogeneity and to reduce tendencies toward the development of internal class differences and heterogeneity in behavior and interests. The taboo on sales of land to outsiders and the tendency toward endogamy made it difficult for outsiders to gain footholds in these villages (Redfield and Tax 1952; Wolf 1955a:457–461).

At the same time, the Crown failed in its attempt to change the Spanish conquerors into passive dependents of royal favors (Miranda 1947). Supported by large retinues of clients (such as *criados, deudos, allegados, paniaguados,* cf. Chevalier 1952:33–38), the colonists increasingly wrested control of the crucial economic and political relationships from the hands of the royal bureaucracy. Most significantly, they developed their own labor force, in contravention of royal command and independently of the Indian communities. They bought Indian and Negro slaves; they attracted to their embryonic enterprises poor whites who had come off second best in the distribution of conquered riches; and they furnished asylum to Indians who were willing to pay the price of acculturation and personal obligation to a Spanish entrepreneur for freedom from the increasingly narrow life of the encysting Indian communities. By the end of the eighteenth century, the colonist enterprises had achieved substantial independence of the Crown in most economic, political, legal, and even military matters. Power thus passed from the hands of the Crown into the hands of local rulers who interposed themselves effectively between nation and community. Effective power to enforce political and economic decisions contrary to the interest of these power holders was not returned to the national level until the victory of the Mexican Revolution of 1910 (Wolf 1955b:193–195).

Alongside the Indian villages and the entrepreneurial communities located near haciendas, mines, or mills, there developed loosely structured settlements of casual farmers and workers, middlemen and "*lumpen*-proletarians" who had no legal place in the colonial order. Colonial records tended to ignore them except when they came into overt conflict with the law. Their symbol in Mexican literature is *El Periquillo Sarmiento*, the man who lives by his wits (cf. Yañez 1945:60–94). "Conceived in violence and without joy, born into the world in sorrow" (Benítez 1947:47), the very marginality of their origins and social position forced them to develop patterns of behavior adapted to a life unstructured by formal law. They were thus well fitted to take charge of the crucial economic and political relationships of the society at a time when social and cultural change began to break down the barriers between statuses and put a premium on individuals and groups able to rise above their traditional stations through manipulation of social ties and improvisation upon them.

The transfer of power from the national level to the intermediate power holders, and the abolition of laws protecting the Indian communities—both accomplished when Mexico gained its independence from Spain (Chávez Orozco 1943:35–47)—produced a new constellation of relationships among Indian communities, colonist entrepreneurs, and "marginals." The colonists' enterprises, and chief among them the hacienda, began to encroach more and more heavily on the Indian communities. At the same time, the Indian communities increasingly faced the twin threats of internal differentiation and of invasion from the outside by the "marginals" of colonial times.

Despite the transcendent importance of the hacienda in Mexican life, anthropologists have paid little attention to this cultural form. To date we do not have a single anthropological or sociological study of a Mexican hacienda or hacienda community. Recent historical research has shown that the hacienda is not an offspring of the *encomienda* (Zavala 1940; 1944). The *encomienda* always remained a form of royal control. The hacienda, however, proved admirably adapted to the purposes of the colonists who strove for greater autonomy. Unlike the *encomienda*, it granted direct ownership of land to a manager-owner, and permitted direct control of a resident labor force. From the beginning, it served commercial ends (Bazant 1950). Its principal function was to convert community-oriented peasants into a disciplined labor force able to produce cash crops for a supra-community market. The social relationships through which this was accomplished involved a series of voluntary or forced transactions in which the worker abdicated much personal autonomy in exchange for heightened social and economic security.

Many observers have stressed the voracity of the hacienda for land and labor. Its appetite for these two factors of production was great indeed, and yet ultimately limited by its very structure. First, the hacienda always lacked capital. It thus tended to farm only the best land (Gruening 1928:134; Tannenbaum 1929:121–122), and relied heavily on the traditional technology of its labor force (Simpson 1937:490). Hacienda owners also curtailed production in order to raise land rent and prices, and to keep down wages (Gama 1931:21).

Thus "Mexico has been a land of large estates, but not a nation of large-scale agriculture" (Martínez de Alba, quoted in Simpson 1937:490). Second, the hacienda was always limited by available demand (Chávez Orozco 1950:19), which in a country with a largely self-sufficient population was always small. What the hacienda owner lacked in capital, however, he made up in the exercise of power over people. He tended to "monopolize land that he might monopolize labor" (Gruening 1928:134). But here again the hacienda encountered limits to its expansion. Even with intensive farming of its core lands and lavish use of gardeners and torch bearers, it reached a point where its mechanisms of control could no longer cope with the surplus of population nominally under its domination. At this point the haciendas ceased to grow, allowing Indian communities like Tepoztlán (Lewis 1951:xxv) or the Sierra and Lake Tarascan villages (West 1948:17) to survive on their fringes. Most hacienda workers did not live on the haciendas; they were generally residents of nearby communities who had lost their land, and exchanged their labor for the right to farm a subsistence plot on hacienda lands (Aguirre and Pozas 1954:202–203). Similarly, only in the arid and sparsely populated North did large haciendas predominate. In the heavily populated central region, Mexico's core area, large haciendas were the exception and the "medium-size" hacienda of about 3,000 ha. was the norm (*ibid.* 201; also Simpson 1937:489).

I should even go so far as to assert that once the haciendas reached the apex of their growth within a given area, they began to add to the defensive capacity of the corporately organized communities of Indian peasantry rather than to detract from it. Their major innovation lay in the field of labor organization and not in the field of technology. Their tenants continued to farm substantial land areas by traditional means (Aguirre and Pozas 1954:201; Whetten 1948:105) and the hacienda did not generally interfere in village affairs except when these came into conflict with its interests. The very threat of a hacienda's presence unified the villagers on its fringes in ways which would have been impossible in its absence. A hacienda owner also resented outside interference with "his" Indians, whether these lived inside or outside his property, and outsiders were allowed to operate in the communities only "by his leave." He thus often acted as a buffer between the Indian communities and nation-oriented groups, a role similar to that played by the hacienda owner in the northern highlands of Peru (Mangin 1955). Periodic work on the haciendas further provided the villagers with opportunities, however small, to maintain aspects of their lives which required small outlays of cash and goods, such as their festive patterns, and thus tended to preserve traditional cultural forms and functions which might otherwise have fallen into disuse (Aguirre and Pozas 1954:221; Wolf 1953:161).

Where corporate peasant communities were ultimately able to establish relations of hostile symbiosis with the haciendas, they confronted other pressures toward dissolution. These pressures came both from within and without the villages, and aimed at the abolition of communal jurisdiction over land. They sought to replace communal jurisdiction with private property in land, that is, to convert village land into a commodity. Like any commodity, land was to become an object to be bought, sold, and used not according to the common understandings of community-oriented groups, but according to the interests of nation-oriented groups outside the community. In some corporate communities outsiders were able to become landowners by buying land or taking land as security on unpaid loans, e.g., in the Tarascan area (Carrasco 1952:17). Typically, these outsiders belonged to the strata of the population which during colonial times had occupied a marginal position, but which exerted increased pressure for wealth, mobility and social recognition during the nineteenth century. Unable to break the monopoly which the haciendas exercised over the best land, they followed the line of least resistance and established beachheads in the Indian communities (Molina Enríquez 1909:53). They were aided in their endeavors by laws designed to break up the holdings of so-called corporations, which included the lands of the Church and the communal holdings of the Indians.

But even where outsiders were barred from acquiring village lands, the best land of the communities tended to pass into private ownership, this time of members of the community itself (Gama 1931:10–11). Important in this change seems to have been the spread of plow culture and oxen which required some capital investment, coupled with the development of wage labor on such holdings and increasing production for a supra-community market. As Oscar Lewis has so well shown for Tepoztlán, once private ownership in land allied to plow culture is established in at least part of the community, the community tends to differentiate into a series of social groups, with different technologies, patterns of work, interests, and thus with different supra-community relationships (Lewis 1951:129–157). This tendency has proceeded at different rates in different parts of Mexico. It has not yet run its course where land constitutes a poor investment risk, or where a favorable man-land ratio makes private property in land nonfunctional, as among the Popoluca of Sayula in Veracruz (Guiteras-Holmes 1952:37–40). Elsewhere it was complete at the end of the nineteenth century.

The Mexican Revolution of 1910 destroyed both the cultural form of the hacienda and the social relationships which were mediated through it. It did so in part because the hacienda was a self-limiting economic system, incapable of further expansion. It did so in part because the hacienda prevented the geographic mobility of a large part of Mexico's population. The end of debt bondage, for example, has permitted or forced large numbers of people to leave their local communities and to seek new opportunities elsewhere. It did so, finally, because the hacienda blocked the channels of social and cultural mobility and communication from nation to community, and tended to atomize the power of the central government. By destroying its power, the Revolution reopened channels of relationship from the communities to the national level, and permitted new circulation of individuals and groups through the various levels (Iturriaga 1951:66).

The new power holders have moved upwards mainly through political channels, and the major means of consolidating and obtaining power in the regional and national level in Mexico today appear to be political. Moreover—and due perhaps in part to the lack of capital in the Mexican economy as a whole—political advantages are necessary to obtain economic advantages. Both economic and political interests must aim at the establishment of monopolistic positions within defined areas of crucial economic and political relationships.

Thus political and economic power seekers tend to meet in alliances and cliques on all levels of the society.

The main formal organization through which their interests are mediated is the government party, the Revolutionary Institutional Party or, as someone has said, "the Revolution as an institution" (Lee 1954:300). This party contains not only groups formally defined as political, but also occupational and other special-interest groups. It is a political holding company representing different group interests (Scott 1955:4). Its major function is to establish channels of communication and mobility from the local community to the central power group at the helm of the government. Individuals who can gain control of the local termini of these channels can now rise to positions of power in the national economy or political machine.

Some of the prerequisites for this new mobility are purely economic. The possession of some wealth, or access to sources of wealth, is important; more important, however, is the ability to adopt the proper patterns of public behavior. These are the patterns of behavior developed by the "marginal" groups of colonial times which have now become the ideal behavior patterns of the nation-oriented person. An individual who seeks power and recognition outside his local community must shape his behavior to fit these new expectations. He must learn to operate in an arena of continuously changing friendships and alliances, which form and dissolve with the appearance or disappearance of new economic or political opportunities. In other words, he must learn to function in terms which characterize any complex stratified society in which individuals can improve their status through the judicious manipulation of social ties. However, this manipulative behavior is always patterned culturally—and patterned differently in Mexico than in the United States or India. He must therefore learn also the cultural forms in which this manipulative behavior is couched. Individuals who are able to operate both in terms of community-oriented and nation-oriented expectations then tend to be selected out for mobility. They become the economic and political "brokers" of nation-community relations, a function which carries its own rewards.

The rise of such politician-entrepreneurs, however, has of necessity produced new problems for the central power. The Spanish Crown had to cope with the ever-growing autonomy of the colonists; the central government of the Republic must similarly check the propensity of political power seekers to free themselves of government control by cornering economic advantages. Once wealthy in their own right, these nation-community "brokers" would soon be independent of government favors and rewards. The Crown placed a check on the colonists by balancing their localized power over bailiwicks with the concentrated power of a corps of royal officials in charge of the corporate Indian communities. Similarly, the government of the Republic must seek to balance the community-derived power of its political "brokers" with the power of other power holders. In modern Mexico, these competing power holders are the leaders of the labor unions—especially of the labor unions in the nationalized industries—and of the *ejidos*, the groups in local communities who have received land grants in accordance with the agrarian laws growing out of the 1910 Revolution.

Leaving aside a discussion of the labor unions due to limitations of time and personal knowledge, I should like to underline the importance of the *ejido* grants as a nation-wide institution. They now include more than 30 per cent of the people in Mexican localities with a population below 10,000 (Whetten 1948:186). A few of these, located in well-irrigated and highly capitalized areas, have proved an economic as well as a political success (*ibid.* 215). The remainder, however, must be regarded as political instruments rather than as economic ones. They are political assets because they have brought under government control large numbers of people who depend ultimately on the government for their livelihood. Agrarian reform has, however, produced social and political changes without concomitant changes in the technological order; the redistribution of land alone can neither change the technology nor supply needed credit (Aguirre and Pozas 1954:207–208; Pozas 1952:316).

At the same time, the Revolution has intensified the tendencies toward further internal differentiation of statuses and interests in the communities, and thus served to reduce their capacity to resist outside impact and pressure. It has mobilized the potentially nation-oriented members of the community, the men with enough land or capital to raise cash crops and operate stores, the men whose position and personality allow them to accept the new patterns of nation-oriented behavior. Yet often enough the attendant show of business and busyness tends to obscure the fact that most of the inhabitants of such communities either lack access to new opportunities or are unable to take advantage of such opportunities when offered. Lacking adequate resources in land, water, technical knowledge, and contacts in the market, the majority also lack the instruments which can transform use values into marketable commodities. At the same time, their inability to speak Spanish and their failure to understand the cues for the new patterns of nation-oriented behavior isolate them from the channels of communication between community and nation. Under these circumstances they must cling to the traditional "rejection pattern" of their ancestors, because their narrow economic base sets limits to the introduction of new cultural alternatives. These are all too often nonfunctional for them. The production of sufficient maize for subsistence purposes remains their major goal in life. In their case, the granting of *ejidos* tended to lend support to their accustomed way of life and reinforced their attachment to their traditional heritage.

Confronted by these contrasts between the mobile and the traditional, the nation-oriented and the community-oriented, village life is riven by contradictions and conflicts, conflicts not only between class groups but also between individuals, families, or entire neighborhoods. Such a community will inevitably differentiate into a number of unstable groups with different orientations and interests.

III

This paper has dealt with the principal ways in which social groups arranged and rearranged themselves in conflict and accommodation along the major economic and political axes of Mexican society. Each rearrangement produced a changed configuration in the relationship of community-oriented and nation-oriented groups. During the first period of post-Columbian Mexican history, political power was concentrated on the national level in the hands of royal officials. Royal officials and colonist entrepreneurs struggled with each other for control of the labor supply located in the Indian communities. In this struggle, the royal officials helped to organize the Indian peasantry into corporate communities which proved strongly resilient to outside change. During the second period, the colonist entrepreneurs—and especially the owners of haciendas—threw off royal control and established autonomous local enclaves, centered on their enterprises. With the fusion of political and economic power in the hands of these intermediate power holders, the national government was rendered impotent and the Indian peasant groups became satellites of the entrepreneurial complex. At the same time, their corporate communal organization was increasingly weakened by internal differentiation and the inroads of outsiders. During the third period, the entrepreneurial complexes standing between community and nation were swept away by the agrarian revolution and power again returned to a central government. Political means are once more applied to check the transformation of power seekers from the local communities into independent entrepreneurs. Among the groups used in exercising such restraint are the agriculturists, organized in *ejidos* which allow the government direct access to the people of the local communities.

Throughout this analysis, we have been concerned with the bonds which unite different groups on different levels of the larger society, rather than with the internal organization of communities and national-level institutions. Such a shift in emphasis seems increasingly necessary as our traditional models of communities and national institutions become obsolete. Barring such a shift, anthropologists will have to abdicate their new-found interest in complex societies. The social-psychological aspects of life in local groups, as opposed to the cultural aspects, have long been explored by sociologists. The study of formal law, politics, or economics is better carried out by specialists in these fields than by anthropologists doubling as part-time experts. Yet the hallmark of anthropology has always been its holistic approach, an approach which is increasingly needed in an age of ever-increasing specialization. This paper constitutes an argument that we can achieve greater synthesis in the study of complex societies by focusing our attention on the relationships between different groups operating on different levels of the society, rather than on any one of its isolated segments.

Such an approach will necessarily lead us to ask some new questions and to reconsider some answers to old questions. We may raise two such questions regarding the material presented in the present paper. First, can we make any generalizations about the ways in which groups in Mexico interrelate with each other over time, as compared to those which unite groups in another society, such as Italy or Japan, for example? We hardly possess the necessary information to answer such a question at this point, but one can indicate the direction which a possible answer might take. Let me point to one salient characteristic of Mexican group relationships which appears from the foregoing analysis: the tendency of new group relationships to contribute to the preservation of traditional cultural forms. The Crown reorganized the Indian communities; they became strongholds of the traditional way of life. The haciendas transformed the Indian peasants into part-time laborers; their wages stabilized their traditional prestige economy. The Revolution of 1910 opened the channels of opportunity to the nation-oriented; it reinforced the community orientation of the immobile. It would indeed seem that in Mexico "the old periods never disappear completely and all wounds, even the oldest, continue to bleed to this day" (Paz 1947:11). This "contemporaneity of the noncontemporaneous" is responsible for the "common-sense" view of many superficial observers that in Mexico "no problems are ever solved," and "reforms always produce results opposite to those intended." It has undoubtedly affected Mexican political development (Wolf 1953:160–165). It may be responsible for the violence which has often accompanied even minor ruptures in these symbiotic patterns. And one may well ask the question whether both processes of accommodation or conflict in Mexico have not acquired certain patterned forms as a result of repeated cyclical returns to hostile symbiosis in group relationships.

Such considerations once again raise the thorny problems presented by the national character approach. Much discussion of this concept has turned on the question of whether all nationals conform to a common pattern of behavior and ideals. This view has been subjected to much justified criticism. We should remember, however, that most national character studies have emphasized the study of ideal norms, constructed on the basis of verbal statements by informants, rather than the study of real behavior through participant observation. The result has been, I think, to confuse cultural form and function. It seems possible to define "national character" operationally as those cultural forms or mechanisms which groups involved in the same overall web of relationships can use in their formal and informal dealings with each other. Such a view need not imply that all nationals think or behave alike, nor that the forms used may not serve different functions in different social contexts. Such common forms must exist if communication between the different constituent groups of a complex society are to be established and maintained. I have pointed out that in modern Mexico the behavior patterns of certain groups in the past have become the expected forms of behavior of nation-oriented individuals. These cultural forms of communication as found in Mexico are manifestly different from those found in other societies (see especially Carrión 1952:70–90; Paz 1947:29–45). Their study by linguists and students of kinesics (Birdwhistell 1951) would do much to establish their direct relevance to the study of complex societies.

A second consideration which derives from the analysis presented in this paper concerns the groups of people who mediate between community-oriented groups in communities and nation-oriented groups which operate primarily through national institutions. We have encountered several such groups in this paper. In post-Columbian Mexico, these mediating functions were first carried out by the leaders of Indian corporate communities and royal officials. Later, these tasks fell into the hands of the local entrepreneurs, such as the owners of haciendas. After the Revolution of 1910, they passed into the hands of nation-oriented individuals from the local communities who have established ties with the national level, and who serve as "brokers" between community-oriented and nation-oriented groups.

The study of these "brokers" will prove increasingly rewarding, as anthropologists shift their attention from the internal organization of communities to the manner of their integration into larger systems. For they stand guard over the crucial junctures or synapses of relationships which connect the local system to the larger whole. Their basic function is to relate community-oriented individuals who want to stabilize or improve their life chances, but who lack economic security and political connections, with nation-oriented individuals who operate primarily in terms of the complex cultural forms standardized as national institutions, but whose success in these operations depends on the size and strength of their personal following. These functions are of course expressed through cultural forms or mechanisms which will differ from culture to culture. Examples of these are Chinese *kan-ch'ing* (Fried 1953), Japanese *oyabun-kobun* (Ishino 1953), Latin American *compadrazgo* (Mintz and Wolf 1950).

Special studies of such "broker" groups can also provide unusual insight into the functions of a complex system through a study of its dysfunctions. The position of these "brokers" is an "exposed" one, since, Janus-like, they face in two directions at once. They must serve some of the interests of groups operating on both the community and the national level, and they must cope with the conflicts raised by the collision of these interests. They cannot settle them, since by doing so they would abolish their own usefulness to others. Thus they often act as buffers between groups, maintaining the tensions which provide the dynamic of their actions. The relation of the hacienda owner to his satellite Indians, the role of the modern politician-broker to his community-oriented followers, may properly be viewed in this light. These would have no raison d'être but for the tensions between community-oriented groups and nation-oriented groups. Yet they must also maintain a grip on these tensions, lest conflict get out of hand and better mediators take their place. Fallers (1955) has demonstrated how much can be learned about the workings of complex systems by studying the "predicament" of one of its "brokers," the Soga chief. We shall learn much from similar studies elsewhere.

SUMMARY

This paper has argued that students of complex societies must proceed from a study of communities or national institutions to a study of the ties between social groups operating on all levels of a society. It then attempted to view Mexico in this light. Emphasis on the external ties between groups rather than on the internal organization of each alone led to renewed questions as to whether these ties were mediated through common cultural forms, and to a discussion of "broker" groups which mediate between different levels of integration of the same society.

NOTE

1. A first draft of this paper was prepared while the author was Research Associate of the Project for Research on Cross-Cultural Regularities, directed by Julian Steward at the University of Illinois, Urbana, Illinois. Parts of it were read before a meeting of the Central States Anthropological Society at Bloomington, Indiana, on May 6, 1955. The author is indebted for helpful criticisms to Julian Steward, to Oscar Lewis of the University of Illinois, and to Sidney Mintz of Yale University.

REFERENCES CITED

Aguirre Beltrán, Gonzalo, and Ricardo Pozas Arciniegas
1954 "Instituciones indígenas en el México actual," in Caso *et al.*, pp. 171–272.

Bazant, Jan
1950 "Feudalismo y capitalismo en la historia económica de México," *Trimestre Económico* 17:81–98.

Benítez, Francisco
1947 "México, la tela de Penélope," *Cuadernos Americanos* 6:44–60.

Birdwhistell, Ray L.
1951 *Kinesics*, Washington, D.C., Foreign Service Institute, U.S. Department of State.

Carrasco, Pedro
1952 *Tarascan Folk Religion: An Analysis of Economic, Social, and Religious Interactions*, Middle American Research Institute Publication 17:1–64, New Orleans, Tulane University.

Carrión, Jorge
1952 "Mito y magia del mexicano," *México y lo mexicano* 3, México, D. F., Porrúa y Obregón.

Caso, Alfonso, *et al.*
1954 *Métodos y resultados de la política indigenista en México*, Memorias del Instituto Nacional Indigenista 6, México, D. F.

Chávez Orozco, Luis
1943 *Las instituciones democráticas de los indígenas Mexicanos en la época colonial*, México, D. F., Ediciones del Instituto Indigenista Interamericano.
1950 "La irrigación en México: ensayo histórico," *Problemas Agrícolas e Industriales de México* 2:11–31.

Chevalier, François
1952 *La formation des grands domaines aux Mexique: terre et société aux XVIe–XVIIe Siècles*, Travaux et Mémoires de l'Institut d'Ethnologie 56, Paris.

Fallers, Lloyd
1955 "The Predicament of the Modern African Chief: An Instance from Uganda," *American Anthropologist* 57:290–305.

Fried, Morton H.
1953 *Fabric of Chinese Society*, New York, Praeger.

Gama, Valentin
1931 *La propiedad en México—la reforma agraria*, México, D. F., Empresa Editorial de Ingeniería y Arquitectura.

Gruening, Ernest
1928 *Mexico and Its Heritage*, New York, Century.

Guiteras-Holmes, Calixta
1952 *Sayula*, México, D. F., Sociedad Mexicana de Geografía y Estadística.

Ishino, Iwao
1953 "The *Oyabun-Kobun:* A Japanese Ritual Kinship Institution," *American Anthropologist* 55:695–707.

Iturriaga, José E.
1951 *La estructura social y cultural de México*, México, D. F., Fondo de Cultura Económica.
Lee, Eric
1954 "Can a One Party System Be Democratic?" *Dissent* 1:299–300.
Lewis, Oscar
1951 *Life in a Mexican Village: Tepoztlán Restudied*, Urbana, University of Illinois Press.
Mangin, William
1955 "*Haciendas, Comunidades* and Strategic Acculturation in the Peruvian Sierra," paper read before the American Anthropological Association, Boston, November 18.
Mintz, Sidney W., and Eric R. Wolf
1950 "An Analysis of Ritual Co-parenthood (*Compadrazgo*)," *Southwestern Journal of Anthropology* 6:341–368.
Miranda, José
1947 "La función económica del encomendero en los orígenes del régimen colonial de Nueva España, 1525–1531," *Anales del Instituto Nacional de Anthropología e Historia* 2:421–462.
Molina Enríquez, Andrés
1909 *Los grandes problemas nacionales*, México, D. F., Imprenta de A. Carranza e Hijos.
Paz, Octavio
1947 *El laberinto de la soledad*, México, D. F., Cuadernos Americanos.
Pozas Arciniegas, Ricardo
1952 "La situation économique et financière de l'Indien Américain," *Civilisations* 2:309–329.
Redfield, Robert, and Sol Tax
1952 "General Characteristics of Present-Day Mesoamerican Indian Society," in *Heritage of Conquest*, Sol Tax, ed., Glencoe, Ill., Free Press, pp. 31–39.
Scott, Robert E.
1955 "The Bases of Political Power in the Caribbean," lecture delivered at the University of Illinois, Urbana, January 14. (Mimeographed.)
Simpson, Eyler N.
1937 *The Ejido: Mexico's Way Out*, Chapel Hill, University of North Carolina Press.
Simpson, Lesley Byrd
1950 *The Encomienda in New Spain: The Beginning of Spanish Mexico*, rev. ed., Berkeley, University of California Press.
Steward, Julian
1950 *Area Research: Theory and Practice*, Social Science Research Council Bulletin 63, New York.
Tannenbaum, Frank
1929 *The Mexican Agrarian Revolution*, Washington, D.C., Brookings Institution.
West, Robert C.
1948 *Cultural Geography of the Modern Tarascan Area*, Smithsonian Institution, Institute of Social Anthropology Publication 7, Washington, D.C.
Whetten, Nathan
1948 *Rural Mexico*, Chicago, University of Chicago Press.

Wolf, Eric R.
1953 "La formación de la nación: un ensayo de formulación," *Ciencias Sociales* 4:50–62, 98–111, 146–171.
1955a "Types of Latin American Peasantry: A Preliminary Discussion," *American Anthropologist* 57:452–471.
1955b *The Mexican Bajío in the Eighteenth Century: An Analysis of Cultural Integration*, Middle American Research Institute Publication 17:177–200, New Orleans, Tulane University.

Yañez, Agustín
1945 "Fichas Mexicanas," *Jornadas* 39, México, D. F., El Colegio de México.

Zavala, Silvio
1940 *De encomiendas y propiedad territorial en algunas regiones de la América Española*, México, D. F., Robredo.
1944 "Orígenes coloniales del peonaje en México," *Trimestre Económico* 10:711–748.

Zavala, Silvio, and José Miranda
1954 "Instituciones indígenas en la colonia," in Caso *et al.*, pp. 29–112.

Brokers and Career Mobility Systems in the Structure of Complex Societies[1]

RICHARD N. ADAMS

Among anthropologists, Richard Adams is exceptional for the degree to which he is concerned with both rigorously specified conceptualization and richly detailed minutiae of social action. In this paper, he develops approaches pioneered by Wolf, Leeds, and others, examines the national social structure of Guatemala in terms of "power," "power domains," and "levels of articulation," and even suggests how the analysis of complex societies relates to the overall process of social evolution.

Richard N. Adams is Professor of Anthropology at the University of Texas. He has conducted a variety of ethnographic and other research in several Latin American countries and has held a number of important offices in professional organizations here and abroad. Among his innovative books are A Community in the Andes (1959), Culture Surveys of Panama-Nicaragua-Guatemala-El Salvador-Honduras (1957), The Second Sowing (1967), *and* Crucifixion by Power (1970); *he is also coauthor of* U.S. University Programs in Latin America (1960), *and* Contemporary Cultures and Societies of Latin America (*1st ed.*, 1965).

From *Southwestern Journal of Anthropology*, XXVI (1970), 315–327. Copyright © 1970 by The University of New Mexico. Reprinted by permission of the author and publisher.

The purpose of this paper is to relate career mobility systems and power brokers with two analytical notions that concern the structure of complex societies, power domains and levels of articulation. Three generally familiar concepts are first reviewed; some modifications are then suggested; finally, interrelations are proposed among them. The proposals are speculative and stem from analyses of the national social structure of Guatemala (Adams 1970).

LEVELS OF INTEGRATION, BROKERS, AND CAREER MOBILITY SYSTEMS

The concept of levels in human society has been used in many contexts and for many centuries. In contemporary anthropology, however, it is especially associated with the work of Steward (1955), and Wolf (1967) has added further thoughts on the subject. While Steward used the concept to refer specifically to "national" and "local" levels, Wolf expanded this to seven "levels and sublevels" for Middle America. But neither author, so far as I know, has directed his attention to a rather central problem: What *is* a level of integration? That is, how do we know when we are dealing with one? How do we know that one may exist, be coming into existence, or possibly be changing? How do we then account for the possible fact that there may be different numbers of such levels in different societies, or in different parts of a single complex society? If these questions cannot be answered, then the concept can never be a satisfactory analytical tool.

"Brokers" has been used to refer to individuals who occupy linkage roles between sectors of a society. "Marriage brokers," as well as "stock brokers," serve to articulate two clients in order to effect an exchange of approximate equivalence. Until a few years ago, this exchange of equivalencies seemed to imply that brokers worked between social equals. Wolf (1956) suggested that this kind of articulatory role could be seen operating in individuals who related social elements which were clearly not equals, where the things being linked were on different levels of the society and, therefore, stood in relatively different positions of power. This extension of the concept has facilitated the conceptualization of the connections and linkages between local levels of a society and the larger system. A problem in the use of the concept, however, is that we have little notion why these "cultural brokers" seem less congenial in some societies than in others and what conditions lead to their appearance or disappearance. A further question is whether the cultural contact between two different levels afforded by a broker is of relevance structurally and, if so, under what circumstances.

"Career mobility systems" refers to a phenomenon that has received little elaboration beyond the case that was presented by Leeds (1965) in Brazil, and the model of spiralism proposed by Watson (1964) for Great Britain. Obviously, in dealing with levels we are also interested in the process of mobility, the devices whereby an individual or party succeeds in moving from one level to another. Societies clearly differ in the degree to which mobility during one's career is possible; and in those societies where mobility is feasible, it usually can be described rather systematically. It is possible, therefore, to speak of career mobility systems as those patterned processes within a given society whereby one moves up or down.

What is sometimes overlooked about these systems is that they are more than merely ways for individuals to move up or down; they also establish linkages between the different levels. Whereas brokers translate the interests of one level into responses at another, in mobility systems those with interests at one level can attempt to move to the next level and to assess their own interests there. In one respect, therefore, career mobility systems parallel the activities of brokers, and the problem posed concerning brokers is equally applicable to them: i.e., under what conditions do these systems come into operation or fall into disuse? Further, do they specifically have some relation to the presence or absence of brokers?

POWER DOMAINS, LEVELS OF ARTICULATION, AND CONFRONTATIONS

The conceptual relations I wish to explore here are derived from trying to understand a series of events covering a twenty-five year period in Guatemala and include matters such as relationships between rural community dwellers, changing national governments, associations of national scope, and the role of foreign powers, specifically Germany, the United States, and Cuba.

Of the concepts central to this discussion, that of the power domain has been discussed elsewhere (Adams 1966). It should be kept in mind that the concept of power used here is not derived from Weber (1964:152–153); i.e., it does not include the totality of influences that make people obey the wills of others. It refers to control over the environment; the environment encompasses any set of events external and relevant to the persons doing the controlling. We are concerned, however, with a particular phase of control, that which one individual may have over the environment of another. Thus, the concept of power being used here diverges from the Weberian in that power is only one of the totality of influences that may exist between two individuals or players. Moreover, we also use a generalized concept of player, one that can include any kind of social operating unit that is coping with the environment. (Adams 1970: 39–53 contains an extended treatment of these concepts.) Thus, a family, a community, a political party, a military establishment, a government may all be operating units, and hence players. A power domain, then, is a relationship wherein one player has greater control over the environment of a second than the second does over that of the first. The domain concept is useful in organizing and examining the dynamics of inequalities in systems of power.

To this, I want to add a remodeling of the notion of levels. To avoid confusion with earlier usages, I am referring to this as "levels of articulation" (see Adams 1970:53–70 for a detailed teatment). A level of articulation comes into being when two players meet in a confrontation. A confrontation takes place when two players find that successfully coping with the environment brings them into a situation where either may stand as an obstacle to the further exercise of power by the other. Confrontations may occur randomly, but they are more commonly foreseen and often actually planned by at least one of the parties. In terms of power, success in a confrontation means that one so uses his power tactically that he eliminates the other or superimposes himself in a domain over the other. This then places them at different levels. Confrontations may, however, be continuing and fairly stabilized, without either party winning. In this case, the parties remain in articulation, to some degree intentionally keeping each other under stress. It is the condition of the continuing presence of balanced confrontations, and the repetition of similar confrontations, that serves to provide some permanence to levels.

It is probably worth noting that the term "confrontation" here is not being used in quite the same manner as in international and local U.S. politics in recent years. This latter usage suggests that a face-to-face meeting necessarily implies a potential conflict and a necessarily violent resolution; e.g., to say that two nations wish to "avoid a confrontation" has become almost synonymous with saying that they wish to avoid a war. In the context of this essay, "confrontation" refers to the fact that two parties are in articulation because one or both are obstacles to the other; it does not imply that they will choose to fight over the issue nor, indeed, that these issues will necessarily ever be resolved.

Levels of articulation become increasingly explicit and important as confrontations become more durable, as more of them occur between parties of equivalent power, and, therefore, as the perception of relative power becomes institutionalized within the society. As such, levels are more than merely loci of confrontations; they also provide a place for many kinds of relationships between parties, ranging from confrontation and competition to cooperation and assimilation. Individuals may find themselves operating at different levels, depending upon which of their various roles they occupy at the moment. Consequently, a consistency tends to emerge among levels of articulation. Instead of ranging over a broad undifferentiated continuum, players tend to bunch where those of roughly equivalent power are maintaining their positions and, consequently, where those who wish to confront them must also congregate. To this should be added the recognition that real players operate in real space. This means that topography and other external features will influence the possibility of confrontations taking place. Because of this, levels in one locale or region need not precisely correspond to those elsewhere. Anything which promotes isolation, be it cultural or physical, may differentiate systems of levels.

In spite of this, however, most complex societies have sets of levels that approximate the following: (1) sub-communal (possibly identified around kin, households, etc.); (2) local (possibly neighborhoods, communities, or sets of small communities); (3) regional (possibly large towns or cities and hinterland, sets of communities, etc.); (4) national (sets of regions or a collectivity of small national scenes); and (5) clearly supranational, the maximal level at which the more powerful nations operate.

The concepts can be illustrated in the Guatemalan cases as follows. Guatemala itself is in a power domain of the United States; its economy is heavily dependent upon actions taken by the United States government, and its political system is explicitly aligned with the policy decisions of the United States and against those of socialist countries. The government of Guatemala, in turn, exercises domain over all Guatemalans in various aspects. And within Guatemala, there are lesser domains of businesses, the church, agrarian enterprises, industries, corporate communities, etc. Levels of articulation can be identified within Guatemala by taking note of the confrontation articulations between individual family heads, of town officials dealing with like officials elsewhere, of ministers of government negotiating with leaders in business and industry or with political figures of distinction, and so forth. They are also evident in the dealings between the Guatemalan government and other governments and in the fact that the United States clearly exercises more power over Guatemalan decisions than the reverse. In this paper, however, we are concerned with the lower levels of articulation, those that operate within the nation.

It is important to recognize that domains and levels are two different ways of conceptualizing the consequences of power operations within a single society. The presence of domains can be examined to see how players with roughly equivalent access to power are aligned horizontally; and the manifestation of levels indicates that the relationship between domains has become somewhat institutionalized. However, the two concepts need differentiation because confrontations may produce domains which are not clearly aligned within a set of levels. The notion to be explored in this paper is that societies, or subsegments of societies, will from time to time place special emphasis on either domains or levels, and that this differential emphasis has consequences for our understanding of brokers and career mobility systems.

APPLICATION OF THE CONCEPTS

Let us now return to the concepts mentioned at the outset. "Levels of articulation" obviously refers to much that is contained in Steward's (1955) and Wolf's (1967) "levels of integration." The new notion, however, is more precise in its referent, allows for cross-cultural correlation of varying forms, indicates the dynamics of the levels, how they come into being, and how they may change. Since they are products of potential conflicts, their locus and systematization must reflect the adaptation to the total environment. Because of these advantages, however, there are some cautions which must also be observed. Since one cannot, a priori, assume that levels found in one locale will necessarily be present or operative in another, they must be sought out empirically. The study of different regional power structures in Guatemala made this quite clear (Adams 1970:219–237). Just as kinship, locality, and political and economic organizations may be assumed to exist in some form, so may levels. But their specific forms must be discovered and described; they cannot be assumed.

The concept of brokers, as a linkage or articulation between levels, has principally been applied in the literature on Latin America to relations between local and national levels. The material from the Guatemalan study suggests that the concept of broker should be modified in two ways. First, it is a term that refers to two quite different kinds of linkages; second, it is a form which seems to be important principally when domain structures are emphasized over levels.

As linkages between local and national levels, various authors have cited instances such as caciques, school teachers, political agents, military recruiting agents, tax collectors, lawyers, labor recruiters, etc. Emphasis generally has been laid on such matters as whether the individual had his origins at the local rather than the national level or whether he represented the interests of one over the other. If it is asked whether brokers act as channels through which power is exercised, however, then we find we must differentiate between two quite different kinds of intermediaries.

Classically in Guatemala, and in many other Latin American countries, the school teacher is a cultural representative of the national system working in a culture different from that within which he is used to operating. While the teacher may serve to make national traits available, he usually has no power himself. He cannot expect firm support from his own Ministry of Education and consequently has little to offer or deny the members of the local group beyond whatever may be inherent in his role. The teacher's weakness at the national level means that he is of little interest to them in any except his specialized capacity. The same may be said for the public health doctor and the agricultural extension agent.

The situation of essential weakness is quite different from that of the cacique, an individual who classically plays the role of intermediary through utilizing his controls at each level to the advantage of the other. He can offer support by the local population to regional or national figures only if he can then be sure that they will respond to his calls for support. His actual control over either sphere depends upon his success in dealing with the other; his controls in one level of articulation provide a basis for controls in another. In addition to the classic cacique, brokers in this sense include political party agents, mass organization leaders, labor union leaders and agents, industrial foremen, local and regional marketeers and credit agents, labor recruiters, lawyers, etc.

It is clear that these "power brokers" differ from those of the first category, for whom we may retain the label "cultural broker." The cultural broker is an individual from one level who lives or operates among individuals of another level. Whatever influence he may have on the other level depends basically not on the power that he can wield but on his own skill and personal influence. Even flamboyant success at one level may have absolutely no effect on his role at the other. The school teacher who is a favorite in a rural school is not necessarily going to be the favorite in the Ministry; and he who "politicks" around the Ministry may fail to gain a following in his own school.

The power broker, on the other hand, specifically wields power at each of two levels, and his power in one level depends upon the success of his operations at the other level. He controls one domain only by virtue of having access to derivative power from a larger domain. It is interesting that so many Latin American governments have, from time to time, attempted to use cultural broker roles in a context where they really needed power brokers. Few governments, however, allow their school teachers or agricultural agents access to power.

The conditions under which each of these brokers appears within a complex society necessarily differ. Cultural brokers are usually sponsored through upper level decisions and are destined to act at lower levels. Their tasks, however, are seldom of first priority, since a failure to realize them is not felt to be a threat to the relative position of power of the parties sponsoring them. Classically, a Minister of Education does not lose his job because he fails to improve national education but because he becomes a political liability. The increase of teachers, public health agents, and agricultural agents varies with changes in national government policy about the importance of these particular areas of life for the government or for the nation. The increase of traveling agents of breweries, shoe salesmen, and wholesale agents depends upon how and when commercial houses decide to improve business operations. In general, I would assume that the importance of cultural brokers varies with the state of the national economy and the particular efforts being made to promote the spread of a national culture.

The incidence of power brokers answers to a different structure. Power brokers link units or actors at different levels, where the difference in power is such that the inferior has no real chance to confront the superior. The 19th-century Guatemalan Indian dealt through the elders or cacique because little could be gained by going directly to officials at the national level. Political party agents operate at the local level to gain voting support for their candidates because it is impossible for the candidate himself to do all the organizing, traveling, and convincing necessary for his election. The military establishment keeps local agents to undertake recruiting because it cannot afford to take up the time of colonels and generals in such a menial task. In all, the power broker holds an important place in the power structure of the country and particularly in the region within which he works.

Since a major feature of the role of power brokers is to mediate where confrontations do not occur, it follows that they should be especially important where domains are dominant. If someone low in a domain wishes to obtain something that is available only to superiors in the domain, he may attempt a confrontation, or he may try to do it through a broker. If he attempts a confrontation, he makes the levels more flexible; if he operates through a broker, he strengthens the domain. Power brokers are important, then, where domains are strong and, correlatively, where levels tend to be rigid. In pre-revolutionary Guatemala (prior to 1944) dictator Ubico allowed no confrontation; similarly, no coffee farmer would allow a show of organized power on the part of his laborers. The major means of handling problems were through elders, caciques, town *intendentes* (government-appointed town mayors), farm administrators, and others who stood in power brokerage positions. At the same time, there was no question as to what levels existed, and each person knew where he stood. Domains were strong and levels were rigid.

During the 1944–1954 revolutionary period, new sources of power opened up, and multiple access to power was made possible by organizing political parties, mass organizations, labor unions, and the like; concomitant with these changes, the incidence of confrontations between organizations and domain superiors increased. As a result, the system of levels became much more flexible, and domains weakened. By the same token, the role of the power broker became ambiguous. As it became increasingly possible for the lower sector to get what it wanted through various new channels, the broker was by-passed if he was not effective. The outstanding case was the manner in which young, politically oriented individuals began to take over control of local governments through the elective process and thereby ignored the traditional channels of local political authority. Indian elders, local *ladino* (mestizo) upper strata, and large farm operators could all be confronted or by-passed completely by virtue of the new access to power of the political party and labor union. (See Adams 1957 for case histories.)

The change bringing about the new emphasis on levels, and the concomitant de-emphasis on domains, did not stop with the end of the revolutionary period in 1954. The increase in confrontations was reduced in important ways, but the new power sources and new channels opened by the revolution began to be used in different ways. Labor courts continued in operation, and, although under severe practical constraints, they were more effective in dealing directly with a farm administrator in extreme instances. Labor unions, while weakened, nevertheless continued to operate, particularly in the capital city.

A contrary case, which tends to demonstrate the proposition here suggested, is that of the labor recruiter. Seasonal migrant labor, which probably numbers as high as 400,000, did not have effective access to new power under the revolution. The labor laws and unions could do little to influence their situation. The means of contracting labor had traditionally been through individuals who would act as brokers between the farm administrations and the laborers of particular towns or villages. These *habilitadores* and *enganchadores*, perfect examples of power brokers, continue to operate up to the present. They serve a purpose for which no readily devisable means of confrontations have been invented. It may be predicted, however, that if and when the labor needs of farms outstrip the availability of the rural population for seasonal labor, then confrontations will begin to take place and the broker will disappear.

Just as rigidity of levels is an aspect of a strong domain system, so flexibility of levels is a concomitant of the weakening of domains. And whereas brokers have a real role in the former situation, this role is replaced by mobility in the latter. In systems where brokers operate, upward mobility is very difficult. Individuals at the lower levels, in the absence of access to derived power, depend upon brokers to provide what little they may get. The weakening of domains and disappearance of brokers is simultaneous with an increase in mobility. Aggressive lower sector individuals reach directly for power themselves; intrasocietal patterns develop whereby confrontations may be made, and the cleverer and luckier individuals and groups will gain more power for themselves and thereby move to higher levels. As was indicated earlier, we are faced with a painful shortage of studies of the mobility processes that have evolved in different societies. Leeds' (1965) description of the career system in Brazil was an important innovative study because here it was made perfectly clear that mobility is considerably more than a set of sociological statistics and that it probably manifests the same diversities that are to be found elsewhere in sociocultural systems.

The replacement of brokerage by mobility suggests that the latter is more than a means of bettering the lot of individuals within the society, that it is also a structural linkage within the system as a whole. Both mobility and brokers enable a social system to continue on its course with only gradual structural change. The difference, quite obviously, is that one keeps people in their appointed roles, whereas the other allows them to change. In both, the role system remains much the same. The increase of confrontations, however, means that individuals and groupings accomplish this mediation by moving out of the lower levels and by obtaining direct access to power (whether derivative or independent).

Another way to look at the contrast between the two situations is to see the broker system as static and the mobility system as dynamic. A broker does not change his position within the total structure by virtue of his activities as broker. Since his power in each level depends upon maintaining his control over resources in both areas, he generally cannot move without losing control over one or both sources. (I say "generally," because there are occasional individuals who are successful in moving out of the brokerage position into higher levels through confrontations. The classic case of the provincial *caudillo* who takes over the central government, as Rafael Carrera did in Guatemala in 1838, does occur. But they are relatively few when compared with the number of brokers in operation.) Consequently, the broker accomplishes linkage within the society by not moving. In a career mobility system, on the other hand, the linkage is accomplished by the individual occupying one position in one part of the society at one point in his career and another position later. He may retain relations at the different levels, but his roles change as he moves up. Time does not change the broker's position, but it extends the roles of the mobile person across various levels of society, and it is the very movement over time that provides the linkage.

THE PROCESS OF WEAKENING AND STRENGTHENING OF DOMAINS

There remains a question as to the reasons that domains vary from weakness to strength and levels of articulation from flexibility to rigidity. Basically a domain may be said to be strong when it has sufficient power within its control to keep subordinates in an inferior position. The circumstances which may affect the relative control of domain superiors are too varied to permit even a cursory review here. They may be illustrated, however, in terms of recent Guatemalan history.

Since levels are defined by the presence of confrontations, it follows that an increased flexibility in levels depends upon an increase in confrontations. Some of the more obvious conditions that produce this include population increase, economic development, and political expansion. Population growth brings about competition over land and other resources, and it results in confrontations which may appear at any level, from the family to the international. Economic development, entailing as it does an increased extraction of resources and production, is inherently a competitive process, both internally and internationally. It, too, may breed confrontations at any level, although they are perhaps better known at higher levels. Political expansion refers mainly to the expansion of nation states or to political movements within nations. These, also, are apparent at higher levels, but they occasionally occur in the form of urban demonstrations and of peasant or Indian movements. Even within the community, the expansion of a family or kin group may be seen in this light.

Because we live in an age where both national growth and economic development, as well as population growth, seem to be in evidence almost everywhere, it may seem harder to find cases where there is a shift from flexible to rigid levels. Indeed, the three processes just described constitute three phases of the major course of contemporary social evolution. Their conjunction is not a convergence of independent variables but a complex whereby each affects the other, and feedback from one increases activities within another.

Given this picture, and assuming reasonably that the course of evolution is unidirectional, it would be easy to assume that flexibility of levels regularly increases. This, however, is erroneous. The changing flexibility of levels and strength of domains is a mechanism within the evolutionary process, not an outcome of it. A major unidirectional change is to increase the number of domains, to increase the amount of power at the top, and, therefore, to increase the importance of larger domains. This inevitably leads to more confrontations and, consequently, to a more complex structure of levels. The specificity of real situations, however, will inevitably lead to a periodic or fluctuating relative isolation of domains; and this relative isolation leads inevitably to fewer confrontations at those points and to a concomitant strengthening of the domain.

To return to the recent history of Guatemala, under the pre-1944 government, the country was a somewhat isolated domain, characteristically a unitary domain, under the general external power of Germany and the United States. Germany was eliminated by World War II, and the United States remained the sole external power of any importance. During the revolutionary period of 1945 to 1954, the internal structure of the country began a drastic reorganization such that internal multiple domains became common and, with this, a sharp increase in confrontations. Levels became flexible, and the internal domains weakened. As the United States became frightened of activity in Guatemala that it considered to be "communistic," it began to provide support to encourage a confrontation between the government and the elements working against the government, a process which culminated in a counter-revolution in 1954. This, in turn, coupled with a steady process of economic development and population increase, led to a severe strengthening of the upper sector, with a concomitant strengthening of and reemphasis on domains and rigidity of levels. In this the United States provided important derivative power crucial to the process. The gradual regeneration of a more virile revolutionary movement in the 1960s, following the Cuban Revolution, led the conservative elements of Guatemala to align themselves (not by any means always to their taste) with United States demands, so that confrontations became parallel at various levels. Not only was the United States in confrontation with Cuba and the socialist world, but the government of Guatemala was in confrontation with some fairly agile guerrilla groups, and in both rural and urban populations there were frequent politically related assassinations. In this way, the increasing activity at various levels initiated a new series of specifically political confrontations. Over the past thirty years, then, Guatemala has shifted from a period of strong domains (pre-1944), to a weakening (1945–1954), back again to strength (1954–ca. 1961), and now again to signs of weakening (ca. 1961 to the present).

Nation states essentially attempt to strengthen their own domain structures. But the fact that they are undergoing economic development and that their populations are usually growing means that inherently the frequency of confrontations increases. Concurrently, levels reassert themselves and become more flexible through confrontations, promoting the appearance of career mobility systems and putting power brokers out of business.

FINAL COMMENT

The intent of this essay has been to relate the process of brokerage and mobility to more inclusive conditions of the total society. It has done this through relating the modes of handling power within a society to the shape and emphasis of the larger social system; it has further suggested that the condition of the larger system sets constraints on the kind of linkages that will emerge within it. As stated at the outset, it has been speculative, and, as such, I hope it will serve to stimulate further inquiry into the relations of the unit activity within a complex society to the world society and to the social evolution of which it is a part.

OTE

1. This is a revised version of a paper read at the 1968 American Anthropological Association Annual Meetings. The Guatemalan work on which it was based was supported by the Ford Foundation and the Institute of Latin American Studies, the University of Texas at Austin.

BIBLIOGRAPHY

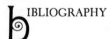

Adams, Richard N.

1957 *Political Changes in Guatemalan Indian Communities: a Symposium.* Tulane University, Middle American Research Institute, publication 24, pp. 1–54.

1966 Power and Power Domains. *América Latina,* ano 9, no. 2, pp. 3–21.

1970 *Crucifixion by Power: Essays in the National Social Structure of Guatemala, 1944–1966.* Austin: University of Texas Press.

Leeds, Anthony

1965 "Brazilian Careers and Social Structure: a Case History and Model," in *Contemporary Cultures and Societies of Latin America* (ed. by D. B. Heath and R. N. Adams), pp. 379–404. New York: Random House.

Steward, Julian

1955 *The Theory of Culture Change.* Urbana: University of Illinois Press.

Watson, William

1964 "Social Mobility and Social Class in Industrial Communities," in *Closed Systems and Open Minds* (ed. by Max Gluckman), pp. 129–157. Chicago: Aldine.

Weber, Max

1964 *The Theory of Economic and Social Organization* (trans. by A. M. Henderson and Talcott Parsons. Ed. with an introduction by Talcott Parsons). Glencoe, Ill.: The Free Press.

Wolf, Eric
1956 Aspects of Group Relations in a Complex Society: Mexico. *American Anthropologist* 58:1065–1078.
1967 "Levels of Communal Relations," in *Handbook of Middle American Indians* (R. Wauchope, general ed., and M. Nash, vol. ed.), vol. 6, pp. 299–316. Austin: University of Texas Press.

Strategies for Survival: The Indians of Highland Ecuador

JOSEPH B. CASAGRANDE

In a different approach to another complex society, Casagrande has chosen to focus on the relationships between "social races" in terms that some would label "symbolic interactionism." By comparing six Ecuadorian communities in different ecological situations, he provides a fruitful sampling of "strategies for survival," which complements Whitten's analysis of such variations within a single community. He also offers some insights into the role of the anthropologist as field worker, within the context of Foster's patron-client paradigm.

Joseph B. Casagrande is Professor of Anthropology and Director of the Center for International Comparative Studies at the University of Illinois at Urbana-Champaign. He has conducted research among several North American Indian groups, including the Ojibwa, Comanche and Navaho. More recently he has been engaged in both field work and archival research on the position of the Indian in Ecuador from colonial times to the present. He is editor of In the Company of Man: Twenty Portraits by Anthropologists (1960) *and author of numerous articles in anthropological linguistics and social anthropology.*

INTRODUCTION

This paper is based on research conducted during the past several years by my students and myself in six Indian communities in Highland Ecuador, each representative of a distinct ecological type.[1] Although dealing with Ecuador, I believe that the general approach we have used in this study, as well as some of the findings, is applicable to other societies in which one finds racial or ethnic groups that are demeaned and dispossessed members of that society or marginal to it.

In what follows I shall first present a brief characterization of the place of the Indian in contemporary Ecuadorian society. I shall then offer a précis of the assumptions and theory motivating the research. This will be followed by

This paper was prepared expressly for this volume.

thumbnail sketches of each group, stressing the differences among them to which our research has been primarily addressed. Finally, I shall describe an experimental field seminar in which informants from our six communities took part.

THE POSITION OF THE SIERRA INDIAN

Like several of its neighbors, Ecuador is characterized by a sharply stratified, dual society in which there is a castelike division between the Indian and non-Indian sectors. Estimates of the Indian population of the sierra vary greatly depending upon the criteria of Indianness employed,[2] but a figure of one million would probably not fall far off the mark. By Ecuadorian standards, some Indians are well off. Nevertheless, the Indian population as a whole bears the classic stigmata that mark them among the dispossessed peoples of the world: poverty, illiteracy, a high infant mortality rate and low life expectancy, a variety of deficiency diseases, low participation in local and national institutions, low self-esteem, and limited opportunities for social mobility. Many mestizos are no better off—the case is comparable to that of rural blacks and whites in the southern United States. However, the Indian's situation is aggravated by his being relegated to the lowest stratum of Ecuadorian society.

In the universal dialectic of racism, the Indian is endowed with the very traits disesteemed by his white superiors. Even the kindliest among the whites tend to look upon the Indian as a child perpetually held at a developmental stage lower than that of a full adult human being, or they regard him simply as a brute little better than any other animal capable of carrying a heavy load. Perhaps most insidious of all is the attitude of benevolent condescension that characterizes the patrón of classic mold and many would-be benefactors. The fact that some Indian groups in Ecuador are singled out for special comment or praise—the Otavaleños, for example, are said to be proud, clean, industrious, intelligent, and so on—is in effect to commend them for having qualities that one is surprised to find among Indians and at the same time to damn other Indian groups with the implication that these are precisely the qualities they *don't* have. Thus most Indians are generally regarded as being lazy, drunken, dirty, stupid, dishonest, or having other flaws of character. And so is fed the stereotype of the Indian that both keeps him at a distance and gives warrant to the ill treatment accorded him.

If in the earlier colonial period there were recognized *caciques* and noble Indian families (some even granted coats-of-arms by the King), these status differences have been leveled off with the passage of time. It is noteworthy, too, that little public honor is paid the symbols of Indian ethnicity. The ingredients are at hand, but neither the Indian nor the nation has constructed a believable history or heritage in which both can take pride and with which the Indian can identify.[3]

In short, racism in Ecuador is institutionalized to a degree that would shock even black Americans. The Indian is constantly and inescapably forced to face the fact of his ethnic stigma and adapt to the profaneness of his own person.[4] There have been very few racial incidents in Ecuador in recent years. In that country Indians and non-Indians have learned their respective roles of dominance and submission extremely well and almost unthinkingy put them into practice. Blacks in the United States would find the Ecuadorian Indians remarkably complacent. They have as yet had no Richard Wright, Eldridge Cleaver, or Stokely Carmichael to fan the fires of their own inarticulate, smoldering indignation. Others, including writers such as Jorge Icaza[5] and the painters Eduardo Kingman and Oswaldo Guayasamin, have spoken in outrage against this oppression, but the Indians have not found their own voice, politically, socially, or economically.

THE RESEARCH APPROACH

Despite the Indian's general low estate, there are marked differences in the adaptive strategies various groups have evolved to defend themselves against the pressures of the dominant society. In our research we have undertaken (1) to describe these differences in full ethnographic detail, (2) to explain the observed differences, and (3) to trace out their consequences with regard to self-image, styles of self-presentation, social mobility, acceptance of innovations, and the like.

It is assumed that a number of modes of adaptation are available to individuals and groups who are relatively powerless, often demeaned or impoverished members of a society or marginal to it. At the most fundamental level these adaptive responses are expressed in the particular social, economic, and political strategies devised to cope with the dominant sector. They are also expressed as dependent variables in the basic stances groups take vis-à-vis the larger society and in the behavioral strategies employed in interpersonal relationships with members of the dominant sector. These behavioral strategies may range from withdrawal or a posture of defensive hostility at one extreme, through strategies of servile deference or feigned ignorance of expected or prescribed behavior, to "realistic" accommodation to and manipulation of the dominant society and its representatives at the other extreme. At the cognitive or conceptual level these differences are expressed in varying notions of one's self and others, of the social structure in which one is enmeshed, of one's life chances, man's fate, and the like. Foster's[6] "image of limited good" is one of the possibilities at this conceptual level.

It is hypothesized that the particular responses chosen, whether at the institutional, behavioral, or cognitive level, are largely determined by, or at least consistent with, a group's particular ecological circumstances. They are workable strategies that both individuals and groups in various social predicaments have evolved to survive in an oppressive society. While there are individual differences, these adaptive strategies are widely shared by members of particular groups. Moreover, individual responses are "summed" as group responses on those occasions when actions or decisions are taken on behalf of a community by a representative group such as the *cabildo* (village council). As we shall see, these adaptive strategies differ, sometimes quite dramatically, from one group to another. Indeed, some behaviors are discontinuously distributed among the six communities that figure in our study. For example, ritualized deference behaviors such as kneeling before and kissing the hand of a secular authority that one may observe in some groups (Atahualpa or San Francisco) are virtually unthinkable in others (Salasaca or Peguche).

Let me now turn to a brief explication of what I regard as the key concept that has guided our research: that of a group's ecological circumstances. By this term I mean, at the most abstract level, the ways in which power[7] emanating from the dominant mestizo–white sector is brought to bear on an Indian community in various domains—economic, political, social, and religious. For many Indians today, as in the past, this domination is mediated by and symbolized in the persons of the parish priest, the *hacendado*, and the *teniente-político*, and by other mestizos such as the *chicheros* and *tinterillos* who live in the towns. In their respective spheres, the priest, *hacendado*, and *teniente-político* (or their alter egos) still wield great power over the lives of the Indians and the fate that befalls them.[8]

Major dimensions of a group's ecological plight are (1) the extent to which it is involved with and dependent on the larger society, (2) the nature of the goods and services exchanged with the outside society, and (3) the degree to which a group has control over the basic resources (land, water, pasture, fuel) necessary to maintain its social and economic integrity at even the minimum level that has for centuries been deemed adequate for Ecuador's impoverished people. With regard to control over basic resources, a major contrast is between those who have long been referred to in Ecuador as *indios proprios* (owned Indians) and *indios libres* (free Indians). Free Indians are those who own their own land, as contrasted with *huasipungueros*, who have usufruct rights to small plots (*huasipungos*) on the large traditional haciendas together with certain perquisites such as access to pasture and firewood, in exchange for their labor on the estate and a small cash wage.

THE SIX COMMUNITIES

PEGUCHE

Peguche is one of the most prosperous of several communities in the canton of Otavalo, Imbabura Province, devoted to weaving.[9] There is evidence that the Indians of Otavalo specialized in weaving even before the Conquest; and until they were outlawed, the textile *obrajes* (workshops in which forced labor was done) were famous just as the products of the present weaving industry are today. It is just and not a little ironic that the Otavaleños have been able to turn to their own advantage the skills learned in the hard schools of the *obrajes*; the communities in which the *obrajes* flourished are precisely those that are best known today for their textiles.

Negociantes (traders) from Otavalo venture as far afield as Venezuela, Puerto Rico, and even the United States to sell their textiles, and they are a familiar sight in the larger cities and weekly markets throughout Ecuador, particularly where tourists are to be found. They do a lively business selling ponchos, scarves, shawls, and the like to passengers and crew members of ships calling at Guayaquil, Ecuador's largest city and principal port. There is a sizable colony of Otavaleños resident in Bogotá, where they weave and sell their wares.

Most younger men and a good many of the older ones have lived outside Peguche for periods ranging up to ten years or so. All are bilingual in Spanish and Quichua.

Virtually all adult men and most boys fourteen and older, as well as many girls and women, are engaged in a cottage weaving industry that has expanded rapidly in the last few decades. The majority are independent weavers, but a significant number are employed as wage workers by Indian entrepreneurs who operate small-scale factories. One man runs a factory in which 60 workers are employed in two around-the-clock shifts. Most of the goods he produces are exported to the United States and sold in large stores such as Macy's in New York City. The more enterprising are quick to accept innovations. Orlon has all but displaced wool, and the traditional hand looms are giving way to power-operated ones. Bright colors and new styles mark the goods now being produced for the growing export market.

Within the limits of his identity as an Indian, the Otavaleño's relationship to those non-Indians with whom he deals is impersonal. He sells the products of his own acknowledged skills, not raw labor. It is the impersonal force of the market that comes to bear upon him, not the personal force of the *hacendado* or *patrón*. The greater freedom and invulnerability of the Otavaleño is readily apparent in his demeanor. His way of presenting himself stands in sharp contrast to the subservience of the hacienda-dominated *huasipunguero* or peon. In the presence of authority the peon stands at a distance, knees bent, hunched over the hat clutched to his breast. The man from Peguche stands proudly erect. Where the peon strings together self-deprecating diminutives and utters them in a voice tuned to supplication, the Otavaleño is forthright and direct. Where the peon may not even be conscious that he is unkempt and dirty, the Otavaleño is impeccably groomed.

Although deeply engaged in the larger society and attuned to many of its values, the Otavaleño nevertheless stands apart and aloof from it; he is in it but not really of it. He tends not to intermarry, and he takes a certain pride in his Indian identity and dress, signaled in part by the braid he wears. Indeed, his Indianness has a commercial value; he uses it as a hallmark of the goods he would sell.

From a secure and expanding economic base, the Otavaleño has evolved what might be described as a strategy of selective engagement. The more affluent have adopted many of the amenities of middle-class Ecuadorian life while still preserving traditional culture forms; for example, the pattern of Indian sociability and participation in fiestas. He must be polite, but he need not be servile, nor is servility expected of him. As an Indian his social mobility is restricted, and there are many doors he cannot enter without mutual discomfiture. He most certainly is not immune to the subtle poisons of prejudice, let alone its grosser manifestations. I was present in a restaurant in Otavalo when a man from Peguche's leading family, Otavalo's wealthiest textile entrepreneur and a complete gentleman, was forced to suffer the loud-mouthed insults of an insignificant town mestizo. Even for a person of his stature, the possibility of such treatment exists. Nevertheless, the Otavaleño does have a large measure of respect if not general acceptance.

ATAHUALPA

Founded by the Order of La Merced in the sixteenth century, Atahualpa is a traditional hacienda located in canton Cayambe, Pichincha Province. A combined residential community and commercial enterprise producing barley, wheat, and potatoes for the domestic market, Atahualpa has a population of about 1,500. Of Atahualpa's largely Indian population 1,237 persons live on 135 separate *huasipungos* averaging 3.7 hectares in size. Another 200 are either squatters along the sides of the roads and ravines or resident sharecroppers whose presence on the estate has long been tolerated. The white administrative, technical, and service personnel all live in the central hacienda compound. One-third of the Indians on the *huasipungos* are *apegados* (relatives "attached" to the *huasipunguero*) who live in 105 separate households on the plots.

Following the expropriation of church lands in the early 1900s, Atahualpa was controlled by a government agency, the *Asistencia Social,* and leased to a succession of individual and institutional patrons, including one of Ecuador's leading breweries. In 1964, in the wake of the Agrarian Reform Law promulgated by the military junta then in power, the *huasipungo* system was abolished and the Indians received title to their small holdings. The hacienda has since been transformed into two cooperatives, one managed by former *huasipungueros* and the other by white ex-employees.

Until very recently, however, in a pattern widely prevalent on other large estates, Atahualpa's Indians were bound to the hacienda in a tightly ordered and relatively self-contained social system presided over by the patron or his surrogate. It was a system sharply divided between those who commanded and those who obeyed. Orders and work assignments flowed down to the workers from the administrator through the *mayordomo* and a number of Indian *mayorales* (overseers).

In encounters between a peon and the patron or other authority figure one could often see acted out a grotesque charade of ceremonial deference as stylized as any ritual behavior ethologists delight in describing. It is a shattering experience to have a man fall on his knees before you, grasp you with a gnarled old root of a hand, and say, with tears streaming down his cheeks, "We who wear the red poncho are nothing. We are animals, brutes who know only how to work. We have nothing. We are poor, poor and ignorant. Look at me!"

Not all Atahualpans are scarred by servitude, however. There are a few exceptional men, including an acknowledged Communist who has visited Cuba and has been in and out of jail in Ecuador. Several of these men have assumed positions of power in the new cooperative. Now they are the *macho* patrons, and they play the part.

However, the simple peon is not defenseless. He has entered into an intricate system of reciprocal relationships for the exchange of various goods and services with kinsmen, *compadres,* and townspeople from Olmedo, the neighboring parish center or *cabecera.* He forms ties of *compadrazgo* with people from the town, and in return for their services as *tinterillos,* intercessors with authorities, and the like, or in exchange for credit extended to him, the peon grazes his *compadres'* animals with his own on hacienda pastures. He also forms sharecropping partnerships with mestizos from the town in a system called *chaqui-*

huasca. The mestizos provide seed and gifts of clothing, *aguardiente,* food, and a small amount of money, and the Indians contribute the land and labor. Both share equally in the harvest. Beyond this, the peon connives with white hacienda employees to illicitly exploit the estate's resources to their common gain.

As long as he fulfills his obligations at some minimal acceptable level, the *huasipunguero* has a certain basic security. His situation and his defenses are not unlike those of the army private. His response to orders may be sullen and grudging; he may feign ignorance of expectations or orders; he may loaf on the job and in other ways test the limits of the system; but he will usually be careful to stay within its limits. Despite his low estate, the *huasipunguero* is well aware that there are others who are landless and worse off than he is. And always lurking in the background is the threat of the brute force that the Indian can apply. Since the hacienda depends so heavily on the Indians' labor, it is vulnerable to work stoppages, particularly at crucial periods during the harvest. The organization for concerted political action is foreshadowed by the hierarchical structure of the hacienda; there are visible targets for the application of force, and there are common grievances to impel revolt. It is not surprising, then, that there has been a history of strikes, work stoppages, and violence—to the point of killing several patrons—on the haciendas of Cayambe.

SALASACA

The Salasaca[10] contrast dramatically with the peons of Atahualpa. About 4,000 of them live in a widely dispersed community of essentially independent subsistence farmers situated about 14 kilometers southeast of the city of Ambato in Tungurahua Province. Although removed from immediate contact with large haciendas (there is one small estate bordering Salasaca that employs about 20 Indians), the Salasaca are almost completely surrounded by small-scale mestizo farmers. Despite their proximity to these mestizos, contacts between the two groups are shallow and occur primarily in the economic sphere. There are virtually no intermarriages. Occasionally they drink together at a local *chichería, cantina,* or fiesta, but the rule of social distance between the two groups still obtains.

The Salasaca have for centuries fended off encroachment by non-Indians. They claim that they are *mitimaes* brought to Ecuador from Bolivia by the Inca conquerors, a belief shared by non-Indians as well. Whether true or not, the story serves to justify the reputation of the Salasaca as a different and distinctive people. Their basic stance against outsiders is aggressively defensive. Strangers who venture off the few main paths and roads open to them are likely to be challenged by an abrupt, "¿A donde va?" ("Where are you going?") and menaced by snarling dogs. Little deference, whether signaled by posture, gesture, or form of address, is shown to whites. The Salasaca's reputation as being *muy bravo* (very fierce) is perpetuated by both themselves and others through a number of oft-told tales of violence. One of these involves the killing of a census taker, another the burning of the Catholic mission, yet another a pitched battle with mestizos over rights to scarce water. Each of these incidents is symbolic in its own way of resistance to various kinds of outside threats. However, Salasaca bravado is perhaps most aptly symbolized by their bulls.

These animals, too, are widely known to be *muy bravo,* and they are eagerly sought for *juegos de toros* (bull-baiting) at local fiestas and even in coastal towns.

The Salasaca pride themselves on not accepting menial jobs as *cargadores* (carriers) or domestic servants, and they are scornful of other Indians who do. In recent years a number of younger men have joined the seasonal exodus of highland Indians to the coast to work on the large plantations there. However, they can work on the coast as comparatively anonymous individuals (they shed their distinctive black ponchos and heavy, broad-brimmed felt hats) and earn what they regard as a decent wage for honorable labor.

Even more significant has been the introduction of commercial weaving. In 1957, with the help of several agencies including the former Point IV Program, three men were taught to weave small tapestries embellished with colorful traditional designs. The original three took on others as apprentices; and today about 200 to 300 Salasaca, mostly young men and boys in their teens, are engaged in weaving and selling tapestries, largely to tourists and for a small export market. In the manner of the Otavaleños, a few of the more enterprising have established small shops in which they employ several weavers who work at piece rates. They have, in fact, albeit in a less sophisticated way, developed many of the same strategies in interethnic relations evident among the Otavalo weavers. In large degree, weaving has displaced the former making of cordage from sisal fiber as a source of cash income, especially for the younger men.

Except for the introduction of commercial weaving, the only agency to gain a solid foothold in Salasaca is the Catholic Church; a Protestant mission has been present for some years, but has gained only a handful of converts. The mission and school that were founded by the Madres Lauritas from Colombia in 1943 have had their own vicissitudes. The *Misión Andina,* an Ecuadorian community development agency, has made several overtures but has been consistently rebuffed. A succession of Peace Corps volunteers has worked in Salasaca. They have had only very modest successes, and these primarily among the weavers. A weavers' cooperative shakily established by one volunteer a few years ago foundered and subsequently failed. Today there are many changes as Salasaca moves increasingly into the larger society, but the basic attitude is, "Leave us in peace." They have learned how to defend themselves effectively, and even today the majority follow an essentially traditional style of life.

SAN FRANCISCO

San Francisco is a nucleated agricultural village of some 540 persons situated on the western rim of the valley of Riobamba in Chimborazo Province. All families own some land, but few have enough to subsist on. What land is available is of poor quality, and much of it is badly eroded. Rainfall is often inadequate, and there is not sufficient water to irrigate regularly. Hail is a constant threat to cereal crops, and a blight called *lancha* is another scourge. Equal inheritance among all heirs has led to great fragmentation of land—some families have as many as 25 or 30 minuscule plots. Such fragmentation does, however, permit the spreading of risks where farming is precarious at best.

Given these uncertainties and the scarcity of land, San Francisqueños are forced to go out of the community to survive. Except for small amounts of produce such as alfalfa, barley, peas, and pyrethrum, a few scrawny sheep, and small baskets woven by the women, they have nothing to offer but their labor in a society where labor is abundant and cheap. Thus about 30 families have a contractual arrangement to provide labor once a week as *ayudas* (helpers) on lands owned by a hacienda in a neighboring valley. In exchange, they are granted access to hacienda pastures for their small flocks of sheep, a ration of potatoes at harvest time, and the like. A number of men are employed as day laborers for periods of several weeks or more on two large estates owned by a wealthy *hacendado* from Ambato. One of these is a sugar-cane plantation on the coast, the other a highland hacienda. The village itself is a sort of collective client for this particular patron.

Others have established individual patron-client relationships with employers in the larger cities. One man who is especially adroit at managing such relationships has patrons in Riobamba, Ambato, and Quito and has used his influence to find jobs for others from San Francisco, including a number of girls employed as domestics. Many have established similar patron-client relationships with mestizo farmers from the nearby town of San Juan. Several have solidified ties with patrons by entering into sharecropping arrangements with them. The Indian supplies the land and labor, the patron *partidario* the seed. Both share equally in the harvest—a bad bargain for the Indian, but a good stratagem to secure an ally. San Francisqueños are frequently forced to mortgage their land at extortionate rates, with half the crop demanded as interest in addition to repayment of the principal.

The patron-client relationship, highly asymmetrical and with strong overtones of dependency, is the prototype for all relationships with authority figures who are potential benefactors, including anthropologists and community development agents. The basic strategy in such a relationship is for the Indian to present himself as a poor, humble, willing, deserving person. Embedded in the relationship, and within the limits of what the patron will tolerate, the Indian employs what might be called a strategy of counterexploitation. In relationships with Ecuadorian patrons the lines are quite clearly drawn, but this is not the case with visiting gringo anthropologists. My role among the people of San Francisco was not sharply defined, nor at the outset did I seek to clarify it or to set limits. I was as a consequence fair game for a variety of exploitative maneuvers, including requests for food, loans, transportation, jobs, and services as intermediary in securing jobs or favors elsewhere. Begging (not the rule in Peguche, Salasaca, or Saraguro) was an especially troublesome problem until I established that I wanted to decide for myself when largess was to be distributed. Perhaps the most poignant example of such behavior was a solemn and tearful leave-taking with a key informant. I count him a true friend, but on parting, and without anticipating any gift I might make him, he asked for my flashlight and a substantial advance against wages for work in a future summer.

The need to establish patron-client relationships can be a source of great competition and envy. I was "captured" early in the game by one man who at first, unbeknownst to me, controlled access to me by his fellow villagers. Jealousy of his relationship with me led to exaggerated stories of the money he got from me, to deep resentment, and to a fight in which he was badly beaten and almost had a thumb bitten off. In San Francisco envy is a gnawing, ever present emotion, and "the image of limited good" is a harsh reality.

GUABUG

Guabug,[11] which lies only a few kilometers to the west across an intervening hill, is like San Francisco in many respects. Yet it has many advantages, and circumstances have conspired to make it a village chosen for progress. Rainfall is more abundant and predictable. The soil is richer and well suited to raising onions, which have become an important cash crop. There have been more and better opportunities for outside employment. A number of men, for example, are employed in a nearby limestone quarry and cement factory established in 1954. There are, moreover, a number of neighboring haciendas which, again in exchange for labor, provide access to their resources and a small cash wage. Although often flagrantly exploitative, such ties are better than none at all, and they are much more regularized than is the case for San Francisco. A number of people have left Guabug, some for well-paying jobs such as school teacher, agronomist, and shopkeeper.

The basic strategies employed in Guabug, both economic and interpersonal, are much like those in San Francisco. The same patterns of deference are shown authority figures and the same sorts of alliances are sought with persons outside the community. San Francisco is, however, much more conservative in its general outlook. The fiesta system that still flourishes in San Francisco has disappeared from Guabug, and many men in the latter community have given up Indian dress for Western-style clothes while still proclaiming their Indian identity. At the field seminar to be described below, for example, the two from Guabug came nattily dressed in tweed jackets and regular trousers while the two from San Francisco wore ponchos and the traditional small round felt hat. In short, Guabug is much farther along the path to cultural mestization and integration into the national culture than is San Francisco.

SARAGURO

Like the Otavaloños in the north, the Saraguro are a large group of more than 10,000 who live in a number of communities in Ecuador's southernmost province, Loja. Both the landscape and the people of Saraguro have a different aspect. There are no snow peaks. Instead there are rolling wooded hills, many of them cleared for fields and pasture, and intensively cultivated valleys devoted largely to corn farming. Unlike the central and northern highlands, there are no large haciendas. Mestizo farms in the area are on the same scale as those owned by the Indians. In fact, the average Indian farmer is at least as well off as his white counterpart. Nor is there the same pressure on the land. The best valley land is expensive, as expensive as corn land in central Illinois, but communal, "free" land is available in the hills for the clearing.

Most important is the fact that the Saraguro have colonized the Oriente (the eastern slopes of the Andes). Since the turn of the century, Saraguro in increasing numbers have settled in the Yacuambi River valley, expropriating the native Jivaro. Here they have cleared extensive tracts for pasture and a few other crops such as *yuca* (manioc), sugar cane, and bananas and have recently become engaged in cattle-raising. Many Saraguro are thus transmigrant, even transhumant, maintaining land and homes in both the Oriente and the sierra. To be sure, these circumstances are exceptional in Ecuador, but the concept of "limited good" would have as little meaning for the Saraguro as it would have had for Andrew Carnegie.

Given the absence of systematic exploitation, the greater abundance of land, and greater economic parity in Saraguro, Indian–white relationships are more egalitarian there than they are in most parts of the sierra. In some communities Indians and whites live side by side at the same level, and cordial relations are maintained between them. There are, in fact, some curious reversals. Poor whites are often employed by Indians as laborers, and there is an institutionalized pattern of whites' begging from Indians. Indians can and do "become" whites (*laichus*, as they are known in Saraguro), simply by changing their costume and, for the men, by cutting their hair. They can change their identity and, unlike most of Ecuador, still openly and unashamedly retain ties with their own Indian families. It is not unusual for one or more children in a family to become *laichus* while their siblings remain Indian, and many genealogies reveal marriages between Indians and *laichus*. Unlike the disavowal of one's racial origins involved in "passing," Saraguro can publicly change their identity and do so without recrimination. The advantage for those who change their identity is that they are able thereby to enlarge their circle of social relations and enter more readily into the world of the whites.

Good farmers, the Saraguro have been quick to accept technological innovations—seed, fertilizer, implements—whatever their source. Their approach to agents of change is pragmatic: "What have you to offer that I can use?" As incipient capitalists and entrepreneurs, they are highly individualistic and little concerned with community development programs unless they have a personal stake in them. In Erasmus's[12] terms, conspicuous ownership takes precedence over conspicuous giving (or, one might add, over conspicuous involvement), and invidious comparison and emulation are important motivating factors. Like the weavers of Peguche, the Saraguro are an open and proud people who confront their white and mestizo compatriots without humility or fear.

THE GUASLÁN SEMINAR

In the summer of 1968 my students and I brought together two men from each of the six communities for an experimental field seminar held at the *Misión Andina's* training center, Guaslán, near Riobamba. Our purpose was to collect additional data, but especially to test some of our hypotheses and interpretations about the differences among the several groups.

For two weeks we lived closely together. We ate together, drank together, socialized and worked together, so that we came to know each other very well. Each morning and afternoon we held formal meetings lasting three hours. We began by asking each pair of men to describe in detail the style of life in their own community—how they earned their living, the political organization, the fiestas celebrated, relations with neighboring villages and towns, and so on. All paid close attention to the presentations and asked a great many questions. We also asked each pair to discuss a series of special topics, such as the nature of interethnic relationships, the terms used to distinguish various social and racial categories, the recent presidential elections, religious beliefs and practices, what they felt were the principal problems in their respective communities, and what the government might do to solve them.

They were also asked to present small sociodramas in which one man took the role of a priest, *hacendado, teniente-político,* or the like and the other that of a simple Indian. The selection of the roles they would play was left largely to the Indians themselves. For example, the two men from Saraguro presented a long and very interesting and entertaining sketch between a Saraguro colonist and a Jivaro; the two from Salasaca acted out an encounter between a *chichero* and an Indian requesting a loan. In similar fashion, we also asked them to give a demonstration of the styles of greeting, in both gestures and words, used in their communities between persons of different social levels.

In many less formal occasions, such as in the dining room or at our small fiestas in the evenings, there were many opportunities to observe differences in behavior among the six groups. For example, the men from Atahualpa, San Francisco, and Guabug showed much more deference to us and to the director of the Guaslán Center than those from Peguche, Salasaca, and Saraguro. The two from San Francisco were shocked when the Salasaca greeted the students by their first names only instead of using a more formal title. When there was hard work to be done such as unloading a truck or killing and dressing a pig for our farewell party, it was those from Guabug, San Francisco, and Atahualpa who volunteered while the others stood idly by as observers. Many similar examples could be cited, but in short, we were able to observe daily in their ordinary behavior many of the differences among the groups that we had hypothesized.

The Indians themselves were sensitive to many of the same differences. In the last day of the seminar we held private interviews with each of the 12 men. Each man was asked to characterize the men from each of the other communities and to compare them with the others. We asked them to tell us which group was most like or most different from themselves, which was the most Indian, the least Indian, the richest, the most "civilized," and so on. In response to such questions, a perceptive and highly intelligent man from Peguche made the following observations:

Question: Which group would you say is most similar to you?

Answer: The group most similar to us are the Saraguros, because they don't have to beg from anyone or ask favors, not from the priest, the *teniente-político*, or the *apu*.[13] They know how to speak directly with anyone, while the others ask someone to speak to the priest or the *teniente-político* for them. The Saraguros aren't afraid. After the Saraguros perhaps the Salasaca are most like us. Those from Guabug and San Francisco are the same and have the same ideas. The Salasaca weren't bothered with *apus*, and they don't beg from the whites.

Question: Are there differences among those from Atahualpa, Guabug, and San Francisco?

Answer: Yes, there are a few differences. Those from Atahualpa work on a hacienda. Those from Guabug and San Francisco work on haciendas without any real benefits, for no more than a few pieces of straw. They get little from their land. Those from Chimborazo have to beg more than the Salasacas; they are used to begging from the *hacendados*, or rather from the white people.

Question: Why do you think they have had to beg more than the Saraguros and you?

Answer: We have always spoken Spanish and can go directly to the priest and the *teniente-político* for what we want. And we haven't been afraid like the others.

Question: Why have they been afraid?

Answer: Perhaps because they don't know how to speak, or because they have always been timid, and because they live under the domination of the hacienda. But we are independent and don't have to look to the haciendas because we have our own industries. The Saraguros also have their own work of cattle-raising and their own industry. They have a lot of cattle and land in the Oriente and they don't have to beg from anyone.

The words of this man eloquently express the essential nature of the differences among the six communities with which we have been concerned. And his insight into the causes of these differences is the best confirmation I can offer of the validity of our own "scientific" explanation of them.

CONCLUSION

The six communities described above represent a considerable range of variation in the degree to which they control essential economic resources, the nature of those resources, and the extent of their involvement in the larger society. Nevertheless, we cannot assume that they cover the full spectrum of adaptive strategies resorted to by the Indians of highland Ecuador. There are other groups—herders who live in the high *páramo* (bleak, barren plateau) and isolated agriculturalists—who presumably have evolved other strategies for survival in their particular, perhaps even harsher, circumstances. I believe, however, that the research approach we have employed is applicable to these groups as well.

Of the six communities we have studied, Peguche, Salasaca, and Saraguro are rather special cases. They are not nearly as representative of the great majority of the Indian population as are Atahualpa, San Francisco, and Guabug. All, however, are changing as the larger society in which they are embedded is itself being transformed, albeit slowly and painfully. These changes can be more fully comprehended if viewed in the context of the adaptive strategies various groups have devised to cope with the vicissitudes of past circumstances and must devise to defend themselves in their present plight.

OTES

1. A preliminary version of this paper was presented at the XXXIX International Congress of Americanists in Lima, Peru, August 1970.

The research has been supported by grants from the National Science Foundation (GS-1224) and the Center for International Comparative Studies of the University of Illinois, Champaign-Urbana. I wish also to acknowledge the contributions of my associates in this research and give them my grateful thanks: Linda and James Belote (Saraguro), Muriel Kaminsky Crespi (Atahualpa), Kathleen Klumpp (Peguche), and Arthur R. Piper (Guabug). Mrs. Crespi's doctoral dissertation, "The Patrons and

Peons of Pesillo: A Traditional Hacienda System in Highland Ecuador," University of Illinois, 1968, provides a full account of the hacienda.

2. The basic question "What is an Indian?" is very difficult to answer. The answers vary depending on whether one uses as the criterion self-identification, categorization of a person as Indian by others both Indian and non-Indian, or some combination of "objective" measures such as knowledge of Quichua, clothing, type of dwelling, or natal community. Physical appearance is not unimportant in Ecuador; many Indians themselves value a light complexion. However, skin color and other physical traits are not the all-but-indelible markers of race they are for blacks in the United States. There are many mestizos and *blancos*, so acknowledged by themselves and others, who are darker in complexion than many Indians. Race in Ecuador is, then, primarily a social and cultural and not a physical category.

For the Indian, clothing (hat, poncho, trousers, skirt, footwear or the lack of it) and hair style (whether the braids of the Otavaleño and Saraguro men or the long-cut hair of the Salasaca) are the public symbols of Indian identity. As elsewhere in the world, costume is used in manifold ways to express one's self-identity, both consciously and unconsciously. One notes a sharp contrast between Otavalo, Saraguro, and Salasaca on the one hand and the Indian from Atahualpa, Guabug, or San Francisco on the other. When asked to pose for a photograph, the former will typically *put on* his best Indian clothes while the latter will divest himself of Indian dress and put on western-style clothes if he has them. In Ecuador one can then, knowing passable Spanish, shed these public symbols of Indianness and slip with little notice into the rural or urban proletariate. Thousands do.

3. On several occasions I took Indians on a tour of the magnificent archaeological collections in the Museum of the Central Bank of Ecuador. My Indian friends evinced only mild interest and saw no connection between themselves and these relics of their past.

4. See Erving Goffman, *Stigma: Notes on the Management of Spoiled Identity*, Prentice-Hall, Englewood Cliffs, N.J., 1963.

5. See especially Icaza's novel *Huasipungo*.

6. George M. Foster, Peasant society and the image of limited good, *American Anthropologist* 67:293–315, 1965.

7. I use the terms "power" and "domain" in the sense employed by Richard N. Adams. See, for example, his article in this book (pp. 82–93).

8. *Hacendado* means owner of a large estate or hacienda; *teniente-político*, a political deputy, the appointed parish civil officer; *chichero*, a man who sells *chicha*, a mildly intoxicating beverage made from fermented corn and brown sugar; *tinterillo*, a kind of legal clerk or scribe who draws up documents, writes letters, and the like.

9. There are upward of 40,000 Indians living in about 75 separate communities in the Otavalo area. While there are many similarities among them, one may observe many of the same differences we have noted for Ecuador as a whole. Thus some groups are primarily agriculturalists; others are part- or full-time artisans making products such as rush mats, pottery, and bricks; and some are strongly tied to haciendas. Otavalo is the best-described area in highland Ecuador. See, for example, Elsie Clews Parsons, *Peguche: A Study of Andean Indians*, University of Chicago Press, 1945; John Collier, Jr., and Aníbal Buitrón, *The Awakening Valley*, University of Chicago Press, 1949; and Gonzalo Rubio Orbe, *Punyaro*, Quito, 1956.

10. The Salasaca are described by Piedad Peñaherra de Costales and Alfredo Costales Samaniego in *Los Salasacas, Llacta* No. 8, Publicaciones del Instituto Ecuatoriano de Antropología, Quito, 1959.

11. For a more complete account of Guabug and the parish to which it pertains, see Joseph B. Casagrande and Arthur R. Piper, "La transformación estructural de una parroquia rural en las tierras altas del Ecuador," *América Indígena*, Vol. XXIX, October 1969, pp. 1039–1064.

12. Charles J. Erasmus, *Man Takes Control: Cultural Development and American Aid*, University of Minnesota Press, Minneapolis, 1961.

13. *Apu:* a lay religious leader and hereditary intermediary for the Indian in his dealings with the priest and *teniente-político*.

Land, Agriculture, and Economics

Latin America is an area of extremes in both natural and social features. Topographic, climatological, and other factors combine to create a wide variety of ecological niches that have been exploited by man in different ways throughout history and prehistory. The importance of economics in Latin America is clear not only in theoretic terms but also in the view of the people themselves.

Anthropologists tend to think of economic behavior as comprising all that people think and do about making a living, that is, ideas and activities concerning production and exchange. A few anthropologists (e.g., Goodfellow, Herskovits, LeClair) appear to have felt quite comfortable applying concepts and definitions from classical economics in new and different contexts among non-Western peoples. Others (e.g., Polanyi *et al.*, Firth, Dalton) have clearly felt that the analytical categories developed in Western cultures cannot be applied to primitive economies.

The early and continued interest in economic field studies in Latin America has resulted in the collection of more detailed data, slightly greater development of theory, and much more work in terms of development than is typical in other major world areas. It has also demonstrated that the approaches of anthropology and economics are by no means contradictory, or even particularly difficult to reconcile, as is illustrated in this section by the articles of Nisbet, and Forman and Riegelhaupt. In general, the anthropologist tends to take a microscopic view, intensively analyzing limited local situations. Illustrative of this tendency in Latin America are studies of regional markets (e.g., Malinowski and de la Fuente 1957, Waterbury 1969, McBryde 1933); of specific communities (e.g., Wagley 1941, Foster 1942, Tax 1953); or even of individual households (e.g., Nash 1961). Another approach is to deal with particular economic institutions (for example: slavery, Aguirre Beltrán 1944; land tenure, Carroll 1965, C.I.D.A.; plantations, Pan American Union 1959, Thompson 1957). By contrast, the economist more often deals with macroscopic patterns, such as inflation, balance of payments, total national production of major commodities, taxation, and so forth (e.g., Eder 1968, Gordon 1950, Wythe 1949, International Bank for Reconstruction and Development). These approaches are clearly complementary, and a number of studies demonstrate how fruitfully they can be integrated (e.g., Kunkel 1961, Glade and Anderson 1963, Mosk 1954, Frank 1967, Fillol 1961, and others).

The papers in this section reflect some of the dominant themes in Latin American economy, as well as provide a sample of the kinds of studies that have been made. In order to set these papers in perspective, I will briefly review the development of studies under four broad rubrics: land and agriculture, wealth and power, systems of exchange, and economic development.

LAND AND AGRICULTURE

Several countries in Latin America have seen widespread and relatively rapid expansion in many sectors of their economies. Despite this fact, the agricultural sector still employs over 40 percent of the labor force in half of the countries in the area. A significant portion of these people is engaged in subsistence farming and participates only slightly in the economic and political life of the nation.

This group includes independent small-scale farmers as well as tenants on haciendas where archaic methods of production persist, depending on massed labor rather than mechanization or other capital investments. Agriculture in such contexts is qualitatively as well as quantitatively distinct from commercial farming; the latter involves different kinds of social relationships as well as production of more (and often different) crops. The hacienda, or uncapitalized latifundium, is often a quasi-feudal estate with unsalaried tenants in some variant of the *colono* system of labor (cf. Feder 1971, International Labor Office 1957). By contrast, the plantation, sometimes called "factory in the field," is highly capitalized, producing for the world market, employing wage labor. This fruitful distinction, similar to that between the *engenho* and *usina* types as described above by Wagley and Harris, has been more fully discussed by Wolf and Mintz (1957). It is a truism that different economic systems are associated with very different cultural contexts, although the relative importance of various factors as "determinants" is by no means agreed upon. The hacienda and the plantation differ not only in terms of production and distribution, but also as entire social systems. The significantly different kinds of communities and their effects on people from the same general cultural milieu are examined in Miller's account of the proletarianization of Peruvian peasants, reprinted in this section.

There is an abundant literature on agricultural methods, and detailed data are available in virtually every ethnographic account or community study. In fact, some of the earliest systematic studies of Latin American communities were conducted under the auspices of the U.S. Department of Agriculture, and the same authors (Hill, Leonard, Loomis, Nelson, Smith, and Whetten) have prepared characterizations of national patterns in which the interests of rural sociology predominate.

The specifics of the annual round, motor habits, tools, and so forth, are clearly important in understanding the life of the local people. Beyond this, some social scientists have attempted to describe and analyze the relation of agriculture to other aspects of the economy at the national and even international levels (e.g., Le Beau in Guatemala [1956]; Hill, Silva, and Hill in Venezuela [1960]); another approach, based on careful analysis of statistical data, is illustrated by the work of Clyde Mitchell and Jacob Schatan, abridged in this section. Whatever reservations one may have about the exactness of such gross national statistics, they are sufficiently consistent and plausible to allow meaningful comparisons through both time and space, and the obstacles to economic development identified in that report conform well with the conclusions arrived at by Erasmus and by Gonzalez, each of whom came at the problem from a very different perspective and used very different kinds of data in their articles reprinted here.

Since a major portion of the population depends for its livelihood on working the land, it is little wonder that these people have developed complex and varied systems of thinking and acting with relation to it. The supposed persistence of some pre-Columbian patterns of man-land relations has long been a focus of attention for Latin American sociologists and social philosophers (e.g., Castro Pozo), and has led to the idealized myth of community, effectively criticized by Adams (1962). Several European institutions were transplanted to the New World, where they underwent peculiar adaptions to local situations, and have persisted for centuries in modified form. Scholars who have contributed to our understanding of these patterns include José Ots Capdequí, François Chevalier, and others. For a long time, even before contemporary patterns of land tenure and related patterns of social relations were systematically studied, they were the subject of novels of social protest in the *indigenista* school (e.g., Alegría 1941, Icaza 1964).

In studies of land tenure, some social scientists tend to introduce an historical perspective somewhat more systematically than in their analyses of some other aspects of culture. This perspective is appropriate to an understanding of how contemporary patterns came to be, and its use in this context sometimes reveals new insights that could not be gained by synchronic study alone, as in Solomon Miller's paper in this section. Because of the jural and political importance of land in European cultures, it is a recurrent subject throughout historical sources—published and unpublished, official and unofficial.

Until recent years, students of land tenure tended to sketch general national or regional patterns (e.g., McBride in Bolivia [1921], Chile [1936], and Mexico [1923]; Martínez in Colombia [1939]. An increasing number of detailed local studies indicate the range of variation around the norm and deal with attitudes and values of the rural populace, as well as with national laws (e.g., Borde and Góngora 1956, Romney 1959, Heath, Erasmus, and Buechler 1969, and others). The widely scattered and diverse studies conducted under the auspices of the Land Tenure Center (by William Thiesenhusen, Ronald Clark, and others) are, in part, summarized by Dorner (1971); those done for the Inter-American Committee on Agricultural Development (by Solon Barraclough, Andrew Pearse, and others) are being published as a monograph on each nation.

Many of the most important values attached to land have no immediate relevance to its productive capacity. In a predominantly agricultural economy, the distribution of wealth is determined largely by control over land, and power and prestige usually accrue to wealthy landowners. Until recent years, nearly all Latin American countries have been characterized as dual[1] societies, in which a small elite long managed to exert economic and political dominance over the ineffectual majority of the populace. Not only do these few seem to control most of the wealth; they often effectively dominate regions and even nations and enjoy privileges denied the majority.

The dual problems of *latifundismo* (concentration of vast areas in the hands of a few) and *minifundismo* (excessive fragmentation of plots among the great majority) are universal in Latin America except in those nations that have undergone large-scale social revolution (Mexico, Bolivia, and Cuba). The traditional degree of concentration of landownership is reflected in the fact that in the middle of the twentieth century almost 90 percent of the cultivated land was still owned by less than 10 percent of the landholders, whereas more than 70 percent of the landowners controlled less than 4 percent of the land. The land reforms that have already taken place in the context of broader national revolutions are important, each in its own right, but it would not be appropriate to take any one country's experience as a model for change elsewhere (cf. Schaedel 1965). Recent experiments in Chile and Peru, involving large-scale changes of land tenure patterns without other wholesale restructuring of the social order, should be informative.

The successes and shortcomings of land reform programs to date indicate clearly that reallocation of land is not enough to markedly increase agricultural production for market; in fact, reallocation sometimes seems to have had the opposite effect. Most analysts agree with the conclusions that Charles Erasmus, in a paper reprinted in this section, draws from the experience of Mexico, Bolivia, and Venezuela—that maximum economic impact can come not from simple *land* reform, but only from a sweeping *agrarian* reform, which should include credit facilities for small farmers, improvement of agricultural techniques, development of transportation and processing facilities, and so forth. Such programs are extremely costly and difficult to administer, and so are understandably rare.

In spite of this, and however much the national economy may suffer, land reform is often sought as a prerequisite to social reform. The idea of land reform as crucial in Latin American social reform is by no means limited to Marxists. Certainly the United Nations, United States, and Alliance for Progress have all been outspoken in support of such a view (see, e.g., U.N., Department of Economic Affairs 1951, International Labor Office 1957, U.S. Agency for International Development 1961, Inter-American Economic and Social Council 1961). Agreement on the principle is widespread, but there is no consensus on how to achieve it. Most North Americans tend to speak in terms of gradual social reform and evolution, whereas many Latin Americans insist that violent revolution will be necessary.

There is one major obstacle to the enactment of economic reforms such as those enjoined by the Alliance for Progress, which include land reform, increase of taxes on income, property and inheritance, and so forth. The problem can be simply stated, but its resolution is not easy; those who control the legislative process are precisely those who would suffer the greatest immediate loss, so that enactment of such reform would appear to be an exceptionally altruistic act. However, among those who consider violent revolution a realistic alternative, or even an imminent one, such philanthropy can be interpreted as a good investment. But this view is not widespread among those who now enjoy political and economic dominance. The writings of Oscar Delgado, Juan José Arévalo, and others cannot be dismissed as merely polemic; not only do they reflect an increasingly widespread and powerful current of thought among Latin Americans, but their interpretation fits the stark historical and social realities of the area. There appears to be strong and growing pressure for major realignment of the distribution of wealth and power, by whatever means may be effective.

WEALTH AND POWER

We have already discussed the reality that is the basis of the stereotype of dual societies in Latin America, with wealth and power concentrated in the hands of a small oligarchy who usually also control most of the land. The papers in this book by Leeds, Strickon, Adams, and others show how tight networks of kinsmen and friends often enjoy an effective monopoly on education, voting, large-scale commerce, and other important activities, while the majority of a nation's population are, at best, second-class citizens, and often serfs or tenant-farmers in a quasi-feudal social order.

The distinction between the "power-prestige sector" and the "work-wealth sector," formulated by Adams (1965) and discussed in the Introduction to the next section, seems both valid and appropriate in many areas. The fact that wealth and power are not precisely correlated is indicated in the recent and progressive growth of a middle sector whose control over wealth has not provided easy access to power and prestige (cf. Beals 1953, J. Johnson 1965). It can also be seen in the Latin American equivalent of "genteel poverty," which seems to be widespread although it has rarely been noted in the literature. Many of the rural gentry are not wealthy—in terms of liquid capital—even in relation to merchants in nearby towns. Their apparent wealth is often in symbols which have only local currency, such as control over unused land, access to laborers, personal leisure, and so forth. Such people seem wealthy because peasants are obliged to work for them where monopolization of land offers no feasible alternative. A surfeit of labor is then one kind of conspicuous consumption appropriate to landlords who cannot afford hard goods, and *hacendados* may live well in terms of the local patterns, even though they command no negotiable assets that would allow them to sell out and move elsewhere. It is possible for such people to enjoy power without wealth largely because the personalistic ethos of Middle and South America emphasizes patronage and clientage (see Foster's article in the following section), and their interpersonal networks provide a quality of social relations that is not directly available to others. The papers by Strickon, Leeds, and Ingham show how patron-client dyads form chains, in which the social status and power of a provincial landlord can be secure within his usual realm of action, even if he has little that is readily negotiable, and would be considered a rustic by the social elite in the capital.

SYSTEMS OF EXCHANGE

One of the most striking features of Latin American economies is the widespread use of money even by those people who retain their indigenous language, dress, and other customs. Although we sometimes speak of peasants operating at a subsistence level, complete self-sufficiency is rare and fast disappearing. Furthermore, the geographic mobility of Latin American peasants is often appreciable, whether they are in quest of seasonal wage-work or on marketing trips. The isolated peasant is at one with the self-sufficient peasant—an unrealistic stereotype, mythical, except in a few very limited areas. A variety of systems of exchange are operative throughout Latin America; a brief review of some of these indicates the degree to which economic activities are integrated with other kinds of interaction.

With reference to rural cultivators who operate on the fringes of a money economy, there are often conflicting interpretations about the relative importance of economic and other values in their ideological systems. This is especially common when some aspects of the peasant culture are strikingly different from hispanic or other Western patterns. Even though Tax made much of the contrasting world views and patterns of social relationships in the Indian and ladino sectors of Guatemala's population (1941), he took pains to dispel the popular view that Indians were unconcerned with profits, showing in detail how they strove as "penny capitalists" (1953). Large expenditures on religious and other festivals, together with exceptional generosity to kinsmen and others, were often misunderstood by some observers who considered them not "rational" (in economic terms). A brief but valuable paper by Evon Vogt, reprinted in this section, shows the constant interplay of economic and other values in one family; his article has the added advantage of showing how the decisions made by specific individuals on specific occasions relate to general propositions about cultural patterns.

The availability of credit is an important feature in the life of small-scale farmers and others whose livelihood is not assured. Charles Nisbet's study of the sources of credit in rural Chile here provides a dramatic illustration of the degree to which patterns of exchange are integrated with other aspects of culture, including social stratification, political organization, and so forth. Manning Nash has written on this aspect of peasant life in Mexico and Guatemala; the relevance of what Foster calls patron-client relations is clear.

Ecological variation is one of the reasons for the regional specialization that is so marked in parts of Middle and South America, especially in mountainous zones where differences in altitude make for different agricultural systems within the radius of a few miles. But custom is also operative, for example, in fairly uniform areas where virtually each village specializes in a particular crop, craft, or service, and communities are interdependent, as in highland Guatemala (McBryde 1947), Bolivia (Bowman 1910), or parts of Mexico (West 1948). Within such networks, special importance attaches to the market, which, in this sense, is as much a distributive mechanism as a place. The article by Shepard Forman and Joyce Riegelhaupt here combines description of a large-scale regional market system with an historical scheme, or typology, and an analysis of how these relate to other ecological considerations. Concerning markets and marketing, as is true of many aspects of culture, descriptions are available in many ethnographic monographs, including community studies. Meticulous quantitative analysis is rare, however, even among those who have paid particular attention to the subject, such as Sidney Mintz, Malinowski and de la Fuente, Sol Tax, and Ronald Waterbury.

Another important system of exchange is the civil-religious hierarchy which is found in many Indian and peasant communities. It is generally expected that each adult male will progress through a series of offices (*cargos*), and the mandatory sponsorship of initiation parties, religious festivals, and so forth, from time to time serve to dissipate or redistribute accumulated wealth. A number of studies suggest that this is an effective means of economic leveling within a closed community (cf. Carrasco 1952, Wolf 1957, Bunzel 1952, and others); the most detailed analysis of a system, however, goes far beyond that simple functional interpretation and offers a number of original and plausible hypotheses, together with abundant data (Cancian 1965).

The analysis of reciprocal labor reflects another kind of economic stabilizer which is effective where the group is limited and social sanctions carry considerable weight, in the "closed corporate community." As such systems have been analyzed by Erasmus (1965), it is clear that they are neither communistic nor even communal, but rather that strict rules govern who helps whom do what and when. Furthermore, it must be emphasized that there is no real fallacy in such a group's "making a living by taking in each other's laundry." Although such a system appears unworkable at any given time, it may be perfectly suitable when one views it as a redistributive system over the period of a year or more.

If we look to the ways in which the economic activities of local communities relate to national institutions and economies, Wolf's paper on "brokers" is again most helpful. Without lessening in any significant measure the urgency of Stavenhagen's denunciation of the widespread pattern of "internal colonialism," it provides guidelines for tracing the linkages between grass-roots producers and ultimate consumers, at whatever level they may be.

Another important aspect of Latin American economics is the international flow of wealth. It is beyond the scope of our discussion to analyze such factors as monoculture, inflation, export of capital rather than investment, and other aspects of large-scale economic systems, but it seems important to note that those features are widespread in the area, and they are of immediate relevance in evaluating problems and prospects for economic development, which is primary among the domestic and international concerns of virtually every Latin American country. Agriculture and mining have long predominated, perpetuating an extractive "colonial" type of economy in which high returns were favored over long-range investment. Industrialization has gained real importance in only a few countries since World War II. It is a telling comment on progress that some early general assessments of problems and prospects for economic development in Latin America remain basically sound (e.g., Hanson 1951, Vries and Medina 1963, and others); more recent judgments, representing a broad spectrum of viewpoints, are offered by Andre Frank, Victor Alba, Raul Prebisch, and others.

Values and attitudes in Latin America have long been cited by North Americans as major obstacles to greater efficiency, the imposition of stricter direction on labor, and so forth, whereas lack of domestic capital has been especially lamented by national critics. Although we do not understand the process very well, we have seen enough examples of abrupt and enthusiastic adoption of commercial-industrial values to seriously question the importance of the stereotypical cavalier-picaresque outlook as severely impeding development, and the regular flight of large amounts of capital to Europe and the United States is well known. Miller's paper, in this section, is very much to the point in this connection, as is the work of Manning Nash, Beate Salz, William Whyte, and others. Foster's discussion of the "image of limited good" is as controversial as it is imaginative.

Increasing experiments in nationalization of major industries provide a discouraging climate for private capitalization (in Bolivia, Chile, and Peru, for example). In a sort of vicious circle, widespread poverty limits the market for manufactured goods, so that new kinds of employment develop only slowly, and the rapid growth of population aggravates unemployment with its associated poverty. Demographic pressures and their important implications for economic development are analyzed in detail by Gonzalez, in this section; it is enough at this point to indicate that the population explosion is progressing in Latin

America at a rate greater than that anywhere else in the world, so that many nations there—even those that are relatively highly industrialized—now have a *lower* income than they did a decade ago, on a *per capita* basis.

Large-scale migration to cities (often called "urbanization") is another major trend in Latin America today, and although it is related to both industrialization and population growth, it should not be considered congruent with either (cf. Hauser 1962, Morse 1971, Violich 1967, and others). As discussed in the following introduction, the reasons for such migration vary greatly, and it should be no surprise that there are significant continuities in life-style between urban and rural dwellers. Migration from densely populated regions to sparsely populated frontiers is only beginning, but may progress rapidly in Colombia, Bolivia, Brazil, Ecuador, and Peru, among other countries.

Throughout the 1950s and 1960s, technical and economic assistance from abroad loomed large in the economies of many Latin American nations. In this connection many North American anthropologists have been involved in "action programs" which require the application of their skills, insights, and knowledge to the solution of practical problems. A diagnostic review of successes and shortcomings is offered by Foster (1973); a general theory of culture was developed by Erasmus (1961) on the basis of his extensive work throughout Latin America. Despite the fact that the impact of foreign aid has often been disappointing to enthusiastic proponents, it has offered a fruitful field for the study of the dynamics of cultural change. An unusual experiment in international collaboration for purposes of improving the welfare of rural farmers is described here by Henry Dobyns. Unlike most such programs, it was administered by social scientists rather than an agency of any government, and long-term research allowed analysis of the resistances, adoptions, adaptations, and rejection of a variety of innovations that were offered.

Domestic and international economic problems are characteristic of all of Latin America. Dissatisfaction over the unequal distribution of wealth and power is finding increased expression among the people, and the slow rate of economic growth is frustrating to officials. These problems are fundamental to understanding the social ferment that characterizes the area today.

OTE

1. Stavenhagen addressed himself to a very different concept in his paper above, when he called the dualistic view of Latin American societies fallacious. I share his stand that two major sectors of the population, although they differ markedly in terms of wealth and power, must be seen as interacting in complementary ways within common national systems rather than as isolated and independent of each other. In a sense, this is what most of the papers in this book are about.

Recommended Readings on LAND, AGRICULTURE, AND ECONOMICS*

Adams, Richard N.
1962 The community in Latin America: A changing myth. *The Centennial Review* 6:409–434.
1965 Introduction [to Social Organization]. In Heath and Adams, 1965.
1967 *The Second Sowing: Power and Secondary Development in Latin America.* Chandler, Chicago.

Aguirre Beltrán, Gonzalo
1944 The slave trade in Mexico. *Hispanic American Historical Review* 24:412–431.

Alba, Victor
1968 *Nationalists Without Nations: The Oligarchy Versus the People of Latin America.* Frederick A. Praeger, New York.

Alegría, Ciro
1941 *Broad and Alien Is the World.* Farrar and Rinehart, New York.

Anderson, Charles W.
1967 *Politics and Economic Change in Latin America.* Van Nostrand, Princeton, N.J.

Arce, Antonio M.
1965 *Desarrollo social y reforma agraria.* Instituto Interamericano de Ciencias Agrícolas, San José, Costa Rica.

Avila, Manuel
1969 *Tradition and Growth: A Study of Four Mexican Villages.* University of Chicago Press, Chicago.

Barraclough, Solon, and Arthur L. Domike
1966 Agrarian structure in seven Latin American countries. *Land Economics* 42:391–424.

Belshaw, Michael
1967 *Land and People of Huecorio: A Village Economy.* Columbia University Press, New York.

Bennett, Charles F.
1967 A review of ecological research in Middle America. *Latin American Research Review* 2, 3:3–27.

Borde, Jean, and Mario Góngora
1956 *Evolución de la propiedad rural en el Valle de Puangue* (2 vols.). Instituto de Sociología, Universidad de Chile, Santiago.

Bourricaud, François
1970 *Power and Society in Contemporary Peru.* Frederick A. Praeger, New York.

Bowman, Isaiah
1910 Trade routes in the economic geography of Bolivia. *American Geographical Society Bulletin* 42:22–37, 90–104, 180–192.

Bunzel, Ruth
1952 *Chichicastenango: A Guatemalan Village.* American Ethnological Society Monograph 22, Seattle.

* This is by no means a comprehensive bibliography on the topics discussed in the Introduction, but is rather a guide to key books and articles that illustrate the approaches and provide a valuable starting point from which any student can further pursue his special interests.

Cancian, Frank
1965 *Economics and Prestige in a Maya Community: The Religious Cargo System in Zinacantan.* Stanford University Press, Stanford, Cal.

Carrasco, Pedro
1952 *Tarascan Folk Religion: An Analysis of Economic, Social, and Religious Interactions.* Tulane University, Middle American Research Institute Publication 17, 1, New Orleans.

Carroll, Thomas F.
1964 Land reform as an explosive force in Latin America. In John J. TePaske and Sydney N. Fisher (eds.), *Explosive Forces in Latin America.* Ohio State University Press, Columbus.
1965 *Land Tenure and Land Reform in Latin America: A Selective Annotated Bibliography* (2d rev. ed.). Inter-American Development Bank, Washington.

Cassady, Ralph, Jr.
1968 Negotiated price-making in Mexican traditional markets: A conceptual analysis. *América Indígena* 28:51–80.

Castillo, Carlos M.
1967 *Growth and Integration in Central America.* Frederick A. Praeger, New York.

Castro Pozo, Hildebrando
1924 *Nuestra comunidad indígena.* El Lucero, Lima.

Chevalier, François
1963 *Land and Society in Colonial Mexico: The Great Hacienda.* University of California Press, Berkeley.

Cochran, Thomas C., and Ruben E. Reina
1962 *Entrepreneurship in Argentine Culture.* University of Pennsylvania Press, Philadelphia.

Cook, Scott
1970 Price and output variability in a peasant–artisan stone working industry in Oaxaca, Mexico: An analytical essay in economic anthropology. *American Anthropologist* 72:776–801.

Dalton, George (ed.)
1971 *Economic Development and Social Change: The Modernization of Village Communities.* Natural History Press, Garden City, N.Y.

Dean, Warren
1970 Latin American golpes and economic fluctuations, 1823–1966. *Social Science Quarterly* 51, 1:70–80.

Delgado, Oscar
1962 Revolution, reform, conservatism: Three types of agrarian structure. *Dissent* 9:350–364.

Diskin, Martin
1969 Estudio estructural del sistema de plaza en el valle de Oaxaca. *América Indígena* 29:1077–1100.

Dobyns, Henry F., and Paul Doughty (eds.)
1971 *Peasants, Power, and Applied Social Change: Vicos as a Model.* Sage Publications, Beverly Hills, Cal.

Dobyns, Henry F., and Mario C. Vázquez (eds.)
1963 *Migración e integración en el Perú.* Editorial Estudios Andinos, Lima.

Dorner, Peter (ed.)
1971 *Land Reform in Latin America: Issues and Cases.* University of Wisconsin, Land Tenure Center, Madison.

ECLA.

1948– *Economic Bulletin for Latin America; Economic Survey of Latin America; Statistical Bulletin For Latin America.* Washington, D.C.

Eder, George J.

1968 *Inflation and Development in Latin America: A Case History of Inflation and Stabilization in Bolivia.* University of Michigan International Business Studies 8, Ann Arbor.

Erasmus, Charles J.

1961 *Man Takes Control: Cultural Development and American Aid.* University of Minnesota Press, Minneapolis.

1965 The occurrence and disappearance of reciprocal labor in Latin America. In Heath and Adams, 1965.

Fals-Borda, Orlando

1955 *Peasant Society in the Colombian Andes: A Sociological Study of Saucío.* University of Florida Press, Gainesville.

Feder, Ernest

1971 *The Rape of the Peasantry: Latin America's Landholding System.* Doubleday, Garden City, N.Y.

Fillol, Thomas

1961 *Social Factors in Economic Development: The Argentine Case.* Massachusetts Institute of Technology Press, Cambridge, Mass.

Firth, Raymond

1969 Social structure and peasant economy: The influence of social structure upon peasant economies. In Clifton R. Wharton, Jr. (ed.), *Subsistence Agriculture and Economic Development.* Aldine, Chicago.

Flores, Edmundo

1961 *Tratado de economía agrícola.* Fondo de Cultura Económica, México.

Ford, Thomas R.

1955 *Man and Land in Peru.* University of Florida Press, Gainesville.

Forman, Shepard

1970 *The Raft Fishermen: Tradition and Change in a Peasant Economy.* Indiana University Press, Bloomington.

Foster, George M.

1942 *A Primitive Mexican Economy.* American Ethnological Society Monograph 5, New York.

1965 Peasant society and the image of limited good. *American Anthropologist* 67:293–315.

1973 *Traditional Societies and Technological Change* (2nd ed.). Harper & Row, New York.

Frank, Andre Gunder

1967 *Capitalism and Underdevelopment in Latin America: Historical Studies of Chile and Brazil.* Monthly Review Press, New York.

Friedrich, Paul

1970 *Agrarian Revolt in a Mexican Village.* Prentice-Hall, Englewood Cliffs, N.J.

Furtado, Celso

1970 *Economic Development in Latin America: A Survey from Colonial Times to the Cuban Revolution.* Cambridge University Press, Cambridge, England.

Germani, Gino

[1969] *Sociología de la modernización: Estudios teóricos, metodológicos y aplicados a América Latina.* Paidos, Buenos Aires.

Glade, William P., Jr.
1969 *The Latin American Economies: A Study of Their Institutional Evolution.* Van Nostrand, Princeton, N.J.
Glade, William P., Jr., and Charles W. Anderson
1963 *The Political Economy of Mexico.* University of Wisconsin Press, Madison.
Góngora, Mario
1960 *Origen de los "inquilinos" de Chile central.* Universidad de Chile, Seminario de Historia Colonial, Santiago.
Goodfellow, D. M.
1939 *Principles of Economic Sociology.* George Routledge & Sons, London.
Gordon, Wendell C.
1967 *The Political Economy of Latin America* (rev. ed.). Columbia University Press, New York.
Griffin, Keith B.
1969 *Underdevelopment in Spanish America.* Massachusetts Institute of Technology Press, Cambridge, Mass.
Hammel, E[ugene] A.
1969 *Power in Ica: The Structural History of a Peruvian Community.* Little, Brown, Boston.
Hanson, Simon G.
1951 *Economic Development in Latin America.* Inter-American Affairs Press, Washington.
Havens, A. Eugene, and William L. Flinn (eds.)
1970 *Internal Colonialism and Structural Change in Colombia.* Frederick A. Praeger, New York.
Heath, Dwight B.
1972 New patrons for old: Changing patron-client relationships in the Bolivian yungas. In Arnold Strickon (ed.), *Patronage and Power in Latin America.* University of New Mexico Press, Albuquerque.
Heath, Dwight B., and Richard N. Adams (eds.)
1965 *Contemporary Cultures and Societies of Latin America* (1st ed.). Random House, New York.
Heath, Dwight B., Charles J. Erasmus, and Hans C. Buechler
1969 *Land Reform and Social Revolution in Bolivia.* Frederick A. Praeger, New York.
Herskovits, Melville J.
1952 *Economic Anthropology: A Study in Primitive Economics.* Alfred A. Knopf, New York.
Hill, George W., José A. Silva M., and Ruth Oliver de Hill
1960 *La vida rural en Venezuela.* Ministerio de Agricultura y Cría, Caracas.
Hirschman, Albert O.
1963 *Journeys Toward Progress: Studies of Economic Policy Making in Latin America.* Twentieth Century Fund, New York.
Holmberg, Allan R. (ed.)
1966 *Vicos: Método y práctica de antropología aplicada.* Editorial Estudios Andinos, Lima.
Horowitz, Irving L. (ed.)
1970 *Masses in Latin America.* Oxford University Press, New York.
Huizer, Gerrit
1972 *The Revolutionary Potential of Peasants in Latin America.* Lexington Books, Lexington, Mass.

Hutchinson, Harry W.
1957 *Village and Plantation Life in Northeastern Brazil.* University of Washington Press, Seattle.
Icaza, Jorge
1964 *Huasipungo: The Villagers.* Southern Illinois University Press, Carbondale.
Interamerican Committee for Agricultural Development
1966– *Land Tenure and Agricultural Development in . . . [various countries].* I.C.A.D., Washington.
Inter-American Development Bank
1967 *Agricultural Development in Latin America: The Next Decade.* I.A.D.B., Washington.
Inter-American Economic and Social Council at the Ministerial Level
1961 *Alliance for Progress: Official Documents.* Pan American Union, Washington.
International Bank for Reconstruction and Development
(A series of monographs on the economies of individual Latin American countries). Johns Hopkins University Press, Baltimore.
International Labor Office
1953 *Indigenous Peoples.* I.L.O., Geneva.
1957 *The Landless Farmer in Latin America.* I.L.O., Geneva.
Johnson, Allen W.
1971 *Sharecroppers of the Sertão: Economics and Dependence on a Brazilian Plantation.* Stanford University Press, Stanford, Cal.
Johnson, John J.
1965 *Political Change in Latin America: The Emergence of the Middle Sectors* (rev. ed.). Stanford University Press, Stanford, Cal.
Kaplan, Bernice A.
1960 Mechanization in Paracho: A craft community. *Alpha Kappa Deltan* 30,1:59–65 (reprinted in Heath and Adams, 1965).
Krauss, Walter, and F. John Mathis
1970 *Latin America and Economic Integration.* University of Iowa Press, Iowa City.
Kunkel, John H.
1961 Economic autonomy and social change in Mexican villages. *Economic Development and Cultural Change* 10:51–63 (reprinted in Heath and Adams, 1965).
1970 *Society and Economic Growth: A Behavioral Perspective of Social Change.* Oxford University Press, New York.
Lamond, Trillis F.
1970 *Lord and Peasant in Peru: A Paradigm of Political and Social Change.* Cambridge University Press, Cambridge, England.
Landsberger, Henry A. (ed.)
1969 *Latin American Peasant Movements.* Cornell University Press, Ithaca, N.Y.
Le Beau, Francis
1956 Agricultura de Guatemala. In *Integración social en Guatemala.* Seminario de Integración Social Guatemalteca Publicación 3, Guatemala.
Le Clair, Edward E., and Harold K. Schneider (eds.)
1968 *Economic Anthropology: Readings in Theory and Analysis.* Holt, Rinehart and Winston, New York.
Leonard, Olen E.
1952 *Bolivia: Land, People, and Institutions.* Scarecrow, Washington.

Lewis, Oscar
1951 *Life in a Mexican Village: Tepoztlán Restudied*. University of Illinois Press, Urbana.
Lipset, Seymour M., and Aldo Solari (eds.)
1967 *Elites in Latin America*. Oxford University Press, New York.
Loomis, Charles P., et al.
1953 *Turrialba: Social Systems and Social Change*. Free Press, Glencoe, Ill.
McBride, George M.
1921 *The Agrarian Indian Communities of Highland Bolivia*. American Geographical Society Research Series 5, New York.
1923 *Land Systems of Mexico*. American Geographical Society Research Series 12, New York.
1936 *Chile: Land and Society*. American Geographical Society Research Series 19, New York.
McBryde, F. Webster
1933 *Sololá: A Guatemalan Town and Cakchiquel Market*. Tulane University, Middle American Research Institute Publication 5, New Orleans.
1947 *Cultural and Historical Geography of Southwest Guatemala*. Smithsonian Institution, Institute of Social Anthropology Publication 4, Washington.
Malinowski, Bronislaw, and Julio de la Fuente
1957 La economía de un sistema de mercados en México. *Acta Antropológica*, Época 2, México.
Martínez, Mario A.
1939 *Régimen de tierras en Colombia* (2 vols.). Talleres Gráficos, Bogotá.
Miller, Solomon
1967 Hacienda to plantation in northern Peru: The processes of proletarianization of a tenant farmer society. In Julian H. Steward (ed)., *Contemporary Change in Traditional Societies, 3: Mexican and Peruvian Communities*. University of Illinois Press, Urbana.
Mintz, Sidney W.
1953 The folk–urban continuum and the rural proletarian community. *American Journal of Sociology* 59:136–143.
[1964] *Peasant Market Places and Economic Development in Latin America*. Vanderbilt University, Graduate Center for Latin American Studies, Occasional Paper 4, Nashville, Tenn.
Morse, Richard M.
1971 Trends and issues in Latin American urban research 1965–1970. *Latin American Research Review* 6,1:3–52; 6,2:19–75.
Mosk, Sanford A.
1954 Indigenous economy in Latin America. *Inter-American Economic Affairs* 8,3:3–27 (reprinted in Heath and Adams, 1965).
Nash, Manning
1957 The multiple society in economic development: Mexico and Guatemala. *American Anthropologist* 59:825–833.
1961 The social context of economic choice in a small society. *Man* 219:186–191.
1964 Capital saving and credit in a Guatemalan and a Mexican Indian peasant society. In R. Firth and B. Yamey (eds.), *Capital, Saving, and Credit in Peasant Societies*. Aldine, Chicago.
1966 *Primitive and Peasant Economic Systems*. Chandler, San Francisco.

Nelson, Lowry
1967 Rural sociology: Some inter-American aspects. *Journal of Inter-American Studies* 9:323–339.
Oberg, Kalervo
1965 The marginal peasant in rural Brazil. *American Anthropologist* 67:1417–1427.
Ots Capdequí, José M.
1959 *España en América: el régimen de tierras en la época colonial.* Fondo de Cultura Económica, México.
Pan American Union
1959 *Plantation Systems of the New World.* Social Science Monograph 7, Washington.
1966 *Latin America's Foreign Trade: Problems and Policies.* Pan American Union, Washington.
1967 *Latin America: Problems and Perspectives of Economic Development.* Johns Hopkins University Press, Baltimore.
Pearse, Andrew
1966 Agrarian change trends in Latin America. *Latin American Research Review* 1,3:45–69.
Poblete Troncoso, Moises, and Ben G. Burnett
1960 *The Rise of the Latin American Labor Movement.* Bookman Associates, New York.
Poggie, John J., Jr., and Frank C. Miller
1969 Contact, change and industrialization in a network of Mexican villages. *Human Organization* 28:190–198.
Polanyi, Karl, Conrad M. Arensberg, and Harry W. Pearson (eds.)
1957 *Trade and Market in the Early Empire: Economies in History and Theory.* Free Press, Glencoe, Ill.
Powelson, John P.
1964 *Latin America: Today's Economic and Social Revolution.* McGraw-Hill, New York.
Prebisch, Raul
1971 *Change and Development: Latin America's Greatest Task.* Frederick A. Praeger, New York.
Quijano, Anibal
1971 *Nationalism and Capitalism in Peru: A Study in Neo-Imperialism.* Monthly Review Press, New York.
Reina, Ruben E.
1966 *The Law of the Saints: A Pokoman Corporate Community and Its Culture.* Bobbs-Merrill, Indianapolis.
Reynolds, Clark W.
1970 *The Mexican Economy: Twentieth-Century Structure and Growth.* Yale University Press, New Haven.
Rivière, Peter
1972 *The Forgotten Frontier: Ranchers of North Brazil.* Holt, Rinehart and Winston, New York.
Romney, D. H.
1959 *Land in British Honduras* (2 vols.). Her Majesty's Stationery Office, London.
Sable, Martin H.
1965 *Periodicals for Latin American Economic Development, Trade and Finance: An Annotated Bibliography.* University of California, Latin American Center, Los Angeles.

1970 *Latin American Agriculture: A Bibliography on Pioneer Settlement, Agricultural History and Economics, Rural Sociology and Population.* University of Wisconsin, Center for Latin American Studies, Milwaukee.

Schaedel, Richard P.
1965 Land reform studies. *Latin American Research Review* 1,1:75–122.
1967 *La demografía y los recursos humanos del sur del Perú.* Instituto Indigenista Interamericano Serie Antropología Social 8, México.

Senior, Clarence
1959 *Land Reform and Democracy.* University of Florida Press, Gainesville.

Silva Herzog, Jesús (ed.)
1961 *La cuestión de la tierra* (4 vols.). Instituto Mexicano de Investigaciones Económicas, México.

Silvert, Kalman H.
1967 The politics of social and economic change in Latin America. In *Sociological Review Monograph* 11, Staffordshire.

Smith, T. Lynn
1963 *Brazil: People and Institutions* (3d ed.). Louisiana State University Press, Baton Rouge.
1967 *Colombia: Social Structure and the Process of Development.* University of Florida Press, Gainesville.

Smith, T. Lynn (ed.)
1965 *Agrarian Reform in Latin America.* Alfred A. Knopf, New York.

Solari, Aldo E.
1971 *Sociología rural latinoamericana.* Paidos, Buenos Aires.

Stavenhagen, Rodolfo
1969 *Las clases sociales en las sociedades agrarias.* Siglo XX, México.

Stavenhagen, Rodolfo (ed.)
1970 *Agrarian Problems and Peasant Movements in Latin America.* Doubleday, Garden City, N.Y.

Stein, Stanley
1957 *Vassaouras: A Brazilian Coffee County, 1850–1900.* Harvard University Press, Cambridge, Mass.

Stein, Stanley, and Barbara Stein
1970 *The Colonial Heritage of Latin America.* Oxford University Press, New York.

Stephens, Richard H.
1971 *Wealth and Power in Peru.* Scarecrow, Metuchin, N.J.

Swift, Jeannine
1971 *Agrarian Reform in Chile: An Economic Study.* D. C. Heath, Lexington, Mass.

Tax, Sol
1941 World view and social relations in Guatemala. *American Anthropologist* 43:27–43 (reprinted in Heath and Adams, 1965).
1953 *Penny Capitalism: A Guatemalan Indian Economy.* Smithsonian Institution, Institute of Social Anthropology Publication 16, Washington.

Taylor, Carl C.
1948 *Rural Life in Argentina.* Louisiana State University Press, Baton Rouge.

Thiesenhusen, William C.
1966 *Chile's Experiments in Agrarian Reform.* University of Wisconsin Press, Madison.

Thompson, Edgar T. (comp.)
1957 *The Plantation: A Bibliography.* Pan American Union Social Science Monograph 4, Washington.

United Nations, Department of Economic Affairs
1951 *Land Reform: Defects in Agrarian Structure as Obstacles to Economic Development.* U.N., New York.

U.S. Agency for International Development
1961 *Latin American USOM's Seminar on Agrarian Reform.* International Cooperation Administration, Washington.

Urquidi, Victor L.
1964 *The Challenge of Development in Latin America.* Frederick A. Praeger, New York.

Vázquez V., Mario C.
1957 Cambios en estratificación social en una hacienda andina. *Perú Indígena* 6, 4–5: 67–87 (reprinted in English in Heath and Adams, 1965).

Veliz, Claudio (ed.)
1965 *Obstacles to Change in Latin America.* Oxford University Press, New York.

Violich, Francis, and Juan B. Astica
1967 *Community Development and the Urban Planning Process in Latin America.* University of California, Latin American Center, Los Angeles.

Vries, Egbert de (ed.)
1966 *Social Research and Rural Life in Central America, Mexico and the Caribbean Region.* UNESCO, New York.

Vries, Egbert de, and José Medina Echavarría (eds.)
1963 *Social Aspects of Economic Development in Latin America* (2 vols.). UNESCO, Paris.

Wagley, Charles
1941 *Economics of a Guatemalan Village.* American Anthropological Association Memoir 58, Menasha, Wis.

Wagley, Charles (ed.)
1964 *Social Science Research on Latin America.* Columbia University Press, New York.

Waterbury, Ronald
1969 Urbanization and a traditional market system. In Walter Goldschmidt and Harry Hoijer (eds.), *The Social Anthropology of Latin America.* University of California, Latin American Center, Los Angeles.

West, Robert C.
1948 *Cultural Geography of the Modern Tarascan Area.* Smithsonian Institution, Institute of Social Anthropology Publication 7, Washington.

Whetten, Nathan L.
1948 *Rural Mexico.* University of Chicago Press, Chicago.
1961 *Guatemala: Land and People.* Yale University Press, New Haven.

Whyte, William F., and Allan R. Holmberg (eds.)
1956 Human problems of U.S. enterprise in Latin America. Special issue of *Human Organization* 15, 3.

Wilkie, Raymond
1971 *San Miguel: A Mexican Collective Ejido.* Stanford University Press, Stanford, Cal.

Wionczek, M. S.
1966 *Latin American Economic Integration.* Frederick A. Praeger, New York.

Wish, John R.
1965 *Economic Development in Latin America: An Annotated Bibliography.* Frederick A. Praeger, New York.

Wolf, Eric R.
1955 Types of Latin American peasantry: A preliminary discussion. *American Anthropologist* 57:452–471.
1956 Aspects of group relations in a complex society: Mexico. *American Anthropologist* 58:1065–1078 (reprinted in Heath and Adams, 1965; also herein).
1957 Closed corporate peasant communities in Mesoamerica and central Java. *Southwestern Journal of Anthropology* 13:1–18.
1966 *Peasants.* Prentice-Hall, Englewood Cliffs, N.J.
1969 *Peasant Wars of the Twentieth Century.* Harper & Row, New York.

Wolf, Eric R., and Edward C. Hansen
1972 *The Human Condition in Latin America.* Oxford University Press, New York.

Wolf, Eric R., and Sidney W. Mintz
1957 Haciendas and plantations in Middle America and the Antilles. *Social and Economic Studies* 6:380–412.

Wolfe, Marshall
1966 Rural settlement patterns and social change in Latin America: Notes for a strategy of rural development. *Latin American Research Review* 1,2:5–50.

Wythe, George
1949 *Industry in Latin America.* Columbia University Press, New York.

Young, Frank W., and Ruth C. Young
1960 Social integration and change in twenty-four Mexican villages. *Economic Development and Cultural Change* 8:366–377.

Young, Ruth C.
1970 The plantation economy and industrial development in Latin America. *Economic Development and Cultural Change* 18:342–361.

The Outlook for Agricultural Development in Latin America[1]

CLYDE MITCHELL AND JACOB SCHATAN

For all the difficulty of defining or measuring "economic development," there are several suggestive indices with respect to agriculture, the predominant industry in most Latin American countries. Using a variety of statistics compiled by international agencies, Mitchell and Schatan unequivocally identify some present and impending problems and make specific positive recommendations. In its broadly comparative scope, this paper illustrates the pervasiveness of some of the obstacles to development identified by Erasmus, Nisbet, Gonzalez, and others.

C. Clyde Mitchell is Regional Advisor on Latin America, United Nations Food and Agricultural Organization. He has served as consultant on economic development and agriculture to several national and international agencies in various countries.

Jacob Schatan is an agricultural economist who has worked with the United Nations and other international agencies in a number of countries.

Agriculture is not properly fulfilling its important role in the development of Latin America. It does not furnish the foods necessary for a good diet for Latin Americans, nor the exports necessary to provide foreign exchange for the developing nations. In recent years such traditionally important agricultural exports as coffee, cocoa, sugar and cotton have run into price and market difficulties because of overproduction. The land and the men who work the land are not properly utilized in Latin America's agriculture. Under current practices some of the land is wasted by wanton destruction, much more is wasted through lack of proper husbandry. And human resources are wasted because millions of farm people are not given the opportunity of improving their farming ability and their incomes.

This severe judgment on the status of agriculture in Latin America must be laid at the doorstep of the governments, the business enterprises, the banks, public and private, and the landowners of the region, more than on the farmers themselves.

The Charter of Punta del Este established minimum goals for economic progress, but agriculture has failed to demonstrate the vitality required to reach these goals. Production in the past fifteen years has increased at a rate slightly greater than population growth, but even this statement obscures a serious deterioration. Total production figures combine both crop and livestock production, and livestock production has failed to keep pace with population.

This failure cannot be explained by a lack of resources. Nature has been niggardly in some continents, where the resources base for progress is simply too

Abridged from *Agricultural Development in Latin America: The Next Decade* (Washington: Inter-American Development Bank, 1967) 45–146; substantial omissions of detail, which do not alter the meaning of the authors, are indicated by suspension points. Abridgement is by the editor; reprinted by permission of the authors and publisher.

narrow. For example, India and Pakistan, with half a billion inhabitants, face a future that is rigidly limited by a lack of land. This does not apply to Latin America, however, if its immense region is considered as a whole. Land and water resources exist there in relative abundance. (See Table 1, p. 130.)

. . .

OBSTACLES TO DEVELOPMENT

1. Concentration of land ownership: Land tenure studies by CIDA in seven countries (Argentina, Brazil, Colombia, Chile, Ecuador, Guatemala and Peru) pointed out that, of a total of 5.4 million farm units, occupying 1.2 billion acres, the large multi-family farms—only 2.6 percent of the total number—controlled 46 percent of the land. These were 138,555 units, with an average size of 4 thousand acres each. At the other extreme, the small uneconomic-sized farms made up 52.7 percent of the total number and controlled only 2.3 percent of the farm area. There were 2,862,662 of these smaller farm families, living on 28.4 million acres, or an average of only 9.8 acres each.

2. The burden of monoculture: In many Latin American countries, agriculture has been organized in plantation systems which in years past have proved to be effective in the economic sense for the production of coffee, sugarcane and bananas. The resulting monoculture has persisted because of the prevailing land tenure system, lack of various services to agriculture which would enable it to diversify, the low purchasing power of internal consumers and the surplus of labor. Monoculture continues to depress the national economies, particularly in light of world overproduction of these traditional products. As a result, diversification has not been able to gain much foothold, and the region remains vulnerable to the fluctuations of world market prices for basic agricultural products. (See Table 2, p. 131.)

3. Low agricultural yields: Concentration of lands in large parcels has not necessarily produced the best results. In one large Latin American country, farmers on family-sized enterprises cultivated 59.8 percent of their land, producing an output value at 881 monetary units of that country for every 2.5 acres. By contrast, the large owners, cultivating only 17.4 percent of their land, had a gross output of only 170 of the same monetary units for 2.5 acres of land. (See Table 3, p. 132.)

4. Inadequate agricultural credit: The medium- and small-size farmer in most countries of the region has never had access to sufficient credit for his agricultural needs. The terms of commercial financing favor principally the large producers. The middle-sized and small units have always needed, but have seldom been able to receive, the technical assistance which must accompany credit.

Agricultural credit organizations in Latin America have in most cases had very little effect on development. This has been due either to the lack of trained personnel, or to the meager financial and physical resources available for the needed loans. All of the countries of the region have had experience in agricultural and livestock credit, but generally the hoped-for increases in production have failed to materialize, both for technical and institutional reasons.

. . .

TABLE 1.* Land Use in Latin America (In thousands of hectares)

Country	Arable Lands[a]	Irrigated	Percent	Cultivated[b]	Percent	Natural Pastures	Percent	Year
Argentina	143,856.0	1,500.0	1.0	33,449.8	23.3	110,406.2	76.7	1960
Bolivia	14,318.6	64.0	0.5	3,091.0	21.6	11,227.6	78.4	1950
Brazil	160,544.0	141.0	0.9	67,976.0	42.3	92,568.0	57.7	1950
Chile	14,539.0	1,363.0	9.4	4,265.2	29.4	10,273.8	70.6	1965
Colombia	19,653.0	226.0	1.2	5,047.0	25.7	14,606.0	74.3	1960
Costa Rica	1,547.0	26.0	1.7	1,010.7	65.3	536.5	34.7	1963
Cuba	7,645.0	60.0	0.8	1,970.0	25.7	5,675.0	74.3	1952
Dominican Republic	1,731.3	135.0	7.8	1,461.2	84.3	270.5	15.7	1950
Ecuador	3,335.5	24.0	0.7	2,081.0	62.4	1,254.5	37.6	1954
El Salvador	1,245.9	–	–	742.3	59.6	503.6	40.4	1961
Guatemala	2,108.9	32.0	1.1	1,566.7	74.3	542.8	25.7	1962
Haiti	870.0	65.0	7.5	370.0	42.5	500.0	57.5	FAO estimate
Honduras	1,718.4	66.0	3.8	895.8	52.1	822.6	47.9	1952
Mexico	103,312.6	3,515.0	3.4	23,817.0	23.1	79,495.6	76.9	1960
Nicaragua	2,599.0	–	–	1,955.5	75.2	643.5	24.8	1963
Panama	1,371.7	14.0	1.0	1,237.0	90.2	134.7	19.8	1961
Paraguay	10,759.0	8.0	0.7	859.0	8.0	9,900.0	92.0	FAO estimate
Peru	11,415.8	1,212.0	10.6	2,596.3	22.7	8,819.5	77.3	1961
Uruguay	16,099.0	27.0	0.2	2,251.7	14.0	13,847.3	86.0	1961
Venezuela	19,177.5	246.0	1.3	5,219.4	27.2	13,998.2	72.8	1961
TOTAL	537,847.7	8,724.0	1.6	161,862.6	30.0	375,985.9	70.0	

* [Editor's note: In the original publication, this was Table I.]

[a] Excludes areas in forest.

[b] Made up of annual crops, permanent crops, cultivated pastures and fallow.

TABLE 2.* Latin America: Rural Population in 1950 and 1960; Rates of Increase of the Total Population, the Gross Domestic Agricultural Product, and the Gross Domestic Non-agricultural Product

Country	Population in 1950 Total (thousands)	Rural (thousands)	Percent	Population in 1960 Total (thousands)	Rural (thousands)	Percent	Annual Rates of Increase Total Population	Agric. Production	Non-agric. Production
Argentina	17,189	6,151	36	20,956	6,795	32	1.8	1.9	2.9
Bolivia	3,013	2,235	74	3,696	2,592	70	2.1	1.2	1.4
Brazil	51,976	35,955	69	70,600	42,800	61	3.0	4.8	5.5
Colombia	11,679	7,426	64	15,468	8,334	54	2.8	3.1	5.5
Chile	6,073	2,560	42	7,627	2,826	37	2.5	3.2	3.8
Dominican Republic	2,243	1,709	76	3,030	2,106	70	3.2	–	–
Ecuador	3,197	2,312	72	4,317	2,818	65	3.2	3.9	5.0
Paraguay	1,397	1,009	72	1,768	1,171	66	2.4	2.5	3.2
Peru	8,521	6,133	72	10,857	6,967	64	2.6	4.0	5.7
Uruguay	2,178	726	33	2,490	726	29	1.2	0.5	1.3
Venezuela	4,974	2,544	51	7,331	2,810	38	3.8	5.7	6.0
Costa Rica	801	569	71	1,171	728	62	4.1	2.8	7.0
Cuba	5,508	2,795	51	6,797	3,088	45	2.1	–	–
El Salvador	1,868	1,351	72	2,442	1,647	67	3.1	3.4	6.4
Guatemala	2,805	2,131	76	3,765	2,598	69	2.9	3.7	5.1
Haiti	3,380	3,040	90	4,140	3,617	87	2.1	1.2	2.3
Honduras	1,428	1,181	83	1,950	1,512	78	3.3	3.3	4.6
Mexico	25,826	14,000	54	34,988	16,248	46	3.2	4.2	6.4
Nicaragua	1,060	762	72	1,477	976	66	3.4	4.6	6.8
Panama	797	510	64	1,055	622	59	3.0	3.9	6.4
TOTAL	155,913	95,099	61	205,925	110,981	53.9	2.8	3.6	4.9

* [Editor's note: In the original publication, this was Table IV.]

SOURCE: ECLA statistics, including ECLA Document E/C No. 12/643.

TABLE 3.* Value of Agricultural Production by Size of Farm Unit, in Various Countries Included in the ICAD Tenure Study[a] (Values in national monetary units)

Country, Year, and Size of Farm Units	Total Value in Thousands	Value of Production: Per Farm Unit	Per Hectare in Farms	Per Hectare Cultivated	Per Farm Worker
Argentina (1960):[b]					
Sub-family-sized[c]	13,806	68.7	2,492	6,185	39.9
Family-sized[d]	55,233	243.7	737	3,171	77.6
Medium multi-family[e]	31,020	915.6	1,267	3,804	145.7
Large multi-family[f]	18,093	4,550.6	304	3,049	192.3
TOTAL	118,152	253.8	718	3,502	80.6
Brazil (1950):[g]					
Sub-family	1,723	3,704	1,498.0	1,721	1,197
Family	11,392	14,114	880.6	1,375	3,481
Medium multi-family	26,412	38,023	361.1	920	5,058
Large multi-family	28,069	226,630	170.0	726	8,237
TOTAL	67,596	29,839	283.8	901	4,883
Chile (1955):[h]					
Sub-family	22,500	404	334	391	268
Family	81,097	1,343	46	126	443
Medium multi-family	117,112	4,794	41	96	828
Large multi-family	299,816	28,876	41	83	1,171
TOTAL	520,525	3,448	24	94	784
Colombia (1960):[i]					
Sub-family	1,503.1	1,943	1,221	1,597	972
Family	3,268.1	8,932	582	1,441	4,067
Medium multi-family	1,384.1	25,193	238	1,347	7,323
Large multi-family	1,081.4	69,736	104	1,273	9,673
TOTAL	7,237.3	5,983	313	1,431	2,731
Ecuador (1954):[j]					
Sub-family	1,678.0	5,800	2,600	3,000	–
Family	2,098.4	46,100	2,200	3,300	–
Medium-multi-family	1,374.6	146,500	1,400	3,300	–
Large multi-family	1,224.9	894,800	700	2,800	–
TOTAL	6,375.9	18,500	1,400	3,100	–
Guatemala (1950):[k]					
Sub-family	31,414	105	63	71	74
Family	13,694	414	35	57	163
Medium multi-family	26,924	5,232	34	87	496
Large multi-family	21,640	41,939	16	59	523
TOTAL	103,672	297	30	70	166

5. Lack of agricultural extension: Extension technicians are necessary to help the Latin American farm operators to become efficient producers. Presently, there are too few of these, and this is a bottleneck for the development of agriculture and the efficient use of credit. This bottleneck must be broken or the agricultural sector will continue to be backward, even when new financial resources are available and tenure conditions improved.

. . .

6. Marketing problems: Latin American farmers, particularly those of middle and small scale, have seldom been able to avail themselves of services and facilities for grading, packing, preserving and selling their products. Trade in exportable products such as coffee, cotton and sugar has, of course, been based on grade, quality standards and up-to-date price quotations. Even in the case of these products, however, it is often the middleman rather than the farmer who is able to benefit most from such refinements. In general, there is a great lack of refrigeration, grain storage and warehousing. This results in large

---

* [Editor's note: In the original publication, this was Table XXI; it is unchanged except for amplification of footnotes.]

[a] The figures represent total value of agricultural production, except in Argentina, where they correspond to value added. . . .

[b] Argentina: value added in 1960 pesos. Total value in millions of pesos; by farm unit and by worker in thousands of pesos. Value per unit of agricultural and cultivated land in pesos.

[[c] Sub-family units are those whose land is insufficient to satisfy the basic needs of one family, in accordance with the local standard of living, not providing remunerative employment during the whole year to the family which is considered to consist of the equivalent of two working men who possess the technical abilities prevalent in the region.]

[[d] Family units are those with sufficient land to satisfy the basic needs of one family and which provide remunerative work for the equivalent of from 2 to 3.9 man-years of labor, with the further condition that the major part of the work is provided by family members.]

[[e] Medium multi-family: units with sufficient land to require the full-time work of from 4 to 12 men, or equivalent.]

[[f] Large multi-family: units which require more than 12 man-years of work per year.]

[g] Brazil: value of the agricultural production in 1950 cruzeiros. Total value in billions of cruzeiros; by farm unit in thousands. Other values in cruzeiros.

[h] Chile: value of 1955 production in 1960 escudos; total value in thousands of escudos; per farm unit in thousands. Other values in escudos.

[i] Colombia: value of 1960 production in 1960 pesos. Total value in millions of pesos by farm unit in thousands. Other values in pesos.

[j] Ecuador: value of production in 1954 sucres. Total value in millions of sucres. Other values in sucres.

[k] Guatemala: production of 9 selected items in 1950 in quetzals. Other values in quetzals.

(–) dependable information was not available.

SOURCE: "La Estructura Agraria en Siete Países de América Latina," S. L. Barraclough and A. L. Domike, *El Trimestre Económico*, Vol. XXXIII, No. 130, Mexico, April-June 1966.

losses of cereals and fruits. Livestock producers cannot take advantage of cold storage to benefit from seasonal price increases.

The lack of organized markets insures that a long chain of intermediaries in the marketing channels exploits both producers and consumers.

. . .

SUGGESTIONS

1. Agricultural Development Planning: The development policies of each country should put emphasis on the preparation of plans and detailed programs of agricultural development which will improve productivity, diversify farming and improve the market both internal and external for agricultural, livestock, forestry and fishery products.

These programs should have, among others, the following objectives:

- To increase the production of a variety of products, including those from livestock, forestry and fishery sources, so as to improve the diet and the levels of living of the Latin Americans and to reduce imports.
- To avoid monoculture, which generates overproduction and helps maintain unjust systems of land tenure.
- To avoid the growth of unemployment or underemployment in rural zones.
- To reduce to the minimum the importation of products which can be produced within the ecological conditions of Latin America.

2. Agrarian Reform: To speed up the programs of agrarian reform, in accordance with the specific needs of each country, agrarian reform should include, among others, the following features:

- Establishment of tenure rights with regard to land and water, for those farmers who, although presently in peaceful possession of the land they work, nevertheless lack title.
- Redistribution of land, to diminish and eliminate both latifundia and minifundia—those distortions of effective land tenure most common in Latin America.
- Colonization programs, which should include the infrastructure necessary for the opening of new areas.
- Cooperatives and assistance, which should supply financial and technical assistance to the farmers.

3. Financial Measures: The magnitude and extent of the agrarian reform programs require a great financial effort, the application of policies which encourage private initiative, and also additional external cooperation which must be available under particularly favorable terms. The following are particularly important points:

- Considerably larger budget must be provided for the increase and improvement of the services related to agricultural development, such as extension, agricultural schools and colleges, development banks, storage and warehousing, grain elevators and cold storage facilities.
- The central banks should adopt policies for the selection of borrowers and distribution of credit in ways designed to channel available resources toward production goals.
- It would be desirable that the system and administrative machinery of land

taxation be improved, in countries where it is necessary, so that land taxes would help bring about production increases and a better distribution of ownership of land and improved land use.

OTE

1. The opinions expressed in this document do not necessarily represent the official views of the Inter-American Development Bank or of the F[ood and] A[gricultural] O[rganization, by whom the authors were employed at the time].

Proletarianization of Indian Peasants in Northern Peru

SOLOMON MILLER

In multi-ethnic societies, contrasting ethnic groups are often identified with distinct ecological niches, in both economic and geographic terms. Miller's brief analysis of the relations between the sierra and the coast in Peru also clarifies some aspects of the relations between Indians and criollos (cf. Patch), between haciendas and plantations (cf. Wagley and Harris), and between peasants and proletarians, in historical perspective.

Solomon Miller is Associate Professor of Anthropology at the New School for Social Research. His studies of social organization among Andean peasants provide meaningful comparisons, in historical perspective, among different regions, as in "The Hacienda and the Plantation in Peru," in Contemporary Change in Traditional Societies, *Julian H. Steward (ed.).*

From late in the nineteenth century when sugar production on the coast of Peru was beginning to recover from the effects of the Chilean war to the mid-1950's when population pressure and a change in sierra production techniques forced many Indians in the sierra to find employment on the coast, sugar planters were chronically plagued with a shortage of unskilled labor. Despite the use of many devices to attract and hold unskilled laborers, plantation managements were consistently driven to recruit Indians from the highlands on a temporary basis by means of loans or salary advances. Often they leased workers *en bloc* from hacienda owners who sent their tenants to the coast for a specified

From *Transactions of the New York Academy of Sciences* XXVII (1965), Series II, 782–789. Copyright © 1965 by The New York Academy of Sciences. Reprinted by permission of the author and publisher.

period of time in exchange for cash. In the 1950's, however, hordes of Indians came flocking to the sugar plantations in search of employment. For the first time in the history of Peru, a large, indigenous, voluntary, unskilled, labor force existed on the coast.

In this paper I shall trace three major phases which occur in the transition of the Indian from highland peasant to coastal proletarian. The first phase or "peasant phase" covers the period when the peasant population in the sierra was relatively stable and when there was little pressure on it to shift to the coast. In the second or "transitional phase," many Indian peasants oscillated between the sierra and the coast. Their ties to the sierra community were considerably loosened, while at the same time their attachments to a coastal community were nebulous. In neither community were they stable, year-around, participating members. In the third or "proletarian phase," the Indian becomes a settled proletarian on the coast.

Certain gross distinctions between peasant and proletarian life are immediately apparent. The peasant owns or controls the land from which he derives subsistence for the entire or, at least, a major part of the year. The proletarian, on the other hand, is landless. Earned through labor, his income is paid in terms of measured time (day, hour, or week) according to the amount produced. The peasant family is an interrelated work unit, and all its members participate cooperatively in the cultivation of the land. The land is the fabric which binds the peasant family with other families in organic interdependence. The proletarian, on the other hand, is engaged in a productive mechanism which separates him from his family. He has an individual relationship to his employer and the productive machine. Authority in the cultivation of land is vested in the working male members, usually the senior male, of the peasant family. When, where, and how the land will be cultivated is determined by the peasant himself. The proletarian has no authority in the production process. His day's labor is wholly circumscribed by the management of the enterprise where he is employed. Finally, the peasant carries through the whole round of production from selecting the seed he plants, to the harvest and distribution of the harvest among family members. The proletarian is involved in a single aspect of a large productive process. He has only one operation to perform as long as he is employed in a given job.

The differences cited above are crucial to an understanding of the peasant and the proletarian in terms of their respective social framework. They are polar differences which refer to social relations in the pursuit of a livelihood. In a specific context the distinctions are obviously more complex.

In Peru, not only have we to describe the polar types, but we have also to describe the transition period which occurred so recently, in which individuals were for a time between "types" so to speak.

The substantive material for this paper was drawn from two communities in northern Peru, which I studied between 1957 and 1959. One was an hacienda community in the highlands where the peasants were tenants, and the other was a plantation community on the coast where the unskilled labor force came mainly from hacienda and other peasant-type communities. I shall call the hacienda Ganadabamba and the plantation Caña Azul.

The discussion of the peasant phase is designed to show that the tenant-peasant at Ganadabamba, for all the abuses inherent in the hacienda system, lived in a relatively stable, integrated society.

Ganadabamba was a typical hacienda community in Peru which was composed almost exclusively of Indians and had a small group of criollo administrators, who governed the hacienda. Its peasant population of some 900 functioned, for the most part, as an independent society.

The tenant on Ganadabamba was in effective control of the land he rented, and on this contingency hinged his role as head of his family, his relations with other families and, to a great extent, his status in the community. He was able to use the land as he pleased without reference to the hacienda administration. What he planted was determined only by the traditional beliefs and customs of the community, for the tenant's belief system regarding the type of crops he could cultivate had significance for the community as a whole. For example, the tenant believed that maize thrived best in the low zones of the hacienda, while potatoes were thought to produce better in the upper zones. The lowest point on the hacienda was about 7000 feet above sea level. The upper limits of the maize line was somewhere near 8300 feet. From 8500 feet upwards, the Indians believed potatoes fared best. Between the two zones the crops were mixed.

Whether from a botanical standpoint this is true or not I do not know. However, the effect of dividing the hacienda into crop zones was to create an economic interdependence between tenants living in the high altitudes with those living in the low altitudes, because they regularly traded the surplus products from their respective zones. This economic interchange was the basis for a variety of social interchanges, which included marriage, compadrazco, and mutual obligations to attend labor bees and household fiestas. Zone cropping had the effect of socially integrating the distant neighborhoods of the hacienda.

While, in fact, the tenant did not own his land, and the hacendado had the legal right to reclaim it, the custom was that the tenant not only used the land as he wished but was free to pass it on to his children according to the traditional rules of inheritance in the community. This point is important because it was one of the economic bases of the tenant's control over his family, particularly his male adult offspring. The tenant also had access to common pasture land which provided a secondary source of subsistence and property. Here, he was able to breed cattle, utilize the beef in times of food shortage and pass the herds on to his children. Normally, cattle were inherited by all the family members. The Ganadabamba tenant was, therefore, fully in control *of* and fully responsible *for* the production and distribution of subsistence for the family. He controlled the round of family life by his grip on the land and his ownership of cattle.

The tenant family articulated with the community as a whole through several community-wide institutions, of which the religious and national fiestas were of first importance. By means of the ostentatious disposal of surpluses during the fiesta, a man and his family gained prestige. The display of affluence and generosity was a public affair and received public recognition. Competition between families was intense, particularly between families from different neighborhoods. An affluent family from a given neighborhood could depend on his neighbors to help him make a good showing against the affluent families from other neighborhoods. It was common procedure to comment negatively on a competitor's display. Such comments often aroused tempers and caused fights. Nevertheless, by the end of a fiesta, both the neighbors and those of other neighborhoods were made fully aware of the prestige and influence of the affluent in the community.

More locally, but equally significant for a family was the small household fiesta which directly involved one's neighbors, friends, and dependents, i.e., subtenants. An example of this type was the cooperative labor bee, or *minga,* as it is called in the highlands. In the minga a man invited the people of his neighborhood to help him with the plowing or the harvest or both. After the day's work, the host was obliged to provide food, drink and entertainment for his helpers and their families. The cost of the festivities was always far in excess of the value of the labor received; however, its purpose was to give a man a chance to display his wealth and to reinforce his prestige.

The range of the community-wide fiestas and the household fiestas was such as to involve ultimately all members of the community. All fiestas, secular and religious, celebrated directly and indirectly the land and its fertility and, above all, supported the status structure of the community.

Marriage in the tenant community was largely endogamous. First cousin marriage was considered too close for comfort, but beyond the first cousin range the field was open. As the community had been in existence for several hundred years, the network of relationships through marriage was enormous. The extensiveness and complexity of these relationships had a two-fold effect: it assured a measure of economic security in the event of crop failure or unexpected shortages in a given family; and it assured a degree of social control in a community where the only negative sanctions on disruptive day-to-day behavior was cold, distant disapproval on the part of relatives and friends. While this closeness of family relations did not eliminate antisocial behavior, it, certainly, put a restraint upon it.

Finally, a word about social stratification on the hacienda. Hacienda society was basically divided into two subsocieties: a criollo subsociety, insignificant in personnel but dominant in certain narrow spheres connected with the hacendado's interests; and the Indian tenants. The latter were clearly stratified. A few of the Indians situated close to the center of the village held very productive land and, in addition, they were small storekeepers who brought in goods manufactured on the coast and abroad. Their stores serviced the criollos as well as the Indians with certain necessities, such as aniline dyes, matches, machetes, plow tips, guitar strings and like items. From the proceeds of their stores and their land, they were able to amass a considerable amount of wealth, which, in turn, gave them a favored position in the fiesta complex. The majority of Indians were simply tenants, and the distinctions among them were only measurable in terms of the size and productivity of their land and their contributions to the fiesta. On the lowest stratum were the subtenants who held no land independently. They usually subleased a small segment of a tenant's land. The last group was in the minority of the Indian subsociety.

Though land and wealth were the basis of stratification, there were no social inhibitions to mobility through the strata. As one Indian had no more marketable or wealth-producing personal skills than another, the accumulation of social capital depended directly upon the accumulation of wealth. A lucky inheritance could conceivably catapult a poor subtenant into the upper stratum of tenant society. This probably never occurred but it was possible theoretically. Social mobility for the tenant, however, was limited to the tenant subsociety because the criollo segment on the hacienda was socially impenetrable.

The tenant community, then, was a self-regulating, closely-knit society at the core of which was the family unit whose social relationships spread in many directions throughout the hacienda. The economic interchange of crops from different zones, the community and private fiestas from which a man and his family achieved prestige and public recognition and community endogamous marriage, all served to create a social interdependence which insulated the society from the outside world.

From the beginning of this century, population growth had forced many members of the poor tenant and subtenant families to earn part of their livelihood as plantation laborers on the coast. This marks the beginning of the second or transitional phase.

Routinely, these sierra Indians spent part of the year on the plantation only to return to the hacienda during the heavy work periods, which also coincided with the fiesta season. The primary loyalty of these Indians was to the tenant community. They considered their work on the plantation a temporary measure to relieve the pressure on the food supply at home.

The characteristics of the transitional phase are the following:

1. The great availability of jobs requiring no skill on the plantations;
2. The instability of the Indian. Not only did many periodically return to the sierra, but those who were permanently estranged from the sierra moved from job to job on the various coastal plantations;
3. Matrifocality of the family. Men frequently had two families, one on the coast and one in the sierra. When the men moved from plantation to plantation, it was usually as isolates for they left their family when they left their jobs;
4. Lack of generation depth and relatives in the Indian subsociety on the coast.

During the transitional phase, the Indians on the plantation formed an extremely amorphous subgroup. Few among them had been with the plantation very long, and many of them had no intention of settling there permanently. The hope of returning to the sierra always lurked in the back of their minds, but, failing that, they were not quite ready for a stable life on the coast, or, more particularly, on any one plantation.

For the Indian who had lately arrived from the sierra, the plantation setting was alien. Unlike sierra communities where the daily activities were mostly determined by the seasons, the plantation regimen was rigorous.

For those Indians who had no refuge in the sierra, there was no alternative to the coast. Their only recourse was to change plantations or to find equally difficult and, to some extent, less rewarding work in the city.

The constant movement of males, naturally, put a severe strain on family life, especially, since some of the moves were expressly for the purpose of changing wives. Of the group of males interviewed, all of whom were married, not a single one was presently living with his first wife. The usual explanations for leaving a wife were that they had become interested in another woman, or that they thought the wife they had left was lazy, tyrannical or morally irresponsible.

From this lack of commitment by males to a single wife and family grew the matrifocal family, characterized by strong devotion of the children for their mother and their siblings. The father was clearly a peripheral figure in the family during the transition phase. To assert that this was purely a plantation phenomenon would be stretching the point, for it also occurred in the sierra hacienda among subtenants who traveled to and from the coast. But, in general, most of the families in the sierra were definitely patricentric, whereas the Indian families on the plantation were mostly matricentric.

Since most of the Indians who were on the coast were relatively recent arrivals and since marriages were unstable, there was neither generation depth nor a network of familial relations which could produce a sense of solidarity in the Indian subgroup. There were no internal mechanisms in the Indian subgroup which overtly or covertly could induce stability or conformity. There were no sanctions *from* or obligations *to* the group as a whole. In short, the individual was an isolate having no long-term relationship to his own subsociety.

In addition to the above, there was no active participation or interest in the political or religious life on the plantation. These were national institutions which were for the criollos. None of the existing social clubs admitted Indians nor did the Indians have any interest in joining them.

Indian social life centered around the chichería (chicha bar) where small knots of those congenial to one another gathered after work. The attachments of chichería mates were necessarily thin because personnel was ever changing.

In general, the Indian's relationship to the criollos during this phase is, at best, tangential. On the job the criollos were the distant management representatives. Off the job, there were no institutions of social intercourse for both criollos and Indians. Indeed, the criollos didn't desire to see any more of the Indian than was absolutely necessary, for they regarded the Indian as degraded and burdensome to the nation.

Thus, in the transitional phase, significant socialization of the sierra Indian in the proletarian context did not occur. Moreover, the Indian who had been expelled from the sierra, and was without a permanent place on a plantation, and had only the thinnest ties to others in the same situation, remained on the coast as part of a large, amorphous group.

In the "proletarian" phase, the Indian subsociety achieves self-consciousness as a social group within plantation society. At the same time, there is an observable tendency *toward* and expression *of* individuality among certain of its members. The change in character of the Indian subsociety is explained by the end of the labor-shortage and the beginning of a labor glut on the coast.

Two basic occurrences can be cited to explain the sudden change from labor shortage to labor glut: the sharp increase in the Indian population on the coast due to large migrations from the sierra; and the tendency among the sugar planters to introduce mechanization of certain field operations which reduced the number of workers needed in the cane fields.

The immediate effect of the labor glut was to halt abruptly the oscillations of the Indians between the coast and the sierra and the random movements between plantations. The Indians began to realize that the market for unskilled laborers was gradually closing, and that competition for jobs was gradually increasing. This produced a greater constancy on the part of the Indians to a single plantation.

The enforced commitment to a plantation had far-reaching consequences for the members of the Indian subsociety. They may be summed up as follows: (1) stabilization of the father's position in the family; (2) intensification of familial associations, particularly between affinals and close relatives which resulted in greater social constraints on the individual; (3) greater opportunities for upward social mobility, for plantation managements began to seek, from the Indian ranks, individuals who seemed to have special aptitudes and potentialities and who could be trained in skills important to the plantation operation. I should like to comment on the implications of these changes in the Indian subsociety on the plantation.

Stabilization of the father's position in the family. The positive identification of a man as the de facto head of his family increased the security and status of his wife and children in the community. Perceptible social goals emerged, especially for the children. The most important goal was to send the younger children to elementary school. This meant, if it was achieved, the eventual criolloization of the children, who, in school, assimilated criollo culture and learned to read and write. Another goal was to arrange a stable marriage for an adolescent daughter, if there was one. To assure a stable marriage, many precautionary measures were taken, the most important of which was to insist on a civil marriage. Thus, a husband could be held liable in case of desertion.

Intensification of intrafamilial associations particularly between affinals and close relatives which resulted in greater social constraints in the Indian subgroup. There was an increase in groups which were socially and economically supportive to their members. There was greater identification with one's family members and greater responsibility to them. The "gang" quality of friend groups, so characteristic in the transition phase, was reduced. A man now had to consider the approval or disapproval of the relative group. This, in turn, changed the character of the friend group.

Selection of individuals by plantation management for skilled jobs. Plantations require an enormous number of skilled people, and the management willingly took the talented from any social stratum. This fed back to the Indian subsociety and fired the ambitions of those Indians who felt their abilities could bring them greater prestige and income. This marked the beginning of internal differentiation of the Indian subsociety on an occupational basis. It also had the effect, to a minor degree, of bridging the caste-like gap between the Indian subsociety and the skilled criollo proletarians. Eventually, changes in the behavior of the skilled Indians became perceptible. At best, however, the skilled Indian could not fully transcend the hardened boundaries which separated him from the criollos. He still did not read or write and his wife, if he had one, was still culturally affiliated to the Indian group, and it was probable that most of his relatives were still unskilled field workers. Furthermore, the management only taught the Indians skills which kept them in the fields, such as the operation of cranes, tractors, locomotives and trucks. They did not interact with criollo proletarians, whose skills mostly kept them in the sugar mill or the machine and repair shops.

The ties enmeshing the Indian subsociety with the larger plantation society and, beyond that, the region and the nation became even more intricate. A most important instrument for broadening the Indians' perspective was the plantation labor union. It came into existence in 1956, and by 1957 it was firmly rooted on the plantation. The significance of the union for the Indians was that it was the first voluntary plantation-wide institution to which members of the Indian subsociety were affiliated. It helped produce a social solidarity within the Indian subsociety and between the Indian and criollo proletarians which was previously unknown. On several occasions in 1958, they had strongly supported each other in their respective demands on management. While membership in the same union did not imply any new extra-union social interaction between the Indians and the criollos, their mutual interests brought them into close working contact. In this situation the Indian's social perspective constantly widened.

The Indian's horizons were broadened even further by the close association between the union and the Apra party. Through the union the Indian proletarians received an education in national politics, and more particularly, in the effect of the national political structure on local conditions. This, for the first time, gave the Indian a national perspective, however limited, that was totally absent before. For the first time, he has become a conscious member of Peruvian society, unlike his relatives in the sierra whose social consciousness does not extend much beyond the local community.

In sum, it can be said that the consequence of the labor glut and the resultant stabilization of the Indian was the change of the Indian subsociety from self-conscious alienation to self-conscious assimilation as proletarians in plantation society.

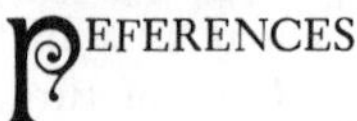EFERENCES

Aranguri, Marcial. 1963. Teoria de la Migracion y Migracion en la Ciudad de Trujillo 1940–1956. Migracion y Integracion en el Peru, Henry F. Dobyns & Mario C. Vasquez, Eds. Lima, Peru.

Erasmus, Charles J. 1956. Culture structure and process: The occurrence and disappearance of reciprocal farm labor. Southwestern J. of Anthropology 12:444–469.

Ford, Thomas R. 1955. Man and Land in Peru. University of Florida Press, Gainesville, Fla.

Mangin, William. 1954. The Cultural Significance of the Fiesta Complex on an Indian Hacienda in Peru. Ph.D. Thesis, Yale Univ. New Haven, Conn.

Mintz, Sidney W., & Eric R. Wolf. 1957. Haciendas and plantations in middle America and the Antilles. Social and Economic Studies 6:380–412.

Smith, M. G. 1960. Social and cultural pluralism. Ann. N.Y. Acad. Sci. 83:763–785.

Wagley, Charles, & Marvin Harris. 1955. A typology of Latin American subcultures. Amer. Anthropologist 57:426–451.

Wolf, Eric R. 1955. Latin American Peasantry. Amer. Anthropologist 57:452–471.

Agrarian Reform vs. Land Reform: Three Latin American Countries

CHARLES J. ERASMUS

"Land to the tiller" has long been a popular rallying cry in those nations where land, wealth, and power are concentrated in the hands of a few families. In comparing the experience of Bolivia, Mexico, and Venezuela, Erasmus stresses that "land distribution by itself cannot effect a revolution," but at the same time he identifies significant links between land tenure and other political, economic, and social aspects of development. His findings complement those of Goldrich, Nisbet, Gonzalez, and Mitchell and Schatan, in ways that often contradict political rhetoric.

Charles J. Erasmus is Professor of Anthropology at the University of California, Santa Barbara. He has done extensive field work in many Latin American countries, and recently in Africa. His books include Las dimensiones de la cultura (1953), *and* Man Takes Control: Cultural Development and American Aid (1961); *he is also coauthor of* Land Reform and Social Revolution in Bolivia (1969).

It has been my privilege to observe at firsthand the results of agrarian reform programs in three Latin-American countries—Bolivia, Mexico, and Venezuela. The experience has left me with mixed feelings on the subject. While the rural populations of most underdeveloped countries obviously need help, the expropriation and redistribution of land cannot by itself eliminate rural poverty. But the phrase "agrarian reform" has come to include much more than we in Anglo-America tend to think of as "land reform." In fact, there is a growing tendency in Latin America to emphasize rural development at the expense of land redistribution, a deliberate policy that reflects an increasing awareness of the limitations and disappointments that attend too narrow a view of rural social problems. In this article I shall frequently make comparisons among the three countries; their problems are similar. But I shall do this in the process of discussing each country in turn, for my focus will be on the special lessons each can teach us about the merits and weaknesses of agrarian reform. Bolivia illustrates the limitations of a program involving little more than the expropriation and redistribution of land. In Mexico, on the other hand, extensive land reform was followed by intensive rural development involving high inputs of capital investment and technological know-how. However, subsequent reconsolidation of land-reform plots into corporately managed farm units has been an unanticipated consequence which largely nullifies the intent of land redistribution. In Venezuela, where land reform has been secondary to technological change and to the development and colonization of new lands, we have the best example of a modern approach to agrarian reform.

From Philip K. Bock (ed.), *Peasants in the Modern World* (Albuquerque, N.M.: University of New Mexico Press, 1969) 9–31. Copyright 1969 by The University of New Mexico. Reprinted by permission of the author and publisher.

BOLIVIA

My study of Bolivia was concentrated in the southeastern departments (states) of Chuquisaca and Tarija. The typical problems of rural Bolivia—high transportation costs, lack of markets and primitive technology—are as severe there as anywhere in the country. Bolivia is ruggedly mountainous with few paved roads, and the dirt highway that connects the southeast with Cochabamba is not negotiable during much of the year. Even if all-weather roads were suddenly provided it would take time for markets to develop. Bolivia's population is overwhelmingly rural, and without accessible export markets most of the agricultural produce gets no farther than the peasant's table. In a year of bumper crops the small urban markets quickly saturate, and prices fall. The peasant finds little opportunity to expand his consumption of manufactured goods through the sale of food surpluses. Geographic and social isolation have resulted in a rural economy that is largely subsistence-oriented.

These very circumstances accounted in large part for the "feudal exploitation" of farm labor against which the 1952 revolution was directed. The large haciendas of southeastern Bolivia gave up two-thirds of their cultivable land in perquisite subsistence plots to serfs in exchange for labor to work the remaining third. Serfs owed their master roughly half the days of the year in free labor to work his fields, build and repair his hacienda house, serve as his domestics, collect his firewood, and sometimes spin his wool and manufacture his *chicha* (corn beer). Even large landowners were limited in the pursuit of wealth by the lack of markets and the difficulties of transportation. They availed themselves of one form of "wealth" made possible through control of the productive land, the human labor which they lavishly and conspicuously consumed in the construction and maintenance of impressive haciendas and in domestic service. To some readers it may seem incredible that a society as feudal as this could have survived as late as the middle of the twentieth century. But similar conditions still exist in parts of Peru and Ecuador.

The Bolivian revolution, and the agrarian reform that followed, gave the serfs the land they had previously held on loan from their hacendados. They no longer owed anyone free labor. In effect the reform simply canceled all "feudal" work obligations and gave the serfs inalienable usufruct of their subsistence plots. As in most cases of land reform, the beneficiaries cannot sell these holdings; the state itself becomes the landowner and sets the conditions of tenure.

North Americans often have the idea that land-reform beneficiaries are radicals with strong Communist leanings. Bolivia demonstrates how mistaken this notion can be. Its rural masses are very resistant to any attempts to organize them into collective farm operations and they jealously defend all inequities in the size of their meager farm plots. On those large properties, where even the portion cultivated by the hacendados was expropriated, this portion was often converted into a "collective" to be worked by all the ex-serfs in collaboration. In nearly all cases these collectives have been divided up by the ex-serfs with or without official permission. As for the plots given them by the reform, no general attempt was made to equalize them. The same striking inequities in size of plots that existed before 1952 have been perpetuated by the reform. But nowhere did peasants I interviewed favor a more equitable redivision of holdings. The very idea fills most of them with alarm.

These reactions of the Bolivian peasantry are paralleled by land-reform beneficiaries in both Mexico and Venezuela. Collectives in Mexico have been a striking failure. Land-reform beneficiaries are strongly opposed to them but none more strongly than former collective members. Mexican authorities usually relax their pressures to maintain collective farms once members become sufficiently persistent and intransigent in their demands to divide the land into family plots. In Venezuela the government has exerted considerably more pressure to maintain its few collective farms. In the case of collective Cascarí, members finally took matters into their own hands and divided the property among themselves. At others I found the majority of members either verging on revolt or strongly opposed to collective operations.

Inequalities in the size of holding have occurred in many land-reform communities in Venezuela where squatting preceded official expropriation. Venezuelan officials feel these inequities are minor compared with the turmoil that would be created by any attempt at reapportionment. In Mexico, plot sizes are usually uniform within the same *ejido* (land-reform association) but often vary enormously between neighboring *ejidos*. But among all but the most disadvantaged *ejidos*, the suggestion of equalizing holdings meets with vigorous opposition. In attitudes of independence and tenure, land-reform beneficiaries are miniature landlords—not militant Bolsheviks.

Given the social—rather than economic—nature of the Bolivian reform, its effect on rural living standards is precisely what one would expect. The decaying hacienda buildings that dot the countryside are reminders of the quaint and lopsided style of life that so recently and so conspicuously provided a small elite with half the working time of their impoverished serfs. The working time has been returned to this labor force, but since the economic situation remains unchanged there are only limited ways in which the additional time can be used to raise living standards. Many peasants migrate to northern Argentina to earn money during sugarcane harvests. Others invest labor in home improvements of their own by installing paved floors and tile roofs in place of the former dirt and thatch. But so far as increased earning power in agriculture is concerned, the same limitations apply as before.

There is no question that the Bolivian peasants appreciate their release from servitude. In this regard their initial reaction to the reform was not unlike that of the Haitian peasantry after the first great land "reform" in the Western Hemisphere—that which followed the Haitian slave insurrection of 1791.

During the early period of Haitian independence under the leadership of Toussaint, Dessalines and Christophe, French plantations were maintained as state farms on which the former slaves continued to work under a system of controls hardly less strict than those of the slavery from which they had nominally been liberated. But with the fragmentation of the great estates begun by Petion (1807–1818) and continued by Boyer (1818–1843), the Haitian farm economy changed drastically in emphasis from one of markets and exports to one of subsistence. Few of the erstwhile slaves had ever had occasion to taste the fruits of the island's highly profitable plantation economy. As consumers they had never acquired the incentives necessary for intensive market production.

Similarly, in Bolivia for a brief time after the 1952 revolution there was a decrease in market produce which created inflationary food prices in the cities. In enjoyment of their new freedom, the peasants concentrated on their own needs while many of the hacendados who had been producing for the urban markets fled temporarily to the cities or abandoned their farms forever. During this period when urban living was most austere many of the professionally trained members of the middle class left Bolivia for jobs in Chile, Peru, and Venezuela. But today Bolivian peasants are satisfying the urban markets and willingly increase their market production when they have the opportunity. They want more radios, bicycles, sewing machines and other manufactured goods of which there are still very few in most rural areas. The pre-reform Bolivian peasants of the mid-twentieth century were far more market-oriented than the newly liberated Haitian slaves of the early nineteenth.

The Bolivian countryside is now ready for an economic revolution, but that will require enormous amounts of capital investment. That land redistribution by itself cannot effect an economic revolution is now admitted by Bolivians. However, some officials are still so much on the defensive about land reform that they deride purely economic appraisals of it as "materialistic" and insist the true measure of its success is "social." Considering the conditions of serfdom that existed in Bolivia before 1952, the point they are making is certainly not a trivial one. But will these social effects be progressive without economic and technological growth?

MEXICO

Mexico has made impressive investments in rural development, particularly in the northwest. In an area that twenty years ago did not even have a paved road connecting it with the capital or the U.S. border, the federal government has invested heavily in dams, irrigation, paved highways and public power. The investments have certainly transformed northwestern Mexico, as anyone knows who has watched the remarkable changes that have transpired in Sonora and Sinaloa since World War II. Although not called "agrarian reform" when they began, these capital investments are today considered an integral part of a balanced agrarian reform program. Mexicans no longer expect land redistribution to raise rural living standards.

The most interesting aspect of the Mexican case is the management problem that arises when land-reform beneficiaries are further benefited by extensive capital improvements. The irrigation districts in the Yaqui and Mayo river valleys of southern Sonora illustrate this problem. In the old days farmers flood-irrigated their land with water provided by the annual inundations of the rivers. Seed was saved from the last harvest, and plowing and cultivating were done with draft animals pastured in adjoining thorn forests. Development of the irrigation districts has greatly extended the area of cultivation and with it the farming population. But now not only is the water taxed, but commercial crop seeds, fertilizers and insecticides have all become increasingly necessary. Moreover, opening the thorn forest to more farm land has left no place to pasture draft animals. Although machinery is available, most farmers cannot afford to own their own; they either rent equipment or contract their plowing and harvesting.

Thus, even for the smallest landowner or land-reform beneficiary, farming must now be financed. The Ejido Bank, which was established to provide land-reform beneficiaries with farm credit, has funds sufficient to help less than a fourth of the land-reform beneficiaries in the Yaqui and Mayo River Irrigation Districts. The rest are forced to rent or sharecrop (the tenant provides the financing and the land-reform beneficiary the land).

According to the Mexican agrarian code, which establishes the conditions of tenure for land-reform beneficiaries, neither renting nor sharecropping of *ejido* plots is permissible. In all three countries the land-reform laws promote personal management of the properties distributed to beneficiaries and discourage their reconsolidation or fragmentation by sale, renting, sharecropping, marriage or inheritance. But the restrictions on renting and sharecropping have long been openly violated throughout Mexico. Recently, when the director of the Ejido Bank for the state of Sonora brought a civil suit against men renting large acreages of *ejido* land within the Yaqui River Irrigation District, the state supreme court refused to hear the case. For all practical purposes this action by the court has now legalized the practice.

Land renting is done by some entrepreneurial farmers on a large scale. Using their own farm machinery they rent large blocks of contiguous *ejido* plots that can be plowed, crop dusted and harvested as a unit. For the same reasons sharecroppers find it more economical to work adjoining parcels, and even the Ejido Bank endeavors to work with groups of adjoining land-reform beneficiaries rather than with scattered individuals. The Bank stipulates the crops to be planted, manages the farming operations and employs land-reform beneficiaries only at manual tasks, mainly during irrigation. These manual labor requirements represent less than ten per cent of the total cropping costs. In such a situation, land-reform beneficiaries working with the Bank are little different from those working with an entrepreneur on a sharecropping basis. They are simply shareholders in a financial venture managed by someone else.

This tendency for redistributed lands to reconsolidate for management purposes when capitalization takes place is strongest in Mexico. In Bolivia, where capitalization of agriculture has been minimal, I observed no cases at all. In Venezuela, in 1964, the sharecropping form was rare but seemed to be spreading.

In Mexico, as in Bolivia, it is difficult to see how land redistribution has lifted material living standards. The relative prosperity of land-reform beneficiaries depends upon the size of their holdings and upon the extent of rural capitalization by the government in their area. For the majority of beneficiaries the holdings are too small to provide anything but a minimal standard of living. In Sonora well over three-fourths must seek supplementary income during the year, usually as field hands and occasionally as unskilled or semiskilled construction laborers in the rapidly growing urban areas. It is the overall economic expansion of this region due to government irrigation and road-building projects that has been most influential in raising living standards. There are more opportunities than ever for small farmers and land-reform beneficiaries to find seasonal and part-time employment to supplement their meager farm incomes. The rising prosperity of the area has also affected the attitudes of merchants toward consumer credit. Rural households find it increasingly easy to buy bicycles, radios and home furnishings with small down payments and no collateral. The pressure of time payments is often an additional incentive to seek part-time employment off the farm.

Many land-reform beneficiaries within the irrigation districts, particularly the Indians, would prefer to plant subsistence crops. They complain of the loss of freedom which has followed the irrigation developments. Forced to seek credit from the Ejido Bank or from sharecroppers to meet the expenses of planting, they become obligated to plant commercial crops such as cotton. Others simply rent their parcels and seek wage labor where they can find it. While all of this is unpleasant to the subsistence-oriented peasant, it has had the effect of forcing him more and more into the market and into a widening sphere of commercial relationships. Outside the irrigation zones many land-reform beneficiaries have changed from subsistence to commercial crops on their own. Sesame seed, for example, does much better under local dry-farming conditions than the traditional food crops. Small farmers have been quick to appreciate the fact that the sesame harvested from their small plots will buy them more corn and beans than they could produce themselves. But the marketing possibilities for commercial crops such as sesame are the result of the overall economic development of the area with the attendant intensification of merchandizing.

The question that comes to mind in considering the Mexican case is whether any purpose is served by making land-reform beneficiaries the nominal, lower-class owners of highly capitalized farm operations which are financed, managed and even worked by other persons. When I suggest to a Mexican official that the land redistribution aspects of Mexico's agrarian reform may already have become an anachronism (to provoke an expression of his attitudes), I usually get a very negative response, and sometimes an angry one. But once the official is reassured that I am just as sincerely concerned with the problems and as perplexed by them as he is, he frequently admits that the time will probably come when Mexico will give land-reform beneficiaries negotiable titles to their plots. However, most informed Mexicans with whom I have discussed this problem do not feel the country is ready for such a drastic move.

On occasion I have suggested that the consequences of such a move would not be as drastic as many people expect. Making *ejido* lands a commodity once again would not have to result in prerevolutionary *latifundismo* (condition of giant land holdings) as long as the present restrictions on maximum farm sizes are retained. For example, in areas of prime land like those in the irrigation districts, one hundred hectares (a little under the average size of U.S. farms) is the most that one person can legally own. Granted that the most able farmers would soon gobble up the rest, this would only mean that for every one who expanded up to this limit, about four or five would eventually be bought out. All farms would then be large enough to afford their owners a middle-class standard of living; the number of competent farm managers necessary to meet the demands of this limit would be a more realistic national goal than the number necessary to make the present *minifundismo* (condition of small land holdings) operate according to land-reform ideology; and finally, the less able managers who sold their holdings would simply go on earning their living as wage laborers as they are already doing.

But to these arguments my Mexican friends reply that the results of such a policy would indeed be drastic. Already people get around the laws restricting the size of individual holdings by buying land in the name of relatives or trusted employees. And many renters now farm thousands of acres of *ejido* lands. Making *ejido* land negotiable would so defeat the ideology of Mexico's agrarian reform that there would be no way left of preserving the existing machinery for helping the rural masses.

In the case of Mexico we come back to the same basic problem we encountered in Bolivia. Land redistribution by itself does not result in material, economic improvements for disadvantaged rural populations. But it has social consequences that seem important. The problem is to determine just how important and beneficial these social consequences really are. Unfortunately, our third case, Venezuela, does not provide any final answers, but its own special circumstances add further dimensions to our question.

VENEZUELA

Compared to Mexico and Bolivia, expropriation and redistribution of land is not a major emphasis of agrarian reform in Venezuela. In Mexico about forty-five per cent of all cultivated land is now in the possession of *ejidatarios* (land-reform beneficiaries), and between two-thirds and three-fourths of Bolivia's cultivated land has nominally changed hands since the revolution. Venezuela's land reform, however, has affected less than six per cent of her cultivated lands. While it is true that the Venezuelan experiment is much younger than the other two, the approach to land expropriation in Venezuela has been much more conservative and cautious. For one thing, the owners of expropriated haciendas in Venezuela are so well reimbursed that more land has been offered for expropriation than the government can afford to buy or could find peasants to occupy even if it did. This is very different from Bolivia where many former landowners are now so destitute that few people in the highlands today are willing to risk capital in the purchase or improvement of agricultural land. In Venezuela the public's confidence in its government's respect for private property is so high that in many newly colonized areas farmers are making heavy investments of labor and capital (dairies, orchards, farm buildings) prior to receiving legal title to their land. In Mexico the farmer-entrepreneur's confidence in his ability to circumvent the law is so great that he often makes expensive improvements on land owned illegally.

Venezuela's agrarian reform has three separate aspects of which land reform is only one. The dominant trend in Venezuela, and one certainly reflected in the attitudes of public officials and high-ranking members of the peasant federations, has been to emphasize the other two aspects—the development of new lands and the "consolidation" of agrarian settlements already established. Unlike Bolivia, where colonization and development of new lands in the tropical lowlands is viewed by government personnel as an alternative or supplement to agrarian reform, Venezuelan officials consider it an integral part of their program. With few exceptions, people employed by government agencies active in agrarian reform favor development of new lands rather than purchase and redistribution of those in production. It is a common opinion that money spent in buying farms would be better invested in roads, irrigation works, and land-clearing projects, etc. Many also feel that *planned* colonization is inadvisable. Peasant families quickly move into areas opened up by roads, and a "natural" selection of colonists results. These are usually better prepared psychologically to overcome new hardships than those chosen by planners.

Venezuela's approach to rural development maximizes new opportunities while leaving for later those problems for which there is no ready solution as yet. The western highlands of Venezuela have a dense and very conservative population with serious social and economic problems. In this region one still encounters archaic haciendas on which tenants equipped with oxen and wooden plows produce for absentee landlords under feudalistic forms of administration. Such haciendas are not expropriated because the land is too steep to meet the standards of the Venezuelan Agrarian Institute. Rather than convert marginal lands of this kind into permanent small plots, government policy is to entice the highland population into the lowlands by creating new opportunities there. As rural productivity and prosperity increase in these lowland areas, the nation can then turn to the solution of agricultural problems that involve the greatest social manipulation. It may then be feasible to take farms on eroded marginal lands completely out of cultivation and plant them to forests or pasture.

The third aspect of Venezuela's agrarian reform, "consolidation," refers to the construction of roads, rural housing, irrigation developments, public power and water distribution systems, as well as the facilitation of farm credit, farm machinery, agricultural extension and adult education programs. These projects are intended to insure the success of settlements formed by land redistribution or colonization. Bolivia has been able to afford very few such programs and even those have been heavily subsidized by United States foreign aid. Mexico, as we have seen, has given extraordinary attention to most of these projects but only recently has begun to advertise them as an integral part of agrarian reform. The income from Venezuela's vast oil deposits has provided her with an unusual opportunity to finance a very investment-conscious form of rural development.

The effects of Venezuela's efforts are evident throughout the countryside. The quantity of expensive consumer goods in rural homes is impressive. Refrigerators, for example, have become relatively common in communities with electricity, but the frequency with which one encounters kerosene refrigerators in remote villages is even more remarkable. Radios are common everywhere and bicycles are numerous in settlements near cities and paved highways.

In Venezuela, as in Bolivia and Mexico, greater personal freedom was frequently mentioned by peasants as a highly desirable result of agrarian reform. To work for oneself and to be the "owner of one's work" was considered far superior to sharecropping for another. But in Venezuela, far more than in the other two countries, peasants associated many material benefits directly with agrarian reform. Among those listed were absence of rent payments, availability of credit, farm machinery, rural housing, water, electricity, rural schools, and the all-important roads to market. Many were buying goods they said they had not even hoped to own before: radios, television sets, furniture, better clothes and a more varied and abundant diet. Children were attending school regularly now that their parents no longer had any reason to be ashamed of their apparel. No Venezuelan government in their memory had ever done so much for "los campesinos" (the peasants).

More striking even than the material evidences of rising living standards has been the effect of Venezuela's development policies on the structure of its rural population. The opening of new lands in the lowland interiors has resulted in considerable population movement. For example, settlements and towns in the progressive states of Portuguesa and Barinas contain families from nearly all parts of the nation. When I had occasion to check, I always found the proportion of out-of-state families greater than that of native born. The results of these population movements are reflected in the dramatic contrast between these dynamic, progressive areas and the static western highlands. Families torn from their old kinship and patron-client relationships form new commercial and political associations. Farmer associations, dairy associations, and credit unions, for example, become the vehicles for more active participation by rural interest groups in their own regional development and in the formation of national policy.

Bringing new lands under cultivation through the development of irrigation projects has had similar population effects in northwest Mexico. I met many families that had moved to Sonora from states farther south because they viewed Sonora as a frontier where they could increase their chances for success. While most find it hard to get land, many have initiated commercial enterprises that have done well. A developing area tends to attract the risk-takers or potential entrepreneurs who have found their own habitat too full of frustration. Here again, these spatially mobile families are much more progressive and much more prone to form new commercial and political associations than the more static, native population.

Even in Bolivia the most progressive and dynamic area is that being colonized around Santa Cruz in the eastern lowlands. Much more typical of Bolivia, however, is the static rural situation where land reform has changed the social order in ways that often seem more nominal than real. Land-reform beneficiaries have been organized into peasant syndicates that correspond to former hacienda boundaries except where serfs of two or more small haciendas form one syndicate. On those haciendas where the *patrón* was allowed to retain a portion of the land, he still lives in the hacienda manor. The ex-serfs still tip their hats to him, still call him "patrón" and often work on his reduced holdings as sharecroppers. The traditional rural social structure of Bolivia often seems remarkably resilient despite its political revolution.

Mexican land-reform associations (*ejidos*) seldom preserve pre-reform hacienda work forces. Not only are an *ejido's* lands frequently scattered but the *ejidatarios* themselves may reside in two or more villages. By cutting across community and ethnic (Indian versus Mestizo) lines, *ejidos* have helped to break down traditional social groupings in rural areas.

In Venezuela many haciendas purchased by the Agrarian Institute have been turned over to a peasant syndicate made up of the original work-force, as was so commonly done in Bolivia. These products of Venezuela's agrarian reform are the most unchanged. At such collectives as La Unión, Loro Pedernales and El

Rodeo, peasants felt the government had become a new *patrón* while everything else stayed much the same. Where land in the highlands had been divided among the beneficiaries in individual plots, the situation closely resembled the expropriation of a Bolivian *latifundio*. Peasants were cropping in a subsistence-oriented fashion or farming for market to maintain their minimal living standards. Family and neighborhood relationships remained intact, and where peasants had not actually withdrawn from the syndicates, their participation was poor. The dramatic improvements in Venezuela's rural living standards already referred to were mainly among the beneficiaries of redistributed and newly opened land in the lowlands near highways and cities. Here one can find many prosperous farmers who were *conuqueros* (slash-and-burn subsistence farmers) only a few years ago. It is in these areas that family heads are most active in peasant syndicates or farmer associations.

Although different in history and emphasis from the agrarian reforms of Bolivia and Mexico, that of Venezuela confirms the major conclusion to be drawn from our comparison. Rural development that accents capital investments and technological improvements is far more likely to produce a significant rise in rural living standards than is land redistribution. Yet there are many Venezuelans, as there are many Bolivians and Mexicans, who believe land redistribution is a necessary part of agrarian reform for social reasons often labeled the "social function" of land reform. These reasons essentially boil down to the reduction of political tensions through a more equitable distribution of political influence. We shall now consider this social problem.

REDISTRIBUTION OF POLITICAL INFLUENCE

The Haitian case is again useful for comparison because the French period preceding independence was an example of unrestrained coercive power. The Negro farm labor that made possible France's lucrative colonial plantations was slave labor. However, the transformation of slaves into subsistence-oriented peasants did not prevent the usurpation of dictatorial powers by heads of state. Haitian history provides clear testimony to the fact that land redistribution does not insure "democracy" as we know it.

The revolution that deposed the French colonial landowners did not immediately change the system of agricultural production. The early Haitian heads of state maintained forced labor through a system of district agricultural inspectors backed by the army. But once the fragmentation of holdings had begun under Petion it became impossible to stop. When Boyer early in his administration attempted to reinstate a forced labor system in his Rural Code of 1826, he was completely unable to enforce it. Today, when Bolivian peasants claim that no change of government could succeed in taking back the land given them or in remaking them into hacienda peons, they are probably right. Moreover, when they say they have gained greater self-respect and "dignity" with their freedom, the Haitian case substantiates this claim as well. Haitian peasants are fiercely independent, and their personality and demeanor have little in common with "Black Sambo" or "Uncle Tom" stereotypes. Despite all the "Papa Docs" of Haitian history, Haitians act more like Sidney Poitier than Stepen Fetchit. But the freedom of the Haitian peasant is the freedom of poverty, hunger, high infant mortality and a short life-span. Slaves and serfs gain considerable "freedom" and self-respect through land redistribution despite few improvements in living standards and despite the concentration of considerable coercive power in urban areas. The greater "freedom" of the post-1952 Bolivian peasant is no guarantee that Bolivia is now immune to coercive or despotic governments.

Elias T. Tuma, in his important book, *Twenty-six Centuries of Agrarian Reform* (1965), compares several important land-tenure reforms from ancient to modern times. One of his major conclusions is that such reforms are more likely to serve the political goals of reformers than the economic and social needs of the people. Certainly the cases examined here confirm the results of Tuma's historical analysis.

The feudal character of Venezuela's haciendas ended with the close of the Gómez dictatorship in 1935. But land-tenure reform did not begin until after the fall of Pérez Jiménez twenty-five years later. It is true that in many parts of Venezuela, during the rule of Pérez Jiménez, squatters were moved off lands owned by the dictator's henchmen. While some token payment was made to the squatters for their "improvements," it was rarely adequate. Upon the downfall of Jiménez the dispossessed peasants rushed back to reclaim their lands. These numerous property "invasions" throughout Venezuela in the early days of the reform led to an exaggerated view of the "social pressure" for land redistribution. Early estimates of the numbers of land-hungry peasants ranged from 300,000 to 500,000 families. But four years after the agrarian reform was initiated only 100,000 families had petitioned for land.

In Mexico, the revolution of 1910 terminated the dictatorship of Porfirio Díaz and led to peasant land invasions in the southern part of the country and to the reform law of 1915. However, large-scale expropriation and redistribution of lands did not really begin until the presidency of Lázaro Cárdenas twenty years later. Cárdenas' desire to strengthen his political influence against that of former president Calles was undoubtedly an important factor in his decision, for he was faced with no widespread urgency to reinterpret the agrarian law.

Bolivia is one case in which land-tenure reform was an integral part of a revolution. Even in Haiti, forced labor on large estates outlasted the slave revolt by more than a generation. However, Bolivia is not really an exceptional case in the sense that social pressures for land reform were general in the countryside at the time it was carried out. Many peasants had to be persuaded and fears of retaliation by the landowners had to be allayed. The southeastern sector was influenced by leadership from outside the area. Cochabamba is believed by some to have been one major point from which revolt spread, and the mining state of Potosí may have been another. Two of the most powerful syndicate leaders in the state of Chuquisaca during the early days of the reform were miners from Potosí.

Organization of the Bolivian peasantry into peasant syndicates became the procedure for initiating the expropriation of hacienda land and simultaneously the means of consolidating the rural masses behind the revolutionary party. Once the formation of peasant syndicates had been justified and implemented through land reform, the party in power could use them at election time to amass the show of votes with which it legitimized its authority.

Many of the characteristics and problems of the peasant federations of

Bolivia, Mexico and Venezuela parallel those of incipient trade union movements in underdeveloped countries. In the first place they are primarily political organizations. Bruce Millen in his study *The Political Role of Labor in Developing Countries* (1963) calls this characteristic "political unionism" to distinguish it from the collective bargaining orientation of U.S. labor unions. Peasant federations are less likely to involve the collective bargaining aspects of unionism than are trade unions. The self-employed beneficiaries of land reform can bargain only with their government. The leadership of both trade and peasant syndicates tends to come from a worker or rural "elite" made up of individuals who are better educated, more ambitious, and more experienced in coping with the larger world than is the average worker or peasant. Since dues in both cases are hard to collect, the unions cannot afford full-time officers without government subsidy. Dependence on outside sources for funds often leads to the compromising of principles and even to corruption.

Despite all their inadequacies and despite the tendency for a ruling party to use them as vehicles for the exercise of power, trade unions and peasant federations provide a vital channel of communication between the masses and the political elites of developing countries. Moreover, the attention and importance that political elites ascribe to these structures as vote-buying mechanisms for the legitimation of their authority does, in effect, transfer political influence to the masses. However, it takes a broader agrarian reform program than land redistribution to maintain peasant unions as vote-buying mechanisms. In this regard Venezuela's peasant federation has undoubtedly consigned more political influence to the rural sector than Bolivia's has been able to do. Because of the Venezuelan emphasis on "consolidation" through programs of farm credit, housing, road building, machinery, etc., local peasant leaders are provided with many goals for rural improvements to which they can redirect their political activities after their request for land has been met. And the more local improvements the rural masses obtain by such measures the more they expect their votes and political support to win them in the future. In short, true redistribution of political influence in the rural sector tends to be associated with the economic and technological developments that progressively lift standards and aspirations—not with land redistribution per se.

In underdeveloped countries where most jobs must be filled from a labor market made up of illiterate, unskilled workers, trade unions emphasizing collective bargaining rather than politics are not likely to develop much power to bargain with. One unskilled worker can so easily replace another that stable, unified union memberships are hard to achieve. Unskilled farm laborers have been the last to successfully organize in the United States, and it is precisely among them that the political overtones of membership are far stronger than in most U.S. unions. This situation not only helps us understand why incipient union movements in such countries must be political, it also illustrates why general economic and industrial development is essential to a permanent and broad distribution of political influence. It is only this kind of development that leads to a permanent diversification of the occupational structure among skilled workers and trained specialists. And it is the diversification of labor skills and labor needs that gives each occupational group its bargaining power vis-à-vis the rest. It becomes harder for any one interest group to control all the rest as it becomes more difficult for each to master all the knowledge and skills of the rest.

Industrialization is the most direct path to the diversification of the occupational structure, including the absorption of farm-labor surpluses created by the mechanization of agriculture. But a country with a class system dominated by a landholding aristocracy is one particularly resistant to the kind of entrepreneurial changes that effect industrialization. Thus land redistribution is viewed as necessary in such situations to destroy the older status-quo ideology. Power taken from the conservative aristocracy is thereby made available to a larger sector of the population. But making political influence available to a target sector does not insure its transfer. Illiterate rural populations, unaccustomed to participation in those kinds of voluntary associations that operationalize political influence, are unlikely to absorb all that is made available to them by a drastic land reform; the surplus is eagerly appropriated by a new elite. Bolivia is a case in point.

When I began my stay in Bolivia I was surprised at being gently reprimanded on several occasions by government officials for using the word "Indian." Instead of "indio" I was instructed to speak of "campesinos" (peasants). The word "indio" was regarded as a term of opprobrium applied by the former landed aristocracy to their peons and therefore a symbol of peonage and inferiority. I was very much impressed by this evidence of an ideological change produced by land reform. Not only did officials and employees of the various government bureaucracies refer to the rural population as "campesinos," they greeted all peasants in direct address as "compañero" (comrade). But despite the impressiveness of this deliberate and practiced alteration of vocabulary, the behavior of the officials employing it often contained a patronizing quality that mitigated the ideological intention. When a peasant, dressed in traditional Indian garb, visited a government office, he was generally treated in a conspicuously egalitarian fashion by a bureaucrat dressed in modern garb. No one observing the egalitarian ritual with which the official embraced his country "comrade" would have had difficulty recognizing which of the two was higher in status. But when a *compesino* and a bureaucrat of higher status were dressed alike, some form of protocol was invariably invoked to make the distinction obvious.

For example, whenever officials travel about the countryside in their pickup trucks they are driven by a "chauffeur" who also serves as mechanic if the car breaks down. Unless the chauffeur has recently soiled his clothes and hands in his role as mechanic, he may be indistinguishable from the higher-status official. Although of *campesino* origins, he may not even differ noticeably in skin color. But when these two individuals, who have been riding side by side all day, stop at a village cafe to eat, the official sits at a separate table. It is soon made clear by manner and conversation which of the two is the official. Physical separation announces the status difference, and subsequent behavior explains who is in charge and who is subservient. Comradeship ends at the crucial point where it might really compromise higher status.

One might argue that this conscious change in vocabulary has been largely nominal since many of the behavioral distinctions between *patrón* and *peón* remain. This point of view is verbalized even by some peasants when they claim the former *rosca* (landed aristocracy—literally "the screw") has been replaced by a *nueva rosca* (the new bureaucratic elite). There would almost seem to be a contradiction here between this recognition of a *nueva rosca* and the peasants' greater sense of self-esteem, noted previously, which they attribute to the reform. But this very contradiction epitomizes the strength and weakness of land reform as an instrument for redistribution of political influence. The peasant has indeed gained greater independence. He can feel the difference and so can the old aristocracy, which complains incessantly of peasant irresponsibilities that at times approach outright sabotage. But the effect is not cumulative as in those parts of Mexico and Venezuela where intensive capitalization of the rural sector has promoted rising living standards. As people grow accustomed to "progress," they expect more and demand more. Distributing small plots of land to peasants may only enhance their freedom to withdraw further from the contest for influence. They have to aspire to something more than a minimal existence.

None of this means that the ideology of land redistribution is meaningless or unimportant. It involves a healthy concern with standards of social justice. In Mexico and Venezuela the number of technicians employed in rural development programs is steadily increasing, as is their dedication and skill. In Mexico, particularly, a great change has taken place in government personnel over the past twenty years. The desire to use an official post as a means of acquiring through graft the capital to start a business or farming venture seems to be much less in vogue. Many able men are making government service a career and taking pride in their reputation for honesty and efficiency. There is a greater tendency today to talk about graft in the past tense. The growing number of skilled and dedicated civil servants has been made possible by the expanding Mexican economy. Land reform has played its part by helping to provide and maintain the justification for rural development. If most of the land in a river valley is owned by a few families, costly irrigation developments by government are much harder to justify in terms of the new social ethic than when those same lands have been redistributed to thousands of poor families. The ideology that accompanies land redistribution can be a much greater catalyst to rural development than the redistribution itself if a country has the resources to follow it up with modern agrarian reform.

CONCLUSIONS

The phrase "agrarian reform" in its broadest sense includes both land redistribution and capital development of the rural sector. I have chosen to contrast these two aspects of planned rural change through a discussion of three national programs I have personally observed. I have come to the following tentative conclusions.

1. Land-tenure reform by itself does not lead to cumulative rural changes. It can give members of a rural population a sense of greater personal freedom and self-respect. It helps provide an ideology critical of asymmetrical standards of social justice, and it helps justify investments in the rural sector that do have cumulative effects.

2. Beneficiaries of land reform tend to be politically conservative rather than politically radical. But this does not mean that land redistributions insure "democracy." Since land reform is more likely to be the product of a politically active "elite" than of a "grassroots" peasant movement, beneficiaries are not simultaneously provided with the knowledge, experience and aspirations to help them consolidate their political influence.

3. When capitalization of the rural sector follows land redistribution, reconsolidation of holdings will tend to take place through corporate management. This follows because modern mechanized agriculture is not economically feasible on tiny farm units and because competent farm managers are not created by fiat. Problems of credit and management will lead government—in the interest of national productivity—to manage the redistributed lands through one of its own agencies or to permit financing and management by private entrepreneurs. In either case the spirit and the letter of the land-reform code may be deliberately disregarded.

4. Agrarian reform programs that increase the spatial mobility of rural populations, as through the development of new lands, will help to break down traditional forms of social structure and make way for the kind of interest-group associations that effect a wider distribution of political influence in the rural sector.

5. Agrarian reform programs that emphasize capitalization of the rural sector will benefit private farmers as well as land-reform beneficiaries. Rural families are more likely to identify with "progress" and begin to link new aspirations with new forms of political participation. In this situation, peasant federations formed by land reform redirect their goals toward other types of rural development as their political experience and influence increase. As broad rural development becomes more and more a national goal, political parties and affiliated associations compete in promoting that goal in order to win the support of the rural sector. Thus, a truly cumulative relegation of political influence gradually becomes a fact.

Penny Capitalists or Tribal Ritualists?—The Relationship of Market Behavior to Ceremonial Life in a Modern Maya Community

EVON Z. VOGT

By recounting in some detail the economic transactions and decisions made by a contemporary Maya-speaker in one (composite) weekend, Vogt convincingly demonstrates that it is beside the point to debate, as some have done, whether the profit motive predominates over symbolic values or vice versa. Taking a cue from an undergraduate's term paper, he suggests that these are complementary rather than mutually exclusive aspects of the world view of many Indians in Middle America.

Evon Z. Vogt is Professor of Social Anthropology, Curator of Middle American Ethnology, and Director of the Harvard-Chiapas Project at Harvard University. He has done extensive field work among the Navaho Indians of New Mexico and the Tzotzil Indians of Mexico. He has written Navaho Veterans (1951), Modern Homesteaders (1955), Zinacantan: A Maya Community in the Highlands of Chiapas (1969) *and* The Zinacantecos of Mexico: A Modern Maya Way of Life (1970), *and is coauthor of* Water Witching U.S.A. (1959), *and* Desarrollo cultural de los Mayas (1964).

When a new field worker first arrives in the modern Maya community of Zinacantan in the Highlands of Chiapas in Southern Mexico,[1] he is shocked to discover that the Indians immediately ask him, and expect him to know very precisely, the price of the Harvard University jeep he is driving, the price of the old field jacket he is wearing, and the current price of corn and beans back home in Massachusetts. The novice field worker never knows the answers to these persistent questions about prices and returns from his first trip to some remote hamlet feeling absolutely stupid and having the impression that the Zinacantecos are obsessed with prices, even to the point of talking about their sacred rituals in terms of the price of candles, incense, and rum liquor.

My students are not unique in forming these impressions about the Indians of the Highlands of Middle America. In her study of Mitla, Oaxaca, Elsie Clews Parsons reported, over 30 years ago, that:

> Mitla is a business town. Trade permeates its whole life; price is of supreme interest to young and old, women and men, the poor and the well-to-do. . . . Money cost enters into the evaluation of things and of experience to a degree I have never found equaled in any other society, including the most plutocratic circles. (Parsons 1936: 12–13).

She adds in her conclusions:

> Price, price, price! Instead of a ritual, a price list! A ritual of price! (Parsons 1936:445).

From *Proceedings [of the] VIIIth International Congress of Anthropological and Ethnological Sciences*, 1968, Tokyo: Science Council of Japan, vol. II, 243–244. Reprinted by permission of the author.

Similarly, Sol Tax, in his study of Panajachel, on the shore of Lake Atitlán in the Highlands of Guatemala, reports that:

> . . . money values are *the* favorite topic of conversation. The typical first question is, "How much did you pay for it?" (Tax 1951:16).

He adds that:

> . . . I find it hard to imagine a people more endowed with the spirit of business enterprise than the Indians. . . . (Tax 1951:18).

And he concludes with a picture of the Indians of Panajachel as having a system of "penny capitalism" in which people have the "capitalist spirit" and their economic transactions are predominantly motivated by a rational desire to maximize their profits in the marketplace.

For the first few years of field work in Zinacantan, I implicitly accepted these views of the Indians as "penny capitalists" for they clearly proved to be as economically astute in business transactions as any group of people I had ever known, and certainly more astute than tribes like the Navahos of the Southwest with whom I had previously worked. I did wonder about why all the very close attention to the details of prices of ritual paraphernalia, like candles and incense and rum liquor, but I passed it off as an aspect of an under-developed economy in which people *must* know prices of everything to survive economically.

Then in the Spring Term of 1967 a bright undergraduate student in my course on Primitive Religion at Harvard set out to reexamine the ethnographic facts reported by Parsons on Mitla. His assignment was to read such theoretical works as those of Mauss, Lévi-Strauss, Leach, Sahlins, Turner, and Wolf and to explore their ideas on "exchange" and on "ritual symbolism" utilizing the data from Mitla. The student, D. Brian Smith, produced a brilliant paper on the "Ritual Exchange of Food in Mitla" (1967) in which he demonstrated that complex systems of exchange of different types of foods were a prominent feature of Mitla life. Furthermore, he had the insight that ritual exchanges in Mitla absolutely depended upon precise knowledge of prices—whether the exchanges are between groups of people, as in weddings, or with the supernaturals, as in funerals. The price-consciousness, which seems like an intrusion from the market, is essential in assuring proper reciprocity in the exchange of ritual gifts. The pricing mechanism has merely permitted the extension of the principle of reciprocity from goods and services of the same kind to goods and services of different kinds.

This insight served to crystallize my earlier questions about the Zinacanteco concern with the minute details of the prices of ritual paraphernalia and is leading to a reexamination of our data on economic and ritual life viewing the transactions that occur as a complex and balanced system of prestations between men, and between men and their gods (See Sahlins 1965). The result has revealed that the Zinacantecos *are* clearly astute "penny capitalists" interested in maximizing profits in the *production* sphere of their economic life. But when it comes to the *distribution* of goods and services the pricing system of the marketplace is utilized less for further profit-seeking than it is to keep track of and to equilibrate transactions in the system of reciprocal prestations.

These abstract statements can best be illustrated by describing the exchanges that occur in the life of typical Zinacanteco. The composite description which follows is fictitious, but each event is drawn from observations we have made in the field during the past ten years.

At sunrise on Saturday morning, Chep?Ok'il (Jose Coyote) accompanied by his wife, Shunka?Akov (Juana Wasp Nest), leaves his thatch-roofed house in the hamlet of Nachih carrying a liter of rum liquor in his shoulder bag. The liquor cost him 4 pesos at a bootleg Chamula distillery where he purchased it the evening before. The couple quietly approaches the house of his elderly neighbor, Romin Tanhol (Domingo Limehead), across the valley. As they reach the patio of the Tanhol house, Chep initiates a dialogue in Tzotzil (Michelle Rosaldo 1967):

"Are you there, mother?" "I am here." "Is the father there?" "Here." "Father, are you there?" "I am here." "May I enter?" "What do you want?" "Just to visit, to talk." "Oh, then, come in." The ?Ok'il couple then enters the Tanhol house, bows to their elders to show respect, and sits down. Then Chep takes the bottle of liquor from his bag, kneels, and as he sets it down, says, "Forgive me, Father, I would like to talk."

As the formal petition unfolds, it develops that Chep and his wife have come to ask the Tanhols to become godparents of baptism for their youngest child in the Cathedral in San Cristobal on Sunday morning. Romin Tanhol does not accept the bottle at once, but pauses to think about the life-long reciprocal obligations that will automatically flow from his becoming a godfather of the child, and hence a compadre of Chep's. He and his wife will each have to purchase one peso white candles for the ceremony tomorrow, but later in the day they will be given a formal chicken meal by the ?Ok'ils. Some months later the Tanhols will have to purchase a special blouse for the godchild, but again they will be fed a chicken meal. More importantly, the compadrazgo will comprise a network of obligations in which each of the persons will have claims on the others for borrowing money, for political aid, for assistance in ceremonial duties. Romin finally accepts the bottle, a young drink-pourer is appointed, and the liquor is drunk in a series of three rounds, accompanied by bowing and releasing, and patterned talk. At the end, the bottle is returned to Chep, the bargain has been sealed, and he and his wife stagger home.

At noon Chep's younger brother, Marian, arrives at the edge of the patio and initiates the same kind of dialogue, entering the house after the appropriate etiquette. This time the tables are turned, and Chep is faced with a request for a loan of 40 pesos from Marian who is out of money to meet his next obligations for a net of tropical fruit that must be presented at the Fiesta of San Lorenzo to the parents of his fiancée. This is part of the bride price that must be paid in the series of prestations and ceremonies that gradually remove the girl from her family and move her into the houses of the ?Ok'il lineage. Chep accepts the bottle, the ritual drinking takes place, and the 40 pesos are provided for Marian so that he will be prepared to continue his courtship on schedule.

At sunset, Chep's older brother, Shun, arrives to talk about their cooperative corn-farming operations in the Lowlands. Shun has a pending religious post, the

Alférez of San Lorenzo, in the Ceremonial Center of Zinacantan. He requested this cargo ten years before and he will be sworn into office in August of 1969. This cargo service costs a total of 9000 pesos, and hence Shun is urgently concerned with how they can improve their farming operations and increase the amount of surplus corn that will be available for sale in the market after the autumn harvest. They decide to try a chemical weed spray they have heard about which will finish the weeding of their fields in four days' time and save the cost of employing five Chamulas for two weeks, thereby making more money available for service to the saints in ceremonies to be performed the following summer. Shun also tells of his plans to rent a tile house with adobe walls—a type of structure that can be larger than a thatch-roofed house with wattle-and-daub walls and, therefore, give ample space for the ceremonies he must host. Furthermore, he has checked in detail on the cost of having the house wired for electricity, thereby being able to illuminate the all-night ceremonies with one 50-watt bulb at a cost of 2 pesos a month instead of using kerosene or gasoline lanterns which can cost as much as 2 pesos a night.

Before the ?Ok'ils leave for San Cristobal on Sunday morning, they dispatch their eldest daughter to the cemetery to burn a 50-centavo white wax candle and offer two avocados, worth 20 centavos each, to the soul of his father, from whom Chep inherited a hectare of land after paying for his funeral and accepting the obligation of caring for the grave in exchange for the land. Each Sunday offerings must be made, and Chep sends either his wife or a daughter to carry out this transaction.

The ?Ok'ils arrive in San Cristobal carrying the new baby and a sack of corn to sell in the market. Since the baptism is scheduled for 10 AM, Chep hurries to empty his corn into a neat pile and begin selling. He is out of cash, after the loan to his younger brother, Marian, and he needs money not only to buy a chicken and liquor to feed the new compadres after the baptism, but also to pay for his share of the chemical weed spray, and for the expenses of a curing ceremony that needs to be performed for his youngest son. His corn is all sold by 9:30 AM to a succession of Ladino housewives, who, after bargaining, have paid him 3½ pesos per cuartilla, the current market price for good corn. He pockets the 84 pesos, and he and his wife hurry off toward the Cathedral. En route, they meet a compadre who tells them a long story about his fiancée's elopement with another man and of his taking the case to the Cabildo in Zinacantan Center early that very morning to force the other man to reimburse him for the 850 pesos he had already invested in the bride price (See Jane Collier 1968).

They finally arrive at the Cathedral as the town clock is striking ten. Following the baptismal ceremony, the ?Ok'ils return home with the Tanhols and feed the new compadres a formal meal of chicken, tortillas, coffee, and rum liquor.

Shortly after the Tanhols have made their departure, Telesh Chochov (Andres Acorn), a shaman who lives nearby, arrives (in response to a request made three days before) to pulse Chep's youngest son, Shun, and prescribe the type of curing ceremony that will be needed. The pulsing discloses that Shun has lost some parts of his inner soul, and the ceremony to recover the soul will require prayers to the ancestral gods at four mountains around the Ceremonial Center. Telesh, following the information he received in his dreams that made him a shaman ten years before, tells Chep that he will need to purchase the following items for the ceremony: two black roosters, one to be sacrificed to the gods, one to be eaten by the patient; 18 50-centavo white candles (three for each of the four mountain shrines, three for the patio cross, and three for inside the house); six liters of rum liquor; two pesos of copal incense; a basket of red geraniums; and enough chicken to serve three meals to the family, the shaman, and the ritual assistants.

As the shaman leaves, agreeing to return in three days to perform the ceremony, Chep calculates that the total cost will be 80 pesos in chicken, 24 pesos in liquor, 9 pesos in candles, 2 pesos in incense, and 1 peso for geraniums, or a total of 116 pesos, not counting the expense for corn to be used for tortillas. Since he has only 60 pesos left in his pocket, he makes plans to return to the San Cristobal market again on Tuesday to sell more corn in order to purchase the ritual materials that will be needed for this transaction with the ancestral gods which, with the aid of the shaman and his expert prayers, he trusts will recover little Shun's complete soul and make him well again.

In conclusion, note how the transactions in this sample of the life experience of a Zinacanteco involve strict attention to price and astute productive behavior seeking to maximize profits. The Zinacantecos, like Parsons' Indians in Mitla and Tax's Indians in Panajachel, *are* "penny capitalists" in the marketplace. But this is only half the story. Their attention to prices does not mean that they are in any sense making their ritual prestations into a "price list" and treating them as secular transactions. On the contrary, note how in each case the transaction involving the distribution of goods and services are significantly embedded in a complex system of prestations between men, and between men and gods, in the ritual cycles which permeate their lives.[2] In a word, these modern Maya Indians in Zinacantan may seem like "penny capitalists" as the observer copes with the price lists, but they are also still very profoundly "tribal ritualists" who have very astutely adapted the market pricing mechanism to express, measure, and keep close track of their reciprocal obligations in the ceremonial round of life.[3]

NOTES

1. My field work in Zinacantan is part of the Harvard Chiapas Project which is sponsored by the Center for Behavioral Sciences and the Peabody Museum at Harvard University and is funded by grants from the National Institute of Mental Health (Grant No. 02100) and the National Science Foundation (Grants No. GS—262, 976, 1524). I am indebted to my students who have done field research in Chiapas, and especially to George and Jane Collier, Gary H. Gossen, and Francesco Pellizzi for their perceptive comments on the first draft of this paper.

2. See Aberle 1967 for a comparable analysis of the modern Navaho case.

3. Unlike Parsons, Tax partly recognized this basic point in his statement that ". . . the pattern of ritual is in part cast after the image of a money-exchange and competitive economy" (Tax 1951:19).

REFERENCES

Aberle, David F., 1967. "The Navaho Singer's 'Fee': Payment or Prestation?" *Studies in Southwestern Ethnolinguistics*, Mouton, The Hague and Paris, pp. 15–32.
Collier, Jane F., 1968. *Courtship and Marriage in Zinacantan, Chiapas, Mexico*. Middle American Research Institute, Tulane.
Parsons, Elsie Clews, 1936. *Mitla, Town of Souls*. University of Chicago Press.
Rosaldo, Michelle, 1967. "Etiquette as Exchange," Anthropology 205 Term Paper, January 1967. Harvard University.
Smith, D. Brian, 1967. "Ritual Exchange of Food in Mitla," Social Relations 112 (Primitive Religion) Term Paper, Harvard University.
Sahlins, Marshall D., 1965. "On the Sociology of Primitive Exchange," *The Relevance of Models for Social Anthropology*, ed. by Michael Banton, A.S.A. Monographs, 1. London, Tavistock Publications, pp. 139–236.
Tax, Sol, 1951. *Penny Capitalism: A Guatemalan Indian Economy*.
Vogt, Evon Z., 1969. *Zinacantan: A Maya Community in the Highlands of Chiapas*. Harvard University Press.

Interest Rates and Imperfect Competition in the Informal Credit Market of Rural Chile

CHARLES NISBET

In recent years there has been increasing and revealing attention paid to microeconomics, the small-scale exchange among individuals that get lost in traditional economic statistics. Nisbet's study of rural credit systems in Chile provides an additional dimension to the understanding of ways in which informal local institutions affect and are affected by formal national ones.

Charles Nisbet is Associate Professor of Economics at the University of California, Los Angeles. He has done research in Chile, Colombia, and Mexico, on credit and other aspects of economic development. He wrote Latin America: Problems in Economic Development (1969), *and compiled* Latin American Economic Development: A Selected Bibliography (*in press*).

It has been asserted that informal credit is usually very expensive in rural areas of underdeveloped countries and that exorbitant rates of interest are

From *Economic Development and Cultural Change* XVI (1967), 73–90. Copyright © 1967 by The University of Chicago. Reprinted by permission of the author and publisher.

possible largely because of the rural lender's semimonopolistic position.[1] This article reports on empirical research designed to test the validity of this assertion for several types of informal credit arrangements in rural Chile.[2]

Specifically, I propose to show that (1) there exists an informal credit market in rural Chile whose nature and mode of operation distinguish it from the formal credit market; (2) informal lenders can be classified, according to their motives for lending, into two basic types: commercial (village stores, itinerant traders, and moneylenders) and noncommercial (friends, neighbors, relatives, and *patrones*[3]); (3) informal commercial lenders exhort usurious real interest rates, whereas noncommercial lenders often lend at negative real rates; (4) there is little or no competition among lenders; and (5) high interest rates on commercial loans are due in large part to imperfect competition.

THE INFORMAL CREDIT MARKET IN RURAL CHILE[4]

The informal credit market in rural Chile consists of regionalized transactions of money, goods, and services among family friends, shopkeepers, itinerant traders, landlords, farm laborers, and moneylenders to facilitate consumption, production, and trade. This market is larger (in number of participants), more heterogeneous (on the supply side), and more imperfect than the formal credit market, and its nature and operation differ considerably from the latter. For example, compared to the formal credit market, loans in the informal credit market are usually smaller, granted on a more personal basis, unsecured beyond a verbal pledge, and much more expensive.

The number of rural people lending and borrowing on an informal basis cannot be precisely determined. Approximately 30 percent of the total rural population are clients of state financial institutions, reform agencies, and private commercial banks. The remaining 70 percent of the rural population do not have access to the formal credit market.

In the field survey, 45 percent of the 200 farmers interviewed operated within the formal credit market, 44 percent operated within the informal credit market, and 25 percent were outside both credit markets. The percentages do not add to 100, since some farmers operated in both markets.

The percentage for the formal credit market is high because the sample was taken in Central Chile, where farmers have greater access to financial institutions and have the most favorable transportation routes in the country and where agriculture is more highly commercialized. If the sample were equally weighted in the Southern and Northern regions, one would expect the percentage dealing with the formal market to fall and the informal to rise, since the above conditions would be reversed. These same factors make it more likely that farm operators could get along without financial assistance than their counterparts in the more remote areas.

In fact, the survey results—that 25 percent of farm operators were outside both credit markets—may not be descriptive of the entire country. Certainly, some farmers interviewed probably preferred not to say they borrowed or needed to seek funds. Probably some farmers applied for credit, and would therefore be included in that market, but were rejected and chose to tell us they did not use credit to avoid admitting failure.

Thus, within the total rural population I would estimate that of the 70 percent outside the formal credit market, 45 to 50 percent participate in the informal credit market at least once a year and 20 to 25 percent are outside both markets.

On the supply side the informal credit market is more heterogeneous than the formal credit market, primarily because of the variety of lender-types, the diverse items lent, and the regionality of credit transactions. To be classified as a lender operating in the informal credit market in this study, a lender must *not:* (1) have facilities for mobilizing liquid funds; (2) have formalized procedures for applying for credit; nor (3) be an urban-based institution.[5] Stated positively, the preceding criteria could be used for the formal credit market. Using these limitations, then, the informal credit market of rural Chile consists of the following suppliers of credit: friends, neighbors, relatives, *patrones,* village stores, itinerant traders, and moneylenders.

The only substantial homogeneity within the informal credit market exists on the demand side or among borrowers. Table 1 reveals some of their socioeconomic characteristics. The typical borrower is from the low-income sector. He might be typified a landless farm operator (i.e., a renter or sharecropper) with less than six years of education operating his farm with animal power and hand tools.

As can be seen in the table, 74 percent of informal credit borrowers are landless or own less than 12.5 acres. Nearly 70 percent of the farm operators, including those operating under all types of tenure, had worked farms of less than 25 acres. Eighty-two percent of the informal borrowers had less than six years of primary education, and 75 percent were operating farms without the use of modern technology.

The 8 percent holding properties over 123 acres and whose farms were heavily mechanized were farmers who had access to and operated within the formal credit market. These farmers continued to borrow from informal sources, because credit from financial institutions was insufficient and/or because informal loans could be had more quickly and with less red tape.

INTEREST RATES AND TYPE OF LENDER

Table 2 shows the distribution of reported interest rates according to type of lender and type of loan. These rates are from actual loans of currency and merchandise expressed in real terms. For example, there were five cases of friends lending currency at a negative 33 percent interest rate and five cases of lending merchandise at a zero interest rate.

The seven types of lenders who extend credit within this market can be divided into two groups: the informal noncommercial lenders (friends, neighbors, relatives, and *patrones*) and the informal commercial lenders (village stores, itinerant traders, and moneylenders). This distinction is based on the lenders' reported reasons for extending credit. Table 2 reflects the low real interest rates of noncommercial lenders and the high real rates of commercial lenders. This difference exists because the former group does not lend for the purpose of receiving a satisfactory return on loan capital, while the latter group lends primarily for this reason.

TABLE 1. Socioeconomic Characteristics of Borrowers in the Informal Credit Market of Rural Chile

(1) *Land tenure*	
Owners of 12.5 or more acres	26.4%
Landless or owners of less than 12.5 acres[a]	73.6
(2) *Farm size*	
Less than 12.5 acres	48.8%
12.5 to 24.6 acres	20.9
24.7 to 49.3 acres	16.3
49.4 to 123.4 acres	5.8
Over 123.5 acres	8.2
(3) *Education*[b]	
None	22.0%
Primary	60.5
Primary and secondary	15.2
Primary, secondary, and technical	2.3
(4) *Degree of farm mechanization*[c]	
None	20.9%
Light	54.6
Medium	15.2
Heavy	9.3

[a] This category includes sharecroppers, renters, commoners, administrators and owners of less than 12.5 acres (*minifundistas*).

[b] Primary represents more than two but less than six years; secondary more than six but less than 12 years; technical schooling means one to three years beyond secondary in some trade like agriculture, masonry, electronics, etc. The majority of those with no education are illiterate; some have a few years of primary education but can only write their name.

[c] None—only a few hand tools, no horses or oxen. Light—hand tools, including up to two horses and four oxen. Medium—complete set of hand tools, horses and/or oxen and some machinery, but not including tractors or trucks. Heavy—complete set of tools and machinery, including tractors and/or trucks.

The variance in interest rates cannot be explained by differences in type of borrower or use of borrowed funds. Nor does the affluence of borrowers explain the different prices, except that the more affluent borrowers had access to the formal credit market, where the rate averaged 18 percent annually.[6] There was some relation between size of loan and interest rate, with smaller loans carrying a higher rate. The three highest rates of interest reported were paid by non-landowners, but all other rates were distributed without distinction as to land tenure.

TABLE 2. The Structure of Reported Rates of Interest with Money Interest Rates Deflated to Real Interest Rates and Rates on Loans in Kind Expressed in Real Terms[a]

Type of lender[b] and type of loan		Interest Rate Distribution (in annual percentage rates)																			Total cases
		−33	−22	−20	−13	−7	−3	0	18	27	30	33	40	46	60	75	90	128	165	360	
(1) *Friends:*	Cash	5	1			1															7
	Kind							5	1												6
(2) *Neighbors:*	Cash																				0
	Kind							4													4
(3) *Relatives:*	Cash	3	1																		4
	Kind							7													7
(4) *Patrones:*	Cash	16																			16
	Kind							3													3
(5) *Village stores:*	Cash	1	1	1	2	1	1							2					1		10
	Kind							9								1	1				11
(6) *Itinerant traders:*	Cash																				0
	Kind										1		1		1	1					4
(7) *Money-lenders:*	Cash									1		1						1			3
	Kind							2					1	1	5	3	2			1	15
Total cases[c]		25	3	1	2	2	1	30	1	1	1	1	2	3	6	5	3	1	1	1	90

[a] All rates are on actual loans for the agricultural year May 1964 through May 1965, and money interest rates were deflated by using the consumer price index. The terms ranged from one month to over one year, so all rates were adjusted to annual figures.

[b] The same lender extends credit to different borrowers, in some cases. The rate of interest charged was at times the same to different borrowers, and at other instances different rates were charged by the same lender on similar loan arrangements.

[c] In seven cases, borrowers did not know the interest rate charged, and there were eight cases of *recargos* (charges in addition to the original sum of value lent).

LOANS IN KIND *VERSUS* LOANS IN CASH

In about 50 percent of the cases of cash loans, the lenders (with the exception of *patrones*) demand repayment in kind. The repayment pattern alters the type of loan; when the loan is made in cash, but repayment is made in kind, the loan is really one in kind and not in cash. In Chile, a country conditioned by nearly 80 years of continuous inflation,[7] this lending condition is understandable, because the people prefer to hold goods rather than money.

Table 2 adjusts for the above mentioned repayment pattern. It is clear from this table that lending within Chile's informal credit market usually occurs in kind and not in currency.[8] This emphasis might be explained by: (1) the lack of well organized markets, which leads to holding of stocks by informal lenders who, given better markets, would hold cash; (2) the reluctance on the part of informal lenders to hold cash as a result of their experience with Chile's inflation;[9] and (3) the unwillingness of noncommercial lenders to charge interest, which means they must lend in kind and/or demand repayment in kind if they are not actually to *lose* by a credit transaction.[10]

With inflation removed from interest rates on currency loans (as in Table 2), most commercial lenders emerge with positive rates ranging from 27 percent to 360 percent, with an annual mean rate of 82 percent. The only exceptions are seven cases of negative rates by village stores, and it is likely that these rates would be positive if we could take into account hidden charges commonly levied with or without the borrowers' knowledge. The effective rates charged by some moneylenders and *patrones* would also increase as a result of hidden charges. It is impossible to know exactly how extensive these practices are, since lenders, naturally, are unwilling to give such information, and many borrowers are unaware of the charges or do not take them into account within the financial arrangement. Some hidden practices encountered during this study are noted below.

(1) *Requiring that the borrower pay a premium for the privilege of receiving credit.* (I.e., a moneylender agrees to lend a farmer $100. Then he discounts $20 from the $100 as the premium and charges the farmer 5 percent monthly on the full amount requested, $100. This was mentioned by two borrowers.)

(2) *Lending in form of a check that must be passed on to a third party, to be cashed for an additional charge when borrower has no checking account.* (I.e., a village store owner has a checking account in Santiago and gives his check as a loan to a farmer from his village area. Because the farmer does not have a checking account in a nearby bank nor in Santiago, he cannot deposit or cash it. If he travels to Santiago, the issuer's bank will not cash it, since the farmer is not known at the bank. Therefore, he must give the check to another person to be deposited in the third party's account. For this favor, the third party often charges up to 10 percent of the face value of the check. This practice is common and was mentioned by several borrowers and also by informants who were not part of the borrower sample.)

(3) *Demanding repayment in kind and undervaluing the commodity received.* (I.e., some moneylenders and owners of village stores make cash loans but demand repayment in wheat. At harvest time these lenders value the crop

at 10 to 20 percent below the previous year's official price of wheat. A majority of borrowers from village stores reported this practice.)

(4) *Demanding labor services for the favor of giving a loan. This occurs primarily with* patrones. (I.e., they ask the sharecroppers to perform extra labor duties on the farm without payment. This way some *patrones* escape apparent negative interest rates on their loans—see Table 2.)

(5) *Giving no receipts so borrower can be required to pay more than the original amount.* (I.e., when farmers charge items at the village store, they receive no receipt for the goods taken on credit. The owner merely makes an entry in a book as to the amount. Most commonly, to escape the negative rates that appeared in Table 2, the owners either take the expected rate of inflation into consideration when they price their goods or charge the borrower the current [readjusted] price at the time of repayment or both.[11] One store owner [who claimed he never followed such practices] told us that many owners simply overcharge the borrower at the time of repayment by putting down any amount they wish. He said that since rural people are ignorant and many cannot read or write, owners can take advantage of this.)

SIZE, TERMS, AND PURPOSES OF LOANS

Table 3 shows that informal loans in rural Chile are quite small, as is thought to be the general case in other underdeveloped rural areas. Our field survey found that 78 percent of the informal credit market loans were for amounts of less than $200, and 97 percent were for loans of less than $1,000.[12] Table 3 indicates that borrowers prefer to solicit smaller sums from commercial lenders and larger sums from noncommercial lenders whenever possible, to take advantage of the latter's more attractive conditions.

While the size of loans is usually smaller in the informal credit market, the term is typically longer.[13] Table 4 gives a breakdown of the terms granted by informal lenders involved in the study. The most typical term was "until the harvest" (from six to nine months), with 40 percent of the loans carrying this term.

Most borrowers cannot repay on a shorter term, since nearly all substantial earnings come from the annual harvest. Nearly 30 percent of the loans carried no expressed term. This means farmers repay whenever they are able, usually after the harvest. This condition is more prevalent with noncommercial lenders,

TABLE 3. Size of Loans Granted

Type of Lender	Amount of the Loan (in dollars[a])			
	Less than $200	$200 to $999	More than $1,000	Total loans
Commercial	47	7	1	55
Noncommercial	34	13	2	49
Total loans	81	20	3	104

[a] An exchange rate of five *escudos* per dollar was used to convert the amount of the loans into dollar figures.

TABLE 4. Terms on Loans Granted

Terms	Type of Lender		
	Commercial	Noncommercial	Total loans
No term	13	17	30
One month	11	3	14
One to three months	4	2	6
Three to six months	2	–	2
Until the harvest[a]	21	21	42
Six to twelve months	1	2	3
More than one year	–	1	1
Unknown	3	3	6
Total loans	55	49	104

[a] The period of harvest ranged from six to nine months.

who offer more favorable conditions. Still, indefinite-term loans from commercial lenders are not infrequent, since these lenders are often satisfied to continue earning interest on the loan and are not concerned with turning their capital over more often. The 11 cases of one-month terms came from village stores. These stores usually do not demand complete retirement of the debt, but only a monthly payment.

Table 5 displays the alleged purposes of the loans received from informal lenders. Half of all loans went for consumption purposes. This emphasis points up the need of these low-income families to sustain themselves over the production period. The majority of loans used for productive purposes were loans of seed, although there were some cases of loans of fertilizer. The mixed category of consumption and production includes all the cases of *patrones* lending to sharecroppers.

Having established the fact that commercial lenders charge very high rates, let us look at the structure of the informal credit market in an attempt to identify factors responsible for these high rates. We will deal here only with the informal commercial lenders, since rates on noncommercial loans are very low or negative.

THE MARKET STRUCTURE[14]

Factors of importance in analyzing structure of the informal credit market are: (1) number of lenders, (2) lenders' and borrowers' degree of knowledge of the market, (3) lenders' degree of market control, and (4) form of competition among lenders.

TABLE 5. Use of Loans Granted

Use	Number of Loans
Consumption	52
Production	27
Consumption and production	25
Total loans	104

1. NUMBER OF LENDERS

This study isolated three types of informal commercial lenders: itinerant traders, moneylenders, and village stores. Numerically the latter two types dominate, since only six cases of lending by itinerant traders were encountered. The itinerant traders were the most heterogeneous group and included wholesalers, peddlers, and renters of farm equipment. Because the majority of them operated on the basis of cash or immediate payment in kind, the remainder of the study considers only moneylenders and village stores.[15]

Moneylenders were found operating in 18 of the 34 *comunas*[16] surveyed. In all cases they lived and operated within their respective *comunas*, and their operations usually were found no more than 1 to 2 miles from a rural village or were confined to the rural neighborhood.[17] Their effective geographical zone of operation, or their "rural credit market area,"[18] then, is much smaller than the *comuna* unit. The number of moneylenders ranged from none to three, with a mean of one within a rural credit market area. In no case did a moneylender operate in an adjoining rural credit market area.

The other principal informal commercial lender, the village store, could be found in each of the 34 *comunas*, but in only 29 *comunas* were the owners actively engaged in credit operations. The village store's range of operation was less uniform than the moneylenders', because it was determined by the distance to neighboring villages and the density of the rural population. In some areas of Chile this means confinement to a 2 to 3 mile radius from the village, while in other areas it includes 15 or 20 miles. Usually, their effective geographical zone of operation or "rural credit market area," like the moneylenders', was smaller than the *comuna* unit. The number of village stores engaged in lending ranged from two to five, with a mean of three per rural credit market area.

In total, the number of informal commercial lenders (moneylenders and village stores) within a rural credit market area ranged from zero to seven, with a mean of two lenders. The areas with zero or one lender were the neighborhoods of dispersed settlements in the countryside, while the areas of five and six lenders were always nucleated population centers. The ratio of borrowers to commercial lenders ranged approximately from a low of 100 to 1 to a high of 1,000 to 1. Thus, empirical evidence gives the range of imperfect competition from monopoly to duopoly to oligopoly.[19]

2. LENDERS' AND BORROWERS' DEGREE OF MARKET KNOWLEDGE

The rural credit market areas are so small that the moneylender and village store owner have intimate personal knowledge of the borrower's circumstances. He knows the size of the borrower's farm, the number of animals he owns, the output of the farm last year, his outstanding debts, the degree of his entrepreneurial skills, etc. This information is common knowledge to most people within the area, since the residents are socially and economically interdependent; however, the informal commercial lenders make it their business to mentally catalog and keep current all such data, to minimize risks.

This degree of detailed knowledge is demonstrated by the rarity of formal contract between lender and borrower and by the absence of financial security in the loan arrangement. We found an exception in one moneylender who required his clients to sign a book with their names (or other identification mark) and indicate the amount loaned and the date of the loan. But the general rule was for monetary transactions to take place on a person-to-person basis, free of any written documents. Furthermore, 66 percent of the loans extended on this informal basis were economically unsecured; that is to say, loans were secured by the verbal promise of the borrower. Borrowers claimed that loan security was "honesty," "friendship," "being known as a good farmer," "being known as a person who honors his obligations," etc.

The farm operators interviewed displayed an appalling lack of knowledge of lenders and of the terms offered. Their ignorance of the lender can be attributed to the regionality of such lending, low levels of education, and economic immobility. Usually a farm operator did not realize the existence of another informal commercial lender in a nearby rural credit market area, let alone know the interest rate charged by this potential alternative source. This was especially true in the case of moneylenders. Since their operations are illegal under Chilean law, transactions are carried out with considerable secrecy. (Only 10 percent of those interviewed could identify another moneylender outside their rural credit market area.) Eighty-three percent of those farm operators dealing with informal commercial lenders had less than six years of primary education. In the 10-province survey, 35 percent of the rural male population could not read or write.[20] The majority of these people were born and raised in the same rural neighborhood where they presently farm,[21] they come from farming families, and their expectations do not call for a future change of occupation. Finally, they have few business or commercial contacts outside their rural credit market area; thus, they receive little information about alternative credit sources.

3. LENDER'S DEGREE OF MARKET CONTROL

The rural commercial lender appears to hold and exercise various oppressive controls over his borrowers. In one *comuna* farmers were afraid to discuss the activities of three moneylenders for fear of losing their only current credit source. Some lenders sell goods to the borrowers, thereby tying the farmers to a particular village store for consumption necessities and farm financing.[22] Some farmers prefer the convenience of selling directly to the "known" person who extends them credit, because they find it difficult and confusing to sell their output in nearby markets. For other farmers the local lender represents the only source for loans in cash and/or in kind. Any attempt to go outside for institutional or noninstitutional credit would endanger their borrowing chances for the next year. Besides, the only really available institutional source is new and unproven (in the case of Instituto de Desarrollo Agropecuario, INDAP),[23] while the informal commercial lender has been around for years. Also, some lenders hold important positions within the rural community which allow them to assert socioeconomic sanctions and moral suasion on individuals who do not cooperate.[24]

4. FORM OF COMPETITION AMONG LENDERS

As previously mentioned, there are two groups of informal lenders within the informal credit market: noncommercial (friends, neighbors, relatives, and *patrones*) and commercial (itinerant traders, village stores, and moneylenders). These groups are essentially noncompetitive. Noncommercial lenders extend credit because of kinship, friendship, reciprocity, tenure traditions, and other reasons aimed at maintaining equilibrium within rural society. Their limited capacity and willingness to extend credit and the absence of full service financing encourages demand for credit to spill over into informal commercial lenders.

No active competition exists, then, between commercial and noncommercial lenders in the informal credit market. Let us now look for competition among moneylenders, among village stores, and, finally, at competition between moneylenders and village stores.

In none of the 200 interviews was there a case where a borrower switched to another moneylender because of price competition (interest rate). In fact, each moneylender's share of the rural credit market area is nearly stationary, with movement occurring only when a borrower defaults or is too far in debt to a lender. The slight fluctuations of interest rates over time are due to demand inelasticities of farmers who face a continuous scarcity of capital.[25]

There are three primary reasons why moneylenders operate on a small scale and do not compete with each other. First, the moneylenders do not have detailed knowledge of a broad market, so their type of business demands a small-scale operation which offers continuous excess demand. Second, because their activities are illegal, they minimize the probability of encounters with legal authorities by restricting their operations geographically in number of clients and volume of credit. The illegality aspect and the separate client market discourage them from competing with a nearby moneylender. Lastly, the moneylenders are principally farmers,[26] whose lending activities do not represent more than 50 percent of their annual gross income. Therefore, unlike the village stores, they lack the capital base to carry on large-scale lending.[27]

Since each rural village generally has two types of stores, their form of competition is different from the moneylenders, who are quite homogeneous. The numerous small-scale stores that carry a few consumption items (coffee, tea, flour, sugar, rice, beverages, etc.) generally operate on a cash basis. The large-scale stores carry a full line of consumption goods, hardware items, and combustibles, and in some cases they own warehouses where they buy and sell farm staples (corn, wheat, potatoes). Usually, stores in the first group are scattered throughout the village and the dispersed settlement areas of the countryside, while the large-scale stores are located around or near the central plaza. We are concerned with the latter group, since they handle the vast majority of credit.

Like the moneylender, the large-scale village store's share of the rural credit market area is stationary, mainly because the clients are tied to the operation through overdue debts or current credit commitments. To be sure, the number of clients and the volume of gross sales move sharply with the cycle of economic activity. For example, the three-month copper strike at the Braden Copper Company in 1966 caused a drastic drop in cash sales for village stores throughout the province of O'Higgins.[28] Here, as with moneylenders, some movement will occur between stores as a result of defaults and/or excessive debt.

With few exceptions, there was little evidence of strong price competition and considerable evidence of uniform pricing within any given village. In some regions, market-sharing arrangements have worked so well that the owners finance each other during the course of the agricultural cycle. For example, in one northern village, the owners of three village stores lend among themselves at 5 percent a month, while charging 10 percent a month to their farmer clients.

Let us look at the competition between the two most important informal commercial lenders, the moneylender and the village store. The moneylender operates illegally, while the village store allegedly works within the law. Because these two sources possess a separate legal status, operate within distinct market areas, and face a similar situation of excess demand for credit, they act as market-sharing duopolists, rather than as competitors. For example, if the moneylender and the village store buy crops before the harvest (*en verde*) as a form of credit extension, they each offer farmers the same price. The purchase price usually represents 50 percent of the crop value, with the loan made about two or three months before the harvest.

In summary, I have demonstrated that the real interest rates existing in the informal commercial credit market are excessive even when inflation is taken into account. I have offered considerable empirical evidence in microeconomic terms supporting the assertion that these usurious rates are due considerably to the high degree of imperfect competition.[29] According to this empirical test, the typical rural commercial lender is either an oligopolist, a duopolist, or an outright monopolist, and his market for loans is confined to the small geographical region in which he lives and operates. The demand curve facing the moneylender is interest-inelastic.[30] Demand is determined by the necessity of farm operators to keep their farms in operation and to support their families until the next harvest, rather than by the farmer's estimate of his marginal efficiency of investment. Lenders possess nearly perfect knowledge of their borrowers, borrowers have little or no knowledge of other lenders, and lenders have nearly complete control over the borrowers' source of funds, with an absence of competition among lenders.

Additionally, the past policies of private and state lending institutions have contributed to the maintenance of imperfect competition in the informal credit market and to the accompanying high rates of interest. Until 1959 there was no important institutional source of credit for the "low-income sectors," and as late as 1964 only 4 percent of the total credit extended by private and state lending institutions went to farmers within this sector.[31] It is precisely the low-income farm operators who negotiate most frequently with lenders of the informal credit market. Thus, historically, commercial lenders have been free from competition and have been assisted indirectly in maintaining their yearly expropriation of monopoly profits. This points out the need for action, but we would not suggest turning the moneylender into a development financing institution, as has been proposed,[32] nor introducing legislation to control usury, as Chile has done.[33] A more reasonable approach could take the form of: (1) introducing alternative sources of credit for borrowers of the informal credit market, or (2) transforming borrowers into potential clients of existing institutional sources. The former approach would create new credit institutions or programs for low-income farmers. To compete successfully with existing informal lenders, such programs would have to depart from traditional Chilean banking practices—i.e., require little or no paper work and no collateral, deliver money or goods without delay, etc. The latter approach would elevate the "creditworthiness" of borrowers, enabling them to compete for credit from existing institutional sources.

This problem has been recognized by the Institute of Agricultural Development, which plans widespread expansion of its credit program for small farmers,[34] and by the State Bank of Chile,[35] which in 1966 opened a new branch to service farmers normally dependent upon noninstitutional credit sources. This recent effort on the part of state lending institutions aims at offering a competitive source to borrowers of informal credit. The effectiveness of these institutions has been hampered because farm operators are (1) reluctant to submit to highly formalized loan procedures, (2) distrustful of the "outside" personnel used by these institutions, and (3) skeptical of the value of new seeds and fertilizers that cost more than substitutes available from informal sources. There appears to be an urgent need for more local administration, involving personnel born and raised in the rural areas who are as knowledgeable as the informal commercial lenders. Under their supervision, for example, farmers could not borrow animals from a neighbor to falsify loan security a few hours before the supervised credit inspector visits the farm. This type of rural shenanigan creates disrespect for the lending institution, which carries over to repayment habits. Some farmers do not feel obligated to repay loans to "these urban bureaucrats," with whom they have no socioeconomic ties, because they believe they are being loaned their own money—money the farmers claim they have paid in taxes to the government.

Lastly, the second approach, transforming borrowers into potential clients of existing institutional sources, demands an agrarian reform program. Such a program includes a combination of redistribution of rural wealth, expansion of extension services, increased emphasis on education, higher quality farm inputs, and greater accessibility to local markets. The Chilean congress in 1967 passed a new land reform bill which, if implemented, will have a profound effect on informal commercial credit in rural Chile.

OTES

Thanks are expressed to the following organizations for their financial and logistical assistance for this study: University of Wisconsin Land Tenure Center of Chile, Santiago; Fulbright Commission of Chile, Santiago; Institute of International Studies and Overseas Administration, University of Oregon; Instituto de Economia, Universidad de Chile, Santiago; Chile-California Program, Santiago; and Agency for International Development, Washington. All views, interpretations, recommendations, and conclusions expressed in this paper are those of the author and not necessarily those of the supporting or cooperating organizations. Special acknowledgment is made to Marion Brown, Rondo Cameron, Raymond Mikesell, and John Strasma for their many comments and suggestions on an earlier draft. Any remaining faults are, of course, entirely my own.

1. See, for example, U Tun Wai, "Interest Rates Outside the Organized Money Markets of Underdeveloped Countries," *Staff Papers of the International Monetary Fund*, Vol. VI (1957–58), p. 124.

2. Very few empirical studies have been undertaken, especially in Latin America, to describe and analyze rural interest rates, the types of informal lenders, the form of competition among lenders, and other characteristics of informal credit transactions. See, for example, the conclusions reached by the Comité Interamericano de Desarrollo Agrícola (CIDA) in *Inventario de la Información Básica para la Programación del Desarrollo Agrícola en la América Latina: Informe Regional* (Washington, D.C.: Secretaría General de la Organización de los Estados Americanos, Union Panamericana, 1963), p. 138.

3. The *patron* has been traditionally the hereditary owner of a farm property, but currently he is any immediate supervisor of farm labor on whom farm laborers are economically dependent.

4. The data on the informal credit market in rural Chile were obtained from a sample field survey of two hundred farm operators (owners, sharecroppers, administrators, commoners, and renters). The sample was selected on a quota basis from 10 of the more prominent agricultural provinces within the 35 provinces of Chile.

5. This classification infers that an informal lender must *not:* (1) receive deposits and/or require membership shares; (2) require written application forms, balance sheets, notarized property deeds, nor inspections by credit supervisors; nor (3) have home offices in Santiago or in other large cities where policies are formulated and where the personnel reside.

6. Interest rates in excess of the current bank rate are illegal.

7. Tom E. Davis, "Eight Decades of Inflation in Chile, 1879–1959: A Political Interpretation," *Journal of Political Economy* (August 1963); David Felix, *Desequilibrios Estructurales y Crecimiento Industrial: El Caso Chileno* (Santiago: Instituto de Economía de la Universidad de Chile, 1958); Frank Whitson Fetter, *Monetary Inflation in Chile* (Princeton: Princeton University Press, 1931); Arnold C. Harberger, "La Dinámica de la Inflación en Chile," *Cuadernos de Economía* (May–August 1965); and "Inflation in Chile," Ch. 3 in Albert O. Hirshman, *Journeys Toward Progress* (New York: Doubleday and Company, 1965), pp. 215–96.

8. The striking exception is the *patron* who grants cash loans to his sharecroppers. The *patron* provides the land and working capital, and the sharecropper provides the tools and labor. The sharecropper normally turns to the *patron* for his financial assistance. *Patrones* often receive the benefit of cheap labor not only of the sharecropper, but of his family. Rates of return to some *patrones* were well over 100 percent on their investment, allowing them to lend without nominal interest.

9. The asset preference of investors for foodstuffs and other primary products under conditions of inflation in underdeveloped areas has been noted recently by Hugh T. Patrick; see "Financing Development and Economic Growth in Underdeveloped Countries," *Economic Development and Cultural Change*, Vol. 14, No. 2 (January 1966), p. 179.

10. For example, Table 2 shows four cases of neighbors lending in kind at no interest. When the money price is increased by an index of wheat prices, the nominal annual rate of interest charged is 42 percent.

11. Higher levels of interest rates resulting from discounting anticipated inflation were also found in Korean informal financial arrangements. See Colin D. Campbell and Chang Shick Ahn, "Kyes and Mujins—Financial Intermediaries in South Korea," *Economic Development and Cultural Change*, Vol. 11, No. 1 (October 1962), p. 63.

12. In contrast, the average size of loan to farmers from the largest commercial bank in Chile was about $10,000 during the agricultural year 1965–66.

13. In the formal credit market the terms range from 30 to 180 days, with some possibility of renewing the loan agreement.

14. The approach used in this section was adopted from an analysis of Southeast Asia and India; see Anthony Bottomley, "Monopoly Profit as a Determinant of Interest Rates in Underdeveloped Rural Areas," *Oxford Economic Papers* (November 1964), pp. 431–37.

15. At the outset of the study, it was hypothesized that commercial informal lenders were obtaining loanable funds from the formal market, thereby providing clear linkage between the two markets. Unfortunately, it was not possible to document this type of linkage. No overt examples of this linkage were observed during any part of the field study. In addition, all farm operators who borrowed from moneylenders were asked where the moneylender obtained his funds. The results were not significant enough to establish this type of linkage. Most said that the moneylender used his own capital, and few indicated he had institutional financing, but no concrete evidence was obtained on this latter assumption.

16. A *comuna* is a minor civil division comparable to the township in the United States.

17. A "rural neighborhood" in this paper refers to a dispersed settlement of farmhouses.

18. The informal credit market is composed of many small "rural credit market areas." The latter vary in size (in the sense of number of commercial lenders and borrowers) and are delineated according to population density, type of terrain, settlement patterns, and available transportation routes.

19. For similar findings in Southeast Asia and India, see Charles Gamboa, "Poverty and some Socio-Economic Aspects of Hoarding, Saving and Borrowing in Malaya," *Malayan Economic Review*, Vol. 3 (October 1958), p. 44; and Report of the Committee of Direction, *All India Rural Credit Survey*, Vol. 2 (Bombay: Reserve Bank of India, 1954), p. 102.

20. Armand Mattelart, *Atlas Social de las Comunas de Chile* (Santiago: Centro de Investigaciones Sociológicas, Universidad Católica, Editorial del Pacífico, 1965), pp. 125–26.

21. See also William J. Smole, *Owner-Cultivatorship in Middle Chile*, Department of Geography, Research Paper No. 89, University of Chicago, Chicago, 1963, pp. 117–18.

22. To cite an interesting example of how village stores tie clients to themselves, a renter of a large farm made an agreement with a large-scale village store for financing the merchandise needs of his 15 sharecroppers. The renter would receive 180-day credit for $1,800 by giving the store owner promissory notes for the $1,800 plus 18 percent official bank interest. In turn, the renter passed on to his 15 sharecroppers, each month, authorization slips worth $20 which they could use only at this particular village store to obtain merchandise on credit. The owner would honor the authorization slips (signed by the renter), but would discount them 10 percent, giving the sharecropper $18 of merchandise. At harvest time the sharecropper would pay back the village store $20 for each of the six slips he exchanged for $18 of merchandise. The adjusted annual interest rate charged by the store owner was 72 percent (18 percent paid by the renter and 54 percent paid by the sharecroppers).

23. The Institute of Agricultural Development was created in 1962 as a government institution offering financial and technical assistance to small and medium farmers.

24. For other methods of securing repayment not usually encountered in Latin America, see Report of the Committee of Direction, *op. cit.*, pp. 171–72, 245–79, and 483; and C. R. Wharton, "Marketing, Merchandising, and Moneylending: A Note on Middleman Monopsony in Malaya," *Malayan Economic Review*, Vol. 7 (October 1962), pp. 34–35. For circumstances in India that approximate those encountered in Chile to reduce risks of default, see B. L. Agrawal, "Risk and Uncertainty in Agriculture: Implications

for Agriculture," *Indian Journal of Agricultural Economics*, Vol. 19, No. 1 (1964), p. 136.

25. The inelastic character of the demand for loans was also found in Southeast Asia; see Department of Census and Statistics, *Final Report of Economic Survey of Rural Ceylon*, 1950–51 (Colombo, 1954), pp. 46–47.

26. In Colombia, I found that rural moneylenders were mainly "professionals"—that farming activities were but a front, and their annual gross income was made up almost entirely from their lending activities. See Charles T. Nisbet, "Banco Estatal, Banco Particular, Prestamista: Alternativas y Preferencias del Agricultor Colombiano," *Agricultura Tropical*, Vol. 22, No. 8 (August 1966), pp. 420–25.

27. Indian moneylenders also were found restrained by limited operating capital; see Frank J. Moore, "Money-Lenders and Co-operators in India," *Economic Development and Cultural Change*, Vol. 2, No. 2 (June 1953), p. 143.

28. Throughout the poorest regions of rural Chile and in the more prosperous regions where farm plots are small, it is typical for younger members of a farming family to work away from the farm in mining, construction, and industry. They are expected to send money home to help support family and relatives.

29. This analysis has not attempted to consider the roles of risk premiums, administrative costs, or opportunity costs in determining interest rates in rural areas that have been stressed by Belshaw, Bottomley, and Schultz. See Horace Belshaw, *El Crédito Agrícola en los Países Economicamente Subdesarrollados* (Roma: Organización de las Naciones Unidas para la Agricultura y la Alimentación, 1959), pp. 102–11; Anthony Bottomley, "The Premium for Risk as a Determinant of Interest Rates in Underdeveloped Rural Areas," *Quarterly Journal of Economics* (November 1963), pp. 637–47; Anthony Bottomley, "The Cost of Administrating Private Loans in Underdeveloped Rural Areas," *Oxford Economic Papers*, Vol. 15 (June 1963), pp. 154–63; and Theodore W. Schultz, *Transforming Traditional Agriculture* (New Haven: Yale University Press, 1964), pp. 85–86.

30. The field survey discovered that the demand curves facing lending institutions of the formal credit market were also interest-inelastic. But in the formal credit market, the real rate of interest has been negative for 10 of the last 14 years. See Julio César Barriga Silva, *Diagnóstic del Crédito Agrícola en Chile*, Memoria, Facultad de Agronomía, Universidad de Chile, Santiago, 1965, p. 55.

31. Instituto de Desarrollo Agropecuario. *Proyecto de Crédito Agrícola al Sector de Bajos Ingresos* (Santiago, 1965), p. 27.

32. Hugh Patrick suggests: "more should be done to explore the possibilities of utilizing these traditional financiers for production purposes, while reducing their monopolistic powers through increased competition"; *op. cit.*, p. 188. See Bert F. Hoselitz, *Sociological Aspects of Economic Growth* (New York: Free Press, 1960), pp. 149–56, for a discussion of the reasons why moneylenders would be unlikely to perform entrepreneurial functions for accelerating economic development.

33. The only result in Chile has been to drive usurious lenders underground. For a similar viewpoint in Asia, see Economic Commission for Asia and the Far East, *Mobilization of Domestic Capital in Certain Countries of Asia and the Far East* (Bangkok, 1951), pp. 41–42.

34. *La Nación*, Santiago, Chile, June 11, 1966.

35. Instituto Chileno de Administración Racional de Empresas, *Moneda y Crédito* (Santiago: Editorial Andrés Bello, 1965), p. 141; and for a good analysis of the government's past performance at financing agriculture through its state bank, see Ernest Feder, "Feudalism and Agricultural Development: The Role of Controlled Credit in Chile's Agriculture," *Land Economics*, Vol. 28–29 (1962–63).

Market Place and Marketing System: Toward a Theory of Peasant Economic Integration

SHEPARD FORMAN AND JOYCE F. RIEGELHAUPT

The role of the peasantry in complex societies has long been a focus of interest for social scientists, especially in Latin America where a majority of the population is farmers who participate in limited ways in national economies. In analyzing the regional marketing system of northeastern Brazil in terms of multiple levels of exchange nexuses with considerable spatial and temporal spread, these two anthropologists not only lay bare the ecology of stratification in a predominantly agricultural society, but also provide a typology of market places and even outline a sequence of stages of development.

Shepard Forman is Assistant Professor of Anthropology at the University of Chicago. His studies include religion and psychological anthropology among North American Indians, as well as decision-making and the interrelations of social and economic factors in Brazil, as described in The Raft Fisherman: Tradition and Change in a Peasant Economy (1970).

Joyce F. Riegelhaupt is Associate Professor of Anthropology at Columbia University. She has done research and written articles on political and economic aspects of peasantry in both Brazil and Portugal.

I. INTRODUCTION

Students of peasant society recognize the importance of the market economy for understanding decision-making processes within the household and the nature of articulation between the peasant sector and the national society.[1] We intend to describe market behavior in Northeast Brazil and to relate such behavior to changes in the agricultural economy in general. The ultimate goal is to understand how peasants are integrated into the national economy as commodity producers and consumers of manufactured goods. By concentrating on the internal marketing system for food staples in Northeast Brazil we hope to refine earlier views of peasants and to suggest a definition of peasantry based on economic integration rather than on partial participation in the national culture.

The Brazilian peasant is not an 'economic zero' who buys little and sells little (Oberg, 1965:1418), but an integral part of national patterns of food production, distribution and consumption. He is deeply involved in regional and national marketing systems and reacts to changes in these systems. In point of fact, development in the marketing sector is often accompanied by the displacement of peasants and local middlemen from the increasingly commercialized rural economy. In Northeast Brazil, we encountered an economy in transition

From *Comparative Studies in Society and History* XII (1970), 188–212. Copyright © 1970 by The Society for the Comparative Study of Society and History. Reprinted by permission of the authors and Cambridge University Press.

in which a highly rationalized internal marketing system is profoundly affecting production, leading to an insufficient supply of food staples to burgeoning urban centers and to widespread discontent in the countryside.

Our research in Northeast Brazil indicates that the simultaneous study of several Market Places at different levels of socio-economic integration is necessary to an understanding of the regional marketing system.[2] We will examine the nature of the relationship between the marketing and production systems for food staples by constructing a typology of Market Places and relating these to marketing patterns in general. That is, by concentrating on the sociology of the marketing system—rather than merely on the ethnography of the Market Place—we hope to clarify the role of the peasant in a dynamic national economy.

Analysis of the peasant Market Place within the rationalizing marketing system also raises several subsidiary problems which we shall discuss, including the functional importance of intermediaries at different levels of the marketing system, the nature of the food supply to rural and urban areas, the effects of consumer demands, and the nature of competition of varying cash crops for land and labor. In describing the regional marketing system, both the role of the peasantry in Brazilian agriculture and apparent trends in land tenure and land usage are clarified. Detailed knowledge of the relationship between peasant producers, middlemen, and consumers interacting in the marketing system adds to an understanding of the system of stratification in this traditional agrarian society and underscores the social structural as well as the economic and ecological implications for future agricultural development in Northeast Brazil.

II

The peasant in Northeast Brazil operates within a capitalist society where land, labor and product all have a market. He is highly valued as a commodity producer and laborer in an agrarian-structured society which exploits commercial export crops on large-scale plantations. Extensive cattle ranches and innumerable smallholdings exist along with the export-oriented commercial enterprises. The small-scale producers supply foodstuffs and labor to the dominant export-centered sector of the economy. Indeed, it can be said that peasant society in Brazil is a concomitant of the internal market mechanism and that the transformation of peasants into modern farmers results from the changing marketing system.

The Brazilian Northeast is well known for its economic and social problems.[3] This area of approximately 800,000 square miles and 25 million inhabitants is roughly divided into three major ecological zones. Along the coast, a number of low humid valleys are exploited for the exportation of partially processed sugar, both on the international market and internally to the large market in southern Brazil. These coastal lowlands, or the *zona da mata,* are characteristically described as comprised of large sugar plantations with their attendant problem of the proletarianization of rural labor. However, this area is also interspersed with a large number of renters and smallholders, some producing sugar cane to supply to the mills, but the majority selling mixed food crops grown on marginal lands not suited to sugar-cane production.

To the west, along the rutted clay roads which traverse the Brazilian Northeast from the coast to the dry hinterland, is a transitional zone, the *agreste*, which is a mixed farming area of food crops, fruits and tobacco, sold locally and exported to other regions of Brazil. The *agreste* is comprised primarily of *minifundia*. As in the coastal lowlands, these peasant homesteads are organized in a variety of tenure systems including ownership, renting, sharecropping, and squatting. They are exploited by paleo-technology and long fallowing.

The *sertão*, or backlands, is probably one of the best known areas of Brazil, popularized through Euclides da Cunha's novel, *Rebellion in the Backlands*, and brought to the consciousness of the world by the reports of the political and religious excesses of its starvation-driven peasants. It is primarily an area of cattle raising. The large cattle ranches are worked by cowboys who until recently herded cattle for a one-quarter share of the stock but are today wage workers. While the former system enabled some cowboys to establish small ranches, the present system leads to proletarianization. Some peasants produce foodstuffs for sale on the internal market in settlements around the many *açudes*, or dams, built to counter the devastating effects of the periodic droughts.

Our research on the role of the peasant in the production and distribution of food staples—corn, beans, rice, and manioc flour—was conducted in the state of Alagoas, a microcosm of the region and, perhaps, the most undeveloped of the traditional sugar-producing states of Northeast Brazil. All three major ecological zones are represented in the state's 27,731 square kilometers. We began our research in two Market Places in the county of Guaiamu, an area comprised of large sugar plantations and a mixed farming zone of smallholdings. Subsequently, we extended the research into the *agreste* and *sertão* through field surveys which covered some ten Market Places in a three-state area.[4] In addition, we visited a variety of agricultural holdings and collected data on the extent of participation in the marketing process. No agriculturalist was found who did not participate to some degree as a commodity producer for the market.

In following the movement of goods and personnel, it became evident that we were not dealing with an agrarian society in which the traditional model of a marketing system was fully applicable. Food staples did not necessarily move upward through a hierarchy of Market Places. There were, as we shall discuss below, clearly distinguishable levels of market activity each with its concomitant functions, but these Market Places did not in themselves constitute the internal marketing system of the region.

The beginning of an internal marketing system in Northeast Brazil was characterized by the presence of *feiras*, or Market Places, which supplied foodstuffs to the growing populations on the expanding plantations and in the coastal cities. Early travel literature is replete with accounts of the movement of produce through market middlemen (Almeida Prado, 1941: 442–43; Koster, 1942: 79, 82, 214 *passim*; Gardner, 1942: 97–98).[5]

The history of the county of Guaiamu provides a view of the development of the peasantry in Northeast Brazil. During the sixteenth and seventeenth centuries the county was an economic satellite of the expanding sugar-cane fields to the north in the province of Pernambuco. Cattle and agricultural produce were sent to the provincial capital of Olinda and dye-woods and hardwood were furnished to the Portuguese Royal Navy (Almeida Prado, 1941: 445–46; Andrade, 1959: 40). By the beginning of the seventeenth century an 'agricultural highway' existed for the transport of goods along the coast of Alagoas through Guaiamu from the São Francisco River community of Penedo north to Olinda (Almeida Prado, 1941: 445–46). This road undoubtedly gave rise to the string of *feiras livres*, or free fairs, found today in the county seats which grew up along the coastal route.

Sugar cane first appeared in the county in the eighteenth century and spread so rapidly that the rich forest resources were put under Royal reserve. Land use in Guaiamu and surrounding counties was restricted to the arid coastal areas where the valuable hardwoods were not found.[6] The heavily furrowed plots now abandoned on the worn-out tablelands attest to the intensified agriculture which was carried on at that time. A nineteenth-century account describes the *municipio* of Guaiamu as 'extremely fertile and containing various sugar mills whose inhabitants annually harvest rich crops of all forms of foodstuffs and transport them to the capital and other parts of the province.' This same account indicates that the county was also 'a refuge for the inhabitants of the interior during the droughts and . . . one of the rich breadbaskets of Maceió, supplying manioc, beans, corn, oil, salt and sometimes even fruits . . .' (Espindola, 1871: 236–37). By 1871, the county of Guaiamu had a total population of 17,117 of whom 78 per cent were freemen and only 22 per cent were slaves.[7] It is important to note that this free majority was engaged in the production of both sugar cane for the *engenhos*, or animal-driven mills, and foodstuffs for the internal market.

The central sugar mill, or *usina*, was built in the county of Guaiamu in 1927 and ownership was transferred to a corporation in 1939. The new owners continued to concentrate the *usina's* landholdings in the county, a trend which started in the last century. Between 1959 and 1965 the mill's share of the county lands stabilized at approximately fifteen thousand hectares,[8] consolidating previously independent, non-contiguous plantations.[9] During the same period, the number of wage laborers at the mill increased from a maximum of 125 in the harvest season (Andrade, 1959: 75) to over 300, and the number of field hands working for the mill increased to over 800. A *feira de usina*, or mill fair, was established at this time.

An important variable in the growth of rural markets is the nature of competition among major farm crops for land and labor. Thus, when sugar became king in the Valley of Guaiamu during the first quarter of this century there was a decrease in the amount of land available for food production. The expansion and growth of the sugar economy in Guaiamu seriously affected food production and the county soon changed from a hinterland breadbasket to a food importer (Andrade, 1959: 81–82). This process continues today. Until recently, land in the county was rented by absentee landowners to peasants who maintained effective control over their plots for long periods. Today, however, tenancy is often of short duration. A peasant may clear the land and retain rights in it for one year only, at which time it reverts to the owner and is usually planted in sugar cane. In such cases, the peasant is hardly willing—even when able—to make any long-term investments in the land. In addition, large tracts of land are utilized for cattle grazing or left as forest, diminishing even further the land available for food production in the county.

At the same time that land appears to be moving out of food production, the rapid urbanization and industrialization of this region makes urgent demands upon the rural sector for increased food supply at lower cost. The years between 1940 and 1960 were marked by tremendous urban growth throughout the nation. Within the state of Alagoas itself the population in and around the capital city, Maceió, grew from 90,523 in 1940 to 170,134 in 1960 (IBGE, 1966: 38). This disparity between decreasing land areas available for food production and increasing non-food-producing rural and urban populations that need to be fed is one of the principal dilemmas of agricultural planning in Northeast Brazil.

III

Brazilian developers often explain the problem of food supply in terms of inadequate production and marketing facilities. Yet, the situation is best described as one in which an archaic production sector is enmeshed in a highly commercialized distributive sector. This does not mean that the traditional peasant marketing system no longer exists. Indeed, we are confronted in Northeast Brazil with the phenomenon of an on-going, increasingly viable system of peasant Market Places which are, at the same time as their peasant participants, well on their way to extinction in a modern world. Before discussing these changes in the marketing system, however, we will describe the traditional Market Place network.

The traditional Market Place, or *feira,* is a periodic market of itinerant sellers housed in non-permanent structures (*barracas*) and convening in a designated place at a set time. A *feira* distributes primary goods and services among rural people who participate both as buyers and sellers. It also serves to distribute finished and semi-finished consumer products in areas in which the lack of liquid capital makes keeping of large stocks impossible. In other words, a *feira* moves goods in a money-poor economy.

At this point the *feira* should be distinguished from other rural commercial establishments which also exist for the distribution of goods but differ somewhat in form, function and the nature of participation. A *feira* is to be contrasted with

1. A market, or *mercado,* which is a permanent daily outlet for goods and services. Large numbers of sellers gather in one location in order to supply a predominantly urban group of consumers. In some large urban centers, the permanent *mercado* has grown up on the site of former *feiras.* On some days, the market is greatly enlarged by the addition of temporary stalls in the surrounding streets. This, in Portuguese, is also referred to as a *feira,* and market days are called *dias de feira.*
2. Warehouses, or *armazens,* which are privately owned or state-operated whole-

salers' facilities for the storage of goods, principally food staples. These are ultimately distributed in part through *feiras.*

3. The general store, or *mercearia,* which refers to a permanent retail outlet with fixed capital goods (i.e., building, equipment and stock). *Mercearias* are usually located in cities and larger county seats where there is a steady consumer market.
4. A shop, or *venda,* which is a rural, small-scale retail outlet. *Vendas* operate primarily on credit, often buying their own goods at the weekly *feira.* A variant of the *venda* is the company store located on plantations.

All of these are to be found throughout the Brazilian Northeast and—with the exception of the *armazen*—within the county of Guaiamu.

There are three types of Market Places in Northeast Brazil: the local Market Place or Rural Buyers' Fair (*Feira de Consumo*), the Distribution Fair (*Feira de Distribuição*), and the Urban Consumers' Fair (*Feira de Abastecimento*). These three types of Market Places do not constitute a developmental typology representing a sequence of stages from one to the other. That is, while the local Market Place is changing, it is not becoming a Distribution Fair, nor is it likely to become an Urban Consumers' Fair, although such developments are not outside the realm of possibility. These types exist simultaneously, and there is not a steady flow of goods or personnel from one to the other. While the typology elaborated below takes in the universe of Market Places (the Market Place network), the internal marketing system of Northeast Brazil is by no means limited to these arenas of exchange.

THE LOCAL MARKET PLACE

The *feira de consumo* is a rural Market Place in which goods and services are distributed in areas of poor access among rural populations with limited capital. Each *feira* is a cyclical market which meets once a week, the day depending largely upon the primary economic activity of the area it serves. For example, fairs in the coastal lowlands are usually scheduled on Saturdays and Sundays in order to take advantage of Friday paydays at the sugar mills. In the *sertão,* cattle fairs may be scheduled any day of the week alternating with regular commodity fairs so that in a given region an entire week may be taken up with one fair or another.

Historically, the *feira de consumo* was characterized by a multiplicity of peasants selling their produce in a central market place. Today, distribution within the *feiras* is carried on by a variety of itinerant traders, called *feirantes* or *cambistas,* peasant retailers and local shopkeepers who sell non-bulk foodstuffs, garden produce, perishables, and manufactured goods. People come to the Market Place both to buy and to sell, and often buyers and sellers are indistinguishable.

The county of Guaiamu has three *feiras de consumo* which serve the needs of some 4,540 townsmen and 18,044 rural dwellers. A *feira livre,* or 'free' fair, takes place at dawn every Saturday on public fair grounds in the county seat. There, over 100 sellers of food staples, meats and notions are housed in a permanent shed surrounded by at least another 250 sellers of perishables and manufactured goods who display their wares in stalls and on the ground. A few women sell cooked food to the participants. A *feira de usina*, or mill fair, is located on privately owned lands in a nucleated settlement of mill workers. This fair attracts more than 350 sellers of foodstuffs, manufactured goods, and services. The sellers, the vast majority of whom do not attend the Guaiamu 'free' fair, begin arriving at the *usina* late Saturday afternoon. The fair peters out by 8 A.M. Sunday. A third fair, somewhat smaller than the other two, services a nearby agricultural colony on Saturday afternoons.

While the form and function of the 'free' fair and the mill fair are essentially the same, there are some distinguishing characteristics. The fact that the majority of residents on sugar-mill lands are wage earners encourages a larger stock of manufactured goods and, thus, a higher degree of capitalization at the mill fair. Since the mill owners provide half-hectare plots to field hands for subsistence agriculture, smaller quantities of perishable goods are sold there. Primarily women deal in fruits and vegetables and men handle drygoods, food staples, and manufactured products. Consequently, greater numbers of men are found selling in the mill fair. In general, the mill fair takes on a highly commercialized bazaar-type atmosphere which is not characteristic of the poorer and slower *feira livre*.

A good deal more socializing takes place at the *feira livre* than at the mill fair. In the county seat, buyers and sellers gather in festive moods for their weekly early morning meetings, often walking two or three hours in the predawn darkness. It is at the Market Place that peasants exchange ideas and define their place in the world outside the restrictive influences of the local setting. Despite the rapid spread of the transistor radio in the past ten years, the fair remains the place where the peasant listens to the troubador spin his tales of culture heroes and newsworthy events. Here, too, he is exposed to the material encumbrances of the Catholic Church encouraging him to replace his rock and shell amulets with golden chains and plaster saints.

At the sugar mill, plantation workers are hauled on flat cars by company tractors to and from the fair grounds so that they can make their necessary purchases. The mills do not appear to dominate economically over the fairs, even in cases where their reputations are marred by the image of the company store. Instead, mill owners prefer to have a fair operate on their premises where behavior can be watched and they can be certain a full crew will be available for work on Monday.

There are three categories of sellers in the local Market Place: (1) A few peasants retail their own produce at the fair, immediately spending their cash income for their own consumer needs; (2) an increasing number of peasants sell their own produce and market goods bought from others; and (3) a large number of middlemen re-sell products purchased elsewhere. The second category represents a growing body of peasants who enter the Market Place as middlemen in order to supplement their cash incomes in an increasingly commercialized rural world.

The fairs are arranged in orderly fashion with specific areas assigned to sellers who specialize in primary or finished goods. A man will deal in wet or dry goods, but not in both. Since manufactured goods (textiles, leather goods, hardware and utensils, etc.) require a greater expenditure of funds, intermediaries dealing in such items are rarely drawn from the peasantry.

Men generally specialize in bulked and processed goods. They occupy the principal areas of the fair grounds, with their large sacks of corn, beans and rice arranged neatly within the protective confines of a large permanent shed. Many who come to sell in Guaiamu travel long distances by truck and mule across several ecological zones trading goods which bring the highest prices in areas of scarcity. Some return to the hinterland carrying quantities of salted fish and coconuts, the specialized food products of the coastal zone. A large section of the outdoor area of the Market Place is occupied by semi-permanent stalls or *barracas,* in which local middlemen sell dry goods. Butchers are located separately from the main part of the fair where they are carefully watched by local tax agents.

While some women work with their husbands at *barracas,* the majority of market women are involved in the more marginal, less capitalized operations such as the sale of green vegetables, fruits, fresh fish and small quantities of salted fish. The dependence of women on the sale of garden produce for incremental earnings can be likened to the Haitian pattern described by Mintz (1959, 1960 a, b) in which lack of alternative employment makes marginal labor amenable to hard work for minimal rewards.

Virtually all retail sales are for cash. Peasant producers with no holding power are ill-prepared to set prices and depend upon information obtained by face-to-face contact at the fair. There are monopolistic controls on certain bulk products such as rice and beans through speculative buying and storing up of large quantities in warehouses. In addition, there are federal and locally fixed prices on certain commodities. Meat prices, for example, are regulated nationally, while the price of fish is set locally by the mayor and the president of the fisherman's guild. Often, information about federal price ceilings are adjusted to the needs of the local community; for example, a new law repealing the paid registration of all vendors and lifting the price ceiling on meat was not communicated to middlemen by local authorities.

Very little haggling takes place at the *feiras,* and there is generally little competition between sellers with regard to price. There is, of course, price variation within established limits, and the process of price-setting often depends upon the relationship between the seller and the means of production. Thus, some vendors are able to sell for a lesser margin of profit than others because they themselves have produced the goods. A female trader and a hired vendor working for a wage both sold lemons at 5 for $100 cruzeiros while a man a short distance away sold lemons at 10 for $100 cruzeiros. He noted that he was able to undersell because he was selling the fruits of his own trees. Another vendor noted that he prefers to sell his own produce because his 'only capital outlay is his own labor.' However, he had his own produce for only two months of the year and was forced to obtain most of his goods from a warehouse after selling off his own harvest.

Likewise, very little hawking is done at the fairs, and vendors usually wait for their regular clients to come along and buy. A good deal of social visiting accompanies these transactions. No special prices are given for the aged, infirm, or for kinsmen, although beggars are often given some small quantity of produce. Buyer-seller relationships are often strengthened by considerable generosity in weights and measures. Very few retail buyers will be afforded credit at the time of purchase.

A sense of competition is present but never exaggerated. Financial ruin of a competitor is not something to be achieved. Many vendors share weighing scales with their neighbor or sell each other's produce with no share being paid when they themselves sell out. One vendor at the *feira livre* wanted to expand his operation to include the *feira de usina,* but waited until a colleague desisted before giving it a try.

Food staples enter the Market Place in several ways. While some produce is grown by peasants and carried to the *feira* for direct sale, the bulk is handled by middlemen who may acquire it for resale either at the farm or from other dealers at local Market Places. However, the major source of supply is now the large hinterland warehouses where goods are stored and sold wholesale.

Regardless of the source, all buying for immediate resale in the local Market Place is done on credit, with payment expected immediately after cash transactions are completed at the fair. Default on payment is not usual, although there are cases reported. Reactions to failure of payment is individual. One man, for example, said he would never again give merchandise on consignment because several people sold goods without paying him for them. In another instance, however, a fish hawker who fell into debt because of heavy losses incurred by over-buying was accepted back by his regular supplier as soon as he was again solvent.

There are no binding contractual arrangements between buyers and sellers in wholesale transactions. These verbal agreements can be entered into or broken at any time. The strength of a wholesale buying relationship is directly correlated with the perishability of the product. Thus, most of the buying of beans is on a first-to-arrive-at-the-farm basis, while fish is handled on a semi-binding relationship between fisherman and fish hawker.

Most vendors carry their merchandise to the fair on muleback or by truck, although some of the more marginal vendors come on foot. Transportation costs are calculated into the prices of goods so that a profit can be made, but there does not seem to be any fixed percentage mark-up above expenditures. Vendors usually stay with kinsmen or sleep by their market stalls under the heavy tarpaulins, and no calculation of maintenance costs enters into the pricing of goods.

Difficulties of transportation and communication facilities are among the keys to the persistence of the peasant Market Place. Lack of access roads from the multiple smallholdings in the Brazilian interior is one of the prime reasons for the persistence of peasant middlemen. Goods produced on small peasant farms connected to rural towns by narrow paths—sometimes not even suited to animal-drawn vehicles—continue to enter the local Market Place. As we shall see, improved transportation and storage facilities allow commercial elites acting both as wholesalers and retailers to penetrate and dominate rural economic life.

Another characteristic of the peasant Market Place is the lack of storable inventory. Furthermore, the rapid turnover of small quantities of goods based on cash transactions militates against the accumulation and concentration of capital. The higher cost of manufactured goods relative to foodstuffs drains capital upward and outward from the local Market Place.

Profits are difficult to calculate, but it can be said that earnings in the peasant Market Place are extremely low. In part this is due to the small quantities of goods being moved and the low buying power of the people. Also, large entrepreneurial profits are difficult to obtain in the arenas of peasant exchange where the producer can still compete as a middleman.

Bureaucratic controls also cut sharply into earnings. Taxes are paid to local, state and federal authorities and entry into the Market Place requires licenses. The mayor appoints tax collectors who regulate all market behavior. License fees and taxes are paid in advance to the mayor's office. Rent for floor space, prorated according to the quality and type of merchandise being sold, is paid on the spot to tax agents. License fees are not so high as to be prohibitive, but together with taxes discourage many people from entering the system and serve to prevent many peasants from marketing their own goods. Fishermen are explicitly prohibited by the mayor's office from selling directly to the consumer 'so as not to make two profits.' Taxes are high, especially for goods which bring the highest margin of profits, such as meat and manufactured items. While such a graduated system has its advantages for the very poor, it also reduces the possibility of capital formation at the levels where it might otherwise be possible. Commercialization at the local level clearly suffers from this excessive taxation, as a troubador sings in the following verse from 'The Lament of the Brazilians over Taxes and Fees':

O pobre negociante
Que tem pouca transação . . .
Paga impôsto e paga renda
E direito do chão

The pitiful vendor
Makes hardly a cent . . .
All he earns goes for taxes,
For fees and for rent.

THE DISTRIBUTION FAIR

Two or three *feiras de consumo* usually form part of a Market Place network. The complete network includes a Distribution Fair to which most middlemen must go for their merchandise. The *feira livre* and *feira de usina* in the county of Guaiamu form just such a network with the larger Distribution Fair in the city of Arapiraca, some four hours away by jeep. However, a Market Place network exists only insofar as it is worked by middlemen. The same personnel need not frequent all of the fairs in a cycle, and some traders may choose to alternate between different Market Places.[10] Thus, while all middlemen in the area of Guaiamu must go to Arapiraca on Mondays to make their purchases and all go to the Sunday mill fair, they may choose between several local *feiras livres* which all take place on Saturdays. The Market Place network, then, is a matter of individual preference and not a pre-fixed cycle of economic trading activities. The *feiras* an individual attends depends on their proximity to one another and nearness to the seller's home. The vast majority of sellers in the local Market Places engage in other activities on non-market days either as agriculturalists working their own lands or as shopkeepers in local *mercearias* and *vendas*.

The *feiras de distribuição* are usually located in hub cities in the transitional mixed-farming areas between the humid coastal lowlands and the drier cattle-raising *sertão*. These fairs are the key links in the distribution network, since they collect various products from different ecological zones and re-distribute them for sale in rural peasant Market Places and in Urban Consumers' Fairs. Their principal distinguishing characteristic is the wholesale buying and selling of goods in bulk for further distribution. This is done through wholesalers who are rapidly coming to dominate the marketing system in Northeast Brazil.

In effect, we find two spheres of activity in the Distribution Fairs, one reinforcing the past and one representing the future. At first glance, we are confronted with a multiplicity of peasant middlemen hustling and bustling in a vastly enlarged *feira de consumo*. Thousands of sellers fill the streets of the city, offering a bewildering display of foodstuffs from stalls and individual sacks on the ground. Not only do these sellers feed the resident population of the hub cities where Distribution Fairs are located, but they carry back goods for resale to local rural populations which are too scattered and without the buying power to attract a single large-scale operator. Much of the food staples were purchased only the day before from the wholesalers whose warehouses stand omnipotently behind the Market Place. It is in these warehouses that perhaps the most important marketing activities take place. Urban retailers also depend on the Distribution Fair wholesalers for their supply of food staples for the city, although they are rarely in evidence on the day of the fair.

The wholesaler who operates in the *feira de distribuição* serves not only as the nexus in a direct line movement of produce from farm to urban areas, but also is the link in the supply of produce back into the countryside. In the first instance, he supplies urban areas with foodstuffs without their passing through the Market Place network. At the same time, he plays a direct role in the Distribution Fair as the starting point for the redistribution of goods to rural areas.[11] It is, then, at the level of the Distribution Fair that the wholesaler plays a vital role in the transitional economy. On the one hand, he supplies the local Market Places and, on the other, he is the center of a rationalized marketing system in Northeast Brazil.

THE URBAN CONSUMERS' FAIR

The third type of Market Place, the *feira de abastecimento*, meets on specific days of the week as part of a large daily market. As an appendage to the permanent *mercado*, this *feira* is comprised almost entirely of retailers who serve large urban populations.[12] On Fair Days foodstuffs fill the streets surrounding the permanent market site. Large numbers of small middlemen join the permanent *mercado* vendors in selling a wide variety of products to the urban housewife (and her maid). Very few peasants sell their own produce in these urban centers. Undoubtedly this is due to the fact that the large port cities of Northeast Brazil are surrounded by fertile sugar lands where almost every available piece of cultivable land is utilized for the production of commercial export crops.

It is precisely because of the specialized export function of Brazilian coastal cities and the concomitant dearth of locally produced foodstuffs that hub cities and their *feiras de distribuição* developed in the transitional agricultural zones settled primarily by small peasant producers. These 'second cities' are truly the back-bone of Brazil. It is from them that goods are supplied to the coastal capitals, either in bulk by wholesalers or in small quantities by middlemen. It is through them that the products of a rapidly industrializing nation are filtered back to the local Market Place.

IV

These rural Market Places, or *feiras*, in Northeast Brazil do not in themselves constitute the internal marketing system of this region. As we traveled the market 'circuit' and spoke with peasants and middlemen about the movement of produce, it became apparent that we were not dealing with an agrarian society in which the traditional model of a marketing system was fully applicable. Such a model posits a hierarchy of Market Places through which goods move both horizontally and vertically, eventually arriving at urban concentrations through the continual change of hands of a variety of middlemen (Mellor, 1966: 341; Chayanov, 1966: 258; Dewey, 1962). The price of goods increases with each transaction, but the margin of profit is in the transfer of goods from place to place and earnings for the primary producer remain relatively small.

Goods and sellers in Northeast Brazil do not necessarily move through a hierarchy of Market Places. There are clearly distinguishable levels of market activity, but the Market Places are not laid out in a 'nested' arrangement where goods move in step-like fashion from lower to higher levels of market integration as they approximate urban centers. In effect, these Market Places are operating within the context of a rationalizing marketing system. With increased urban demands on the food supply and with the opening up of transportation and communications facilities, the function of the *feira* has been altered. Traditionally, the peasant producer entered the system through the local Market Place which was the starting point in the upward flow of primary produce. Now, food staples have begun to follow the model of commercial export crops in a funnel-like movement from producer to consumer through large warehouses. Wholesalers go to the farm to buy produce in bulk. In this way, crops by-pass the traditional peasant Market Place which comes to serve primarily as a mechanism for the horizontal movement of foodstuffs and the terminal point in the downward flow of manufactured goods. In other words, the peasant Market Place has become a buyers' rather than a sellers' market.

The foregoing ethnography of the different types of Market Places in Northeast Brazil points up the dichotomy between the traditional market network and the developing marketing system. Because of the urban demands for more food at lower cost, the marketing system tends to do away with the multiplicity of middlemen and to reduce rather than increase the number of effective entrepreneurs.

Within the interlocking network of rural Market Places, the proliferation of middlemen is a necessary ecological and social adjustment to small and widely scattered centers of production and consumption and to the scarcity of transportation and storage facilities. This important point, made by Bauer for West Africa (1954), is also relevant in the Brazilian context. The large number of middlemen in Brazilian *feiras* provide the greatest possible spread and distribution of goods on the local level. These middlemen are functional as distributors of goods in small quantities among money-poor peasants and do not compete with the large wholesalers.

Peasants realize the utility of large numbers of middlemen. A single individual with minimal capital cannot incur substantial risk. He is unable to handle large quantities of goods and the prospect of large losses. This is particularly true for middlemen dealing in perishables which demand rapid movement.

The important question to be asked is not why such middlemen persist but what is their sociological significance in an economic situation which can only be described as extremely marginal. It must be pointed out that alternative employment opportunities in rural Brazil are virtually non-existent. At the same time, the improving transportation and communication facilities bring to the hinterland quantities of manufactured goods which quickly become consumer needs. The appearance of manufactured goods in the remotest weekly Market Places causes rises in expectations which are not easily met. The worker and the peasant are constantly being exposed to a wide variety of consumer commodities from clothing to plastic flowers. Thus many peasants are forced into the Market Place as the only means by which they can acquire money to meet their families' new demands. They no longer return to the farm after selling off their own crop but begin to buy and sell the produce of others. As one peasant put it: 'Nobody wants to work; everyone wants to be in business!'

Apparent minimal earnings are not an indication of the non-existence of entrepreneurial talent on the local level. Indeed, the peasant middleman is a highly effective operator, taking full advantage of the Market Place situation. For example, one man comes weekly to the *feira* selling from a single sack of beans which he purchases at a *feira de distribuição* for $25,000 cruzeiros. Over a two-week period he managed to sell the beans for $30,000 cruizeiros, an increment of 20 per cent, or $5,000 cruzeiros which equals 2.5 days wage labor. When asked about the efficiency of his small-scale operation, the man said that he had neither the capital to buy nor the clientele to whom to sell in larger quantities. At the same time, he indicated that despite the harsh effects of inflation, taxes and fees, his expenditures of time and energy were worth the additional income which he needed to satisfy the pressing consumer demands of his large family.

Nevertheless, there is virtually no possibility for such a middleman to become an effective entrepreneur in a rationalized marketing system. As we have indicated, socio-economic impediments in the form of sometimes arbitrary imposition of taxes and fees, the lack of access to strategic resources such as information, credit, patron, or family connections, and a consumer audience with limited buying power restricts the vertical mobility of these small, independent middlemen.

Small-scale vendors do not group together in cooperative endeavors in order to operate in economies of scale as do the *baliks* in Java (Dewey, 1962: 88–89 *passim*). The Market Place in Northeast Brazil is an arena of individualistic behavior where other forms of self-protection prevail. Thus, middlemen attempt to diversify their capital in the form of their own labor. One man sells corn and beans at the market and manioc flour from his house. He also works as a trucker but not a jobber of wood and rice. He does not serve as a middleman for these products because he is certain of their freight income and this serves as a buffer which permits his speculative buying of other primary produce.

There is one instance of middlemen grouping together in a marketing cooperative to sell fish. However, this endeavor failed because, lacking adequate refrigeration and transportation facilities, the cooperative was unable to move large quantities of fresh fish as a single unit to the urban consumer market.

Entrepreneurs operating in economies of scale do appear, along with a proportional decrease in the number of intermediaries in the ever-shrinking chain between peasant producers and consumer market, but they grow out of a rural commercial class which is in a strategic position to control 'the flow of capital goods in exchanges between groups' (Firth, 1963: 22). The multiple middlemen who move minimal units of goods as highly functional components of the peasant Market Place network are replaced by wholesalers who have the capabilities of moving produce in bulk. Few peasant middlemen have the capital necessary to maintain large stocks of goods in warehouses for months at a time and to pay cash for produce at its source. Indeed, it is from these wholesalers that local middlemen are themselves forced to buy during non-harvest seasons or when their own produce is in short supply.

The wholesalers also funnel food staples to the city from the countryside. The trend is clear. In the state of Alagoas from 1964–5 alone the number of wholesale warehouses increased from 89 to 125, and for the first time two refrigeration facilities were constructed (Anuário Estatístico, 1966: 230). With the appearance of these warehouses crops began to by-pass the traditional peasant Market Place, thus reducing the number of transactions in the movement of food staples to the cities. While we were unable to gather statistical evidence for this statement given the time and resources available to us, a study undertaken by the Latin American Market Planning Center at Michigan State University in conjunction with the Agency for the Development of the Northeast (SUDENE) amply documents this trend.[13] In a comparative study of two bean-producing regions of the same urban food shed, they describe the effects of the changing marketing system:

> The market structure is changing slowly as competitive pressures force the smaller, less efficient firms out of business. This appears to be taking place more rapidly in the Irece [Bahia] than in the Al-Pe [Alagoas] area (LAMP 1968. Chapter 9-A, page 35). The Al-Pe channel has more different types of buyers who handle smaller market shares and perform more specialized services. Irece, on the other hand, has fewer types of buyers handling larger market shares . . . An average of 3.4 transactions is involved in the movement of beans from producers in the Al-Pe area through the large urban wholesalers. This compares with less than three transactions for beans moving from the Irece area in Bahia . . . The Irece channel appears to have eliminated the need for many small assemblers who still survive in the Al-Pe channel (pp. 12–13).

According to the LAMP study, this same process is occurring in the rural marketing system for rice in the São Francisco River region of the state of Alagoas (1968, Chapter 9-B).

Prices for processed and bulked food staples are fixed by the wholesalers who are able to store large quantities against the time when supply is short. They withhold goods from the market and control prices both on and off season. Wholesalers often buy from peasants and middlemen whom they intercept on their way to the Market Places. This process, called *por atacado*, brings a lower price to the peasant producer, but enables him to avoid the risks inherent in Market Place sales.

Increased transportation facilities are now permitting wholesalers to go directly to the source to buy produce which they acquire with cash. The peasant prefers to sell for a lower cash price to wholesalers than to sell on credit to local Market Place middlemen. The wholesalers coming into the countryside make the peasant aware of market conditions. As one peasant noted, 'the warehouses set the prices!' Local Market Place middlemen also derive their price information from the speculative activities of wholesalers. For example, one vendor adjusted his own prices upward when he was informed that four trucks were buying up beans on the road to the Market Place. In a sense, the wholesalers set the purchase price to suppliers and the sales price for retailers.

A characteristic problem of peasant societies is that they are communications poor. Such lines of communication as do exist are uni-directional—they come down to the peasant from the elite sectors of society. Where a patron-client relationship has not been established, this communication flow takes place through indirect links. Oftentimes these links are the intermediaries in the marketing system. Since wholesalers have storage facilities and better information about the size of crops and commodity supplies, they are in a far better position than the peasant or the local middleman to take advantage of buying and selling opportunities.

The penetration of wholesalers into the countryside has far-reaching effects, way beyond mere price setting and commodity control. It reaches into the very heart of the system of land tenure and land usage. As urban demands increase and access roads are built into the hinterland, wholesalers extend their commercial operations. The LAMP study confirms our research findings that wholesalers find it advantageous to deal directly with large producers rather than to engage in numerous transactions with small peasants (1968: Chapters 9-A–B). In effect, food crops become commercial crops and those producers who can provide bulk shipments are placed in a favored economic position.

Interestingly, this process of commercialization of food staples reinforces the sharecropping arrangements characteristic of export crop production in Brazil. Throughout this paper we have been discussing those peasants who have the right to independently sell their own produce. We have not dealt with the large numbers of sharecroppers whose produce has liens upon it through a variety of contractual arrangements. The routes by which sharecroppers' goods enter the marketing system is well known. Even his own share of the crop is turned over to the landlord at a pre-determined price, often far below the going market price. Large landowners—often absentee—serve as central collecting agents for wholesalers. Goods bulked in this fashion do not enter the local Market Place directly.

The relationship between the large landowner and the wholesaler is beyond the scope of this paper. However, it should be pointed out that as in the case of commercial export crop production, wholesalers furnish credit in exchange for exclusive rights to food crops, and, consequently, exercise an important influence over the production sector of the rural economy.

There is a greater concentration of capital on the higher levels of the marketing system where transportation and storage facilities and ready cash are required. This is indicative of development in the agrarian sector (Belshaw, 1965: 82). Such development is occurring largely because of the urban demands for agricultural produce which have stimulated a process of rationalization of the internal marketing system in Northeast Brazil.

The resultant commercialization in agriculture has serious consequences for production and land tenure. Peasant farms are viable and competitive as commodity producers given the Market Place network as a means of distributing minimal quantities of goods. However, atomistic peasant producers and middlemen are in themselves incapable of meeting increased urban needs. Commercial elites, attracted to the marketing system by high middleman profits, are better able to insure a steady and continuous supply of food staples if they can buy in bulk at the source. Larger productive units can more efficiently fulfill this need if increased profit margins make capital investment advantageous. When the marketing system begins to involve fewer intermediaries and higher rates of capitalization, it appears that consolidation of farms occurs.

Given the structure of Brazilian agrarian society, we believe that the influx of capital into the countryside through modern marketing procedures will result in further concentration of landholdings and the increased proletarianization of the rural masses. In addition to attracting commercial elites to the marketing system, high food prices also drive up the value of the land. The peasant is neither able to compete for new land nor make capital investments for improvements in the land he already owns. Despite the fact that the peasant has always been the principal producer of food staples, he finds today that his mode of production is not adequate to meet current demands. In sharp contrast to the large landowner, the Brazilian peasant has extremely limited access to sources of credit.[14] In a highly competitive rural economy, the government leaves him largely to his own devices.

The data from Northeast Brazil suggest that there is a point at which capitalization in the distributive sector of a rural economy requires like commitments of capital in the production sector, leading to the displacement or transformation of a peasantry. Such a change need not be beneficial to the society as a whole. Despite increased commercialization in Brazilian agriculture, a crisis in food supply persists. In part this can be explained by the competition between food staples and export crops for land and capital investments. The beneficiaries of an increased food market are the intermediaries and not the producers. Thus, newly concentrated landholdings may be utilized for increased production by wage labor of commercial export crops supported by government incentives (CIDA, 1966: 106–07 *passim*). In other instances, land is acquired as a speculative hedge against inflation and utilized for the extensive grazing of cattle (*ibid.*, 24).

While the stated aims of the Brazilian government are to stimulate the development of a 'middle-class' agriculture, by grouping small properties into cooperatives and modernizing and democratizing medium and large plantations (Cantanhede, 1967: 8), land speculation and concentration of landholdings continues throughout Northeast Brazil. Commercialization in agriculture outpaces government planning; peasants are being evicted from their lands thus 'abandoning subsistence agriculture which supplies foodstuffs to the Market Places . . .' (*Jornal do Comercio*, 8/13/67: 13).

SUMMARY

We have presented a body of data which describes the traditional system of peasant Market Places in Northeast Brazil and the changes which are currently occurring in the distributive sector of the rural economy. We will now present schematically a series of stages designed to show the integrative effects which a rationalizing marketing system has had on the Brazilian peasantry over time.

It must be remembered that these forms of peasant-marketing integration in the supply of food staples may exist simultaneously but represent a continuum of development. We have delineated five stages in the process of rationalization of the regional marketing system in Northeast Brazil.

Referring to the table [see next page]:

Stage 1. The peasant retails his own goods in the local Market Place. This is an ideal stage, representing near perfect competition (Belshaw, 1965: 57, 77), which is unlikely to have existed in such pure form in Brazil. Indeed, the early travel literature reports the buying of bulk goods by wholesalers and strict controls over the marketing of certain produce.

Stage 2. The incipient upward flow of goods by peasants who sell to middlemen. This occurs primarily at the local Market Place but also at Distribution Fairs. Most sales to middlemen are done on credit, the producer being paid immediately after the cash resale has been transacted.

Up to this point both stages are characterized by labor intensive operations in both production and distribution.

Stage 3. Middlemen go to the source to buy in larger quantities and sell either in the Market Place or, occasionally, to wholesalers. Again, the initial transaction is usually done on credit, while subsequent sales are for cash. At this stage the economic system is labor intensive in agriculture and industry although there is increased capitalization in the marketing of goods, particularly manufactured items. The cost of both primary produce and finished goods is high. The growth of the local Market Place is stimulated by the appearance of manufactured goods and increasing horizontal exchanges.

The marketing system in the county of Guaiamu and in the state of Alagoas is now transitional between this stage and the stage below.

Stage 4. Wholesalers begin to by-pass the middlemen and go directly to the peasant producer. Since they pay cash, the peasant producer is willing to sell on a first come first served basis, often at a lower price. This stage is marked by development of the infrastructure, although a lack of information prevails at

Stages in the Marketing System

Stage	Participants	Predominant types of markets	Marketing inputs	Production inputs
1.	pp—co	Local Market Place	Labor intensive	Labor intensive
2.	pp—mm—co	Local Market Place and Distribution Fair	Labor intensive	Labor intensive
3.	pp—mm—W—co	Distribution Fair with increased growth in local Market Place	Increased capitalization through wholesaling	Labor intensive
4.	pp—W—co	Distribution Fair and Urban Consumers' Market	Increased capitalization on all levels of distribution	Labor intensive
5.	alternatives:			
	(a) P—W—co	Urban Consumers' Market	Capital intensive	Capital intensive
	(b) pp—Wmm—co	Marketing cooperatives for urban areas	Capital intensive	Capital intensive
	(c) Ppp—W—co	Urban Consumers' Market	Capital intensive	Capital intensive through voluntary cooperation

pp = peasant producer
co = consumer
mm = middlemen
W = wholesalers
P = large-scale producers

the local level. A high degree of capitalization is required in the distributive sector. Prices for the entire system are controlled at this level by the wholesalers. The stage has many of the characteristics which Chayanov describes as a 'sweat shop system' of agriculture (1966: 257).

Between stages 4 and 5a transition occurs in which market demands require adjustments in the agrarian structure. This leads to a number of possible alternatives.

Stage 5.

(a) The prevailing tendency in Northeast Brazil is for wholesalers operating in highly capitalized economies of scale to want to deal directly with large-scale producers who assure a steady and continuous supply of food staples at a central delivery point. Purchases are made on credit to privately owned, large-scale farms.

(b) Another form of supplying urban areas with quantities of foodstuffs grown on small individual plots is through marketing cooperatives. However, these are rare in Northeast Brazil.[15]

(c) Peasants group themselves into cooperatives for the production and sale of goods to wholesalers. A number of experimental cooperatives which furnish technological and educational assistance to their members are now found in Northeast Brazil. It is this 'vertical concentration' of small farms through cooperatives that Chayanov thought would enable the Russian peasant labor farm to compete successfully on the market (1966: 266).[16] It is important to note that cooperatives are viable only at this level. We feel that cooperatives are a concomitant of this stage of development and not a catalyst to development.

We believe that Northeast Brazil now finds itself in the critical transition between Stages 4 and 5, and it is precisely this state of affairs which is largely responsible for the tensions which exist in the rural society. We are not suggesting that the rationalization of the marketing system presupposes a particular system of production, nor will we speculate on the comparative benefits of the apparent alternatives.[17] We cannot predict here the type of land tenure system which will develop in any one nation. This involves a complex set of ecological, demographic, social structural, economic and political considerations beyond the scope of this paper (Moore, 1966; Warriner, 1965). We are calling to mind the fact that agricultural development is a two-part process: the marketing system will lead to a restructuring of the production system when the latter is unable to meet consumer demands.

OTES

The field research upon which this paper is based was conducted in the summer of 1967, supported by grants from the Agricultural Development Council to Professors Riegelhaupt and Forman and from the International Affairs Center at Indiana University (Ford International II) to Professor Forman. In addition, Professor Forman did anthropological fieldwork in the same region from 1964–5 under an NDEA-Related

Fulbright–Hays Award. The authors are indebted to Marc Hoffnagel, Leona Shluger Forman and Edward I. Riegelhaupt for their assistance in the research and writing of this paper. We would like to thank Professors Robert Birrel, Matthew Edel, Ernestine Friedl, Daniel Gross, Allen Johnson, Sidney Mintz, Marvin Miracle, Sydel Silverman, and Eric Wolf for their critical examination of an earlier draft of this paper.

1. There is a large body of research and literature by anthropologists on peasant Market Places and traditional marketing systems. The works of Tax (1953), Mintz (1955, 1957, 1959, 1960a, 1960b, 1961), Katzin (1959, 1960), Bohannan and Dalton (1965), Dewey (1962), Belshaw (1965), Nash (1966), Skinner (1964), Wolf (1966), and Ortiz (1967) have all dealt with marketing institutions. Economists are well aware of the role of the market—particularly in Western economic systems. Oddly, they neglect the relevance of the market to peasant economies. With few exceptions, economists have studied the peasantry only in relation to its role in aggregate economies. Only recently have they begun to ask questions vital to peasant economy itself (Georgescu-Rogen, 1960; Dandekar, 1962; Schultz, 1964; Mellor, 1966 among others). The recent translation of A. V. Chayanov's *The Theory of Peasant Economy* (1966) has greatly enriched the literature in this field, even though he did not examine the nature of the feedback effects of the market on peasant agriculture.

2. Throughout this paper, Market Place refers to the physical locus for the periodic exchange of goods and services in rural areas. A Market Place network refers to a number of such loci which are connected through the movement of goods and personnel. The marketing system refers to the regional or national movement of goods between rural and urban centers.

3. For an interesting but controversial treatment of the manner in which the very 'underdevelopment' of Northeast Brazil is tied to the 'development' of southern Brazil, see A. G. Frank, "The Myth of Feudalism in Brazilian Agriculture," in *Capitalism and Underdevelopment in Latin America* (New York: Monthly Review Press, 1967), pp. 331–77.

4. Certain commodities produced in the county of Guaiamu, such as straw baskets, extend beyond this marketing radius, being sold in urban centers like Rio de Janeiro, Salvador, etc. (Forman, 1966). Sugar cane, of course, moves out into the international market. However, we followed only the movement of food staples in the internal marketing system.

5. Koster (1942: *passim*) refers to weekly markets in interior cities of Pernambuco during his voyage through Brazil in 1816. We believe that further historical research will document the earlier existence of rural Market Places. We know that warehouses existed in urban areas during the colonial period, but we can only assume that difficulties of transport and communications between coastal cities and widely scattered hinterland suppliers necessitated a multiplicity of Market Places.

6. A Royal decree of 1798 states that 'The lands more or less concentrated adjacent to the sea as well as those bordering on all woodlands judged to be useless for the Royal Navy will be set aside for the agriculture of the people' (Vilhena, 1921: 804–05).

7. In 1847, the Province of Alagoas had 207,766 inhabitants of which 167,976, or *ca.* 80 per cent were freemen, and 39,790 were slaves (Espindola, 1871: 93).

8. Further concentration was limited by salt marshes and tide lands to the east, by the mill owners' own cattle ranches to the west, and by quotas which cut into potential production.

9. Distorted statistics are obviously highly functional in traditional agrarian societies toying with the idea of land reform. According to the latest cadastral survey ordered by the President of the Republic in 1967 as part of his overall land reform, the county of Guaiamu has a total of 850 rural establishments with a land area of 81,140 hectares.

Of these, 593 are *minifundia*, representing a land area of 10,839 hectares, or approximately 13 per cent. 245 establishments are listed as *latifundia* with a total land areas of 62,216 hectares. Twelve properties with a land area of 8,084 hectares are listed as rural business (IBRA, 1967: 42). Based on the IBRA data, we are at a complete loss to explain the whereabouts of the 15,000-hectare single-property sugar mill.

10. Daniel Gross reports a similar randomness in attendance at fairs in the interior of the state of Bahia. 'There are trucks on Friday which go to Coité, a Distribution Fair, and on Saturday which go to both Valente and Santa Luz. On Sunday there is a *feira* here, but most people come on foot or mounted. In Monte Santo, people could attend the Distribution Fair in Euclides da Cunha on Saturday, then go to Cansanção on Monday, Pedro Vermelha on Tuesday, and Monte Santo on Friday' (1968: personal communication).

11. There is more than just food staples flowing back into the countryside from the Distribution Fairs. A large proportion of handicraft products, such as metalwork and leather goods, have their origins in these market towns.

12. In the state of Alagoas, there are two Urban Consumers' Fairs serving the capital city of Maceió (150,000 people) and the city of Penedo (32,000 people).

13. Michigan State University in cooperation with the Brazilian Agency for the Development of the Northeast (SUDENE) conducted research in the Recife foodshed area from 1966–7. Over 80 people participated in this large research endeavor. We are indebted to Professor Kelly Harrison, Chief of Party, and Dr. Harold Riley, Latin American Market Planning Center, for their cooperation.

14. The exact nature of debt-credit relationships in peasant economies is one of the most urgent research tasks confronting anthropologists, since data of this kind is crucial to a full understanding of changing rural social stratification in transitional agrarian societies.

15. The one example we have of this type of marketing organization is the fish hawkers' cooperative.

16. Chayanov (1966: 268–69) noted that even in a system of cooperatives, the pervasiveness of market pressures effects the forms that cooperation will take, leading eventually from selling to processing and ultimately to production cooperatives.

17. A fourth alternative for the consolidation of production units might be the grouping of peasants on collective farms with the distribution of foodstuffs through state agencies. Such a system becomes capital intensive through the mobilization of labor; however, it may lead to decreases in production. There is no such system presently in operation in Northeast Brazil, and its development would appear unlikely given the prevailing political ideology.

REFERENCES

Almeida Prado (1941), *Pernambuco e as capitanias do norte do Brasil 1530–1630*, Tomo II, Rio de Janeiro: Brasiliana.

Andrade, Manuel Correia de (1959), *Os Rios-do-Açucar do Nordeste Oriental*, Vol. IV (Os Rios Coruripe, Jiquia e São Miguel), Recife: Instituto Joaquim Nabuco de Pesquisas Sociais.

Bauer, P. T. (1954), *West African Trade*, Cambridge: Cambridge University Press.

Belshaw, C. (1965), *Traditional Exchange and Modern Market*, Englewood Cliffs: Prentice-Hall.

Bohannan, Paul, and George Dalton (1965), *Markets in Africa*, Garden City: Doubleday and Co.

Cantanhede, Cesar (1967), *Palestra proferida na Escola Superior da Guerra,* Rio de Janeiro: Institute Brasileira de Reforma Agraria.

Censo Escolar (1964), *Estado de Alagoas,* Maceió.

Chayanov, A. V. (1966), *The Theory of Peasant Economy,* Homewood, Ill.: Irwin (first published in Russian in 1925).

Comité Interamericano de Desenvolvimento Agricola (1966), *Posse e Uso da Terra e Desenvolvimento Socio-Economico do Setor Agricola,* Washington, D.C.: Pan American Union.

Dandekar, V. M. (1962), 'Economic Theory and Agrarian Reform,' *Oxford Economic Papers,* 14: 69–80.

Dewey, Alice (1962), *Peasant Marketing in Java,* Glencoe: The Free Press.

Espindola, Tomas (1871), *Geographia Alagoana ou descripção physico, politico, e historico da provincia das Alagoas,* Maceió.

Firth, R. (1963), 'Capital, Saving and Credit in Peasant Societies: A Viewpoint from Economic Anthropology,' in *Capital, Saving and Credit in Peasant Societies,* Raymond Firth and B. S. Yamey, eds., Chicago: Aldine Publishing Co.

Forman, Shepard (1966), *Jangadeiros: The Raft Fisherman of Northeast Brazil,* Ph.D. Dissertation. New York: Columbia University.

Frank, A. G. (1967), 'The Myth of Feudalism in Brazilian Agriculture,' in *Capitalism and Underdevelopment in Latin America,* New York: Monthly Review Press, pp. 331–77.

Furtado, Celso (1965), *The Economic Growth of Brazil,* Berkeley: University of California Press.

Gardner, George (1942), *Viagens No Brasil,* trans. by Albertino Pinheiro, Ed. Nacional, from *Travels in Brazil,* London, 1849.

Georgescu-Rogen, N. (1960), 'Economic Theory and Agrarian Economics,' *Oxford Economic Papers,* 12: 1–40.

Instituto Brasileiro de Geografia e Estatistica (1966), *Anuario Estatistico do Brasil,* Rio de Janeiro: IBGE-Conselho Nacional de Estatistica.

Instituto Brasileiro de Reforma Agraria (1967), *Cadastro de Imoveis Rurais—Alagoas,* Rio de Janeiro.

Katzin, Margaret F. (1959), 'The Jamaican Country Higgler,' *Social and Economic Studies,* 8(4): 421–35.

——— (1960), 'The Business of Higgling in Jamaica,' *Social and Economic Studies,* 9: 267–331.

Koster, Henry (1942), *Viagem ao Nordeste do Brasil,* trans. by Luiz da Camara Cascudo, Ed. Nacional, from *Travels in Brazil,* London, 1816.

LAMP (Latin American Market Planning Center) (1968), *Market Processes in the Recife Area of Northeast Brazil.* Research Report, Michigan State University, mimeographed.

Mellor, John W. (1966), *The Economics of Agricultural Development,* Ithaca: Cornell University Press.

Mintz, Sidney (1955), 'The Jamaican Internal Marketing Pattern: Some Notes and Hypotheses,' *Social and Economic Studies,* 4(1): 95–103.

——— (1957), 'The Role of the Middleman in the Internal Distribution System of a Caribbean Peasant Economy,' *Human Organization,* 15(2): 18–23.

——— (1959), 'Internal Market Systems as Mechanisms of Social Articulation,' *Proceedings of the Annual Spring Meeting, American Ethnological Society,* pp. 20–30.

——— (1960a), 'Peasant Markets,' *Scientific American,* 203(2): 112–18.

——— (1960b), 'A Tentative Typology of Eight Haitian Market Places,' *Revista de Ciencias Sociales,* 4(1): 15–58.

——— (1961), 'Pratik: Haitian Personal Economic Relationships,' *Proceedings of the Annual Spring Meeting, American Ethnological Society*, pp. 54–63.
Moore, Barrington, Jr. (1966), *Social Origins of Dictatorship and Democracy*, Boston: Beacon Press.
Nash, M. (1966), *Primitive and Peasant Economic Systems*, San Francisco: Chandler Publishing Co.
Oberg, K. (1965), 'The Marginal Peasant in Rural Brazil,' *American Anthropologist*, 67(6): 1417–27.
Ortiz, Sutti (1967), 'Colombian Rural Market Organization: An Exploratory Model,' *Man*, n.s., 2:393–414.
Schultz, T. W. (1964), *Transforming Traditional Agriculture*, New Haven: Yale University Press.
Skinner, G. W. (1964), 'Marketing and Social Structure in Rural China,' *Journal of Asian Studies*, 24(1): 3–43. (Also Parts II and III.)
Tax, Sol (1953), *Penny Capitalism*, Institute of Social Anthropology, No. 16, Washington, D.C., Smithsonian Institution.
Vilhena, Luiz Santos (1921), *Recopilação de noticias soterpolitanas e Brasilicas*. Bahia (1802).
Warriner, Doreen (1965), *Economics of Peasant Farming*, 2nd ed., New York: Barnes and Noble.
Wolf, Eric (1966), *Peasants*, Englewood Cliffs: Prentice-Hall.

The Cornell-Peru Project: Experimental Intervention in Vicos

HENRY F. DOBYNS

Social scientists have not only studied cultural change as a phenomenon but some have also been actively engaged in trying to direct it toward specific ends. One of the most ambitious ventures in this connection is already famous as "the Vicos project," conceived by Allan Holmberg as a long-term experiment in "participant intervention." Representatives of Cornell University assumed the dual role of researchers and managers of an hacienda for several years in collaboration with the Peruvian government. By briefly chronicling some successes, Dobyns provides a small part of the still-unwritten history of that controversial undertaking. Whyte's analysis of alternate roads to development chosen by Peruvian peasants is especially pertinent by way of contrast.

Henry F. Dobyns is Professor of Anthropology at Prescott College, and a former Research Coordinator of the Cornell-Peru Project. He has conducted research for the Hualapai, Havasupai, Papago and Gila River Pima-Maricopa Indians of Arizona, and has studied various Indian communities in Peru, Bolivia and Ecuador. His books include The Social Matrix of Peruvian Indigenous Communities (1964), *and a series of*

This paper was prepared expressly for this volume.

brief monographs on U.S. Indians; he is coauthor of Migración e integración en el Perú (1963), *and* Peasants, Power, and Applied Social Change: Vicos as a Model (1971).

Anthropologists at Cornell University in 1947 launched a broad comparative study of processes of postwar cultural change among southwestern U.S. Indians, coastal Nova Scotians, farm villagers on India's Gangetic Plain and Thailand's Mekong Delta, and Indians and mestizos in Peru's high Andes mountains. Allan R. Holmberg chose to study sample populations in Peru's Callejón de Huaylas whose lives he expected would change because of a large hydroelectric generating plant that was then under construction. In 1949 Holmberg launched two of his Peruvian students on studies of Marcará, a mestizo trading center and district capital, and Vicos, a hacienda with Indian serfs six kilometers distant.

In 1951 the Peruvian corporation that was leasing Vicos offered to sublease it to Holmberg. Meanwhile, however, a flood destroyed the hydroelectric project and with it the anticipated change stimulus. Holmberg therefore seized the opportunity to introduce his own changes at Vicos for the benefit of its serfs as well as the study. This paper very briefly summarizes some important consequences of what Holmberg thought of as anthropological "experimental intervention" at Vicos.

ANDEAN AGRARIAN PRODUCTION UNITS

The hacienda constituted one type of rural food-producing unit in the central Andes in 1951. Other units included "factories in the field," usually corporate, that utilized commercial bank short-term credit, were mechanized, and hired unionized wage laborers. Such *plantations* on the Pacific coastal littoral (rarely in the eastern jungles) were the most productive units and obtained high yields of crops for world markets, including sugar, rice, cotton, coffee, and bananas. *Ranches* at high altitudes above the limit of mountain agriculture produced wool and meat.

Family *farmers* with smaller properties and less capital produced a wider range of cash crops. Because they did not have the resources of the plantations and were unable to afford their own technicians, they depended more on government banks for credit and government technicians for technical assistance.

Millions of *peasants* cultivated minute plots using primitive tools and methods; for them, little or no credit was available. While they owned their land, many belonged to indigenous communities and their ownership was not absolute. They constituted the largest unskilled labor reservoir in the region and made up most of the massive stream of rural to urban migration.

More millions of serfs cultivated *manors* (haciendas), the least productive food-growing units in the central Andean area. Had the obligatory labor costs of these serfs been charged against sales income, many manors would have operated at a financial loss. The social prestige that went with managing other men kept many landlords in business. Serfs cultivated their own plots or grazed their stock, using the simplest technology and the least capital of any food producers in the region.

VICOS AS SAMPLE MANOR

When Holmberg leased Hacienda Vicos, he assumed direction of a manor—both its lands and the Indians who occupied and tilled them. Like most Andean manors, Vicos extended over a large land area. Yet, for all their size, such manors were overpopulated, since the populations they could comfortably support were limited by traditional food production technology. The manor's principal value to renters lay in its large labor force, not in its land per se.

In 1952, 363 Vicos men (or grown boys or adult females acting as substitutes) were required to labor for the manor three days each week, or 156 days per year, in return for a token payment of 20 Peruvian centavos daily (long in arrears) and a family house lot and garden plots. Other manors exacted even more serf labor. Obligatory labor could be applied anywhere the management wished, in Vicos or outside, on fields or in factories. None of the payment outsiders made for the rental of Vicosino labor went to the workers; they had no more say in the matter than oxen.

The 363 families in Vicos at the beginning of 1952 utilized some 85 percent of the area of cultivable land. The manor farmed the remaining 15 percent of the cultivable area for profit, using serf labor. Despite the high proportion of the estate the Vicosinos used, they did not support themselves from it in 1952. Serfs knew so little about agricultural techniques that their potato crops failed because unprotected plants succumbed to blight, and the men had to seek outside jobs on nonobligatory days to earn cash to buy food.

Vicos renters seldom exercised enough control over manorial lands to eject a serf or reassign the plots to different serfs. The 1952 land tenure pattern was, therefore, the result of a long-standing serf land-tenancy system centered on patrilineal *castas*. Serfs cultivated extremely fractionalized fields. No one has yet counted all the small plots, but they apparently number about 10,000 identifiable parcels. Each Vicosino cultivated a few square meters in four to seven areas, at distances ranging from a few yards to several kilometers from his farmstead. Such gardening predominates in the Andean mountains, at least in numbers of cultivators. The least productive form of food production, such gardening absorbs the energies of the vast majority of the rural populace.

The serf was inefficient not only because he was ignorant but because he lacked the motivation to be productive. Almost the only property he could accumulate was livestock and a few changes of homespun clothing in the local traditional style. To own and pasture animals on most manors, he had to pay a grazing fee in cash or labor. Owning animals gained a serf social prestige and economic power. Livestock could be sold at almost any time for cash because of the constant urban demand for meat. The serf who had cash or livestock could significantly ameliorate his position on a manor, at least as long as he escaped managerial notice or wrath. He could dominate others who did not own any livestock by lending them oxen for plowing or cash to pay for marriages, cures, and funerals. The serf borrower accepted socioeconomic subservience to the lender, responding to demands for help with the lender's gardening rather than risk making himself ineligible for future loans.

The manorial system exemplified by Vicos included at least two other features that influenced agricultural development. Parish priest and landlord typically charged a group of local serf authorities with responsibility for everyday religious instruction and even some rituals. In addition, landlords held these same serf authorities responsible for carrying out certain kinds of maintenance and repairs—to the chapel, to bridges, even to roads. Other repairs were made during the serfs' obligatory work days. If manor maintenance was neglected, the results were serious; for example, farm-to-market access roads developed hard, high centers fatal to motor vehicles, and prehistoric terraces collapsed for lack of annual renewal.

Manorial production for the commercial market was reduced further by systematic theft. Even after intervention began at Vicos, the serfs reburied half the potato yield for their wives to glean later, and women who shelled maize left the warehouses with their pockets bulging. Thievery stemmed from the serf's view that he competed with the manor for a relatively fixed amount of agricultural production from manorial fields. The Vicos subculture emphasized doing someone else out of his share for one's own benefit, instead of augmenting production so as to increase the supply of food and other scarce goods. Consequently, serfs stole from one another as well as from the estate. They beseiged manorial overseers to adjudicate disputes concerning ownership of rustled livestock or damage to crops caused by strayed (or deliberately misherded) animals. At harvest time, Vicosinos erected tiny thatched huts near their crops; here they spent the night guarding the mature products against man—and stayed awake during the day to drive birds out of the grain fields.

No matter how restrictive the economic situation, the serf had some need to obtain goods not produced on the manor. To purchase *coca;* salt, pepper, distilled liquor, cloth, and festive bread, and to pay for services, the serf had to sell something on the outside or work for wages. Typically protein food sales constituted the most important source of cash. Livestock, chickens and other barnyard fowl, eggs, and cheese were sold, while Vicosinos consumed a largely vegetarian diet. Guinea pigs furnished most of the animal protein they consumed.

To earn cash, serfs tried to find work outside the manor on days that were not taken up with obligatory labor. But, because they were unskilled and because there were not enough jobs to go around, even when they did work they earned very little. Furthermore, while the able-bodied men were working or seeking jobs outside the manor, the cultivation of their subsistence plots was left to the women and children. Since they worked the plots at something less than optimal levels, productivity remained low.

In sum, members of manorial labor forces lived lives of relative physical and emotional deprivation, in what researchers came to regard as a culture of repression.

EXPERIMENTAL INTERVENTION

Allan R. Holmberg of Cornell University and Carlos Monge Medrano, President of the Peruvian Indian Institute, set up the Cornell–Peru Project late in 1951. This bination organization intervened in the manor serf world at Hacienda Vicos with a twofold objective. First, the project sought to improve the standard of living of the Vicos population. Second, it set out to determine scientifically what actions would be effective in increasing agricultural and human productivity among Indian serfs.

Cornell University leased the manor for a five-year period so as to change the situation of the serfs and thus to change them. Leasing placed the project in the position of manor manager. It might have instituted sweeping innovations by employing the coercive power that manorial managers wielded at the time. In fact, one widely held opinion has it that the project was able to change the Vicos subculture only because it coerced the serfs.

Traditionally, Andean manorial managers employed severe sanctions. The manors operated private jails, and overseers wielded whips and forceably seized both person and property of serfs. The national policemen were at the beck and call of the landlords and leasing exploiters. And the national judiciary, which was drawn largely from the landed elite, cooperated with manorial managers to suppress serf resistance to domination.

In contrast, members of the Cornell–Peru Project seldom directly coerced anyone, even though they occupied a social role that had inherent coercive power. Power of another kind constituted the key to the project's success in changing the Vicos subculture. The project eschewed power that was backed up by severe deprivation and instead relied on the power of persuasion.

The project director chose to persuade serfs to change by enlightening them, educating them, and giving them new experiences. The project exposed Vicosinos to egalitarian and decision-making experiences that afforded them new knowledge with which to perceive new needs and desires and fashion novel ways of satisfying both.

Questioning by project staff early revealed that the Vicosinos did not particularly object to working the obligatory three days weekly, but that they did regard as extremely irksome the additional unpaid assignments as stableboy, houseboy, nursemaid, cook, and so on that were traditionally imposed by manorial managers. The project director therefore abolished that form of unrecompensed service and hired Vicosinos to perform such tasks for wages when needed. The director retained the pattern of obligatory labor for four reasons: (1) to keep social transition somewhat gradual, (2) to allow commercial fields to function as demonstration plots for gardening practices previously unknown to the serfs, (3) to produce additional capital for reinvestment in local improvements, and (4) to permit him to train serfs in social decision-making behavior with which they were unfamiliar. Thus, when innovations in crop production technology were introduced on the Vicos commercial fields, the specter of coercive power brought ready serf acceptance. The project undertook, however, to persuade serfs—not coerce them—to apply those innovations to their own fields.

The Vicosinos could easily have ignored new crop-growing techniques as something that those apparently rich and slightly crazy *gringos* could afford to use on commercial fields, but that poor and uneducated Indian serfs could not. The project therefore offered improved seed potatoes, fertilizer, and appropriate fungicides and insecticides to serfs who would agree to try them on their own garden plots on a sharecropping basis. Because they suffered recurrent crop failures, the Vicosinos had at times obtained new seed from local merchants by sharecropping on terms fairly disadvantageous to them. The project allowed

Vicos gardeners to keep a larger portion of the harvest than had local merchants, and the charge was high enough to convince the Indians that the offer was serious and not foolish.

One rule that was put into effect early was that those using new techniques for the first time do so under project supervision. Peruvian anthropologist Mario C. Vázquez assumed the role of agricultural instructor and supervisor. Every day for several months during the first season he devoted nearly full time to visiting 17 cooperating serf potato growers. A similar procedure was repeated during the next four growing seasons.

The supervised credit program of the Ministry of Agriculture and the Agricultural Development Bank continued instruction in modern crop production after 1956. The bank began to lend money to Vicos for crop production each year it was required. A decade after initial intervention, efficiency reached the point where knowledge of modern potato production techniques became generalized among Vicos "new peasants," and in 1962 they purchased their own land.

The increased productivity of the Vicosinos can be measured, at least roughly. When intervention began in 1952, only 7.7 percent of the serf families at Vicos owned 11 or more head of livestock. Vicosinos viewed 11 head as a sufficient number of animals to give a family effective freedom of economic decision making plus power over less well-off families. Within a decade, some 22.3 percent (103 of 461 families of new peasants) averaged a cash income of $36.04 per season by selling home-grown potatoes on the national wholesale market through the community organization. These same families also sold additional potatoes, and more families sold tubers on local and regional markets. Thus truck farming competed with livestock as the main source of cash income, and the proportion of well-to-do Indians had at least tripled. In other words, mountain peasant truck gardening in Vicos not only became increasingly commercialized from 1952 to 1962, but also specialized in producing a single cash crop just as plantations did in Peru's irrigated, well-developed coastal valleys. (In the Ica Valley, for example, farmers planted 81.8 percent of the cultivated area to cotton and 6 percent to grapes in 1956).

Although the Cornell–Peru Project staff avoided wielding power backed by severe deprivation within Vicos, the fact that the project occupied a potentially powerful position was of fundamental importance for Vicos self-determination. The project was in a position to exclude other wielders of power from Vicos long enough to allow the former Indian serfs to accumulate economic and political power sufficient to make them capable of defending themselves. By establishing its power domain over Vicos, the project excluded other power domains that traditionally weighed upon the Vicosinos. By asserting the legitimacy of its power over Vicos serfs, even without making much use of it, the project allowed them enough freedom of choice and freedom of action to achieve meaningful liberty as a community of cooperating new peasants.

The Cornell–Peru Project power domain expelled from Vicos for five years the traditional renter, who was concerned with obtaining maximum profits without regard for conserving either human or natural resources. The project power domain brought conservation-minded scientific managers to initiate forestation as well as to teach Vicosinos how to bolster their crop production. In large measure that power domain also excluded literate non-Indian mercantile exploiters of rural Indians.

Following the projects' five-year change program, the Peruvian Indian Institute prevented the return of Vicos to an exploiter who submitted the highest bid at public auction for the privilege of profiting from Vicos land and people for a period of years. This protection left the Vicosinos free to run their own community production enterprise until 1962, when they purchased Vicos. With that purchase the Vicosinos acquired most of the attributes of power that accompany land ownership in Peru. At the same time, they still benefited from a measure of central government protection against would-be provincial exploiters, at the cost of some exploitation by low-level bureaucrats.

Experimental intervention by social scientists allowed the one-time serfs of Vicos a decade of cumulative enlightenment and experience in the democratic conduct of their own affairs, including a large crop-growing business. During this decade they developed into a technologically competent peasant production unit not insignificant in its contribution to the total national product. Intervention guided Vicosinos in establishing direct relationships—like those of other citizens of Peru—with national institutions such as the armed forces, civilian government ministries, and courts, ending manorial control of nearly all aspects of life except marketing.

From 1957 to 1962, the Vicos community production enterprise hired independent truckers to carry its potatoes to market. Then it purchased its own truck to symbolize its newly won freedom and to allow the shipment of produce without delay when price quotations were highest. Several years of experience with hiring truck drivers and mechanics outside Vicos convinced the governing council that its truck purchase was a premature venture into mechanization, and it reverted to the earlier type of trucking arrangement.

A decade after initial intervention, not only had the proportion of well-off Vicosinos greatly increased, but the general standard of living had risen markedly. The project director had founded a school hot lunch program that introduced eggs and tropical fruits into the diet, as well as a manor garden demonstration program that materially augmented the amount of green leafy vegetables grown and consumed locally. In addition, more than a hundred new peasant families earning almost $40 in potato sales per season grew them on fields that had not been productive enough to feed the serfs in 1951. By the time they purchased their land, the Vicos new peasants marketed first- and second-grade tubers only, consuming third-grade potatoes they grew or received in payment for their labor on the community's fields. The community also grew grain adequate to supply Vicos internal demand, charging nominal prices. Thus Vicosinos improved their diet and at the same time lessened their dependence on town merchants, who had charged the impoverished serfs high prices for grain in the past.

While over a fifth of the new peasants sold potatoes in Lima, many Vicosinos continued to sell all their truck produce on the regional and local markets. Some rode tramp trucks along the highway to Huaraz, the departmental capital. Others kept a social anchor out against adversity by maintaining their ritual kinship ties with merchants in Marcará. Strikingly, a decade after intervention, Vicos new peasants not only produced enough to feed themselves, but were able to decide for themselves whether to sell locally, regionally, or nationally.

While the Vicosinos were paying off half their mortgage in three annual installments, they encountered competition from coastal plantations that kept their potatoes in cold storage and brought them to market at the same time as the Vicos crop. The new peasants then began to diversify their truck gardening by growing maize.

Even during the initial five-year experimental intervention, Vicosinos began to sell garden produce for cash. Ever since then, buying and selling commodities for cash has been the Vicos norm. Cash has been the means of escape from the traditional Indian subservience and interpersonal dependence that characterizes the manorial system. In the Andes, social subservience has long involved personal service. The serf or peasant with cash need no longer pay with personal service for favors rendered. For example, a poor Vicosino had had to beg cattle owners to stake their animals on his fields because he could not otherwise fertilize his crops. This kept him under the domination of the few well-to-do cattle owners. But within a decade after intervention the Vicos new peasant was selling his field crops and could purchase fertilizer with cash. This freed him of the need to plead for favors that would later have to be paid for with a measure of his freedom. In a parallel social change, a Vicosino who owns no oxen can now hire them for cash when needed, rather than beg their use at the owner's convenience. For several years during the 1960s a Vicos gardener could on occasion even borrow the powerful tractor given to the community by members of the U.S. National Farmers Union.

The Cornell–Peru Project began teaching women to sew on machines in 1960. Increased purchasing power led to the acquisition of more than twenty new sewing machines. Owners purchased dry goods directly from Huaraz merchants, at times for wholesale prices. The Peruvian National Plan for Integrating the Aboriginal Population made sewing instruction a continuing part of its adult education program in Vicos. Consequently, Vicos dependence upon mestizo tailors and seamstresses diminished rapidly during the 1960s as more and more women learned to make clothing. This trend directly decreased Vicos subservience to mestizo artisans as well as to actual or potential employers, whose wages Vicosinos needed less and less.

Interpersonal relations between Vicosinos became much more egalitarian as intervention converted serfs into peasants. The mestizo population outside Vicos also simultaneously accorded increasing respect to Vicosinos as the latter acquired technical skills in crop production, new affluence, formal education, and, in 1962, land.

Structurally, technical and legal changes resulting from intervention at Vicos ended its long history as a hacienda. Intervention resulted neither in expropriation nor in forceful seizure that could have brought about violent repression. Nor did intervention result in giving Vicos to its inhabitants. They bought it; and instead of dividing the land up into smallholdings, the Vicosinos elected to maintain the estate as a commercial production unit, communally managed and worked for the common good.

RESEARCH DESIGN FOR POLICY SCIENCE PROTOTYPING

Were the sort of social and economic transition that experimental intervention by social scientists triggered in Vicos to spread widely over the Andean region, many of its gravest political and social difficulties would be likely to disappear. Were the agrarian problems of Andean republics resolved, the region's whole population could participate in the processes that produce an industrialized, relatively affluent, and in many ways more egalitarian society such as is evolving in coastal cities and even among coastal and some jungle-colony proletariats. Experimental anthropological intervention at Vicos, even though it provided only a single prototype, generated tremendous policy science implications.

The Cornell–Peru Project demonstrated that a strategic assault on the regionally common problem of less-than-subsistence production by serfs and peasants, planned and led by social scientists, could rapidly increase such production. Intervention at Vicos showed that a change from less-than-subsistence production to growing a commercially marketable surplus could be made in five years by (1) teaching gardeners new technical skills and (2) augmenting production incentives through land tenure reforms that converted serfs into peasants who produced in their own interest.

Anthropological intervention at Vicos indicated that this transition could be achieved for a development investment of thousands of dollars, rather than the millions required for irrigation projects that benefit a few score farmers. Further, the Vicos program involved the producers in none of the human travail of massive jungle-area resettlement attempts.

Initial intervention at Vicos squarely confronted the erroneous assumption that agricultural extension efforts reaching plantations somehow automatically trickled out to Indian producers across rigid social, ethnic, and linguistic barriers. By focusing on augmenting local productivity while launching a full-scale elementary school system, the Cornell–Peru Project also avoided creating the urban problems that result from forcing large numbers of cultivators off their land before they were educated for industrial employment or prepared for urban life. Experimental social scientific intervention at Vicos won immediate regional attention because it asserted that social and technological means were already available to deal with many of the social and economic problems that plagued the Andean area.

The anthropological intervention in Vicos has several kinds of significance for areas outside the central Andes. The successful transformation of starving Vicosinos into commercial truck-gardeners holds out hope for any country whose food deficits stem from grossly unequal social structures that keep peasants or serfs so subordinated as to have little motivation to produce more by acquiring technical skills.

The pattern of experimental intervention at Vicos provides a practical model for generating funds for rural community development while augmenting urban food supplies and helping to keep food prices low.

In scientific terms, experimental intervention in Vicos proved feasible one prototype for an extremely rare but methodologically desirable research design. Unlike the vast majority of social scientists, who must attempt to identify causation *ex post facto*, Cornell–Peru Project researchers knew with certainty what caused numerous changes among Vicosinos. As participant interveners, the researchers themselves carried out or instituted actions whose consequences they first predicted and then observed. Anthropological intervention in Vicos provided, in other words, the nearest approach to truly experimental research design that social scientists seem likely to achieve for some time to come.

In policy science terms, the intervention further demonstrated that such elaborate research designing by social scientists becomes feasible, with marked direct benefits for the population studied and for policy makers, when exceptionally visionary policy makers such as Carlos Monge Medrano cooperate in the design.

SUGGESTED READING

The references utilized in this paper may be found with numerous additional guides to the reports of the Cornell–Peru Project in the bibliography appearing in *Peasants, Power, and Applied Social Change: Vicos as a Model*, edited by Henry F. Dobyns, Paul L. Doughty, and Harold D. Lasswell (Sage Publications, Beverly Hills, Cal., 1971). The volume itself reports much additional information about the course of the intervention at Vicos.

Some Effects of Population Growth on Latin America's Economy

ALFONSO GONZALEZ

The "population explosion" and resultant problems were recognized in most Latin American countries several years ago, especially in connection with the "Alice-in-Wonderland effect"—impressive gross gains in food production, industrialization, housing, welfare, and other areas of social development have been more than offset by increases in population, resulting in net losses on a per capita basis. Gonzalez's analysis of demographic obstacles to development is forceful in its emphasis on ample and pertinent statistics rather than rhetoric. In documenting the nature and extent of such problems, this approach complements those of Lewis, Mitchell and Schatan, Mangin, and others.

This paper has been substantially revised for this volume from an earlier version, "Some Effects of Population Growth on Latin America's Economy," which appeared in *Journal of Inter-American Studies* IX (1967), 22–42. Copyright © by the Pan American Foundation. The present version, updated by the author to include data through 1970, is printed here by permission of the author and The University of Miami Press.

Alfonso Gonzalez is Associate Professor of Geography at the University of Calgary in Canada. He has conducted research on population, land-use, and socioeconomic development in Mexico. He not only writes on these subjects, but has also been involved in related action projects.

The stability of Latin America rests essentially on the solution of two interrelated problems—population growth and economic development. A further corollary, and an extremely significant one, will be the social distribution of the benefits accruing from economic betterment. Latin America is both the fastest growing world region in population and also the most advanced of the underdeveloped regions of the world (in terms of the death rate, literacy, and per capita income). It is also the only region of the underdeveloped world that had evolved from political colonial status prior to World War II. This region, therefore, has had the longest history of endeavoring to solve directly many of the problems that plague the more than 70 percent of mankind that lives in the underdeveloped countries.

Since mortality is lower in Latin America than in the other underdeveloped regions, and birth rates vary less than death rates, the rate of natural increase is higher in this region than elsewhere. Latin America serves as a harbinger of conditions that will soon prevail in the other underdeveloped regions as modern medical technology is diffused and mortality rates continue to decline. The pressure of population on resources will increase in all the underdeveloped regions because mortality continues to decline, resulting in an ever widening gap between births and deaths in the absence of significant fertility control.[1]

In mid-1970 the estimated population of Latin America was 283 million, with a forecast for 1980 ranging from a low of 362 million to a high (based on continuing demographic trends) of 383 million.[2] This means that by the end of the century the population of Latin America may be between 532 million and 686 million. The range of population estimates varies with the assumptions regarding the timing of declines in fertility, because a continued trend in the decline of mortality is highly likely. The fundamental reason for this rapid increase in population is the same factor that has accounted for the rapid increase in the world's population since the advent of the industrial revolution, viz., control of mortality. In the 1945–1950 period the crude death rate (number of deaths per 1000 population) for Latin America was 17–19 and by 1955–1960 it had declined to 13–15. Further but slower declines continued into the 1960s, with an average of 10–11 in the early part of the decade and 9 by 1970.[3] This represents an overall decline of approximately 40 percent in the post-World War II period. Since the crude birth rate (number of births per 1000 population) has remained consistently high (41–43), the rate of population growth has increased from 2.5 percent annually in the late 1940s to about 3 percent in the 1960s (Table 1). At present growth rates the population of Latin America will double in less than a quarter century. The fastest growing world subregion is undoubtedly mainland Middle America, where every country in the 1963–1968 period increased at least 3 percent annually and the overall sub-regional average was 3.5 percent (meaning that the population will double within two decades).

TABLE 1. Latin America: Population Characteristics

	Population(m) 1970[a]	Est. 1980[b]	Current % Annual Pop. Increase[a]	Birth Rate[abc]	Death Rate[abc]	Infant Mortality Rate[abc]
Mexico	50.7	71.4	3.4	43	9	63
Guatemala	5.1	6.9	2.9	45	16	92
Salvador	3.4	4.9	3.4	47	13	63
Honduras	2.7	3.7	3.4	49	16	44
Nicaragua	2.0	2.8	3.0	47	16	55
Costa Rica	1.8	2.7	3.8	45	7	70
Panama	1.5	2.0	3.3	40	10	43
Cuba	8.4	10.1	1.9	28	8	38
Dominican Rep.	4.3	6.2	3.4	48	15	80
Haiti	5.2	6.8	2.5	45	20	190
Venezuela	10.8	15.0	3.4	46	9	46
Colombia	21.4	31.4	3.4	44	11	78
Ecuador	6.1	8.4	3.4	47	13	90
Peru	13.6	18.5	3.1	44	12	62
Bolivia	4.6	6.0	2.4	44	20	77
Paraguay	2.4	3.5	3.4	45	12	84
Chile	9.8	12.2	2.3	33	10	100
Argentina	24.3	28.2	1.5	22	9	58
Uruguay	2.9	3.3	1.2	24	9	43
Brazil	93.0	124.0	2.8	39	10	93
LATIN AMERICA[d]	283	378.4[e]	2.9	38	9	81

[a] *World Population Data Sheet:* 1970. Population Reference Bureau, Inc., April 1970.

[b] *Datos Básicos de Población en América Latina,* 1970. Pan American Union, Department of Social Affairs, Washington, D.C.

[c] *Demographic Yearbook:* 1968. United Nations, Department of Economic and Social Affairs.

[d] Totals usually include figures for other territories in addition to the countries listed in the table.

[e] *World Population Prospects as Assessed in* 1963. United Nations, Department of Economic and Social Affairs Population Studies No. 41, 1966, Tables A3.8, A3.2.

Improved health conditions have increased life expectancy over much of tropical Latin America (to about 61 years at present-day trends); if projected to the end of the century, this would increase to 73 years (approximately present-day levels in the advanced regions of the world). The Latin American infant mortality rate (number of deaths of infants less than one year of age per 1000 live births), which in combination with life expectancy at birth comprises the best index of health conditions, has improved from about 102 in the late 1940s to about 63 in the mid-1960s.[4]

The differences in natality between Latin America and the other underdeveloped regions are insignificant, especially if the low fertility countries of Latin America (viz., Argentina and Uruguay) are discounted. However, the mortality rate of Latin America overall is from one-third to one-half less than in the Afro-

Asian regions, and it is this differential that accounts for Latin America's greater rate of population growth. The Afro-Asian underdeveloped regions are increasing at more than 2 percent annually while Latin America is increasing at about 3 percent. Current Afro-Asian mortality rates prevailed in Latin America during the 1940s. Mortality in Latin America began to decline slowly about 1920, with the post-World War I health programs, but declined precipitately with World War II programs, and the decrease was especially marked during the 1950s. The decline in mortality was most significant among the younger age groups due to the application of programs combating infectious diseases and malnutrition (especially among children).

The factors behind the high fertility of Latin America are readily apparent: (a) The large family is an ingrained trait of the national ethos,* (b) women in reproductive ages represent a relatively high proportion of the total population, (c) women enter consensual union at an early age, (d) a large percentage of women are married (either legally or by common-law), and (e) family planning is rare—even among the urban and better-educated sectors of the population.

The rate of population growth in the near future will be at least as great as at present because of the presumed continued decline in mortality over practically all of Latin America. Fertility, on the other hand, is under effective control only in Argentina and Uruguay, with significant declines now discernible in Cuba and Chile.

DEMOGRAPHIC CONSEQUENCES

There are a number of demographic consequences of considerable importance to economic development resulting from past and present population characteristics. These features are also to be found in the other underdeveloped world regions. One of these consequences is the youth of the population, resulting from high natality. Slightly more than 40 percent of the population are under 15 years of age, but, due to relatively high mortality, only about 3 percent of the population are over 65. The net result is that only about 55 percent of the population of Latin America are in the economically productive ages, in contrast to about 60–65 percent in the developed countries. Only in Argentina and Uruguay, where birth rates have been less than 30 since at least the 1930s, are about two-thirds of the population in the productive ages. In Cuba and Chile, where fertility is intermediate between the high levels prevailing in most of Latin America and the low levels of Argentina and Uruguay, slightly less than three-fifths of the population are in the productive ages. In the remaining countries the proportion is 55 percent or less. The result is that in most Latin American countries only about one-third of the population are economically active, whereas in the developed countries of the world the proportion is 40–45 percent. Thereby, the dependency ratio (number of persons dependent upon each thousand of the economically productive age population) is higher in Latin America (and underdeveloped countries generally) than it is in the

* [Editor's note: The widespread positive evaluation of a large family among Latin Americans has been questioned only recently (but convincingly). The success of birth control clinics in a few countries seems to substantiate massive evidence based on attitude surveys indicating that many adults no longer want large families.]

developed regions. Even more critical is that the dependency ratio in Latin America will actually increase from a 1960 level of 818 (contrasted with about 500–650 in developed countries) to 855–887 in the 1970–80 decade.[5]

A further demographic handicap that Latin America is facing, and it will become even more severe in the near future, is that increasingly larger groups of males will enter the labor force so that employment opportunities should be provided. In the period 1965–1980, the labor force in Latin America will expand from 77 million to 120 million. During that period, nearly 3 million jobs will have to be created annually if unemployment is not to mount even higher and pose an increasing threat.[6]

The youthful structure of the population virtually ensures a continued high rate of population increase in the near future. By 1975 there will be 50–60 percent more women of childbearing age than in 1960, so that, unless social patterns change significantly by that time, the absolute population growth (as well as the rate of growth) will be prodigious.[7]

POPULATION PRESSURE ON RESOURCES

The pressure of a rapidly expanding population is being exerted with increasing impact on the resource base of Latin America. This pressure of absolute numerical increase is being compounded by the "revolution of rising expectations" that is sweeping the world. The demand for a better livelihood now is augmenting the rising demand that results from demographic increase, and the combination of these two elements is severely straining the limited resources of an already politically unstable region.

The rate of economic expansion in Latin America overall varies significantly according to sectors, and Latin America does not compare favorably with the rate of economic development in the underdeveloped world generally (Table 2). The one major category in which Latin America clearly excels is the rate of population growth, and this obviously has a detrimental effect in terms of production increments on a per capita basis.

AGRICULTURE

Population pressure on available resources in Latin America is most critically apparent in agriculture. Although the density of population based on cultivated land for Latin America is comparable to that for the world (332 inhabitants per square kilometer of cultivated land in 1962, compared with the world average of 340), this relatively low figure for Latin America is due essentially to low densities prevailing in the three leading agricultural countries of the region (Brazil, Mexico, and Argentina). The median density for Latin America (479–500) is between one-third and one-half greater than the world average, and this density is exceeded by few of the major agricultural countries of the world (viz., Japan, United Kingdom, West Germany, United Arab Republic, China, Indonesia, East Germany, and the Philippines).[8]

The actual pressure of population on the cultivated land in Latin America becomes even clearer if consideration is given to the yields obtained from the land under cultivation. Although the yields obtained in Latin America are the highest of the underdeveloped world (using cereals as an index and excluding

TABLE 2. Population & Economic Indexes: 1967 (1960 = 100)

	Latin America	Underdeveloped World	Developed World	WORLD
Population[1]	122	116	108	114
Gross Domestic Product[2]	139	138	140	140
Agriculture[3]	122	120	120	119
Manufacturing[4]	143	148	148	148
Foreign Trade Exports[5]	127	146	162	158

[1] Based on data from *Demographic Yearbook:* 1968. United Nations, Department of Economic and Social Affairs, Table 1.

[2] Based on data from *Statistical Yearbook:* 1968. United Nations, Department of Economic and Social Affairs, Table 4. Excludes Communist countries of Eastern Hemisphere.

[3] Based on data from *Production Yearbook:* 1968. Food and Agriculture Organization of the United Nations, Table 7. Excludes China (Mainland).

[4] Based on data from *Statistical Yearbook:* 1968, op. cit., Table 9. Excludes Communist countries of Eastern Hemisphere.

[5] Ibid., Table 14. Excludes Communist countries of Eastern Hemisphere.

Japan from the Orient), Latin American yields are now significantly below the world average and are only about 50–60 percent of those obtained in the highly advanced world regions (Table 3). The net result is that the number of inhabitants per unit of arable land (and giving weight to yields) in Latin America is about comparable to that of the Middle East, and these two regions are exceeded only by the Orient among the world's regions.

The cropland-yield densities (Table 4) prevailing in virtually all the Latin

TABLE 3. World Regions: Comparative Population & Agricultural Data (1967)*

	Population (m)	Arable Land (m ha)	Arable Land Density[a]	Cereal Yields (100kg/ha)[b]	Arable Yield Density[c]
Latin America	259.3	119	218	13.84	252
Middle East	213.9	108	198	10.05	315
Orient	1876.6	384	489	14.15	553
Africa (Sub-Saharan)	225.2	182	124	8.78	226
Europe	451.3	150	301	25.16	191
U.S.S.R.	235.5	242	97	27.50	120
Anglo-America	219.7	220	100	12.96	58
Oceania	18.1	42	43	11.74	59
WORLD	3499.6	1447	242	16.01	242

[a] Number of inhabitants per square kilometer of arable land.

[b] Average of 1966–67.

[c] Figure for "Arable Land Density" is divided by ratio of the region's cereal yields to the world cereal yields.

* Based on data from *Food and Agriculture Production Yearbook:* 1968.

TABLE 4. Latin America: Economic Characteristics

	% of Economic Active Pop. in Agric. (1965)[1]	Cropland-Yield Density[2]	Calories per Capita (1966)[3]	GNP per Capita (1967, US $)[4]	GDP Growth Annually per Capita (%) (1961–69)[5]	Agric. Prod. 1967–69[6] (1957–59 = 100) Total	Per Capita	Mfg. Prod. 1968[7] (1958 = 100)
Mexico	52	428	2550	490	3.2	147	105	223
Guatemala	64	629	2220	310	1.9	159	116	153
Salvador	59	614	1840	270	2.2	139	101	229
Honduras	65	448	2010	240	2.0	143	103	176[a]
Nicaragua	59	868	2350	360	3.4	182	134	181
Costa Rica	48	583	2610	410	2.3	146	103	181[a]
Panama	43	753	2500	550	4.3	148	108	335
Cuba	39	445	2730[b]	330		103[c]	84[c]	
Dominican Republic	57	582	2290	260	−0.8	104	74	126[a]
Haiti	79	2684	1780[b]	70	−0.6	81	64	126[a]
Venezuela	29	768	2490	880	1.1	170	120	215
Colombia	47	630	2200	300	1.5	127	93	163
Ecuador	52	626	2020	210	1.1	145	105	212
Peru	47	827	2340	350	2.3	120	90	225
Bolivia	65	992	1980	170	2.6	111	89	203
Paraguay	51	564	2520[d]	220	1.4	123	92	109
Chile	26	488	2830	470	1.7	115	92	174
Argentina	18	179	2920	800	1.9	115	97	126
Uruguay	17	430	3170	550	−1.1	107	94	100
Brazil	48	303	2690	250	1.9	137	102	203
LATIN AMERICA	48[e]	382	2420[f]	320[f]	1.9	134[g]	100[g]	203[f]

[1] *Food and Agriculture Organization Production Yearbook*: 1968, Tables 5, 6.

[2] Number of inhabitants per square kilometer of cropland divided by the ratio of cereal yields obtained to the average world cereal yields. Cropland computed from the summation of crop data available in *Food and Agriculture Organization Production Yearbook*: 1963.

[3] *Food and Agriculture Organization Production Yearbook*: 1968, Table 136.

[4] 1970 *World Population Data Sheet*. Population Reference Bureau, Inc., April 1970. Data obtained from International Bank for Reconstruction and Development.

[5] *Socio-Economic Progress in Latin America*. Social Progress Trust Fund, 9th Annual Report (1969), Table 1 (p. 2).

[6] Based on data from: *The Agriculture Situation in the Western Hemisphere*. Review of 1969 and Outlook for 1970. United States Department of Agriculture, Economic Research Service, Washington, D.C., 1970, Table 2.

[7] Based on data from: *Statistical Bulletin for Latin America*. Vol. III, No. 2 (September 1966), Table 27; Vol. V, No. 2 (September 1968), Table 16; *Socio-Economic Progress in Latin America*, op. cit., Table 5 (p. 15).

[a] 1961 = 100.

[b] 1959–61. *Western Hemisphere Agricultural Situation*. Review of 1966 and Outlook for 1967. Department of Agriculture, Economic Research Service, Washington, D.C., 1967. Probably a significant decline has occurred during the 1960s.

[c] 1966–67 (1956–57 = 100). Based on data from *Food and Agriculture Organization Production Yearbook*: 1968, Tables 10, 12.

[d] 1960–62.

[e] % agricultural population of the total population.

[f] Median.

[g] Except Cuba.

American countries (the notable exceptions are Argentina and Brazil) are considerably above the Latin American average. In four Latin American countries (Haiti, Bolivia, Nicaragua, and Peru) the cropland-yield density exceeds that of the most dense of the major agricultural countries of the world (Sudan: 791). An additional eight Latin American countries have a density exceeding that of the tenth leading major world country in density (Pakistan: 521). It is clear that population pressure on agricultural productivity in Latin America is already formidable.

Agricultural development is being given considerable attention widely in Latin America, and one very fundamental reason is in order to cope with the rapidly expanding population. In addition, the rising expectations for greater food consumption, and the necessity for greater export-surplus in order to secure foreign exchange to further economic development, give rise to further pressures for increased agricultural productivity. Broadly speaking, increased productivity is being achieved in Latin America by increasing both cultivated land and yields, with the former more significant.

The area devoted to the major crops in Latin America increased overall between the 1948–1952 period and 1962–1963 by 32.2 percent, somewhat less than the overall population increment (38.3 percent) for the same period.[9] The cultivated area of cereals (which account for approximately 56 percent of all the cultivated area in Latin America) increased by 58.8 percent (comparable to the growth of population, 58 percent), while overall production increased by 65.3 percent (between the 1948–1952 and 1966–1967 periods). The improvement in agricultural yields overall in Latin America has been relatively small in the post-World War II period. The yields for maize and wheat (the two leading crops by area) increased by one-quarter; in contrast, in the same period, maize yields in Anglo-America nearly doubled and in Europe they increased by a third, while wheat yields increased by nearly one-half in Anglo-America and by nearly two-thirds in Europe. Generally, the greatest improvements in agricultural yields in the post-World War II period have occurred in the more advanced regions of the world. The net result is that Latin America's maize yields have declined relatively, from 68 percent of the world's average in the 1948–1952 period to 57 percent in 1966–1967.

The endeavor to increase yields can be measured by the notable increase in commercial fertilizer consumption in Latin America. The use of nitrate, phosphate, and potash fertilizers increased 6–8 times between the 1948–1952 and 1966–1968 periods in Latin America. The production of commercial fertilizer in Latin America remains insignificant by world standards, however, and is virtually limited to Chile, Peru, Mexico, and Brazil. The use of commercial fertilizers is still abysmally low in Latin America compared with the more advanced regions, so that West Germany, with only about one-fifteenth the arable land of Latin America, consumes nearly the same quantity of nitrates, more phosphates, and about two and a half times the potash that Latin America does. The same holds true for the mechanization of agriculture; the number of tractors in all Latin America quadrupled between 1950 and 1967, yet West Germany alone has nearly two and one-half times more tractors.

The combined increase in cultivated area and improvement in yields resulted in a notable increase in crop production since the 1950s in Latin America.

Between the 1948–1952 and 1966–1967 periods, maize production more than doubled and comparable or greater relative increments in production occurred for rice, cassava, tomatoes, beans, bananas, the oilseeds, and the palms. With regard to livestock, only swine have increased faster than the human population, and meat production throughout Latin America has fallen in per capita terms.

The result is that overall net agricultural production between the 1948–1952 and the 1966–1967 periods increased in Latin America by two-thirds. This rate slightly exceeds the world overall increment, and this prodigious increase represents an average annual increment of 3.3 percent in agricultural production.[10] Of the major Latin American countries, Mexico and Venezuela exhibited the greatest average annual increments (5.1 percent) and would rank among the world's leaders in the rate of agricultural expansion. (By comparison, the average annual increment in the United States during World War II when governmental policies encouraged augmented production was less than 3 percent.[11] Despite the rapid expansion of agricultural production in Latin America, population growth was such that the increased annual agricultural output *per capita* during the same period amounted to only 0.5 percent. In a number of countries there was an actual decline in per capita output, viz., the Dominican Republic, Uruguay, Chile, Paraguay, and probably Cuba and Haiti. During the decade of the 1960s total agricultural production and population growth expanded overall at comparable rates; i.e., 3 percent annually.[12]

Despite the overall rapid expansion of agricultural production during the 1950s and 1960s, the agricultural sector has only been able to maintain parity with population growth during the period. Therefore, in the late 1960s food production per capita in Latin America overall was little different from that of the 1950s. No other underdeveloped region is performing so poorly in agricultural output with relation to population growth as is Latin America. The fundamental reason is that population growth is more rapid in Latin America than elsewhere, so that improvements in agricultural output are instantaneously eroded away by further population increases.

Several Latin American countries have even suffered a significant reduction in per capita food production during this period; the situation is most acute in Uruguay, the Dominican Republic, Cuba, El Salvador, and Haiti, and it is only somewhat better in Chile, Paraguay, and Peru. The greatest relative improvements (despite large population increments) have occurred in Ecuador, Nicaragua, Mexico, Venezuela, and Bolivia.

The pressure of population can be seen in the more rapid increments accruing to crop and livestock production in Latin America destined for domestic consumption rather than for the export market.[13] This has necessitated a curtailment of the expansion of the export trade and constitutes a serious problem for Latin America's further economic development.[14] This lagging sector restricts the accumulation of necessary foreign exchange and presents serious balance-of-payments problems to most of the countries of the region.

In comparing the period around 1960 with that of 1966 (data for Cuba, Haiti, and Paraguay are not available) only six countries (El Salvador, Honduras, Colombia, Bolivia, Uruguay, and Brazil) experienced a decline in the caloric content of food available per capita.[15] There were eight countries consuming less than 2400 calories per capita daily in 1966, and undoubtedly Haiti must be added to this list (Table 4). (Presumably Cuba should now be added to the food-deficit countries of Latin America.) Only in Uruguay and Argentina is the food consumption level comparable to that of the more advanced regions of the world. Overall for Latin America the daily caloric consumption is probably slightly in excess of 2500 calories, which would represent a deficiency of about 500–600 calories daily in comparison with Anglo-America or Western Europe. In view of the existing sociopolitical instability of the region, it is questionable how long Latin America will be able to endure such food consumption levels (especially in view of the rate of population growth) without serious political upheavals.

INDUSTRY

The pressure of population growth on industrial output (mining, manufacturing, and utilities) is both less critical and less urgent in Latin America. This sector is growing appreciably faster than the population, and, since large segments of the peoples of Latin America are in basically subsistence or local economies, food necessities are of more overriding immediate importance than is access to manufactured goods. However, the industrial sector must maintain a very high rate of expansion in order to ensure employment for the rapidly increasing population. Traditionally, Latin America (like other underdeveloped regions) has been basically agricultural, with about three-fifths of the economically active population engaged in agriculture in the pre-World War II period. However, the proportion had declined to 56 percent overall for Latin America by 1945, and by 1955 agriculture was exceeded by the nonagricultural sectors.[16] In 1965 the nonagricultural sectors accounted for 55 percent of the economically active population. Since World War II the agricultural labor force has been increasing at only one-half the overall rate for the total economically active population. With the agricultural sector declining relatively, and with the labor force increasing annually by between two and three million (probably about one-fifth being females), the burden of employment falls increasingly on the industrial sectors of the economy, especially manufacturing. It is questionable how long the Latin American economies can sustain a relatively high proportion engaged in services, with a relatively small industrial base.

As is the case with the economically active population, so the sector origins of the gross domestic product (GDP) reflect a decreasing share being contributed by agriculture and the opposite trend for manufacturing and (to a much smaller degree) mining. In fact, the latter two activities (along with services) are the only sectors that rather steadily and significantly increased their share of the GDP in Latin America overall during the 1950s.[17] During the 1960s, in a decade of slower economic growth (except for construction), only manufacturing and the utilities were able to significantly increase their share of the GDP.[18]

In Latin America overall, the manufacturing sector exceeded the agricultural beginning in the late 1950s. Manufacturing already contributes a greater share of the GDP than agriculture in Mexico, Cuba, Venezuela, Chile, Argentina, and Uruguay. In both Brazil and Peru, manufacturing was relatively close to parity with agriculture by the mid-1960s.

The industrial sector has been expanding faster in Latin America than the agricultural. Whereas the agricultural sector of the GDP increased overall in Latin America by slightly more than 3.5 percent annually during the 1950s and 1960–1967, the manufacturing sector expanded by 6.8 percent annually during the 1950s and 5.9 percent in the 1960s. All the Latin American countries for which data are available (excludes several small countries plus Cuba) had a more rapid rate of industrial expansion than agricultural growth during both the 1950s and 1960–1967 (except the Dominican Republic for the 1960s).[19] Due to the appreciably greater growth rate, the industrial sector in Latin America has been in a much more favorable relationship to population than has agriculture. During the 1950s all countries attained at least parity between industrial expansion and population growth, and in the 1960s period only Uruguay, Paraguay, and probably the Dominican Republic failed to expand industrially at a rate comparable to the demographic increase.

SOCIAL SERVICES

Improvement in social services was an important cornerstone of the Alliance for Progress, and a change in U.S. policy about 1958 has resulted in considerably expanding social services in Latin America. The betterment of social services can help ameliorate some existing problems should another sector of the economy falter in its developmental plans.

The pressure of population growth, however, aggravates existing pressures on the already meager social services in Latin America. Notable material progress has been made in recent years in education, housing, and public health. Education now accounts for approximately 20 percent of national budgets overall, and public health between 10 and 15 percent. Also many new housing units have been constructed in Latin America due to public, private, and Alliance efforts. The infant mortality rate (probably the best gauge for determining existing medical and health conditions) has declined by as much as one-third between the late 1940s and late 1960s, but still remains three or four times greater than the rate prevailing in the advanced countries of the world. It may take another decade or two for most Latin American countries to attain the level prevailing now in Puerto Rico (less than 30 infant deaths per 1000 live births), which is slightly better than that of the nonwhite population of the United States. No Latin American countries are in that category now (Table 1), but in the 1930s Puerto Rico's infant mortality rate (132 in 1932) was typical of Latin America. Improvements in sanitation and potable water supplies, antimalarial campaigns, health clinics, and other public health measures are undoubtedly having considerable effect in reducing mortality and thereby increasing population totals. But nutritional problems are of a different nature because a fundamental improvement in agriculture is necessary, despite food aid programs. These programs must increase considerably in the future to keep pace with population growth (not to mention improvement in the per capita food consumption), but U.S. domestic policy and foreign assistance have notably decreased the available surplus food stocks in the United States.

Considerable expansion of the educational facilities in Latin America has also occurred in recent years. The elementary school enrollment in Latin America (excludes Cuba) increased from 25 million in 1960 to 41.5 million in 1969.[20]

Despite the very rapid increase (3.2 percent annually) of the school-age population in Latin America, the region overall during the 1960–1969 period was able to increase elementary school enrollments at an 81 percent faster rate. Nevertheless, in 1969 about 40 percent of all children in the elementary school ages (5–14) were still not attending school, and only 20–25 percent of those attending were able to complete the sixth grade. If the very rapid rate of school enrollment expansion continues through the 1970s (more rapid growth is not expected), more than 30 percent of school-age children will still not be attending school by 1980, because of the very rapid population increase. The deficit in higher education is also critical. Latin America has a population about one-quarter larger than that of the United States but has less than a seventh of the students attending universities and advanced technical teaching centers.

A substantial and critical housing deficit also exists in Latin America (probably at least 20 million units), and the housing shortage has been increasing since 1950.[21] The annual rate of new housing construction (for the few countries for which data are available) represents only about 0.5 percent of existing housing units and so is far below the 2–3 percent construction rate that characterizes the advanced countries (which also have far slower rates of population growth). The net result is that the combination of poor existing housing with the rapidly expanding population (especially in urban centers) creates a virtually insurmountable gap between the needs for adequate housing facilities and actual accomplishments. Approximately 3 million units should be constructed annually during the coming decade, and probably only about a third as many are actually being constructed.

ALTERNATIVE POLICIES AND OUTLOOK

Only during four years (1964, 1965, 1968, and 1969) did the Alliance for Progress achieve its objective of an annual per capita product increment of 2.5 percent for Latin America overall despite an annual population growth of 2.9 percent.[22] In the 1961–1969 period only four countries (Panama, Nicaragua, Mexico, and Bolivia) achieved overall the Alliance objective of development growth. The other nations have been economically expanding at less satisfactory rates, with three countries (Haiti, the Dominican Republic, and Uruguay) actually experiencing overall declines in per capita output for the 1960s. Under the stimulus of the Alliance, central planning agencies were established in all Latin American countries.

Industrial growth overall appears to continue at a more satisfactory rate of expansion, with Mexico having achieved an 8.8 percent yearly increment for 1960–1967, the highest rate among the major Latin American countries. Agriculture, however, continues as a major problem area despite a significant production increase during the 1960s. Despite nearly a 15 percent increase in agricultural output since the Alliance began in 1961, per capita food production improved little during the decades because of rapid population growth.

The major endeavor of most Latin American countries is to improve the livelihood of their inhabitants, and with this objective in mind the various governments, with varying degrees of U.S. and international assistance, are attempting to utilize domestic resources more fully to further socioeconomic development. Two general approaches or programs are available to Latin America (and to the other underdeveloped regions) in their process of development: (1) increased productivity (including the application of improved technology)—the objective is to expand and improve the economic base in order to increase the volume of output of goods and services; and (2) population control—the objective is to restrict population so that per capita output will rise more rapidly and increasing productivity will not be nullified by population increases. Heretofore, Latin America has relied almost exclusively on increasing productivity and the application of improved technology as the solution to the problem of living conditions, although it would appear from recent developments that the role of population control may take on added importance.

INCREASED PRODUCTIVITY

Latin America continues to rely on the expansion of the economic base and the application of improved and more advanced methods in order to augment per capita output and thereby to raise the levels of living. Agriculture remains a serious impediment to rapid economic development despite significant increments in production. Much of the increase in agricultural output has been from the increase in cultivated area rather than from higher yields. In the case of maize, by far Latin America's leading crop (accounting for almost one-third of the total cultivated area), about two-thirds of the augmented production between the 1948–1952 and 1966–1967 periods is attributable to increased cultivated area. How long Latin America will be able to expand output in this fashion is questionable, but increasing pressure on the land will force more farmers onto marginal and submarginal lands or into the already overcongested urban centers. Between 1960 and 1970 the urban population of Latin America increased by 4.3 percent annually, representing some of the most rapidly urbanizing areas on earth. In 1965 the urban population of Latin America probably exceeded the rural for the first time.

Food output is currently about keeping pace with population growth and there may be increasing demands in the near future for consumption levels higher than the 2500 calories daily per capita presently available. The crux of the problem remains: to increase land and labor productivity, and this will require considerable outlays of capital and rural credit facilities for improved seed, fertilizers, pesticides, irrigation projects, and the like, along with more widespread training of farmers in more advanced techniques. The incentives under present conditions are inadequate to effectuate large-scale improvements due to fluctuating world commodity prices, heavy indirect taxation of agriculture, direct and indirect governmental price controls, and, the most serious of all, the land tenure system. As of about 1950, only 1.5 percent of Latin American farms accounted for fully 64.9 percent of the total farmland, while 72.6 percent of the farms contained only 3.7 percent of all farmland.[23] The agrarian problem in Latin America involves both attendant problems of latifundia and minifundia. The overall changes of the land tenure system since 1950 (except in Bolivia and Cuba) are insignificant because, despite reform legislation in virtually all the Latin American countries, little land has actually been redistributed (and most of that in Mexico, Bolivia, and Venezuela).

Rural conditions contribute in a major way to the mass migrations into Latin American cities, especially the larger centers. This reduces the agricultural labor supply (in a region where mechanization is not widespread), places greater strain on the remaining farmers to supply the rapidly increasing urban population, and creates serious employment problems in the most politically explosive environment, the cities.

Agricultural output is also closely tied to another major problem sector of the Latin American economy—foreign trade. Overall foreign trade has expanded only slightly faster than population growth, and Latin America's share of world trade has been gradually declining since the 1940s. The export market must expand rapidly in order to sustain a rising import demand of capital equipment so necessary for any further development. Production of agricultural commodities must thereby increase sufficiently to satisfy both the growing domestic market and the necessities of exportation.

Industrial growth appears to present a less pressing problem, although there is doubt whether this sector can expand fast enough to provide employment opportunities for the very rapidly expanding urban populace. Inadequate supplies of capital, skilled labor, and raw materials, along with restricted local markets, will also present problems. However, governmental development emphasis in Latin America is most frequently oriented toward industrialization, and nearly three-quarters of all U.S. direct investments are in the industrial sector (notably mining). Expansion of industrial output will also place increasing pressure on raw material production, and so further restrict the export trade.

Two basic requirements for rapid increase in productivity are capital and education, and the latter is dependent in large part on the former. There are various sources of capital available for Latin America and all are used to varying degrees: (a) domestic savings, (b) foreign trade, (c) foreign investments, and (d) foreign assistance.

Domestic savings have traditionally been the major source of investment funds in Latin America, but this source has been expanding inadequately. The annual per capita income in Latin America in the late 1960s was less than $400, and income distribution is markedly uneven. For those countries where data are available, the top 5 percent of the population in income account for 25 to 40 percent of the total national income. The rate of fixed capital formation in most Latin American countries is 13–20 percent, probably as high as can be expected considering the existing levels of living and the socioeconomic structure. The encouragement of domestic savings is seriously hampered by the fact that, on a regional basis, Latin America has the highest rate of inflation on earth.

Although modest tax reforms in several Latin American countries have resulted in the improvement of tax collections, there still is a considerable flight of local capital to the United States and Europe. As a result, in 1968 Latin American investments in the United States alone amounted to $7.2 billion and have been increasing at a rate about 50 percent faster than U.S. investments in Latin America.[24]

As indicated previously, the export market has not been expanding at a rate to warrant encouragement for expanded sources of capital from this direction in the near future.

Since Castro's accession to power, foreign investment in Latin America has been disappointing; in 1962, U.S. direct investments (probably almost 80 percent of all foreign investments) were less than withdrawals, with a net outflow of $32 million. U.S. investments began a very modest improvement in 1963, however, but Latin America has become a less and less significant region for U.S. direct investments (which had fallen to only about 20 percent of the world total in the late 1960s).

Since 1961 the annual flow of U.S. direct investments into Latin America has averaged less than one-half the annual Alliance objective of $300 million. Consequently, U.S. assistance has become that much more important to Latin America. Nonmilitary assistance to Latin America has increased appreciably both absolutely and relatively since 1960 and amounted to nearly $700 million annually (almost one-fifth of the world total) in the 1961–1969 period. This aid is concentrated in Brazil (more than one-quarter of Latin America's total) with significant portions to Chile and Colombia. However, the proportion of net U.S. assistance to Latin America has declined steadily since 1961, and about one-tenth of this net aid is military.

Fundamental changes in long-range productivity and lessening of sociopolitical pressures due to existing conditions could be effectuated by basic structural reforms, viz., agrarian reform, effective progressive tax structure, social welfare programs for redistribution of wealth, and drastic curtailment of military expenditures (one-tenth to more than one-quarter of the national budgets of practically all Latin American countries). Some of these measures were the founding principles of the Alliance when originally conceived in 1961, but have been relegated to a very minor role in recent years.

The net overall result is that, in attempting to rely almost entirely upon increased productivity for the solution to its serious problem of raising levels of living and absorbing a rapidly expanding population, Latin America is beset with difficulties of the greatest magnitude. All the pressures described above are manifested in an increasing sociopolitical instability that has already brought about serious repercussions for individual Latin American countries, the United States, and the O.A.S.

POPULATION CONTROL

The other major alternative, control of fertility, has been virtually ignored in Latin America (except for Argentina and Uruguay, with Cuba and Chile demonstrating a transitional stage). With the population now increasing at 2.9 percent annually, and the prospect that the rate may increase still further with additional reductions of mortality which appear inevitable, the pressure on available resources (despite notable economic development) is considerable and will undoubtedly increase. Barring widespread adoption of some "miraculous" birth control device, it does not seem likely that Latin America will be able to reduce its fertility significantly before the 1980s or 1990s, and by 1980 (assuming declining fertility—which at present does not appear likely) the population of Latin America will be more than 40 percent greater than in 1965. The Puerto Rican example (which, because of its special political status, may not be valid as an example for Latin America generally) suggests, however, that the birth rate could be reduced by one-quarter in less than 25 years.

Several countries of the underdeveloped world, faced with basically the same problems and limited alternatives, have recently begun active programs in the field of family planning. Because of the Latin American ethos, including religious considerations, this alternative until very recently had not even received widespread discussion, much less support. However, former President Fernando Belaunde Terry of Peru may have been the first Latin American chief executive to recognize publicly the formidable problem that population growth poses when he established a center for demographic study in December 1964. Only since the latter half of the 1960s have family planning information and birth control services attained significance in Latin America. Virtually all countries now have some family planning services available, although facilities are still quite limited. The Agency for International Development (AID) in the 1960s expanded its operations and assistance in the field of population planning, although it still cannot make unsolicited recommendations and proposals. Also, numerous private organizations have been active in this field in Latin America.

Governments have generally endeavored to avoid this approach so far, and the Roman Catholic Church has reaffirmed its opposition to mechanical and chemical methods of birth control. There is no question that Latin American fertility will be reduced, regardless of the attitude of the Church, for the historical examples of European Catholic countries, the U.S. Catholic population, Puerto Rico, Argentina, and Uruguay are clear. Presumably, improved education and changes wrought by the industrialization and commercialization of the economies will provide social changes that will make birth control widely accepted.

At the heart of the struggle between population growth and economic development are basically two conflicting schools of thought: the technologists who believe that improving efficiency and technology will supply sufficient goods and services for the population (notwithstanding rapid demographic growth); and the neo-Malthusians who envision the population exceeding the available resources (despite technological innovations), with the only solution remaining that of fertility control. Latin America must of course decide for itself as to which approach is right—or, to be safe, it can use both approaches simultaneously—but Latin America's capital and energies are (like those of all regions) limited, and some decisions and some sacrifices must be made and soon.

NOTES

1. The discussion on population in this paper is based on the assumption that there will be no nuclear war, general political disintegration, or widespread adoption of any spectacular fertility control technique.

2. 1970 *World Population Data Sheet*, Population Reference Bureau, Inc., Washing-

ton, D.C., April 1970. *World Population Prospects as Assessed in 1963*, U.N. Department of Economic and Social Affairs, Population Studies No. 41, 1966, Tables A3.4, A3.3.

3. *Economic Bulletin for Latin America*, United Nations, Vol. VIII, No. 1 (October 1962), Statistical Bulletin. *Demographic Yearbook: 1966*, United Nations, Table 17. *Datos Básicos de Población en América Latina*, 1970, Department of Social Affairs, Pan American Union, Washington, D.C., p. 5.

4. Based on the median of 16 countries for both periods from the *Demographic Yearbook: 1966* (Table 14) and *Demographic Yearbook: 1968* (Table 17).

5. Based on data from *World Population Prospects as Assessed in 1963*, op. cit., Table A2.1.

6. *Socio-Economic Progress in Latin America*, Social Progress Trust Fund, 9th Annual Report, 1969, Inter-American Development Bank, Washington, D.C., 1970, p. 161.

7. Irene B. Taeuber, "Population Growth in Latin America: Paradox of Development," *Population Bulletin*, Vol. XVIII, No. 6 (October 1962), p. 129.

8. Major agricultural countries are here defined as those having more than 5 million hectares of arable land according to the *Production Yearbook: 1963*, Food and Agriculture Organization of the United Nations, Table 1. The countries of sub-Saharan Africa (except South Africa) are excluded because of the incompleteness of data regarding cultivated land.

9. Cultivated area is based on summation of area cultivated for all crops given in the *Food and Agriculture Organization Production Yearbook: 1963*. Some significant crops are excluded from the totals (because areas are not given), viz., the deciduous mid-latitude fruits, citrus, the palms and some tropical fruits. The population estimates are also those provided by the same Food and Agriculture Organization source.

10. *Economic Progress of Agriculture in Developing Nations: 1950–68*. U.S. Dept. of Agriculture, Economic Research Service. Washington, D.C.: 1970. Table 3.

11. *Foreign Agriculture*, U.S. Dept. of Agriculture, Foreign Agricultural Service, III, No. 50 (December 13, 1965), 4.

12. *Socio-Economic Progress in Latin America*, op. cit., Table 4 (p. 10).

13. *Economic Survey of Latin America: 1963*, Chapter III.

14. "Latin America at Mid-Decade," *Latin American Business Highlights*. XV, No. 3 (Third Quarter, 1965), 8–9.

15. *The Western Hemisphere Agricultural Situation: Review of 1966*, Table 1 (p. 40). A daily caloric consumption of only 2400 calories would appear insufficient in view of the 3000 calories or more consumed in Anglo-America, Western Europe, European Oceania, and even Argentina and Uruguay.

16. *The Economic Development of Latin America in the Post-War Period*, Table 23.

17. *Economic Survey of Latin America: 1963*, Table 17.

18. *Economic Survey of Latin America: 1967*, Table 2.

19. *Yearbook of National Accounts Statistics: 1968*, Vol. II, Table 5B.

20. *Socio-Economic Progress in Latin America*, op. cit., Table 3 (p. 141).

21. *Economic Survey of Latin America: 1963*, Chapter VII; *Alliance for Progress Weekly Newsletter*, November 15 and December 6, 1965; *Socio-Economic Progress in Latin America*, op. cit., p. 101.

22. *Alliance for Progress Weekly Newsletter*, August 16, 1965, January 24, 1966, and January 22, 1968; *Socio-Economic Progress in Latin America*, op. cit., p. 2.

23. Thomas F. Carroll, "The Land Reform Issue in Latin America," in Albert O. Hirschman (ed.) *Latin American Issues: Essays and Comments* (New York: 20th Century Fund, 1961).

24. David T. Devlin and Frederick Cutler, "International Investment Position of the U.S.: Developments in 1968." *Survey of Current Business,* U.S. Dept. of Commerce, XLIX, No. 10 (October 1969).

Social Groupings and Authority

The papers in this section have been chosen to illustrate important aspects of social organization in Latin America, to reflect traditional anthropological interests, and also to illustrate some exciting recent trends in research. One of the principal concerns of social scientists, wherever they work, is with the ways in which people relate to each other, as individuals or as groups; and it is clear that sometimes social relations are based on judgments about social categories, or on networks of interpersonal bonds, neither of which reflect any sort of integral group.

Some authors make much of the distinction between *social* anthropology (emphasizing society, or social structure) and *cultural* anthropology (emphasizing culture, or patterns of thought and action). Among contributors to this book, such a distinction seems superfluous. For example, in the first paper reprinted in this section, Eva Hunt offers a meticulously detailed explication of the kinship terminology of a Mexican community (sufficient to please almost any social anthropologist) and also discusses at length the role expectations and behavioral dynamics of individuals who are in those relationships, that is, the cultural expression of kin relationships. In discussing social classes, Norman Whitten's contribution to this section makes it clear that individuals are able to move from class to class, and indicates something of the range of behaviors that is appropriate to each.

In order to set these papers in historical and intellectual context, I have briefly outlined the development of work by social scientists in Latin America in terms of six broad headings: demography; family and lateral systems; class, ethnicity, and mobility; migration and urbanization; community and nation; and power and authority.

DEMOGRAPHY

Before one can assess the meaning of kinds of social groups or categories within any population, it is important to know the nature of the overall population, in terms of such fundamental variables as numbers, age, and sex; for certain analytic purposes, other variables are important (such as occupation, geographic distribution, and so forth). Anthropologists have traditionally compiled detailed data on small local populations among whom they worked. However, it is obvious that large-scale demographic trends within regions and nations often have significant impact on local patterns. For example, the age-pyramid of national population affects opportunity for employment, education and other social services; in most Latin American countries, a large portion of the population are too young to be economically productive and yet they are "consumers" of costly schooling, health services, and so forth. Similarly, differential population densities not only reflect but also affect migration; the growth of urban concentrations affects all of those, and has a rapid and appreciable determining effect with respect to the allocation of national resources.

Much has been said about the worldwide "population explosion," and Central America has the most rapidly expanding population in the world. The article by Alfonso Gonzalez, reprinted in the previous section, provides a useful compilation of relevant statistics which dramatically document the nature of population dynamics throughout the area, and relates them to economic and other social indices. The crux of the problem is that population growth has outstripped all kinds of production in many Latin American countries, resulting in a decreasing standard of living in terms of the usual economic measures. It appears in the early 1970s that this disproportionate growth may be lessening as a result of widespread adoption of various techniques of family planning. This has come about in spite of outspoken opposition, in some areas, on the part of Roman Catholic leaders and also in spite of the traditional value of numbers of children as reflecting a man's *machismo* (masculinity). Research by J. M. Stycos, the United Nations, and others are pertinent not only in offering statistical data but also in discussing associated attitudes and behavior.

FAMILY AND LATERAL SYSTEMS

In the same way that attitudes about *machismo* have long affected the size of Latin American households, attitudes about *personalismo* affect the radius within which special relationships are extended. A concern with kinship and social structure has long been fundamental in anthropological studies, and the importance of these relationships as subjects for research is in large part a reflection of their importance in the lives of individual people.

One of the most widespread reference groups in all human societies is the family, comprising a varying range of persons who recognize significant degrees of relationship through consanguinity ("blood") or affinity ("marriage"). The composition of the family varies from one society to another, and even within a single society through time, in terms of differing conceptions about what constitute "significant degrees of relationship."

There are contexts in which the most dramatic contrasts are not between two things which look different, but rather between things which superficially appear to be similar and yet reveal profound differences in their workings. It is this latter kind of contrast that Anglo-American readers should recognize in Eva Hunt's account of a Mexican kinship system in which the terminology is homologous with their own, but the quality of social relationships implied is very different.

Despite the traditional sociological and anthropological focus on groups, there are many kinds of interpersonal relations that can be only partially understood in terms of unique ego-centered sets of linkages. In contrast with the "British structuralist" approach, Adams (1960) made an early appeal for analyzing family structures in terms of component dyads, and George Foster went even further, proposing "the dyadic contract" as a model for social relationships in Tzintzuntzan, where each person "is the center of his private and unique network of contractual ties, a network whose overlap with other networks has no functional significance" (1961, 1963). Although not all observers share his atomistic view as the norm for Latin American peasant communities, most recognize that this early approach toward what is now called "network analysis" allows one to understand patterns of belief and action that defy interpretation in terms of more traditional structural-functional analysis. Foster's article, reprinted in this section, focuses on asymmetrical "patron-client" dyads and goes far toward explaining how informal secondary systems can operate fast and effectively in the same setting where formal systems are slow and ineffectual. For example, the caudillo, political strong-man with a personal following whose loyalty is based more on patronage than ideology, is a familiar figure in Latin American history and literature (Wolf and Hansen, 1967), and the personalistic bureaucracy described by Aron-Schaar elsewhere in this book is typical of small towns throughout the area.

A patron often serves as a "culture broker" for his clients, as described by Wolf and Adams in articles elsewhere in this book, and studies in terms of patronage have become important recently, not only in Latin America (e.g., Strickon, et al., 1972) but also in southern Europe, eastern Canada, Southeast Asia, and elsewhere. One of the most widespread and least understood of social relationships other than those based on kinship and patronage is friendship: Foster's earlier article on colleague contracts is helpful in this connection, as is the work of Ruben Reina on friendship in a Guatemalan town (1959). Another way of extending bonds of social reciprocity is through *compadrazgo* (or, *compadrinazgo*, i.e., co-parenthood), often called "ritual kinship," or "fictive kinship." Most Latin Americans who are at least nominally Roman Catholic ask others to serve as godparents to each child, at least at baptism, and often at confirmation, marriage, or other ritual occasions. The important new relationship is ostensibly that between godparent (*padrino*) or godmother (*madrina*) and the godchild (*ahijado, -a*), but in practice, there is often no link that endures beyond the ceremony. The situation is very different, however, with respect to those of the same generation: the godparent of one's child is one's own coparent (*compadre, comadre*), and vice versa (the parent of one's godchild is also one's co-parent). Between co-parents, who are normally of the same generation, there is often a lifelong relationship—egalitarian when *compadres* are chosen from the same social stratum, or asymmetrical when people use this as a means of allying themselves as clients to a wealthier or more powerful patron; John Ingham's article reprinted here shows how this latter process operates in one Mexican community.

It is not only the poor who seek to extend their circles of relationship for their advantage. One man's patron is another man's client, in chains that range along a broad hierarchy of wealth or power, with dyadic contracts, of the sort characterized by Foster, linking those at adjacent levels. Anthony Leeds demonstrates, in an original contribution to this book, how this works in urban Brazil, and Arnold Strickon's paper, in another section, shows how Argentines act out and articulate the same process, with what are quite literally interlocking directorates, friends in court, and so forth. The importance of affinal kinsmen ("in-laws") is illustrated in this connection, lending substance to the folkwisdom that "those who control things are all related."

CLASS, ETHNICITY, AND MOBILITY

The Latin American nations are, with a few exceptions, states with highly differentiated plural societies. Most sociologists and anthropologists have been limited in their analyses of such societies because of their tendency to focus on cultural differences as the bases for distinguishing among components, rather than on social relations. An understanding of the real complexity of plural systems is often hampered by the inappropriate use of terms derived from other kinds of systems. Among the widespread confusions are those surrounding the terms "caste," "race," and "class."

In the 1940s it was common for social scientists as well as laymen to characterize most Latin American societies as divided into "castes," usually "Indian" and "white," sometimes with a third group ("mestizo," "criollo," or "ladino," depending on the region) usually called intermediate but treated more as a residual category. The early work of Melvin Tumin, John Gillin, Sol Tax, and others, is instructive in this connection. The reality of social mobility was amply documented, however, and that mobility combined with a number of other factors to discredit uncritical use of the Asiatic "caste" model.

By the 1950s some anthropologists were focusing on individuals who had changed their identity from one social category to another and on communities in which this change occurred with some frequency. Some observers were quick to label this a shift from "caste" to "class" as the dominant principle of social organization and to interpret it as a new flexibility that would foster growth of a progressive middle class. This faith in a "new middle class" is one of the popular fallacies that Stavenhagen dismissed at the beginning of this book, but it was a focus of considerable attention. There was confusion and controversy over the relevant criteria of class identification (cultural, occupational, economic, or other) and over the applicability of an historical model derived from northern Europe, as exemplified in the compilation by Crevenna (1951) and books and articles by John Johnson, Claudio Veliz, and Lipset and Solari. Ralph Beals's (1953) review of systems of social stratification in Latin America is remarkably cogent today, even though research emphases have shifted (see Iutaka 1965).

One of the few new insights on the subject was offered by Richard Adams in the first edition of this book (1965), where he attempted to avoid the confusion of multivariant uses of the term *social class* by referring instead to two sectors that are differentiated in terms of the contrasting bases for ranking that are recognized within them. A lower, or *work-wealth* sector, is internally stratified in terms of things that can be bought, whether we refer to sewing machines or radios or to positions in the ceremonial hierarchy of an Indian community, and the only way to gain such wealth is through work. The upper, or *power-prestige* sector, is based on specific prestige symbols, access to which is more dependent on power than on wealth, and which specifically exclude most kinds of work. This approach, more fully developed in a later book (Adams 1967), addresses itself directly to the dualism that is the most striking fact of social stratification throughout Latin America. It should not be confused with the fallacious view of dualism that Stavenhagen appropriately challenged, since the goal of this approach is to demonstrate how these sectors interact within the encompassing complex society, rather than treating them as independent entities.

The fact of social mobility within each sector and of the ideological gulf between the sectors is illustrated in very different ways in a number of the articles included here, notably those by Whitten, Patch, and van den Berghe. The latter two also point up another terminological confusion, that surrounding "race." Pierre van den Berghe musters demographic evidence of widespread shifts in ethnic membership in Guatemala, and Richard Patch traces the decisions and actions through which an individual Peruvian actually made such a shift. Both demonstrate the phenomenon of "social race" identified by Wagley (1959), who recognized that so-called racial categories are socially rather than biologically defined, that the criteria vary from region to region, with different emphasis given to ancestry, physical appearance, or sociocultural factors, and that different structural arrangements for race relations prevail. Patch's article shows how much variation there is with respect to such usages and related stereotypes, even within a limited area, where geographic mobility is often linked with social mobility. "Passing" from one social category to another involves considerable relearning in behavioral terms, and often also requires major shifts in one's relationships with others. It is an oversimplification to speak of such a complex process as "acculturation" or "assimilation," but the same dynamics are relevant.

The superficially simple question, "What is an Indian?" had been answered in a bewildering variety of ways, by tax-collectors, census-takers, and administrators, long before anthropologists began to wrestle with it. The bases for designation as ladino or mestizo have been even more confused and confusing over the years, as is documented in the research of a few scholars who are beginning to throw light on the question, in historical and ethnographic terms (e.g., Magnus Mörner, Eric Wolf, Angel Rosenblat, Alejandro Lipschutz, and others).

Following the prevailing biological analogy, many authors have identified a third major "racial" component in the population of Latin America, usually labeled "Negro," "African," or "Afro-American." Studies of the cultures of black populations in Middle and South America were pioneered by Melville Herskovits, Roger Bastide, and others; in recent years, a number of others have contributed significantly, and the emphasis has shifted from the content of culture to definitions of ethnic boundaries and the nature of group relations.

The concept of social race is just as pertinent with reference to Afro-Americans as it is with respect to Indians, mestizos, or whites. An enormous literature exists on Brazil alone, not merely because that country comprises half of the population of South America, but also because Brazilians enjoy world-wide renown for their egalitarian ethos. A number of local studies (e.g., by Donald Pierson, Marvin Harris, Seth Leacock, Edison Carneiro, and others) demonstrate that practice often differs from the ideal, and Fernandes's chapter elsewhere in this book may surprise many by describing an early movement in which the organizing strategy was not to strive for any major change in ways of thinking, but rather to seek greater behavioral conformity with values that were already popularly expressed.

Afro-American populations in other areas of Latin America have received less attention, but have not been totally ignored: the "Bush Negroes" or "Black Caribs" of Guatemala and the Guianas have been studied by Herskovits, Peter Kloos, Nancie Solien Gonzalez, Raymond Smith, and others; black populations of Ecuador by Whitten; enclaves in the Andes by David Preston; scattered populations on the Caribbean coast of Central America by Michael Olien, Mary Helms, and others; and a community in Mexico by Aguirre.

Other components of the populations of mainland Latin America have only rarely been subjects of research, and their relatively small numbers are often ignored in general discussions of the area. Among such groups are descendants of Chinese in Peru and Central America, recent Japanese and Ryukyuan immigrants in Bolivia and Brazil, East Indians in Surinam and Guyana, and Europeans, North Americans, and Levantines throughout the area.

It is worth emphasizing again that a cardinal strength of many recent studies of class, ethnicity, and mobility in Latin America is their recognition that social categories are neither static nor unitary. In complex or plural societies, ethnic identification is largely a matter of subjective perceptions that include conceptions of the self, of one's own reference group, and of socially significant others. As such, ethnic identification is clearly relational and refers less to uniformities within groups than to differential participation between groups. It is in this sense that Stavenhagen questions the dual view of Latin American society; it is not that each of the plural components of a complex society has its own institutions, but rather that they participate in different ways in many institutions that they share with others.

URBANIZATION AND MIGRATION

In the last few pages I have occasionally referred to *mobility* in the sense that sociologists would distinguish as "vertical," that is, along a hierarchy of relative social status. Another significant kind of mobility, called "horizontal" by the same social scientists, refers to actual movement through space and is also important in terms of Latin American social organization.

The explosive population growth that characterizes most countries in the area creates disproportionate social and economic problems because of the uneven pattern of demographic distribution, with extremely dense populations in some regions and exceptionally sparse settlement in others. It is obvious that ecological considerations play a major role in this connection, but the fact that human culture in large part determines the relative importance of ecological alternatives is sometimes ignored.

Geographic mobility is often directly associated with social mobility, sometimes as an indispensable prerequisite; examples of this linkage are reprinted here by van den Berghe and Miller as well as Patch. The stereotype of peasants who have never been out of the valley in which they were born reflects one part of Latin American reality, but there is another part in which migration over considerable distances, at least for certain seasons of each year, is a long-standing tradition. In Guatemala, Kekchi men annually go from their highland villages to work on the lowland coffee plantations; the Mayas of nearby Mexico often grow different crops in fields near their homes and in their own or rented farmlands in "hot country" several days' walk away; Quechua mountaineers are an important component of the work-crews who harvest sugarcane at Peruvian coastal plantations; Aymara farmers from around Lake Titicaca play an important role in the labor-scarce yungas area of Bolivia; much of Argentina's sugarcane is harvested by migrant workers; while herders, miners, vendors of salt or of pottery, and others in many countries habitually spend months away from home.

The practice of seasonal migration does not necessarily pave the way for a permanent shift of residence. In some instances, however, relocation does become a popular pattern, with changes in life-style of the migrants reaching significant proportions, as in the proletarianization of Peruvian peasants described above by Miller.

Another kind of migration, also involving changes in work habits but still within the pattern of small-scale subsistence farming, is taking place with increasing frequency, especially in Brazil and in the Andean nations. "Homesteading" is probably a more meaningful label for North American readers, although "colonization" is frequently used in direct translation from its Spanish and Portuguese cognates. The idea of opening "new frontiers" has special appeal to politicians who see this as inevitably stimulating economic development (although experience does not dramatically substantiate that hope) and to venturesome peasants who have little hope otherwise of getting more than minifundia in densely populated regions. The psychic and social costs are great, and the economic costs would be also, if the investments in infrastructure that are generally recommended were actually made. Only rarely has such migration led to the large-scale increments of national or even familial wealth and welfare that have been predicted, but they may serve as an important "safety valve" on exploding populations.

The term "urbanization" is used in very different but related senses in the social sciences. In an historical sense, it refers to the dynamics of the city as a social artifact—what happens when the density of human population results in qualitative differences in the style of life, such as markedly increased division of labor with full-time specialists, permanent architecture, social stratification, and so forth. In a sociological sense, "urbanization" often also refers to what happens to the population in relation to growing cities—both in demographic terms, with respect to geographical distribution and other factors, and in sociocultural terms, with respect to the adjustments that migrants make in shifting from a rural or small town ambience to an urban one.

This is not the place to trace the derivation of the anti-urban bias that seems to have played an unconscious role in coloring sociological and anthropological interpretations of the city until a few years ago. Redfield's "folk-urban" contrast included evaluative connotations, clear even if implicit, favoring the former, and the importance of Oscar Lewis's early work in Mexico City is reflected in his iconoclastic title, "Urbanization without breakdown" (1952). Having demonstrated that religious concerns, bonds to kinsmen, and other aspects of traditional morality were not abandoned when migrants went from a village to the city, Lewis devoted his efforts subsequently to revealing what such people actually do feel and how they come to terms with poverty in an urban setting.

In Latin America a majority of the population lived in rural areas until a few years ago, but the few cities have exerted enormous influence because each one is the commercial and administrative center for so large an area. The explosive growth of population in the cities is a compound result of both normal demographic processes within the urban population and increasing migration to the cities. One of the most visually dramatic aspects of this rapid growth has been the proliferation of squatter settlements, variously called *favelas* in Brazil, *barriadas* in Peru, *callampas* in Chile, and other names in other areas. Unfortunately, a considerable amount of what has been written about such communities is based on little more than surface appearances, so there is a large corpus of myth which has only recently been challenged by those who have undertaken substantive research among the people in such communities, including William Mangin, Anthony Leeds, José Matos, and others. Mangin's review of the literature on this subject, reprinted in this section, reveals that not only has the composition of these populations been grossly misjudged, but also their social organization and values.

Special kinds of insight into life in the squatter settlements are also available, including the autobiography of a *favelada* (Jesus 1962), and a study of politicization, reprinted here, in which Daniel Goldrich provides quantitative support for many of the generalizations offered by Mangin. Another strength of Goldrich's paper is the partial explanation it affords for the political apathy that is often reported as integral to "the culture of poverty" but that clearly can be overcome when the needs felt by the people are made a focus of concern. Politicization is an important process in rural as well as urban areas, with long-term implications that are difficult to foresee in detail, inasmuch as it broadens the perspectives of major portions of the populace. It holds promise of effecting significant changes not only in the view of the individuals themselves but also in terms of social organization and the distribution of power, at every level from the local community to the nation.

COMMUNITY AND NATION

In an earlier introduction I have already noted that community studies played an important role in the early spread of cultural anthropology in Middle and South America. That role was so important that Robert Redfield devoted an entire book to exploring the several ways in which "the little community" could fruitfully be approached (1955).

Nevertheless, Richard Adams was justified in noting in a context like this that "most students have looked at the community as a place in which things happen, and not as an entity in itself, . . . that set of relationships that is territorially identified and named" (1965). The abundant literature on "community development" is generally disappointingly doctrinaire rather than analytic. However, the kind of work that is recently being done by Adams, Casagrande, Leeds, Strickon, Whitten, and others, is beginning to provide important insights about how the local systems relate to the national and other more encompassing systems. As is often the case with respect to significant developments in Latin American studies, a germ of this approach can be identified in Redfield's writings, notably in his differentiation of "the Great Tradition" and "the little tradition." But his insights were not phrased in terms that were readily adaptable to research methods, and it was probably Wolf, as much as anyone, who provided the stimulus for the fruitful approaches that those people and others are now using. My earlier discussion of pluralism in a complex society is pertinent in this connection, as is Stavenhagen's treatment of "internal colonialism," a useful characterization of some aspects of the relationship between local and larger systems as it typically operates in many Latin American countries.

Although social scientists have often written about individual communities as if they were relatively isolated and self-contained social systems, this approach appears generally to have been only a heuristic device and does not necessarily reflect any lack of awareness or basic misunderstanding of the community's relationship to the nation. Especially with respect to the economic and political realms, the articulation of the local community with the rest of the nation is often explicitly recognized and sometimes insightfully analyzed. A good example of this is Frederic Hicks's study, reprinted here, of the role of the priest in a small Paraguayan town; he serves as broker not only between his parishioners and the Church, but also between the community and political groups at various other levels.

The feeling of powerlessness that is so often reported as pervading communities in Latin America may not even need to be subjected to profound scrutiny in psychological terms, since it appears to be wholly realistic in terms of the prevailing patterns of social grouping and authority. This is not to say that those patterns are in any sense ideal or immutable, but that the sociology of power should not be ignored.

POWER AND AUTHORITY

It has been easy for those doing research at the grass-roots level of society to ignore the distribution of power at other levels, just as it has been easy for many political scientists studying laws and administrative decisions to ignore the effects that those laws and decisions have on the workaday lives of rural farmers and others. It is a heartening sign of the maturity of the social sciences that some students are bridging that gap from both directions, as exemplified in the work of Adams, Goldrich, and others. The paper by Adams that is included in this book could well serve as an introduction to the imaginative book (1967) in which he examines the broad question of Latin America's development from the perspective of power.

Others have approached the subject in terms of relevant categories of those who share differentially in access to power, such as: elites, the military, the Church, labor unions, campesino syndicates, and political parties.

Many of the stereotypes about Latin American nations are substantially true, in at least a relative sense, in comparison with Anglo-America. One such *relatively* accurate stereotype is that of oligarchic government, as contrasted with more broad-based participant democracy. The articles by Anthony Leeds and Arnold Strickon that are reprinted here show how intricate networks of personalistic relationships—many of them based on the reciprocal advantages of patronage and clientage, although Foster's usage is not specifically followed—allow a relatively few individuals to play many roles, sharing and trading advantages to which others have no access. These are the people, aptly termed "elites," who had long been the focus of research and reporting on Latin America (e.g., Lipset and Solari 1967). An unusual strength of Samuel Stone's study in this section is that it adds both quantification and historical depth to the popular stereotype that "a few families" effectively dominate the nation, in terms of the distribution of wealth and power, even in Costa Rica, which is generally considered to have one of the most open societies in Latin America.

Another category that has been pertinent with respect to power throughout the history of the area is the military. In some countries, professional military leaders have tried in recent years to shift their role—or at least their image—from that of "defenders of the oligarchy" to one of professional nationalists willing to use what they proudly call "clean force" for the good of the nation as they judge it from the perspective of technocrats not constrained by obligations of patronage or clientage. Such a role is not, of course, universally possible, nor does the image always reflect reality. And, of course, there is by no means full consensus among military men themselves concerning what their role should be. Changing views on the military in Latin America can be traced in the writings of Gino Germani, John Johnson, Martin Needler, José Nun, Kalman Silvert, and others.

Another major institution that has loomed large throughout Latin American history is the Roman Catholic Church. Like the military establishment, the Church is also torn by internal dissension, and for many of the same reasons. Like the military, the Church has traditionally been viewed, whether accurately or not, as a tool or, at least, a friend of the oligarchy. And, also like the military, some of the church officials are impatient supporters of major reforms, favoring increased social welfare at the cost of elite dominance, whereas others range all the way to reactionary conservatism. Iván Illich, Helder Cámara, and Camilo Torres (reprinted in another section), are articulate spokesmen for liberalization within the Church; historical perspectives are offered by J. L. Mecham, Frederick Pike, Ivan Vallier, and others.

During the early decades of the nineteenth century, representatives from a number of international socialist movements had uneven success in promoting labor organizations in many Latin American countries. The distinctiveness of national histories and cultures was not always recognized, so that local outcomes sometimes took unforeseen directions. Among the contrasts that many Anglo-Americans find most striking are the widespread predominance of "white-collar" over "blue-collar" unionization, and the frequent links between unions and governments. Among those who have written widely on the subject are Robert Alexander, Ben Burnett, Moises Poblete, and others.

In recent years, a very different kind of popular organization has been taking place in a number of Middle and South American countries, the formation of campesino syndicates (sometimes called peasant leagues or farmers' unions), organizations of small-scale agriculturalists. The ostensible function of such a syndicate is to serve as a lobby for making the farmers' wants known to politicians; sometimes it is expanded to serve as a credit union, a buying or selling cooperative, and so forth. In practice, syndicates vary enormously even within a single country, but often they are little more than local cells of a political party, ad hoc land companies formed as corporate entities merely to carry through expropriation procedures against large-scale landholders, or representatives of other special interests. In Bolivia, one can find campesino syndicates that fit each of the above descriptions, whereas those in Brazil and Venezuela seem to be more uniformly concerned with the social and economic welfare of their members. Studies by Charles Erasmus, Henry Landsberger, Dwight Heath, and others are pertinent.

Political parties constitute another kind of group intimately involved in plays for power. With noteworthy exceptions, however, parties in Latin America have tended to be less ideological and more personal than is the case even in Anglo-

America. Alliances shift; names change; dissident factions form new parties; and it is sometimes difficult to follow when, as in Bolivia, as many as eighteen parties may compete in a single election. It is in this arena of social action that patronage and clientage are most clearly operative, although a researcher must have special rapport before he can enjoy the full confidence of those whose competition for high stakes makes frank discussion difficult. It is problematic enough to get straight answers from politicians in a small town, as Aron-Schaar's paper illustrates; most of the political analysis that has been written is based on very different kinds of data from those used in the study of other realms of social organization. A few of the outstanding authors who have contributed to this difficult field are Richard Adams, Robert Alexander, Kalman Silvert, and James Wilkie.

Recommended Readings on SOCIAL GROUPINGS AND AUTHORITY*

Adams, Richard N.

1956 *Encuesta sobre la cultura de los ladinos en Guatemala.* Seminario de Integración Social Guatemalteca Publicación 2, Guatemala.

1956 Cultural components of Central America. *American Anthropologist* 58:881–907.

1960 An inquiry into the nature of the family. In Gertrude E. Dole and Robert L. Carneiro (eds.), *Essays in the Science of Culture.* Thomas Y. Crowell, New York.

1962 The community in Latin America: A changing myth. *The Centennial Review* 6:409–434.

1965 Introduction [to Social Organization]. In Heath and Adams, 1965.

1967 *The Second Sowing: Power and Secondary Development in Latin America.* Chandler, Chicago.

Adams, Richard N., et al.

1970 *Crucifixion by Power: Essays on Guatemalan National Social Structure, 1944–1966.* University of Texas Press, Austin.

Aguirre Beltrán, Gonzalo

1946 *La población negra de México, 1519–1810: Estudio etnohistórico.* Fuente Cultural, México.

1958 *Cuijla: Esbozo etnográfico de un pueblo negro.* Fondo de Cultura Económica, México.

1967 *Regiones de refugio: el desarrollo de la comunidad y el proceso dominical en mestizo América.* Instituto Indigenista Interamericano Ediciones Especiales 46, México.

Alba, Victor

1968 *Nationalists Without Nations: The Oligarchy Versus the People of Latin America.* Frederick A. Praeger, New York.

Alexander, Robert J.

1965 *Organized Labor in Latin America.* Free Press, New York.

1970 *Political Parties in Latin America.* Frederick A. Praeger, New York.

Anderson, Charles W.

1967 *Politics and Economic Change in Latin America.* Van Nostrand, Princeton, N.J.

Azevedo, Thales de

1961 Famila, casamento e divorcio no Brasil. *Journal of Inter-American Studies* 3:213–237 (reprinted in English in Heath and Adams, 1965).

Bagü, Sergio

1959 *Estratificación y movilidad social en Argentina.* Centro Latino-Americano de Pesquisas em Ciências Sociais Publicação 6, Rio de Janeiro.

Balan, Jorge

1969 Migrant–native socioeconomic differences in Latin American cities: A structural analysis. *Latin American Research Review* 4:3–30.

* This is by no means a comprehensive bibliography on the topics discussed in the Introduction, but is rather a guide to key books and articles that illustrate the approaches and provide a valuable starting point from which any student can further pursue his special interests.

Bastide, Roger
1971 *African Civilizations in the New World*. Harper & Row, New York.
Bates, Margaret (ed.)
1957 *The Migration of Peoples to Latin America*. Catholic University of America Press, Washington.
Beals, Ralph L.
1953 Social stratification in Latin America. *American Journal of Sociology* 58:327–339 (reprinted in Heath and Adams, 1965).
1961 Community typologies in Latin America. *Anthropological Linguistics* 3:8–16.
Bell, Betty (ed.)
1967 *Indian Mexico: Past and Present*. University of California, Latin American Center, Los Angeles.
Beyer, Glenn H. (ed.)
1968 *The Urban Explosion in Latin America: A Continent in Process of Modernization*. Cornell University Press, Ithaca, N.Y.
Billig, Otto, John Gillin, and William Davidson
1947–1949 Aspects of personality and culture in a Guatemalan community: Ethnological and Rorschach approaches. *Journal of Personality* 16,1:153–178; 16,2:328–368.
Bonilla, Frank, and José A. Silva Michelina (eds.)
1968 *The Politics of Change in Venezuela* (2 vols.). Massachusetts Institute of Technology Press, Cambridge, Mass.
Bourricaud, François
1970 *Power and Society in Contemporary Peru*. Frederick A. Praeger, New York.
Brooks, Rhoda, and Earle Brooks
1965 *The Barrios of Manta*. New American Library, New York.
Burnett, Ben G., and Kenneth F. Johnson (eds.)
1968 *Political Forces in Latin America: Dimensions of the Quest for Stability*. Wadsworth, Belmont, Cal.
Cancian, Frank
1965 *Economics and Prestige in a Maya Community: The Religious Cargo System in Zinacantan*. Stanford University Press, Stanford, Cal.
Carneiro, Edison
1968 *Ladinos e crioulos: Estudos sobre o negro no Brasil*. Civilização Brasileira, Rio de Janeiro.
Casagrande, Joseph M., Stephen I. Thompson, and Philip D. Young
1964 Colonization as a research frontier: The Ecuadorian case. In Robert Manners (ed.), *Process and Pattern in Culture*. Aldine, Chicago.
Chaplin, David
1968 Peruvian social mobility: Revolutionary and developmental potential. *Journal of Interamerican Studies* 10:547–570.
Chilcote, Ronald H. (comp.)
1970 *Revolution and Structural Change in Latin America* (2 vols.). Hoover Institution, Stanford, Cal.
Cline, Howard F.
1952 Mexican community studies. *Hispanic American Historical Review* 32:212–242.
Colby, Benjamin N., and Pierre van den Berghe
1961 Ethnic relations in southeastern Mexico. *American Anthropologist* 63:772–792.

1969 *Ixil Country: A Plural Society in Highland Guatemala.* University of California Press, Berkeley.

Cotler, Julio
1968 *The Mechanics of Internal Domination and Social Change in Peru.* Studies in Comparative International Development 3:038, Sage Publications, Beverly Hills, Cal.

Council on Foreign Relations
1960 *Social Change in Latin America Today.* Harper & Row, New York.

Crevenna, Theodore (ed.)
1951 *Materiales para el estudio de la clase media en la América Latina* (6 vols.). Pan American Union, Washington (mimeo).

Davis, Harold E. (ed.)
1958 *Government and Politics in Latin America.* Ronald Press, New York.

Davis, Kingsley
1972 *Population Studies in Latin America.* Columbia University Press, New York.

Deshon, Shirley
1963 Compadrazgo on a henequen hacienda in Yucatan: A structural reevaluation. *American Anthropologist* 65:574–583.

Dew, Edward
1969 *Politics in the Altiplano: The Dynamics of Change in Rural Peru.* University of Texas Press, Austin.

Diaz, May Nordquist
1966 *Tonalá: Conservatism, Responsibility, and Authority in a Mexican Town.* University of California Press, Berkeley.

Diegues Junior, Manuel
1952 *Etnias e Culturas no Brasil.* Ministerio de Educação e Saude Os Cadernos de Cultura, Rio de Janeiro.

Diegues Junior, Manuel, and Bryce Wood (eds.)
1967 *Social Science in Latin America.* Columbia University Press, New York.

Dobyns, Henry F.
[1964] *The Social Matrix of Peruvian Indigenous Communities.* Cornell–Peru Project Monograph, Department of Anthropology, Cornell University [Ithaca, N.Y.].

Dobyns, Henry F., and Mario C. Vázquez (eds.)
1963 *Migración e integración en el Perú.* Editorial Estudios Andinos, Lima.

Edelmann, Alexander T.
1965 *Latin American Government and Politics: The Dynamics of a Revolutionary Society.* Dorsey Press, Homewood, Ill.

Erasmus, Charles J.
1965 The occurrence and disappearance of reciprocal labor in Latin America. In Heath and Adams, 1965.

Fagen, Richard R., and Wayne A. Cornelius, Jr. (eds.)
1970 *Political Power in Latin America: Seven Confrontations.* Prentice-Hall, Englewood Cliffs, N.J.

Fals-Borda, Orlando
1969 *Subversion and Social Change in Colombia.* Columbia University Press, New York.

Fernandes, Florestan
1965 *A integração do negro á sociedade de clases* (2 vols.). São Paulo (partially translated as: *The Negro in Brazilian Society*, Columbia University Press, New York, 1969).

Field, Arthur J. (ed.)
1970 *City and Country in the Third World: Issues in the Modernization of Latin America.* Schenkman, Cambridge, Mass.

Fillol, Thomas
1961 *Social Factors in Economic Development: The Argentine Case.* M.I.T. Press, Cambridge, Mass.

Foster, George M.
1961 The dyadic contract: A model for the social structure of a Mexican peasant village. *American Anthropologist* 63:1173–1192.
1963 The dyadic contract in Tzintzuntzan, II: Patron–client relationship. *American Anthropologist* 65:1280–1294 (reprinted herein).
1965 Peasant society and the image of limited good. *American Anthropologist* 67:293–315.
1967 *Tzintzuntzan: Mexican Peasants in a Changing World.* Little, Brown, Boston.
1969 Godparents and social networks in Tzintzuntzan. *Southwestern Journal of Anthropology* 25:261–278.

Frank, Andre Gunder
1967 *Capitalism and Underdevelopment in Latin America: Historical Studies of Chile and Brazil.* Monthly Review Press, New York.

Freyre, Gilberto
1956 *The Masters and the Slaves: A Study in the Development of Brazilian Civilization* (rev. Eng. ed.). Alfred A. Knopf, New York.
1966 *The Mansions and the Shanties: The Making of Modern Brazil.* Alfred A. Knopf, New York.

Friedmann, John
1970 *The Future of Urbanization in Latin America.* Studies in Comparative International Development 5:059, Sage Publications, Beverly Hills, Cal.

Fujii, Yukio, and T. Lynn Smith
1959 *The Acculturation of the Japanese Immigrants in Brazil.* University of Florida, Latin American Monograph 8, Gainesville.

Furtado, Celso
1965 *Development and Stagnation in Latin America: A Structuralist Approach.* Studies in Comparative International Development 1:011, Sage Publications, Beverly Hills, Cal.

Galjart, Benno
1964 Class and "following" in rural Brazil. *América Latina* 7:3–24.
1968 *Itaguai: Old Habits and New Practices in a Brazilian Land Settlement.* Centre for Agricultural Publishing and Documentation, Wageningen, Netherlands.

Germani, Gino
1961 El proceso de transición a una democracia de masa en la Argentina. *Política* 16:10–27 (reprinted in English in Heath and Adams, 1965).
[1969] *Sociología de la modernización: Estudios teóricos, metodológicos y aplicados a América Latina.* Paidos, Buenos Aires.

Germani, Gino, and Kalman Silvert
1967 Politics, social structure and military intervention in Latin America. In Wilson C. McWilliams (ed.), *Garrisons and Government: Politics and the Military in New States.* Chandler, Chicago.

Gillin, John P.
1951 *The Culture of Security in San Carlos.* Tulane University, Middle American Research Institute Publication 16, New Orleans.

Goldrich, Daniel
1965 Toward the comparative study of politicization in Latin America. In Heath and Adams, 1965.
1966 *Sons of the Establishment: Elite Youth in Panama and Costa Rica.* Rand McNally, Chicago.
Gomez Rosendo, Adolfo
1964 *Government and Politics in Latin America* (rev. ed.). Random House, New York.
Góngora, Mario
1960 *Origen de los "inquilinos" de Chile central.* Universidad de Chile, Seminario de Historia Colonial, Santiago.
Gonzalez, Nancie L. Solien
1969 *Black Carib Household Structure: A Study of Migration and Modernization.* University of Washington Press, Seattle.
González Casanova, Pablo
1970 *Democracy in Mexico.* Oxford University Press, New York.
Hamill, Hugh M., Jr., (ed.)
1965 *Dictatorship in Spanish America.* Alfred A. Knopf, New York.
Hammel, E[ugene] A.
1969 *Power in Ica: The Structural History of a Peruvian Community.* Little, Brown, Boston.
Harris, Marvin
1956 *Town and Country in Brazil.* Columbia University Press, New York.
1970 Referential ambiguity in the calculus of Brazilian racial identity. *Southwestern Journal of Anthropology* 26:1–14.
Hauser, Philip M. (ed.)
1962 *Urbanization in Latin America.* UNESCO, New York.
Havens, A. Eugene, and William L. Flinn (eds.)
1970 *Internal Colonialism and Structural Change in Colombia.* Frederick A. Praeger, New York.
Heath, Dwight B.
1973 New patrons for old: Changing patron–client relationships in the Bolivian yungas. *Ethnology* 12:75–98.
Heath, Dwight B., and Richard N. Adams (eds.)
1965 *Contemporary Cultures and Societies of Latin America* (1st ed.). Random House, New York.
Helms, Mary W.
1972 *Asang: Adaptation to Culture Contact in a Miskito Community.* University of Florida Press, Gainesville.
Horowitz, Irving L.
1967 *The Rise and Fall of Project Camelot: Studies in the Relationship Between Social Sciences and Practical Politics.* M.I.T. Press, Cambridge, Mass.
Horowitz, Irving L. (ed.)
1970 *Masses in Latin America.* Oxford University Press, New York.
Horowitz, Irving L., Josué de Castro, and John Gerassi (eds.)
1969 *Latin American Radicalism: A Documentary Report on Left and Nationalist Movements.* Random House, New York.
Hotchkiss, John C.
1967 Children and conduct in a ladino community of Chiapas, Mexico. *American Anthropologist* 69:711–718.

Illich, Iván D.
1970 *Celebration of Awareness: A Call for Institutional Revolution*. Doubleday, Garden City, N.Y.

International Institute for Labor Studies
1965 *Bibliografía sobre los movimientos obreros en la América Latina: 1950–1964*. I.I.L.S., Geneva.

International Labor Office
1953 *Indigenous Peoples*. I.L.O., Geneva.

International Population Census Bibliography
1965 *Latin America and the Caribbean*. University of Texas, Population Research Center, Austin.

Iutaka, Sugiyama
1965 Social stratification research in Latin America. *Latin American Research Review* 1,1:7–34.

Jesus, Carolina Maria de
1962 *Child of the Dark*. E. P. Dutton, New York.

Johnson, Allen W.
1971 *Sharecroppers of the Sertão: Economics and Dependence on a Brazilian Plantation*. Stanford University Press, Stanford, Cal.

Johnson, John J.
1964 *The Military and Society in Latin America*. Stanford University Press, Stanford, Cal.
1965 *Political Change in Latin America: The Emergence of the Middle Sectors* (rev. ed.). Stanford University Press, Stanford, Cal.

Jorrin, Miguel, and John D. Martz
1970 *Latin American Political Thought and Ideology*. University of North Carolina Press, Chapel Hill.

Kantor, Harry
1969 *Patterns of Politics and Political Systems in Latin America: Bureaucracy and Participation*. Rand McNally, Indianapolis.

Kantor, Harry (ed.)
1968 *Latin American Political Parties: A Bibliography*. University of Florida Library, Gainesville.

Kloos, Peter
1971 *The Maroni River Caribs of Surinam*. Humanities Press, New York.

Konetzke, Richard
1965 *Die Indianerkulturen Altamerikas und die Spanisch–Portugiesische Kolonialherrschaft*. Fisher Weltgeschichte 22, Frankfurt am Main.

Kubler, George
1952 *The Indian Caste of Peru, 1795–1940: A Population Study Based upon Tax Records and Census Reports*. Smithsonian Institution, Institute of Social Anthropology Publication 14, Washington.

Lambert, Jacques
1967 *Latin America: Social Structures and Political Institutions*. University of California Press, Berkeley.

Lamond, Trillis F.
1970 *Lord and Peasant in Peru: A Paradigm of Political and Social Change*. Cambridge University Press, Cambridge, England.

Landsberger, Henry A. (ed.)
1969 *Latin American Peasant Movements*. Cornell University Press, Ithaca, N.Y.

Leacock, Seth
1971 *Afro-Brazilian Religion: New Saints and Old Songs.* Bobbs-Merrill, Indianapolis.

Leeds, Anthony
1969 The significant variables determining the character of squatter settlements. *América Latina* 12,3:44–86.

Leonard, Olen E., and Charles P. Loomis (eds.)
1953 *Readings in Latin American Social Organization and Institutions.* Michigan State College Press, East Lansing.

Lévi-Strauss, Claude
1963 *Structural Anthropology.* Basic Books, New York.

Lewis, Oscar
1952 Urbanization without breakdown: A case study. *The Scientific Monthly* 75:31–41 (reprinted in Heath and Adams, 1965).
1959 *Five Families: Mexican Case Studies in the Culture of Poverty.* Basic Books, New York.
1961 *The Children of Sánchez.* Random House, New York.
1964 *Pedro Martínez: A Mexican Peasant and His Family.* Random House, New York.
1969 *A Death in the Sánchez Family.* Random House, New York.

Lieuwen, Edwin
1963 *Arms and Politics in Latin America* (rev. ed.). Frederick A. Praeger, New York.
1964 *Generals vs. Presidents: Neomilitarism in Latin America.* Frederick A. Praeger, New York.

Lipschutz, Alejandro
1967 *El problema racial en la conquista de América y el mestizaje* (2 da. ed.). Andrés Bello, Santiago.

Lipset, Seymour M., and Aldo Solari (eds.)
1967 *Elites in Latin America.* Oxford University Press, New York.

McAlister, Lyle N.
1966 Recent research and writings on the role of the military in Latin America. *Latin American Research Review* 2,1:5–36.

McCorkle, Thomas
1965 *Fajardo's People: Cultural Adjustment in Venezuela and the Little Community in Latin America and North American Contexts.* University of California, Latin American Center, Los Angeles.

Maier, Joseph, and Richard W. Weatherhead (eds.)
1964 *The Politics of Change in Latin America,* Frederick A. Praeger, New York.

Mangin, William
1967 *Las comunidades alteñas en América Latina.* Instituto Indigenista Interamericano Serie Antropología Social 5, México.

Mangin, William P. (ed.)
1970 *Peasants in Cities.* Little, Brown, Boston.

Marshall, C. E.
1939 The birth of the mestizo in New Spain. *Hispanic American Historical Review* 19:161–184.

Martínez, Héctor
1961 *Las migraciones altiplánicas y la colonización del Tambopata.* Ministerio de Trabajo y Asuntos Indígenas, Plan Nacional de Integración de la Población Aborígen, Lima.

Martz, John D.
1965 *The Dynamics of Change in Latin American Politics.* Prentice-Hall, Englewood Cliffs, N.J.
1971 Political science and Latin American studies: A discipline in search of a region. *Latin American Research Review* 6,1:73–99.
Masur, Gerhard
1966 *Nationalism in Latin America: Diversity and Unity.* Macmillan, New York.
Matos Mar, José
1966 *Estudio de las barriadas limeñas.* Universidad Nacional Mayor de San Marcos, Lima.
Midlarsky, Manus, and Raymond Tanter
1967 Toward a theory of political instability in Latin America. *Journal of Peace Research* (Oslo) 3:209–227.
Miguens, José Enrique
1970 *The New Latin American Military Coup.* Studies in Comparative International Development 6, Sage Publications, Beverly Hills, Cal.
Miller, John, and Ralph A. Gakenheimer (eds.)
1970 *Latin American Urban Policies and the Social Sciences.* Sage Publications, Beverly Hills, Cal.
Miller, Solomon
1967 Hacienda to plantation in northern Peru: The processes of proletarianization of a tenant farmer society. In Julian H. Steward (ed.), *Contemporary Change in Traditional Societies, 3: Mexican and Peruvian Communities.* University of Illinois Press, Urbana.
Miner, Horace
1952 The folk–urban continuum. *American Sociological Review* 17:529–537.
Mintz, Sidney W.
1953 The folk–urban continuum and the rural proletarian community. *American Journal of Sociology* 59:136–143.
Mintz, Sidney W., and Eric R. Wolf
1950 An analysis of ritual co-parenthood (*compadrazgo*). *Southwestern Journal of Anthropology* 6:341–368.
Monteforte Toledo, Mario
1969 *Bibliografía sociopolítica latinoamericana.* Universidad Nacional Autónoma de México, México.
Mörner, Magnus
1967 *Race Mixture in the History of Latin America.* Little, Brown, Boston.
Mörner, Magnus (ed.)
1969 *Race and Class in Latin America.* Columbia University Press, New York.
Morse, Richard M.
1958 *From Community to Metropolis: A Biography of São Paulo, Brazil.* University of Florida Press, Gainesville.
1971 Trends and issues in Latin American urban research 1965–1970. *Latin American Research Review* 6,1:3–52; 6,2:19–75.
Nash, June
1970 *In the Eyes of the Ancestors: Belief and Behavior in a Maya Community.* Yale University Press, New Haven.
Nash, Manning
1957 The multiple society in economic development: Mexico and Guatemala. *American Anthropologist* 59:825–833.

Needler, Martin C.
1968 *Political Development in Latin America: Instability, Violence, and Evolutionary Change*. Random House, New York.
1968 *Latin American Politics in Perspective* (rev. ed.). Van Nostrand, Princeton, N.J.

Nun, José
1965 *A Latin American Military Phenomenon: The Middle Class Military Coup*. University of California, Institute of International Studies, Los Angeles.

Nutini, Hugo G.
1968 *San Bernardino Contla: Marriage and Family Structure in a Tlaxcalan Municipio*. University of Pittsburgh Press, Pittsburgh.

Olien, Michael
1969 The city and pluralism in Limon, Costa Rica. In Henry Pauly (ed.), *Anthropological Studies of the City*. University of Georgia Press, Athens.

Pan American Union
1959 *Plantation Systems of the New World*. Social Science Monograph 7, Washington.
1970 *Datos básicos de población en América Latina*. Washington.

Parsons, James J.
1968 *Antioquia: Colonization in Western Colombia* (rev. ed.). University of California Press, Berkeley.

Payne, James L.
1965 *Labor and Politics in Peru: The System of Political Bargaining*. Yale University Press, New Haven.

Peattie, Lisa Redfield
1968 *The View from the Barrio*. University of Michigan Press, Ann Arbor.

Petras, James
1970 *Politics and Social Structure in Latin America*. Monthly Review Press, New York

Pierson, Donald
1942 *Negroes in Brazil: A Study of Race Contact at Bahia*. University of Chicago Press, Chicago.

Pike, Frederick B. (ed.)
1967 *Freedom and Reform in Latin America* (rev. ed.). University of Notre Dame Press, Notre Dame, Ind.

Pike, Frederick B., and V. D'Antonio
1964 *Religion, Revolution and Reform: New Forces for Change in Latin America*. Frederick A. Praeger, New York.

Poblete Troncoso, Moises, and Ben G. Burnett
1960 *The Rise of the Latin American Labor Movement*. Bookman Associates, New York.

Powelson, John P.
1964 *Latin America: Today's Economic and Social Revolution*. McGraw-Hill, New York.

Preston, David A.
1965 Negro, mestizo, and Indian in an Andean environment. *Geographical Journal* 131:220–234.

Quijano, Anibal
1971 *Nationalism and Capitalism in Peru: A Study in Neo-Imperialism*. Monthly Review Press, New York.

Rabinovitz, Francine F. (ed.)
1970 *Urban Development and Political Development in Latin America.* Sage Publications, Beverly Hills, Cal.

Ranis, Peter
1971 *Five Latin American Nations: A Comparative Political Study.* Macmillan, New York.

Ray, Talton F.
1969 *Politics of the Barrios of Venezuela.* University of California Press, Berkeley.

Redfield, Robert
1947 The folk society. *American Journal of Sociology* 52:293–308.
1955 *The Little Community.* University of Chicago Press, Chicago.
1956 *Peasant Society and Culture.* University of Chicago Press, Chicago.

Reina, Ruben E.
1959 Two patterns of friendship in a Guatemalan community. *American Anthropologist* 61:44–50.
1966 *The Law of the Saints: A Pokoman Corporate Community and Its Culture.* Bobbs-Merrill, Indianapolis.

Richardson, Miles
1970 *San Pedro, Colombia: Small Town in a Developing Society.* Holt, Rinehart and Winston, New York.

Rosenblat, Angel
1954 *La población indígena y el mestizaje en América* (2 vols.). Nova, Buenos Aires.

Rozman, Stephen L.
1970 The evolution of the political role of the Peruvian military. *Journal of Inter-American Studies* 12:539–564.

Sable, Martin H.
1967 *A Guide to Latin American Studies* (2 vols.). University of California, Latin American Center, Los Angeles.
1970 *Latin American Agriculture: A Bibliography on Pioneer Settlement, Agricultural History and Economics, Rural Sociology and Population.* University of Wisconsin, Center for Latin American Studies, Milwaukee.

Sayres, William C.
1956 Disorientation and status change. *Southwestern Journal of Anthropology* 12:79–86.
1956 Ritual kinship and negative affect. *American Sociological Review* 21:348–352.

Schaedel, Richard P.
1967 *La demografía y los recursos humanos del sur del Perú.* Instituto Indigenista Interamericano Serie Antropología Social 8, México.

Schmitt, Karl M., and David D. Burks
1964 *Evolution or Chaos: Dynamics of Latin American Government and Politics.* Frederick A. Praeger, New York.

Sigmund, Paul E. (ed.)
1970 *Models of Political Change in Latin America.* Frederick A. Praeger, New York.

Silvert, Kalman H.
1966 Leadership formation and modernization in Latin America. *Journal of International Affairs* 20:318–331.

Simmons, Ozzie G.
1955 The criollo outlook in the mestizo culture of coastal Peru. *American Anthropologist* 57:107–117 (reprinted in Heath and Adams, 1965).

Smith, M[ichael] G.
1965 *The Plural Society in the British West Indies*. University of California Press, Berkeley.
Smith, Raymond T.
1956 *The Negro Family in British Guiana: Family Structure and Social Status in the Villages*. Routledge and Kegan Paul, London.
Smith, T. Lynn
1970 *Studies of Latin American Societies*. Doubleday, Garden City, N.Y.
Stavenhagen, Rodolfo (ed.)
1969 *Las clases sociales en las sociedades agrarias*. Siglo XX, México.
Stavenhagen, Rodolfo (ed.)
1970 *Agrarian Problems and Peasant Movements in Latin America*. Doubleday, Garden City, N.Y.
Stephens, Richard H.
1971 *Wealth and Power in Peru*. Scarecrow, Metuchin, N.J.
Strickon, Arnold
1962 Class and kinship in Argentina. *Ethnology* 1:500–515 (reprinted in Heath and Adams, 1965).
Strickon, Arnold, and Sidney M. Greenfield (eds.)
1972 *Structure and Process in Latin America: Patronage, Clientage, and Power Systems*. University of New Mexico Press, Albuquerque.
Stycos, J. Mayone
1968 *Human Fertility in Latin America: Sociological Perspectives*. Cornell University Press, Ithaca, N.Y.
Tax, Sol
1937 The municipios of the midwestern highlands of Guatemala. *American Anthropologist* 39:423–444.
1941 World view and social relations in Guatemala. *American Anthropologist* 43:27–43 (reprinted in Heath and Adams, 1965).
Taylor, Douglas M.
1951 *The Black Carib of British Honduras*. Viking Fund Publication in Anthropology 17, New York.
Tomasek, Robert D. (ed.)
1966 *Latin American Politics: Studies of the Contemporary Scene*. Doubleday, Garden City, N.Y.
[Torres, Camilo]
1971 *Revolutionary Priest: The Complete Writings and Messages of Camilo Torres* (John Gerassi, ed.). Random House, New York.
Tschopik, Harry
1948 On the concept of creole culture in Peru. *Transactions of the New York Academy of Sciences* 2,10:252–261.
Tumin, Melvin M.
1952 *Caste in a Peasant Society*. Princeton University Press, Princeton, N.J.
Ugalde, Antonio
1970 *Power and Conflict in a Mexican Community*. University of New Mexico Press, Albuquerque.
United Nations
1954 *The Population of Central America (Including Mexico): 1950–1980*. Population Studies 16, New York.
1955 *The Population of South America: 1950–1980*. Population Studies 21, New York.

Vallier, Ivan
1970 *Catholicism, Social Control, and Modernization in Latin America.* Prentice-Hall, Englewood Cliffs, N.J.

Vaughan, Denton R. (comp.)
1970 *Urbanization in Twentieth Century Latin America: A Working Bibliography.* Institute of Latin American Studies, Population Research Center, University of Texas, Austin.

Vázquez V., Mario C.
1957 Cambios en estratificación social en una hacienda andina. *Perú Indígena* 6, 4–5:67–87 (reprinted in English in Heath and Adams, 1965).

Veliz, Claudio (ed.)
1967 *The Politics of Conformity in Latin America.* Oxford University Press, New York.

Violich, Francis, and Juan B. Astica
1967 *Community Development and the Urban Planning Process in Latin America.* University of California, Latin American Center, Los Angeles.

Von Lazar, Arpad, and Robert R. Kaufman (eds.)
1969 *Reform and Revolution: Readings in Latin American Politics.* Allyn & Bacon, Boston.

Wagley, Charles
1959 On the concept of social race in the Americas. *Actas del 33 Congreso Internacional de Americanistas,* T. 1:403–417. Lehmann, San José (reprinted in Heath and Adams, 1965).

Wagley, Charles (ed.)
1964 *Social Science Research on Latin America.* Columbia University Press, New York.

Wagley, Charles, and Marvin Harris
1968 *Minorities in the New World: Six Case Studies.* Columbia University Press, New York.

Whiteford, Andrew H.
1960 *Two Cities of Latin America.* Logan Museum of Anthropology, Beloit, Wis.

Whitten, Norman E., Jr.
1965 *Class, Kinship, and Power in an Ecuadorian Town: The Negroes of San Lorenzo.* Stanford University Press, Stanford, Cal.

Whitten, Norman E., Jr., and John Szwed (eds.)
1970 *Afro-American Anthropology: Contemporary Perspectives.* Free Press, New York.

Wilkie, James W., and Edna Monzón de Wilkie
1969 *México visto en el siglo XX: Entrevistas de historia oral.* Instituto Mexicano de Investigaciones Económicas, México.

Wolf, Eric R.
1955 Types of Latin American peasantry: A preliminary discussion. *American Anthropologist* 57:452–471.
1956 Aspects of group relations in a complex society: Mexico. *American Anthropologist* 58:1065–1078 (reprinted in Heath and Adams, 1965; also herein).
1957 Closed corporate peasant communities in Mesoamerica and central Java. *Southwestern Journal of Anthropology* 13:1–18.
1959 *Sons of the Shaking Earth.* University of Chicago Press, Chicago.
1966 *Peasants.* Prentice-Hall, Englewood Cliffs, N.J.
1969 *Peasant Wars of the Twentieth Century.* Harper & Row, New York.

Wolf, Eric R., and Edward C. Hansen

1967 *Caudillo* politics: A structural analysis. *Comparative Studies in Society and History* 9:168–179.

1972 *The Human Condition in Latin America*. Oxford University Press, New York.

Wolfe, Marshall

1966 Rural settlement patterns and social change in Latin America: Notes for a strategy of rural development. *Latin American Research Review* 1,2:5–50.

The Meaning of Kinship in San Juan: Genealogical and Social Models[1]

EVA HUNT

In view of the fact that anthropologists have paid what many people consider an inordinate amount of attention to kinship, it may seem strange that this selection is the first formal analysis of Spanish kinship terms that has been published. Hunt goes far beyond genealogical terminology and relationships and examines kinship in terms of "folk models" (cf. Strickon) and actual networks of social interaction as well, to demonstrate various ways in which this approach can be useful in understanding life in a Mexican village.

Eva Hunt is Associate Professor of Anthropology at Boston University. She has conducted ethnographic and historical research on a number of Indian groups in Mexico and has written several articles on social and political organization.

Bohannan (1963: 54–55) has suggested that there are three distinct referents of "kinship relationships": a genealogical, a social, and a terminological one. As we see it, the first refers to a network of birth and mating connections, with which all cultures handle the legitimization of the gene flow in the population. The second refers to a network of prescribed, preferred, or accepted interactions, with which all cultures handle the legitimization of some roles in terms of the symbolic flow of social relationships. The third refers to a linguistic code, by which persons are tagged in terms of either or both of the two networks in any particular society. From here on we will refer to these as the genealogical network, the social network, and the terminological code.

In traditional kinship analysis, since the days of Morgan (1871) and Rivers (1901, 1924) the genealogical network and the social one have usually been assumed to be isomorphous, and both have been conceived as being reflected in the code which anthropologists call the kinship terminology. In general terms, they have been handled analytically as if the three components or referents formed a single system of relationships, one of which (the terminology) maps the other two linguistically. This kind of construct—what Kuhn (1962) would call a scientific paradigm—proved very useful for a time to treat evidence from societies in which kinship as a genealogical net had extreme prominence as an organizational basis for the society (cf. Parsons 1966), especially those which utilized the terminological code to make genealogical unilineal discriminations in social relationships. Eggan (1950) can be cited as a prime example of the value of such approach. Lacks of congruency (so-called deviations, extensions, and so on) between the use of the code in the genealogical and social networks have been treated as logical *faux pas* of the folk system: metaphorical extensions, fuzzy boundaries, fictitious or pseudo-kinship, ritual relationships, etc. These "anomalies" have become increasingly prominent as anthropologists have

From *Ethnology* VII (1969), 37–53. Reprinted by permission of the author and publisher.

shifted the focus of their interests to nonunilineal or cognatic codes (cf., for example, Marshall 1957). They can be perceived, however, even in the most classical examples of unilineal code usage, such as the Hopi, Zuni, or Tiv (Titiev 1967; Schneider and Roberts 1956; Bohannan 1954).

Our data from the Mexican mestizo town of San Juan, in Oaxaca, suggests that Bohannan's three logical distinctions are in fact separate empirical realities, and should be treated as independent models. Our data specially point out, moreover, that the genealogical and social aspects may be two separate models not only analytically but in the minds of the carriers of a culture (i.e., they have distinct psychological reality as models for thought). Furthermore, the manner in which San Juaneros handle the kinship terminology suggests that the two models are independently activated, and that anthropological assumptions about isomorphism, congruency, and extension of the use of the term code are not always supported by the cultural reality. In fact, each model is based on different principles of recruitment, maintenance, and termination of relationships, and each has to be analyzed as a separate and distinct universe (Hunt 1967).

The independence of the models needs qualification. Both models are by definition within culture, and in this sense cannot be independent, inasmuch as culture is a system. But as cultural constructs they are independent as (a) analytical categories in the scientist's mind, and (b) distinct "maze-ways" in the native's mind (cf. Wallace 1956). A simple but not totally accurate solution would be to claim that (a) the genealogical model is primarily ideational (a cultural view of genealogical linkages based on ethnobiology); and (b) the social model is primarily an empirical pattern of what people "do on the ground" (a cultural view of ethnosociology). This, however, is not absolutely true. First, both models are ideational because they are cognitions in the natives' minds. Second, feelings and cognitions both produce significant social discriminations between kin, which are followed as well as follow the functioning of the two models at the empirical level. Third, both are equally abstract (or concrete) in terms of actual behaviors and neither explains by itself the total structure of San Juan kinship. We consider them independent because they are psychologically distinct and because they lead to the formation of different groups, on the basis of distinct principles and activated for different social goals. Obviously, independence would be out of the question if one were dealing with an undifferentiated socio-cultural realm of phenomena. But our treatment follows a Parsonian view of the action system. We do not, however, axiomatically assign culture or any other of the subsystems to a higher cybernetic level or as an independent variable (Parsons 1966: 9). The analytical advantages of separating the social and cultural realms in anthropological analysis have been clearly illustrated (e.g., Geertz 1957; Spiro 1961).

Finally, our work points out that, contrary to the assumptions of some anthropologists (e.g., Lounsbury 1965), culture carriers may adjust the perception of the genealogical network to accord with the social network, rather than the reverse. This point has been made theoretically, and in slightly different phrasing, by Leach (1958), but he focuses upon the structural reality rather than the psychological validity for the culture carriers.[2] We think we are not taking a theoretical stand (although in the long run this may be the case) but instead are making an empirical observation. However, the Leach-Lounsbury controversy, in the context of our data analysis, is not truly relevant. For the San Juanero, both dimensions have primacy, depending on context. In this sense, the kinship term code, which is utilized for the two models, serves a double function—to tag bio-genealogical "kinship" and interacting members of a descent group—and kin terms do not have the same semantic space for each model, although the words used are the same. This is what Schneider and Roberts (1956: 17) call "the role designating and classifying functions of any given kinship term." The total meaning of the term is the sum of its alternative, complementary, and partial meanings. Neither usage is purely an extension of the others as Lounsbury believes, nor are social groupings or patterns of social exchange always dominant. Which meaning of the code dominates may depend on the context in which it is used, and a term can only be meaning-specific in the cultural setting in which it occurs.

The San Juan genealogical model can be presented most economically with the now standard methods of componential analysis (cf. Hammel 1965).[3] Since the genealogical networks are based primarily on genealogical grids, biological or pseudo-biological principles explain the distribution and usage of terminology. In San Juan these can be accounted for by principles of Kroeberian type (Kroeber 1909). Added to these we have fertility, which is a crucial principle, not for recruitment but for the maintenance of the spouse relationship, in many cultures as well as that of San Juan.

The principles functioning in the San Juan terminology are: (1) absolute generation,[4] (2) sex of the referent (sex of the speaker is never applied), (3) linearity *vs.* collaterality, (4) three degrees of collaterality, (5) relative age or seniority, and (6) number of mating links. Five generations are distinguished terminologically, two above and two below Ego, for all consanguineal kin. Nine are distinguished for lineals, three for affinals. Sex of the referent is universal. Linearity and collaterality function to place exclusive terms in zero, 1+, and 1− (adjacent) generations to Ego. All terms imply the distinction of lineal *vs.* nonlineal. The code applied to the genealogical network for consanguineals consists of eight morphemic stems (*-adre, herman-, hij-, niet-, ti-, pri-, sobrin-, abuel-*), which form the linguistic core of the code. All other positions in the genealogical net are tagged by modifications of these roots. The same is true for the affinal net code. That is, the core of the terminology (which is also the address terminology) is complemented by derivative code items. Manipulation of suffix and prefix changes, and the combination of these roots, give rise to all other terms by simply modifying gender and number according to the grammatical rules of Spanish (see Chart 1).

The principle of degree of collaterality is, ideally, infinite in application. San Juaneros, however, close the system at the third degree, indicating the three relevant distinctions by adding to a core term the words *segundo* or *tercero* (second and third). These degrees are measured by the number of links between two positions. Two or three links indicate first degree; four or five links, second degree; six and seven links, third degree. Mating links apply only to the affinal terminology, and only two degrees are counted: kin related through one mating link, and kin related through two marital links. Collateral affinality thus distinguishes only two degrees (as distinct from collateral consanguineal), tagged by the prefix *con* in combination with the stems for affinals.

CHART 1: San Juan Kinship Terminology Applied to the Genealogical Network (Consanguineals)

The Kinsmen (El Parentesco—La parentela)

Absolute Generation	sex of referent							
	male	female	male	female	male	female	male	female
+4	tatarabuelo	tatarabuela						
−4	tataranieto	tataranieta						
+3	bisabuelo	bisabuela				parientes lejanos		
−3	bisnieto	bisnieta						
+2	abuel(it)o	abuel(it)a	tioabuelo	tiabuela				
−2	niet(ecit)o	niet(ecit)a	sobrinonieto	sobrinanieta				
+1	padre (papá)	madre (mamá)	tío	tía	tío segundo	tía segunda	tío tercero	tía tercera
−1	hij(it)o	hij(it)a	sobrino	sobrina	sobrino segundo	sobrina segunda	sobrino tercero	sobrina tercera
>0	hermano* mayor	hermana mayor	primo	prima	primo segundo	prima segunda	primo tercero	prima tercera
<0	hermano menor (hermanito)	hermana menor (hermanita)						
	direct or lineals		1st degree collaterals		2nd degree collaterals		3rd degree collaterals	
	near kin (parientes cercanos—marriage forbidden)				far kin (parientes lejanos—marriage permitted)			

– – – La mera familia (nuclear family) ⌜ Core terms (Address terminology)

* Siblings are not lineals but co-lineals. Mexican law treats them as a special kind of collaterals. San Juaneros merge them with lineals. We have included them with lineals because of design problems in a two-dimensional paradigm.

Relative age (*mayor* and *menor*), which is also implied by the generational distinctions, is used exclusively for the senior-junior differentiation between individuals of zero generation, and serves to refine the generational principle by adding a more subtle differentiation among a person's contemporaries (see Chart 2).

The use of the terminology with the genealogical network serves several functions. First, it tags Ego's genealogical personal kindred, as a category of persons related to Ego (Freeman 1961: 202–03). Three Ego-centered, circumscriptive kin groupings are formed, each further removed from Ego (Murdock 1960: 5): the nuclear family (*la mera familia*), the near kin (*los parientes cercanos* or *la familia cercana*), and the far or removed kin (*los parientes lejanos*). All these together form the *parentesco* or *los parientes*, that is, all the individuals with whom genealogical connections exist, are traced, and are terminologically tagged by Ego. Second, the model provides the primary frame for the application of incest regulations. Primacy here means most important as defined by San Juaneros. Informants clearly indicated that incest relates first and foremost to sexual relations between blood kin (*parientes de sangre*), and that it is most "horrifying" when it occurs between close blood kin, especially in the nuclear family. All individuals who occupy positions classified as lineals or first degree collaterals (i.e., by the eight core terms) and who belong to the near kin (*mera familia* and *parientes cercanos*) are forbidden to marry each other.

The *mera familia* and *parientes cercanos* of some particular Egos also serve as the genealogical base from which members of the descent group may be recruited. However, this genealogical base, as we will show, is not the only prerequisite for descent group formation or membership, nor necessarily a criterion for membership in all cases.

These regulations, which are always stated in normative terms by San Juaneros (*se debe or no se debe*: "one ought to" or "one ought not to") exhaust the analysis of the terminology as it applies to the genealogical net. Wallace and Atkins (1960) and Schneider (1965) among several authors,

CHART 2. San Juan Kinship Terminology Applied to the Genealogical Network (Affinals)

Absolute Generation	sex of referent					
	male	female	male	female	male	female
+1	suegro	suegra	consuegro	consuegra		
−1	yerno	nuera		parientes	políticos	
0	esposo (marido)	esposa (mujer)	cuñado	cuñada	concuñado	concuñada
	direct or lineal		collateral			
	one marital link				two marital links	

NOTE: The marital link is always on zero generation.

however, have often pointed out that componential analysis only deals with one domain of kinship and leaves a large residue of evidence in terms of kinship relationships (as well as excluding connotations from the semantic space occupied by denotative terms). That is, important relevant information on the kinship system cannot be retrieved by the use of the terminological paradigm. For part of this residue we must turn to an analysis of the social network. Before we complete this task, however, it is necessary to describe briefly the social structure in which these networks function in San Juan.

San Juan is a mestizo (Mexican, non-Indian) town of Spanish speakers in the state of Oaxaca, Mexico. The town is located in a narrow valley surrounded by a mountainous Indian hinterland, and is a major center of agricultural and enterpreneurial activities for its local region. Most San Juaneros are involved both in agricultural tasks, primarily for the production of cash crops in the national market, and in business activities involving trade with the Indian hinterland and the larger urban centers of Mexico.

Differences of wealth, education, and political power are indicated by multiple social markers and give rise to three social classes, which are recognized and named by all San Juaneros.[5] There is a small elite (*la gente de categoría, la clase alta*) comprising approximately 10 per cent of the population of 2,500 inhabitants, a middle class (*la clase media, los de medio pelo*) of slightly larger size, and a majority of the lower class (*los peones, los de menos*). The Spanish terminology to distinguish between the classes is extensive and rich in synonyms and quasi-synonyms and is the first way in which a person's social status is defined in terms of the community.[6]

Social interaction between classes is highly restricted (both normatively and in practice) to formal contexts through the regulation of a set of norms collectively called *igualarse* (literally, to make oneself equal). The process of *igualarse* refers to social mobility and to permissible behavior between members of different classes. *Igualarse* norms are reminiscent of caste restrictions. They involve such behaviors as unidirectional visiting patterns, differential use of space in households in which one is not a member, unidirectional exchanges of certain foods in terms of quality, order of placing and serving on public occasions, asymmetrical greeting, nonsharing of alcohol outside ritual occasions, etc. A complete description of its workings is difficult to present here for reasons of space, but here suffice it to say that behavior in violation of these norms is equivalent to social deviancy and evokes negative sanctions from both members of one's own class and others. *Igualarse* restrictions impinge upon the kinship system by (a) imposing restrictions on permissible or preferred marital partners, and (b) excluding as recognized kin, for interaction and as members of the descent group, individuals who do not belong to the same social level, even though they may be genealogically connected and are known to be so. Ideally, in this system, women and men circulate horizontally in the class scale, but it is permissible for women to marry upwards, or men downwards, if social distance is not extreme in terms of class rank. In practice, the upper-class males usually marry down, and elite females either do not marry, marry outside of the community, or are faced with a downward marriage which immediately jeopardizes their class position and their kinship statuses. Part of the contradiction between norm and behavior is easily explained by the restricted number of possible mating partners within the upper class. Partly it can be explained because of further applications of the *igualarse* restrictions, based on political factionalism.

Criss-crossing class boundaries, San Juan has two old political factions which are based on two separate, similar, and competitive networks of economic allegiances, represented by two coalitions of patron-client sets. These function in terms both of the local economy and of political support for incumbents of local and state offices of the PRI party (the official party of the Mexican Revolution, now in power). The reasons why politics and economics go hand in hand in San Juan is discussed elsewhere (cf. Hunt 1965). The two networks, however, are defined by membership at the top. Each one of these antagonistic politico-economic factions is headed by a few families of the local elite, who are in actual control of the town's economic and political life, and in their wake follow the other classes through the patron-client network.

The economic might of the elite is based on business enterprises which control land, irrigation water, credit, and wholesale and retail commerce for the town, and which are nuclear family corporations headed by the eldest male in the family. These enterprises, however, collaborate with each other within each political faction, primarily to protect and expand their control. In a sense, although the enterprise is inherited exclusively from one nuclear family through another by monoinheritance of a son, and to succeed through time it must be a centripetal institution, its needs for communication with the larger world of business and politics of Mexico make it a centrifugal one (see Hunt 1965). Connections of the enterprise with the outside world are effected through the institution of the *familia*.

The *familia* in the social network is not the personal kindred as it was defined in the context of the genealogical network. Instead, it is a corporate descent group, a stem kindred (Davenport 1959). Its core is a small group of related males, their spouses, and children. Attached to this core are some selected collaterals and affinals and some nongenealogically connected individuals with whom business and political connections are maintained by the group. It is a prerequisite for membership that approximately the same social rank be maintained. Individuals who fall out of the upper classes, and/or belong to opposite political factions, are not included in the elite *familia*, even though logically, in terms of the genealogical model, they belong within its boundaries; indeed San Juaneros believe that they should be in it, if the blood were followed, since *familia* limits are, genealogically, a function of collateral distance.

Recognition as a member of a *familia* is indicated by the use of its *apellido* (surname), which is inherited from male lines. Even though a person may be connected through female links, and thus carry a different personal surname, he is identified by the *familia* surname rather than his own. Five of these *familias* distributed in eighteen households (only those resident in San Juan) make up the elite.

The genealogical bases of *familia* formation are three different forms of marriage, *amasiato* (or *unión libre*), civil, and/or religious marriage, and three different classifications for offspring: nonrecognized legally (*bastardos*), recognized through the civil register but without legal marriage of parents (*ilegítimos*), and fully legitimate children (*legítimos*) who are both recognized and born within legitimate wedlock. These three types of legitimization of marriage and offspring are ranked in status and usually occur at different times in the life cycle of a parental set, especially in the life cycle of elite males. Thus many males of the San Juan elite initiate adulthood with a casual union which produces *bastardo* offspring, later enter into a common-law union whose children are recognized but not legitimized, and finally establish a legal marriage with legitimate offspring. The last two may be with the same or different females, and both may be maintained through time in separate households, the famous *casa chica* of Mexico.

Nutini (1965) has pointed out that there are distinctions which separate common-law spouses from lovers or mistresses in Mexico. The *casa chica* in some cases in San Juan involves a common-law union, in others is purely a concubinage arrangement, but the two are socially distinct. The expression is usually confined to concubinage, while *amasiato* is preferred to describe a common-law union. Common-law marriages are legitimized through a special ceremony involving the parental set of the female and the new couple, called the *pedida de perdón* (the asking for forgiveness), which takes place after an *amasiato* has been initiated by elopement (*robo* or *huída*). If one desires to give a name to this pattern, it can be called ranked serial polygamy. Spouses of any of the three forms of marriage can be incorporated into the *familia,* as long as they are of close class status and belong to the same political faction. Both legitimate and illegitimate children may be also incorporated in the elite, but *bastardos* are not. The latter may not marry into the elite, but both *ilegítimos* and *legítimos* can do so.

These regulations delineate *familia* membership. Hence the *familia* does not incorporate new members in a symmetrical genealogical fashion nor as a function of collateral distance, but according to class, politics, and the kind of legitimization of marriage and descent. Since both marriage and descent legitimization are ranked in terms of prestige, the core of a *familia* tends to contain legitimate children and spouses exclusively, but when these are absent (or not dominant) it may incorporate lower ranked relationships, as long as class and political faction requirements are met.

Added to these restrictions are those imposed by the expectations of proper behavior in a *familia* member. Personal misdemeanors, if serious enough (e.g., homicide or alcoholism among the elite) exclude a person from rights to enter a *familia* group or maintain membership in it. If a person is declassed (e.g., by marrying an Indian), changes political allegiances, becomes impoverished, marries across factions, or otherwise misbehaves in terms of *familia* norms, he is ostracized and loses his status as *pariente*. That is, the kinship connection is severed from the social point of view, and the kinship relationship is terminated. His descendants are thus erased from the genealogy. This, of course, presents a contrast with the genealogical kin network, in which only divorce or death terminates a relationship.

Looking at the social network from the point of view of the terminological code, it becomes apparent that the principles which affect kin term usages are to a large extent different from those applied to the genealogical net (see Chart 3).

First, genealogical connections, although the basis of some social acknowl-

CHART 3. San Juan Kinship Terminology Applied to the Social Network

Continuum of Respeto	Age Rank	Same Class or Faction				Different Class or Faction	
		High Interdependency		Low Interdependency		positive affect	neutral or negative affect
		males	females	males	females	either sex	either sex
mucho respeto	+2	abuel(it)o	abuel(it)a	⟶		parientes de saludo* (prefer to use name rather than kin term)	medio-emparentados (use names only)
menos respeto	−2	niet(ecit)o	niet(ecit)a	⟶			
mucho respeto	+1	padre (papá)	madre (mamá)	tío	tía		
menos respeto	−1	hij(it)o	hij(it)a	sobrin(it)o	sobrin(it)a		
(un poco respeto)	>0	hermano mayor	hermana mayor	primo (grande)	prima (grande)		
iguales	<0	hermanito	hermanita	primo (chico) (primito)	prima (chica) (primita)		
		imperative behaviors		expected-voluntary behaviors		occasional unexpected exchanges	no contacts
		near kin (la familia)				far kin	

*When the kin term is used (in reference) these are always "kinsmen in second degree."

NOTE: Diminutive forms (in parenthesis) indicate more affection or marked age differences within the age range.

edgment of kinship, are neither sufficient nor the only determinants. Individuals as well as whole branches of a *familia* are given kin terms, while other kinsmen are not terminologically named. Ego-centered kindred not incorporated in the *familia* are called *parientes de saludo* and referred to as well as addressed by name rather than by the appropriate genealogical term in the kinship code. *Parientes de saludo* (literally, greeting kin) are individually selected (personal kindred), while *familia* members are non-Ego-centered in recruitment. Individuals cannot, for personal reasons of likes or dislikes, exclude kin who are considered *parientes* by other *familia* members. Only those relationships based on same class, political sympathy, economic cooperation, and integration into the corporate institution of the *familia* and socially recognized connected nuclear families are perceived as real *parientes,* and called by kin terms.

Second, among those who are called by kin terms, the terms themselves may be transposed in relation to the genealogical network. Kin terms do not indicate in the social network genealogical connections of absolute generation, but exclusively of relative age. Thus individuals are moved terminologically in the genealogy to fit their age range, and the terms utilized may not correspond with absolute generation positions. The simple equivalent in English would be to transpose a PaBr into the category of cousin because he is too young to be called uncle. These switches are usually not individualistic, but are determined by the use established by the core generation in each *familia* group; juniors follow with the appropriate junior term, according to the use of kin term selected by their senior. Secondarily, degree of collaterality and linearity may be modified. Thus, although siblings may be excluded from a *familia* by virtue of being impoverished or because of inheritance conflicts, and not assigned kin terms or considered kin, zero *generación* cousins, even far removed ones, can be relocated as *hermanos* and assigned *hermano* terms. The closer two kinsmen are in terms of their common economic and political loyalties within the *familia,* the more likely that they will be assigned genealogically lineal rather than collateral terms. Again, individuals who genealogically are far kin (*parientes lejanos*) are reclassified as close kin if the actual social relationship is a tight one. The reverse, however, is not true. That is, individuals whose social position promotes kinship distanciation are not moved to further positions but are not assigned kin terms at all, and are usually removed from the *familia.* The code apparently carries the implication that positive, nonantagonistic relations exist between users, and cannot be utilized for negative tagging.

These regulations affect not only collaterals, but even primary relationships: parents, siblings, offspring. Moreover, they allow for the incorporation into the *familia* and the use of kin terms towards individuals with whom no kinship connection is demonstrable, as long as they are incorporated into the economic and political network of a particular *familia.* These, San Juaneros maintain, are real *parientes* (kin), not fictitious or "ritual" ones, and they show discomfort when questioned about the validity of their classification.[7]

One major consequence of this distribution is that terms which in the genealogical net are used as exclusive for specific positions (e.g., *madre* as genetrix) in the social network may be occupied by either several individuals or none. Thus the term *madre* as a person performing a mothering role (cf.

Schneider 1961: 2, 5) can be given to more than one woman. Variations in the form of the word serve to indicate differences between *madres,* so that a younger and an older one may be addressed as *mamá chica* and *mamá grande* (small and large). Another consequence is that asymmetrical uses of kin terms occur when a set of dyadic relations is seen *in toto.* Thus, a child may call *mamá* and *papá* two individuals who call each other *papá* and *hija* or *hermano* and *hermana,* and who could never be expected to be husband and wife to each other. Again, a person may call *madre* and *abuelo* two people who are married to each other (this is common when a woman is raising a son's offspring). When nuclear family kin are excluded (become ex-kinsmen), genealogies contain holes where kinsmen who are not acknowledged should be listed. Illegitimate sons incorporated into the *familia* of the *padre,* whose genealogical mother is not a spouse of the *padre,* appear not to have a mother at all, or an unknown or socially "dead" mother. This is an obvious social fiction, which happens even if the biological mother is alive, and occasionally leads to serious interpersonal conflict.

The principles affecting the application of kin terms in the social network are: (1) types of legitimization of marriage and offspring, (2) sex of the referent, (3) relative age, (4) class membership, (5) faction membership, and (6) proper role performance. This last principle is in fact a complex one, a set of criteria about proper role performance rather than one principle, and includes several variables. First, there is a distinction between terms which imply that role performance of a certain sort is imperative expected behavior (*de por fuerza;* literally, by force), and those which imply that it is expected but voluntary behavior (*de voluntad*). For example, in the first set one expects that command and obedience exist in a relationship, or flow between the kin using the terms. In the other, advice and compliance should flow instead. In one case economic responsibility or dependency are implied. For example, persons tagged as *padre, madre,* or *hermanos mayores* are responsible for providing economic support in childhood and in times of stress during early adulthood, making decisions about the junior's career, approving of a chosen marital partner, etc. Persons classified as *tíos,* however, are expected to do the same only if they wish to do so; the behavior is only a voluntary part of their performance in the kinship role, in the absence of "closer" kin. Whereas the absence of imperative behaviors terminates (or endangers) a relationship, the absence of expected but voluntary ones does not.

Second, code terms applied to social roles rather than genealogical positions indicate three different degrees of the folk criterion of *respeto.* One degree (*de mucho respeto*) implies respect in English, and indicates deference, courtesy, and a certain formality in the presentation of the self, lack of intimacy (sharing of personal confidential information), and obedience of commands given by the senior. The *menos respeto* category implies authority of the speaker over his junior, a sense of protectiveness, permissible practical joking, unsubmissiveness, and a dignified (although not necessarily formal) presentation of the self, involving being stern. For the third, *iguales,* kin terms under this category imply in fact the absence of any degree of *respeto* or social distance; they connote a person of similar relative age in a relationship conceived as involving equivalent and highly informal reciprocal roles (cf. Diaz-Guerrero and Peck 1964 for a comparative statement). In fact, elders may receive some deference within zero generation (even in informal interaction), normatively characterized as "a little bit" of *respeto* and tied to the importance of age-rank rather than to other duties or rights.

Since the criteria overlap (i.e., produce a certain amount of redundancy) in their application, there are two others which are not included in the paradigm but are significant in allocating tags to kin. One is the category of intimacy, independent of the respect dimension. Roles are distinguished from each other at least three ways. First, with the least intimacy, parental roles; second, other individuals of +1 and of alternate generations; and, third, individuals of Ego's generation. The second is the category of authority-obedience and responsibility-dependency, which can be analytically separated from *respeto*, but which in terms of its distribution San Juaneros merge, except that it fades out in alternate generations.

The application of all kinship terms in the social network is determined by these role demands incorporated into the folk principle which we call proper role performance and the others listed above, rather than by all the biological or pseudo-biological ones which distribute the terms in the genealogical model.

It is clear, at this point, that, from an analytical point of view, we have in fact two models. This, however, does not justify claims as to the separate empirical reality of these two models in natives' cognitions. For these, our informants rather than ourselves take primacy. San Juaneros probably do not go about thinking of model transformations or principles when they relate to those whom they call kinsmen. They are, however, very ready to discuss the matter in their own words, and to make predictable choices in the abstract as well as when faced with concrete examples. First, they recognize, like Laura Bohannan (1954), that there are two distinct manners in which one perceives kin: by blood and by deed. Second, they are perfectly willing to indicate which are the active principles by which the assignments of kin terms are made in the two networks. Names for all the principles which we have discussed exist in Spanish and are known and used by San Juaneros. Third, informants can pinpoint the rules of transformation between term usages from one model to the other, and, moreover, they can indicate when the two models are not only different but incongruent.

The most characteristic example of the last point is the application of incest regulations in the social network. Although incest regulations are said by San Juaneros to apply primarily to the genealogical grid, kin who are reclassified in the social network as close kin are excluded from marriage even though their marital union may be permissible in terms of the biological network. The other side of this coin is that, because many close kin in the genealogical network are excluded from the *familia* in each generation, there is a constant fear, expressed in Oedipal and sibling incest fantasies, that incestuous relations might be established without the marital partners being aware of a prohibiting biological relationship. This is, of course, related to the high rate of illegitimacy in the society (60 per cent of all births) and the lack of kinship recognition which follows many births, and it is a common fantasy in Mexican society, not merely in San Juan.[8]

Thus San Juaneros perceive kinship as two distinct forms of relationships:

one set by bio-links, another by personal and group allegiances. The kinship terminology in the second model tags marriage rank, birth legitimization, class status, economic and political co-operation, proper role performance, and positive affect, not bio-links nor even normative descent.[9] And it is upon these principles that the recognition of descent links and kinsmen in the social model is based, not the genealogical principles. It seems clear to us that the San Juan system is highly specialized in a functional sense. The whole system of kin recognition is dominated by the economic-political structure of the town and region, even to the point that biological links are frequently perceived only in terms of the social network.[10] Conflict between the two models is partially resolved by the use of a single terminological code which can be adjusted to changing social relationships and membership in groups.

It is our hypothesis that many kinship systems other than the one in San Juan may be functionally specialized as well, that is, that kinship terminologies may carry different semantic and functional loads in different societies. Some systems may emphasize actual genealogical links, some may not. San Juan specializes in a direction which requires two separate models to operate. The Javanese, for example, focus on status inequality, which is a major organizational principle in the society, and the code used within genealogical kinship is also utilized outside this domain (H. Geertz 1961; Koentjaraningrat 1957, 1960). The code, then, does not reflect (is not exclusively isomorphous with) genealogical linkages, nor does it reflect behavior or interaction differences in particular relationships, but only indicates certain general classes of statuses and roles which have certain privileges in a relationship.[11] Whether one of the models is an extension of the other is a problem of the frame of analysis as well as of the nature of the data. But Javanese evidence indicates that the code can only be called a kinship terminology because it is first learned to be applied in the context of the *kulawarga* or nuclear family (as I interpret Lounsbury, he assumes this to be true in all kinship systems), not because the terms specify exclusively birth or marriage links, or behavior in kinship relations, or any attribute of Javanese kinship as separate from any other domain of social action.[12]

Among the !Kung Bushmen (Marshall 1957) it appears that regulations of incest according to the naming pattern carry a heavy functional load. The !Kung have two sets of terms used in dyadic relationships between any two individuals in the society, all of which are "kin terms" in the traditional view. Of these terms, one set is applied exclusively among consanguineals and affinals, the kinship model for these being built on the application of the code to a genealogical network. The other set of terms in the code, however, applies not only to the genealogical model but to a social network of name-exchanges between paired individuals, who may be affinals, consanguineals, or persons not connected genealogically. In this case, the terms apply to the genealogical model to differentiate some exclusive genealogical connections (e.g., parent and child in the nuclear family), but a separate (linguistically derivative) code applies to a different model based on name allocations, which functions to regulate marriage, permissible joking, and the definition of insiders and foreigners in terms of territorial groups.

These examples are, of course, simple illustrations of the possibility that a cross-cultural search may provide a final solution in terms of discovering (a) the range of application of each model, (b) the range of possible variations in application, and (c) the extent to which what we call kinship terminologies are actually codes which apply primarily to genealogical constructs, or to define roles in descent groups, or to carry some other symbolic load.

In summary, we have tried to show the Bohannan's logical distinction between social and biological networks in kinship is important empirically, and that considerations of genealogical linkage, descent, or social interaction may vary from society to society (or from context to context) in delimiting the use of kin terms and their basic meanings. A start has been made in the componential analysis of the roles involved (what is usually called kinship behavior) in terms of principles. These include such items as kind of marriage legitimization, dominance, positive affect, economic interdependency, etc. The San Juan system is built with a very heavy functional load on social rather than genealogical solidarity, and it is suggested that other systems be reanalyzed from this point of view to determine to what degree they are also so specialized. This may offer a new strategy to solve a usually ignored basic problem of analysis.

NOTES

1. The field work on which this paper is based was carried out during parts of 1963 and 1964. This research was sponsored by the National Science Foundation, Grant #GS-87, for which we wish to express our gratitude. A long previous acquaintance with the Mexican kinship system derived from previous work and personal (rather than anthropological) experience has been incorporated. This paper would never have been written, however, without the intellectual prompting of Paul J. Bohannan and Robert Hunt. The first also provided the author with a post-doctoral fellowship of the Center for Social Science Research of Northwestern University, during the holding of which much of the thinking done for this paper was initiated. The second has contributed to the ideas expressed here to the extent that I cannot, with any certainty, separate the sources. I feel, however, tradition bound to free them from any responsibility for this statement. Professor David Schneider read a draft of this paper and raised some useful criticisms. I hope finally to have resolved some of the ambiguities. A shorter version of this paper was read at the annual meeting of the Central States Anthropological Society, Chicago, 1967. A longer version, in monograph form, is in preparation. Many points barely outlined here will there be made explicit and amply illustrated with examples.

2. In the case of Lounsbury it seems that some sort of psychological reality determining primacy of the genealogical network (especially for terms of closely connected kin) is assumed. His statements, however, allow the interpretation that his analysis is about the primacy of scientific and structural (rather than psychological) permutations. Since in San Juan children learn the use of the code in both networks simultaneously, one is faced with an impossible task in determining primacy, or any sort of ranking of primary versus secondary use of the code. We suppose that counting the instances in which terms are used in one or the other network, and determining frequencies, could be considered a weighting technique. But this misses the point that the functional load carried by particular symbols may be highly significant even though its manifestations in data may be rare.

3. We do not give the preliminary algebraic treatment, because anyone interested in it

can easily reconstruct the traditional genealogy from the information provided in text and paradigm. This genealogy is itself an abstraction. Given the realities of San Juaneros' handling of the kinship system, genealogical data gathering with traditional methods was curtailed. In its classic form it soon proved insufficient to deal with the phenomena observed or even to gather the relevant information. Final genealogies of specific informants were built from information from multiple others: friend and foe, kin and nonkin, life histories, observations of uses of the code in everyday and special contexts, etc., and also by probing with individuals their own awareness of the meaning of terms and the uses to which they put them in connection to both real persons and abstracted genealogical or social positions. It is only because our San Juan informants were acutely aware of the problems involved (in their own lives) that they could bridge for us the gap between datum and anthropological abstraction.

4. We call this absolute generation to distinguish from folk generation, which may lump together individual positions which genealogically are at different levels. Goodenough (1951), in his treatment of Truk kinship, merges them. Using the folk constructs may be more useful to explain the specific system, but it curtails the comparative value of componential analysis, in terms of principles, in a cross-cultural context (Hunt 1967).

5. A division of classes by occupation in the manner of American sociologists (cf. Lipset and R. Bendix 1959) is misleading. Differences of class in San Juan would be blurred on the basis of this criterion because San Juaneros all do the same things. What makes for a difference, occupationally, is how much land or capital is invested and what the return profit is. Specialization, except for a handful of professionals (the two doctors, a judge, and a federal engineer who is temporarily posted in San Juan), is only a part-time engagement. Markers indicating class differences which are significant in San Juan are style of clothing, diet, dialect, housing, visiting patterns, types of preferred leisure activities, expenditure in certain rituals, sources of savings, knowledge and connections outside the community, etc. That is, outside the economic base, what Weber (1966: 422–429) would call social status (mode of living, prestige, etc.) are the markers of the class.

6. Since class is a crucial structural variable, synonyms and quasi-synonyms are abundant. We give a few of the many forms in the text. Some refer to the different wealth of classes, some to their ethnic origin, some to their prestige; a complete presentation requires a separate analysis of the class code. Within classes, further differentiation is also acknowledged. The elite, for example, is divided into the Spanish elite (families who have recently had a living head who was or is a Spanish immigrant) and the old Mexican elite (descendants of the colonial, pre-revolutionary upper classes of Mexican extraction). These internal differences, however, do not function to curtail interaction since both groups are represented in all families and across political factions and are tied by multiple, recognized, legitimate, affinal ties. Each of these claims to have higher prestige than the other within the class.

7. Older informants faced with questions about this nongenealogical incorporation of kinsmen give complex "explanations" on why or how a case occurred (in one specific instance a man was incorporated because he was once engaged to, but did not marry, one of the *familia* young women). Younger *familia* members actually do not know that genealogical links may be lacking, and merely assume that it is the intermediate links which have been forgotten.

8. Among other examples, it is a frequent theme in Mexican novels, theatrical plays, and magazine stories. Cf. for example, Carballido (1956), Cordero León (1960), Fernandez Bustamante (n.d.), Gamboa (1956), Lozano Martinez (1960).

9. By normative descent we mean that implied in the genealogical network use of the code, which San Juaneros define normatively as bilateral, symmetrical, and fading in the

the third degree. This descent rule, however, is not the one applying to the formation of socially recognized descent groups. However, since San Juaneros do not distinguish abstractly between kinship and descent, such dichotomies as are presented by Scheffler (1966) are not applicable in this paper, except as an exercise in metalanguage refinement.

10. We include the region because members of a *familia* in San Juan may also have socially recognized kin who are resident in nearby towns and, among the elite, many reside in the larger cities of Mexico.

11. We are extremely grateful to the commentaries Dr. Hildred Geertz made on an earlier, unpublished paper of ours, partially based on her Javanese data.

12. This generalization excludes some few collateral terms (e.g., cousin terms), which are exclusively genealogical and are treated as such among the elite (*prijaji*).

BIBLIOGRAPHY

Bohannan, L. (under nom de plume of Elenore Smith Bowen). 1954. Return to Laughter. New York.

Bohannan, P. J. 1963. Social Anthropology. New York.

Carballido, E. 1956. La danza que sueña la tortuga. Teatro Mexicano del Siglo XX 3:135–206. México.

Cordero León, G. 1960. Tres tragedias rurales: Dies irae. Catálogo del Teatro Mexicano Contemporáneo 2:32. México: Instituto Nacional de Bellas Artes.

Davenport, W. 1959. Nonunilinear Descent and Descent Groups. American Anthropologist 61:557–572.

Diaz-Guerrero, R., and R. F. Peck. 1964. Respeto y posición social en dos culturas. Anuario de Psicología, Universidad Nacional Autónoma de México 1:37–63.

Eggan, F. 1950. Social Organization of the Western Pueblos. Chicago.

Fernandez Bustamante, A. 1960. Judith. Colección Teatro Mexicano Contemporáneo 2:40. México.

Freeman, J. D. 1961. On the Concept of Kindred. Journal of the Royal Anthropological Institute 91:192–220.

Gamboa, F. 1956. La venganza de la gleba. Colección Teatro Mexicano del Siglo XX 1:185–240. México.

Geertz, C. 1957. Ritual and Social Change: A Javanese Example. American Anthropologist 59:32–54.

Geertz, H. 1961. The Javanese Family: A Study of Kinship and Socialization. Glencoe.

Goodenough, W. H. 1951. Property, Kin, and Community on Truk. Yale University Publications in Anthropology 46:1–192.

Hammel, E. A., ed. 1965. Formal Semantic Analysis. American Anthropologist 67:v, pt. 2 (Special Publication).

Hunt, R. C. 1965. The Development Cycle of the Family Business in Rural Mexico. American Ethnological Society, Proceedings of the Annual Spring Meeting: Essays in Economic Anthropology, ed. J. Helm, pp. 54–79.

——— 1967. Toward a Componential Analysis of Interaction. Paper read at the annual meeting of the Central States Anthropological Society in Chicago.

Koentjaraningrat. 1957. A Preliminary Description of the Javanese Kinship System. Yale University South East Asia Studies, Cultural Report Series 4.

——— 1960. The Javanese of South Central Java. Viking Fund Publications in Anthropology 29:88–115.

Kroeber, A. L. 1909. Classificatory Systems of Relationship. Journal of the Royal Anthropological Institute 39:77–84.
Kuhn, T. 1962. The Structure of Scientific Revolutions. Chicago.
Leach, E. R. 1958. Concerning Trobriand Clans and the Kinship Category *Tabu*. Cambridge Papers in Social Anthropology 1:120–145.
Lipset, S. M., and R. Bendix. 1959. Social Mobility in Industrial Society. Berkeley and Los Angeles.
Lounsbury, F. G. 1965. Another View of the Trobriand Kinship Categories. Formal Semantic Analysis, ed. E. A. Hammel, pp. 142–185. American Anthropologist 67:v, pt. 2 (Special Publication).
Lozano Martinez, T. 1960. El doctor es mi padre. Catálogo del Teatro Mexicano Contemporáneo 2:83–84. México.
Marshall, L. 1957. The Kinship Terminology System of the !Kung Bushmen. Africa 27:1–25.
Morgan, L. H. 1870. Systems of Consanguinity and Affinity of the Human Family. Smithsonian Contributions to Knowledge 17:1–590.
Murdock, G. P. 1960. Cognatic Forms of Social Organization. Viking Fund Publications in Anthropology 29:1–14.
Nutini, H. G. 1965. Polygyny in a Tlaxcalan Community. Ethnology 4:123–147.
Parsons, T. 1966. Societies: Evolutionary and Comparative Perspectives. Englewood Cliffs, New Jersey.
Rivers, W. H. R. 1910. The Genealogical Method of Anthropological Inquiry. Sociological Review 3:1–12.
——— 1924. Social Organization. New York.
Scheffler, H. W. 1966. Ancestor Worship in Anthropology. Current Anthropology 7:541–551.
Schneider, D. M. 1961. Introduction. Matrilineal Kinship, ed. D. M. Schneider and K. Gough, pp. 1–29. Berkeley.
——— 1965. American Kin Terms and Terms for Kinsmen. Formal Semantic Analysis, ed. E. A. Hammel, pp. 288–308. American Anthropologist 67:v, pt. 2 (Special Publication).
Schneider, D. M., and J. Roberts. 1956. Zuni Kin Terms. University of Nebraska Laboratory of Anthropology Monographs, Note Book 3:i, 1–23.
Spiro, M. E. 1961. Social Systems, Personality, and Functional Analysis. Studying Personality Cross-Culturally, ed. B. Kaplan, pp. 93–127. Evanston.
Titiev, M. 1967. The Hopi Use of Kinship Terms for Expressing Sociocultural Values. Anthropological Linguistics 7:v, 44–49.
Wallace, A. F. C. 1956. Revitalization Movements. American Anthropologist 58:264–281.
——— 1965. The Problem of the Psychological Validity of Componential Analysis. Formal Semantic Analysis, ed. E. A. Hammel, pp. 229–248. American Anthropologist 67:v, pt. 2 (Special Publication).
Wallace, A. F. C., and J. Atkins. 1960. The Meaning of Kinship Terms. American Anthropologist 62:58–80.
Weber, M. 1966. The Theory of Social and Economic Organization. New York. (First edit., 1947).

The Dyadic Contract in Tzintzuntzan, II: Patron-Client Relationship[1]

GEORGE M. FOSTER

One of the best things that one can say of a social scientist's interpretation is that it not only "rings true" but also "makes sense" out of some things that the reader had not previously been able to understand; such a reaction is commonplace with respect to George Foster's writings. One of the most influential is this article, focusing on the virtual absence of corporate ties in a peasant community and showing how dyadic relationships predominate. The continuing quest of some for patrons (to buttress one's security), and of others for clients (to extend one's "power domain," in Adams's terms) fits with the ethic of personalismo *that pervades so much of Latin culture. The motivations and reference groups of brokers (cf. Wolf) can also be better understood in terms of the dyadic contract.*

George M. Foster is Professor of Anthropology at the University of California, Berkeley. He has contributed to the development of applied anthropology in many countries throughout the world, although his ethnographic and historical research has consistently focused on Mexico and Spain. Apart from several seminal articles, he has also written Empire's Children: The People of Tzintzuntzan *(1948),* Culture and Conquest: America's Spanish Heritage *(1960),* Tzintzuntzan: Mexican Peasants in a Changing World *(1967),* Applied Anthropology *(1969),* Traditional Societies and Technological Change *(2nd ed., 1973), and other books.*

The inhabitants of the mestizo peasant village of Tzintzuntzan, Michoacán, lie near the bottom of the Mexican socioeconomic pyramid. Individually and collectively they have limited power, influence, and economic security. They see themselves facing a hostile and dangerous world, from birth until death, in which the good things of life are in short supply, and in which existence itself is constantly threatened by hunger, illness, death, abuse by neighbors, and spoliation by powerful people outside the community. Society and culture provide Tzintzuntzeños with formal institutions and behavior patterns within the framework of which they struggle to "defend" themselves and their families in this essentially unequal battle. When asked how things are going, a man may reply, "*Pues, me defiendo,*" that is, "I am managing to defend myself." Or, in the face of a near-hopeless situation, he may ask, often a bit belligerently, "*Con qué me defiendo?*" That is, "With what do you think I'm going to defend myself?"

To defend one's self means, in the narrow economic sense, to be able to make both ends meet, to have enough to house, clothe, and feed a wife and children. But in the wider sense the expression implies the ability to face up to all of the natural and supernatural threats that fill the peasant villager's world,

---

From *American Anthropologist* LXV (1963), 1280–1294. Copyright © 1963 by the American Anthropological Association. Reprinted by permission of the author and publisher.

to have effective means to counterattack in the face of any specific emergency. To be able to defend one's self, then, means to have the wit and knowledge to take the right step at the right time, to remain on top of the situation.

The goal—the ideal—of successful defense is to be able to live *sin compromisos,* to be strong, masculine, independent, able to meet life's continuing challenges without help from others, to be able to live without entangling alliances. "*Quiero vivir sin compromisos,*" "I want to live without being obligated," is a feeling frequently voiced by hard-working family heads. Yet, paradoxically, the struggle to reach this goal can be made only by saddling one's self with a wide variety of obligations. Strength and independence—success in defending one's self—in fact always depend on the number and quality of the contractual ties one has incurred.[2] Hence the whole course of life consists of manipulating and exploiting the institutions and behavior forms one knows to achieve desirable obligations, to tap social resources so that life's dangers will be minimized and its opportunities maximized.

In an earlier paper (Foster 1961) I proposed the *dyadic contract* as a model to explain how a Tzintzuntzeño incurs and maintains the obligations that are essential to his "defense." Briefly, it was suggested that adults[3] enter contractual relationships of a special type with a wide variety of classes of people (or beings): fellow villagers, friends of comparable socioeconomic status from other communities, individuals of superior power and influence, and supernatural beings such as Christ, the Virgin Mary, and the saints. I called these ties dyadic since normally they bind pairs of contractants, rather than groups. The importance of this distinction is illustrated by the fact that in Tzintzuntzan there are no voluntary associations or institutions in the usual sense in which ego has comparable obligations to two or more people. Each person is the center of his private and unique network of contractual ties, a network whose overlap with other networks has no functional significance. That is, *A*'s tie to *B* in no way necessarily binds him to *C*, who also is tied to *B*. *A* may have a contractual relationship with *C* as well as *B*, but this does not give rise to a feeling of association or group. Ego conceptualizes his obligations and expectations as a two-way street, he at one end and a single partner at the other end.

Dyadic contracts are based on the principle of, and are validated by, reciprocal obligations expressed in the exchange of goods and services. Each partner expects to receive something he wants from the other partner, at times, in ways, and in forms that are clearly understood by both. Each partner, in turn, acknowledges his obligation to give something to the other, again at times, in ways, and in forms that are a function of the type of relationship involved.

Depending on the relative positions of the partners, and on the kinds of things they exchange, two basic types of dyadic contract may be recognized. *Colleague* contracts[4] tie people of equal or approximately equal socioeconomic status, who exchange the same kinds of goods and services. Colleague contracts are phrased horizontally, and they can be thought of as symmetrical, since each partner, in position and obligations, mirrors the other. *Patron-client* contracts tie people (or people to beings) of significantly different socioeconomic status (or order of power), who exchange different kinds of goods and services. Patron-client contracts are phrased vertically, and they can be thought of as asymmetrical since each partner is quite different from the other in position and obligations.

In the earlier paper colleague contracts only were described. It was pointed out that these are informal, or implicit, since they lack ritual or legal basis, and since they are not based on the idea of law, they are unenforceable through authority. Rather, the existence of a contract of this type is recognized when two people exchange goods and services over a period of time—when they maintain an exchange relationship. A functional requisite of the colleague contract is that an even balance between the two partners never be struck. Since the contract is recognized only when exchanges continue, canceling of debits and credits would, in effect, cancel the contract. Colleague contracts, therefore, are all *continuing,* whether for several months or for many years, in the sense that a single exchange between two people does not, in itself, constitute a contract. Colleague contracts are terminated only when an exchange relationship is allowed to lapse, and never by a single act,[5] or the delivery of a specific good or service.

In this paper I complete the analysis of the dyadic contract model by describing patron-client relationship patterns found in Tzintzuntzan.[6] The Spanish word *patrón* ("patron") has several related meanings: an employer of workers, a ceremonial sponsor, a skipper of a small boat, the protecting saint of a village or parish, the protecting saint to all people who bear his (or her) name. All of these definitions are correct for Tzintzuntzan. A patron, it is clear, is someone who combines status, power, influence, authority—attributes useful to anyone—in "defending" himself or in helping someone else to defend himself. But a person, however powerful and influential, is a patron only in relationship to someone of lesser position—a client who, under specific circumstances, he is willing to help.

Tzintzuntzeños all look up to a number of patrons. Each recognizes the saint whose name he bears as *mi santo patrón,* and everyone knows San Francisco is patron of the village. All accept the Virgin of Guadalupe as patron of America and Mexico, and consequently as their patron as well. In addition, many adults refer to people in Pátzcuaro, Morelia, and other towns as *mi patrón,* because of employer-employee or other relationships in which they assume the position of the subordinate partner. Tzintzuntzeños have no corresponding word for themselves as clients. Since they represent near-bottom in the Mexican socioeconomic hierarchy, they rarely if ever look down upon others from the lofty position of patron, and they do not think of the relationship as one in which a person may be either patron or client, depending on relative position and power.

Analytically, two basic types of patrons may be distinguished in Tzintzuntzan: (1) human beings, and (2) supernatural beings. The former include employers, politicians and government employees, town and city friends, godparents or cogodparents (*padrinos* or *compadres*) of superior status, influence, or special abilities, and church personnel, especially the local priests. The latter—the supernatural patrons—are God, Christ, the Virgin Mary, and the saints, the last three in any of their geographical and advocational manifestations. Even the devil is a potential patron. Almost all human patrons, except the local priests, are from outside Tzintzuntzan, since the status differences that are essential for a patron-client relationship are lacking within the community. Supernatural patrons are those associated with the local churches or with family altars, as well as those found in more distant communities.

As is true of colleague contracts, the partners' recognition of mutual obligations underlies and validates the patron-client system. There are, however, two important differences in exchange patterns. First, the patron and client exchange different kinds of goods and services, and second, whereas all colleague contracts are continuing, a significant part of patron-client exchanges are noncontinuing, or short-term. That is, a particular good or service offered by a prospective client requires an immediate and specific return from the potential patron. If the offer is reciprocated, the patron-client contract is established, but the act of reciprocation either simultaneously terminates the contract or establishes conditions for termination in the near future. To be more specific, patron-client relationships involving human beings are like colleague contracts in that goods and services are exchanged over time, with no attempt to strike a balance, since this would cancel the contract. In some instances in which the patron is supernatural, the relationship continues over time, with no attempt to strike an exact balance. But in many other instances, and particularly those in which a supplicant asks for help in time of sickness or other crisis, the expectation is that the granting of the request is canceled out, or balanced off, by the supplicant's compliance with his vow. Hence, no contract exists until the request is granted, and no contract exists after the supplicant complies. This type of patron-client contract is terminated by striking what is recognized as an even bargain between the contractants, the very act that is zealously avoided by colleague contractants so that their relationship *will not* be terminated.

These distinctions should become more clear in the following discussion, where patron-client relationships involving humans only, and humans and supernatural patrons, are dealt with in turn.

PATRON-CLIENT RELATIONSHIPS BETWEEN HUMAN BEINGS

Tzintzuntzeños, recognizing their humble position and lack of power and influence, are continually alert to the possibility of obligating a person of superior wealth, position, or influence, thereby initiating a patron-client relationship which, if matters go well, will buttress the villagers' security in a variety of life crises that are only too certain: illness, the sudden need for cash, help in legal disputes, protection against various forms of possible exploitation, and advice on the wisdom of contemplated moves.

Exploitation of the compadrazgo system (Foster 1961: 1181–83) is one of the most obvious ways to gain a patron, and wealthy city relatives, local ranchers (of whom there are only a few), and storekeepers in near-by Pátzcuaro with whom one may have commercial relations are common targets. When Pedro Castellanos' youngest son, Lucio,[7] was married, his wife's nephew, who had become a successful Pátzcuaro doctor, agreed to be marriage godfather (and his wife automatically became godmother). A pre-existing family tie was thereby strengthened, and the new godfather was under strong obligation to help with free medical attention, possible loans, and advice that the greater wisdom of a town-dweller makes possible. Pedro and his wife, in return, expect to take presents from time to time to their nephew, to invite him to family fiestas and meals in Tzintzuntzan, and perhaps to drum up trade among ill villagers. Macaria Gómez persuaded a distant bachelor cousin, Isaac Mendoza, whose mother controls one of the few remaining haciendas in the neighborhood, to be baptismal godfather to her eldest daughter, Laura. Isaac, in addition to the general prestige he sheds on Macaria, has loaned her money to help with her chicken ranching, and he gave her a considerable sum when she underwent a serious operation. His return is less clear. When he visits Tzintzuntzan, on rare occasions, he is fawned on and made over in extravagant fashion, and perhaps in a land where large landowners are not popular, it is good to have villagers who speak well of one.

The most striking example of a compadrazgo patron-client relationship occurred in 1961 when the governor of the state of Michoacán agreed to stand as godfather to Tiburcio Zúñiga, a rising young potter. Beginning some years earlier, when he held a lesser office, the official began to stop at Tiburcio's pottery stand to buy ware as he passed through the village, thus becoming acquainted with the big Zúñiga family. They, when in the state capital, Morelia, stopped at his home and presented him with Tzintzuntzan pottery, and he in turn helped them find other buyers. By the time of the marriage Tiburcio's father, Victor, felt the friendship had reached a point where he dared ask his patron, now governor, to be godfather. With some trepidation he traveled to Morelia, asked the question, and to his relief and delight, was accepted. As matters turned out, the governor was unable to attend the wedding, but he sent his wife and a brother-in-law as stand-ins. The governor has a leading citizen in Tzintzuntzan who speaks well of him, and in addition he is deluged with presents of attractive pottery. He, in turn, will aid his compadre and godson when needed.

I, as a visiting anthropologist, and obviously a fabulously wealthy and influential man, am continually deluged with requests to be a compadre. My interest in and knowledge of the subject is obvious to the villagers, and they assume that, if snared, I will be bound to honor all obligations to the hilt!

Patron-client compadrazgo relationships, although formally identical to those binding socioeconomic equals, are in fact recognized as quite distinct by all participants. This is especially apparent in linguistic usage. Compadres of the same status, as is well known, are extremely formal with each other—in theory at least—dropping the familiar second person singular personal pronoun "*tu*" in favor of the formal "*Usted*." Client compadres, of course, are extremely formal with their patron compadres (as with all other human patrons), but patron compadres, almost without exception, address their village compadres with the familiar "tu," so that the relative status of the two partners is never in doubt. Isaac Mendoza, for example, is considerably younger than Macaria Gómez; yet, because of his superior status, it is taken for granted by both that he will address her as "tu," while she will address him as "Usted."

Although the compadrazgo institution is an excellent way to establish a patron-client relationship, less formal acts also work well. One day while I sat with Silverio Caro in his roadside pottery stand, a small car drove up with three people. Silverio greeted the driver, "*Buenos días*, doctor," in such a way that it was clear they had had previous contact. After buying several pieces of pottery, the doctor and his friends left. Silverio then explained that this was a relatively new doctor in Pátzcuaro whom he had consulted several times, and it became clear to me that he was carefully building a relationship with him. The regular price of the merchandise selected was 16.50 pesos, but Silverio had charged only 13.00. If, on future visits to Pátzcuaro, the doctor shows a bit more consideration than usual, or goes out of his way to show friendship in some other way, Silverio will take presents of pottery and feel that his relationship with the doctor is good health insurance.

On another occasion Silverio invited me, in a rather vague way, to come to his house and look at his storeroom of pottery. Since I had done this many times previously, the reason was obscure. After inspecting and praising the quality of the ware, and accepting a small ash tray as a gift, I was about to leave when Jovita, his wife, invited me to sit down on a chair. Presently the design came out: would I not, she wondered, bring a used television the next time I drove from the United States to Mexico, which they would buy from me at cost? I explained that, as a tourist, I could not bring merchandise other than personal effects into Mexico, and that customs officials are always very unpredictable and best not crossed. Silverio and Jovita accepted this in good grace, and it was clear that the ploy had been attempted in a "nothing ventured nothing gained" mood. When nothing specific came of the attempt they were not upset, nor did our friendship suffer.

The establishment of the Unesco CREFAL community development training center in Pátzcuaro in 1952, and the subsequent attention given to Tzintzuntzan for several years, multiplied village contacts with people of superior power, and nearly every faculty member and student who visited the village became patron to a number of people. The patrons received presents of pottery, fish, eggs and chickens, and free meals on occasion, and in return offered medical help, tools, and a variety of technical and personal services.

Within Tzintzuntzan, although there are wealth differences, there are no social distinctions that justify the use of the patron-client concept to describe personal relationships, with the single exception of the two priests. Both are reluctant to accept compadrazgo ties, although both have done so on rare occasions, thereby establishing patron-client bonds. But other less specific ties exist. The priests need supporters and helpers to maintain church ritual, to arrange flowers and candles on altars, to clean the buildings, and to supply them with a good deal of their food. They, in turn, can confer extra spiritual blessings on their supporters, and they can, because of their education and knowledge of the world, give temporal advice as well. So, it seems to me, it is proper to think of the priests as participating in exchange relationships with the villagers, in which they are patrons and the villagers are clients.

Both similarities to and differences from the colleague dyadic contracts are apparent in these examples. On the one hand, the relationships are continuing, and neither patron nor client attempts to strike an immediate balance, which both recognize would terminate the contract. On the other hand, the asymmetrical nature of the relationship emerges. Unlike colleague contracts, the partners are not equals, and they make no pretense to equality. Even in the nominally equalizing compadrazgo relationship, differential forms of address reveal this to be true. Asymmetry also is evidenced in the different kinds of goods and services exchanged. It is, in fact, the ability to offer one's partner something distinct from that which he offers that makes the system worthwhile. Within the village, local contractual ties provide a man with all he needs, at peak periods of demand, of the kinds of goods and services to which he has access, and which he can provide when call is made upon him.

At first glance the patron-client compadrazgo, which is formally as well as informally contractual, appears to contradict the dyadic principle: in its important forms it binds a minimum of five and a maximum of eight people (e.g., for baptism, the child, parents, and godparents; for marriage, the godparents, the couple, and the parents of both bride and groom). The contradiction, however, is more apparent than real, since the *meaningful exchange-based* ties which underlie the formalities of the system seem normally to involve dyads only. Above all, the patron is always an individual. In the case of the governor, for example, he in effect has two distinct ties: one with the father who approached him, and whose petition he accepted, and another with Tiburcio, his godson. Tiburcio's bride does not really participate in a contractual relationship with the governor, and even less so do her parents (in theory, however, she could establish her own relationship with him by taking presents and otherwise playing the game). Similarly, Isaac Mendoza, godfather to Laura Prieto, is patron both to her and her mother, by means of two distinct ties. The basic, implicit, informal contracts bind two people, and though they may appear to "blanket in" others, there are no doubts in the minds of the participants as to the nature of the relationship.

PATRON-CLIENT RELATIONSHIPS BETWEEN HUMAN BEINGS AND SUPERNATURAL BEINGS

Supernatural patrons are finite in number, but none-the-less numerous. God, and Christ and the Virgin Mary in their many local *advocaciones*, or manifestations, are of course patrons to all mankind, while the Virgin of Guadalupe, as patroness of America and especially Mexico, is turned to by nearly all Mexicans. Just as the individual casts about among human beings for patrons, so he turns to the saints, to the various manifestations of Christ and the Virgin, and even to the devil, testing their willingness to enter a contractual relationship with him (i.e., by helping, by responding to overtures). Some of the resulting dyadic contracts are, like all those previously described, continuing, in that an even balance in the exchange is never struck. Other contracts are rather different, in that they are called into being for a specific crisis, in response to the supplication of a human being. If the contract is made, i.e., if the supernatural being grants the request of the supplicant, the latter is obligated, at his earliest convenience, to fulfill his part of the bargain, to strike the balance by complying with his offer. This terminates the contract. An individual may try to renew the contract at a later time for a new crisis, but, as will be seen, he often will attempt a contract with a different patron on each new occasion.

Continuing patron-client contracts with supernatural beings are best seen in the pattern of daily prayers and lighting of candles practiced by most villagers. Every home has one or more simple altars, usually a shelf with a few wilted flowers and guttered candles beneath several pictures of Christ, the Virgin, and an assortment of saints. This low-pitched daily homage is believed to gain the protection of the beings invoked, not specifically for crises, but against the thousand and one unthought daily dangers that lie in wait for the unwary. In the room in which Laura Prieto sleeps and sews, the wall altar holds pictures of the Virgin of Guadalupe, Our Lady of Perpetual Help, the Virgin of Lourdes, and San Martín de Porras, a Peruvian saint about whom she learned from a radio soap opera. When she sits down to sew, or at other times when she "just feels like it," she lights a *velador* (vigil light) "to all of them." She is paying her respects, asking them to continue to watch over her in return for this attention. Her mother pays little attention to this altar, but she prays to the Virgin of Guadalupe before arising in the morning, and Divine Providence is the object of a credo before she goes to sleep. In return, the mother hopes to receive her "daily necessities." Laura's stepfather is addicted to Souls in Purgatory and Our Lady of Perpetual Help, to both of whom he prays daily. In other homes the pattern is similar.

A noteworthy point in this pattern is that altars are not really centers of family rites, even though several members may light candles. Each member of the family has his special responsibility toward the patrons he has elected, who he feels favor him. No one, except upon special request, is responsible for acts of deference and respect for other family members. If Laura is away for a day or two on a pilgrimage, her mother feels no compulsion to light candles to Laura's patrons, although she will certainly ask her own patrons to care for her daughter. In the continuing type of relationship with supernatural patrons, the dyadic pattern that characterizes other village relationships is the rule.

Attendance at Mass on prescribed days can be thought of as man's obligation to the supreme patron, God. At first thought this may look like a group, or family rite. Yet upon closer examination, the solitary aspects of the rite are what strike one. Daughters may accompany their mothers to the church, but men rarely walk with their families. Once inside, men hurry to their place on the left side of the nave, and women pass to the right. Tiny boys kneel with their fathers, who teach them to cross themselves, as mothers teach young daughters. But parents usually are made nervous by squirming children, often strike and threaten them when they talk or cry, and are only too happy when they reach the age of six or seven, when they can join their age mates in the front of the nave, under the watchful eyes of the Daughters of Mary and other catechism teachers. In Mass, as in other religious situations, each worshiper experiences a unique and personal relationship with his supreme patron, almost unmindful that others simultaneously are undergoing the same experience with the same patron.

Apart from what may be called "obligatory" patrons—God, Christ, and the Virgin—how does one select continuing patrons? There is no rule; one simply follows hunches or whim, as in the case of Laura who decided to add San Martín de Porras after hearing about him on the radio. Manuel Herrera, with impeccable logic, says he supposes the Virgin is really the most powerful. After all, "*Ella tiene más parentesco con el Mero Jefe*," "She is the closest relative of the Big Boss."

Other patrons who logically fall in the "continuing" category are relatively unimportant. San Francisco, patron of Tzintzuntzan, has never shown the "miraculous" qualities a village likes to see in its patron, and his fiesta is most perfunctory. One's name saint likewise receives little attention, although his day itself is often marked by the equivalent of an American birthday party. Occupational patrons—San Isidro for farmers, for example—also receive short shrift in Tzintzuntzan. The devil as patron is more theoretical than real; no one, of course, admits to this relationship. Yet stories are told, usually about people in nearby villages, in which a petitioner becomes wealthy by selling his soul to the devil. "Don Lucifer" is patron and the petitioner is client.

Non-continuing or short-term contracts with supernatural patrons are best seen in the pattern of votive offerings. When an individual faces a crisis, such as illness or accident, or an unusual need for money, he (or she) makes a *manda* or *promesa,* a vow or solemn promise to a saint or one or another of the many images or manifestations of Christ or the Virgin, to do some pious act known to be pleasing to the patron. In the simplest pious acts, for rather minor crises, the petitioner lights a candle and prays, or hangs a silver *milagro* at the altar of the patron invoked. The silver (sometimes base metal) votive offerings are small representations of parts of the body such as an arm, a leg, eyes, breasts, or even an entire body, or of pigs, goats, sheep, horses, or cattle. The one selected depends, of course, on the nature of the supplication: a pig for a lost or sick sow, and an arm for a sore arm.

In more serious crises the client promises the patron to wear a *hábito,* a plain religious garment, for a number of months, and to refrain from all kinds of public entertainment if the request is granted. At other times, and particularly when a person finds himself in sudden, grave peril, he commends himself to one of the advocations of Christ or the Virgin, and if he is saved, he orders a *retablo,* in classic form a painted metal sheet which graphically portrays the danger, shows the patron floating in the sky, and at the bottom has a line describing the details. For other grave crises, or in the hopes of very special favors, a supplicant promises Christ, in the form of the Santo Entierro (an Ecce Homo in the Soledad Church in Tzintzuntzan), to assume the role of a penitent during one or more Easter Week observances, by carrying a wooden cross around the village or by hobbling with leg irons from cross to cross in the streets. In other cases—usually illness—one appeals to a "miraculous" saint or image of Christ or the Virgin in another town, promising to go on a religious pilgrimage to fulfill the vow if the request is granted. Some *mayordomías* are also accepted in response to a vow.

Several examples will show how the system works:

Valentín Rivera on two occasions has taken silver votive oxen to the church of San Antonio in Morelia, for aid in finding lost animals. San Antonio is patron of animals, and he is also very skilled in helping people find things such as, for farmers, lost animals, and—for young maidens—husbands. Benigno Zúñiga has taken silver eyes and a silver leg to the altar of Señor del Rescate (a painting of Christ) in the Tzintzuntzan parish church, both times for personal illness. Few if any adults have not, at some time or other, made use of ex-votos.

Laura Prieto was afflicted with giant urticaria which caused her great suffering. She visited a Pátzcuaro doctor, who prescribed medicine, and then she appealed to the Virgin of Health ("the most miraculous Virgin in Pátzcuaro"), promising to wear the Virgin's "habit" for six months if she were relieved. Within a week she was much improved, so Laura bought the costly, heavy scratchy wool, made the dress, wore it six months, and faithfully abstained from all public recreation. The doctor received no credit.

Most painted retablos in Tzintzuntzan are dedicated to the "miraculous" painting of Señor del Rescate, whose extraordinary powers were noted in 1900 when he was credited with saving the villagers from extermination by smallpox. A few are also placed on lateral altars dedicated to the Virgin of Guadalupe and Our Lady of the Sacred Heart. One, showing a painting of Christ on the cross, with a woman kneeling below, bears the legend "I give thanks to the very miraculous Señor del Rescate for having saved my life in a dangerous operation April 10, 1950, from which I nearly died. I offer myself with all my heart to El Señor. Glafira Ceja who resides in Ciudad Júarez, Chihuahua." A second, large, framed, hand-lettered script without picture says simply "A miracle which the Señor del Rescate did for me. I give my most sincere thanks to our Señor del Rescate for having saved my life when I was a prisoner in the Pátzcuaro jail in 1919. Eligio Carrillo." A third, modern retablo, consists of three framed postcard size photographs, the first of which shows a man about to descend from a roof on a ladder, the second the man sprawled on the ground, and the third the victim being swathed in bandages. The caption reads "Estanislado Alvarado. I give thanks to Christ Crucified for saving me from this horrible fall. Zamora, July, 1961."

Of the 19 retablos hanging in 1961, 12 were related to health, and seven dealt with personal problems such as finding a lost animal, delivery from prison, drunkenness, avoidance of military service, and the sparing of animals from the hoof and mouth disease. All except one were placed by the individual who was in danger or great need; the exception was a man who gave thanks for his wife's restored health. Curiously, only one of the retablos was hung by a Tzintzuntzeño: a widow who thanks Our Lady of the Sacred Heart for the "miracle" of making it possible for her to have a house. Why this discrimination? As far as Señor del Rescate is concerned, Benigno Zúñiga probably speaks for the village when he says that this Christ "*es casi de la familia,*" is almost a member of the family, and can be approached successfully in a number of simpler ways, particularly with silver votive offerings. It looks as if it is a case of distant fields looking greener. San Juan de las Colchas, and San Juan de los Lagos, says Macaria, is where Tzintzuntzeños like to hang retablos.

Although a person usually vows to be a penitent at times of serious illness, other grave matters may also be resolved in this fashion. Bartolo Zúñiga, for example, bought a used truck from his *bracero* savings, but he did not know how to drive it, and he greatly feared wrecking it. He promised the Santo Entierro that he would be a *penitente* for two Easters, wearing leg irons, if the patron would help him learn to drive by "putting skill in my hands." The truck was spared, and Bartolo complied with his vow.

Illustrating the pilgrimage pattern, Manuel Herrera, while working as a bracero in California, fell ill, not gravely, but enough so he feared he would lose work time, a critical matter for a man on a short-term contract. He promised the Virgin of the Rosary of Coeneo, Michoacán, about 50 miles from Tzintzuntzan, that if she cured him quickly he would make a pilgrimage to her church to light a five peso candle in her honor. He recovered without lost time, and shortly after his return to Mexico he visited Coeneo as promised.

A man often accepts a religious mayordomía—an obligation called *cargo* (hence he is a *carguero*) in Tzintzuntzan—in order to gain prestige, but not infrequently the acceptance is the consequence of a manda. In fact, Tzintzuntzan's biggest annual fiesta, the "function" in honor of Señor del Rescate, began in that way. Guadalupe Estrada, sacristan in 1900 during a terrible smallpox epidemic, remembered an old painting of Christ half hidden behind an altar and, casting about for help in the eclectic fashion of the villagers, he turned to it and cried out, "*Ay, Señor, porque no rescates a tu pueblo?*" ("Ay, Señor why don't you rescue your people? If you do I promise to establish a cult in your honor.") The epidemic quickly died down, the painting came to be called "del Rescate" because it saved the village, Guadalupe served as carguero until the fiesta was well established, and San Francisco, the official patron, slipped into near obscurity, since he had done nothing for his clients.

The way in which non-continuing, short-term contracts with supernatural patrons differs from continuing contracts should be apparent from the examples given. Except for the offering of ex-votos and candles and prayers, *the vow or promise is conditional upon the patron granting the request.* The offering of the would-be client, the promise of a pious act, must be carried through only if the patron in fact fulfills his (or her) part of the bargain, which is the act that brings the contract into being. Laura would not have worn her habit if she had not greatly improved; the retablos would not have been hung if the favors requested had not been granted; Manuel would not have gone to Coeneo if he had become seriously ill; and Bartolo would not have worn leg-irons as a penitente if he had had an accident in learning to drive, since no contract would have been established. "Thus, we really lose nothing," says Laura's very practical mother, in explaining how the system works. Neither patron nor client is under long-term or continuing obligation to his partner as a consequence of a successful exchange. The relationship is a one-time one-subject affair, and with the striking of an exact balance of obligation, both partners are free to go their own ways, perhaps but not necessarily coming together at a future time.

Although Christ and the Virgin may be appealed to in any manifestation, and any saint may be approached, some are recognized as especially powerful or "miraculous" (like the Virgin of Health in Pátzcuaro), while others are particularly efficacious for certain things. San Judas Tadeo, for example, helps people find lost objects, and some villagers have his small framed picture in their homes, which upon request they loan to neighbors as well. If he is appealed to, by lighting a candle, and fails to help, his picture is turned to the wall or placed face down on a chair. Both San Anacasio and San Antonio also help in finding lost objects although the latter, unlike the indignity heaped upon him in other parts of Mexico when he fails, is not hung upside down in a well until he grants a request.

In general, though, an eclectic approach is utilized in seeking special aid. When Macaria Gómez feared a gall-bladder operation, her daughter Victoria promised to wear the habit of the Virgin of Health for three months if the operation were not necessary; her daughter Laura promised to make a pilgrimage the 400 miles to the famous Virgin of San Juan de los Lagos (two neighbors had told her this virgin was "especially miraculous"); one friend promised the Virgin of Counsel in Santa Clara de los Cobres to bring Macaria with her on pilgrimage; another friend promised the Virgin of the Rosary in Coeneo to bring Macaria with her; while her stepdaughter simply vowed alms to Señor del Rescate. Macaria avoided the operation, but is in some doubt as to who receives the credit. Her husband, Manuel, in addition to the Virgin of the Rosary in Coeneo, has at some time appealed to Señor de la Misericordia in Capula, to Santiago, patron saint of Capula, to San Juan de los Conejos, near Uruapan, to Señor de la Exaltación in Sante Fe, to the Holy Virgin in the abstract, and to most of the saints and pictures in the Tzintzuntzan churches.

Several points in the manda complex require further discussion. Can a well-wisher make a vow that implicates another person, so that that person must comply? At first glance, it looks as if Macaria was implicated by her friends. However, if the person implicated refuses to comply, the responsibility bounces back to the one who made the vow, and he or she must extract himself from the predicament. It is hard to tell how often this kind of manda is made; not often, probably, because the priests say that it is wrong to make a manda in the name of another person.

Actually, except for major vows, supernatural patrons are not choosy about who completes a manda; the important thing is that it be completed, almost in mechanical form. If, for example, one makes a minor manda to Señor del Rescate to light a candle and it isn't convenient for the petitioner to comply, he or she gives the candle to a child, with the promised alms, and sends the little messenger along to do the job. Manuel once bought a house that turned out to be haunted. Twice he wrestled with the ghost before he realized it was a soul in purgatory; then he asked it what it wanted and was told it had died before lighting a 50 centavo candle to the Virgin of Light in San José Church in Morelia. Manuel promised to light the candle, which he did, and the ghost departed, his contract fulfilled.

Can a person make a vow or promise to more than one potential patron for a single reason? Some informants say no. When I asked Laura Prieto she mumbled "yes," looked embarrassed, and acted as if maybe it were really cheating a bit to do so. In fact, there seems to be a number one object of the request, but, following the usual pattern of trying to maximize potential help in every situation, a number of people make secondary requests, hoping that these acts will slide by unnoticed by the major object of attention.

Do two or more people jointly petition a single patron? For example, might two daughters say to the Virgin of Health of Pátzcuaro, "*We* promise to wear your habit if our mother is restored to health"? All of the evidence I have indicates that this is not done. No informant ever used a plural personal pronoun in describing a petition; no informant ever suggested that anyone else was equally implicated in fulfilling a vow; and no informant ever suggested that his responsibility was shared with another. In all nineteen retablos, the petitioner who fulfills the terms of his vow is invariably a single person. Several people may take action in the face of a single calamity threatening a family, but each action is dyadic, independent of the others, involving a single petitioner and a single patron. Patron-client relationships are enormously personalistic, and the benefits that accrue from a successful contract are not willingly shared by a client. It rather looks as if the bounty of a supernatural patron, like all other good things in life, is looked upon as a limited and precious commodity, and to the extent one shares it with others, so in that degree is one's portion reduced. Two petitions to a single patron will not produce twice the bounty; they will simply dilute and divide a finite quantity. Where this point of view prevails, it is clear that several people individually appealing to several patrons is a more logical policy, offering greater potential help, than the same people appealing collectively to a single patron.

Basic to an understanding of patron-client relationships, both between human beings alone, and with the supernatural, is the concept of *palanca,* or "lever." Broadly speaking, the palanca is *a way of access to a patron,* someone with "leverage." "For example," says Macaria to me, "I want something from you, but I don't want to ask you directly, so I ask Mariquita (Mary Foster) to approach you. She is my palanca." And again, "When I ask an intimate friend to help, I say '*Que me hagas una palanca*' ('You be my lever')." A palanca, then, is a go-between, someone with whom ego feels on reasonably close terms, who is helpful in getting to the real patron. A palanca, perhaps, is a semi-patron as well as a patron. He can help in himself, but his real value resides in his ability to favorably influence the ultimate source of power.

As previously pointed out, priests are reluctant to accept compadrazgo ties with villagers. Consequently, their nieces are deluged with requests to be godmothers, and they often accept. The nieces are looked upon as palancas. The relationship with them is not particularly valued in itself, but it is assumed that via them the client can more easily gain the ear of the priest in time of need; they are the lever, the device to achieve the desired end.

Although the term palanca is used only for human beings, it is clear that this concept of power structure is equally applicable to the supernatural. In trying to work out the pattern, I commented to Macaria that the person who wants to get ahead looks for palancas, tries to get them in debt by offering a meal or doing some other favor, but one is merely trying; and until the potential palanca comes through, one doesn't know. Nevertheless, a person keeps searching for the best palancas. "*Es la misma cosa con los santos,*" said Macaria with considerable feeling—"It's the very same thing with the saints." One continually tries different saints, shopping around, hoping to find the most influential ones, or the ones that can help the petitioner to the greatest extent. When I suggested to other informants that saints were really palancas, most were shocked; but a few, not too upset to speculate, said, in effect, "Yes, that's really the way it is."

The concept of the palanca also helps us in understanding the real nature of the patron-client relationship with saints. The saints, and the Virgin Mary as well, in one sense are patrons in that the contract is made with them, but ultimately they are palancas, or go-betweens. "*Cuando Diós no quiere, los santos no pueden,*" the saying goes ("When God doesn't wish it, the saints can't do it"). The saints and the Virgin are, then, advocates, special pleaders, whom one can approach more readily than God. They will handle your case when presented with it, but only if they are successful must the fee be paid, must the petitioner "comply" with the terms of the manda.

SUMMARY

In this, and the earlier paper, the model of the dyadic contract is suggested to explain and tie together a considerable segment of Tzintzuntzan social behavior. Tzintzuntzeños, like other peasants, lead a precarious life, largely devoid of power, influence, and economic security. Existence depends on success in tapping as many as possible of the sources of help and security which are potentially available to villagers. The manner in which this is done can be studied in terms of formal social, political, economic, and religious institutions, but underlying and cross-cutting formal institutions is a network of contractual ties between pairs of individuals which provides the basic vigor of the system. Contractual ties, of course, are found in all societies. The significant point in Tzintzuntzan (and many other peasant communities, I am sure) is the absence or near absence of corporate ties. Meaningful contracts occur almost exclusively between pairs; they form a dyad and do not bind larger groups.

Every Tzintzunzeño tries, tests, and manipulates all potential contractual situations which he feels will be helpful to him. Over time he builds contractual relationships with fellow villagers and friends in other communities, occasionally dropping those that no longer serve and developing new ones that offer promise. Every villager works out, or tries to work out, similar ties with human patrons, and every villager binds himself to supernatural patrons from whom he expects continuing support. In times of special crisis, villagers look for special aid from supernatural patrons (and from colleagues as well, of course), thereby establishing, or attempting to establish, short-term contractual relationships. The approach both to colleague and patron-client relationships is eclectic, based on trial and error, and on a spirit of "nothing ventured nothing gained." Ego looks for ways to interest and obligate potential partners, both colleagues and patrons, whom he feels can help him, and in so doing, commits himself to carry out the terms of the bargain with those that, in effect, accept his offer. By means of a great number of dyadic contracts, with both colleagues and patrons, the villager maximizes his security in the uncertain world in which he lives.

OTES

1. The periodic field trips 1959–1962 which supplied the data on which this paper is based were supported by grants from the National Science Foundation and the Research Committee of the University of California (Berkeley). I have pictured Tzintzuntzan as of 1945–1946 in *Empire's Children: The People of Tzintzuntzan* (Foster 1948).

2. One is reminded of the modern American business system in which the entrepreneur's success is measured, not by his bank balance, but rather by his credit rating, the amount of money the financial world permits him to owe.

3. Although the model was described in terms of adults, contractual ties characterize adolescence, and, doubtless, childhood as well.

4. In the earlier article, the term "colleague" was not used to describe this type of contract.

5. At least not by a non-hostile act. I suppose a sudden and unexpected fight would effectively terminate a contract.

6. Patron-client patterns in Spain have been ably described by Michael Kenny (1960). Although basic patterns are very similar, Professor Kenny visualizes the Spanish system as a pyramidal structure at the top of which is God, the supreme patron, rather than in terms of dyadic relationships.

7. Fictitious names are used for all living Tzintzuntzeños mentioned in this article.

REFERENCES CITED

Foster, George M.

1948 Empire's children: the people of Tzintzuntzan. Smithsonian Institution, Institute of Social Anthropology, Publication No. 6, Mexico City.

1961 The dyadic contract: a model for the social structure of a Mexican peasant village. American Anthropologist 63:1173–1192.

Kenny, Michael

1960 Patterns of patronage in Spain. Anthropological Quarterly 33:14–23.

Brazilian Careers and Social Structure: A Case History and Model

ANTHONY LEEDS

Only in recent years have more than a few anthropologists begun to study bureaucrats and other "white collar" urbanites. Leeds's paper was a pioneering analysis in terms of relationships among individuals rather than among social groups or categories. The "networks of mutual obligation" that he uncovered are chains of dyadic contract relationships (cf. Foster) that are more important than formal tables of organization; his idea of career mobility systems is further developed by Adams. He even offers a plausible explanation of the functional value of poverty in Brazil (cf. Lewis).

Anthony Leeds is Professor of Anthropology at the University of Texas. His studies, especially in Brazil, have yielded several papers on ecology, ethnohistory, inter-ethnic relations, urban anthropology, linguistics, and other topics; he is also coauthor of Man, Culture, and Animals: The Place of Animals in Human Ecological Adjustment (1965).

I

The research reported here is interesting not only for the data, which are novel and have a certain intrinsic fascination, but also because they confirm what was already suspected from theoretical reasoning and a few dissociated observations. I had in fact already "described" my field results before I went to the field. It

This paper was prepared expressly for the first edition of this book; a slightly expanded version appeared in *American Anthropologist* LXVI (1964), 1321–1347.

will be of interest to review briefly how this came about and consider its broader implications later.

I have for some time been looking for a typology of state-organized societies which would be based on a synoptic view of the function, total structure, and trajectory of the societies rather than, as in certain previous typologies, on one or a few traits or symptoms (cf. Steward 1949; Bennett, ed. 1948; Meggers, *et al.* 1956). The aim of such a typology is to permit comparisons for inquiry into regularities of developmental sequences for search for general laws of sociocultural development. Examining only unique cases prohibits generalizing from processes or mechanisms described for that case and excludes prediction.

The ideal types of state-organized societies characterize the later phases of cultural evolution, at least until the very recent present. I call these the "static-agrarian society" and "the expansive-industrial society."[1] The former is represented by such cases as Feudal Europe, pre-conquest India, the great oriental despotisms, several Near Eastern countries, possibly Haiti, and so on; the latter by today's Germany, U.S.S.R., U.S.A., England, and the like. Preceding the static-agrarian type of society is to be found the "expansive-agrarian society," all of whose examples, such as the early Mesopotamian empires, are extinct. One may hypothesize that a "static-industrial" type of society will follow the presently encountered expansive-industrial ones and one may attempt to delineate characteristics of such societies and the world in which they will be predominant (cf. Guardini 1956).

Briefly, the static-agrarian society may be described as deriving all of its fundamental resources and wealth from, and organizing its basic allocations of labor, technical equipment, and so forth, around agriculture. Consequently, all major social features—the division of labor, management and supervision, community structure, communications, the social structure of warfare and power, the state itself—are shaped by the basic broad agrarian technology. The crops produced constitute the sources of major wealth and power.

With the given technology, agrarian and communicational, the social order is necessarily markedly structured around localities and localized communities. Therefore, face-to-face, kin, pseudo-kin, and other personal ties, often highly ritualized, appear as major organizational mechanisms of the total society.

The expansive-industrial society derives its fundamental resources and wealth from and organizes all its basic allocations around industry. In the early stages of such societies, agriculture becomes subordinate to industry, economically, politically, and ideologically, and, later, itself becomes industrialized in technology and organization. All major social features are shaped by the basic technological relationships to the diverse resources necessary for industrial production, among which crops are important as non-food matériel. The fundamental ecological pattern is multiregional, tending toward global, and consequently, the societies tend to be exocentric, politically and economically; to maximize trans-local relationships at the expense of locality and community relationships; and to operate through highly organized supra-local institutions and associations. Without such necessary ties, the production-consumption system would not operate.

Maximizing trans- and supra-local institutions and associations causes these societies to expand politically and economically—the so-called growth-after-

"take-off" pattern (cf. Rostow, 1960). In expansion, they display characteristic institutions of policy such as colonialism, foreign investment, foreign aid, creation of common markets, and the like.

Historically, the pristine appearance of the expansive-industrial society is an evolutionary outgrowth, through various phases, of Western feudalism. Once the pristine development has occurred, all sorts of juxtapositions with earlier societal forms may occur in acculturation situations. Thus, well or partly developed expansive-industrial societies may find themselves in varying kinds of accultural contact with static-agrarian societies at various stages of development or with early post-static agrarian phases brought about by independent evolution.

We may, from these remarks, consider several hypotheses.[2] First, where cultures of these distinctive types are in long-term and vigorous structural contact, institutions of both will be found operating in some characteristic interlocking network. One should expect to find characteristic expansive-industrial organizational features linked with typical static-agrarian ones. One would expect to find those social and contractual-status[3] entities of industrial organization functionally related to the technology penetrating into the static-agrarian society, to be linked by characteristic "feudal" modes of interaction such as blood and affinal kin; ritual kin; friendship; man—patron, master—apprentice, *guru*—student relationships; and a variety of nonformalized interpersonal face-to-face contacts, either qualitatively or quantitatively different from the relationships found in industrial society. Examples of introduced entities include corporations, agencies, syndicates, managerial systems, vocational and professional schools, etc.

A second hypothesis relates to the transformational expansion of socioeconomic opportunities. Where two (or more) large, complex cultures, respectively at earlier and later stages of evolution, are interposed, a rapid and continuous multiplication of new economic sectors, occupations, and statuses occurs in the less-evolved societies, such as most so-called underdeveloped countries today. It follows that, in such conditions, one would expect a continual shortage of personnel for filling the emerging positions of the expanding opportunity structure, because training institutions would be absent or inadequate. Various solutions to this problem may be hypothesized:

1. The importation of personnel
2. The internal creation of new personnel more or less at haphazard, especially by self-instruction, or "autodidactism," until training is curricularized
3. The multiplication of positions held by any given individual

Personnel importation is intrinsically limited by the supply and by the cost of importation, though it may accommodate a modicum of new positions. This solution is temporary and unreliable, since it is not institutionally built into the social system itself. Most frequently, one would expect either the filling of positions by self-trained or partially self-trained persons, or the filling of a number of often diverse positions by single individuals—frequently autodidacts.

As a corollary, one would expect multiple position holding and autodidactism to be complementary, since a man in position A, in some organization, seeing an available new position B, for which no candidate exists, may train himself to fill position B. Given the nature of social links mentioned in the first hypothesis, it is to his interest to maintain connections with the first organization through his incumbency in position A, while establishing new connections through position B. Furthermore, there may actually be pressures not to leave A, since other incumbents are unavailable for that position. A second corollary is that entering into position A may be seen as a preliminary for entry into position B, or may prepare such a connection even where it is not foreseen. That is, A may serve as the springboard for leaping to B. Entry into position A may even involve the invention and creation of position A as a prelude to leaping into B.

The pilot research carried out in Brazil during June and July of 1962 was intended not only to confirm the existence of institutions described in the hypotheses, but also to get case histories to illustrate how these institutions function—how organization operates.

II

We may now turn to the research itself. During a fortnight's stay in Brazil in 1961, repeated use of the word *autodidato* began to register in my awareness, suggesting that the autodidact was an important phenomenon, as it turned out to be in other Latin American countries. It appears to be a function of the absence of what we may call curricularized training and careers so characteristic of advanced expansive-industrial societies as routes into statuses (in the general sociological sense)[4] and careers.

In asking about the Brazilian autodidact and his genesis, the phenomenon of multiple job holding, which permeates the entire Brazilian society and for certain types of which Brazilians have a word, *cabide de emprego*,[5] or "employment hanger," began to assume more and more theoretical importance.

Intuitively, the two phenomena appeared to be significantly linked, and both related to an acculturationally induced, rapidly expanding opportunity structure. In such a condition, there tend to be more positions than there are candidates. Both the autodidact and the *cabide* phenomena appeared to be functions of this situation, highly adapted to it, and of great use in the subtler operations of the society, despite many moralizing statements, especially about the *cabide* and its abuses as a system of operation.

On hypothesis, the *cabide* is a social link in a society in rapid transition from a characteristic static-agrarian to a characteristic, fully developed expansive-industrial condition. As we have remarked, in the former, the links of status (in Maine's sense), such as those of kinship, pseudo-kinship (*compadrasco*, vassalage), and a variety of personalized ties, are standardized, while in the latter, links of a contractual kind predominate.

In the intermediate society, where contractual links have not yet developed or become organized, the *cabide* serves both status and contractual ends, combining essential features of each in single individuals, who, in effect, maintain informal and contractual relations with themselves in different positions.

Since hypothetically, the *cabide* appears to be a major social link, the question arises as to how the *cabide* gets to be one and how, when he becomes one, he operates to tie together various organized entities in Brazilian society;

entities such as bureaucratic agencies, new bits of universities, managerial structures, public services, etc., largely borrowed from the highly industrialized societies. It was to reject or confirm the hypotheses and to answer this question that the research was undertaken.

Since, however, neither the organization nor the interrelationships of the community recognized situses of the society such as the bureaucracy, the military, the Church, the business world, etc., have been adequately described for Brazil, it was necessary to develop some sort of operating model against which to assess the activities of the autodidact and the *cabide*. Teixeira's model (1962, and conversations) was useful for this. The model (cf. Fig. 1) *structurally* was compatible, by its very disjointedness, with the *cabide* phenomenon. I conceived of the *cabides*, at any one moment, as linking these oligarchies,[6] providing their internal organization, and generally weaving a network among the various above-mentioned situses of the society. At the same time, they provide the social nodes whose complex interconnections create the division between what, for convenience, we may call the "classes" and the "masses."

Here, we are chiefly concerned with the internal structure and dynamics of the classes, and more specifically with the entry into, and operations of, the higher ranks within the classes. The masses are sufficiently separate from the classes so that their internal organization and dynamics, for the present, are irrelevant to the description of the classes. They require a separate description.[7]

III

Since the general hypotheses stated that the connections among organizations, the links among oligarchies, and the inner organization of the classes are maintained by various kinds of personal connections, and also that one would expect movement from position to position and the holding of many positions by a single incumbent, it followed that the most incisive way to discover the intimate workings of the system was to trace the histories of individuals as they moved through their careers, establishing connections and moving from organized entity to organized entity. Consequently, the primary research technique consisted of interviews with selected informants having *cabide*, and often autodidact, characteristics and representing all the major situses and oligarchies.

Several representatives from each generation were to show the increase in curricularization in any situs once such a situs has become established.

Third, given the relatively great autonomy of Brazilian provinces and states in many significant matters and their ecological, economic, and historical variety, it follows that their social structures, in themselves and as contexts for careers, would differ considerably. In fact, they might be ordered on a developmental scale so as to give a spatial representation of the development of Brazilian social organization, while careers studied in a selection of such states would reflect this developmental ordering by a corresponding increase in curricularization.

We chose the cities of São Paulo, Rio, Belo Horizonte, Recife, and Salvador as purportedly representing a series of states decreasingly developed in an industrial, financial, and political sense, or, conversely, increasingly archaic in behaviors, customs, and ideologies. We also included Brasília in our sample, since as

FIGURE 1. Teixeira's Model of the Brazilian Power Structure: With Reference to Political Pressure Groups

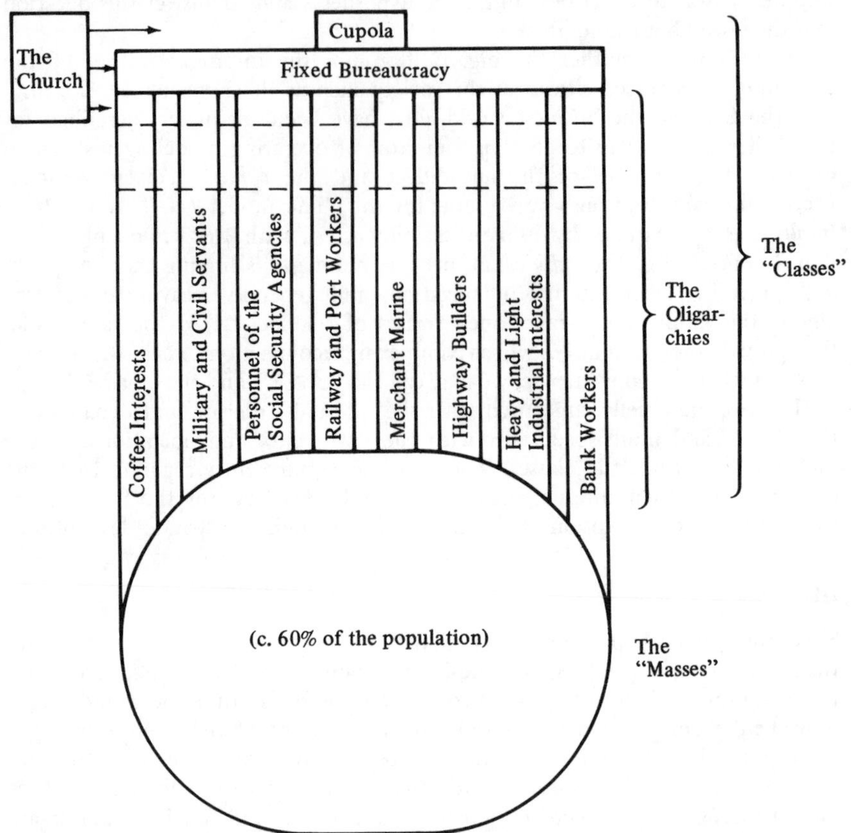

N.B. It may be noted that each column represents a pressure group or oligarchy which is described as operating on the cupola above it. It should also be noted that the *individuals, qua* individuals, who compose the oligarchies are not necessarily in the least at comparable income, prestige, or power levels: these common stratification criteria are social-structurally irrelevant here. Dotted lines represent "strata" levels within the oligarchies.

the seat of national power, no Brazilian reality can be understood without a searching look at the *cúpola*.

In each city, we made contact with at least one, and generally more, well-informed citizens of some prominence who were prevailed upon to give us lists of the important local *cabides* with as much information as possible about each as regarded his connections. Lists of *cabides* gotten from two or more independent sources were always in substantial agreement. Thus we were able to get for each a kind of thumbnail sketch of his career and his "social genealogy." By "social genealogy" I mean a mapping of his personal connections not only through kin but also through friendships, ties of mutual obligation, and so on—a web of non-kin quite analogous to the web of kinship known from the standard ethnographic genealogy.

Whenever possible we tried to get a personal, or at least a written, introduction or to have appointments made by intermediaries who knew both us and the informant. With such contacts, cooperation never failed. Where, however, we had to present ourselves, we were often turned aside. The authority of personal introductions and of intermediaries was one of the best evidences of the significance of personal ties in Brazilian society, since it was strong enough to open doors leading to considerable intimacy even among utter strangers.

I initiated each interview by explaining what we were trying to discover and asking for the informant's cooperation. At some point in this introductory exchange, the informant invariably introduced some aspect of his own experience. We used this as an entry to move into the entire life history. An ideal interview consisted of several sessions, separated by a few days to give us time to review our notes and to formulate further questions. Some interviews had to be done in a single session. These are invariably full of lacunae.

The research team, consisting of two Brazilian psychologists and myself, was able in the six weeks to gather fifteen full interviews, several shorter ones, and one or two quite detailed career reports about certain persons from their acquaintances. Wherever possible, we tried to check respondents' data with reports from other informants who knew them and from whom we also usually got substantial additional data.

Three other sources of data provided a check on each other and on the interviews. I systematically clipped the newspapers, first, for data relating to the oligarchies and social spheres and, second, for data on careers. Unwittingly, the newspapers were useful sources for career material: career stories are very often published in most Brazilian papers.

Second, we sought informants who appeared well acquainted with the local economic, social, and political organization and the incumbent personnel. From these persons, we tried to get as much information about the local social operations as possible through cases and through reports on the behavior of the personnel concerned. This sort of information often turned out to be very rich indeed, since, for reasons to be explained below, so many of the operations become known throughout the upper circles despite their ostensible privacy—a privacy which is, in fact, always potentially, and purposively, public.

The third source of information was published material, such as studies in Brazilian politico-economic organizations; the Congressional *Diário Oficial;* analyses of bureaucratic organizations; of studies of electoral behavior; books with ulterior motives such as Niemeyer's eulogy of Jucelino Kubitschek written under guise of discussing his experiences in Brasília (1961), and magazines whose feature articles are paid for by interest groups.

IV

I present only a synopsis of our findings and discuss their implications; fuller presentation of the data must await later publication.

First, the concept and word "*cabide*" occur only in informal communication. In the course of the research, moreover, I discovered that there was a whole language, also existing only in informal communication, of the career and its structural aspects. The career and the *cabide*, however, were not the only structural units to be described in the informal discourse, familiar to everyone. I also "discovered" the *panelinha* ("little saucepan"), whose relation to careers and *cabides* no one has noted previously. For the moment, the *panelinha* may be defined as a relatively closed, completely informal primary group, held together in common interest by personal ties and including a roster of all key socio-politico-economic positions.

The fact that these social structural units which are so vital in Brazil are known only in informal discourse is itself a reflection of the lack of curricularization and formalization of the social fabric of Brazilian society. Without knowing this informal organization, one cannot understand how Brazil functions, economically or politically.[8]

Schematically, the career consists of a continual branching out into new activities—sometimes multiplications of old ones, sometimes in new situses. The main problem is to establish the first step, to create a *trampolim* or springboard, as they say. The variety of techniques for this is numerous and sometimes used singly or in combination. I mention only a few, such as notable activity in university student associations, especially in the law schools flamboyantly joining Communist or Fascist groups; making public stands in favor of policies not in favor with the entrenched powers; marrying rich girls; being helped by one's own or one's spouse's family; being helped by one's godparents; being helped by a *pistolão* ("a friend in the right place or position to give a hand"); journalism; making a name in sports; entering into politics in lower political positions; entering into a small bureaucratic office from which upward and outward ties can be established.

The significant thing about each of these connections, as the careerist ideal-typically uses them, is that none of them is intrinsic to the career's end as such, but rather to the creation of a *nome* ("name"), the beginning of *uma promocão* ("a self-promotion"), the eliciting of *projecão* ("a presence growing in time").

As a rule, many such steps to new connections are achieved through immediate consanguineal or affinal kin connections. Plainly, large families are highly functional under such conditions and are, indeed, universally operative among the Brazilian, and the Latin American, "classes." Any one of a multitude of relatives may be in a status from which he can either provide a position for his kin-client or can persuade others, through networks of mutual obligation, to provide such positions or helping hands. The most immediate place for this sort of help, for example, is the family firm in which the parent provides loci for the early career-operations of his sons, in fact, more or less sets forth the major outlines of the career at its outset. The connections may be established through less immediate, connecting kin with nepotistic relatives of more distant degrees. The most characteristic linking relatives are parents and spouses, usually wives, the patron relative being, then, mainly an uncle or father-in-law and sometimes, by extension, a cousin. Such relationships figured in a number of our cases from quite varied fields, e.g., a politician, an industrialist-business man, a politician-real estate man, and an educator.

Still wider kin connections may be called upon occasionally, but these do not generally figure as major ties in the career trajectory. Nevertheless, even distant kin may provide a needed link, may help open a door, and in any case constitute a basis for immediate entering into relationship which is not otherwise available. Hence the importance of mapping out genealogical ties as quickly as possible and wherever practicable. A Brazilian, arriving in a community new to him, with utmost speed acquires an intricate mental map of all the significant personages of the town, both kin and non-kin, who may number into the scores or hundreds, as well as of their significant relatives in other localities. By this mapping, he has also explored for points at which he himself might be connected either by ties of consanguinity, affinity, or friendship with persons on the "genealogical" map. Kin and non-kin connecting points provide steps to advance interests or establish new relationships.

The initial moves of the career must be made known in the right places, since the young careerist may be called on to support, assist, or form alliances with others of his own age or more advanced in their careers than he. Letting the moves be known gives information about the young careerist's capacities and his connections. But the divulgations cannot be too open, because, first, one wants to have a selective response, and, second, some of the dealings are perhaps a bit shady. In short, from the beginning of the career on, there is a constant emission of cues which are intended to convey information about the state of man's career—that is, about his positions, hence the range of his connections, the kinds of influence he possesses, the probable kinds of deals he can carry out, and also the people who can be reached through him.

It is my conviction, confirmed by the extraordinary ability, intelligence, and variegated activities of most of our informants who were not selected on these criteria, that in this whole process there is an intense selection for those persons with keener perceptions, with sharper abilities to see more meanings behind the cues, and with the energy and drive to follow up and use the information so acquired.

The mechanisms for cue emission are highly institutionalized, albeit largely informal. Perhaps the most important is journalism. The variety of techniques involved is enormous. The rector of the University of X keeps a stable of reporters in part-time employ. Through them, he can keep a daily diet of magnificent rectorship before the public, especially the politicos with whom he has extensive dealings. Most persons of considerable position can publish in a newspaper by sending in their contributions. They can contact reporters who, they know, will publish statements for or about them. They can perform some public act, a reporter's presence having been arranged. Relations of reciprocal obligation and dependence between a careerist and a reporter are not infrequent, since the reporter, too, may be advancing in his *own* career by the contact.

The newspapers present an extraordinary variety of contexts of cue emission: notices from municipalities in the interior, including the most wretched society columns; business facts columns; the political columns; private ads. All list connections. All are suggesting new connections or advertising the potentialities and willingness of their writers or the persons written about to make new ties. Significantly, almost every career we studied showed some major connection with a newspaper. Similarly, in most, some major connection with political life or with public office provided a key. Clearly, journalism and public life are central institutions in Brazilian society and to individual Brazilians of the classes.

The *futing* ("promenading [with one's ears open]") is another technique important to information flow and making connections. The *futing* provides the opportunity for exploratory meetings which occur at coffee houses, in bookstore doorways, etc., and are cast in informal conversations about the city's social scene in such a way as covertly to emit opinions and to show knowledge and connection.

Today, TV and radio are also providing channels for cue transmission for that small portion of the personnel of the society which has access to them.

Gossip is another vital mechanism. Brazilians *listen* to gossip and store it up, in contrast to Americans whose main purpose is to project into it, pass it on, and then forget it. One case is reported of a Brazilian who even keeps a card file of gossip items and other information on a large number of people in public and private life.

Meeting in social clubs also provides a means of distributing cues which is of special significance because of its exclusiveness. The circle within which cues are to be disseminated is sharply defined and restricted.

V

The main function of cue transmission and manipulation is the maintenance of boundaries between mutually exclusive informal groupings of persons and the arrogating of prerogatives and rewards to some of these groups while denying them to others. One may look at the entire communications system as a means of diffusing only certain kinds of information in certain codings to only certain categories of people. Awareness of the codes and of the relevant kinds of information is taught by those who know them to their congeners and successors. Teaching takes place primarily in the family circle, but also in the socially proper non-kin contacts among like-minded families, as in the social clubs, cliques, and groups of friends. Access to the information which is carried in newspapers and magazines, on radio and TV, and in coffee-house gossip requires a certain minimum of resources on the part of participants. They must have been able to become literate. They must be able to buy the newspapers consistently or own a radio or TV if it is to be of continuing use. They must be able to visit the coffee shops, and so on.

Total exclusion from, or even a merely partial and highly sporadic access to, the information transmitted by these agencies renders the personnel involved virtually quite ineffective in all those operations with respect to which the cue transmission is important, that is, to all significant, organized, economic and political control, planning, and decision making. This point will become clearer below in my discussion of the *panelinha*.

It is plain that institutionalized poverty would be highly functional in the maintenance of such a system, since it automatically and effectively excludes the poor, whether totally or in significant degree, from access to cue-transmitted information. The institutionalization of poverty in Brazil includes an inflation which, especially at the lower levels, consumes virtually all wage raises given, but which, at the same time, is used by the moneyed to increase their own income. It includes a school system so constructed in various ways as to foster privilege and extrude the poor as early as possible, from the higher elementary grades, by requiring special, paid tutoring to go on (cf. Leeds 1957: Ch. 5; 1962; Teixeira 1957, 1958, 1960?). It also includes an extraordinary array of informal institutions of which the cue-transmission control I have just discussed is one.

Poverty, too, entails its own outward symbols, especially dress, speech, and manners, so that its informal institutionalization easily includes differential treatment by all, both rich and poor. The techniques are legion, the consequences ineluctable.

Further, communications, more broadly defined, enter into the control of the poverty-stricken. The, in effect, institutionalized malfunctioning of virtually all Brazilian urban telephone networks (except in highly organized São Paulo) and of the so-called "Nacional" telegraph system guarantees major difficulties in organizing, both in terms of the ability to overcome problems of the spatial distribution of persons and in terms of time needed for organizing. Only the personnel of the state, politicos, and wealthier, well-connected private citizens, who have access to private or state-owned radio transmitters or to the expensive "Western" or "Radional" telegraph and telephone systems, or to rapid personal transportation, chiefly by airplane, are excepted from the slow pace of telephonic organization. Significantly, all these operate very effectively indeed on a *nation-wide* basis. In passing, it is worth pointing out that the institutionalized malfunctioning of systems of communication affects the masses of the poor totally, but it also extensively affects all the middle ranges of status and income levels of the "classes," and acts upon them, too, as a system of social control exercised by the holders of the central positions of the society.

In summary, then, cue transmission in itself, its control, the broad flow of other forms of information, the control of that flow, and all the formal and informal institutions arising from those controls create and sustain highly impermeable boundaries between two major groups—which I have called the "classes" and the "masses"—and only relatively permeable boundaries among hierarchic subgrouping in the "classes."

It must be noted that the "masses" and "classes" of such social systems as Brazil's are in quite viable functional relationship to each other. These masses are not symptoms of "disorganization" or "dysfunction" or of an "unhealthy" society. Because power, wealth, prestige, and decision making all rest with the "classes," who are vastly advantaged by them, the system tends to perpetuate itself. Furthermore, the great degree of control exercised over the masses tends to force them to look to the classes for support, thus reinforcing the system structurally and ideologically through institutions generally described as "paternalistic."

VI

Returning to the internal structure of the classes, we may examine the role of communications in leading the new careerist into significant relationships with persons of coordinate status and the kind of informally institutionalized and societally focal group into which he enters. The result of cue transmission and manipulation is an ever-widening series of connections, memberships, and positions held. Thus one twenty-six-year-old informant, who controls a social columnist by doing occasional favors for him such as paying off gambling debts or debts contracted because of women, has already become involved in a *panelinha,* has connections in Rio, and has even been made a member of various boards of directors without even being asked. That he also has specialized training in a nonacademic field is generally known and plays a role in his being selected.

The early and middle stages of the career, perhaps lasting ten to fifteen years, are characterized by multiplying the sources of support, first, so that there may be no retrogression; second, so that there be a permanent set of *trampolims;* third, so that there exist variegated sets of connections, among which, for strategic reasons, the careerist may move to advance his later career.

Perhaps our best example is a man who concurrently built a career as lawyer, academician, politician, and journalist. When defeated for political office, he had three other active sets of interests and connections to continue his *projecão,* as the Brazilians say. He had divided his academic life between native and foreign soils. When he became scandalously involved with a lady other than his wife, he found convenient temporary refuge in Europe from whence he continued his journalism. He then returned to reactivate the political pillar and to resume his academic role.

Connected with this multiplication of the sources of support is the device of surrounding oneself with a tactical corps of supporters, a kind of coterie, called in Brazil a *rotary* or *igrejinha* ("little church"). Such *igrejinhas* are especially useful if the members have journalistic or other communicational connections—as they so often do. They are carriers of information, transmitters of cues, promoters and boosters of the master careerist to whom they are attached. He reciprocates in a typical complementary relationship by using his influence to get them jobs, to advance their careers, to variegate their *bicos*[9] by mobilizing his connections, especially as a *cabide* and particularly in an upward direction.

Thus, the *igrejinha* is in fact a mutual career promotion, a web of mutual obligations, between a person with greater *projecão* or *nome* in his career, on one hand, and his supporters, on the other. Such *igrejinhas* may, if in the same domain of interests, compete for rewards of a very broad range of statuses often entirely outside the interests of the *rotary.* Such competition may be particularly sharp if the opportunity structure is not an elastic one. This seems to be especially true in the case of literary coteries. Concerning one of the most important of these in Brazil, it is reported that its central figure arranged the position of cultural attaché for one of the claque by mobilizing his own upward connections.

When a man has reached a certain point in his career, marked by the possession of desirable contacts, of a certain *nome* in his area or areas, and maybe of an *igrejinha,* he may be asked to join a *panelinha.* The asking may be explicit or may be carried out by a kind of unexplicit verbal assaying. *Panelinhas* can cover all sorts of activities, but, for our purpose, the politico-economic, rather than, say, the literary or academic, *panelinhas* are of most interest, though it must be recalled that all *panelinhas* are at least partly concerned with political ends.

The politico-economic *panelinha* characteristically consists of a customs official, an insurance man, a lawyer or two, businessmen, an accountant, a municipal, state, or federal deputy, and a banker with his bank. No formal commitment is made among these parties; no formal meetings are held. They are identifiable only by informants' reports or by the observation in various contexts over long periods of time of associative behavior among the persons involved. Often such cooperative behavior is not easily visible.

Each *panelinha* maintains its internal relations at any given level by certain very simple potential sanctions. The man who would leave a *panela* automatically would lose his connections therein. Since the *panela* in the locality is also a clique concerned with mutual protection—its members are virtually immune from the law because of the pressures which can be brought through *panela* connections—the apostate would lose his protections, unless, of course, he had already aligned himself with another *panela.* In other words, as a member of a *panela,* he both gives and receives.

The banker who leaves, loses the business and deposits of his *panela* members—and sometimes the combined assets of a *panela* may amount to eight or ten billion, or more, cruzeiros—would have difficulty finding substitutes, since most interesting prospects are already connected with some other bank. Because of the bank's dependence, it does not tend to be the predominating force of the *panela,* whose members are more or less in equivalent power status to each other.

Similarly, the deputy depends on the *panela* for his election (and his good salary)—he is their man. Yet, in turn, they depend on him because he supplies the links with the government which are so necessary to the resolution of a host of problems defined by *panela* members.

This is particularly true when there is a question of links reaching upward to the politico-administrative cupola, since every *panela* has its ties with the juridical political hierarchy up to the president, who is the keystone of the whole structure. These ties go through Rio de Janeiro, especially through Rio law firms, high Rio bureaucrats, ministry officials, federal deputies and senators, and so on, whence the ministers can be reached. The ministers make the contacts with the president where necessary, especially in such matters as may involve appointing officials or making highest-level decisions regarding the allocation of funds. In recent years, ultimate cupola decisions affecting *panelas* at lower politico-administrative levels have shifted to Brasília and will do so more rapidly hereafter.

Panelinhas, however, are not wholly in a dependent relationship with the president and other high authorities, since these, in turn, need the *panelinhas* which they have favored for return favors. This is especially true as regards local-level political support either in elections or in effecting policy decisions in state and municipal political bodies. Alienation of a *panelinha* is not good politics. The relationship between higher- and lower-level *panelinhas* is reciprocal, just as relationships within the *panelinha*, though in a different way, are reciprocal, and individual connections with groups and organizations on the part of the *cabide* are also reciprocal in their obligations and exploitations—a vast network of mutual, personalized obligation.

The state-level *panelinha* also reaches down to the lowest political level, establishing contact with the municipal *panelas* just as it does with federal-level *panelas*. Similar reciprocal relations are established here. Persons who can move in both are at an advantage, but tend to move permanently into the higher-level one, replacing the "egalitarian" reciprocal relations of a participant in the lower-level one with the hierarchical complementary relations of a participant in a higher one with respect to a lower one and with the "egalitarian" reciprocal relations of a participant in the higher-level one.

The number of *panelas* in a city or state is proportional to the level of its economic, political, or social advancement. Thus, states like Piauí and Maranhão probably have only one or two; Bahia, several; Minas, a number; São Paulo, a great many. Under an expanding opportunity structure, apparently the *panelinhas* generally do not often fight each other, especially locally. A fight which might be destructive to one *panelinha* is not joined, the losing *panelinha* preferring to attach itself to the winning one. Only for great contracts do genuine competitive battles go on, but these battles tend to be passed up the *panela* chain of command to be fought out at the highest bureaucratic, even ministerial, level.

VII

It will be seen that the *panela* is a self-maintaining group which serves a great number of ends. First, it serves to select talent of a certain kind, although it may also protect ineptitude for internal political reasons. The leading members, however, are mostly persons of great skill, indicated in such terms of admiration, almost of endearment, as *furador* ("one who worms his way in"), *cavador* ("burrower"), *absorvente* ("sops things up"), *paraquedista* ("serendipitist by intention"), etc. Inclusion by invitation gives a certain guarantee that such personnel will be brought in.

The obverse of this is that mediocre careerists tend to be excluded and all possible persons who wish to rise, to move up socially, are in effect controlled from above, even if they are already in the "classes." The control over upward mobility from the "masses" is much more severe and will be described at another time.

In brief, the *panelinha* and the *cabide* are two major structural entities (or nodes) of organization (cf. Leeds 1967) that, linked or not,[10] create in Brazil an almost totally impermeable boundary between the two groupings of people whom I have called the "classes" and the "masses." The term "class," in the Marxian sense, may be applied to these more or less organized groupings.

Within each of these groupings, vaguely delimited hierarchic layerings occur. The layers might perhaps best be called "strata," though they correspond to what in common American popular and sociological usage are called "classes" (cf. Bohannan 1963: Ch. 11, esp. 171–179). They arise from partial impermeabilities created by *panelinhas* and other structural entities. The boundaries between strata are not fully impermeable because of the hierarchic relationships among the *panelinhas,* because of the *igrejinhas* attached to *cabides,* and because the lower strata comprise an ever-present pool from which personnel selection from above takes place or can take place. Selection means not only taking some in, but also excluding others, and the term "partial permeability" describes this duality. The impermeability between strata is especially marked near the very bottom and at the top. These strata are by no means integrated, much less self-conscious, groups for which the Marxian term "class" would be appropriate.

In sum, Brazil displays internal stratification in at least one of its two classes; the other is just becoming known, but also appears to be stratified (cf. footnote 7; Leeds 1957: Chs. 4 and 5).

Second, the *panelinha* serves a number of economic ends. It is a capital-pooling and controlling group keeping a large part of its money in liquid form. This permits its members to lay hands on large sums of money easily by short-circuiting most of the legal restrictions and requirements and facilitates winning contracts, especially when these are being given out on bids, or making large-scale purchases or various speculations.

In various ways, the *panelinha* operates to assist its members to resist taxation by, for example, moving goods from one to another without paying turnover taxes or by introducing foreign goods as contraband or with much-reduced import taxes through the agency of their customs house members. Through their political and banking members, the *panelinha* attempts to take advantage of the government-controlled exchange rates in order to counter the inflation and to take advantage of it for the increase of capital and liquidity—and of course of personal wealth. At the same time, through the varied interests and activities of its members, a *panelinha* tries to control a very large proportion of the economic goods within the political unit in which it is operating, since control may have major political repercussions, may even be a political device, as in the recent withholding of basic foods from the urban markets with the accompanying political maneuvers at all levels.[11]

So much for the *panelinha* and its *cabide* components; we return to the career. Ideally, it should pass through a hierarchy of *panelinhas,* mainly identified with the *município*, state, and federal political levels. As a man grows in connections, activities, experience, and wealth, and contracts more vertical relationships upward and more supporters behind him, his career tends to reach into the next higher level *panelinha.* From the career point of view, he gradually universalizes or nationalizes himself (*ele se universaliza*) in the sense that his name, his influence, and his activities become geographically national in scope. That is, his *projecão* always broadens in socio-geographic range. It is made structurally firm by downward ties with various state and municipal *panelinhas,* by his *cabide* ties in several disparate types of endeavor, by his *rotary,* and by his geographically dispersed interests and activities. For example, one of our cases has his political strength in a northeastern state; his most influential associational ties and a large number of his business connections in Rio de Janeiro; his central business activities in Brasília; and a set of relatives in the national Congress and the state and municipal legislatures.

The final stage of a career is international *projecão*, but the society's positions for this are extremely limited in number, as are the highest national politico-bureaucratic positions. It is at this highest level, where the otherwise expanding opportunity structure suddenly contracts sharply, that the fiercest conflict is to be observed in Brazil.

Both national and international *projecão* are aided most significantly by access to, or control of, the means of communication and of transportation. The former aids in establishing contacts, keeping appropriate information flowing, and so on, while the latter permits the continuous maintenance of important relationships and the execution of vital maneuvers in critical, high-level competitive situations. Both together permit a relatively instantaneous control over problems needing resolution which is not at all available to the masses and only feebly so to the lower levels of the classes. In fact, the control of both of these technologies by the upper levels is one of the major mechanisms of maintaining the impermeable boundary between the classes and the masses, especially, but also of the semi-permeable boundaries between the topmost and lowest strata of the classes.

VIII

A few points with respect to this synopsis. First, the division of the Brazilian politico-economy into sub-spheres or situses such as business, education, industry, bureaucratic agencies, public services, etc., has, at best, analytic value, but really does not make much sense structurally at their higher levels. They are all so very closely articulated by *cabides* whose positions lie in several situses. This is especially true in the later and "higher" phases of career development, i.e., at the higher levels of effective decision making.

Brazilian social divisions are, in fact, more along the oligarchic lines described by Teixeira, evidences of which came into the life-history materials repeatedly. The oligarchies tend to cross-cut the more conventional analytic sectors or situses. They seem to be more advanced in the states of São Paulo and Minas than in Bahia and Recife. At the highest levels within each oligarchy, the boundaries begin to fade because of the number and intensity of crossties among the personnel incumbent in the highest positions or because persons, especially highly placed politicos, enter into relationship with several oligarchies at once.

For the most part, at these highest levels, ultimate ends of all concerned are relatively uniform so that there are at present few significant generic policy cleavages at the cupola in Brazil (cf. Leeds 1964). The cleavages appear to revolve about specific policies for implementing generic policy aims and about access to control of the entire system and its rewards at the topmost point—the presidency and its dependencies. I should represent the situation of total Brazilian social organization somewhat as in Fig. 2.[12]

Second, some comments regarding the research technique. It can readily be extended to all other significant groups in the society, e.g., the middle ranges of

FIGURE 2

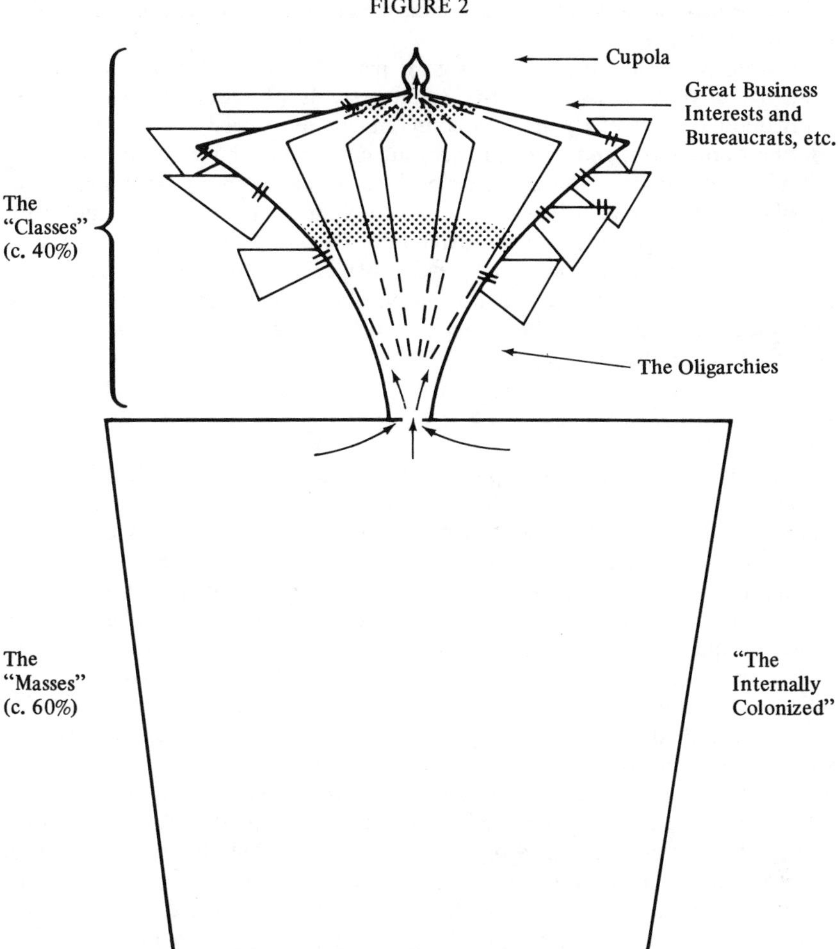

N.B. Slanting vertical lines represent expansion and contraction of the opportunity structure. Arrows represent upward mobility. Dashed lines represent indefinite or poorly defined boundaries. Dotted layers represent strata divisions. Dashed-line triangles represent rather amorphous interest groupings or categories not significantly attached to the major vested interest groupings, the "oligarchies." The symbol /=/ represents channels through which connection is made with the great oligarchies. These groupings or categories, in my present view, include such as the churches, primary and secondary teachers, self-employed professionals, some unions, some types of associations, etc.

status and income levels and the "masses," including union presidents, skilled workers, and the like. In view of reported indicators of the existence of *panelinha*-like organization in the masses and lower levels of the "classes," research of this sort would be most revealing as to social structure, social barriers, social mobility, and the mechanisms of social organizing in and beyond any sort of locality.

In fact, the technique can, for a great many important features, be used in the qualitative description of the social systems of cities of any size—the intimate operations of the city economy and polity as well as their dependent stratification system, and so on. Indeed, the outcome of the technique is to map out a kind of kin and non-kin "genealogy" of all the significant groupings in the population of a city as well as of many of the individuals concerned, and at the same time one also describes the dynamics of social organization. It is important to note that the mapping reveals structures not usually visible and generally not accessible to observation using the ordinary categories of information gathering, such as demographic, statistical, occupational, and common stratification indicators.

IX

In conclusion, I should like to point out, first, that by route of describing the structure of careers in Brazil, it has been possible to describe several most fundamental aspects of Brazilian national social structures: social institutions which are carried out by national and locality groupings concomitantly. The description is not limited by the artificial boundaries created by the so-called community study method, or worse, by the plethora of studies of localities which are not even communities but are embedded in national social structures.

The community or locality-study method has always prevented seeing the integrating connections of the community with the larger social order by which it is so profoundly affected. Insofar as communities in national societies are social units at all, they exist in constant and active relation with the national institutions which are rarely described by anthropologists. Communities may conflict with the national institutions; coexist with them, as it were; actively participate in them; or, respecting different aspects of community life, do all of these at once in differing degrees and at different times. In the literature, the community appears, because of the method, as a kind of monad whose external dynamics and whose trajectory cannot be grasped more than obscurely. The method suggested here permits at least an approach to the analysis of both the whole and the part at the same time because they are seen as basically made up of the same social units.

Second, it can be seen that the overwhelmingly important kinds of informal organization I have described for Brazil are highly flexible under circumstances of rapid techno-economic change now being experienced, but where the existent technology of transport and communications and the rather rudimentary industrialism still create great difficulties for long-term organization over large distances. Under such conditions, the relative autonomy and geographical and social atomism of social units of all kinds are functional since they permit the units, *qua* units, to have greater ranges of response. The *panelinha*, the semi-public-semi-private autarchy, the semi-detached oligarchy, the notably autonomous states, and even sometimes municipalities, and even such bodies as the universities, the schools, and some of the churches, have a considerable flexibility because of their autonomy and atomism.

They may be contrasted with the ossified and rigid monolithic fixed bureaucracy. The flexible social units I have described here may move quickly, seize opportunities, reformulate policies, change strategies, and so on, without themselves changing much. In short this rather atomized, loose type of organization, without a juridical foundation, is highly adaptive for societies in which a juxtaposition of their own static-agrarian past and an expansive-industrial future is occurring.

Third, hypothetically, the case described here provides a model for all similar societies. Thus, in general, one would expect Middle Eastern, Southeast Asian, some African, and other Latin American countries to conform to the model except insofar as the variable factors are more or less influential in each case.

Put another way, the various expectations deduced from the model and even the model itself are in fact predictions. The use of a model permits predictions of two kinds. First is the prediction of field situations, that is, the prior description, as it were, of what sort of sociocultural conditions one will find in an unknown sociocultural system such as, say, Yemen or Bhutan. Departure from the expected conditions would lead one to modify the theoretical principles upon which the model-construction was based, as well as to modify the model by redefining the relationships of the variables, whereas finding the expected conditions would tend to confirm both the principles, the model, and the defined relationships among the variables.

Second, the use of the model permits one to make reasonable predictions about future states of the society under consideration and even of specific events. From the model and its variable elements one may logically derive variant consequent models by describing changed relationships of the variable. Such models would constitute a range of possible trajectories and outcomes for a society under divers conditions. Where a given outcome did not correspond to the expectations of the model constructed on the basis of variables whose values for the society are known, one would be obliged and in a position to extract new significant variables from the data, thus refining and making more powerful the theory.

Finally, it may be pointed out that the model I have been discussing has been framed mainly in terms of a juxtaposition of an already existing expansive-industrial structure with a static-agrarian one. It is incumbent upon us to ask what sort of a model we should construct for structures intermediate between the two when an expansive-industrial structure does not yet exist. This refers, of course, to the pristine development of the expansive-industrial society out of the static-agrarian. Would the model be quite different? Would it be substantially the same? Would some of the variables be extensively affected? Surely the variable of *rate* would be significantly different, since the pressure to condense the total time of transformation from one state to another is absent in the pristine sequence. Plainly, too, the variable of direct or indirect *coercion* present in the juxtaposition must needs be absent. Patently, the variable of *guidance* in transformation on the part of the acculturating body would be lacking. How do such differences affect the model? Do they suggest, for example, that the pristine development may have been more diverse, while the acculturational outcomes are likely to be relatively more like each other?

Such questions remain for future research. Answers to them might involve retrodictions of conditions that one would expect to find having happened in the pristine development (in Western Europe). For example, one might predict the occurrence, especially in the eighteenth century, of something resembling the autodidact phenomenon. Departure from the retrospective models would require modification of principles, models, and variables while discovering the conditions predicted would confirm them.

OTES

1. These concepts were originally developed in a lecture to the School of Advanced International Studies, Johns Hopkins University (cf. Leeds 1961) and subsequently expanded in Leeds (1961, Ms; 1962, Ms).

2. These hypotheses were in part *induced* from having noted the existence of the Brazilian autodidact and the multiple position holder, discussed below. They are presented here as deduced from more general evolutionary principles, since they are intended as more general models for this "transitional" type of society. That is, on the basis of theory and the derived hypotheses, we should expect to find similar or related phenomena in other societies transitional from static-agrarian to expansive-industrial both in acculturation situations and also in the evolutionary sequence itself. The hypotheses presented below should be testable in European history in, say, the sixteenth to nineteenth centuries. If the data confirm the hypotheses, the theoretical argument is strengthened; if not, one may first investigate the consequences of asserting that the evolution of a pristine system and the acculturation between two evolutionary levels are not the same things, so that different outcomes are to be expected from each. Such figures as Michelangelo, Rubens, and Goethe, however, suggest confirmation of the hypotheses.

3. The term status, role, etc., follow the usage in Leeds (1963), pp. 73 ff., and more fully defined in the version of the paper (1963, Ms) from which the published paper was abridged.

4. The famous article by Davis and Moore (1945) deals in fact with the channels of entry and curricularization of various sorts, not with stratification at all.

5. Though the usage is not strictly correct, I shall refer to the phenomenon of multiple job holding by this term for convenience' sake. The term is used mainly for "high-level" personnel and may refer to either the person or the collection of positions he holds. Each job individually is called a *bico* ("beak, spout, nipple").

6. The Portuguese word used by Dr. Teixeira was *oligarquias*, which is perhaps best translated as "vested interest groupings," since, in his conception, the entities he referred to include not only "the few" but those of "the many" who are organizationally attached to the former. Since, in contrast to the "masses," the total vested interest group numerically comprises only "a few," I shall retain the word "oligarchies." Teixeira has also used the expression "pressure groups" for these entities. (Cf. Teixeira 1962.)

7. Cate (1962, 1963, and conversations) has recently discovered an extremely complex organization of the masses in Recife, its surrounding hinterlands, and, by extension, other major cities. Similar structures were found in Maceió and Salvador, and seem indicated at least for Belém and Rio de Janeiro. The most central institution of this organization of the masses comprises the Carnaval dance organizations, such as the Escolas de Samba.

8. Indeed, any modern state society, like the United States or Germany, etc., will display

analogous structures. *Panelinhas* of the type described in this paper, however, seem more restricted in number, membership, and general accessibility; seem to control much vaster resources relatively and absolutely, and much less to permeate the entire weft of society as a fundamental social form. Another way of saying this is that America is highly organized, operating more fully through jural channels, charters, contracts, and other formal devices, including schedules and curricula, than is the case in countries like Brazil. The *cabide* phenomenon in the U.S. appears mainly at the highest level of decision making, while at levels of execution or administration and of production not only is specialization present but also effectively only single job holding. The *cabide* as a social node, a type of entity serving as a major form of social tie in the society, like the *panelinha* to which it is complementary, permeates the social order of a country like Brazil. Furthermore, the autodidact phenomenon has virtually disappeared from the United States. It is hard to think of cases. The sharp quantitative differences between societies like Brazil and those like the United States with regard to those social units, in addition to qualitative differences in their contexts, appears to me to indicate types of total societies also qualitatively quite different.

9. See footnote 5, supra.

10. There are several other nodes. Most recent, of course, has been the massive burgeoning of large-scale voluntary associations and bureaucratic agencies, but these represent an emerging trend occurring at the expense of such older and still highly important types of social nodes as the family, the inadequately described and defined unit referred to by the term "paternalism," and its special, territorially linked subclass, referred to by the term "*coronelismo*," which is presently in desuetude. Jointly all these types of units link land, labor, capital, occupational specializations, politics, and so on, into a single dynamic system.

11. In June and July of 1962, acute shortage of all major staples was experienced in south-central Brazil, especially in the Rio area. Promises were constantly being made and ineffectual action taken to alleviate the situation, until, first, 5,000,000 sacks of rice were "discovered" "hidden" in Rio Grande do Sul, and, second, a food riot in Duque de Caxias, State of Rio de Janeiro, brought about an almost instantaneous reappearance of almost all staples in adequate supply in the stores. During the riot, all houses were damaged or broken into *except* a deputy's. The riotous mob considerately left his house untouched!

12. This paper was prepared for this volume. The field work on which it is based was supported, for the writer, by the Pan-American Union, Department of Social Affairs, and for his two colleagues and certain special costs by the Instituto Nacional de Estudos Pedagógicos of Brazil. The work would have been impossible without the support of Dr. Anisio Teixeira of I.N.E.P. and the Social Affairs Department, P.A.U.; without the collaboration of my two co-workers, Prof. Carolina Martuscelli Bori, Chairman, Department of Psychology, Faculdade de Filosofía, Rio Claro (São Paulo) and Prof. Nilce Mejias of the same department, and without the extensive aid and cooperation of various indispensable persons in the several cities we visited. The present version is considerably abbreviated from the presentation read before the Anthropological Society of Washington, D.C., October 16, 1962.

REFERENCES CITED

Bennett, W. C., ed., *et al.*

1948 *A Reappraisal of Peruvian Archeology*, Memoir 4, Society for American Archeology, Menasha, Wis.

Bohannan, P.
1963 *Social Anthropology*, New York, Holt, Rinehart and Winston.
Cate, K. R.
1962 "Final Report to the Technical Secretariat of the OAS Fellowship Program," July 15. (Typescript.)
1963 Letter to Dr. Vera Rubin, Dir., Research Institute for the Study of Man, September 11.
Davis, K., and W. E. Moore
1945 "Some Principles of Stratification," *American Sociological Review*, 10:2:242–249.
Guardini, R.
1956 *The End of the Modern World*, New York, Sheed and Ward.
Leeds, A.
1957 *Economic Cycles in Brazil: The Persistence of a Total Culture Pattern: Cacao and Other Cases*, Ph.D. Thesis, Columbia University; Ann Arbor, University Microfilms.
1961 Talk, "Cultural Patterns in 'Traditional Societies,'" to School of Advanced International Studies, Johns Hopkins University, lecture series "The United States in a Changing World Environment," Washington, D.C., October 31.
1961 "The Family in Static-Agrarian Societies and Its Transformation." (Manuscript.)
1962 "Borderlands and Elite Circulation in Latin America—Locality Power vs. Central Power Institutions," paper read at annual meeting, American Anthropological Association, Chicago, November. (Manuscript.)
1962 "Fatôres culturais em educacãe: Brasil, India, Estados Unides, União Soviética: Alguns problemas de antropologia aplicada," *Educação e Ciências Socialis*, 7.20:9–68.
1963 "The Functions of War," in J. M. Masserman, ed., *Violence and War, with Clinical Studies*, Vol. 4 of *Science and Psychoanalysis*, 4, New York, Grune and Stratton.
1963 "Toward an Analysis of the Functions of War," revised version of paper read at annual meeting, American Association for the Advancement of Science, December 1962. (Manuscript.)
1964 "Brazil and the Myth of Francisco Julião," in Maier and R. W. Weatherhead, eds., *Politics of Change in Latin America*, New York, Praeger.
1967 "Some Problems in the Analysis of Class and the Social Order," in A. Leeds, ed., *Social Structure, Stratification, and Mobility*, Washington, D.C., Pan American Union.
Meggers, B. J., *et al.*
1956 "Functional and Evolutionary Implications of Community Patterning," in R. Wauchope, ed., *Seminars in Archeology*, 1955, Memoir 11, Society for American Archeology, Menasha, Wis.
Niemeyer, O.
1961 *Minha experiência em Brasília*, Rio de Janerio, Editorial Vitória.
Rostow, W. W.
1960 *The Stages of Economic Growth: A Non-Communist Manifesto*, Cambridge, Cambridge University Press.
Steward, Julian
1949 "Cultural Causality and Law: A Trial Formulation of the Development of Early Civilizations," *American Anthropologist*, 51:1:1–27.

Teixeira, A. S.
1953 *Educaçacão e um direito,* Thesis, Rio de Janeiro. (Mimeographed.)
1957 *Educaçacão nao e privilégio,* Rio de Janerio, Jose Olympio.
1960(?) "The Brazilian School and Social Mobility." (Typescript and mimeo.)
1962 "Revolução e Educaçacão." (Mimeo.)

Serrano and *Criollo,* the Confusion of Race with Class

RICHARD W. PATCH

Ethnic stereotypes are as commonplace in Latin America as elsewhere, and social or cultural attributes are often mislabeled "racial." For that matter, even emotionally loaded terms have different meanings in different contexts, as illustrated in this discussion of usages around the produce market in Lima, Peru. Data such as these reveal the limits of earlier anthropological views which treated "a society" as a unitary group of individuals who shared "a culture," and also of sociological concerns about "assimilation" or "passing" (cf. Berghe).

Richard W. Patch is Professor of Anthropology at the State University of New York, Buffalo. He has spent many years conducting research in Bolivia and Peru, and his excellent papers on industrialization, migration, agrarian reform, politics, economics, and a wide range of topics have appeared frequently in American Universities Field Staff Reports *and elsewhere.*

The people of the Terminal* are very sure about who is a *criollo* and who is a *serrano* and what the difference is between the two. It is the nature of this subjective distinction which gives us a view into the social realities behind the confusion of race with class in the Andean countries.

The stereotypes of *criollo* and *serrano* are simple to describe. The criteria used are three and are supposed to coincide: geographical origin, ethnic extraction, and cultural traits such as language and mannerisms. By these measures, the *criollo* is a person from the coast, a *mestizo* who speaks Spanish and is ignorant of indigenous languages, and is *vivo*—a latter-day Gil Blas. The *serrano* is of the highlands, an Indian who speaks Quechua or Aymará and perhaps some Spanish, and is *torpe*—a bit stupid. The mixture of criteria which

* [Editor's note: This article is a continuation of the author's report[1] on field work conducted in La Parada ("the Terminal"), which is not only the principal marketplace of Lima, Peru, but also a slum neighborhood of lower class vendors and the underworld.]

From *Fieldstaff Reports,* West Coast South American Series, Vol. 14, No. 2 (New York: American Universities Field Staff, 1967). Reprinted by permission of the author and publisher. The title used here was originally subtitle to "La Parada, Lima's Market: Part II."

are present at birth (geographical origin and attributed intelligence) with those which are acquired later (culture) gives the impression of an inherent distinctiveness present from birth, making social mobility between the two groups impossible and preserving the outworn belief of the ethnic apartness of speakers of indigenous languages.

An earlier report has shown that social mobility from "Indian" to *criollo* is possible in rural areas of the coast.[2] Interviews in the Terminal show that such mobility is also possible in the capital city and into groups which are self-consciously and defensively the epitome of *criollismo*. Mobility into this lowest urban class with its sharply drawn lines is a major demonstration of the permeability of urban classes and the fiction of the ethnic difference of the "Indian" or *serrano*.

The Terminal, however, is not a place where *serranos* in large numbers can learn urban ways and move into the normal structure of urban classes. Most remain . . . identifiably *serranos* and either eventually return to the sierra or incorporate themselves into Lima as domestic servants, factory hands, or stall or street vendors around the Terminal. Their children . . . become *criollos*. Since the *criollos* of the Terminal are so near the bottom of the social hierarchy, they bolster their position by finding a group lower than themselves. The *serranos* serve this function, and *criollos* do not ease the path of upward movement for them. On the contrary, they attempt to impede adjustment and maintain the stereotypes of difference, even though the stereotypes are not convincing to the *criollos* themselves, for they are surrounded by cases of *serranos* who have become *criollos*.

One difficulty in holding the *criollo* line is an ambiguity in the word itself. For the people of the Terminal, *criollo* is a cohesive social class. A more common meaning, however, is "that which is typically Peruvian," with the qualification "of the coast" understood. Peruvian coastal foods, music, dances, and beliefs are *criollo*, and a foreigner after some years in the country may find himself congratulated on having become *criollo*, meaning appreciative of Peruvian coastal customs. *Criollo*, as class, shades into a meaning of national identification. The same ambiguity can be seen in the word "Yankee" as used in and outside the United States.

Neither *criollo* nor *serrano* is an emotive word. *Cholo* and *indio*, on the other hand, are strongly emotive words in the Terminal and are used with care. They may be used as deliberate insults to *serranos*, but the use of such clumsy, direct terms is considered childish. In addition, the *criollo* who calls a *serrano* "*cholo*" may in turn be called "*cholo*" by the *limeños*. A word presently in vogue for *serrano* is *nacional*. Generally in the Terminal the words *indio* and *indígena* are not used, while the more vague and ambiguous *cholo* is used only with circumspection.

At this point it should be clear that *criollo* cannot be defined sensibly in a strict sense by denotation. The meaning of the word lies in its connotations, and the complexity of the connotations can best be indicated by attempting to render in English the words of the interviewers themselves. The interviewers obviously consider themselves *criollos*, and their remarks are largely self-images:

> The people of Lima [*los limeños*, which is a nice distinction in itself] apply the term *criollo* to the people who live in the poorer sections [*barrios populares*]. These people

[the *criollos*] are very high-spirited [*muy alegre*] and have as a custom the celebration of many fiestas: birthdays, weddings, baptisms, the first haircut, etc. The women are friendly and have the ability to present themselves well in conversation with strange men who make them compliments [*dicen piropos*]. They [the *criolla* women] answer in the same manner, or with a smile. On the other hand, the *serrana* women respond to these manifestations with ugly words [*lisuras*] or even acts of violence.

Women are *criollas* when they know how to dance the new dances, when they know how to dress according to the season, and when they know how to talk with different kinds of people of different classes.

Men are *criollos* when they can act with great dexterity in the poorer sections [*desenvolverse con gran vivasidad dentro del ambiente popular*], when they know how to dance, play football, and have meetings of friends which end in great drunken fights in the bars. They must know how to fight [*mecharse*] and speak slang.

The people of Callao [*los chalacos*—inhabitants of the port of Lima] have a stricter definition of *criollo*. They think of *criollos* as being only those people who live in *corralones y callejones* [special kinds of slum multiple-dwelling units], who are high-spirited, and who are very valiant in provoking fights and in defending themselves.

The Negroes of Callao are considered the most *criollo* of all [*los chalacos morenos son los considerados criollazos*]. They enjoy the respect—and the fear—of the *serranos* and the *limeños* [inhabitants of Lima in general].

The thugs and thieves [*hampones y rateros*] only call *criollo* those persons who do not allow themselves to be robbed [*no se dejan timar*] and who speak the same slang that they themselves do. All the rest of the *limeños* and *chalacos* they call *giles* [*sonsos*, or "blockheads"]. They call *serranos* "*chontiles*" [a special deprecation for *cholos*], and they are the objects of confidence games and robberies.

The *serrano* needs at least three or four years to become a *criollo*, correcting his accent, cutting his hair right, wearing clothes according to the season and the fashion, and, above all, living in the *callejones*—where, after an infinity of jokes and insults, he learns how to dance, fight, and conduct himself with dexterity in the streets.

The Chinese and Japanese, in spite of their great difficulty with Spanish, become friends with the *criollos* because they have such businesses as barbershops, whorehouses, billiard parlors, bars, and hotels. There they become intimate with the *criollos* who play jokes on them and give them nicknames. [In other words, first-generation Chinese and Japanese do not themselves become *criollos*.]

The children of Chinese and Japanese become *criollos* when they live with the poor people. They often become good football players. But they have problems when they fall in love with Peruvian girls. The Japanese parents are conservative and do not like to mix their race with the Peruvian.

Some Japanese married to Peruvians have had to renounce their parents and friends. The *criollos*, on the other hand, think of Japanese and Chinese girls as good-looking, but the *criollos* do not have much luck with them because the girls are usually engaged to men of their own race.

Thus we see that, depending upon the speaker and his context, *criollo* may mean nothing more than "Peruvian," in the same way that "Yankee" may be applied indiscriminately to any person from the United States. Or it may mean a Peruvian from the coast. Or it may have a very special meaning of a particular class in the urban slums of the coast. It is this last meaning which concerns us here, because its use is an excellent illustration of the confusion in the Andes between class and race. In this sense, *criollo* has an ideal and supposedly denotative sense in which the individual is racially distinct from the *serrano* because the former is a "*mestizo*" and the latter is an "Indian." However, the material given above makes it amply clear that *criollo* has no real racial meaning—for Chinese, Japanese, and even the so-called *serranos* may become *criollos* by acquiring certain modes of behavior. Throughout the Peruvian social hierarchy there is an attempt to reinforce the abnormally rigid class structure by the attribution of racial distinctiveness. The upper classes appropriate for themselves the appellation of "white" (*blanco*) to differentiate themselves both from the supposedly "*mestizo*" *criollos* and from the supposedly "Indian" *serranos*. The illogicality of the *blancos* is revealed in conversations in which some Peruvians are, in certain situations, proud of their "pure white" ancestry, while in other situations—usually after a discussion of the glories of the Incan Empire—they claim that they are descendants of the Incas.

The lesson here is that in Peru—as elsewhere in the world where rigid class lines are drawn to prevent upward mobility through achievement—the class lines are fortified by the attribution of an ethnic distinctiveness to the classes. Actual mobility is ignored. Definitions become circumstantial.

THE LIFE OF A CRIOLLO IN THE TERMINAL

One of the interviewees had lived in the Terminal for several years. His own description of existence there adds flesh to the bones of the generalizations above. His own selection of a pseudonym was "Carlos Zapata," and he was about seventeen years old at the time he describes.

Carlos was more aware than most persons of the vagaries of the distinction between *criollo* and *serrano*. He had been born a good *criollo* in Lima's port of Callao. His father, a seaman, abandoned the family, and Carlos was sent, at the age of eight, to live with distant kin in the sierra. He lived and went to school there in the *mestizo* town of Cajamarca which, although it is in the northern sierra and is the setting for Ciro Alegría's novel of indigenous life, *Broad and Alien Is the World*, is not a place where the Quechua language is often heard; nor is it nearly so typically Indian as the central and southern Andes of Peru. Nonetheless, Carlos became accustomed to sierra ways, the manner of speaking, and views of life. For three years he rather enjoyed life there and unconsciously adopted the sierra accent in speaking Spanish. After he finished his primary education, however, his mother required him to return to Callao, and it was a considerable shock for him in the first year of "intermediate" school to find that he was considered a *serrano* by his *criollo* classmates. According to his statement, it took about two months to lose his sierra accent, resume the coastal accent, and readapt his ways to those of the slums of a large coastal city. No doubt his ability to outfight his hecklers was largely responsible for a rapid reacceptance of his *criollo*-ness.

Equally important was Carlos' step-by-step entrance into the underworld. By this time he was eleven years old, and he had a bicycle. He enlisted the services of a less fortunate sub-teenager, and the two formed a team of purse-snatchers. They would roam the streets of Callao looking for some well-dressed woman who was walking alone and carrying a purse. Carlos' accomplice would grab the purse, then hop on the bicycle as Carlos rode by. If enough money was seized they would rest for several days, but if pickings were slim they would steal another purse at least once a day. Several months passed before they were caught, and then they were released with only a beating and a reprimand by the police.

Carlos Zapata's mother was able to make her influence felt by requiring the boy to go to work when he was thirteen years old. He began as a construction worker, doing a man's job, and unfortunately (as he said) associating with men of all sorts. Two *sambos* persuaded him to join them in their robberies of dwellings, and thus Carlos graduated from *carterista* (purse-snatcher) to *ratero* (thief or hoodlum). He did not, however, become a thug, or *hampón,* because he did not carry weapons and only broke into unoccupied houses.

These three *rateros* committed robberies with such frequency that the probable soon happened. They had climbed the wall around a house in a fashionable part of Lima after observing the departure of the owners. A neighbor saw them climbing into the garden and telephoned the police. Carlos' associates were captured, but he himself had scrambled up a tree and succeeded in hiding from the *tombos* (police). The other two members of the gang were convicted and sentenced without having informed on Carlos; but the boy was understandably concerned that he might be implicated and did not return to the rooms he had occupied with his mother. Instead, he lived for a time with a friend who was maintained by two prostitutes. Then he himself spent a year with one of the women. His life was enmeshed at every turn with criminals; he was aware of this and eventually grew to loathe it. Breaking with his woman, he sought sanctuary—if such it may be called—in the Terminal.

The "Hotel Roti" was a hotel of sorts (*hotelucho*), which Carlos described as "third class," in the ninth block of the *jirón* Humboldt. The ground floor of the two-story building was taken by a "transportation agency"—an office receiving and dispatching passengers and produce between the provinces of the central sierra and the Terminal. The "hotel" itself consisted of some rooms on the second floor and eighteen wooden cubicles built atop the roof. In Lima, a city without rain, the roofs of many buildings are thus converted into aerial tenements.

The establishment, with its sign all but hidden behind a huge advertisement for the transport office, belonged to a Chinese of "advanced age" (sixty years old), who was called Don Juanito by his "clients." He employed three *serranos* to do the cleaning and washing: Manuel, always called Mañuco; Valentín, called Cahuide; and one whose real name was lost and was known only as Cholo Malo (roughly, "Bad Halfbreed"). *Criollos,* as Carlos Zapata explained, would not accept this kind of work, nor the pay (or lack of it) offered by the Chinese owner. Only *serranos* recently arrived in the Terminal from the highlands would agree to such demeaning employment. It consisted of working fourteen hours a day, seven days a week, for barely enough money to eat, buy second-hand clothing, and sleep in a shabby bed. In the Terminal, however, there are a huge number of *serranos* willing to accept any conditions in order to live. Carlos blamed their presence for the depression of wages for work acceptable to *criollos*.

The hotel guests were referred to as "clients" because the Roti was not a transients' hotel—except during the day when beds were rented out by Don Juanito, each for a few sweaty minutes. The regular clients were "known persons": that is, they were well known both to Don Juanito and to the police. The *tombos* (police) made visits to the Roti every Monday and Friday looking for hoodlums and pimps (*cabrones*); but, through an understanding between the police and Don Juanito, the premises were not disturbed on Saturdays and Sundays, and Don Juanito's "known persons" were not subjected to scrutiny despite their lack of identification papers. This was the sanctuary that Carlos Zapata—or "Babyface" as he became known in the Terminal—found.

Carlos rented Room 39, one of the wooden cells on the roof, measuring 9 by 12 feet. It contained a bed, a nightstand, a chair, and a hook for clothes. The youth did not complain of the sparseness, for he was alone, had no more clothing than the single hook would hold, and used the room only to sleep in at night. He compared his lot favorably with that of families in other cells at the Roti, who had to accommodate two or three children in bunks and cook within the crowded confines of their rooms. Don Juanito extracted a daily rent of 15 soles (about 60 cents) from Carlos.

Life was not without its complications in the boy's first months in the hotel. The *serrano* employees made only a gesture of washing the sheets. The mattress "smelled like a sty" and harbored such a quantity of fleas that sleep was almost impossible. Carlos also had difficulty with the neighbors on both sides of his room. The partitions were little more than screens, and every conversation and movement on either side was perfectly audible. Two *serrano* youths lived on one side, retiring early enough, but rising at six in the morning—an impossibly early hour for Carlos. He complained that they talked about "stupidities" (his actual word is untranslatable and unprintable), such as "their women [*cholas*], their homeland, and their ideas for making money." Worse still, they turned on their radio at full volume and "instead of playing popular music [*de la nueva ola*] they played *huayñitos*." (In Peru *huayños* are traditional dances of the sierra.) "Can you imagine," complained Carlos, "being awakened every morning at six by 'Despertar Andino'?" ("Despertar Andino" is the early program of a Lima station which plays only records of *huayños* and is meant for the early-rising *serrano* population of the city.)

The boy was impartial in his complaints. His neighbors on the other side were *criollos:* a prostitute and her "husband" (the word *marido* was amended to *cabrón* in the interview). "Willy and Nena would come from the bordello at four or five in the morning, and then I would have another problem. The evening before I had moved my bed from the noisy *serrano* side to the quiet side—next to that occupied by Willy and Nena." At the return of Willy and Nena, however, this "quiet side" became a sounding board for sexual activities which did little to help Carlos to sleep. Still, in the Terminal one becomes accustomed to almost everything, and Carlos remarked, "Frankly the first days were very difficult, but I became used to it in time, and tried to improve the condition of my room." He goes on to describe his *criollo* activities in and about the Terminal:

I worked in Tacora as a *cachinero* [a person who buys and sells stolen articles or the goods of people who have died]. I would get up at half-past eight in the morning and go to my *pensión* for breakfast. There I had a *criolla* girl named María, although she was called Mary, who worked for the owner of the *pensión*, Señora Carmen, whom we called "Tía" [aunt]. This servant, Mary, liked me very much and saw that I got the best food. Tía Carmen noticed this but said nothing because I always paid, while the other *cachineros* who ate there would skip out on their weekly bill [do the *perro muerto* or *cabezaso*].

Mary was worried about me because the other *cachineros* and *rateros* tried to force their attentions on her, even with a knife [*la punta*], not knowing that she went with me. Mary realized that they came to the *pensión* of Tía Carmen only because of her [Mary], for she was very buxomly beautiful [*mamasita*]. She was afraid they would scar my face or beat me nearly to death [*sacarme el alma*].

But nothing of this sort happened to me because I was well known [among the *criollos*], they were my friends—and besides there lived in my hotel some real toughs [*capazotes*] who would have taken revenge. These *capazotes* would sometimes give me some of their stolen goods to keep in my room, because I was not *parca* [known by the police]. The rooms of the others were constantly searched by the *tiras* [detectives].

My work began at nine in the morning when some women would begin coming to me with blankets, sheets, coats, or plates and service which had been used by a person recently dead. It is the custom to sell these in Tacora. I would also buy some things from a few thieves, but not things which were of much value or which were large—because these would be noticed by the *tiras*, or the police, or by their owners.

Everyone knows that Tacora is the thieves' market, and many persons who had been robbed would come there to look for their goods. A few would find their articles, but most were unsuccessful because of the wall of silence that surrounds the *cachinero*. Few people in Tacora talk [*cantan*—or "sing"] to an outsider because of the law of the *criollo* thugs [*la ley del hampa criolla*]. Because of the danger, however, the *cachinero* always asks the thief he is buying from if the goods are *con roche* [recently stolen]. If they had been recently stolen, I would change their appearance or keep them until they were *sin roche*.

Each day I would begin with a capital of 150 to 200 soles [$6 to $8] and would earn between 100 and 150 soles. Saturdays were *de raya* [of most profit], when I would earn between 200 and 250 soles [$8 to $12].

My specialty was clothing because there were many other *cachineros* specializing in *bobos* [watches], *rieles* [shoes], *garras* [bedding], and records. I was one of about 300 *cachineros* in Tacora, not counting the *tangueros* [shills]. The *tangueros* served the *cachineros* in the following way: I, for example, would have a suit which cost me 80 or 100 soles, which I could get so cheap because the seller needed money. I would shake it out and press it in my room, then take it out and ask 350 soles for it—saying that it cost 1,200 in the stores and was almost new. Curious and interested people would begin to gather around, which was when the *tanguero* (a friend of mine) would appear. He would come closer and say, "Hey, I'll give you 300 soles for the suit because that's all I have, but the suit is *bacanaso* [very good quality]." I'd tell him, "No, you're crazy to offer so little." Then I would hand it to another person who showed interest, and he would offer me 320 soles. I'd think it over, and finally accept, while the *tanguero* looked disappointed. Afterwards I would congratulate myself on having cleared 220 soles, but I would have to give 20 soles to the shill for his shill-work [*tanga*].

At two o'clock in the afternoon I would go to the *pensión* of Tía Carmen and afterward to sleep at the hotel from three to five. Later I would take Mary to the movies—but, of course, not every day. Many evenings I would go to *timbiar* [play cards, craps, or pool].

With the money I earned in *la cachina*, I would pay Don Juanito his 15 soles a day, or sometimes for a whole week in advance, and would pay Aunt for my board [*pensión*]. My clothing was always nearly new, although I had only two or three trousers and shirts. But I would wear them for a while, then press them, sell them in Tacora, and buy others.

The smell of the hotel bedding was overwhelming, and the money I saved went to buy my own sheets, pillowcases, blankets, a suitcase, and a spray gun for the fleas. I even bought some cardboard to cover the walls which had been punctured by *sapos* [people who wished to see activities in the adjoining rooms] and painted the walls, ceiling, chair, nightstand, and cot. I bought some wire to hold together the steel webbing of the cot because the mattress was falling through almost to the floor. Finally, mine was the best arranged and cleanest of all the rooftop rooms, and the only one inhabited by a single person.

But one day I returned to the hotel at noon, instead of at my usual time of three in the afternoon. Everything was in disorder, and especially the bed was a mess. It was only then that I realized that Don Juanito had been renting out my room to couples in the mornings, charging 30 soles an hour. After that I bought a padlock for the door and continued to live in the room for two and a half years without further trouble. During the time I lived at the hotel I made many friends—and many observations.

The dwellings on the rooftop of the hotel were a sorry sight. There were only two lavatories, one for the men and one for the women. Between seven and eight in the morning, lines would form of up to fourteen persons. The women had poles and clotheslines for their washing, but the soot from the kerosene stoves blackened not only the rooms of those who cooked inside them, but also made it impossible to have sheets, clothes, and diapers which were both dry and clean. The floor below [the second story of the structure] was more decent. It was expensive and only for transients staying one or two days.

On this floor, at the head of the stairs, was Don Juanito's office. It contained an iron box which looked like a safe, but was not—being secured only by a large padlock. Recently Don Juanito was registering two *sambos* at three o'clock in the morning. One put a knife to Juanito's throat and then they beat him unconscious. They took the key from him, opened the box, and stole 15,000 soles in cash, jewelry, and other articles to a total of 50,000 soles [somewhat less than $2,000]. The next day Don Juanito began enclosing his office with steel plates and bars, leaving only a little window where clients could register and pay. He moved his bed inside, placed a knife and a club near at hand, and installed a bell on the street door, which could only be opened by pulling a rope from inside the cage to lift the latch. Most hotel owners of the Terminal protect themselves in this way.

Among many others I observed in the hotel was a man and his wife, who was called Raquel. The husband earned little in his factory job and the children were ill, causing great medical expenses. Señora Raquel fell a month behind in her payments to Don Juanito, who threatened to throw the family out of the hotel and keep their goods as payment. But this was not his real intention—he wanted Raquel, who was one of the prettiest women in the building, but very faithful to her husband. She ignored the importunities of the Chinaman until a month and a half had gone by without payment. Then the Chinaman told her to get out, and she had to submit to him—who was old and ugly.

One could have very good women in the hotel [*se comía muy buenas mujeres del hotel*]. They would tell me of their adventures. There was much infidelity there when the husbands would go to work. The wives would take advantage of the time to cheat on them [*sacarle la torna*]. [Such matter-of-fact comments were common among the *criollo* interviewees. Comparable reports were very uncommon among the *serranos*.]

Don Juanito would also accept homosexuals and men bringing in little girls, charging them more than the going rate because he did not want trouble.

SOME PERSONS ESCAPE

The interviewee, Carlos Zapata, changed tone in reports on his interviews and observations when he described how Willy and Nena, the couple living next to him in the Hotel Roti, succeeded in escaping from the entanglements of their situation. "Willy" was now more respectfully referred to as "Willfredo," and the intensely deprecatory *cabrón* (pimp) gave way to such terms as *caficho* and *mangasón* (both meaning a protector rather than an exploiter of prostitutes). The latter usually become the common-law husbands of the prostitutes and have children by them. Such was the case of Willfredo and Nena, and Carlos Zapata came to realize the difference:

During the months I was living in the hotel, I could hear that the couple living next to me were doing everything possible to leave this place where they had found themselves. To this end the young man, Willfredo, who did not like to drink or gamble [*timbiar*], saved all the money he could from Nena's daily takings in the bordello—about 400 soles a day, and more on Saturdays, Sundays, and holidays. He did not act like some other *cafichos*, who drink, gamble, dress as best they can, and take advantage of other prostitutes. Every night Willfredo would take Nena's money and then deposit it next day in the bank. His hope was to buy a used car and work as a taxi driver, and thus get Nena out of the bordello. Many things complicated his plan, especially when one of their children became ill and it took a great deal of money to cure the boy.

The owner of the *pensión* who fed them, Señora Rosa, gave them special things to eat—milk, beefsteak, juice, and toast—and the same for lunch. Nena claimed to work in a hospital to account for her suspicious hours.

In fact, Willfredo took Nena to the bordello every day at six in the morning, and then he returned to their room in the hotel to sleep or listen to music until three in the afternoon. At that hour he would have the children wash themselves and he would go to the bordello to retrieve Nena. This is a precaution that most *cafichos* take, for there is never any lack of men anxious to take their places, nor of thieves who prey on prostitutes leaving their places of work. Some of the *hampa* try to kidnap the prostitutes, cutting their faces, arms, and legs if they resist.

In the hotel I could hear Willfredo and Nena talking, although they spoke very low. I was surprised that they had great love for one another, and were making plans for themselves and their children.

The relative decency of Willfredo and Nena [in the Terminal] caused invidious comments among the neighbors, who never tired of talking of the *puta* and her shameless keeper [*sinvergüenza*]. After eight months, when the child was well at last, Willfredo bought a car and began to work. He and Nena found a house in La Victoria and moved from the hotel. Other residents of the roof shacks were sad and probably envious.

From the conversations on the other side of my room, I found that the two *serranos* were *paisanos*, both coming from the Department of Cuzco. They earned their living by selling apples, imported from California and Chile, as street vendors with carts. One earned only up to 50 soles a day, but the other earned 80 to 100 soles, and he would lend money to his less fortunate fellow-lodger. They were planning to put together a little capital, buy some of the small manufactured goods and textiles which are relatively cheap in the Terminal and expensive in the sierra, and then take the goods from Lima to one of the regional fairs in the mountain communities near Cuzco, sell them, and return to the Terminal with the profits to begin again on a larger scale.

Unfortunately, one of them, Teófilo, did not return to the hotel to sleep one night. His companion went out the next day to look for him and learned from one of Teófilo's fellow vendors that the police had rounded him up, along with many others of age for military service, and drafted him into the army. [This is the common draft procedure in Peru, when at a certain time of year the cities are combed for men of military age who do not have their papers in order. Persons with financial resources or family are usually able to escape this system, but the poor have no recourse.] The companion sold his own cart and the remainder of his apples and asked a woman to go to the Zona Militar to ask for Teófilo. He was afraid to go himself for fear that he might also be impressed. The woman returned saying that Teófilo had been taken and had already been transferred to a distant camp. The companion, alone, could no longer pay the rent to Don Juanito, so he bought a few things with what money he had and took passage atop a trunk returning to Cuzco. He arrived there little better off than when he had first left, but he counted himself lucky not to have been impressed into the army and also to have been able to sell his cart and apples. Often street vendors are drafted into the army without being allowed even time to dispose of their goods, which become the property of the Municipality.

NOTES

1. See Richard W. Patch, *La Parada, Lima's Market, A Study of Class and Assimilation, Part I: A Villager Who Met Disaster* (RWP-1-'67), American Universities Field Staff Reports, West Coast South America Series, Volume XIV, No. 1, February 1967.

2. See Richard W. Patch, *The Role of a Coastal Hacienda in the Hispanization of Andean Indians* (RWP-2-'59), American Universities Field Staff Reports, West Coast South America Series, Volume VI, No. 2, March 1959.

Ethnic Membership and Cultural Change in Guatemala

PIERRE L. VAN DEN BERGHE

Guatemala has a higher proportion of Indians in her population than almost any other country in Latin America, but that proportion has undergone steady and relatively rapid decline during this century. Where vital statistics fly in the face of popular use of the term

From *Social Forces* XLVI (1968), 514–522. Copyright © 1968, University of North Carolina Press. Reprinted by permission of the author and publisher.

"caste system" to characterize relations between superordinate ladinos and subordinate Indians, van den Berghe provides clues to the delineation of ethnic boundaries, and to related phenomena such as "social race," "passing," and "biculturalism."

Pierre L. van den Berghe is Professor of Sociology at the University of Washington. His broad perspectives on interethnic relations, politics, and change reflect a variety of research in Africa and Meso-America, documented in his books Caneville: The Social Structure of a South American Town (1964), South Africa: A Study in Conflict (1965), Race and Racism: A Comparative Perspective (1967), Race and Ethnicity: Essays in Comparative Sociology (1970), Intergroup Relations (1972); *he is also coauthor of* Africa: Social Problems of Change and Conflict (1965), Ixil Country: A Plural Society in Highland Guatemala (1969), *and* Race and Ethnicity in Africa (*in press*).

Guatemala, a country of 4.2 million (1964 Census), is one of the least Westernized countries of the Hemisphere.[1] Its population is divided into a dominant group of Spanish-speaking Ladinos (who constituted 56.7 percent of the total in 1964), and various subordinate Indian groups speaking related Maya languages. Four of these, Quiché, Mam, Cakchiquel and Quecchi, include over 100,000 people each. The Indian population is heavily concentrated in the western and central highlands of the country, where the elevation is highest and the soil among the poorest and most difficult to cultivate. The coastal zones, the Petén, and the east, including the capital city, are predominantly Ladino.

Ethnic relations in Guatemala have been the object of considerable study, mostly by North American anthropologists.[2] Most studies have been of small local communities, and few attempts have been made to incorporate ethnic relations in the study of the whole of Guatemala as a complex plural society. Within the relatively small area of Guatemala, local ethnic situations vary greatly in such factors as demographic ratios, local dominance of Ladinos versus Indians, and degree of conflict between the two groups. Such comparisons as have been made have seldom gone beyond stating differences in ethnic situations between local communities, and suggesting *ad hoc* "explanations" for the differences.

DEMOGRAPHIC CHANGES IN ETHNIC COMPOSITION

The purpose of this paper is to account for two seemingly paradoxical sets of facts concerning ethnic membership in Guatemala:

1. While several community studies stress the rigidity of ethnic boundaries and while some authors go so far as to describe the Ladino-Indian distinction as a caste system,[3] there has been a steady decline in the relative size of the Indian group (Table 1). This decline, as we shall see, must be attributed mostly to "passing."

2. Although the Ladino-Indian distinction has been described as largely cultural rather than racial, actual hispanization and ladinoization by Indians does not seem to affect the rigidity of the ethnic line at the local level. A number of "social Indians" are in fact strongly hispanicized.

TABLE 1. Ethnic Composition of Guatemalan Population (1774–1964)

Year	Percent Indian	Percent Ladino
1774	78.4	21.6
1880	64.7	35.3
1921	64.8	35.2
1940	55.7	44.3
1950	53.6	46.4
1964	43.3	56.7

The decline in the relative proportion of the Indian population could, of course, be due to several factors besides cultural assimilation, notably foreign immigration, a change in the definition of ethnicity by the census, and differential rates of net reproduction. In the last censuses, "ethnic group" has been consistently defined in terms of "social estimation in which a person is held in the place where the census is taken." Migration to and from Guatemala is on much too small a scale to account for a significant proportion of the change in ethnic ratio.

This leaves differential net reproduction rate as a possible determinant of the ethnic change. This factor, however, is also minor. There are no good vital statistics by ethnicity. It might be expected that both infant and adult mortality are somewhat higher for Indians than for Ladinos because of the latter group's better economic position. On the other hand, the disproportionate concentration of Ladinos in the low altitude regions with malaria, intestinal parasites, and other tropical diseases may cancel out the Ladinos' slight economic advantage. The birth rate is quite high for both groups, leading to a 3.1 percent annual population growth between the 1950 and the 1964 census. Statistics by *departamento* (or province) indicate that the net reproduction rate for Indians and Ladinos is nearly equal. There is no clear relationship between the rank-order of Guatemala's 22 *departamentos* in the percentage of their Ladino population and in their rate of population increase (Table 2). (The Spearman rank correlation is +.19. If one excludes the five *departamentos* which increased at rates considerably above the national average because of high rates of in-migration from other *departamentos*, the rank correlation becomes −.18.)

The relative decline in the Indian population is thus largely a result of gradual cultural and social assimilation to the dominant Ladino group. On the average, some 15 to 20,000 Indians probably "pass" as Ladinos each year. In fact, the rate of ethnic mobility at the national level is probably comparable to that of class mobility within the Ladino group. Can one then speak of Guatemalan ethnic relations constituting a "caste system"? The answer is clearly "no" at the national level, but, in many local communities with a predominantly Indian population, the two ethnic groups closely approximate the three basic criteria of Kroeber's definition of caste, namely endogamy (accompanied by extensive interethnic concubinage), hierarchy, and ascribed membership by birth and for life. Methodologically, this discrepancy highlights the danger of extrapolating from the local microcosm to the larger society.

Assuming that changes in ethnic ratios reflect mostly cultural assimilation, an

TABLE 2. Population Increase and Ethnicity

	Percent Yearly Population Increase 1950–1964	Rank Order in Rate of Population Increase	Percent Ladino 1964	Rank Order in Percent Ladinos
Izabal	5.3	1	88.5	7
Escuintla	5.1	2	92.9	4
Guatemala	4.2	3	89.7	5
Petén	4.0	4	75.1	8
Retalhuleu	3.8	5	66.1	9
Quetzaltenango	2.7	8.5	46.0	14.5
Suchitepéquez	2.7	8.5	46.0	14.5
Quiché	2.7	8.5	15.3	19
Baja Verapaz	2.7	8.5	47.7	13
Santa Rosa	2.7	8.5	99.1	3
Totonicapán	2.7	8.5	4.6	22
San Marcos	2.5	12.5	39.5	16
Huehuetenango	2.5	12.5	32.5	17
Alta Verapaz	2.4	14	8.1	20
Progreso	2.3	15	99.6	1.5
Zacapa	2.2	16.5	88.6	6
Jutiapa	2.1	16.5	99.6	1.5
Chimaltenango	2.0	18	23.9	18
Sacatepéquez	2.0	20	54.4	11
Sololá	2.0	20	7.3	21
Jalapa	2.0	20	57.4	10
Chiquimula	1.8	22	50.4	12
Total Guatemala	3.1	–	56.7	

examination of statistics by *departamento* reveals wide regional differences in rates of assimilation (Table 3). Two main factors seem to affect the situation. The first one is relative size of Indian population. In all of the heavily (75 to 95 percent in 1964) Indian *departamentos* (Totonicapán, Sololá, Alta Verapaz, Chimaltenango and Quiché), the ethnic ratio remained quite stable. In all five *departamentos*, there was a large absolute increase in the Indian population, and in Quiché there was even a slight relative increase of 0.6 percent between 1950 and 1964. The other four *departamentos* showed a relative decline of only 1.1 to 1.5 percent. With the exception of Chimaltenango, these *departamentos* were also remarkably stable between 1940 and 1950. In short, there has been little change in ethnic composition of the heavily Indian western and central highlands for the last quarter century.

On the other hand, in four of the seven *departamentos* where Indians numbered only 10 to 20 percent of the population in 1950, the decline has been rapid. In Jutiapa, the percentage of Indians declined from 19.6 to 0.4, and absolute members went from 27,249 to 840; in Progreso, from 9.4 to 0.4 and from 4,482 to 240; in Santa Rosa, from 9.4 to 0.9 and from 10,294 to 1,460. Escuintla experienced an absolute decrease from 19,660 to 17,880 and a relative one from 15.9 to 7.1 percent. Of the seven *departamentos* with Indian popula-

TABLE 3. Changes in Ethnic Composition by *Departamento* (1940–1964)

Departamento	Percent Indian			Change in Percent Indian		Rank-Order of Change in Indian Population	
	1940	1950	1964	1940–1950	1950–1964	1940–1950	1950–1964
Izabal	19.0	17.2	11.5	− 1.8	− 5.7	13	16
Escuintla	18.9	15.9	7.1	− 3.0	− 8.8	8	8
Guatemala	19.5	18.1	10.3	− 1.4	− 7.8	14	11.5
Petén	32.3	27.9	24.9	− 4.4	− 3.0	4.5	17
Retalhuleu	56.3	51.9	33.9	− 4.4	−18.0	4.5	2
Quetzaltenango	69.8	67.6	54.0	− 2.2	−13.6	10.5	4
Suchitepéquez	66.9	67.7	54.0	− 2.2	−13.7	10.5	3
Quiché	84.8	84.1	84.7	− 0.7	+ 0.6	17	22
Baja Verapaz	60.4	58.5	52.3	− 1.9	− 6.2	12	13
Santa Rosa	10.5	9.4	0.9	− 1.1	− 8.5	16	9
Totonicapán	96.1	96.8	95.4	+ 0.7	− 1.4	20	20
San Marcos	73.8	72.5	60.5	− 1.3	−12.0	15	6
Huehuetenango	76.5	73.3	67.5	− 3.2	− 5.8	6.5	15
Alta Verapas	93.9	93.4	91.9	− 0.5	− 1.5	18	18.5
Progreso	16.1	9.4	0.4	− 6.7	− 9.0	3	7
Zacapa	30.9	19.2	11.4	−11.7	− 7.8	1	11.5
Jutiapa	22.2	19.6	0.4	− 2.6	−19.2	9	1
Chimaltenango	86.6	77.6	76.1	− 9.0	− 1.5	2	18.5
Sacatepéquez	54.8	51.6	45.6	− 3.2	− 6.0	6.5	14
Sololá	93.3	93.8	92.7	+ 0.5	− 1.1	19	21
Jalapa	49.5	50.5	42.6	+ 1.0	− 7.9	22	10
Chiquimula	61.0	61.9	49.6	+ 0.9	−12.3	21	5

tions of less than 20 percent in 1950, only Izabal, Zacapa, and Guatemala retained Indian minorities in excess of 10 percent. Where Indians are in minority, especially in the eastern part of the country, they are becoming rapidly absorbed into the Ladino group. Ethnic ratios by *departamento* account for approximately 32 percent of the variance in rate of assimilation. (The Spearman rank correlation between Indian percentage in 1964 and relative decline of Indian population between 1950 and 1964 is −.54.)

There are, however, five *departamentos* which had Indian majorities of 52 to 73 percent in 1950, and which nevertheless experienced large declines of between 18 and 12 percent between 1950 and 1964. With the exception of Chiquimula, those *departamentos* are located in the southwestern zone of large-scale coffee, sugarcane and cotton plantations. San Marcos, Quetzaltenango, Retalhuleu and Suchitepéquez are all rapidly growing due to the steady influx of agricultural laborers. It might be thought that the Indian population declines relatively (despite a slow rate of absolute growth) because of Ladino in-migration. Such is not the case, however, because much of the in-migration consists of Indians coming from the adjacent western highlands. If it were not for assimilation, the Indian proportion should rise rather than decline as a consequence of in-migration into that zone. The region of large-scale commercial agriculture is probably, with the capital city, the one where "passing" takes place most rapidly and on the largest scale. The fifth *departamento* with a relatively large but rapidly declining Indian population, Chiquimula, does not resemble the other four. Its rate of population growth is the lowest in the Republic indicating considerable out-migration. Its location in eastern Guatemala is probably the main factor accounting for the rapid Indian decline. Chiquimula is surrounded by predominantly Ladino *departamentos* and is also relatively accessible to the capital city. A number of Indians probably emigrate to neighboring Ladino areas and become assimilated.

FACTORS OF SOCIOCULTURAL CHANGE AND STABILITY

What then are the conditions making for ethnic fluidity in some parts of the country and great rigidity in other parts? "Passing" across the ethnic line is largely a function of geographical mobility. The Indian who stays in his village or town of birth almost never "passes"; the one who goes to work in a larger city or on a large coffee, cotton or sugarcane plantation frequently becomes accepted as a Ladino after a few years. The *departamentos* where the Indian population is in greatest relative decline also tend to be those which, through in-migration, increase fastest in total population. Since most of the migrants are Indians from the western highlands, this Indian migration is clearly accompanied by considerable ladinoization.[4]

In short, the more isolated, rural, economically stagnant parts of Guatemala with a predominantly Indian population have a stable ethnic situation; conversely, the larger urban centers, specially the capital city, and the zones of large-scale commercial agriculture which attract a mobile rural proletariat and where the Ladino population is larger are characterized by more fluid ethnic boundaries. Any comprehensive view of ethnic relations and culture contact in Guatemala or indeed anywhere must analyze the entire country as a differentiated system, rather than compare a series of small local "peasant" communities.

The second apparent paradox is that, at the local level, in the more stable part of the country, the ethnic line remains quite rigid in spite of considerable hispanization of the Indian population. Local Indians who are literate, speak fluent Spanish, dress as Ladinos, live in town, and practice nontraditional occupations, are still frequently regarded as Indians by both Indians and Ladinos. Actual acculturation of Indians often seems to have no perceptible effect on the permeability of the local ethnic line. This situation only appears paradoxical, of course, if one accepts the common statement that the criteria of ethnic membership in Guatemala are cultural. At this point we must examine more closely the definition of Guatemalan ethnic groups.

Most North American authors dealing with Latin America in general and Guatemala in particular have stressed the nonracial character of group distinctions in that part of the Western Hemisphere.[5] Some Latin-American and European authors, on the other hand, have argued that there is at least some racism in Spanish America and certainly in Brazil.[6] With the exception of a few atypical individuals, racism in Spanish America is at most a residual phenomenon. There is a clear priority of sociocultural criteria in the definition of group boundaries.

Although Guatemalan informants occasionally mention physical traits as distinguishing characteristics between Ladinos and Indians, the division is almost entirely nonracial.[7] Any attempt to divide the population phenotypically would, to be sure, overlap with ethnicity somewhat above the level expected by chance. However, most working-class Ladinos look undistinguishable from Indians, and a few Indians are genetically mestizos and phenotypically caucasoid-looking. To most Guatemalans, physical appearance is of little significance except perhaps as a crude indicator of ethnicity. The most commonly used and most discriminating criteria of group membership are home language and clothing, especially footgear or its absence. There are a number of other cultural correlates of ethnicity such as literacy, the practice of orthodox versus syncretistic Catholicism, diet, house architecture, and standard of living; these characteristics taken individually are not completely reliable but, used in combination, they leave little ambiguity as to a person's ethnic status.

Yet, the possession or nonpossession of certain objective cultural characteristics does not give one a complete picture of ethnic boundaries and mobility. Thus, for example, the asymmetry in the assimilation process also makes for an asymmetry in ethnic definition. In terms of objective characteristics, many Indians exhibit various degrees of biculturalism and bilingualism, whereas very few Ladinos do. Ladino status, then, is not only determined by knowledge of Spanish but also by ignorance of any indigenous tongue, while conversely biculturalism and bilingualism are associated with Indian status. This resolves the apparent paradox noted above. An Indian may acquire most of the cultural attributes of Ladinos and still be regarded as an Indian in his local community.

It might be expected that this rigidity would result from the reluctance of Ladinos to accept persons of known Indian ancestry into the superordinate group. Although some Ladinos are exclusivistic, the dominant attitudes of Ladinos (and the officially sanctioned policy of the government) are assimilationist. Most Ladinos regard indigenous cultures as backward and inferior to their own, and, hence, conclude that hispanization of the Indians is an improvement to be encouraged, and that it contributes to national integration and progress. To the extent that ethnic attitudes are a determining factor, the rigidity of the ethnic line is probably more a function of the Indians' lack of desire or motivation to "pass," than of Ladino rejection. Many Indians show strong ethnic solidarity, and only regard certain material and technological aspects of the dominant culture as desirable. Furthermore, Indians in some of the more remote parts of the highlands have locally retained sufficient political and economic autonomy from the larger society and from local Ladinos to make "passing" unattractive. The achievement of relative wealth, primary education, high political office in the municipality, and upward class mobility is often locally possible for an Indian without becoming assimilated to the Ladino group. High prestige through religious office in traditional Indian organizations such as the *cofradias* can only be achieved by remaining Indian.[8]

THE CULTURAL DYNAMICS VERSUS THE SOCIAL STRUCTURE OF ETHNIC RELATIONS

In practice, "passing" takes place overwhelmingly in three kinds of cases:

1. When Indians move outside of their home area;

2. When Indians are adopted or serve as domestic servants in Ladino households from childhood or adolescence on;
3. In cases of interethnic marriage or concubinage, when one of the spouses adopts the way of life of the other. In this last instance, there are some cases of Ladinos who become Indianized, as well as the more common reverse situation. The ethnic affiliation of mestizo children is generally determined by the dominant culture of their family orientation, or, in the case of illegitimate children, by the ethnic affiliation of the parent who brings them up. Some local communities, however, recognize an intermediate category of mestizos.

A common feature of all three situations leading to "passing" is that the persons involved are partially or totally removed not only from their cultural milieu, but, even more importantly, from their *socially significant groups* and from their traditional networks of interaction with kinsmen, friends, and acquaintances. Migration and adoption are, of course, facilitating factors in cultural assimilation and change, but they also mark an abrupt severance of social ties. It is useful here to distinguish between the *cultural dynamics* of ethnic situations and their *social structure* in terms of networks of relationships. Ethnicity is defined just as much by membership in a specific group which has distinct structural properties and social boundaries, as by sharing of a cultural heritage and speaking of a common language.

Most American anthropologists working in the Western Hemisphere have stressed the cultural aspect of ethnicity and have approached "passing" from the point of view of acculturation theory. European anthropologists studying similar phenomena in Africa, on the other hand, have adopted a more structural approach, focusing their analyses on social roles or on networks of interaction.[9] The Mexican anthropologist, Aguirre Beltrán, has adopted elements of both approaches and has thereby presented one of the most cogent analyses of culture contact and change in Meso-America.[10]

First, "passing" and "acculturation" are not one-way phenomena. This is true not only in the sense that members of the dominant group sometimes become assimilated to the subordinate group, but also in the more interesting sense of "cultural commuting." Acculturation and "passing" are not only continuous phenomena where individuals gradually move from one group and from one culture to another. A number of people exhibit various degrees of biculturalism and bi-ethnicity, and abruptly shift or "commute" back and forth in cultural and social space.[11]

This phenomenon is especially common among the migrant *Lumpenproletariat* in agriculture and industry. Thus, in Guatemala, the highland Indian who goes to work on the coastal plantations or takes a trip to the capital often dresses indistinguishably from Ladinos while away from home, uses Spanish as his *lingua franca,* and temporarily ceases to be readily identifiable as an Indian. When he returns home, he or she resumes wearing the local dress and again becomes more visibly Indian. The ladinoized Indian who is fluent in Spanish can and does accommodate to the Ladino world for reasons of convenience and expediency, or simply to remain inconspicuous, or perhaps even to avoid discrimination. At home where he is known, he cannot "pass," but in alien territory he frequently "passes" temporarily, shuttling back and forth between two cultural and social universes. Since many more Indians than Ladinos are bicultural, most people involved in this commuting are Indians. The nearly total absence of phenotypical differences between Ladinos and Indians makes "passing" in transitory, segmental and public forms of interaction (such as the employer-employee or the merchant-customer relationship) relatively easy.

Cultural and social commuting raise of course the problem of what a person "really" is. A census-taker using the criterion of local definition of ethnicity may classify the same person as a Ladino in one place and an Indian in another. Ethnic fluidity is not only a function of long-range, irreversible movement across the ethnic line, but also of the repeated and sometimes quite rapid oscillations on both sides of it. Clearly, this commuting has both a cultural and a social dimension, and the latter is frequently the more important or relevant one.

The social structural approach to ethnicity leads us to a second phenomenon, namely asymmetry in the subjective perception of ethnic membership by the dominant and the subordinate groups. In somewhat oversimplified terms, Ladinos tend to have a dichotomous view of their country's ethnic structure, while Indians tend to have a more fragmented one. To most Ladinos, Guatemala consists basically of Indians and Ladinos. This does not mean, of course, that Ladinos are not aware of the existence of differences between Indians; these differences are so obvious as to strike even the most casual tourist. However, Ladinos tend to ascribe a distinctly secondary importance to ethnic distinctions between Indians, and they view the country as divided into the two significant groups. To most Indians on the other hand, any concept of common "indianness" is of little or no significance. The local town or *municipio* or at most the language community is the basic membership and reference group, so that most Indians will refer to themselves by locality (e.g., as people of Cobán, San Cristobal, or Sacapulas) or as speakers of a given language (e.g., as Quiché, Mam, or Cakchiquel). Other Indians are, to be sure, distinguished from Ladinos, but typically treated as ethnic strangers, and sometimes collectively referred to by a single generic term denoting any nonlocal Indian.

These two "models" of Guatemalan social structure are, of course, meaningfully related to the respective positions of Ladinos and Indians. Ladinos are indeed a culturally homogeneous group and a single-speech community. Although social class distinctions between Ladinos are important, Ladinos are nevertheless a meaningful national group whose frame of reference is the State of Guatemala, and, in the case of the upper class, even Central America or the entire Spanish-speaking world. Many high-status Ladino families have kinship and friendship ties which extend over the entire country and even beyond. Nothing comparable is found among Indians who belong to localized groups without extensive outside ties, and are surrounded by culturally distinct ethnic groups speaking related but frequently not mutually intelligible languages. Nor is there any significant political consciousness of common Indian status vis-à-vis Ladinos to overcome ethnic diversity, as there is for example between Zulu, Sotho and Xhosa in South Africa.

Given the reality of ethnic differentiation among Indians, and the fragmented perception of that reality by most Indians, the close relationship between "passing" and geographical mobility becomes almost inevitable. Physically separated from his group of origin, the Indian finds other Indians almost as alien as Ladinos, and has little or no prospect of acceptance into the local Indian group. On the other hand, to the extent that he already speaks Spanish, he will use that language almost exclusively in his dealings with both Ladinos and other Indians, unless he also happens to know the local Indian tongue. In order to be less conspicuous, he will abandon his own ethnic dress, and, if only for reasons of economy, he will dress as a Ladino rather than as a local Indian. (Handwoven Indian clothes typically cost at least twice as much as cheap machine-made Ladino clothes.) In the absence both of strong resistance to assimilation by Ladinos and of an Indian solidary group to help maintain one's separate identity, the outcome is almost inevitably assimilation to the dominant group. Social benefits accruing from acceptance as a Ladino may not be very great in some areas, but they are sufficient to determine the main direction of assimilation, in much the same way as, for example, European immigrants to Canada predominantly assimilate to the English rather than to the French group even in Quebec where the French are a numerical majority.

CONCLUSION

In conclusion, an adequate understanding of the dynamics of ethnic relations requires a partial shift of focus from the conventional approach used by most North American anthropologists who worked in Meso-America. More specifically:

1. Local communities are not simply microcosms of the national society, nor is the national society simply a conglomerate of diverse ethnic groups. As Aguirre Beltrán, de la Fuente, and other Mexican anthropologists have noted, ethnic relations must be understood within the larger regional and national context.[12] In Guatemala, the picture which emerges from the macrocosmic view is radically different from that conveyed by the local community in the heavily Indian areas. Yet, the two perspectives complement each other, and the apparent paradoxes disappear if one analyzes local communities within the context of the larger society.

2. The analysis of ethnic relations must not be focused exclusively nor even primarily at the cultural level; ethnic relations cannot satisfactorily be accounted for simply in terms of cultural differences, culture contact and acculturation between groups. It is important to distinguish analytically the structural elements of ethnic relations from the cultural ones. The dynamics of group membership, solidarity and conflict, and the network of structured relationships both within and between groups are at least as essential to an understanding of ethnic relations as the cultural dynamics of group contact. People are not only "carriers of culture," they are also members of structured groups. Insofar as systems of ethnic relations are largely determined by structural asymmetries in wealth, prestige and power between groups, an inventory of cultural differences gives one a very incomplete picture of group relations. Cultural differences are frequently symptoms rather than determinants of intergroup behavior, even in systems where the distinguishing criteria of group membership are predominantly cultural.

NOTES

1. The field work which led to this paper was made possible through a summer research grant of the Graduate School of Arts and Sciences, University of Washington, for which I want to express my gratitude. In the course of eight years of professional collaboration in Meso-American research, I have greatly profited from my exchanges with Benjamin N. and Lore Colby. I am also indebted to Ernest T. Barth and John F. Scott of the University of Washington who criticized an earlier draft of this paper, and to my Mexican colleague Gonzalo Aguirre Beltrán with whom I discussed problems of culture change and ethnic relations in Meso-America.

2. See Richard Adams, *Political Changes in Guatemalan Indian Communities, A Symposium* (New Orleans: Tulane University, 1957); Ruth Bunzel, *Chichicastenango, A Guatemalan Village* (Locust Valley, N.Y.: Augustin, 1952); Allain X. Dessaint, "Effects of the Hacienda and Plantation Systems on Guatemala's Indians," *Practical Anthropology*, 10 (July–August 1963); John Gillin, *The Culture of Security in San Carlos* (New Orleans: Tulane University, 1951); John Gillin, "Race Relations without Conflict: A Guatemalan Town," *American Journal of Sociology*, 53 (November 1948), pp. 337–343; Jackson Steward Lincoln, *An Ethnological Study of the Ixil Indians of the Guatemala Highlands* (Chicago: University of Chicago Microfilm, 1945); Marvin K. Mayers (ed.), *Languages of Guatemala* (The Hague: Mouton & Co., 1966); Manning Nash, *Machine Age Maya*, American Anthropological Association, Memoir 87, 1958; Robert Redfield, "The Relations between Indians and Ladinos in Agua Escondida, Guatemala," *America Indígena*, 16 (1956), pp. 253–276; K. H. Silvert, *A Study in Government, Guatemala* (New Orleans: Tulane University, 1954); Sol Tax, "Ethnic Relations in Guatemala," *America Indígena*, 2 (1942); and Melvin Tumin, *Caste in a Peasant Society* (Princeton: Princeton University Press, 1952). The principal works in Spanish are the series of publications of the *Seminario de Integración Social Guatemalteca* (Guatemala: Ministerio de Educación Pública).

3. See esp. Tumin, *op. cit.*

4. There is of course nothing unusual or surprising about the relationship between geographical mobility and a breakdown of social barriers between ascriptive groups that are not phenotypically distinguishable. The Hindu caste system is also being undermined by horizontal mobility and urbanization, but the motivation and mechanics of "passing" are quite different in India and Guatemala. The low-caste Hindu who claims higher status is deliberately trying to "cheat" in order to evade onerous disabilities. Many Hindus who went overseas as indentured laborers, for example, "passed" by changing their names. See Pierre L. van den Berghe, *Caneville, The Social Structure of a South African Town* (Middletown, Conn.: Wesleyan University Press, 1964), p. 191. In Guatemala, on the other hand, there is relatively little opposition by Ladinos to assimilation and little desire by Indians to become assimilated. "Passing" there is largely a gradual consequence of interaction. In the Guatemalan context, Mario Monteforte Toledo notes the importance of internal migration for acculturation. See his *Guatemala, Monografía Sociológica* (México: Universidad Nacional Autónoma de México, 1959), pp. 105, 107.

5. Cf., for example, Charles Wagley and Marvin Harris, *Minorities in the New World* (New York: Columbia University Press, 1958).

6. Monteforte Toledo, for example, claims that the Ladino-Indian distinction in Guatemala is based at least partly on a social conception of "race," *op. cit.*, p. 116. The presence of at least mild racism in Brazil is unquestionable. Cf. Roger Bastide and Pierre

van den Berghe, "Stereotypes, Norms and Interracial Behavior in São Paulo, Brazil," *American Sociological Review*, 22 (October 1957), pp. 689–694. In Spanish America, however, there is a clear predominance of cultural criteria of group membership over phenotypical ones. Beyond the expression of mild esthetic preferences for certain physical traits, one is hard put to encounter any evidence of racism in Spanish America, although there was some anti-African prejudice in Colonial days. See Pierre L. van den Berghe, *Race and Racism* (New York: John Wiley & Sons, 1967).

7. For example, in a sample of 40 Ladinos in the town of Nebaj, in the *departamento* of Quiché, where I conducted field work in the summer of 1966, 33 mentioned only cultural differences when asked what distinguished Ladinos from Indians. Six respondents mentioned both cultural and physical traits. None listed physical traits only. (One person did not reply.) Benjamin N. Colby and I [have presented] the results of our study in a monograph, *Ixil Country, A Plural Society in Highland Guatemala* (Berkeley: University of California Press, 1969).

8. *Cofradias* are religious brotherhoods with ranked officeholders who devote themselves to the cult of a saint. The statues of the saints are carried around in elaborate processions, and the *cofradias* are the center of much ritual in the syncretistic Maya-Catholic religion of Guatemalan Indians.

9. See, for example, Philip Mayer, *Townsmen or Tribesmen* (Cape Town: Oxford University Press, 1961); and his article, "Migrancy and the Study of Africans in Towns," *American Anthropologist*, 64 (1962), pp. 576–592.

10. See Gonzalo Aguirre Beltrán, *El Proceso de Aculturación* (México: Universidad Nacional Autónoma de México, 1957).

11. For a discussion of similar problems and a critique of acculturation theory in the African context, see Pierre L. van den Berghe (ed.), *Africa, Social Problems of Change and Conflict* (San Francisco: Chandler Publishing Co., 1965), Introduction.

12. See Aguirre Beltrán, *op. cit.*, and Julio de la Fuente, *Relaciones Interétnicas* (Mexico: Instituto Nacional Indígenista, 1965).

The Ecology of Race Relations in Northwest Ecuador

NORMAN E. WHITTEN, JR.

Afro-American adaptations differ not only from one area to another, but also through time. Whitten's long-term work in coastal Ecuador reflects changes both in the local situation and in the anthropologist's approach. His focus on ecology and ethnicity invites a variety of comparisons—with highland Indians in the same country (*Casagrande*), *with*

This paper was written expressly for this volume. It incorporates substantial revision and updating of data reported (in Spanish) in *América Indígena* XXX (1970), 345–358; and (in French) in *Journal de la Société des Américanistes de Paris* (forthcoming). Both publishers have granted permission for this expanded and revised version, written in English by the author.

Afro-Americans in Brazil (Fernandes, Willems), with methodologically similar studies of other groups (Leeds, Strickon).

Norman E. Whitten, Jr., is Associate Professor of Anthropology at the University of Illinois at Urbana-Champaign. Besides field work in Ecuador, he has also worked in Colombia, Nova Scotia, and North Carolina on various projects dealing with Afro-American adaptations. He is author of Class, Kinship, and Power in an Ecuadorian Town: The Negroes of San Lorenzo *(1965), and* Afro-Hispanic Culture: Black Frontiersmen in Western Ecuador *(forthcoming), and coeditor of* Afro-American Anthropology: Contemporary Perspectives *(1970).*

INTRODUCTORY REMARKS

This paper attempts to portray changing ethnicity in a sector of a slowly developing nation. By ethnicity I refer to patterns of human interaction which form the basis for categorical social relationships with observable or projected economic consequence. "Race relations" pertains to interactions between people in contrasting or complementary social categories, where the categories are sometimes conceived of in biological terms. Charles Wagley (1959, *in* 1968:155–156) established the basis for such a perspective in Latin America:

> . . . the way people are classified in social races in a multiracial society tells us much about the relations between such groups.

Wagley was concerned with the *varied bases* of racial concepts held by diverse people in the Americas, and he noted the social relational aspect of such concepts. As time passed in the acceleration of economic change in the New World, ideas about social race, or ethnicity, have tended to become increasingly generalized, and social categories have become more abstract. While North American racial ideation swung to the extreme of seeing the entire world in binary white–nonwhite classes, Latin Americans generalized in comparable manners, but did not establish the extreme binary constructs. (See Harris 1964 and Mörner 1966, 1967 for details on changing race relations in Latin America.) It is in the increased ideational abstraction of various ethnic categories that the seeds of social, economic, and political exclusion may lie. Ethnic exclusion is manifest when exchange patterns making up personal networks and structural relations parallel, or reflect, abstract ethnic categories. (See Southall 1961:1–46, Mitchell 1966:52–53, Banton 1967, Whitten and Szwed 1970b: 43–48, Whitten and Wolfe: in press.)

One of the clearest statements about a framework for ethnicity in social context has more recently been set forth by Marvin Harris. In a review of Michael Banton's book, *Race Relations* (1967), he states (Harris 1968:204):

> A theory of race relations must be a sub-case of a theory of social stratification, which in turn must be a sub-case of a theory of sociocultural evolution. It must be able to answer the question of how access to wealth and power is regularized; how groups achieve specific adaptations to each other; and how intergroup relations evolve along general and specific trajectories as determined by general and specific conditions.

In this paper I am concerned with specific relationships between ethnic categories in northwest Ecuador, under specific conditions, which fit a more general picture of the evolution of "black–white" categorical relationships in the contemporary world. I suggest that northwest Ecuadorian society may be in a stage of pre-segregation, by which I mean that the *criteria for eventual exclusion on the basis of color are accumulating.* I speak of the ecology of race relations to suggest the environing situation to which cultural and behavioral patterns of black aggregates will increasingly have to adapt.

This brief presentation reports ongoing research in the northern sector of the Province of Esmeraldas, the specific locus being the growing port town of San Lorenzo.[1] Since my first visit in 1961 San Lorenzo has continued to grow and is beginning to develop. Regarding the concepts of growth and development I follow Carneiro (1967:240) and regard *growth* as the "quantitative change of like units" and *development* as "the emergence of new kinds of units and new types of arrangements between units." Both growth and development patterns in San Lorenzo have contributed to various processes of sociocultural change, one of the most significant of which falls into the domain of generalized ethnicity. One convenient manner of demonstrating these assertions is to set forth some crucial factors of emerging ethnicity by reference to a model of social structure.

CHANGING SOCIAL STRUCTURE

A few years ago I constructed a model of socioeconomic mobility based on data from San Lorenzo (Whitten 1965:1969) in an effort to abstract the myriad behavioral strategies being played daily by my informants and friends. The 1965 version saw San Lorenzo as divided into three local economic classes, based on family income for *costeños* and individual income for highland *blanco–metizos* and for coastal people from the south. Prestige factors, including ethnicity, contributed to economic standing; and politics, defined by personal relationships as well as party alliances, also contributed significantly to economic success. I presented the social structure through processes of mobility, arguing that, for natives of the northern coast, lower-class personal kindreds aided members in spatial mobility and subsistence economics, whereas middle-class stem kindreds contributed to socioeconomic mobility from the lower to the middle class. The middle-class stem kindreds were classified as "small rising," "corporate established," and "larger disintegrating," representing action-sets in the second, third, and fourth generations of socioeconomic mobility. The third-generation stem kindred was crucial in providing personnel to unite cash and subsistence economics and to function as brokers in highland–coastal transactions.

More recently (Whitten 1969) this model has been elaborated to argue that the sequence of strategies allowing for mobility can encompass a structure in which peasant organization transforms to proletarian organization and successful proletarian organization evolves into the activities of the local entrepreneurs. Crucial to this model was the idea that black *costeños* had thus far maintained a measure of control over their life chances by strategically manipulating social and political capital to maximize access to new resources during economic boom periods.

On my return to the town in 1968 I found that, in spite of a doubling of population from 3,000 to 6,000, the sequence was still meaningful, but that additive growth patterns combined with a few new social units have changed some of the *functions* of social and political relationships. Because of this the expected *relative* economic success (not absolute economic standing) of black *costeños* had altered. Crucial factors in such change include increased "rationalization" in timber exploitation, and the expansion of *blanco–mestizos* in pivotal, local middle-class positions in *town* economics and politics. Frequency interpretations (Erasmus 1961:22–23) made by the increasing *numbers* of white and mestizo newcomers on black behavior, together with the newcomers' desire to use non-Negro cultural brokers to buffer highland–coastal transactions, have altered the character of race relations particularly in terms of the *effect* on aggregates of black *costeños*. From observations made during the month of June 1968, I see increased stiffening of racial lines which resemble those previously reported from larger towns (Limones, Esmeraldas; Whitten 1965) and comparable to those alluded to by Julian Pitt-Rivers (1967). I should like to set forth some of the causes and consequences of an emerging disenfranchisement of black *costeños*.

NEW FACTORS

The following has taken place between 1965 and 1968 (mostly occurring during 1967–1968).

—— Timber exploitation has been rationalized by large-scale operations, and increased expansion is imminent.

—— Large-scale (for the area) plantations are developing, run by resident bosses representing highland *blanco–mestizo* subculture and south coast *blanco–mestizo* subculture.

—— Policies of modernization introduced by the *Junta Militar* in 1964–1966 led to the abandoning of the malaria campaign, which in turn led to malarial outbreaks of epidemic proportions along hinterland rivers.

—— With the coming of the *Junta Militar* the Catholic church-based "conservative" party virtually disappeared. "Liberal" church priests merged, politically, with the military. Both opposed "socialist," "communist," "Velasquista," and other "independent" movements.[2]

—— Funds from Catholic missionaries and the Ecuadorian government (under military dictatorship) facilitated the development of a hospital and new trade schools in carpentry for men and home economics for women.[3]

—— Policies of modernization allowed the development of banking facilities controlled by the local Catholic church, administered through the church's various formal organizations.[4]

—— The possibility of increased linkage of north coast and Sierra, together with continued economic depression in the rural sectors of the Sierra, stimulated increased in-migration of highland laborers as well as *petit bourgeois* merchants and shopkeepers who successfully competed with the shops of the black *costeños*. They bought out those of the stem kindred dominant in 1963–1965 and either purchased or forced out of business the saloon and *cantinas* owned by rising second generation kin sets competing for dominance in 1963–1965.[5]

—— Highlanders have contributed money to facilitate the building of new saloons and shops which exploit sudden inputs of cash.

—— Lumbermen and plantation owners add inducements to keep men out of town on weekends; these include bringing liquor, music, and imported women into the camps and onto the plantations.

These factors have altered the sociopolitical environment for black *costeños*. As such, a new ecology of race relationships in and around San Lorenzo has developed, and the mobility sequence has taken on new functions in the new political economy. In brief, this is what seems to be unfolding.

NEW FUNCTIONS

—— Black in-migrants forced out of their riparian niche by malaria come from some of the least accessible hinterland regions in the area—from north of the railroad near the Ecuadorian–Colombian border. They locate on the fringes of town and have themselves more than doubled the community's area in the last two years. Many new self-contained *barrios* have developed. They are self-sustaining and named after the place of origin of the settlers; each has an identifiable locus, with an elected "*jefe*." The process of localization discussed in 1965 seems greatly speeded up, and the "ruralization" of the black sectors of the town is quite obvious to all.

—— Budding households and expanding families in the old areas are moving out over the water, beginning to build networks of houses connected by catwalks. As older families move in with children their land-based center-of-town houses become occupied by highland and coastal *blanco–mestizos*.[6]

—— Young black men are encouraged into the Catholic carpentry school and young women into home economics school where they are taught the basis of home construction and maintenance and warned about engaging in political processes. They are advised of the desirability of upward socioeconomic mobility, but are given no means other than as-yet scarcely needed skills to achieve mobility.

—— The church–government banking facility overtly favors lending money to women and is clear about denying requests by most men as a matter of policy. The argument made by the controlling clergy is that women are "more stable in the community." They do not, presumably, spend money on drink or on political bribes.[7] Furthermore, they *remain in the community* on a more or less full-time basis, attending to their homes and to church-approved (and government-approved) affairs, whereas men tend to move about in the forest and in search of wage labor.

—— The clergy teaches young women means of making budgets and figuring credit on a strictly monetary basis. They are also instructed in the nature of banking, lending, and saving procedures. Men, by contrast, either are taught to build houses with tools and materials which they cannot afford to buy or are encouraged to work on a wage-labor basis for a timber company or on a plantation.

—— Women still have a relatively steady income based on shellfish gathering, and the gathering of *conchas* (mussels) has greatly expanded. But the marketing of the *conchas* is now almost exclusively in the hands of highland *blanco–mestizo* merchants. The *blanco–mestizo* merchants, who have access to the railroad officials resident in Ibarra, have been more successful in gaining concessions, loans, and credit from the railroad than have local black people in San Lorenzo, who must deal with local highland administrators within the town. Some local black men have journeyed to Ibarra to ask for credit and concessions to market the *conchas*, but have met with no success there.

—— First generation settlers find the most ready cash (for men) away from the residential locus, in the forest, and on plantations. Women tend to cluster in the new town *barrios*, aided by the shellfish business and the priest's bank. This leads to a conspicuous absence of men between ages 25 and 40, except those with an investment in upward socioeconomic mobility. A new strategy of investing time and energy in church-sponsored change, including housing projects and work for the church, has developed. Acting in accord with this strategy means severing most local political contacts, and often changing the residential locus from kinship-dominated *barrio* to the "new town."[8]

—— Newcomers from the riparian hinterland represent an expanding labor force for forest and plantation. Special attention is paid to them by those controlling the expanding resources. The Catholic clergy feels that they have "stronger family ties" than the town-dwellers. We could say that the newcomers are at first unaccustomed to the proletarian role, and therefore are more readily exploited by those in search of cheap rural labor. Eventual self-awareness of this proletarianization often occurs *outside the town niche* instead of within it. It is within the town niche that strategies of adaptive mobility are most effective (see Whitten 1969).

—— Those proletarian and entrepreneurial black people well adapted to combining town and rural life (who have long served as cultural brokers) meet resistance from lumbermen, priests, and officials. Their obvious abilities of maneuver within rural *and* urbanizing contexts are feared. They are labeled *comunistas*. Such labeling indicates that the organizational format of Afro-Hispanic culture in this zone is insufficiently understood by present outsiders. Such outsiders, in an effort to explain the existence of a black power structure, tend to project outward. Such projection, set in today's world of gross dichotomies of political ideology, results in pejorative labeling rather than understanding. Attaching the "communist" tag to black strivers makes black maneuver all the more difficult for such people and increases the potential for confrontation politics.

—— In terms of my earlier model, there are still linked action-sets in the form of stem kindreds which are crucial to internal politicking in San Lorenzo. But *blanco–mestizos* now compete with the nodes of black action-sets in acquiring brokerage and patronage roles. A consequence of this is a strengthening of any light-skinned member of Afro-Hispanic culture and a tendency to include those whom I earlier called light-*costeño* as *blancos* or *mulatos* for some purposes. Such classification gives inordinate weight to phenotypic characteristics, even over cultural and behavioral characteristics. In terms of our definition of ethnicity, we can say that the economic consequence of such ethnic (ideational) asymmetry is seriously eroding the developmental sequence of previously adaptive mobility strategies.

—— Now, as earlier, individuals representative of dominant kindreds within a *barrio* must manifest respectability symbols acceptable to the Catholic church. But this now includes allowing indoctrination of young men and women by the priests and nuns through their school. Among other things, this makes polygyny more covert and increasingly difficult for the upward-mobile.

—— The rising groups of kinsmen who actively compete with *blanco–mestizo* brokerage find that the accusation of "leftist politics is readily applied by church and governmental officials. Tagging black entrepreneurs with the designation "leftist" (*izquierdista*) may carry a stigma ramifying to their kinsmen and to others with whom they carry on regular mutual cooperation.

—— Because of such specific communist-accusations based on generalized communist-fear, many local upper-class *blanco–mestizos* formerly dependent on such black entrepreneurs, together with many first and second generation rising strivers, have become leary of overt exchanges symbolizing alliance with the accused. In other words, the political label of "leftist" serves to make upward strivers poorer risks as brokers, at the very period in their economic rise when the broker role, together with its political functions, becomes most crucial for continued mobility. Such blockages in the mobility process lead those with rising expectations to turn to new strategies, such as leftist politics, in attempting to achieve felt needs.

—— Finally, we can say that the linkages between local middle-class entrepreneurial black and lower-class, upward-mobile proletarian blacks are weakened by the introduction of *blanco–mestizo* brokers, unidentified with black aggregates, into the local mobility processes. The possible necessity of interethnic linkages between complementary proletarian and entrepreneurial black role sets may eventually separate various black *costeños* into contrasting class-conscious sectors. With the parallel growth of self-conscious ethnicity, class-consciousness may possibly be inimical to more general strategies of adaptation played by black *costeños* while favorable to the asymmetric ethnic strategies of the new "*blancos*." Banton's (1967:138–139) proposition is relevant. Writing about black–white categorical relationships in the southern United States following Reconstruction, he says:

> . . . the patterns of countervailing checks and balances characteristic of community relations is distorted where there are cleavages and one category of people cannot adequately press its claims. When this happens, those who gain most immediately from their rivals' weakness acquire a strategically advantageous position. They press their short-term sectional interests at the expense of the long-run interests of their social category, and, indeed, of the whole regional society.

Later in the same work (Banton 1967:336) he adds, "When to class differences is added racial difference, the likelihood of fundamental cleavage is increased."

What this sketch adds up to in northwest Ecuador is this: As men make more money in the rationalized lumber and plantation industries, women become more economically and politically important to *blanco–mestizo* buyers and brokers and to the church-controlled system of social honor in the residential community. The *incidence* of woman-centered households probably has not altered significantly, but *its function has changed.* Rather than directly serving black *costeños* in their processes of economic rise and in spatial mobility, they now represent relatively autonomous loci for family relations. As the church-sponsored "family stability" campaign expands, the actual kinship and family system is made less functional to black male–female relationships in the contexts of political, social honor, and economic gain. The black family becomes more an adjustive response to increased white dominance. Though men may be relatively better off economically, they are clearly powerless. They are aware of this situation and vocal about such powerlessness. The old game of mobility is still played, and *barrio* organization is what has been previously reported for larger towns such as Buenaventura and Tumaco in Colombia and Esmeraldas in Ecuador. The investigator with a model of four-generational mobility would understand the various strategies played by black *costeños.* But to understand the growing sense of frustration and tension, he would have to analyze the more general processes of black disenfranchisement now taking place. Some black *costeños* are already making such an analysis.

From the standpoint of *blanco–mestizos,* who seem to be making frequency interpretations about their black townsmen, a rather appalling previously established cultural image is becoming reinforced. Based on folk-observations made by highland *blanco–mestizos,* in and near the center of town, in the framework of the mechanical (as opposed to lunar) day, and fortified by highland attitudes toward highland blacks, mestizos use such nouns as *sucio, vago, tonto, montubio, incivilizado, bruto, infrahumano, feo* (i.e., dirty, lazy, stupid, rural bumpkin, without "national culture," brute, subhuman, ugly [in terms of racial features]) to depict black *aggregates,* but not *specific individuals.* When one wishes to project these attributes onto a specific individual it is sufficient to use the term *negro* vis-à-vis that individual.

There is a reinforcement of these stereotypes through discussion in which those people "typifying" black ethnicity agree to two or three characteristics, usually discarding one or two of the above attributes. Since the retaining and discarding of attributes through debate results in inconsistent denotations, the entire complex of loose pejorative connotations attaches itself to the term *negro.* The general drift of such racist-reinforcing discussion follows this line: Black men are oversexed and primarily interested in dancing and drinking; black women are all interested in lighter men and in having lighter babies. *Blanco–mestizos* with considerable time on the coast (or coastal whites) dispute the highland stereotype that the black man is oversexed and point out the virtual absence of a *machismo* complex amongst blacks. They argue that black men would as soon drink and dance as fornicate, and so the black man's woman is easy prey for whites or mestizos who would take her, leaving him with his rum and his dancing to find another sexual partner when the mood moves him. This last frequency interpretation, I would submit, arises from the fact that, in saloon contexts, where alliance of individuals and groups for short-run gain is often symbolized, women *are* equivalent tokens to a shot of rum or a dance; but only as a brief dancing partner.[9] At any rate, frequency interpretations are reinforcing previously established racist tendencies on the part of *blanco–mestizos,* but not on the part of blacks themselves, except at the black *costeño*–

black *serrano*, or black *Ecuadoriano*–black *Colombiano* level.[10] Indeed, white standards of beauty, but not behavior, seem to characterize the black *costeños*.

SUMMARY AND CONCLUDING STATEMENT

In 1965 I failed to take into account the possible effects of increasing *numbers* of *blanco–mestizos* falling into the category, or potential category, "whiteness," where blackness and whiteness are seen to contrast for particular purposes. Black aggregates still manipulate newcomers from the Sierra to the coast and play their generalized games of exploiting their natural and sociopolitical environment. Adaptable though they may be, however, consideration must increasingly be given to the changing function of interpersonal relationships with the development and growth of the north Ecuadorian coastal economy. In terms of growth, the addition or expansion of like units has multiplied the racist-based frequency interpretations by mestizos and whites about black behavior, giving a new affect to old stereotypes. Development of a *new social unit*—"*negro*"—"nonwhite," "non-Indian," "nonmestizo," has emerged. I suggest that the stereotypic contrast implied by this unit may block access to basic, or strategic, incoming resources. In fact, treating the black as invisible in terms of social planning for land redistribution, something not discussed in this paper, may also block access to basic resources which black people today do control.[11]

The processes sketched above are not unfamiliar as a concomitant of world industrialization (cf. Smith 1962, Hunter [ed.] 1965, Thales de Azevedo 1966, Banton 1967). If I may speculate on the not-so distant future, I suggest that present development of west Ecuadorian society may be entering a phase of preadaptation to contemporary industrial economy, where segregation along color lines is one relatively convenient means of sorting aggregates into access classes. By preadaptation I follow Fried (1967:154).

> I take this to refer in sociocultural evolution to aggregating minor changes which themselves exert only small visible effects on the *status quo*, but suddenly occupy quite different functional roles when the society is transformed.

With the signing of a contract with Georgia-Pacific Lumber Company for full-scale exploitation of timber; with the impending construction of an oil pipeline by Texaco–Gulf from the Ecuadorian *Oriente* (Montaña) through the *Litoral;* with the increased number of North American whites entering the region for short-run gain; and with the rising racism of *blanco-mestizos* and concomitant compartmentalization and disenfranchisement of black *costeños*, we have additional reinforcements to the cumulative forces sketched briefly in this paper. It will not be long before the natural resource base of northwest Ecuador will be inadequate to sustain the balanced adaptation to cash and subsistence economics which I have described elsewhere.[12] Decrease in the natural basic resources and increased reliance on introduced economic and sociopolitical resources would seem, at this time, to set ethnic aggregates in competition with one another. The segregated society with racism directed against black aggregates so common in the United States now seems imminent in the Pacific littoral of northern Ecuador, and by implication north through the same natural and similar sociopolitical environment in Colombia.

NOTES

1. This study is part of a larger project designed to understand internal colonialism, economic opportunity, and changing ethnicity in the lowlands of Ecuador. Fieldwork is now being carried out in the eastern rainforests with the "Lowland Quechua." Much of this analysis parallels that of San Lorenzeño Bolívar Arisala, who contributed considerably to this work during my 1968 return to the town. My decision to return to northwest Ecuador in 1968, and to focus on changing race relations (as processes of ethnicity), came about through conversations and communication with a number of people, among whom Charles A. Valentine, Thomas J. Price, Alvin W. Wolfe, Joseph A. Kahl, Julian Pitt-Rivers, and Lee Rainwater were most persuasive. Dorothea S. Whitten and Robert C. Hunt constructively criticized earlier drafts of the paper. All faults, of course, are attributable only to the author.

The original plan for this volume was to bring this work up to date by including materials from a field trip in the summer of 1970. However, work with another ethnic category with comparable asymmetric position vis-à-vis emerging *blanco* society of the lowland Andean escarpment—the Lowland Quechua near Puyo and the Bobonaza, Curaray, Napo River areas—prevented such work on the west coast. Second-hand information on San Lorenzo gained through informants, however, indicates that my analysis fits the 1970 picture on the north Ecuadorian coast.

It should be noted here that the research in eastern Ecuador with a lowland Indian segment of Ecuadorian pluralism contributes to an understanding of strengthening ethnic lines in the white–nonwhite (black, Indian) sectors. A subsequent paper will document the increased ethnicity of Indian–*blanco* differentiation in the face of new opportunities in the money economy.

Research in 1968 was sponsored by NIMH program No. 1 PO1 MH 15567-01 and funded by Washington University toward the end of the field season. A Latin American Committee grant at Washington University provided funds for the beginning of the field work. In 1970 research with the Lowland Quechua was begun under National Science Foundation Grant No. GS-2999. Both these grants facilitated analysis and writing of the material in this paper.

2. Following my earlier analysis (Whitten 1965:170–183) "Conservative," and "Liberal" parties were usually allied through the *Consejo Parroquial* which, ostensibly, should represent only one party. "Socialist," "Independent," and "Communist" parties frequently allied in opposition to the *Consejo*. Harmony among several parties came about in 1963, when ". . . Liberal and Socialist parties act in concert. This harmony is reached when members of the upper class initiate action indirectly, through formal organizations, supported by ritual kinship ties with organization members" (Whitten 1965:194). Bringing together of socialist and liberal strands of political ideology involved reinforcement of black *costeño* and "light *costeño*" kinship and affinal ties. Such reinforcement could occur when conservative and liberal alliances formed to resist ever present opposition. It was also argued that failure of political goal-oriented behavior tended to underscore ethnic, kinship, and class lines. With the power of the military regime co-opting the strength of the Catholic church through economic grants, and with the merger of liberal and conservative parties, no *costeño*-sponsored goal-oriented behavior seems to have succeeded since 1963. The result seems, indeed, to be an under-

scoring of ethnic, class, and kinship lines with the possible result of schismatic factionalism and a muddling of political purpose across such lines (cf. Beals and Siegel 1966). By 1970 the national situation had further crystallized as Velasquistas became part of the new military–church–one-party establishment.

3. The specific Catholic order referred to is a German one, called in Ecuador *Misión Comboniana Arquidiócesis de Munich*. All its priests and nuns are Italian in Esmeraldas province.

4. The Ecuadorian *Banco de Vivienda*, which is the institution here referred to, was originally begun as a U.S.A.I.D.-sponsored agency to stimulate the development of rural housing. Such housing really got started under military dictatorship when the *Junta Autónoma de Ferrocarril Quito–San Lorenzo* (agency responsible for the development of the area around the Quito–San Lorenzo Railroad, the development of San Lorenzo, the development of the port, and the establishment of modern facilities in the northern sector) transferred the land for a new town to the *Misión Comboniana* and agreed to transport building materials without charge. The mission together with the *Junta Militar* provided funds for the *Banco de Vivienda* in San Lorenzo, which was administered exclusively through the Catholic church.

5. For a preliminary analysis of the processes of colonization and internal migration in Ecuador see Casagrande, Thompson, and Young (1964:281–325) and Gillette (1970). The former state (1964:282), "The theoretical interest in studying colonization lies both in the processes whereby an already established sociocultural system is extended, replicated or reintegrated, and in colonization as a *creative process*, since colonists frequently must accommodate themselves to a new ecological situation, and to novel sociopolitical and economic arrangements." In an earlier work (Whitten 1965) I also took this approach to San Lorenzo, focusing mainly on the internal structure of black *costeños*, and thinking of colonists as having to adapt to the new local scene. But in the view taken here, another important creative process of internal colonization from the high Andes to tropical lowlands is the transposition of *blanco* ethnic values, reinforced through demographic shifts, causing local peoples classed as "*negro*" or "*indio*" to face a new socioeconomic environment, one with an effective ideational block to strategic resources growing within their niche.

As highland mestizos descend the Andes they enter zones which lack the contrasting upper-class "*blanco*" category and, it seems, in the absence of that contrast assume membership in the category themselves. As a consequence, those who would be "*cholo*" or "mestizo" in the Sierra become "*blanco*" on the coast and eastern slopes. "Blanco-ness" is reinforced by generalizing the non-*blanco* ethnic contrasts—lumping Negroes into one pejorative category and lowland Indians into another. In eastern Ecuador, Indians have been forced completely out of the town niche in some places, though economic dependence on towns increases.

These processes are complex and need much more attention. Suffice it to say here that the present paper complements the Casagrande, Thompson, and Young analysis. The altered ethnicity of the lower-class peasant, proletarian, and entrepreneurs moving from highland to lowland contexts, and the new strategies they play in the town niches, will be the subject of a subsequent paper.

6. The appearance of San Lorenzo is taking on a remarkable similarity to its northern forerunners in development, Tumaco and Buenaventura, Colombia. Esthetically, a coconut blight combined with the depressed effect of overcrowding have nearly destroyed the picturesque setting of only a few years ago. More serious than the esthetics—which may result in a loss in tourism—is the effect of the coconut blight itself. The coconut groves have for some time formed a security basis for second, third, and fourth generation settlers. Briefly, small groves provide a steady small income for those kindreds with sufficient settlement time and sufficient social capital to maintain and harvest them.

Mature groves of 15 to 20 properly planted trees produce about one coconut per day, worth one to two *sucres* per nut. Average groves have 20 to 50 trees. The analysis of the significance of these groves, which I minimized in earlier analyses, will be part of a forthcoming monograph, tentatively entitled "Afro-Hispanic Culture: Black Frontiersmen in Western Ecuador and Colombia."

7. Following my previous discussions (1968, 1969) such spending was an essential aspect in continuing economic security within the fluctuating cash economy.

8. The "new town" is described in Whitten (1965). In 1963 it was a source of considerable amusement. By 1964 some development had begun on the basis of economic loans secured by one priest from the *Junta Militar*. In 1968 I was amazed at the growth and development. The *Junta Militar* supported the priest in his development plans. Today there are schools, a hospital furnished with the discarded equipment of a New York City Catholic hospital, and a number of housing projects—and an advanced high school (*colegio segundario*), which will make San Lorenzo the center of blacksmith training and wood-cutting specialties in the nation, is being planned.

9. Whitten (1968:59–60) states: "In the context of the saloon a dance and a drink are equivalent tokens of exchange. . . . A drink and a dance are prestations with implied contingencies for reciprocity, while verbal personal compliments and proffered thanks for a drink and a dance are terminal (closed) exchanges. By accepting a shot of *aguardiente* . . . and/or by dancing with a proffered woman without returning thanks, the recipient indebts himself to the donor. . . . The network of personal ties established in saloons is apparent primarily when there is economic gain to be had for group labor on a short-term basis. The social relationships themselves are long term, but they are activated only on the basis of short-term group labor . . . men intensify the potential for cooperation among themselves by the exchange of dance partners and *aguardiente* as tokens for future economic cooperation."

10. To elaborate a bit on black stereotypes, let me say here that black *costeños* will use all these pejorative terms to depict the "racial quality" of black highlanders, particularly those from the Chota Valley of north highland Ecuador. Also, light *costeños* will hold forth at great length on the story of Illescas and the shipwreck of Negroes off the coast of Esmeraldas where African *bozales* seized their freedom, married Indians, and came to propagate a race of *zambos* with such political power that they ascended to rule over the entire province in the sixteenth century. The introduction of *negro* elements, it is said, is recent and from Colombia. Again, all the pejorative connotations will be applied to the stereotypic Colombian blacks by black Ecuadorians, never identifying specific individuals or even, in this context, groups of individuals. The only exception to this would be an obstreperous crew of Colombian blacks, transient in port and threatening physical violence—they would become *negro* when a fight became imminent. In Colombia, self-derogation in towns such as Tumaco and Buenaventura allows black men to apply pejorative categories to their own *barrio*, but not to themselves or to specific individuals.

11. There are recent verbal proposals in Ecuador to place Cayapa Indians on a reserve and to get Negroes "off Indian land" and "off government land." One such proposal has actually reached at least one United States funding agency. During my field work in 1963 I repeatedly found inhabited areas to be classified as "uninhabited" by developers. Even dense areas of town settlement (such as *barrio Las Tres Marías*) in San Lorenzo is still regarded as unoccupied, and lots are now and then sold in Quito. Unfortunately for the black *costeños*, they are not classed as "*Indígenas*" and so must purchase or inherit their land, and the latter condition is demonstrable only through "papers."

12. See Whitten (1965, 1969). This adaptation forms the core of a book previously mentioned. The differential adaptation made by black and Indian aggregates is set forth in a manuscript, "River Indians of Ecuador," written by Milton Altschuler.

REFERENCES

Altschuler, Milton
N.D. River Indians of Ecuador: A study of Cayapa law and personality. Ms.

Azevedo, Thales de
1966 Cultura e Situacão Racial no Brasil. Editôra civilizacão Brasileira, S.A. (Retratos do Brazil 42: Rio de Janeiro).

Banton, Michael
1967 *Race Relations*. Basic Books, New York.

Beals, Alan R., and Bernard J. Siegel
1966 *Divisiveness and Social Conflict: An Anthropological Perspective*. Stanford University Press, Stanford, Cal.

Caneiro, Robert L.
1967 On the relationship between size of population and complexity of social organization. *Southwestern Journal of Anthropology* 23 (3):234–243.

Casagrande, Joseph B., Stephen I. Thompson, and Philip D. Young
1964 Colonization as a research frontier: The Ecuadorian case. In Robert Manners (ed.), *Process and Pattern in Culture: Essays in Honor of Julian H. Steward*. Aldine, Chicago.

Erasmus, Charles J.
1961 *Man Takes Control: Cultural Development and American Aid*. University of Minnesota Press, Minneapolis.

Fried, Morton H.
1967 *The Evolution of Political Society: An Essay in Political Anthropology*. Random House, New York.

Gillette, Cynthía
N.D. Problems of colonization in the Ecuadorian Oriente. M.A. thesis, Washington University (St. Louis, Mo.), deposited in Olin library.

Harris, Marvin
1964 *Patterns of Race in the Americas*. New York: Walker.
1969 Review of Michael Banton, *Race Relations*. *Current Anthropology* 10 (23):103–104.

Hunter, Guy (ed.)
1965 *Industrialisation and Race Relations: A Symposium*. Oxford University Press, London.

Mitchell, J. Clyde
1966 Theoretical orientations in African urban studies. In Michael Banton (ed.), *The Social Anthropology of Complex Societies*. Praeger, New York.

Mörner, Magnus
1966 The history of race relations in Latin America: Some comments on the state of research. *Latin American Research Review* 1 (3):17–44.
1967 *Race Mixture in the History of Latin America*. Little, Brown, Boston.

Pitt-Rivers, Julian
1967 Race, color, and class in Central America and the Andes. *Daedalus* 96 (2): Proceedings of the American Academy of Arts and Sciences.

Smith, Raymond T.
1962 *British Guiana*. Oxford University Press, London.

Southall, Aidan (ed.)
1961 *Social Change in Modern Africa*. Oxford University Press, London.

Wagley, Charles
1959 The concept of social race in the Americas. *Actas del XXXIII Congress Internacional de Americanistas.* I:403–417. San José, Costa Rica.
1968 *The Latin American Tradition: Essays on the Unity and the Diversity of Latin American Culture.* Columbia University Press, New York and London.

Whitten, Norman E., Jr.
1965 *Class, Kinship, and Power in an Ecuadorian Town: The Negroes of San Lorenzo.* Stanford University Press, Stanford, Cal.
1968 Music and social relationships in the Pacific lowlands of Colombia and Ecuador. *Man:* Journal of the Royal Anthropological Institute of Great Britain and Ireland 3 (1):50–63.
1969 Strategies of adaptive mobility in the Colombian–Ecuadorian littoral. *American Anthropologist* 71 (2):228–242.
N.D. Afro-Hispanic culture: black frontiersmen in western Ecuador and Colombia. Ms. (mimeo).

Whitten, Norman E., Jr., and John F. Szwed (eds.)
1970a *Afro-American Anthropology: Contemporary Perspectives.* Free Press, New York; Collier-Macmillan, London.
1970b Introduction. In Whitten and Szwed (eds.), *Afro-American Anthropology: Contemporary Perspectives.*

Whitten, Norman E., Jr., and Alvin W. Wolfe
in press Network analysis. In John J. Honigmann (ed.), *Handbook of Social and Cultural Anthropology* (Chapter 23). Rand McNally, Chicago.

Latin American Squatter Settlements: A Problem and a Solution

WILLIAM MANGIN

A dramatic focus of popular attention about population growth and urbanization has been the proliferation of "squatter settlements" in and around major cities throughout Latin America. In this wide-ranging review article, Mangin effectively discredits many of the widely accepted myths that relate to such communities and also demonstrates some of their positive values. Complementary perspectives on some of the same populations are offered by Morse, Goldrich, Leeds, and Lewis.

William Mangin is Professor of Anthropology at Syracuse University. He has combined research with applied anthropology in Peru, Ecuador, and New York, including service with Peace Corps, mental hospitals, and public schools; he edited Peasants in Cities *in 1970, combining the major themes on which he has written abundantly.*

Abridged from *Latin American Research Review* II (1967), 65–98. Copyright, 1967 by Latin American Research Review. Reprinted by permission of the author and publisher.

Squatter settlements have formed around large cities throughout the world, mushrooming particularly since the end of World War II. In an excellent preview to a forthcoming book, Turner (1966) has discussed some common features among squatter settlements in Latin America, Asia, Africa, and Europe. Morse (1965a) has also referred to squatter communities and to general characteristics of Latin American urbanization. . . .[1] Without repeating the work of Turner and Morse I would like to present a preliminary survey of Latin American squatter settlements with a model of their formation, growth, and social development that contradicts many views held by planners, politicians, newspapermen, and much of the general population, including many residents of the settlements themselves.

Several writers have referred to various local names given to squatter communities: *colonias proletarias* in Mexico, *barriadas brujas* in Panama, *ranchos* in Venezuela, *barriadas* in Peru, *callampas* in Chile, *cantegriles* in Uruguay, *favelas* in Brazil, and, in other places, marginal areas, clandestine urbanizations, *barrios* of invasion, parachutists, phantom towns, etc. There are no general works on the subject, but some good descriptions of local conditions do exist. The major sources used are listed by country in note 2. Not many sources are available and, unfortunately, several appear only in mimeographed form. The reports point out that squatter populations consist mainly of low-income families but all of the authors distinguish between squatter settlements and other types of lower-class housing in tenements, alleys (*callejones*), shack yards (*coralones, jacales*), and rented slum buildings. They agree, sometimes to their own surprise, that it is difficult to describe squatter settlements as slums. The differentiation of squatter settlements from inner-city slums is, in fact, one of the first breaks from the widely shared mythology about them. (See, for example, Patch, 1961; Mangin, 1965.) The purpose in noting this mythology is not merely to set up a straw man for the paper. A review of the "Chaos, Crisis, Revolution and Whither Now Latin America" literature, or, of most governmental, United Nations, or AID reports, or, of most newspapers and magazines in Latin America will show that it is the predominant position on squatter settlements.

The standard myths, not all incorrect and by no means mutually consistent, are, with some variation among countries, as follows:

1. The squatter settlements are formed by rural people (Indians where possible) coming directly from "their" farms.
2. They are chaotic and unorganized.
3. They are slums with the accompanying crime, juvenile delinquency, prostitution, family breakdown, illegitimacy, etc.
4. They represent an economic drain on the nation since unemployment is high and they are the lowest class economically, the hungriest and most poorly housed, and their labor might better be used back on the farms.
5. They do not participate in the life of the city, illiteracy is high and the education level low.
6. They are rural peasant villages (or Indian communities) reconstituted in the cities.
7. They are "breeding grounds for" or "festering sores of" radical political ac-

tivity, particularly communism, because of resentment, ignorance, and a longing to be led.

8. There are two solutions to the problem: (a) prevent migration by law or by making life in the provinces more attractive; or (b) prevent the formation of new squatter settlements by law and "eradicate" (a favorite word among architects and planners) the existing ones, replacing them with housing projects.

The myths are embodied in writings ranging from the ridiculous—for example, a North American M.D. from the ship *Hope* (Walsh, 1966), reflecting the views of many of his Peruvian medical colleagues, says of a barriada near the city of Trujillo,

> In this enormous slum lived some 15,000 people many of whom had come down from the mountains, lured by communist agitators. Why starve on a farm the agitators asked, when well-paid jobs, good food, housing and education were waiting in Trujillo? This technique for spreading chaos and unrest has brought as many as 3,000 farmers and their families to the barriadas in a month. Once they arrive (on a one-way ride in communist-provided trucks) they are trapped in the festering slums with no money to return to their farms.

to serious observations by responsible people—for example, a North American sociologist (Schulman, 1966) who worked in a Colombian *tugurio* for nine months writes of squatter settlements,

> It is the rudest kind of slum, clustering like a dirty beehive around the edges of any principal city in Latin America. In the past two decades poor rural people have flocked to the cities, found no opportunities but stayed on in urban fringe shanty-towns squatting squalidly on the land. . . . Living almost like animals, the tugurio's residents are overwhelmed by animality. Religion, social control, education, domestic life are warped and disfigured.

A familiar theme of anti-city feeling and rural, small-town bias runs through much of the European and North American commentary on squatter settlements.[3] Latin American academics and politicians, on the other hand, tend to be anti-countryside and pro-city, considering the latter to be the repository of all that is good and beautiful in Spanish and Portuguese culture. In a strange way, both points of view reinforce each other in condemning squatter settlements as disorganized products of outside agitation, and in suggesting eradication and shipment back to the rural areas as a solution.

It is probably apparent from the tone of the above remarks that my own views differ from those mentioned. In discussing the eight myths, I believe that I can portray a very different picture. Other myths, however, influence my own thinking so not all of the observations to which I refer are mistaken. They are biased, but they do reflect an aspect of reality. In presenting a different, and I believe a more hopeful and realistic, view, I do not mean to minimize the problems of overpopulation, rapid urbanization, poverty, prejudice, and lack of elementary health and social services that play such an important part in squatter settlement life.

William F. Whyte (1943) provided an effective counter to the anti-city literature by revealing strong informal institutions created by people in a Boston slum to serve their own needs. Since then many studies have drawn similar conclusions, including a recent study of the same area (Gans, 1962) that shows stability through change Turner (1963, 1966) and I (1963, 1964, 1965) have noted similar kinds of institutions in squatter settlements, viewing them as solutions to difficult social problems rather than as problems in themselves.[4] The formation of squatter settlements is a popular response to rapid urbanization in countries that cannot or will not provide services for the increasing urban population.[5] In their study of the Polish peasant in Europe and America, Thomas and Znaniecki (1920) viewed situations of great change and disorganization not as "a mere reinforcement of the decaying organization," but as ". . . a production of new schemes of behavior and new institutions better adapted to the changed demands of the group; we call this production of new schemes and institutions social reconstruction." I, too, see the squatter settlements as a process of social reconstruction through popular initiative.

FORMATION OF SQUATTER SETTLEMENTS

In two studies I have described the planning of a barriada invasion (Mangin, 1963) and constructed a composite history of a barriada in Peru (1960). The process is also discussed and photographed in a UN film, *A Roof of My Own*, advised by John Turner in the International Zone series. Subsequent investigation has indicated that strikingly similar sequences have occurred in other countries.

As a general pattern the majority of residents of a settlement have been born in the provinces and have migrated from farms or small towns. They have also come largely from tenements, alleys, and other slums within city limits where they settled upon arrival. According to a census of a typical Lima barriada in 1959, the average time of residence in Lima for heads of families originally from the provinces was nine years, and practically none of them had been in Lima less than three years. [Barriadas may now contain 400,000 of Lima's population of two million as opposed to 45,000 in 1940 (Abrams, 1965).] Frieden (1964) writes that in a 1958 census in Mexico City more than half of the residents of metropolitan tenements were of rural origin and that they were the squatters in the colonias proletarias. The colonias have two million inhabitants and may occupy 40 percent of the land area of the Federal District by 1970 (Harth Deneke, 1966). Cortén (1965) reports that the majority of squatters in Santo Domingo are from the provinces and that not a single rural immigrant in his sample settled directly in a newly formed squatter settlement. Cuevas (1965) notes that in Guatemala City, where the squatters comprise 10 percent of the population, "the great majority of the inhabitants (73 percent) are economically displaced from the city itself," and that they are originally from the provinces or the rural areas of the Department of Guatemala. Lopez et al. (1965) corroborate this finding. In Venezuela, where squatters in ranchos comprise about 35 percent of the population of Caracas and 50 percent of that of Maracaibo, . . . Talton Ray's study (1966) shows that most rancho residents are migrants but that "close to 100 percent come from barrios within the city, not from the countryside." C. B. Turner (1964) and Usandizaga and Havens (1966) describe the same circumstances in Bogotá and Barranquilla,

Colombia. Lutz (1966) found the same situation in Panama City, Bon (1963) in Montevideo, and Leeds (1966) in Rio de Janeiro, where favelas contain more than 500,000 people. Rosenbluth found that this relationship obtained for the callampas in Chile (1963) (6 percent had come directly from the provinces only since 1960, 12 percent before 1930). In the callampa sample of Goldrich, Pratt, and Schuller (1966) the residents are from rural areas but only 6 percent had been in Santiago less than three years, and 80 percent had been there 12 years or more. They estimate that about one-tenth of Santiago's population of two million are in callampas; [other estimates go as high as] 25 percent.

The establishment of the community varies with local conditions, geographic and political. They arise on vacant land, usually uncultivated and owned by a governmental entity, on the outskirts of cities, or on undesirable land within the city, e.g., on steep hillsides, swamps, river beds, and dumps. Where there has been no active opposition from governments, settlements have been formed in an unorganized fashion by a few families drifting onto a site or, as in Guatemala, Guayaquil (Vitale, which I have personally observed), and parts of Lima, augmenting a group of families relocated by the government after a natural disaster. More common, however, is an organized invasion in the face of active opposition from the police. In countries not noted for governmental efficiency some of the invasions have been remarkably well organized. In Lima, after months of planning, thousands of people moved during one night to a site that had been secretly surveyed and laid out. They arrived with the materials to build a straw house, all their belongings, and a Peruvian flag. They were determined and, in several cases, returned to sites two and three times after police burned their belongings and beat and killed their fellows (reported in the Peruvian bimonthlies, *Caretas* and *Oiga*, 1963, for example). Police opposition to organized occupations has also been encountered in Brazil, Santiago de Chile (Clark, 1963), Cali (Powelson, 1964), Bogotá, Acapulco, and other places. Very little data is available on the organizers of invasions outside Peru. In Peru, evidence from my own experience and that of many Peace Corps volunteers and other observers indicates that the organizers were generally residents of the barriada of invasion. They often sought help from outsiders such as engineering students, lawyers, and, at least in two cases, army officers. The situation most closely approximating the often alleged agitation by outsiders involved men who helped form invasion groups on several occasions apparently because they thoroughly enjoyed and gained status from the meetings and the excitement. Land speculators have been involved in several countries, but they generally appear after the invasion.

The migrants come from rural provinces but many of them are from towns rather than farms. In Peru they come from a variety of settings and economic levels (Matos, 1961). In Chile 65 percent of the migrants to Santiago had lived in towns of more than 5,000 as of 1946 (Herrick, 1966). Sixty percent of the migrants to Buenos Aires studied by Germani (1961) had fathers who did manual labor, but many had shopkeeper fathers. Many of the migrants in countries where the data are available have lived for a time somewhere between the rural setting and the metropolis. Of migrants studied in villas miserias, Germani (1961) notes that 15 percent had migrated from areas of less than

2,000 population, more than a third from settings with 2,000 to 20,000 inhabitants, and 50 percent from large towns.

INTERNAL ORGANIZATION OF THE SQUATTER SETTLEMENTS

In the barrios formed by organized invasion, the original organization is strong at first. In those formed by other means, organizations are established to defend the community and advocate its cause to the government. The only exception is the Dominican Republic in which Cortén (1965) suggests that the lack of organizations was due to the dictator Trujillo and that since his regime they have been formed in new squatter settlements. In Lima the invasion organizations lose their power as the barriada becomes integrated with the city, but in some places they remain important as intermediaries with the government and as organizers of mutual aid public works. In most of the barriadas studied, orderly, unofficial elections were held annually, and the importance of the organization depended largely on the personality of the elected leader. National politics had a part in many of the elections, but regionalism and personal charisma played a greater role in the elections I observed. Goldrich et al. (1966) compare political organizations in barriadas and callampas in Lima and Santiago and find the Chilean callampa organizations to be more permanent because they are able to change their function from invasion and defense to that of "output agencies mediating between the community and the government." Lutz (1966) emphasizes that practically the only political activity in the barriadas of Panama is the barriada organization. In the papers by Leeds, Hoenack, Wygand, and Morocco (1966) on Rio's favelas, the degree of organization in the favela associations is striking. They have organized everything from private water systems, markets, labor division, and groups to raise money to buy the land on which they live, to Carnaval dance groups essential to the famous Rio festival. In Lima and Rio, national political parties figure somewhat in squatter settlement politics, while in Venezuela, according to Ray (1966), they play a larger role. Nevertheless, the internal organization of a Venezuelan rancho is strong and, despite the struggles over plots of land during the original occupation of the rancho, the residents show great respect for each other's lot once they begin construction.

Membership in the associations varies but there are always nonmembers. In most cases membership doesn't imply participation but it appears that in squatter settlements there is at least as much and probably more participation in local politics than in other parts of the countries. The associations have trouble enforcing rules and often fail in their dealings with the bureaucracy. They do seem to be able to control, to a certain extent, who will be the members of the invasion group and the new residents; they favor nuclear families with an employed male as head. Associations frequently manage to get some assistance in installing sewers, water, roads, etc., and they provide a low-level, unofficial court for minor disputes. Most important, associations often give people a feeling of controlling their own destinies. This is frequently illusory, and distrust of local leadership is present almost from the start. The association does, however, have a major accomplishment that is visible at all times, namely, the invasion and successful retention of a piece of land.

SQUATTER SETTLEMENTS AND SOCIAL DISORGANIZATION

In Rio and Lima, many people warned me not to go into barriadas or favelas because they were full of criminals. Other scholars have had the same experience in other countries. In fact, however, squatter settlements are overwhelmingly composed of poor families who work hard and aspire to get ahead legitimately. Petty thievery is common, low-level tax evasion a national pastime; disputes occur over land titles, children annoying or damaging others' property, small debts, dogs, etc. Wife and child beating are frequent, at least in Lima and Rio, and drunkenness is common. Assault outside the family is rare. Organized crime is practically nonexistent.

. . .

Empirical evidence does not indicate that crimes occur with more frequency within squatter settlements than outside. In the only comparative study I could find (Rotondo et al., 1963) the rate of delinquency in a central city slum of Lima was high and varied, while that of a barriada was low and unvaried—primarily complaints of wives against husbands and petty thievery.

. . .

Goldrich (1966) writes of callampas in Chile and barriadas in Peru,

> In the face of their reputation for social disorganization, these settlers reveal remarkably little of it; crime, promiscuity, broken homes occur infrequently, particularly in comparison to the bridgehead settlements and traditional city slums. Though born as illegal invasions, these communities display a prevailing orientation toward law and order.

Family and kinship relationships are strong and provide a degree of crisis insurance. Rotondo, referring to a Lima barriada (1965) and a slum (1963), notes greater involvement with kin and much less social pathology in the barriada. Pearse (1961) discusses kin-group controls on behavior in favelas. The importance of the family cannot be overestimated. The information on all the squatter settlements indicates that by far the greatest number of households consist of nuclear, bilateral families with resident fathers. The exceptions are Buenaventura, Colombia, where Mallol (1963) found a large number of female-based households, and Puerto Rico, where Safa (1965) encountered a similar situation. Grandparents and other relatives are also prevalent but the populations are generally younger than the already young national population averages. Since some squatter settlements have been in existence for 20 years there is variation in the age levels and one can see a family cycle (see Hammel, 1961, 1964). As Turner (1966) points out, the invader spends several years consolidating his building lot and constructing a house. This provides a start for his children. Desertion and early death of males are probably about the same as outside the settlement, but the widow or abandoned wife has the assets of a house and lot to make her an attractive marriage or common law partner.

. . .

Family relationships are as ambivalent in the squatter settlements as outside. Gordon Parks' account of violence and bitterness within a favela family (1961) could be duplicated inside and outside squatter settlements throughout Latin America and inside and outside slums throughout the world.[6] Padilla (1958)

. . . reports social disorganization among Puerto Rican migrants to New York but emphasizes that parents integrate and sacrifice for their children. Lewis (1966a), in a much more intensive study of fewer people, reports some integration and sacrifice for children but emphasizes disorganization, bitterness, and violence. Lewis notes the same conditions among rural migrants to Mexico City (1960) but many observers have taken issue with him (for example, Butterworth, 1962; Paddock, 1961; Bendiner, 1967), and in other studies (Lewis, 1952, 1959, 1965) he, too, emphasizes very different sorts of migrant behavior in Mexico City. Fried (1959) and I (1960, 1964) describe family attitudes in a Peruvian barriada in very different terms. He found and stressed pity and pessimism; I encountered and stressed self-help and optimism. As I have pointed out (1967), we are both correct in stressing apparently contradictory aspects of reality that exist in the same population. Lewis and Butterworth are both right. Lewis and Wakefield are both right about Puerto Rico. Bonilla (1961) says that Camus, in his film *Black Orpheus*, and Parks in his *Life* photographic essay, "each fasten on separate phases of the emotional cycle of the favela." The film stresses favelados as ". . . carefree, full of boundless energy and rhythm, with an unfettered zest for life." Parks' family is ". . . a proto-human band, weakened by chronic illness, callously indifferent to each other's suffering, living in a monotone degradation punctured only by flashes of violence." Both exist in favelas, barriadas, colônias proletarias, and outside.

. . .

Discussions of alienation and the quality of urban life probably digress too far from the purpose of a survey article, but I believe existing evidence indicates that inhabitants of squatter settlements are less alienated from the national state and more involved with each other than are residents of central city slums. Although reports are not explicit on the subject, one of the reasons for this difference is that squatters can constantly see around them a major accomplishment of their own, i.e., the seizure of land and the creation of a community.

THE ECONOMIC CONDITION OF SQUATTER SETTLEMENTS

Just as traditional economists have difficulty with peasant economics, they have difficulty in evaluating the contribution (or lack of it) of squatter settlements to national and city economies. Obviously one major contribution is that millions of people have solved their own housing problem in situations where the national governments were practically unable to move. On the other hand, as Abrams (1965), Turner (1963), and many governmental planners have pointed out, by so doing they have occupied land that might have a more "logical" use in a city, and they have made the provision of services such as water, sewage disposal, electricity, and paved streets much more expensive than if the land were empty. This dilemma, unfortunately, is only a dilemma for planners. People who need housing can't be kept in the pipeline for years as a plan can. Clearly the land invaders want services and, in most cases, have shown themselves to be quite willing to pay for them. They are not, however, willing to wait for them on the basis of a governmental promise. The result has been the creation of many unsanitary communities with expensive private water and electric arrangements and poor internal transportation. One of the rational considerations weighed by potential residents in established squatter settlements as well as by invaders is the balance between the economic advantages of paying no rent, "owning" your own home, and joining a community, on the one hand, and having few services, building your own house, risking great loss if dislocated, and taking unpopular and often illegal political action, on the other. Since some squatter settlements are located close to the dwellers' places of employment, this is also a consideration. The central city slums are also close to employment but they are expensive and undesirable. The few governmental attempts to build new projects (Peru, Brazil, Venezuela, Argentina) have chosen sites that are much too far from work and have proved to be much too expensive for the squatters.

Squatter settlements make four kinds of contributions to national economies. First is the investment in housing and land improvement mentioned above. The literature on types of houses is extensive (see Turner, 1966) and includes many photographs since the settlements tend to be very photogenic. Housing is often temporary and, of necessity, hastily built upon the first occupation of the land through invasion or other means. The residents then put a good deal of the capital, which would have been used to pay rent, into constructions that may take as long as ten years to complete. Most of them live on the sites in temporary houses or shells during this period but a few don't move in until they have completed an elaborate house. Land titles play a major role in investment in housing, and in places where a title or some assurance of permanence is thought to exist constructions are more elaborate than in those without titles. Even with the land title problem the vast majority of squatter residents are owner-occupiers. In no report does the percentage of renters go higher than 46 percent (in colonias proletarias in Mexico City) and it usually is closer to 4 or 5 percent (Venezuela, Peru, Brazil). The older the settlement, the higher the percentage of renters. One of the reasons for hesitancy to invest in housing in favelas is that so many of them are on private land and are frequently threatened with eviction. In Lima and Mexico City, although each city has known evictions and pitched battles between squatters and police, constructions are substantial because most of the land occupied is state land and some provisional titles have been granted. The construction of houses, stairways, streets, water systems, water control dikes and spillways, etc., in the Rio favelas amounts to millions of dollars, despite the threat of eviction (Leeds, Smith, 1966; Pearse, 1961).

The second contribution is in the job market. Unemployment figures are difficult to evaluate because of the large number of marginally employed and self-employed people. Rosenbluth (1963) estimates a high of 27 percent unemployment in Chilean callampas. Herrick (1966) writes that migrants to Santiago are in about the same proportion in callampas as in the city, and that migrants are much more active economically than they were in their places of origin. The BEMDOC (1965) study of a favela in Rio indicates that 12 percent of family heads are unemployed. Usandizaga and Havens (1966) give 8 percent as the unemployment figure for squatters in Barranquilla. In the Bucaramanga, Colombia, study (Pinto, 1966) a population of about 10,000 had 60 percent stable employment and 40 percent casual employment. Matos (1961) notes that 71 percent of the active population of Lima's barriadas (in 1956) had stable employment, 27 percent casual employment, and 2 percent unknown. These studies and many others (Bon, 1963; Germani, 1961; Leeds et al., 1966; SAGMACS, 1960, for example) cover a wide variety of occupations ranging in income from gardening and garbage collection, through skilled and unskilled factory work, through service jobs in restaurants, police forces, armies, government offices, and banks, to store owners, teachers, lawyers, and doctors. In the barriada Pampa de Comas in Lima the membership of the residents' *Club John F. Kennedy a Favor de Comas* included a medical doctor, a bank branch manager, a police lieutenant, two university students, a lawyer, several store and bar owners, and two resident Peace Corps volunteers. Squatter settlements are seldom one-class communities.

In addition to the jobs held outside the settlements (the ones that appear in national employment figures) many people work full and part time within the settlement. Construction workers particularly find a great deal of part-time work. Turner (1966) reports that the owner-occupiers often provide only the unskilled labor value on their houses and that the difficult, skilled, and expensive work, such as roof building, is done largely by local construction workers. Hoenack refers to burden carriers in favelas. Rosenbluth and Bon mention different kinds of jobs in callampas and cantegriles.

In a version of Foster's (1965) image of limited good, upper- and middle-class Latin Americans accept an 18th-century view of "the poor" and see no way to raise their income because the economy won't stand it unless the money comes from the wealthy. They also believe that poverty is always with us, part of the natural law of life, and millions of poor people join them in this belief (Miller and Rein, 1964). In very few Latin American countries is there a clear relationship between merit, hard work, and success. This serves to keep aspiration levels rather low. Many persons know of cases in which poor people win lotteries, or rise to wealth through athletic ability, entertainment skills, or possibly through the military.

Unions have been strong in some countries but a number are often influenced by management, political dictators, U.S. unions, or communists to take actions quite apart from those that would further the welfare of their members. They have seldom moved outside the specific labor dispute area, although a few unions in Peru assisted their members in developing squatter settlements in Arequipa (graphic arts union) and Chimbote (steel workers).

A very important area of economic development where people have created capital on their own, and where hard work and ability have demonstrably paid off is in the growth of small businesses in squatter settlements. This third contribution is the least known outside the settlements and extremely important monetarily. There is a tremendous proliferation of small enterprise. When a squatter settlement has become more or less established and accepted by the government, banks appear (mobile banks in panel trucks appear long before this point), movie houses are built, chain stores open, horse race lottery shops open, etc. Even from the outset, however, the local people begin buying and selling to and from each other at a great rate. In a Lima barriada of approximately 1,500 houses, we counted more than 100 houses where something was sold. Converting the room that faces the street into a store is a very common pattern in rural Peru and is followed in barriadas. Some had very low stocks of merchandise, others did a booming business. Leeds (1966) and Hoenack (1966) describe large numbers of stores and restaurants opened by favelados in Rio, and Hoenack points out that owners of small stores often oppose change in favela conditions in order to protect their businesses. Bars, restaurants, garages, repair shops, barber shops, school supply stores, bakeries, groceries, fruit stores, and newsstands are reported in all of the squatter settlements. Bus companies are among the first groups to be formed if the established companies won't serve the community. Some people charge admission to watch their television and use the proceeds to make the time payments on the set. Peattie (1966) makes a similar point about investment and small business in the ranchos of Caracas.

Markets grow up within squatter settlements and hundreds of peddlers go back and forth from central markets to the settlements by bicycle, tricycle, bus, and taxi carrying produce for resale. Bradley (1966) discusses the involvement of barriada dwellers in Lima's wholesale market, La Parada. Hoenack (1966) describes in detail many of the problems of supplying and selling in Rio favelas. In Lima, the arrival of market inspectors and tax collectors is not exactly welcomed but they do abet those who stake out market stalls by attempting to drive off peddlers who display their limited wares on the ground around the market itself. Tax collection is often tolerated as a sign of recognition from outside and can be the final confidence builder needed to encourage permanent construction. I have never seen a barriada or a rural store in Peru that did not keep a special set of books for the tax collector. Hoenack notes the same procedure in favelas.

Real estate speculation takes place as does considerable buying and selling of land with very elaborate, and generally totally illegal, titles changing hands. Renting is forbidden in some settlements but is found in all. Money lenders thrive in squatter settlements in Rio and Mexico City but are seldom found in Peruvian barriadas where the residents go to kinsmen or *compadres* for money. Credit unions exist in many of the settlements, often promoted and sometimes funded originally by outside capital from a national credit cooperative, a church group, or a U.S. aid group.

The fourth contribution—intangible social capital invested in the creation of a community—is not exclusively economic and I shall continue to discuss it in the next section. The community makes possible investment in housing and neighborhood improvements and investment in the numerous small enterprises. The community also involves the inhabitants of a squatter settlement in the life of the nation with a small but increasingly effective power base. Leeds (1966) discusses social investments in neighborhood, family and kin groups and their economic consequences in favelas, making more or less the same point that the considerable economic contribution to the city is directly related to the social relationships that led to the invasions. Another socio-economic aspect of squatter settlements is that they are beginning to attract world-wide attention as possible focuses of direct economic aid and community development. Foreigners from the U.S., Europe, and the United Nations view them in this light because they have already developed active communities with high morale and have created conditions for further economic and social development.

PARTICIPATION IN CITY AND NATIONAL LIFE

The data on social participation vary. Economic participation is at a high level and most of the adult men are away from the settlements working in the city on week days. Women work as domestic servants, waitresses, and factory workers and are often in the city. Men and women go to and from markets, stores, churches, and places of amusement. Children go to high schools and private schools in the city. Most settlements seem to have their own state primary schools, often built by the residents, and some have private schools. A few do not have primary schools in the settlement and bus their children to other locations in the city. I have met a few women in Lima barriadas who lived within sight of the bright lights of downtown yet had never been there; they had, however, been to the wholesale market area and to the nearby sections of the city. Similar cases are noted in other studies.

Not only do squatters do much of the service work of the city, but they also patronize the movies, bars, soccer games, musical tent shows, TV broadcasts, and other amusements. They attend Catholic and Protestant services. They also buy from city merchants, borrow from and deposit money in city banks, and maintain a constant flow of traffic to and from governmental offices.

People have relatives in all parts of the city and make friends at work. Visiting kinsmen, a common Latin American pastime, is an important activity for squatters who travel throughout the city to make their visits. In Lima we found people from one barriada working in practically every section of the city, some with a commuting time of almost two hours. [Various authors] point out that favelas are not social enclaves isolated from the city and Morocco (1966) describes the intense involvement of the favela-based samba schools in the life of Rio.

The lack of social participation among squatters is frequently attributed to their illiteracy and ignorance. The data do not support this assertion. Without exception education ranks near the top of the list of *desiderata* for children in every country referred to in this survey. In several places, particularly in Peru, the squatters have provided their own school buildings and, in some cases, hired their own teachers. In Guatemala, Cuevas (1965) writes, "In spite of all the inconveniences, the index of literacy (80 percent) is appreciably higher than that which exists in the urban and suburban areas of origin of the adults of the families." He adds that the great majority of the children of squatters attend school regularly. Matos (1961) notes that in Lima barriadas, ". . . 86 percent of the population above the age of 5 years had received or were receiving an education and only 10 percent were illiterate." Paredes (1963), in a survey of Lima's most urbanized barriada, found an even higher literacy rate. It is higher than the literacy figure for Lima as a whole and considerably higher than that for the whole country. In the barriada in which I worked intensively the great majority of the illiterates were older people, primarily older women. Goldrich (1966) found 10 percent and 7 percent illiteracy in two Chilean callampa samples. . . . Rosenbluth (1963) found 29 percent illiteracy in callampas and reports that 45 percent of callampa children do not attend school. This high figure is not reflected in the Goldrich study of two callampas. The SAGMACS study and Leeds' material on Rio's favelas describe variations among favelas, but a keen interest in education, many schools, and a high literacy rate. On the other hand, the BEMDOC (1965) study of a favela noted an illiteracy rate of 34 percent, the highest reported figure. The 16 percent illiteracy rate in cantegriles in Uruguay (Bon, 1963) is high for Montevideo but not for parts of rural Uruguay and it is concentrated in the population over 40.

Newspapers and magazines sell in large numbers in squatter settlements, and transistor and plug-in radios are in practically every house. TV aerials abound in almost any photo of a settlement and we counted more than 50 sets in a ten square block area of the Pampa de Comas in Lima. Abrams (1964) writes that 30 percent of Venezuelan rancho homes have TV sets. Musical programs, dramatic serials, and sports are the most popular fare but the owners also listen to political and other local news shows in Lima and Rio, the only places for which I have information. Involvement of squatter settlement residents in national and city life through newspapers, radio, and TV is a carry-over from life in the city and is also increasingly common in the rural areas of most countries. Many of the migrants to the city who eventually go to the settlements have passed through rural towns and provincial cities, where they have been exposed to mass media and have developed what Reina (1964) has described in Peten, as ". . . a strong urban style of life in the absence of a true city."

Finally, it should be stressed again that the particular conditions created by the squatter settlements forcibly involve them with the cities. They are compelled to acculturate strategically in order, as they so frequently point out, to defend themselves. They keep up with news, become sophisticated about how to manipulate the national and international bureaucracies, play off political parties, and become real estate and legal specialists. We were constantly surprised by the large numbers of "ordinary" barriada residents in Peru who were conversant with the legal number and the content of complex laws dealing with land titles, etc. Jobs, marketing, schools, and kinship and voluntary associational ties keep most people in close touch with the city.

SQUATTER SETTLEMENTS AS RURAL COMMUNITIES RECONSTITUTED IN THE CITY

Since most of the adult residents of the squatter settlements are from rural areas they do bring rural customs with them. Since they also usually have more space in the settlements than they had in the city centers they are likely to supplement their diets and incomes by raising small animals or cultivating gardens. Combine this practice with the sight of a few people wearing rural clothes, particularly rural Indian clothes, and, in Peru, where many barriadas are carved out of steep hillsides, the impression of a rural Andean community is very strong.

The rural-urban differences are greater in countries with large Indian populations because they often involve basic cultural differences, but non-Indians as well as Indians live in rural areas and the non-Indians seem to be more likely to migrate to cities. Indians who do move to squatter settlements probably have spent years in the city and have become acculturated to the national culture (Mangin, 1967; see also note 7).

. . .

Extended family bonds and godparenthood are important in squatter settlements, just as they are outside, so their presence has little to do with the rural or urban character of the communities. . . . The kinship bonds and use of godparenthood for mobility and for cementing kinship and other relationships carry over into squatter settlements. Many individuals, however, say that they migrated from rural areas to escape kinship ties, godparenthood, and religious obligations.

. . .

In most of the studies, the kinship, godparent, regional, and voluntary associational ties existing in squatter settlements tie them to the rest of the country rather than create rural communities in the city (see, for example, Mangin, 1959).

With the exception of Buenaventura (Mallol, 1963) and Puerto Rico (Safa, 1965) where a matri-centered family is frequently found, the Latin American city kinship pattern is bilateral. Whitten (1965), in his study of Negroes in an Ecuadorean town, makes a statement that seems to describe the squatter settlement situation: "Unlike the unilineal and bilineal kinship systems that tend to break down in societies undergoing intercultural contact and economic rationalization, the cognatic descent system, based on personal and stem kindreds, seems highly adaptable to expanding and changing functions."

Formal religious activity may be more intensive in cities than in rural areas because of the larger number of priests and ministers, but fiesta activity probably declines. Data are scarce on the subject. In Peruvian barriadas and to a larger extent in Rio's favelas (Willems, 1966) evangelical sectarian Protestantism flourishes. Wakefield and Padilla comment on the same development among Puerto Ricans in San Juan and New York. In Peru, most of the Catholic priests working in barriadas are North American, Irish, or French, and offer temporal programs based on social action rather than the Peruvian and Spanish emphasis on reward in heaven. They also share with the evangelists and adventists a much more egalitarian ideology and have far greater appeal. This phenomenon occurs when the same groups of foreign Catholics and Protestants operate in rural areas, so it does not reflect the creation of rural communities in the city. It is, however, a mark of general cultural change.

The feature most frequently cited to support the country-in-the-city view is the presence of mutual aid house construction and public works. Both are common. I have seen mestizo squatters, migrants from Peruvian coastal cities and plantations, working on roads and sewer trenches in barriadas on Sundays and saying that they were working in *minga* groups just like the Incas. Most of them had never heard of mingas before they read about them in newspapers. Nonetheless, the inspiration for cooperative work organization may well be a rural pattern re-created in the city. Cooperative labor is noted for every country in the survey and is often referred to by the authors and squatters as a carry-over from rural culture.

Rural people retain many elements of rural culture in the city and in the squatter settlements. The settlements are, however, urban phenomena resulting from sophisticated urban decisions made by long-time urban residents, and the internal political organization is new, following no rural pattern.

POLITICAL ACTIVITY, RADICAL AND OTHERWISE, IN SQUATTER SETTLEMENTS

In their book on housing in Latin America, Koth, Silva, and Dietz (1964) write of squatter settlements and slums, "Probably most importantly, political agitators in urban slum areas find fertile ground for spreading doctrines of conflict and social disorder and efforts to improve housing may decrease conflict." Schmitt and Burks (1963) state that

> Unemployed and unskilled workers have clustered into shanty-towns called ranchos, particularly around Caracas, and as elsewhere in Latin America they are vulnerable to the blandishments of radical agitators and revolutionaries.

Trevor Armbrister of the *Saturday Evening Post* called a Lima barriada a "red seedbed." A Peruvian Catholic magazine, *Accion*, in January of 1963 [claimed] that 3,000 migrants a month arrived in Trujillo in communist trucks. *Accion* informed its readers that the reason they didn't see their police and army officer friends and relatives on New Year's Eve was because they had all been alerted and had thus prevented an attack on upper-class parties in private homes and clubs by "the people of the barriadas."

Other more sophisticated views of the squatter settlements as hovering presences menacing cities could be cited. Again, the facts, scarce as they are, portray quite a different situation. Turner (1966) states that the assumption that squatters are political radicals is universal, while the opposite is actually true. He writes, "If development of marginal areas (squatter settlements) ceases the upper-class prophecy could become self-fulfilling." He adds that most squatter settlements are "slums of hope rather than slums of despair," (a distinction made by Charles Stokes, 1962, and used by Peattie in reference to Venezuelan ranchos) in comparing them to Watts and Harlem (see also Jones, 1964). Myron Wiener (1966) has also demonstrated that slum voting in general is often more conservative than mddle-class voting.

For most Latin American squatters the *only* communal political action they perform is the original invasion and defense of the settlement.

. . .

My own impression from the studies cited and my experience in Lima is that a paternalistic ideology, combined with a "don't let them take it away" slogan, would be more appealing than a revolutionary "let's rise and kill the oligarchy" approach. Probably not many inhabitants of the squatter settlements would have regrets if someone else took the latter action, but they themselves are too busy. Of the many reported instances of confrontations with, and often subsequent violence by, the police during invasions and attempts to dislodge settlers, only one seems to have involved organized radical political parties. This case appears to refer to home-grown, non-ideological communists.

Clark (1963) describes a police cordon and siege of a callampa in Santiago in

1957 where the squatters were led by elected communists. When Clark returned four years later he found that there were six communists, three socialists, and one Trotskyite on the committee of the callampa and that the Trotskyite considered the communists not sufficiently revolutionary.

. . .

Turner and I reached a similar conclusion about Peruvian barriadas in 1959 after considerable contact with attempts at organizing communities for various purposes. The dominant ideology of most of the active barriada people appeared to be very similar to the beliefs of the operator of a small business in 19th-century England or the United States. These can be summed up in the familiar and accepted maxims: Work hard, save your money, trust only family members (and them not too much), outwit the state, vote conservatively if possible, but always in your own economic self-interest; educate your children for their future and as old-age insurance for yourself. Aspirations are toward improvement of the local situation with the hope that children will enter the professional class. All of the above statements pertain perfectly to favelas.

A somewhat puzzling factor must be noted in these populations that have achieved so much. Despite their own problem-solving efforts they seem to believe that the only answer to their problems lies in outside solutions from the government, the United States, the United Nations, etc. This is also the assumption of practically every governmental report I have read on squatter settlements. We asked our sample in a Lima barriada how the problems of the barrio could be solved. Only 11 of more than 70 replied that they could do anything to solve their own problems. In the sample were heads of families, many of whom had taken part in the invasion and were at the time active in the local association working on water, sewage disposal, and legal problems.

Aspiration levels for many of the adult migrants are relatively low and many of them feel that when they have a steady income, a house of their own, and their children in school, they have achieved more than they had believed possible. If mobility is blocked and their extremely high aspirations for their children are not satisfied, as they almost surely will not be, then some change may occur in the political climate. At present they seem capable of mobilization only as a group to defend their homes.

"SOLUTIONS" TO THE PROBLEM

[Most people seem to feel that any "squatter settlement" poses] a problem, yet my major thesis has been that the squatter settlements represent a solution to the complex problem of rapid urbanization and migration, combined with a housing shortage. The problem is the solution is the problem.

. . .

Attempts to displace the squatter settlements, when modest in scale, providing land, sewers, water, technical assistance, and possibly house shells, and allowing people to build at their own pace, has worked at least once in Valdivieso, Lima (Turner, 1963). That effort, however, used unoccupied land and did not involve eradication. The many proponents of eradication assume an investment of almost nothing in straw and scrap construction instead of the investment of millions of dollars in labor and so-called "noble" materials actually involved in most of the settlements.

As Turner notes (1963), the governments of Peru, Chile, and Colombia have experimented with housing cooperatives, credit programs, and minimal aid programs with some success on a very small scale. Meanwhile thousands of people have applied what he calls the "unaided self-help solution." In Venezuela, where resources are vast, the housing projects and "Superbloques," have scarcely touched the housing need. Turner (1966) reports that the thousands in the Superblocks have had no effect on migration to Caracas or on population expansion in the ranchos. The satellite cities of Ventanilla (Lima), Ciudad Kennedy (Bogotá), and Vila Kennedy and Vila Esperança in Rio (joint national government-AID housing programs) have proved to be heavily subsidized and extremely expensive developments. They have met the needs of some of the more affluent working-class and white-collar members of the population, but have had no effect on and provided only negative solutions to the housing shortage problem.

AID and government officials, in the Salmon report (1966) and the Wagner, McVoy, Edwards report (1966), are beginning to recommend a third solution that seems to reflect a greater degree of ethnographic and political reality. The report by Wagner et al. stated that the Rio satellites were too far from places of work and that residents complained of losing jobs because of transportation problems. Zoning and planning regulations prevent the growth of local enterprise. Salmon points out that the mortgage payments are too high, particularly if an emergency arises, since people live so close to the margin economically. He also notes that a number of ex-favelados felt safer on the streets of the favelas because there were more people around and they knew everyone. Lance Belville, in *The New York Times*, November 21, 1965, reports identical feelings in Vila Aliance, another satellite city near Rio, and quotes a resident who formerly lived in a favela overlooking Botafogo Bay, close to his place of work,

> I hate it here . . . they brought me to this place in handcuffs . . . it's too far from any work . . . my old shack had plenty of room for me and the family . . . and the shack didn't leak . . . I'm too far from the beach to go find crabs . . . sometimes I just can't make the payments on the house . . . the house can wait. My children cannot wait.

. . .

The solution under *consideration* in Peru, Brazil, Colombia, Venezuela, and Chile is to check the growth of new squatter settlements by providing cheap land and services for those who want them, and to rehabilitate rather than eradicate most existing squatter settlements. The AID report of Wagner et al., (1966) states, "Generally speaking, the cost of upgrading the favelas will be less than the cost of relocation of favela dwellers in new housing construction." With regard to upgrading favelas, Juan de Onis writes,

> Many favelas have schools, meeting houses, churches, stores and small shops; they also have self-help-constructed water and electricity distribution systems, and in some instances sewer systems. Small industries operated by individual owners or as family enterprises are scattered throughout most favelas. A good many houses are of perfectly sound construction. (*The New York Times*, August 12, 1966.)

Latin American rural people are so accustomed to being cheated and dispossessed by banks and mortgage holders that the very concept of a bank loan or a mortgage is suspect.

. . .

At least one source from every country surveyed stated that the squatters were more satisfied with their present housing and economic situation than with what they had had in the rural areas, small towns, and in the central city. This includes even the Argentine situation (Germani, 1961) where the squatters are of a somewhat different character (see note 5). Herrick (1966), referring to migrants to Santiago and not exclusively to callampa residents, noted that return movement was rare.

Of these migrants, all of whom had moved to Santiago within the last ten years, only one-seventh know anyone who had come to Santiago to live and who had subsequently returned to his place of origin for any reason.

In my study of a barriada in Peru, only two families from the sample moved out in two years, one to return to the mountains, one to go to a house in the city. I heard of very few families returning to the country. The city growth and the squatter settlements are permanent developments.

Few would now agree with the Guatemalan government official who stated at an international meeting in 1964 that "The sudden growth of shanty towns is in many cases the consequence of the lack of a firm attitude on the part of governmental and municipal authorities." Interested persons are much more aware that migrants come to cities for economic and other reasons; that central city slums are expensive, often unpleasant places in which to live, and provide no opportunities to invest in the future; that national governments (even with U.S. aid) cannot provide housing; and that people must go somewhere. There are also small indications that a few governments are beginning to find it more productive to work with popular initiative than to fight it.

In conclusion, I suggest that despite the talk about urban anthropology, anthropologists have done very little urban work. Other than those on East Africa the number of studies has been very small and mostly unpublished. The few anthropologists, architects, sociologists, and political scientists (Latin and North American) who have worked in squatter settlements have to a large extent been responsible for some of the policy changes noted above. Whether or not influencing policy is anyone's goal, the need for more research on squatter settlements is apparent. To fully appreciate the intense personal and familial histories presented by Lewis for Mexico and Puerto Rico, we need to understand a great deal more about migration, squatter settlements, and the relationship of urban social organization to squatter settlements. Simmons (1952) suggested that Peruvian barriadas, and by inference squatter settlements in other countries, provided a cheap and efficient way to study the ethnography of the whole country since they contained migrants from every province. The settlements also present a unique community formation that is important in the development of cities all over the world. As places to study institutional development they are singularly useful. Finally, as a special inducement to anthropologists, who might be dissuaded by my previous comments that barriadas are not rural communities reconstituted in the city, let me add that they do have many of the characteristics of small communities. Considerable face-to-face interaction takes place and people feel part of a community, if only because they are so often under attack. In addition, local institutions have some influence on behavior, thereby enabling the residents to relate to the outside world as a community.

NOTES

1. There are several good sources on Latin American urbanization. The sources I have consulted as background are Hauser (1961), a report on a UN seminar on urbanization in Latin America; Dorselaer and Gregory (1962); and T. Lynn Smith (1960) on population studies; Rycoft and Clemmer (1963); the special issue on urbanization of *Scientific American* (Sept. 1965); and Charles Abrams' book (1964) on world housing problems.

2. I refer specifically to studies in the text when I discuss matters in detail. When I refer to Peru without giving a specific source I am using my own experience based on more than six years of field work. I do, on occasion, refer to "the studies in the survey," "all the reports," or say "the sources all agree," etc. Following is a list of the major sources I consulted by country. Mexico: Frieden, 1964, 1965; Lewis, 1959, 1960; Harth, 1966; Butterworth, 1962. Guatemala: Cuevas, 1965; Lopez y otros, 1965. Dominican Republic: Cortén, 1965. Venezuela: Ray, 1966; Peattie, 1962, 1966; Jones, 1964. Colombia: C. B. Turner, 1964; Usandizaga and Havens, 1966; Pinto, 1966; Mallol, 1963; Bernal, 1963. Panama: Gutierrez, 1961; Lutz, 1966. Puerto Rico: Lewis, 1966a; Safa, 1964, 1966. Uruguay: Bon, 1963. Argentina: Germani, 1961; Wilson, 1965. Brazil: SAGMACS, 1960; Pearse, 1961; BEMDOC, 1965; and an invaluable set of mimeographed reports of chapters in a forthcoming book on favelas by Hoenack, Leeds, Modesto, Morocco, O'Neil, Smith, and Wygand, 1966. Peru: Turner, 1963, 1966; Matos, 1961; Hammel, 1961, 1964; Rotondo y otros, 1963; Rotondo, 1965; Mangin, 1960, 1963, 1964.

3. For an analysis of some of the anti-city literature in U.S. social science, see Mills, 1943. For a discussion of urbanism in Latin America, and elsewhere, see Morse, 1965b.

4. Lima and other cities have always grown through the formation of squatter settlements. In *Relación del virrey Conde de Superinda*, Documento C1312, Biblioteca Nacional del Peru, a report from 1746 denounces the formation of barriadas in present-day Rimac, notes that they are unsanitary, and that the people should be sent back to the mountains (I am indebted to John Te Paske for calling my attention to the document). Schaedel (1966) points out that pre-Spanish, and pre-Incaic cities on the Peruvian coast used the same sorts of land for housing that are presently being used by barriadas, and he refers to this type of use as "characteristic of indigenous America at its highest point of development," and "resolving urban living problems better than the imported Spanish variety."

5. [It is generally agreed that the] fastest rates of urbanization now are occurring in societies with relatively low levels of urbanization. Wingo (1966) has made [that affirmation specific to] Latin America, and he separates Argentina, Uruguay, and Cuba from other countries on the basis of their more advanced urbanization. Migration to cities has slowed down, and squatter settlements reflect a pushing out of the least competitive members of the society rather than an outlet for the pressures of rapid urbanization. Silvert (1966) has made the same division, adding Costa Rica, and making a

similar point. The Argentine material does suggest a difference from the others. Germani (1961) points out that delinquency is higher in squatter settlements than in tenements and that recent migrants are more apt to be found in squatter settlements. This contradicts the information from other countries and may be due to the distinction made by Wingo and Silvert. Wilson (1965), however, says that squatters are very much like other Argentines and are in the settlements because of the housing shortage that affects the total population of Buenos Aires. The Uruguayan situation is not described in sufficient detail, but it appears to fit the general, rather than the Argentine, pattern. I could find no information on squatter settlements in Cuba or Costa Rica.

6. The concept of the culture of poverty developed by Lewis, as described in the introduction to *Children of Sanchez* and revised in *Scientific American*, October, 1966, is an important idea that is applicable to certain older squatter settlements, but more so to central city slums. I would take issue with the term "culture," since a change in employment or sudden acquisition of wealth *may* change an individual's "culture" if it is the culture of poverty. Carolina María de Jesús (1962), from a Rio favela, and the people Lewis describes in La Esmeralda, a Puerto Rican squatter settlement, fit the concept perfectly, and sudden wealth does not necessarily change their culture. I do feel that the concept has no particular application to the majority of the residents of the majority of squatter settlements. Despite their poverty in relation to that of poor people in the United States, the fantastic disparity in wealth and power between the squatters and their own upper and middle classes, and the ambivalent attitude of the national governments reflected in the violence of the army and the police toward the squatters coupled with half-hearted attempts to assist them with housing, they are not alienated, hopeless people caught in a vicious circle of poverty. For most of the adults their condition in the squatter settlements is the best of their lives and a marked improvement on their previous two or three houses. I am always suspicious of the characterization of any population as apathetic, and it is certainly an inappropriate term for squatter settlements.

7. Arias (1965) points out that Indians migrate to cities much less frequently than Ladinos in Guatemala. This situation prevails in Peru. This statement, however, presupposes a cultural definition of Indian, and a man who leaves an Indian community in adolescence and lives for several years on a plantation or in a small town becomes a national Peruvian or Guatemalan. He might then migrate to the capital and, for purposes of classification, not be counted as an Indian. By the time he moves to a squatter settlement, after years of residence in the city, he is not an Indian. As I have pointed out (Mangin, 1964) there is a very small number of older women, and even fewer men, who speak no Spanish in barriadas. Barriadas do have ethnic and racial tensions, however, and light-skinned coastal people are generally richer and more powerful than darker skinned, shorter *serranos* (mountain-people). But this is not, by any means, always the case, and serranos often join together to elect one of their own to a barriada presidency. Rotondo and I have noted serrano-Negro hostility both in and out of barriadas. In the few favelas I visited in Rio it seemed that whites had the majority of the best houses in the best locations, and that the majority of those in the poorer houses nearest to sewers, mud flats, etc., were Negroes.

BIBLIOGRAPHY

Abrams, Charles
1964 Man's Struggle for Shelter in an Urbanizing World. Cambridge, Mass.
1965 The use of land in cities. Scientific American. September. 151–161.

Arias B., Jorge
1965 La concentración urbana y las migraciones internas. In: Problemas de la Urbanización en Guatemala. 19–45. Ministerio de Educación.
Bemdoc (Brasil Estados Unidos Movimento de Desenvolvimento e Organização de Comunidade)
1965 Vial Proletaria da Penha. Rio de Janeiro.
Bendiner, Elmer
1967 Outside the kingdom of the middle class: La Vida by Oscar Lewis. The Nation. January 2.
Bernal A., Hernando
1963 Ritmos de vida en Buenaventura. Revista Colombiana de Antropologia. 12:331–355.
Bon Espasandin, Mario
1963 Cantegriles: Familia, Educación, Niveles Económicos—Laborales, Vivienda y Aspectos Generales que Componen el "Collar de Miserias" de Montevideo. Montevideo.
Bonilla, Frank
1961 Rio's favelas: the rural slum within the city. American Universities Field Staff Report. August.
Bourricaud, Francois
1964 Lima en la vida política peruana. América Latina. October–December.
Bradley, John
1966 The market system and urbanization in Lima. (Mimeographed.)
Butterworth, Douglas
1962 A study of the urbanization process among the Mixtec migrants from Tilantongo in Mexico City. América Indígena. 22:257–274.
Caretas
1963 Enero-Febrero.
Clark, Gerald
1963 The Coming Explosion in Latin America. New York City.
Cortén, Andre
1965 Como vive la otra mitad de Santo Domingo: estudio de dualismo estructural. Caribbean Studies. 4:3–19.
Cuevas, Marco Antonio
1965 Análisis de tres áreas marginales de la ciudad de Guatemala. In: Problemas de la Urbanización en Guatemala. Ministerio de Educación.
Davis, Kingsley
1965 The urbanization of the human population. Scientific American. September. 41–50.
Dorselaer, Jaime, and Gregory, Alfonso
1962 La Urbanización en América Latina. Oficina Internacional de Investigaciones Sociales de FERES. Bogotá.
Foster, George
1965 Peasant society and the image of limited good. American Anthropologist. 67:293–315.
Fried, Jacob
1959 Acculturation and mental health among migrants in Peru. In: Culture and Mental Health. Marvin Opler, ed. New York City.
Frieden, Bernard
1964 A program for housing and urban development in Mexico City. (Mimeographed.) AID. Washington, D.C.
1965 The search for housing policy in Mexico City. Town Planning Review. 35:July.

Gans, Herbert
1962 The Urban Villagers. New York City.
Germani, Gino
1961 Inquiry into the social effects of urbanization in a working-class sector of Buenos Aires. In: Urbanization in Latin America. Philip M. Hauser, ed. 206–233. UNESCO. New York City.
Goldrich, Daniel
1965 Toward the comparative study of politicization in Latin America. In: Contemporary Cultures and Societies of Latin America. 1st ed. Dwight Heath and Richard Adams, eds. 361–378. New York City.
Goldrich, Daniel, Pratt, R. B., and Schuller, C. R.
1966 The political integration of lower class urban settlements in Chile and Peru. (Mimeographed.) Annual Meeting of American Political Science Association. New York City.
Gutierrez, Samuel
1961 El problema de las barriadas brujas en la ciudad de Panama. Instituto de Vivienda y Urbanismo.
Halperin, Ernst
1965 The decline of communism in Latin America. Atlantic Monthly. May. 65–70.
Hammel, Eugene A.
1961 The family cycle in a coastal Peruvian slum and village. American Anthropologist. 63:989–1005.
1964 Some characteristics of rural village and urban slum populations on the coast of Peru. Southwestern Journal of Anthropology. 20:346–358.
Harth Deneke, Jorge
1966 The colonias proletarias of Mexico City, low-income settlements on the urban fringe. Master's thesis in City Planning. Massachusetts Institute of Technology. Cambridge, Mass.
Hauser, Philip M., ed.
1961 Urbanization in Latin America. UNESCO. New York City.
Heath, Dwight, and Adams, Richard, eds.
1965 Contemporary Cultures and Societies of Latin America. 1st ed. New York City.
Herrick, Bruce H.
1966 Urban Migration and Economic Development in Chile. Cambridge, Mass.
Hoenack, Judith
1966 Marketing, supply and their social ties in Rio favelas. (Mimeographed.) *
Jones, Emrys
1964 Aspects of urbanization in Venezuela. Ekistics. 18:109.
Koth, Marcia, Silva, Julia, and Dietz, Albert
1964 Housing in Latin America. Cambridge, Mass.
Leeds, Anthony
1964 Brazilian careers and social structure: an evolutionary model and case history. American Anthropologist. 66:1321–1347.†

* Papers presented at 36th International Congress of Americanists. September 1966. Mar del Plata.

† Reprinted in Contemporary Cultures and Societies of Latin America. Dwight Heath and Richard Adams, eds. New York City. [Editor's note: This refers to the first edition (1965) of this book; they are not included in the second (revised) edition.]

Leeds, Anthony, and others
1966 The investment climate in Rio favelas. (Mimeographed.) *
Lewis, Oscar
1952 Urbanization without breakdown. Scientific Monthly. 75:31–41.†
1959 Five Families. New York City.
1960 The Children of Sanchez. New York City.
1965 The folk urban ideal types. In: The Study of Urbanization. P. Hauser and L. Schnore, eds. New York City.
1966a La Vida: A Puerto Rican Family in the Culture of Poverty. New York City.
1966b Even the saints cry. Trans-Action. November. 18–23.
1966c The culture of poverty. Scientific American. October. 19–25.
Lopez T., Jose, and others
1965 Barrios Marginales. Informe Sobre La Colonia "La Verbena," Ciudad de Guatemala. Dirección de Obras Públicas.
Ludwig, Armin K.
1966 The planning and creation of Brasilia. In: New Perspectives of Brazil. E. Baklanoff, ed. Nashville, Tenn.
Lutz, Thomas
1966 Some aspects of community organization and activity in the squatter settlements of Panama City. (Mimeographed.)
Mallol de Recassens, Maria Rosa, Y Recassens, Jose
1963 Estudios comparativos de los niveles de vivienda en Buenaventura y Puerto Colombia. Revista Colombiana de Antropologia. 12:295–328.
Mangin, William
1959 The role of regional associations in the adaptation of rural population in Peru. Sociologus. 9:21–36.†
1960 Mental health and migration to cities. Annals of the NY Academy of Sciences. 84:17:911–917.†
1963 Urbanization case history in Peru. Architectural Design. August.
1964 Sociológical, cultural and political characteristics of some rural Indians and urban migrants in Peru. Wenner-Gren Symposium on Cross-Cultural Similarities in the Urbanization Process. (Mimeographed.)
1965 The role of social organization in improving the environment. In: Environmental Determinants of Community Well-Being. Pan American Health Organization.
1967 Las Comunidades Alteñas en la América Latina. México.
Maria de Jesus, Carolina
1962 Child of the Dark. Translated from Portuguese by St. Clair Drake. New York City.
Matos Mar, Jose
1961 Migration and urbanization: the barriadas of Lima. In: Urbanization in Latin America. Philip M. Hauser, ed. 170–190. New York City.
Miller, S. M., and Rein, Martin
1964 Poverty and social change. The American Child. March.
Mills, C. Wright
1943 The professional ideology of social pathologists. American Journal of Sociology. 49:165–180.
Modesto, Helio
1966 Favelas-reflexoes sobre o problema. (Mimeographed.) *
Morocco, David
1966 Carnaval groups-maintainers and intensifiers of the favela phenomenon in Rio. (Mimeographed.) *

Morse, Richard M.
1965a Urbanization in Latin America. Latin American Research Review. 1:1:35–74.
1965b The sociology of San Juan: an exegesis of urban mythology. Caribbean Studies. 5:45–55.
Nehemkis, Peter
1964 Latin America: Myth and Reality. New York City.
Olga
1963 Enero.
O'Neill, Charles
1966 Some problems of urbanization and removal of Rio favelas. (Mimeographed.) *
Paddock, John
1961 Oscar Lewis's Mexico. Anthropological Quarterly. 34:129–149.
Padilla, Elena
1958 Up from Puerto Rico. New York City.
Paredes, Ernesto
1963 Fuentes de la población de la barriada Fray Martín de Porres. In: Migración e Integración en el Perú. H. Dobyns and M. Vasquez, eds. Lima.
Parks, Gordon
1961 Freedom's fearful foe: poverty. Life. June 16.
Patch, Richard W.
1961 Life in a callejón. American Universities Field Staff Report. June.
Pearse, Andrew
1961 Some characteristics of urbanization in the city of Rio de Janeiro. In: Urbanization in Latin America. Philip M. Hauser, ed. 191–205. New York City.
Peattie, Lisa
1962 A short ethnography of La Laja. (Mimeographed.)
1966 Social issues in housing. Joint Center for Urban Studies. (Mimeographed.) Cambridge, Mass.
Pinto Barajas, Eugenio, ed.
1966 Control y Erradicación de Tugurios en Bucaramanga. Santander, Colombia.
Powelson, J. P.
1964 The land-grabbers of Cali. The Reporter. January 16.
Ray, Talton
1966 The political life of a Venezuelan barrio. (Mimeographed.)
Reina, Ruben E.
1964 The urban world view of a tropical forest community in the absence of a city, Petén, Guatemala. Human Organization. 23:265–277.
Rodwin, Lloyd
1965 Ciudad Guayana: a new city. Scientific American. September. 122–132.
Rosenbluth L., Guillermo
1963 Problemas Socio-Económicos de la Marginalidad y la Integración Urbana: El Caso de las Poblaciones Callampas en el Gran Santiago. Santiago, Chile.
Rotondo, Humberto
1965 Adaptability of human behavior. In: Environmental Determinants of Community Well-Being. Pan American Health Organization.
Rotondo, Humberto, and others
1963 Un estudio comparativo de la conducta antisocial de menores en áreas urbanas y rurales. In: Estudios de Psiquiatría Social en el Perú. Lima.

Rycroft, W. Stanley, and Clemmer, Myrtle
1963 A Study of Urbanization in Latin America. United Presbyterian Church. New York City.
Safa, Helen
1964 From shantytown to public housing: a comparison of family structure in two urban neighborhoods in Puerto Rico. Caribbean Studies. 4:3–12.
1965 The female-based household in public housing: a case study in Puerto Rico. Human Organization. 24:135–139.
SAGMACS
1960 Aspectos Humanos de Favela Carioca. Report of Mission of Father Lebret. Special Supplement to O Estado de São Paulo. April 13.
Salmon, Lawrence
1966 Report on Vila Kennedy and Vila Esperança. (Mimeographed.) Cooperativa Habitacional (COHAB).
Schaedel, Richard P.
1966 Urban growth and ekistics on the Peruvian coast. 36th International Congress of Americanists. 1:531–539. Sevilla.
Schmitt, Karl, and Burks, David
1963 Evolution or Chaos: Dynamics of Latin American Government and Politics. New York City.
Schulman, Sam
1966 Latin American shantytown. N.Y. Times Magazine. January 16.
Silvert, Kalman H.
1966 The Conflict Society: Reaction and Revolution in Latin America. American Universities Field Staff. New York City.
Simmons, Ozzie G.
1952 El uso de los conceptos de aculturación y asimilación en el estudio del cambio cultural en el Perú. Perú Indígena. 2:40–47. Lima.
Smith, Nancy
1966 Eviction in a Rio favela-leadership, land tenure and legal aspects. (Mimeographed.) *
Smith, T. Lynn
1960 Latin American Population Studies. University of Florida. Gainesville.
Stokes, Charles J.
1962 A theory of slums. Land Economics. 38:3.
Thomas, William I., and Znaniecki, Florian
1920 The Polish Peasant in Europe and America. Chicago.
Turner, Charles Barton
1964 Squatter settlements in Bogotá. (Mimeographed.) CINVA. Bogotá.
Turner, John F. C.
1963 Dwelling resources in South America. Architectural Design. August.
1966 Asentamientos Urbanos No Regulados. Cuadernos de la Sociedad Venezolana de Planificación. 36.
Usandizaga, Elsa, and Havens, Eugene
1966 Tres Barrios de Invasión. Facultad de Sociología. Bogotá.
Wagner, Bernard, McVoy, David, and Edwards, Gordon
1966 Guanabara Housing and Urban Development. AID Housing Report. July 1.
Wakefield, Dan
1959 Island in the City. Boston.
Walsh, William, MD.
1966 Yanqui, Come Back! The Voyage of the U.S. Hope to Peru. New York City.

Whitten, Norman E., Jr.
1965 Class, Kinship and Power in an Ecuadorean Town: The Negroes of San Lorenzo. Stanford, Calif.

Whyte, William Foote
1943 Street Corner Society. Chicago.

Wiener, Myron
1962 Urbanization and Political Extremism. (Mimeographed.) Cambridge, Mass.

Willems, Emilio
1966 Religious mass movements and social change in Brazil. In: New Perspectives of Brazil. E. Baklanoff, ed. Nashville, Tenn.

Wilson, L. Albert
1965 Voice of the Villas. Foundation for Cooperative Housing. Washington, D.C.

Wingo, Lowdon, Jr.
1966 Some aspects of recent urbanization in Latin America. Resources for the Future. (Mimeographed.) Washington, D.C.

Wygand, James
1966 Water networks: their technology and sociology in Rio favelas. (Mimeographed.) *

Political Organization and the Politicization of the Poblador

DANIEL GOLDRICH

One of the most visible changes in many Latin American countries during the past decade has been the widespread and rapid diffusion of political awareness and involvement among poor people who had traditionally been ignored by politicians and parties alike. Goldrich's imaginative surveys in Chile and Peru suggest how and why this change occurred. They also support Mangin's high estimation of urban slum-dwellers, and have obvious implications about the relative feasibility of "evolution vs. revolution."

Daniel Goldrich is Professor of Political Science at the University of Oregon. Having conducted research on political economics and development in Chile, Peru, and Central America, he is author of Sons of the Establishment: Elite Youth in Panama and Costa Rica (1966), *and coauthor of* The Rulers and the Ruled (1964).

This is a study of the effect of organization on the politicization of the poblador in some Santiago and Lima settlements. A poblador is an urban

From *Comparative Political Studies* III (1970), 176–202. © 1970 by Sage Publications, Inc. Reprinted by permission of the author and publisher. A brief "Postscript" has been added by the author to bring the article up to date.

squatter or resident in a government settlement. The themes addressed are: variations in community-politicization patterns by national political structural factors, and by the stage of the community in the quest for housing security; the effect of sanctions on politicization, and the role of partisanship and party organization in assuaging that effect; the role of particular parties in promoting politicization, especially the Chilean Marxist parties in land-invasion situations; the special effect of these parties in the maintenance of solidarity after the attainment of housing and urban facilities, and in the shift in focus of politicization to economic needs. A conglomerate case history is presented of the political organization of the homeless in Santiago by the Communist Party. This illustrates the interaction of organization in a situation of acute need to politicize previously apolitical adults, intensely and for a considerable period, despite severe hardship and sanction. The general significance of political organizations in relation to acute needs as politicizing factors is then considered, with additional reference to the Cuban revolutionary situation.

If the definition of political socialization is taken to be "the process by which an individual learns politically relevant attitudinal dispositions and behavior patterns" (Langton, 1969: 5), then the link here between the study of political socialization and that of politicization is the focus on the effect of a set of political factors (such as party organization and the political structuring of the ways of meeting needs) on the political involvement of the poblador. Any significance this study may have derives from two considerations: (1) political socialization generally has been studied in relation to childhood and early youth, whereas the present report focuses on adult socialization; (2) most theoretical and research attention has been given to such relatively nonpolitical politicizing agents as the family and school, while the present study focuses on political organization and political situations as politicizing agents.

BACKGROUND[1]

This is a study of residents of four lower-class settlements on the urban periphery of Santiago, Chile, and Lima, Peru. All four have been recently established, are permanent, and have obtained or are in the process of obtaining legal title to the land. Three have their origins in squatter invasions. The fourth is a government housing project, partly composed of invaders and of applicants who successfully qualified through a "normal" administrative process. These areas are commonly stereotyped by more prestigious elements within the nation as slums, but they are in reality being improved and consolidated, and as such should be sharply distinguished from deteriorating areas or true slums.

The data are derived largely from interviews conducted with samples of lower-class male adult residents of the four communities during the period of May through July, 1965. Additional background information and case material were collected during 1967–1969.

In the two Santiago areas, a very recent census was available from which households and respondents within them were randomly selected. In the two Lima barriadas, block and dwelling maps were used to assign areas to interviewers, who selected households and respondents by availability, although care was taken to disperse the selection throughout the area. The representativeness of our sample in the El Espíritu barriada is indicated by its close congruence in important respects, such as education, with the sample characteristics of another, more systematically designed study done there in the same year (Instituto de Investigaciones Económicas, 1965).

THE FOUR RESEARCH COMMUNITIES

The two barriadas on Lima's outskirts originated in organized invasions of undeveloped state-owned land. Pampa Seca was thus founded without active opposition in 1957, while El Espíritu's origin in 1962 was violently confronted by the police. Though both have made considerable physical progress, Pampa Seca is the much more established of the two. Its population at the time of the study was about 30,000; that of El Espíritu, about 14,000.

In 1960, 3 de Mayo (May 3) was established by invasion with little public notice in the Santiago periphery. After years of negotiation the settlement won a presumption of legal permanence from the government, and expected future large-scale assistance in home construction and urban facilities for its approximately 1,200 residents.

Santo Domingo was created in 1961 as one of the new low-cost government housing projects in the periphery of the working-class districts. It has two main types of residents, those recruited through normal administrative processes (about 70%), and those who invaded public lands and were then transferred to the project (about 30%). Legal title will be given to the residents upon completion of relatively low monthly payments on a long-term mortgage. Santo Domingo had about 12,000 residents and the best physical facilities of the four communities.

The great majority of people in these communities have had years of metropolitan experience, though originally rural and provincial. Educationally and occupationally they represent a range of urban lower-class situations, but rank well above the bottom typically. Compared to their fathers, the men in these samples are considerably more educated and better off occupationally.

POLITICIZATION: CONCEPT AND MEASUREMENT

In this study, the concept of politicization refers to the individual's awareness and psychological involvement in politics, his image of himself as an active or passive agent in it, the accessibility to him of channels leading to political decision-making, and his participation directly in politics. The four components, then, are salience, sense of efficacy, access, and participation. The measure of this relationship to politics is the politicization scale.

A typology of politicization was constructed on these four bases with survey data. (The subscales are described in the Appendix.) Since active participation is here considered the behavior that has most impact on the political process, and a logical culmination of political involvement, the highest type, D, is defined thereby. It is assumed that active participants also have some medium attitudinal or access resource, and in fact that is the case. Pobladores of the D-type are referred to also as activists or demand makers. Type C includes those who are relatively highly politicized but have not actively participated; they may be moderately politicized on all four dimensions, or highly politicized on salience, efficacy, or access dimensions. Type B includes those who show medium politicization along two or three dimensions. Type A, the lowest, is characterized by either a total lack of development on any dimension, or medium development on a single one of them. For present purposes, relationships among the dimensions will be ignored. Suffice it to say here that activism is undergirded by varying patterns of salience, efficacy, and access. There is a strong monotonic relationship in each community between each of these dimensions and activism. Activism does not occur without at least medium development of some other dimension. Except for El Espíritu, 90% to 95% of the sets of activists show more than medium development along at least one of the dimensions.

THE POLITICIZATION OF THE POBLADORES

In three of the four cases, there is a higher incidence of activism than noninvolvement, demonstrating the distinctiveness of these settlements—despite their poverty and relatively poor physical conditions—from the archetypal slum with its attendant apathy. The high level of social organization, with which Mangin (1967) characterizes Latin American squatter settlements generally and which has also been cited for these four communities (Goldrich et al., 1967), has its reflection here in political terms. In the one case where there is a relative abundance of the A-type, the El Espíritu barriada, the phenomenon seems a probable consequence of a set of political factors to be analyzed, not of low socioeconomic resources.

Politicization varies along national lines, the Chilean pair of poblaciones having more residents in the higher categories than the Peruvian pair. Thus there is an association between the structure and content of national politics (the major partisan competition between the Christian Democrats and the FRAP, and the prominence of economic- and social-policy issues such as popular housing) and the response of the poblador.

The least physically developed, least legally established, and socioeconomically lowest of the settlements, 3 de Mayo, is by a substantial margin the most politicized. Four of every ten men are activists, and there are four times more

TABLE 1. Levels of Politicization, by Community

	Politicization Type, in Percentages					
	A (low)	B	C	D (high)	Total %	n
Lima						
Pampa Seca	20	28	28	24	100	(127)
El Espíritu	31	25	24	20	100	(119)
Santiago						
Santo Domingo—Total	15	19	40	27	101	(191)
Invaders	15	15	36	34	100	(59)
Noninvaders	14	20	42	24	100	(132)
3 de Mayo	11	21	28	40	100	(98)

of the D- than the A-type. Since the national political structure is the same for both Santiago settlements, and the partisan distribution is about the same in each, the critical factor seems to be the fact that the priority need of the pobladores, housing, is highly concrete in the Chilean context, with two of the major political forces having defined alternative solutions and fiercely competing for the support of this sector. Thus, need, the seizure of land, and responsive political organizations seem to have had far more effect as politicizers than physical and social deprivation as impediments.

That the factor of relative need alone is insufficient for high politicization is indicated by the low profile in El Espíritu, the Peruvian counterpart to 3 de Mayo in the sense of being the much-less-developed settlement of the pair.

Santo Domingo's politicization profile is higher than the Peruvians' but not nearly so high as 3 de Mayo's. Given the relative similarity in background between the two Santiago sets of pobladores, and the key role of the housing political process, a reasonable assumption is that Santo Domingo's politicization may once have been as high as 3 de Mayo's and has now diminished to its present level. Regarding the two types of residents (according to the process by which they acquired a place in the settlement), it may be expected that higher initial risk, internal organization, external support, and cost were involved for the invaders than in the case of those recruited through normal administrative processes. The hypothesis is that such an invasion process is an especially politicizing experience.

In fact, the proportion of activists among the Santo Domingo invaders is higher than among the other residents, approaching that of 3 de Mayo. Even after the provision of urban facilities and the acquisition of definitive housing, the invaders still show relatively high political involvement. But it is still notable, nevertheless, that the politicization level does not equal that of those not yet benefited. Why hasn't the demand level been sustained or escalated? All needs are not felt equally, and the housing problem was a case of a particularly deeply felt need. Housing is a highly tangible matter, the attainment of which is easy for the poblador to visualize; and the major political competitors in Chile had made this an issue, detailing alternative, plausible means of meeting the need. In other areas of severe need, such as sheer economic want, alternative courses of action were not so easily conceived nor so plausibly structured by the various sets of political leaders. This last factor will be examined subsequently regarding economic needs.

THE LAGGING POLITICIZATION OF EL ESPIRITU

This barriada lags behind all the rest in politicization. There are no educational-, occupational-, income- or migrational-background differences between this and other settlements that might account for this profile. What does vary between El Espíritu and the other communities are the external and internal political circumstances surrounding their establishment. The response by the authorities to the original invasions varied. The 3 de Mayo seizure occurred quietly, and the government came later to negotiate a settlement between invaders and landowner. The invaders who later won a place in Santo Domingo were subjected to close police surveillance and constraint but not to violent suppression, though they were forcibly removed from the first site they had originally seized. Pampa Seca also was invaded without provoking a violent government reaction. El Espíritu, on the other hand, was the scene of a series of pitched battles between troops and squatters, involving some loss of life and property. In addition, the armed forces ringed the area for some time after the initial invasion so that the squatters were under constant fear that attacks would be launched to drive them off the land.

We have some survey evidence bearing on this matter for the two barriadas. The respondents were asked what problems they encountered in establishing themselves. Only 8% of the Pampa Seca sample referred to traumatic experiences with police or soldiers, but 42% of the El Espíritu sample mentioned the fighting, the encirclement, the necessity for posting night guard, and so on. In the context of this kind of background and survey data on the four settlements, we conclude that El Espíritu suffered a distinctively severe sanction.

One test of the impact of these special circumstances is the comparison of politicization profiles between original invaders and latercomers in the two barriadas, and between the invaders (the first actual residents) and duly administratively recruited residents of Santo Domingo.[2] Given (1) the typical preparation of groups planning invasion, including the important matter of taking into account the probable reaction of the relevant authorities; and (2) the heightened politicization of the immediate postinvasion period when essential services and legitimacy must be sought—entailing relatively intense dealing with officials—it is expected that the original invaders would be more politically involved than the latercomers.

The profiles are as expected in two of the three cases. Especially in Pampa Seca, but also in Santo Domingo, the original invaders are more politicized. In El Espíritu, however, there is essentially no such internal difference. Furthermore, its original invaders are much more heavily weighted toward the lowest end of the scale than the Pampa Seca counterparts.

TABLE 2. Politicization of Original Invaders versus Latercomers[a] in Three Poblaciones

	Politicization Type, in Percentages					
	A	B	C	D	Total %	n
Pampa Seco						
Original Invaders	13	36	28	23	100	(61)
Latercomers	42	21	15	21	99	(33)
El Espíritu						
Original Invaders	30	26	24	20	100	(89)
Latercomers	26	26	26	22	100	(27)
Santo Domingo						
Original Invaders	15	15	36	34	100	(59)
Latercomers	14	20	42	24	100	(132)

[a] In the case of the two barriadas, the total does not equal total sample size because two sets of respondents were eliminated from the particular analysis: those who failed to give sufficient information to permit assignment to one or another category, and those whose responses were too ambiguous to permit clear-cut assignment.

If severe negative sanctions depoliticize, how do they do so and whom do they most affect? One of the distinctions noted above in original invasion circumstances was the degree of external support. In the two barriadas, there was none, at least in any overt organized fashion. But the invaders who finally achieved sites in Santo Domingo went through a protracted struggle for it, during which considerable support was organized, principally by the Communists and Socialists, but also by Christian Democrats. We expect that external support at a time of great stress contributes to the capacity to withstand that stress without subsequent depoliticization. We can test this in the case of support by parties by comparing the politicization of nonaffiliated versus partisan affiliates among the invaders.

The hypothesis is that sanctions particularly depoliticize those unaffiliated with outside political groups. Organization should help to withstand sanctions. If so, the nonaffiliated should show the least politicization in El Espíritu where the most severe sanctions occurred, the most in Pampa Seca where no sanctions occurred, and medium in Santo Domingo where moderate sanctions occurred. The evidence supports this, both in absolute comparisons among the three sets of nonaffiliates, and in a comparison of the strength of the relationship within each community between affiliation and politicization. El Espíritu's nonaffiliated are the least politicized of the three sets, and fall the farthest behind the affiliates; Pampa Seca's nonaffiliates are the most politicized, and the closest in politicization to the affiliates.

TABLE 3. Politicization of Partisan Affiliates and Nonaffiliates Among Original Invaders in Three Communities

	Politicization Type, in Percentages					
	A	B	C	D	Total %	n
Pampa Seca						
Nonaffiliates	18	43	27	12	100	(33)
Party Affiliates	7	29	29	36	101	(28)
El Espíritu						
Nonaffiliates	54	33	9	4	100	(46)
Party Affiliates	5	19	39	37	100	(43)
Santo Domingo						
Nonaffiliates	42	21	21	16	100	(19)
Party Affiliates	2	12	43	43	100	(40)

That sanctions can be withstood through organization is no surprise. What was unexpected is the almost equal support provided by party affiliation among the El Espíritu invaders compared to the Santo Domingo invaders, when in the latter community party politicians were so much in evidence, whereas in El Espíritu, there was little overt organized help. This suggests that the merest organizational tie-in to the establishment, to the powerful, is a strong psychological support for the poor in a time of political stress.

PARTIES, PARTISANSHIP AND POLITICIZATION

The general importance of parties in the politicization of the pobladores has already been indicated. This factor will now be examined more directly. A brief description of the party system provides background.

During the study period, both countries had popularly elected governments and multiparty systems. Chile had a wide spectrum ranging from Socialists on the farther left to Communists; the two allied in the FRAP coalition, Christian Democrats, Radicals; and on the farther right, the Nationals. Frei and the Christian Democrats did very well in the 1964 and 1965 elections. Since then, competition from the FRAP has kept pace, and there has been a resurgence on the right. Both the FRAP parties and the Christian Democracy (CD) have highly developed programs for political, social, and economic change. They vary between a seeking for more independence of the United States in foreign policy and economic matters, and total rejection of United States dominance. The FRAP wants to move toward a nationalized economy, while the CD, though ideologically committed to "communitarianism," is much more ambivalent about the role of private capital. However, the CD government has moved from joint state-United States company control of the copper mines to nationalization. Both the FRAP and the CD concern themselves with massive housing plans, agrarian reform, and educational expansion.

The major Peruvian parties cannot be arrayed so readily on a programmatic basis. Acción Popular of President Belaúnde (elected in 1963) had an image of progressiveness and of a technician-directed attack on underdevelopment. Its program was diffuse and its organization weak. APRA (American Popular Revolutionary Alliance) has long been led by Haya de la Torre, one of Latin America's major politicians. The APRA has been the best-organized party, once quite radical and the bête noire of the Peruvian establishment, now moderated to the point of conservatism in an effort to win the presidency and be allowed to govern by its traditional military opposition. The third party is the Unión Nacional Odriista (UNO), the traditionally, personalistically styled following of former dictator Manuel Odría. UNO and APRA coalesced after the 1963 election, and together controlled the legislature, preventing Belaúnde from carrying out much of his program. A fourth, small Peruvian party was Christian Democracy. Its support of Belaúnde was crucial in the 1963 election. The party had some substantial political leaders, but lacked impetus and organization; it split in two.

The inability of the Belaúnde government to forestall an economic crisis, its apparently compromised position regarding nationalization of the symbolically potent International Petroleum Company, and its internal division, making likely an APRA victory in the 1969 elections, prompted the military coup of October, 1968.

The greater programmatic focus on the poor of the Chilean Christian Democrats and Marxist parties is reflected in the receptivity of the pobladores. With the slightest exception, they affiliate only with these parties, and a much higher proportion affiliates than in the Peruvian communities. The Christian Democrats have recruited far more successfully than any of the other parties, a success demonstrated at the polls in the 1964 presidential and 1965 congressional elections. The design of this study has not generated data adequate to explain their appeal, but the fact that their program included a strong appeal to the poor and that the gains were projected without coercion, conflict, and disorder may account for their differential appeal compared to the FRAP, especially given the fact that the pobladores have just achieved, or are about to, property ownership for the first time in their lives.

The partisan politicization profiles indicate that any party affiliation tends to support political involvement. As noted previously regarding the El Espíritu case, even the Acción Popular and APRA in Peru seem to function in this

TABLE 4. Politicization by Party in the Four Communities

	Politicization Type, in Percentages						
	A	B	C	D	Total %	n	% of tot. samp. affil. w/ea. party
Pampa Seca							
Nonaffiliated	30	33	24	13	100	(70)	55
Acción Popular	11	25	25	39	100	(28)	22
APRA	8	23	23	46	100	(13)	10
UNO	9	18	45	27	99	(11)	9
Other	–	–	–	–	–	(5)	4
El Espíritu							
Nonaffiliated	55	32	8	5	100	(63)	53
Acción Popular	0	17	37	46	100	(24)	20
APRA	0	9	36	55	100	(11)	9
UNO	11	22	44	22	99	(18)	15
Other	–	–	–	–	–	(3)	3
Santo Domingo							
Nonaffiliated	34	25	25	15	99	(67)	35
Christian Democracy	4	18	54	24	100	(83)	44
FRAP	3	9	40	49	101	(35)	18
Other	–	–	–	–	–	(6)	3
Santo Domingo—Invaders							
Nonaffiliated	42	21	21	16	100	(19)	32
Christian Democracy	4	18	52	26	100	(23)	39
FRAP	0	7	33	60	100	(15)	26
Other	–	–	–	–	–	(2)	3
Santo Domingo—Noninvaders							
Nonaffiliated	31	27	27	15	100	(48)	36
Christian Democracy	3	18	55	23	99	(60)	46
FRAP	5	10	45	40	100	(20)	15
Other	–	–	–	–	–	(4)	3
3 de Mayo							
Nonaffiliated	28	28	22	22	100	(32)	33
Christian Democracy	2	24	41	33	100	(42)	43
FRAP	4	8	13	75	100	(24)	24

regard though lacking a programmatic focus on the barriadas' problems; the FRAP parties with their more direct involvement in this area and their zealous activity in invasion cases seem to promote politicization most effectively. The apparent weakness of the Christian Democrats as a politicizing agent is somewhat offset by a consideration of their unsurpassed recruitment success. A part of that success may have been their capacity to mobilize for electoral purposes relatively apolitical people.

If indicators of local politicization are extracted from subscales of the overall politicization scale, rescored,[3] and combined into a local politicization scale, it provides a more refined reflection of the manner in which party organization tends to operate in these settlements.

The most outstanding aspect of the local profile is the high level of involvement of the FRAP invaders compared to all other groups. The significance of the association between FRAP organization and the invasion experience as a politicizing agent is indicated by the differentially high local involvement of FRAP invader groups compared to (1) FRAP noninvaders, and (2) Christian Democrat and nonaffiliated invaders, who either do not develop or do not sustain high local politicization. The interaction between party organization and the situation of homelessness leading to invasions is described in some case material (see Table 5).

TRANSITION IN POLITICIZATION FROM HOUSING TO ECONOMIC NEEDS: THE ROLE OF THE PARTY

Dwelling and urbanization politics is characterized by the immediacy of the need, the tangibility of the goal, and the relative feasibility of the alternative solutions proposed by the major political competitors. Other objectively significant areas of need, such as economics and education, lack some or all of these characteristics. Consequently, politicization may be less likely to develop in these areas, and may subside when the more acute dwelling and urbanization needs are met.

One way of assessing whether the poblador's politicization is likely to be sustained is to see what areas of potential demands, for example, are reflected by those who have already exhibited a high level of politicization. To the extent that they reveal little orientation toward other problem areas, it may be projected that their presently high degree of politicization will probably diminish. This would seem particularly the case in those poblaciones where dwelling and urbanization needs have been most fully met—particularly Santo Domingo, and then Pampa Seca.

Potential demands are measured here by a question asking "What could you do if you wanted to get the government to do something? What sorts of problems could you deal with this way?"[4]

By a considerable margin, Santo Domingo activists (37%) lead all others in indicating they could make demands concerning their economic and educational needs; they are followed by Pampa Seca (23%), 3 de Mayo (18%), and far behind, El Espíritu (4%). Thus in both the Santiago and Lima cases, there is evidence among the activists of a greater shift in focus from housing to broader economic (and educational) problem areas in the more established

TABLE 5. Local Politicization by Party

	Local Politicization Score[a] in Percentages					
	0	1	2	3+	Total %	n
Pampa Seca						
Nonaffiliated	53	24	17	6	100	(70)
Acción Popular	50	25	25	0	100	(28)
APRA	23	62	0	15	100	(13)
UNO	27	46	18	9	100	(11)
El Espíritu						
Nonaffiliated	51	36	11	2	100	(63)
Acción Popular	12	54	12	21	99	(24)
APRA	9	64	18	9	100	(11)
UNO	28	67	0	6	101	(18)
Santo Domingo—Total						
Nonaffiliated	64	27	8	2	101	(67)
Christian Democracy	60	27	11	2	100	(83)
FRAP	31	31	23	14	99	(35)
Santo Domingo—Invaders						
Nonaffiliated	58	26	11	5	100	(19)
Christian Democracy	57	26	13	4	100	(23)
FRAP	20	20	27	34	101	(15)
Santo Domingo—Noninvaders						
Nonaffiliated	67	27	6	0	100	(48)
Christian Democracy	62	26	10	2	100	(60)
FRAP	40	40	20	0	100	(20)
3 de Mayo						
Nonaffiliated	44	41	9	6	100	(32)
Christian Democracy	43	45	10	2	100	(42)
FRAP	25	17	21	37	100	(24)

[a] Two items concerning participation in the local association and discussion of politics with friends and neighbors provide the basis of this measure. Leadership in the local association was given two points, membership one point; frequent political discussion was given two points, occasional discussion one point.

poblaciones. But since activists in both the more and the less established Santiago poblaciones evidence this shift more than their Lima counterparts, it seems that Chilean politics is also a factor.

A closer inquiry into the basis of the relatively pronounced development of economically oriented potential demands of Santo Domingo activists reveals that neither the factor of the high level of physical development of the settlement nor a general "Chilean politics" factor accounts for the phenomenon. There is an extremely powerful partisan factor, without which the level of economically based potential demands would fall to about that of the Pampa Seca activists. Some 59% of Santo Domingo activists affiliated with FRAP conceive of taking economic or educational problems before officials for help, compared to only 20% of the Christian Democrats.

Furthermore, the same indication occurs in 3 de Mayo. Though it is in far more precarious housing and urbanization circumstances than Santo Domingo, and therefore the potential demands of its activists are heavily weighted toward that area of problems, there is an extreme partisan difference regarding the substance of political discussion engaged in by these activists. Fully half of the FRAP affiliates report discussing economic issues, compared to but 7% of the Christian Democrats.[5]

No Peruvian partisan group shows an economic potential beyond that of the Chilean Christian Democrats. Though both parties ideologically stress economic issues as they affect the poor, it is only the FRAP that seems to socialize the poblador activist to think specifically about these matters in demand terms. And it is only the FRAP that has seemed to effect the transition in the politicization of the activist from the immediate, pressing housing need to a focus on more fundamental problems.

PROSPECTS FOR SOLIDARITY, AND THE ROLE OF PARTY

During the initial stage of poblacion establishment and conquest of basic urban services, a process that may last many years, there is a strong impetus to cohesive action. Toward the end of this stage, it becomes problematic whether the pobladores either can or will find reason to maintain their solidarity. To the extent that it lapses, they are much less likely to have an impact on the economic and political situations which they may want to affect. In the following, then, we focus on the general disposition of the pobladores to work collectively on the problems they face, and on the manner in which this factor is associated with politicization, education, and partisanship. The data came from responses to the question, "Do you believe that (1) families can resolve their problems by themselves; or (2) that they have to work with others and depend on one another to resolve them?" The first alternative is taken as an indicator of an individualistic orientation to problem-solving, and the second as indicating a disposition to work collectively.

There is really no variation of significance within pairs of poblaciones regarding disposition to work collectively; the major difference is a national one, the Peruvian barriadas displaying more of this disposition. Given the national differences in extent to which the governments have taken responsibility for meeting housing-urbanization needs of the poor, the greater emphasis on collective action in Peru is not so surprising. If anything is to be won, it must be primarily through the residents' own efforts.

There is a relationship in all communities between politicization and disposition to work collectively, though it varies in strength and there are minor deviations. Apparently, as the poblador becomes more aware of and involved in politics, he comes to perceive that some degree of interdependence promotes the resolution of his problems.

Given this relationship, however, the most highly politicized Santo Dominicans show much less collectivity disposition than any other set of D scorers. This is significant because Santo Domingo is the community among the four that has come closest to attaining the full complement of housing and urbanization facilities. Thus, the relatively low collectivity disposition of its highly politicized may augur a general decline in this orientation with increasing urbanization, at least on the part of the politically most demanding group, the activists. To the extent this is so, the poblador sector is likely to lose political impact in the degree to which its needs—narrowly defined in housing-urbanization terms—are fulfilled. The remaining fundamental economic problems, for example, would not be the object of the solidary action tending to occur in the case of the other needs.

Once again, however, as in the case of the poblador's transition of political focus from the housing-urbanization syndrome to the economic, there is a party

TABLE 6. Disposition to Work Collectively, by Community, Education, and Party

	Pampa Seca	El Espíritu	Santo Domingo	3 de Mayo
Percentage disposed to work collectively	60	65	42	48
Percentage disposed to work collectively by politicization level:				
A	42	69	29	9
B	63	57	42	29
C	69	61	46	59
D	61	75	45	62
Within D level, percentage partisans disposed to work collectively:[a]				
Christian Democrats	–	–		–
FRAP	–	–		–
Percentage disposed to work collectively by education:				
0–2 yrs. primary	68	67	49	37
Intermed. primary	52	70	49	52
Complete primary	58	61	42	48
Any secondary	68	64	26	54
Within D level, percentage disposed to work collectively by education:[b]				
Less than secondary	–	–	53	–
Any secondary	–	–	23	–
Within secondary-education level percentage disposed to work collectively by party:[c]				
Christian Democrat	–	–	13	–
FRAP	–	–	50	–

[a] N of D-level Christian Democrats on which percent is based = 20, of FRAP, 17.

[b] N of D-level secondary educated on which percent is based = 13, of less than secondary, 38.

[c] N of secondary-educated Christian Democrats on which percent is based = 15, of FRAP = 8.

factor here. Among the highly politicized Santo Dominicans, the FRAP adherents show a markedly greater collectivity disposition than the Christian Democrats. As before, one notes the differential political socialization of the activist poblador, such that the parties of the FRAP tend to promote transition in focus to other problem areas, and maintenance of the collective orientation toward problem-solving.

Education may be a crucial factor with regard to disposition to work collectively. There is growing awareness in a country such as Chile that the effect of secondary education is to inculcate middle-class values in the young poblador, for which secondary education typically fails to provide the means of implementation, but which also psychologically removes the mobile, advantaged youth from any identification with his poblacion (Gurrieri, 1966).

There is no general relationship between education and collectivity orientation in the four communities. In three of the communities, the secondary educated either show more of this disposition or about the same degree of it as those less educated. However, in Santo Domingo the high school educated stand out as the least collectively oriented in their community, and compared to their relatively highly educated counterparts in the other communities, they are a great deal less disposed to work with each other. Furthermore when one looks at the effect of secondary education within the D-politicization stratum in Santo Domingo, one sees that it strongly offsets the previously mentioned tendency of the more highly politicized toward a collectivity disposition. Even though the numbers are small, it seems extremely noteworthy that among the D's only 23% of the high school educated are disposed to work collectively, compared to 53% of the less educated.

The significance of this lies in its indication that the most educated (also both scarce and potentially most socially effective) pobladores may become increasingly individualistic in pursuit of their goals once the housing-urbanization needs are close to being met. Furthermore, though it is widely assumed that the increasing access of the poor to high school education is a progressive and totally desirable phenomenon in Latin America, this pattern suggests a consequence that is dysfunctional to the political solidarity required for breakthroughs in fundamental problem areas.

Here again there is evidence of a distinctive partisan factor, the consistency of which tends to override my caution because of the small numbers on which this analysis is made. Fully half of the high school educated affiliated with the FRAP are disposed to work collectively, compared to only 13% of the Christian Democrats at the same educational level. In their function as agents of political socialization, the parties of the FRAP seem able to offset the individualizing impact of high school education, in strong distinction to Christian Democracy. Though both parties at the leadership level promote ideologies valuing organization and collective action of the poor, only the FRAP seems to effect the internalization of this principle in its poblador adherents.

The survey data provide evidence that any organizational affiliation helps support the poor through a taxing process of making a political demand. Affiliation even with parties as unrelated to the general problems of the poor as the Peruvian ones is associated with a relatively high degree of politicization, though the more direct, on-the-scene character of the FRAP parties is reflected in the even higher politicization of the invader groups they supported. Beyond this, the Chilean data provide evidence that the activist poor who support the FRAP tend to maintain a sense of solidarity and make the transition, in their thinking, about politics from the acute housing need focus to the equally acute but less vulnerable set of economic needs.

But this solidarity and disposition to consider economic demand-making has not been reflected in action. Why not? The housing needs were acute, a line of easily imaginable action existed through which to meet the needs, involving an organization through which to mobilize the people themselves and external support. But for economic needs, the situation is different. Few clear-cut lines of action have been formulated by the FRAP or any other party leadership indicating what the poor might do to change their economic condition other than to give them electoral support. This point will be raised again in the concluding section.

This analysis of the marked effectiveness of the FRAP in politicizing the pobladores derives from survey data collected at one point in time. A less systematic but more dynamic description of the manner in which the FRAP relates to the housing needs of the poor and mobilizes their political participation adds a different kind of evidence about its functioning.

THE POLITICIZATION OF "LOS SIN CASA"

The situation of many "los sin casa" (homeless) groups in greater Santiago provides evidence calling for a reconsideration of political socialization theory.[6] The los sin casa are extremely poor, young families who in increasing thousands as organized collectivities pressure the government for a housing solution. They engage in a political process of demand-making and complex pressure-building over an intense period of sometimes two years, which may culminate in an illegal act of land invasion frequently met with force—in any event, involving severe hardship. Throughout, their political behavior demonstrates a capacity for organization, discipline, and purposeful sacrifice (Giusti, 1968). Key factors seem to be an acute need, and a perceived way of meeting this need through political organization. The political and theoretical significance lie therein too, since the phenomenon shows that thousands of people, ordinarily considered to be lacking the experiences and resources to sustain concerted political action, learn to do so where their needs can be met. The focus then should shift to the general question, under what conditions is such behavior elicited?

The los sin casa are the following: families, perhaps having recently come from the provinces, living with relatives in a room; those dispossessed from center-city rooms scheduled for demolition for urban improvements; squatters on marginal lands; and renters of costly, cramped, inadequate quarters. The demand on government has also been reinforced by the fact that since so much of the lower class live in government projects, their married children and other relatives temporarily living with them come to expect an expansion of public efforts in their own behalf.

Typically the formation of a demand for housing is the first protracted political experience for the homeless. Most have only a primary education and have therefore been outside the politicizing environment of the secondary school. Nor does any union affiliation seem to involve the young men politically by this stage in their lives. Many hold marginal jobs, and the level of unemployment among them is high.

The seizure of land for homesites is a common third-world and Latin American occurrence (Abrams, 1966). In the greater Santiago area, organized land invasions on a large scale have been increasing in number ironically as successive governments have devoted increasing resources to popular housing problems. The Alessandri administration (1958–1964) engaged in large-scale construction of housing settlements for the poor, but the cost of this approach of providing definitive housing and urbanization was too great for either a conservative government such as Alessandri's, or even a reformist government such as Frei's; the latter largely discontinued the program. Frei shifted to Operación Sitio, a plan of providing sites with minimal housing and urban facilities to be developed in stages, with savings and auto-construction by the residents, with official supervision. The Frei government stands out in Latin America in the degree of its commitment to finding housing solutions for the poor. An indicator of its unparalleled accomplishments in this regard is the fact that in 1969 the last of the squatter settlements were almost totally eradicated from metropolitan Santiago, their residents having found a location in an Operación Sitio settlement.

Nonetheless, there is evidence that the program is too static and too isolated in conception to be adequate to popular needs even in the near run. With urbanward migration, natural increase, and metropolitan redevelopment, the number of poor people seeking the minimal Operación Sitio solution is growing faster than even a reformist government's capacity to acquire land in the urban periphery, urbanize it minimally, and place the needy on it.

As a consequence both of the growing need for low-cost housing solutions and growing governmental involvement in the field, demand on government has also increased. The failure of the program to keep pace has provided the Marxist-coalition opposition parties with an opportunity. Major Santiago-area land invasions by the poor with FRAP help have increased from a rate of single large-scale seizures in 1947, 1957, 1960, 1961, 1965 to two in 1967, and six major and several minor ones in 1969; more are likely in the near future. A premium is now put on organization of those seeking a housing solution from the government. The administrative process involves application for Operación Sitio (or other plans) and the opening of an account in a state bank in which quotas are deposited, representing savings for the future place in a program (Sanders, 1969). The leaders of the committees of homeless help organize the necessary documentation and quota purchases and negotiate the arrangements with the bureaucracy.

The number of committees organized to push Operación Sitio demands is very large. Some attain their goals sooner, some later, and some are delayed through what seem to the members to be political reasons.

In any case, the Communist Party and its newspaper have increasingly emphasized organization of this social sector, particularly those who encounter substantial delay in resolving housing problems. The party has only in 1969 been able to develop municipality-wide associations of homeless in the poorer metropolitan districts, plus a metropolis-wide association organized under the auspices of the major labor central, itself dominated by the FRAP. For the first time a march of the homeless of greater Santiago was carried out by the coordinating body.

THE HISTORY OF A FRAP-AFFILIATED LOS SIN CASA COMMITTEE[7]

The first step is the drawing together of an aggregate of people needing housing. Little is presently known about this stage, but it involves many grass-roots leaders and participants who have no previous public political experience. Increasingly these are becoming amalgamated into a municipality-wide organization sometimes representing several thousand families. A preliminary meeting with a representative of the housing ministry will result in a general plan, but at any stage the committee experiences irritating delay contacting the "right" bureaucrat. At some point the ministry will make a commitment to find a particular solution within a roughly specified period, assuming the fulfillment of a set of conditions by the committee. There follows a protracted period of committee activity to promote quota purchases by the membership and the maintenance of collective spirits for the difficult savings effort. From time to time, the committee returns to the officials with a progress statement in an effort to nail down the official commitment. Frequently it is difficult to locate the same official, who is "at a meeting" or "out of town," so that the committee leadership composed of working people lose pay and time. To minimize this loss, their delegations may include a congressional deputy known for his support of the homeless. If even this fails, visits are made to the communist newspaper or a popular daily that tends to make brief reports on such situations. Finally a specific set of commitments will be won.

When the committee comes close to meeting its end of the bargain, it again tries to meet with the officials to make certain that due dates will be respected. If doubt arises on this score, frequently the case, given the overextendedness of the ministry, variations in marshaling pressure are tried. In some cases marches are held to dramatize the plight of the homeless and evasion by the officials. Frustration wells up when deadlines are missed, as the cramped and desperate situation of the people is felt to be no longer supportable. A massive sit-in in the ministry has been used to stop all other official business and virtually force the bureaucracy to deal with the committee. At that juncture, feelings are so high that any anger or disdain shown by officials toward the people vastly increases the intensity of the demand, and the legitimacy felt by the committee is reinforced by their sense of broken promises. Sometimes such forced meetings reveal that the minister or key official is crucially misinformed about the nature of the "deal" between the committee and the government; in fact he may even assume from internal reports that the problem has already been resolved. Such revealed slippage also reinforces the insistence of the committee. Further steps may include a history of the process in the communist or socialist paper, an attempt to petition the president directly, and the threat to invade land as others before have done.

With the passage of a reset deadline, and after intensified organization and even a rehearsal by the committee, a land invasion occurs, usually in the early morning hours. Materials sufficient to throw up a scanty shelter are carried near the site, and at a signal the homeless rush onto the field, raise flimsy tents, each with a national flag; then comes the tactical squad of the police. Warnings will be given, entreaties made by the committee leadership together with supporting FRAP congressmen and local FRAP councilmen. Frequently the police attack to dislodge the invaders. Infrequently a few deaths occur, but there are always the injured, and tear gas, stones thrown, and a melee to create scenes of horror for the children. The people will be pushed off to the side of the road and allowed to stay there temporarily. Sometimes the matter will be resolved within days, but months may also be consumed in negotiations. The insalubrious conditions of the camps bring sickness; in winter up to forty children have died of bronchopneumonia contracted in the soaking, frigid postinvasion conditions. Food, scarce under normal circumstances, becomes even more so for lack of money and access to markets. This is made worse by the upsurge of unemployment, resulting from job loss as the men stay on the invasion site to protect their families.

In these crisis circumstances, the high level of organization achieved by the FRAP-supported (particularly the communist) committees shows itself from the outset. Discipline in the camps is tight, liquor barred, vigilance-committee assignments made, a central headquarters with loudspeaker is set up, a provisional first-aid station established; if necessary, a common soup kitchen is started. The Communist Youth is mobilized to collect food, money, and medicine. Frequently from the first day on, folksingers affiliated with the party (sometimes Chile's finest) arrive to perform, showing outside solidarity with the "heroic" invaders. Almost immediately the camp will take a symbolically potent name, such as either the date of the invasion, or a martyr created during the first invasion stages. The establishment newspapers that ignore the situation of the poor will publish stories emphasizing the breakdown of law and order and communist manipulation of the ignorant poor.

In the end, the determination and obvious suffering of the people, their large numbers, the relative legitimacy of their claims, and the furor created by FRAP congressmen and municipal officials encourage the government to negotiate a solution. After additional time necessary to minimally urbanize a site, the invasion group is transferred to their land.

The extreme hostility generated by the confrontation means that subsequent governmental assistance in urbanization will be extremely slow in coming. Nonetheless there are recent signs that the morale generated by the successful invasion and the high level of organization of the invaders carry over to animate community development efforts (Portes, 1969). Their success becomes legend in communist efforts to organize other los sin casa committees. Leaders who have arisen in the course of the experience become officers of new, more inclusive organizations of the poor. Folk singers, recruited from the invasion-established community, perform before other committees and propagate an obvious example. The community is cited repeatedly in political propaganda, which reinforces its pride and augments the meaning of its experience. Partisan follow-up may include summer vacation art classes for the children where they draw pictures of the actual invasion scenes, and parks may be established in adjoining grounds named for heroes of international communism, such as Ho Chi Minh, to promote a broader radical perspective. Foreign delegates may visit the site. Within months come announcements that so many hundred new recruits have joined the Juventud Comunista from the new invasion community. Though some undoubtedly were oriented in this direction prior to the committee experience, newspaper interviews suggest that many others were politicized and radicalized in the course of it.

CONCLUSION

This description of political processes involving the homeless does not demonstrate but provides evidence in accord with the proposition that adults, previously inexperienced and uninvolved in politics, learn to engage in and sustain complex political demand-making under certain circumstances. The most important of these seem to be a sense of acute needs, a perception of a strategy of action adequate to meeting the needs, and the availability of an organization to channel the action.

This reading of the experience of the homeless should be related to a recent study of political participation based on large-scale comparative-survey analysis. One of its principal findings was that people involved in organizations may be politically active even though they lack certain psychological bases (such as efficacy, informedness, attentiveness) frequently considered requisites of political action. Regarding organizations, the authors (Nie et al., 1969: 813) suggest that:

> Apparently mobilization opens direct lines to participation, or provides attitudinal resources relevant to specific problems only. There might be, for instance, group-initiated political discussion, group-organized contacts with political authorities, or group-related political information relevant to a specific issue.

This seems to fit the experience of many of the homeless extremely well. Moreover, the cynicism with attendant disinterest expressed by many of the poor toward government and politics seems a function of the general lack of relevance of the latter to their needs, despite much propaganda to the contrary. But when a political organizational channel exists through which an acute need can be met, then apparently information is generated, consumed, and carefully planned political efforts are made, even over a relatively long period of time.

That organizations meeting the needs of the poor are relatively rare does not excuse the tendency on the part of social science to ignore their efficacy as agencies of rapid, intense political socialization. It is precisely through the development of such organizations that the lack of political involvement of the poor may be most efficiently overcome. In fact, the analysis of survey data collected from former invader groups that had had a roughly similar experience to those of the los sin casa indicates that such organizations, after demonstrating their efficacy in meeting an acute need, proceed generally to politicize the people. The high level of politicization reflected by the FRAP invader groups is such evidence.

We have tended to look at the process of political socialization in too unstructured a fashion, the primary model being one of gradual learning by children of political information, attitudes, values, and practices through the family and school, with the national environment as a diffuse factor. The poor or lower-status sectors do tend to be politically socialized to passive, relatively apolitical roles in a polity such as ours. But increasingly numerous revolutionary cases call attention to the extraordinary amount of mass political socialization of adults, as well as children, through organizations designed to produce new men by channeling their behavior.

A consideration of recent Cuban experience shows that an extremely high level of political participation can be mobilized and sustained among the previously apolitical poor when organizations are created and officially promoted for this purpose, and when governmental policies are so directed to the needs of the poor that support is generated. The Cuban government has gone a long way toward providing security for the poor regarding housing (low rents), food, medical care, and employment. Furthermore, schooling has been vastly extended, and more than anywhere else in Latin America, equal opportunity has become the basis for recruitment to postprimary education. From all accounts I have seen, the degree of support of this government by the poor, especially the youth, has been high, as evidenced by volunteer labor, participation in the militia or Committees of Defense of the Revolution, attendance at political events, obedience to the law and to the spirit of the law, and community development efforts, even discounting substantially for political and peer-group pressures (Fagen, 1969; Hochschild, 1969; Yglesias, 1968; Trans-action, 1969; Zeitlin, 1970), and notwithstanding recent sizes of exhaustion and demoralization.

The previously mentioned comparative study of social structure and political participation finds that economic development promotes political participation by increasing the proportion of middle- and upper-class people in the society, because upper status promotes attitudinal resources and learning situations fostering participation. But even in economically developed nations, "the majority of citizens do not participate very actively in politics and do not have the attitudinal resources which lead to citizen control of public policies" (Nie et al., 1969: 825–826). Since, as previously cited, political participation also flows importantly from organization, participation can be fostered:

> It appears that the richness and complexity of organizational life might be altered somewhat independently of economic development. Deliberate governmental policies, for instance, can increase the number of citizens who are politically active. Mobilization parties . . . are one example of how this might happen [Nie et al., 1969: 826].

The further point is necessary that such deliberate participation-expanding policies may be designed to elicit participation in politically relevant activities that directly promote economic development. The multiple organized efforts of the Cuban government to recruit the citizens, including many of the young and poor, for volunteer labor such as cane-cutting or carrying literacy campaigns to the uneducated throughout the island, or the agricultural development of the Isle of Pines, are designed both to promote economic development and to transform the political culture through involvement in collective activities.

This study has focused on the way in which political organizations can relate to needs to politicize socioeconomically deprived people. In the study of political socialization, those of low status are typically found to be, and generally considered to be, low in politicization, without analyzing the power structural factors that result in this condition. By inference, the low politicization of the poor, especially in the United States, is considered normal.[8] To the extent our analysis is valid, it suggests that the politicization of the poor, or anyone else, depends crucially on organization relevant to their needs. Where such organization does not exist, the politicization of the poor will be low. Where it can function, their politicization will be higher, and where it functions with official sanction and can define as political and strive to meet a wide range of needs, their politicization will be even higher. And as the Cuban case indicates, such participation can be promoted so as to bear vitally on the work of economic development.

POSTSCRIPT

The increasing organizational effectiveness of the FRAP noted throughout this study no doubt contributed to its 1970 presidential electoral success. Throughout the preelection period the rate of land seizures intensified, and the FRAP worked hard to benefit by them. Thus the housing demands on the new administration will doubtless be heavy. Now the Allende "people's" government will be challenged to work toward a more adequate balance of citizen benefits and responsibilities than that achieved by its predecessors. It will find housing an extremely costly welfare program, particularly in competition with its economic structural-change goals. Whether it will be able to transform poblador impatience about housing needs into supportive comprehension of its overall development strategy, and whether it will be able to deal with land seizures, some of which are almost inevitable, in more constructive ways than its predecessors are crucial problems.

OTES

AUTHOR'S NOTE: *Support for this reported research came from the Ford Foundation and from the Social Science Research Council.*

1. For further description of the study and background on these communities and their urbanization context, see Goldrich et al. (1967).

2. Equivalent data distinguishing between original invaders and latecomers were unfortunately not collected in 3 de Mayo.

3. The scoring method refines that used on the general scale in that it not only segregates local indicators, but reveals intensity of local involvement rather than its mere existence.

4. This item was used to form part of the Political Efficacy Scale, a component of the overall Politicization Scale, but since we are dealing here only with the activist politicization type, no particular bias intrudes when the data are analyzed regarding area of political problem that the poblador could present to one or another governmental office.

5. In neither case is this disparity a function of the primarily FRAP control of the labor unions, which might be assumed to promote an economic problem orientation among

poblador workers. There is no difference in proportion of union members among activists of Christian Democratic or FRAP affiliation.

6. A more precise test of these propositions through natural experiments to control levels of politicization among the homeless prior to and after the demand process culminating in invasion will be, unfortunately, extremely difficult to carry out. Such a research strategy almost necessarily means a panel study, in turn requiring identification of subjects by the researcher. Since invasion is obviously illegal, and secrecy critical to its success, and since such social-research techniques are unfamiliar and such social science stigmatized by the left as a United States plot, the obstacles appear enormous.

7. The observations on which this section is based were made during relatively brief field work periods in 1965 and 1967, and an eighteen-month period in 1968–1969. During the last period, depth interviews were carried out with a small number of leaders of past and present los sin casa committees, some of whom participated in invasions. In addition, newspaper files were compiled, periodic visits made to invasion sites, meetings of los sin casa committees were attended, and interviews were held with party and ministry officials concerned with the problem. Data were collected from at least some participants affiliated with all of the relevant political parties. The description generally is drawn from the experience of six major invasions in the 1967–1969 period.

8. On the politicization potential of the American working and poorer sectors, see Lipsitz (1970).

REFERENCES

Abrams, C. (1966) Man's Struggle for Shelter in an Urbanizing World. Cambridge, Mass.: MIT Press.

Fagen, R. (1969) The Transformation of Political Culture in Cuba. Stanford, Calif.: Stanford Univ. Press.

Giusti, J. (1968) "Rasgos organizativos en el poblador marginal urbano latinoamericano." Revista Mexicana de Sociología 30 (Enero–Marzo): 53–77.

Goldrich, D., et al. (1967) "The political integration of lower-class urban settlements in Chile and Peru." Studies in Comparative International Development 3: 1–22.

Gurrieri, A. (1966) "Situacion y perspectivas de la juventud en una poblacion urbana popular." Revista Mexicana de Sociología 28 (Julio–Septiembre): 571–602.

Hochschild, A. (1969) "Communism on Treasure Island: Cuba's Isle of Pines." Liberation 14 (December): 15–21.

Instituto de Investigaciones Económicas. (1965) Estudio Socioeconómico de una Barriada Lima: Universidad Nacional Mayor de San Marcos.

Langton, K. (1969) Political Socialization. New York: Oxford Univ. Press.

Lipsitz, L. (1970) "On political belief: the grievances of the poor." P. Green and S. Levinson, eds., Power and Community, pp. 142–172. New York: Vintage.

Mangin, W. (1967) "Latin American squatter settlements: a problem and a solution." Latin American Research Rev. 2 (Summer): 65–98.

Nie, N., B. G. Powell, Jr., and K. Prewitt. (1969) "Social structure and political participation: developmental relationships, II." Amer. Pol. Sci. Rev. 63 (September): 808–832.

Portes, A. (1969) Cuatro Poblaciones: Informe Preliminar sobre Situación y Aspiraciones de Grupos Marginados en el Gran Santiago. Santiago: Programa Sociología del Desarrollo de la Universidad de Wisconsin.

Sanders, T. (1969) "Juan Pérez buys a house." American Universities Field Staff Reports, West Coast South America Series 16, 2: 1–17.

Trans-action (1969) "Cuba: ten years after." (special issue) 6 (April).
Yglesias, J. (1968) In the Fist of the Revolution. New York: Pantheon.
Zeitlin, Maurice. (1970) Revolutionary Politics and the Cuban Working Class. New York: Harper.

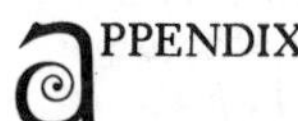PPENDIX

CONSTRUCTION OF THE POLITICIZATION SCALE

The scale is based on four subscales, the first three of which are simply aggregative. High, medium, and low scores were made on each subscale.

Salience. This is measured by an item on interest in what government does, two open-ended opinion items in which the expression of an opinion is considered an indicator of political salience, and an open item about anything that has happened in politics the respondent considers to have affected his life very much.

Sense of Personal Political Efficacy. This is based on two items, one of which concerns whether one's role is only as a passive recipient of government action or an active agent that can influence government action; and an open item about what one might do to get government to act or cease acting in a given way.

Access. Channels of access into decision-making processes are indicated by affiliation with a political party, membership in unions and the local association of the community, and knowing someone who can help one make use of government programs.

Participation. Unlike the previous subscales, participation is not merely aggregative. High participation is defined as having discussed politics in at least two contexts (described below), plus having directly tried to get government to do something, or having attended political meetings, or having taken part in demonstrations. Medium participation is defined as either discussion in two contexts, or at least one of the more concerted activities, while low participation is defined as having done neither of those. The discussion contexts are defined as at least occasional discussion of politics with family, or friends, or coworkers, or politicians, or, a separate item, any discussion of the Dominican Revolution, a major international event that occurred just prior to the survey.

Politics, Power, and the Role of the Village Priest in Paraguay

FREDERIC HICKS

Much of what has been written about "the Church in Latin America" is strongly partisan, praising or condemning its role, whether as a monolithic obstacle to progress or as a breeding-ground of social discontent. Controversy among priests and church officials

---

From *Journal of Inter-American Studies* IX (1967), 273–282. Copyright © Pan American Foundation 1967. Reprinted by permission of the author and the University of Miami Press.

over what they ought to do is heated enough; this paper is one of the few studies that tells what a cleric in a politically strategic position actually does. Although he might not understand the term, it is clear that this Paraguayan priest often serves as a crucial "culture broker" for his parishioners (cf. Wolf).

Frederic Hicks is Associate Professor of Anthropology at the University of Louisville, Kentucky. His published articles include reports on archeological research in Mexico and on political anthropology in Paraguay, where he taught as a Fulbright-Hays Fellow.

I

The parochial priests in small Paraguayan towns are generally reputed, in Paraguay, to exercise an extraordinary amount of power and influence over the people of their parishes—to a greater extent, it would seem, than in most other Latin American countries. This is, moreover, despite the fact that the church, as an institution, is considerably weaker, economically and politically, than in all but a handful of such countries. Therefore, what power the individual priest may have can not be viewed as simply an extension of the power of the church. Most urban Paraguayans, including at least some members of the church hierarchy, are inclined to attribute this situation to the alleged superstitious or credulous nature of the Paraguayan peasants. The rural people themselves, on the other hand, are apt to explain the influence of their own local priest, at least, as due to his personal qualities or strength of character, as did the Services when referring to the prestige of the local priest of Tobatí.[1]

In this paper, an alternative explanation will be offered, one based on the social and political structure of rural Paraguayan towns. It will be suggested that this structure is such as to provide a role—that filled by the village priest—which offers its occupant extraordinary opportunities to achieve a position of very high prestige, power, and influence. Merely by occupying this role, the priest, given a certain minimum of natural ability on his part and an inclination to take advantage of the opportunities his role affords, may in many cases be virtually forced into a position of community leadership.

The analysis which follows is based on observations in one Paraguayan town. Capiatá, which is located in the relatively densely populated central part of Paraguay, 20 kilometers from Asunción.[2] Since there was no opportunity to make comparative studies, the analysis can not be applied automatically to Paraguay generally, but as will be seen, the forces affecting the priest's role in Capiatá are of such a nature as to be present and operative in other towns as well.

II

The town of Capiatá has a population of about 2,000, although its entire *distrito*—a unit somewhat comparable to a large New England township or a small county—has a population of about 23,000, according to the latest census figures. The resident priest, who serves the whole *distrito*, is a native of Capiatá. As is typical for this part of Paraguay, the landholding pattern is one of small, family-owned or family-managed plots; there are no large plantations. Some large landholdings do exist, but they are worked by sharecroppers or squatters, much as if they were constituted of small holdings. Neither the church nor the priest is a landowner, and this also is typical. The principal, and practically the only source of employment in the vicinity is the *Compañía Algodonera Paraguaya, Sociedad Anónima* (CAPSA), a factory located one kilometer from the town, which, financed largely by Uruguayan capital, manufactures vegetable oils, animal feed, solvents, fertilizers, and other by-products of local raw materials, and which employs between 250 and 600 workers, depending on the season. Most of the workers come from Capiatá, but the managers live in Asunción.[3]

Before describing the priest's role, it is necessary to describe the social and political structure which gives rise to the distinctive features of that role. Of primary importance, in this regard, is the near universality of membership in one or the other of the two traditional political parties, Liberal and Colorado. Virtually all Paraguayans, above all in the rural areas, consider themselves as belonging to one or the other of these two parties.[4] This pattern has considerable time depth. Both parties were founded in 1887; the Liberal party was formed first by a group of businessmen and their intellectual and professional allies to defend their interests against a clique which, with the support of the government, threatened to monopolize economic opportunities. In response, members of the ruling clique formed, later in that same year, the *Asociación Nacional Republicana,* also called the *Partido Colorado* after the red banner it adopted as its emblem (the Liberals adopted the color blue).[5]

Through a network of friendships, personal loyalties, and group interests, membership in one or the other of these two parties spread throughout the country, involving people of all social classes. Today, their respective numerical strength is estimated to be approximately equal for the country as a whole, although there are communities or regions in which one predominates over the other. The basis for party affiliation was not, and still is not, ideological. To the extent that the parties had or have any ideological content, they could both be characterized as "liberal" in the 19th-century sense. The significance of this is that neither party is markedly more pro-clerical than the other; they were formed at a time when economic liberalism was in its ascendancy, and the church, its power effectively broken during Francia's dictatorship (1814–1840), was not sufficiently powerful for either incipient party to seek its support.[6]

The parties grew and flourished because of their function as mutual aid societies and pressure groups, through which members hoped to increase their economic advantages. In other words, the two traditional parties are patronage parties, designed to serve the individual interests of their clients. Probably as a result of this function, both parties tend to become divided into factions, on either the national or the local level, particularly when in power.

Especially in the rural areas, everyone must have a party affiliation—a commitment to one or the other party, or to one of the factions within the party if such exist. This commitment must be made known, because one can not deal normally with a person without knowing what his commitment is. One doesn't know how to interpret what he says, or how one's own statements will be interpreted. Paraguayans are very adept at seeing the functional relations between politics and other aspects of their culture, and practically everything has its political significance. Neutrality is socially impossible. If someone were to try to maintain an attitude of neutrality or aloofness, it could only mean that he had something to hide, and he would be viewed with suspicion. He might be a spy, or an informer, or a "communist"—that is, someone who works secretly toward vaguely evil ends. There are people who would prefer to "stay out of politics," that is, to remain neutral, generally for business or professional reasons, but they find this difficult. The author knows of one case, that of a doctor newly arrived in Capiatá from Asunción to take charge of the local health center, who attempted to keep out of the factional dispute within his (Colorado) party, but the result of his efforts was that neither faction trusted him until he accepted identification with one of them. Once an individual's commitment is known, then, even if he belongs to the opposition, one can deal with him in a normal, friendly manner.

One must remain loyal to his party, as well as to his particular party faction. To "turn corners," that is, to switch parties, is viewed as a betrayal of a set of personal loyalties and obligations built up over a long period of time and often extending several generations into the past. In individual cases, there may arise compelling reasons for switching, almost always to the party in power, for considerations of personal advantage or material gain, such as employment opportunities or greater freedom of activity. But since it is not considered likely that one could change parties because of a change in his ideological convictions, but only for reasons of self-interest, a person who would do so is naturally regarded as untrustworthy.

The political system of Paraguay has been, ever since the late 19th century, of the "caudillo" type, in which leaders who acquire a large following by means which include the use of traditional party loyalties, jockey for positions of political power, supported by followers who expect a share of the spoils if he succeeds. This is the basis for the formation of factions, for dissatisfied elements often get together to try to unseat the leader. Political office, from the presidency on down, is sought for the power it brings, chiefly through the opportunities to bestow patronage. Since the Colorado party is presently in power, it is expected that the economic opportunities that arise will go to Colorados rather than to Liberals.

On the local level, the political activity of party members is coordinated by units called *comités* in the case of the Liberals and *seccionales* in the case of the Colorados. Each such unit is composed of a president, a series of minor officials, and a dozen or so members at large, chosen at regular intervals in elections supervised by the party leadership in Asunción. These local officials are expected to look after the welfare of party members within their area, and this includes seeing to it that as large a share as possible of the relatively scarce economic opportunities are used so as to benefit fellow party members, especially those that are most loyal. Since it is the Colorado party that is in power, the president of the *seccional* is aided and encouraged in his efforts by the national government, and he is therefore likely to be a very powerful figure. The Liberal leader is at a definite disadvantage; but by virtue of their numbers, the Liberals can, if organized as a bloc, exert a certain amount of economic and political pressure.

The president of the *seccional* shares in the municipal government with the *intendente*, or mayor, and the *comisario*, or police chief, both appointive offices (that of *intendente* was made elective late in 1965). Although the *intendente* is theoretically the chief municipal official, he is likely to be overshadowed in actual power by the president of the *seccional.* The spoils system operates on the national level, so these offices, as well as all others, are held by Colorados, regardless of local sentiment; in Capiatá, for example, it is estimated that the population is from 60 to 75 percent Liberal.

Because of the nature of the political system and the character of the two traditional parties, it is expected, in Capiatá as in other towns, that if community matters—whether these are disputes between individuals, fund raising activities, or relations between the community and outside groups—are channeled through the officially constituted authorities, political considerations will prevail over what is generally regarded by the community as its best interests. To insure the smooth functioning of the social system, therefore, some mechanism is needed for achieving a balance between conflicting political interests, and for by-passing the constituted authorities when their aims and obligations would seem to come into conflict with the welfare of the community. The priest, it is here suggested, provides that mechanism.

III

The duties of a resident priest in any small Latin American community are such as to make him a relatively prominent figure. He officiates at mass, and his presence is required at baptisms, funerals, and other important occasions. Under any circumstances, he would probably figure among the dozen or so most prominent men of the community. But in Paraguay, there is often another factor that helps to give him still greater power. He is expected to be, and generally is, politically neutral. Moreover, he is the only one in the entire community who is expected, or even permitted, to be neutral. He is therefore in the truly unique position of being able to mediate between rival interests without being suspected of political favoritism. He is the only one who can, potentially, gain the confidence of all villagers, of whatever political affiliation, to an equal degree.

The nature of the priest's role as a political neutral, and the way in which this gives him power and influence, are illustrated by the following examples.

A common way of effecting local civic improvements in Paraguay is through the formation of a *comisión*, composed of prominent citizens of the community. The responsibilities of the *comisión* are to collect money, labor, and equipment from members of the community who are able to provide them and, when necessary, to solicit the cooperation of the appropriate government agency. Improvements which have been effected in this way in Capiatá in recent years include an addition to the local government health center, an extension of the electrical lines, the beautification of the church plaza, and road improvement. In other communities, such things as road construction, school construction and repair, or drainage works may be involved.

In Capiatá, as in other communities, political factions, and especially the Colorado *seccional* president and his followers (with encouragement from the national party leadership), frequently seek to dominate the *comisiones* in order to have a decisive voice in the use of the collected funds and equipment, and to guide their use so as to benefit their own followers, regardless of whether the stated project is realized—something those not benefited by such maneuvers try to prevent. It is generally held, therefore, that the *comisión* will have a greater chance of success in achieving its stated objective if "politics is kept out of it," which in effect means that the *comisión* should be politically "balanced." It should include representatives of both parties and be dominated by neither, lest members of the other party be reluctant to cooperate with and contribute to the *comisión*. In order to achieve a balance between political interests, however, the president of the *comisión* should ideally be politically neutral, and the only prominent person in the community who has this qualification is likely to be the priest. In Capiatá, the priest turns out to have been the president of every *comisión* that has achieved its aim, and the people of Capiatá give him credit for most of the civic improvements in their community in recent years.

In an underdeveloped, non-industrialized country like Paraguay, salaried jobs are scarce. Employment, therefore, is an excellent form of reward for political loyalty or minor political services, and since the Colorado party is in power, the *seccional* is expected to try to secure such rewards. In Capiatá, the CAPSA factory is the only large employer, and the *seccional* naturally makes efforts to obtain employment there for its loyal party workers. It is here that the private employer, necessarily concerned with efficient management of the business and responsible to its stockholders (in this case, largely foreign), regardless of personal political preferences, may be caught in the middle. For business reasons, he prefers that "politics be kept out of it." This requirement is understood by the officials of the appropriate branches of the national government. On the other hand, these same officials also expect the local *seccional* president to perform his own job well, and they know he is doing so when he pressures local employers on behalf of loyal party members.

Some mechanism is needed whereby the factory can maintain effective relations with the community, while still placing efficiency above politics and exercising some control over its hiring practices. But it must be some mechanism which does not involve the national government, whose officials would be obligated to side with the *seccional* president should a dispute arise between the *seccional* and the factory. The priest provides that mechanism; he has become the principal intermediary between the factory and the community. He is the only one through whom the factory can maintain good relations with the whole community, all factions included. He is the only one from whom the factory management can receive a recommendation for employment and not suspect it of being politically motivated. This position as intermediary naturally enhances the priest's power in the community, but it is a position he can only hold because of his political neutrality. If he were openly Liberal, the factory could not deal with him for fear of antagonizing a segment of the community with ties to powerful government officials—and Paraguayan communities are always alert to signs of political favoritism. If he were openly Colorado, he would be overshadowed in importance by the *seccional* president.

An example of the priest's use of his power and influence is provided by his role in the formation of the union of CAPSA workers (Paraguayan law permits only company unions, although they are grouped into the government-controlled *Confederación Paraguaya de Trabajo*). The factory had long opposed the formation of a union, and any attempt by an employee to organize one was grounds for his dismissal. Eventually, however, the employees succeeded in organizing a union by working very rapidly, one Saturday afternoon after leaving the plant, and so were already in a position to exert pressure on the management by the time work resumed on Monday. To show their strength, the leaders of the union wanted to stage a two-and-a-half-hour strike on that Monday and a rally in front of the factory. The priest opposed this plan—arguing that a strike should be reserved for a last resort—because he thought it would exacerbate relations between the management and the local workers, but he was unsuccessful (some union leaders were from neighboring towns, not so subject to the influence of the Capiatá priest). The factory managers, at home in Asunción, got word that something was afoot and, fearing the worst, such as an attack on the factory, had a large number of police sent to Capiatá from Asunción. By Sunday morning, the town was bristling with police.

At this point, the union leaders went to the priest to ask his advice. He went to the police officer in charge and was driven in a police vehicle to the Asunción home of one of the principal directors of the factory. He told the director that the workers were determined to form a union and to stage a strike that would completely paralyze factory operations. He advised that by accepting the union and not firing the organizers, the management could probably avoid a strike, or at worst have only a short symbolic one. This was agreeable; presumably the management wished to avoid antagonizing the priest. The police, seeing the priest's ability to control matters and his influence among all concerned, agreed to remove their forces from Capiatá, leaving only a small detachment stationed at the factory. The priest was then able to persuade the union to call off its rally at the factory and simply stay home for the two-and-a-half-hour strike period.

As stated at the outset, we have no evidence that the power the village priests are reputed to have in other Paraguayan communities is due to the same factors that operate in Capiatá, but the significant structural features are present also in most other towns. It may be hypothesized that a priest in a "one-party" parish would not exercise the same kind of power that the priest of Capiatá does. There are very few one-party communities. Some neighborhoods or *compañias* (outlying parts of *distritos*) are inhabited exclusively by members of one or the other political party, but in rural areas they do not have their own resident priests. The writer made the acquaintance of the priest in charge of the church in Barrio Presidente Stroessner, a new low-cost suburban development on the outskirts of Asunción. The 182 households of this community were all solidly Colorado. The community was administered by, and had originally been developed by, three military officers (all Colorados, since a military career is open only to members of this party at present). Though none of the three was a resident, one of them tended to be regarded as responsible for and to the community in a paternalistic way. In such an environment, the politically neutral priest has virtually no place. The priest (who happens to be a Spaniard by nationality, which introduces a new variable) was decidedly not in a position of influence; he was unable to elicit support and cooperation in at least one civic project he tried to promote, and indeed, was the subject of a variety of malicious rumors.

The question arises as to how neutral the native Paraguayan priest really is.

He is the product of a culture in which political affiliation is expected, and his family presumably adheres to these norms. In Capiatá, for example, the priest is known to come from a Colorado family, and his brother is presently active in local Colorado politics. It should be kept in mind, however, that to adopt a position of neutrality would not normally involve giving up any ideological convictions. Many Paraguayans would prefer to be neutral, but social pressures work against this. The priest, on the other hand, is subject to social pressures which work in the opposite direction. So great is the need in the community for a prominent neutral figure and the desire to cast the priest in that role, that the people may even overlook occasional indications that the priest is perhaps not totally neutral in sentiment. The people of the community, including Liberal political figures, want him as a neutral, and he will apparently be accepted as such if he does not act to the advantage of one party or faction over another. From time to time, the priest in Capiatá is accused of political favoritism, but significantly, all factions of both parties have made such accusations, and it is always a rival group he is supposed to be favoring.

It is quite possible, of course, that an individual priest may choose not to take advantage of the opportunity to be politically neutral, or because of his political antecedents he may be unable to do so. I am informed that in the town of Luque, the chief chaplain of the Paraguayan army has been serving as priest, and he is militantly Colorado. However, it is said that many people of Luque have a very cynical attitude toward him, refusing to attend confession, and his influence in local civic affairs appears insignificant. He is gradually being replaced by a younger priest who is politically neutral, and this younger priest is evidently more favorably received.

The purpose of this paper has been to offer an explanation for the power and influence attributed to the priests of rural Paraguayan towns. The situation in the town of Capiatá was described, and it is suggested that the same or similar factors may be found to operate in other towns as well. The Paraguayan political structure is such that a prominent individual who is politically neutral is needed in the community to serve as an intermediary in a variety of situations. There is no reason why the individual who assumes this role must necessarily be the priest, but if there is a priest in the town, he is the one most likely to have the necessary qualifications. The priest may not always take full advantage of the potentialities of the role, but there are pressures on him to do so, and if he does, the role is such that, given just a minimum of natural ability, he can become a very influential and powerful person.

OTES

1. Elman R. Service and Helen S. Service, *Tobatí: Paraguayan Town* (Chicago: University of Chicago Press, 1954), pp. 84–85.

2. Field work in Capiatá was carried out intermittently between April and August, 1965, while the author was a lecturer in anthropology at the Universidad Nacional de Asunción, under the Fulbright-Hays program. Dr. Egidio Picchioni, of the Ministerio de Salud Pública y Bienestar Social, collaborated in the field work.

3. Frederic Hicks and Egidio Picchioni, "Algunos aspectos de la industrialización en una comunidad paraguaya," *Suplemento Antropológico de la Revista del Ateneo Paraguayo*, Vol. II, núm. 1 (Diciembre 1966), pp. 31–54.

4. Two other political parties which have legal status in Paraguay at present are the Febrerista and the recently-formed Demócrata Cristiano. However, their membership is small and is concentrated among the urban bourgeoisie. While occasional members are to be found in the rural areas, the parties themselves do not function there in the same way as do the traditional parties.

5. Efraín Cardozo, *Paraguay independiente* (Barcelona: Salvat Editores, 1949); pp. 287–288; Carlos Centurión, *Historia de la cultura paraguaya* (2 Vols. Asunción: Biblioteca "Ortiz Guerrero," 1961), I, 408 ff.

6. This has not always been understood by North American writers, and deserves some clarification. In recent years, the Colorado Party has consciously sought to identify itself with such traditional conservative parties as the Blancos of Uruguay and the Conservadores of Colombia, but this is not an old tradition of the party, and one suspects it is intended today primarily to obtain foreign good will. Occasionally also, toward the end of the period of Liberal dominance (1904–1940), opposition Colorado propagandists sometimes took stands against Liberal principles, which were by then becoming outmoded. However, when the actual behavior of the two parties in government, particularly during their formative decades, is examined, the liberalism of both is apparent.

The Asymmetrical Implications of Godparenthood in Tlayacapan, Morelos

JOHN M. INGHAM

The Roman Catholic institution of godparenthood, widespread and important in Latin America, has social implications apart from its theological basis. Most analysts have stressed its function as a means of extending the coparents' range of reciprocal obligations, by establishing quasi-kin relationships through ritual means. In this paper, quantitative data from a Mexican community forcefully support the complementary transactional view of compadrazgo *as a way of affirming patron-client contracts (cf. Foster).*

John M. Ingham is Associate Professor of Anthropology at the University of Minnesota. His studies of Mexican peasants have been focused on physical and mental health, world view, and social organization.

Social hierarchy takes on mystery and legitimacy when dressed in spiritual rhetoric and ritual. Social position may be further enhanced with acts of

From *Man* (new series), V, (1970), 281–289. © Royal Anthropological Institute 1970. Reprinted by permission of the author and publisher. The author has made minor editorial revisions.

patronage, that is, when persons give economic assistance in return for deference, prestige, and ritual acknowledgement of their higher social status (Leach 1961; Homans 1961; Blau 1964). The aim of this article is to show that in the Mexican village of Tlayacapan, and perhaps throughout Latin America, *compadrazgo* (co-parenthood) is asymmetrical in the sense that godparent selections are not reciprocated, and that the rights and obligations based upon this relationship are not precisely the same for each co-godfather and family. This asymmetry may or may not entail differences in social status; when it does, we may regard *compadrazgo* as a patron-client relationship couched in a religious idiom (Foster 1963). Statistical data from Tlayacapan indicate that hierarchical, or patron-client, *compadrazgo* occurs far more often than one would expect by chance, and conversely that horizontal *compadrazgo*, although common, is less frequent than would be predicted on *a priori* grounds. Moreover, the ethnography suggests that the selection of social equals as *compadres*, which otherwise seems inconsistent with the asymmetrical aspects of the institution, can be understood in terms of the structural implications for *compadrazgo* of status inequality.

Compadrazgo has become a pervasive feature of rural society in Latin America since several Catholic rites of passage are felt to require the selection of a godfather (*padrino*) and/or godmother (*madrina*) to sponsor the godchild (*ahijado-a*). The godfather and godmother become respectively *compadre* (co-father) and *comadre* (co-mother) to the child's father and mother; between *compadres* (godparents and parents) these terms are used reciprocally. When two people have become *compadres* they address each other with the respectful *Usted* form of the personal pronoun, and the bond is deemed so sacred that adultery or marriage between them is regarded as incestuous. In addition to mutual respect, this relationship involves prestations and counter-prestations, including the godparent's act of sponsorship, a fiesta given in his honour, and informal exchanges of food and drink, loans, work and favours in return for political alliance (Friedrich 1958; Foster 1961; 1963; Ravicz 1967).

Godparenthood can be said to mirror social hierarchy if people select godparents of higher status. Although Foster (1953: 9; 1961: 1182; 1969: 265–67) states that most *compadres* are social equals, other investigators generally report that the selection of superiors occurs frequently, and that the primary motive in making such a choice is the expectation of personal benefit.[1] In Latin American communities which have a caste structure of Ladinos at the top and Indians at the bottom, godparenthood is asymmetrical in that Indians select Ladinos, but the latter rarely choose the former (Gillin 1951: 61; Reichel-Dolmatoff 1961: 172; Martinez 1963: 129–30; Reina 1966: 231; Osborn 1968: 593; Vogt 1969: 31). Many studies find that just as, in the expectation of help, the parent of lower status seeks a godparent of higher status for his child, the godparent receives prestige in return, and this prestige is augmented by the number of children he sponsors (Redfield & Villa Rojas 1934: 99; Gillin 1951: 62; Wagley 1953: 157; Wolf 1956: 208; Stein 1961: 135; Martinez 1963: 138).

Tlayacapan is a village of 3,000 Spanish-speaking and apparently *mestizo* people in north-central Morelos which nevertheless preserves features of a closed, corporate, Indian community, including communal lands, an elaborate fiesta system, resistance to immigration, and the persistence of the Nahuatl language in its surrounding hamlets and among some aged people in the village itself. Before the revolution of 1910, the village had a caste structure of a small *criollo/mestizo* elite and a larger population of Indians. Members of the elite were not sponsors of village or neighbourhood fiestas and thus did not redistribute their wealth in this way. But they were often godparents to the humbler people; and those who owned stores gave expensive Christmas parties (*posadas*) to which all were invited.

Today, *compadrazgo* ties permeate Tlayacapan's social fabric and in many instances unite villagers with wealthy people in larger communities outside. A child acquires godparents of baptism, first communion, confirmation, and marriage; these are the most significant and are known together as godparents *de sacramento*. But there are other types of *compadrazgo* of lesser importance. Indeed by the time a man's child has become an adult, the father may have more *compadres* than he can easily remember.

When villagers pass one another on the street they usually exchange perfunctory greetings. However, *compadres* (especially a *compadre* and a *comadre* or two *comadres*) stop to shake hands and exchange pleasantries. Formerly, a parent paid respect to his child's godfather by kissing his hand, particularly if the latter were his social superior. This custom is rare today, although one often sees godchildren kissing the hands of their godparents, and adults sometimes kiss the hands of their parents' godparents. When asked what is important about *compadrazgo*, most villagers say 'respect.' In addition to the show of deference to the *padrino* and of mutual respect between parents and godparents, the relationship involves the reciprocal obligation to give gifts and pay expenses for ceremonies which may absorb a substantial portion of a family's annual income. The godfather's first responsibility is sponsorship of his godchild's religious rite. A marriage *padrino* selected by the groom's family may spend several thousand *pesos* on a wedding fiesta. The marriage godparents become *compadres* to other godparents of the bride and groom, since they are co-parents to the same people; thus, in theory, ties are greatly ramified, and the economic obligations of the marriage *padrinos* are compounded. Moreover, the marriage godfather is expected to sponsor the baptism of the couple's first child. If he does so, he purchases new clothes for the godchild, pays the priest, and throws coins to children waiting on the church steps. For the small fiesta given in his honour by the parents, he brings one or two bottles of rum, an expensive luxury for most Tlayacapenses. Some days later he and his wife return with food to show their appreciation for having been chosen as godparents. As the godchild grows older, the godparents are expected to aid the parents economically if the child becomes ill, and they also assume responsibility for the costs of his funeral if he dies, and adopt him if he is orphaned.

The expenses to godparents who sponsor confirmation or first communion may be even greater initially since the clothes they must buy for their godchildren are expensive. On these occasions also parents give a fiesta in honour of the sponsor, who reciprocates with gifts of rum and food. In general, *padrinos de sacramento* are expected to look after the spiritual welfare of their godchildren, aid them in negotiating their marriages, and help them, after marriage, to iron out quarrels and maintain wedding vows.

The non-*de sacramento compadrazgo* relations generally involve fewer and less costly obligations. On graduation from the sixth grade in school a student acquires a godparent, who gives his godchild a present. When a girl turns fifteen, a fiesta *de quince años*, a kind of coming out party, is given for her at which she acquires another godparent who pays for a special mass held at this time and bears the cost of the music and part of the food for the fiesta. Twelve *compadres de evangelios* (of blessings) may be selected to help to cure a child suffering from *susto* (an illness attributed to soul-loss). They take the child to the priest to be blessed, and buy him a religious pendant and a suit of clothes. Having little lasting significance, these *compadres* are humorously referred to as 'sunflower *compadres*.' People who buy a house, store, or tractor give a fiesta and select a *compadre de estreno* (of breaking in), who pays the priest to bless the new possessions and to prevent the bad luck which newness is thought to bring. A *compadre de la cruz* (of the cross) may be sought by a member of a bereaved family in order to help to defray the costs of a funeral.

I have described the first duties of *compadres* in Tlayacapan; following these, the relationships formed are sustained over time by many small exchanges of gifts and favours. *Comadres* often send each other food, and in emergencies men turn to *compadres* for loans since they have more trust (*confianza*) in them. Sometimes *compadres* help one another with farm work, and when a man gives a fiesta, he customarily invites his *compadres*. Exchange behaviour and mutual respect are found in all categories of *compadrazgo*, yet we note that the relationship is asymmetrical in some respects. Financial obligations are heavier for the *padrino*, whereas the godchild and his parents treat the *padrino* with greater respect. Symbolically, the superordination of godparents is implied by the notion of 'spiritual' parents.

If the ethnographic description given above is accurate, the asymmetry in *compadrazgo* should be reflected in patterns of selecting godparents; that is, we should find that social superiors are frequently chosen, and that choices are not reciprocated. To test this proposition, I gathered data in 1966 in Tlayacapan on the selection of baptismal godparents. On the assumption that information on economic status would be more reliable, I limited my examination to 155 children who were three years of age or younger. (Of 186 children in this age group, ten had not been baptised, and 21 others were excluded because it seemed desirable to include only one child per family.[2]) The scaling of the economic statuses of parents and godparents was done by giving a point for each of the following: ownership of a home; each room above one in the house (e.g. three points for four rooms); electric power in the home; gas stove; sewing machine; radio; television set; and one point for each store-bought bed.

One manifestation of asymmetry in these selections is the striking absence of reciprocated choices; only one of the 155 families whose choices were examined was also chosen by a family they had selected. (This statement is based on all baptismal selections by the families under consideration and is not limited to those made during the three years before the census was taken.) The lack of

TABLE 1. Status of Parents and Godparents

Status of parents	Status of godparents				
	0–4	5–8	9–12	13+	Out-of-town
0–4	6	28	13	2	10
5–8	5	29	19	4	9
9–12	2	9	11	1	5
13+	0	1	1	0	0

reciprocated selections cannot be construed to mean that there is no inclination to reinforce existing *compadrazgo* relations since 21 percent of all choices made for second and subsequent children were repetitions of previous selections. Both initial selection, and reinforcement of existing linkages, are asymmetrical. Further evidence of asymmetry is that Tlayacapenses may serve as *padrinos* to families in nearby hamlets, but there is no indication of the reverse. By contrast, 15 percent of baptismal godparents selected by residents of Tlayacapan itself live in larger towns or cities.[3]

A convincing demonstration of the hierarchical character of *compadrazgo* is provided by the frequency with which people choose godparents of higher socioeconomic status than their own. Table 1, which compares the status of godparents with that of the families which selected them, reveals many upward choices. However, it is important to note that since the poor outnumber the rich in a stratified population like Tlayacapan's, the question turns not only on the percentage of upward choices, but on the difference between the *a priori* probability of a selection pattern (given the population's distribution by status), and the actual distribution of selection by status level. A random model of godparent selection would predict that the distribution of choices should be proportional to the distribution of potential godparents. On the other hand, if hierarchy exerts an influence on selection, a deviation should occur between the distribution of choices by status categories, and the distribution of a measure of potential godparents, say, all village households (see Table 2).[4] A sensible statistic for testing the difference between two sample distributions is their maximum deviation. The asymptotic distribution of this statistic has been derived and tabulated by Smirnov (1948); its value in the present case is 28.1 and occurs in column 0–4. For sample sizes of 131 and 503 this value has significance at $P<.001$, and demonstrates that the selection of social superiors far exceeds the level of expected frequency.

TABLE 2. Deviation Between the Status Distributions of Godparent Selections and Households

Status	0–4	5–8	9–12	13+	N
Percentages of godparent choices	9.9	51.2	33.6	5.8	131
Cumulative percentages	9.9	61.1	94.7	100.0	
Percentages of total households	38.0	42.3	16.5	3.2	503
Cumulative percentages	38.0	80.3	96.8	100.0	
Deviations of cumulative percentages	28.1	19.2	2.1	0.0	

Even though the data show hierarchy to be a major determinant in selection, it must be allowed that many families select godparents among social equals or inferiors. The question therefore arises as to why upward selection does or does not take place. I suspect that the selection of social equals can be deduced from the institution's asymmetry, that is, from the accumulation of prestige by one family and economic aid by the other. Villagers will choose superiors when they need economic support; they will cease to follow this pattern of selection if they feel the economic advantages are not worth the added deference and allegiance due to a *compadre* of superior status. Empirical support for this interpretation appears in a tendency, shown in Table 1, for wealthier families to choose equals or inferiors more often than do poor people.[5]

What, then, are the structural implications of these various selection patterns? By choosing a superior the rich would reinforce the status differences between themselves and the families chosen, and at the same time undermine their own status aspirations. If a wealthy villager chooses an inferior, on the other hand, his poorer *compadre*, unable to be a real patron, cannot command greater deference. Similarly, the selection of social equals must lead to exchanges of favour and respect which are more nearly equal and reciprocal. The poorer villager may resolve the dilemma the other way since for him the potential economic advantages of having wealthy patrons weigh more heavily. Yet here too there are counterbalancing obligations which discourage unlimited upward selection; not only must greater deference be paid to wealthy *compadres*, but also fiestas given in their honour should be proportionally more elaborate. Further, although ideally it is bad form to refuse to be a godparent, in practice this may happen since there are limits to the patronage even a rich man can bestow, or because the potential godparent may feel he will not receive sufficient respect. Inasmuch as wealthy parents are also expected to give more expensive fiestas for godparents, several devices are employed by all villagers to reduce the costs of *compadrazgo*. One is to intensify previous relationships which, as a result, carry little additional burden; thus some baptismal godparents represent repetitions of earlier selections, and 16 percent of all those chosen are relatives. To avoid expenses, parents may delay baptisms, confirmations, and first communions on the grounds that 'there is not enough food in the house.' Or, within a family, one child may be baptised and another confirmed on the same day, and in this manner one fiesta instead of two is given for the two sets of godparents.

I want now to examine the transactional structure of *compadrazgo* from a comparative perspective, that of Latin American ethnography. Paul (1942: 72) long ago commented on the crucial differences between fictive and actual kinship systems. Godparenthood is flexible and does not limit relationships to specific persons in the way that a kinship system does; the network of fictive kin may be extended or restricted. In the terminology of Lévi-Strauss (1969), *compadrazgo* is a 'complex' exchange system, which may also assume a more restricted form similar to what Lévi-Strauss calls generalised exchange (see Schwartz 1963: 125, Hammel 1968). Like generalised exchange, *compadrazgo* is asymmetrical. Leach (1961) has offered the further observation that while generalised exchange is compatible with equals marrying in a circle, the relation between any pair of wife-givers and wife-takers is unilateral and that this fact lends itself to expressing status differences between lineages or classes of lineages. Similarly, it has been established that even when *compadres* are economic equals their relationship is asymmetrical with respect to rights and obligations, and also because a selection by one of them is not reciprocated by the other.

Due to the flexibility of godparenthood as an institution, the structural homology between it and matrilateral cross-cousin marriage may be still more precise as Hammel (1968) has suggested in his study of Serbian *kumstvo* (godparenthood). In rural areas, *kumstvo* is an asymmetrical relationship (i.e., it is hierarchical and choices are not reciprocated) between agnatic groups which endures across generations, whereas in economically developed regions it occurs between social equals. Hammel observes that Middle American Indian cultures tend to have agnatic groupings, and speculates that godparenthood will conform to the Serbian model in areas of agnatic grouping, low mobility, and economic backwardness. Vogt (1969: 237) has indeed found evidence that *compadrazgo* is used to cement and perpetuate alliances between lineages in the highland Chiapas community of Zinacantan. Reina (1966: 228–36) describes what appear to be asymmetrical alliances that persist between given families across generations in his account of *compadrazgo* in the Guatemalan Indian village of Chinautla. In Tlayacapan, a village that was once both more Indian and more economically isolated than it is today, *compadrazgo* seems to have what may be vestiges of an asymmetrical system which persisted between families over time. These include: (1) an obligation on the part of children to kiss the hands of their parents' *padrinos;* (2) an expectation that the marriage *padrino* will sponsor the baptism of the first child; (3) a fair percentage of redundant choices; and (4) the custom that the parents of both the godparents and their *compadres* should address each other as *compadres.*

If *compadrazgo* on the Serbian model once existed in Tlayacapan, it has now developed into an extensive number of different varieties. This seeming paradox—a combination of restriction and extension—may be a consequence of Tlayacapan's former caste system. Despite some exceptions, in the Indian communities of highland Chiapas a greater variety of *compadrazgo* categories is related to prosperity and increased exposure to Ladinos (Laughlin 1969: 168, 169; Villa Rojas 1969: 219), and it has been observed that Ladinos tend to have more extensive ties than poor Indians or *mestizos* (van den Berghe & van den Berghe 1966). In the *barrios* and hamlets, Tlayacapan was an Indian community, while a Ladino-like elite lived near the plaza. Several types of *compadrazgo* with lesser importance (i.e., sixth-grade graduation, fifteenth birthday, and new store) were doubtless restricted to the elite since others rarely graduated from school or owned stores. The fiesta *de quince años* as a coming-out party has obvious aristocratic connotations and was perhaps practiced only by Ladinos at some time in the past.

Recent ethnography, then, provides support for Mintz & Wolf's (1950) idea that economic mobility encourages more extensive *compadrazgo* linkages, but it does not sustain their particular hypothesis that vertical selection results from economic mobility. On the contrary, it demonstrates that *compadrazgo* is traditionally asymmetrical (in the manner indicated above) and often, but not always, hierarchical in both *mestizo* and Indian communities. In fact, substantial economic mobility must make permanent asymmetrical arrangements—especially those with continuity across generations—unstable. In another sense, too, asymmetry is undermined by industrialisation and economic change; as prestige becomes associated with consumption rather than giving, the basis for exchange in patron-client relationships diminishes. I think this explains why godparenthood is less important and more horizontally structured in urban environments (Redfield 1941: 219–28; Service 1954: 174, 182–83; Harris 1956: 153), and why modern economic conditions have caused shifts from vertical to horizontal godparent selection on Puerto Rican sugar plantations (Mintz 1956: 389–90; Padilla 1956: 295).

As Lévi-Strauss has proposed, a generalised kinship system may integrate more people than a restricted one. Yet in peasant societies kinship is an insufficient basis for necessary exchange arrangements, although peasants, living at near subsistence levels, are as inclined as other pre-industrial peoples to give prestige to those who are generous. In the non-market sectors of a complex pre-industrial civilisation, then, one finds highly generalised exchange systems involving ritual giving and sponsorship. Such complex exchange can be brought about by redistribution (fiesta sponsorship), by affinal alliance, or through fictive kinship. The crux of my argument is that *compadrazgo* may have a restricted expression (like the Serbian model), or as economic conditions warrant it may expand into a more extensive network which, if not consisting entirely of patrons and clients, is nonetheless asymmetrical in traditional contexts in the sense that to give as a godparent is more blessed than to receive as an earthly parent.

OTES

The fieldwork for this article was done under a grant from the Foreign Area Fellowship Program of the Social Science Research Council and American Council of Learned Societies. The Department of Anthropology at Rice University provided funds for computer analysis. I am grateful to Professors Edward Norbeck, Edwin Harwood, Frank Hole, William Martin, and David H. Nissen for their helpful suggestions. I am responsible for any errors in the article.

1. See Redfield 1941:63, 64; Paul 1942:72; Beals 1945:40; Villa Rojas 1945:90; Gillin 1947:108; Lewis 1951:48, 350, 351; Taylor 1951:92; Wagley 1953:157; Service 1954: 290; Stein 1961:136; Schwartz 1963:120, 125; Reina 1966:23; Vogt 1969:233.

2. Not in the sample are godparent choices made for children who died before the census was taken (about 60), but I have not found any reason to suspect this has biased my results. If a household had more than one child of three years of age or under, only the godparent choice for the eldest was considered.

3. Given discussions about the relation between mechanical and statistical models, it is of interest that Tlayacapenses do not articulate as an ideal that one should not reciprocate choices, whereas in another Morelos village—Chiconcuac—villagers do have an asymmetrical rule about godparent selection; see Schwartz (1963:119).

4. Out-of-town choices have not been included in this test since it would be inappropriate to compare them with potential intra-village choices. Out-of-town choices may be considered upward choices since they are almost always made into larger towns than

Tlayacapan, and because those selected usually have higher status occupations than Tlayacapan villagers. It should be noted then that by leaving them out the test in Table 2 is made more conservative, and this should increase confidence in its results.

5. It could be argued that those of higher status choose inferiors more often than others because of *a priori* probability, but since I have demonstrated that the *a priori* model has relatively little effect on the whole sample, it is doubtful that this is the sole explanation of the pattern.

REFERENCES

Beals, R. 1945. *Ethnology of the western Mixe* (Univ. Calif. Publ. Am. Archaeol. Ethnol. 42:1). Washington, D.C.: Smithsonian Institution.

Berghe, P. L. van den & G. van den Berghe 1966. Compadrazgo and class in southeastern Mexico. *Am. Anthrop.* 68:1236–44.

Blau, P. M. 1964. *Exchange and power in social life.* New York: John Wiley.

Foster, G. M. 1953. Cofradía and compadrazgo in Spain and Spanish America. *SWest. J. Anthrop.* 9:1–28.

——— 1961. The dyadic contract: a model for the social structure of a Mexican peasant village. *Am. Anthrop.* 63:1173–92.

——— 1963. The dyadic contract in Tzintzuntzan II: patron-client relationship. *Am. Anthrop.* 65:1280–94.

——— 1969. Godparents and social networks in Tzintzuntzan. *SWest. J. Anthrop.* 25:261–78.

Friedrich, P. 1958. A Tarascan cacicazgo: structure and function. In *Systems of political control and bureaucracy in human societies,* (ed.) V. F. Ray. Seattle: Univ. of Washington Press.

Gillin, J. 1947. *Moche: a Peruvian coastal community.* Washington, D.C.: Smithsonian Institution of Social Anthropology Publication No. 3.

——— 1951. *The culture of security in San Carlos: a study of Guatemalan community of Indians and ladinos.* New Orleans: Tulane Univ. Press.

Hammel, E. A. 1968. *Alternative social structures and ritual relations in the Balkans.* Englewood Cliffs, N.J.: Prentice-Hall.

Harris, M. 1956. *Town and country in Brazil.* New York: Columbia Univ. Press.

Homans, G. C. 1961. *Social behavior: its elementary forms.* New York: Harcourt, Brace & World.

Laughlin, R. M. 1969. The Tzotzil. In *Handbook of Middle American Indians,* Vol. 7, (ed.) R. Wauchope. Austin: Univ. of Texas Press.

Leach, E. R. 1961. The structural implications of matrilateral cross-cousin marriage. In *Rethinking anthropology.* London: Athlone Press.

Lévi-Strauss, C. 1969. *The elementary forms of kinship.* Boston: Beacon.

Lewis, O. 1951. *Life in a Mexican village: Tepoztlán restudied.* Urban: Univ. of Illinois Press.

Martinez, H. 1963. Compadrazgo en una comunidad indígena altiplánica. *Am. indíg.* 23:127–39.

Mintz, S. W. 1956. Cañemelar: the subculture of a rural sugar plantation proletariat. In *The people of Puerto Rico* (ed.), J. H. Steward. Urbana: Univ. of Illinois Press.

——— & E. R. Wolf 1950. An analysis of ritual co-parenthood (compadrazgo). *SWest. J. Anthrop.* 6:341–68

Osborn, A. 1968. Compadrazgo and patronage: a Colombian case. *Man* (N.S.) 3:593–608.

Padilla, E. 1956. Nocorá: the subculture of workers on a government-owned sugar plantation. In *The people of Puerto Rico*, (ed.) J. H. Steward. Urbana: Univ. of Illinois Press.
Paul, B. D. 1942. Ritual kinship; with special reference to godparenthood in Middle America. Unpublished Ph.D. dissertation, Univ. of Chicago, Chicago.
Ravicz, R. 1967. Compadrazgo. In *Handbook of Middle American Indians*, Vol. 6, (ed.) R. Wauchope. Austin: Univ. of Texas Press.
Redfield, R. 1941. *The folk culture of Yucatan*. Chicago: Univ. of Chicago Press.
——— & A. Villa Rojas 1934. *Chan Kom, a Maya village* (Carnegie Instn Publ. 448). Washington, D.C.: Carnegie Institution.
Reichel-Dolmatoff, G. 1961. *The people of Aritama*. Chicago: Univ. of Chicago Press.
Reina, R. E. 1966. *The law of the saints*. New York: Bobbs-Merrill.
Schwartz, L. R. M. 1963. Morality, conflict and violence in a Mexican mestizo village. Thesis, Univ. of Indiana, Bloomington.
Service, E. R. 1954. *Tobatí: Paraguayan town*. Chicago: Univ. of Chicago Press.
Smirnov, N. 1948. Table for estimating the goodness of fit of empirical distributions. *Annls math. Sci.* 19:279–81.
Stein, W. 1961. *Hualcan: life in the highlands of Peru*. Ithaca, N.Y.: Cornell Univ. Press.
Taylor, D. M. 1951. *The Black Carib of British Honduras* (Viking Fd Publ. Anthrop. 17). New York: Wenner-Gren Foundation for Anthropological Research.
Villa Rojas, A. 1945. *The Maya of east central Quintana Roo* (Carnegie Instn Publ. 559). Washington, D.C.: Carnegie Institution.
——— 1969. The Tzeltal. In *Handbook of Middle American Indians*, Vol. 7, (ed.) R. Wauchope. Austin: Univ. of Texas Press.
Vogt, E. 1969. *Zinacantan: a Maya community in the highlands of Chiapas*. Cambridge, Mass.: Harvard Univ. Press.
Wagley, C. 1953. *Amazon town: a study of man in the tropics*. New York: Macmillan.
Wolf, E. R. 1956. San Jose: subculture of a 'traditional' coffee municipality. In *The people of Puerto Rico*, (ed.) J. H. Steward. Urbana: Univ. of Illinois Press.

Aspects of Power Distribution in Costa Rica

SAMUEL Z. STONE

Another popular stereotype about Latin America is that of oligopoly, the concentration and retention of wealth and power in the hands of "a few families" throughout the history of each country. Far from reflecting any North American prejudice or misunderstanding, this view is most often expressed by people within those countries, who firmly believe, without precise substantiation, that "all those in power are relatives."

This paper was prepared expressly for this volume. It was based on the author's 1968 doctoral dissertation in sociology at the Université de Paris, "Los Cafetaleros: Une Etude des Grands Planteurs de Café au Costa Rica"; more detailed genealogical data

Through imaginative and meticulous use of genealogies, Stone demonstrates the degree to which this statement has proved to be true in Costa Rica, which is often cited as being unusually democratic. As a case study in the relationship between political power and economic preponderance, this paper gives historical depth to the approaches of Adams, Leeds, Strickon, and others.

Samuel Z. Stone is Professor of Sociology and Director of the School of Political Science of the Universidad de Costa Rica. He brings an unusual combination of economic, historical and sociological perspectives to bear on problems in his country.

The most important factor in the economic development of Costa Rica has been coffee cultivation. This activity was first undertaken on a large scale by a small group of planters shortly after Independence from Spain in 1821. By mid-century their entrepreneurial ability had stimulated progress to a degree where the country emerged from having been the most miserable economic quagmire on the continent to a position of prosperity far surpassing the other nations of the Central American isthmus. Coffee has allowed subsequent growth to a point ranking high on any scale designed to measure economic development in Latin America.[1]

Tracing the ancestries of the first members of this planter group to the beginning of the Spanish Conquest makes it evident that they were descended from a colonial political and economic elite; following their lines of descent into the twentieth century reveals a significant portion of those who have occupied political posts even to this day. In fact the ascending and descending lines of consanguinity and affinity among the planters from the beginning of the colonial period to the present reveal a political class[2] whose members have exercised the functions of government in the executive, legislative, and judicial branches to a far greater extent than any other group in Costa Rican society.

The foregoing gives rise to a number of questions. One of these concerns the circumstances which permitted the class to survive the transition from colony to independent republic without losing its dominant position. Another has to do with the basis of power during the various stages of the nation's social evolution. A third and more general problem is the relationship between political power and economic preponderance in Costa Rica. The continuing importance of coffee in the economy, however, leads to the more immediate issues surrounding the role of the planters in society today and poses an important question regarding the present status of the political class within the national social structure.

The following pages attempt to provide an insight into this aspect of Costa Rican society through an examination of the relationship between kinship and political power. The method used is that of a genealogical analysis; the subjects are the presidents and congressmen, a significant portion of whom appear in the lineages of a few important families who settled in Costa Rica during the first century following the Spanish Conquest. The lines of consanguinity and affinity

---

are available in his "Algunos aspectos de la distribución del poder político en Costa Rica," Revista de Ciencias Jurídicas (San José, Costa Rica) 17:105–130, *con suplemento*, 1971.

among the descendants of those six "first families" are presented within the context of the social setting in which their class emerged and developed. While this approach is useful in casting light on the emergence of the planter group from the class after Independence, its greatest value lies in discovering the significance of the many divisions which have been taking place within the ranks of the class during the nineteenth and twentieth centuries. This in turn allows the formulation of a hypothesis concerning the structure of modern national society.

THE SPANISH CROWN AND THE BIRTH OF THE POLITICAL CLASS

During the sixteenth and seventeenth centuries Spain created a pattern of power distribution which still continues to determine the nature of Costa Rican politics. It reserved access to political posts to *Conquistadores* and *hidalgos* (nobles),[3] thus giving control of the province to a small group of families by virtue of their descent. This monopoly of power, enhanced in many instances by wealth, enabled the elite also to monopolize cacao cultivation, the most profitable activity of the colonial period. The group stood in contrast with the rest of the population, which subsisted on a primitive type of agriculture.

Two factors account for the organization of an almost exclusively agricultural economy. At the same time, they help explain the presence of a population consisting primarily of small farmers under the political tutelage of a landed gentry instead of ambitious and avaricious fortune-seekers such as existed in many other parts of Latin America. One of these factors was the absence of sufficient Indians to constitute an important labor force. This consideration alone seriously limited the scale of any type of activity and practically restricted the choice to agriculture. As a result, a majority of the settlers, who had been attracted (principally from the working classes of Andalucia[4]) by the idea of becoming landowners under special incentives offered by the Crown during the seventeenth century, had arrived with the intention of working their newly acquired lands by themselves. The other factor was the scarcity of gold, which not only ruled out mining but also had the effect of attracting farmers of both noble and plebeian stock instead of ambitious adventurers. Even before undertaking the journey to Costa Rica, all the settlers had known that the province of their choice offered neither glory nor riches.

This evokes an irony of history arising from the origin of the name of Costa Rica. On his fourth voyage, Columbus discovered the area which actually comprises the northeastern section of Panama and southeastern Costa Rica. Upon seeing the natives' display of golden objects his dreams were fulfilled and he baptized his paradise with the name of Veragua. People thus came to talk of the entire east coast of the Isthmus as the *costa rica*—the rich coast—of Veragua,[5] until it became necessary to distinguish the region which forms the present Republic of Costa Rica from the territory of Veragua claimed by the Admiral's heirs.[6] In reality, the riches of meridional Central America are still part of Columbian mythology. Early in the Conquest the legend of the *costa rica* attracted a few ambitious Spaniards, but they soon left and in their footsteps followed the farmer.

The elite continued as a small group of closely related families during the colonial period, inheriting power from generation to generation. Its predominance was greatly facilitated by the small size of the society[7] and by the isolation of the territory. Approximately three months were required to travel by horse from Costa Rica to Guatemala, the seat of its colonial government. The effect of such isolation on the population can be appreciated by considering that the bishop in charge of the province, who resided in Nicaragua, was able to pay only 11 visits to the unfortunate territory between 1607 and 1815, the intervals between visits ranging up to 33 years.[8] Such seclusion kept the inhabitants unaware of social and political trends which in other parts of the isthmus defied the positions of ruling classes.

By the eighteenth century the policies of the Crown and Guatemala had resulted in complete economic stagnation to the point where even cacao had to be abandoned. The Church and piracy are also to be blamed. The *hidalguía,* or elite, while retaining its political power, was forced to lower its standard of living, thus leading to a discrepancy between its modest manner of life and its high social and political rank. Even governors had to work their own land. By Independence, this economic leveling had favored an approaching of the social categories to a point where society presented a notably equalitarian aspect. The elite was there, however, and thanks to its political power would soon become the motor of economic expansion, finding its fuel in coffee. The group was to become, after Independence, that of the coffee planters.

The considerations have an important bearing on modern national society. The resulting land distribution into small parcels has been closely related to political stability. For lack of Indians to convert, the territory had a small clergy. It is not by coincidence that the Church has never been the focal point of violent political struggles as in other parts of the continent. For lack of Indians to conquer, the province never had a significant army (which may in part account for the continued absence of enthusiasm for the military). Finally, there could never have existed feudal structures such as the ones that developed in other parts of Central America where there were large autochthonous populations—powerful aristocracies, equally powerful clergies, classes of functionaries, and the like. The simple needs of a simple society never even gave rise to a class of artisans in colonial Costa Rica.

EMERGENCE OF THE ENTREPRENEURIAL PLANTER GROUP

In 1821, with Independence, the colonial political class inherited the leadership of the new nation and began to concentrate on finding an activity which would allow its members to raise their standard of living to a level in keeping with their political and social positions.[9] Among the many agricultural products tried was coffee. This had been cultivated since the first half of the eighteenth century but, as with other crops, the absence of an accessible market had limited production to an almost insignificant scale. An opportunity came in 1833 when a German immigrant was able to effect a small shipment to Chile,[10] thus allowing many to foresee the possibility of further exports. Land was taken by assault and many members of the class took advantage of their positions of power to acquire the best areas of the fertile central plateau. Costa Rica, however, was on no important trade route, nor was it a regular port of call, and for these reasons exports could not be relied upon. Furthermore, coffee was processed in Chile and shipped to Europe, where it was sold as Chilean coffee at prices which appeared exorbitantly high to the Costa Rican planters. The disillusionment brought on by their not having direct access to European markets was aggravated by being obliged to work through intermediaries. The group therefore began to neglect cultivation until, quite by chance, a British shipowner gave them direct access to the English market in 1845.[11]

From this time on, national society began to undergo a transformation. The first exports had been financed by the wealthier planter families; but, as the volume of business increased following the opening of the London market, these sought credit in England on future crops. This accentuated the division of labor between modest coffee farmers from the lower social category and the growing export planters from the political class. The latter, by negotiating the sale of their own crops as well as coffee purchased from the former, soon came to control the situation. A new social category arose when partnerships of export planters began offering credit to small producers. When these could not meet their obligations their lands went to their creditors, thus giving birth to the large plantation as well as to the social class of peons, or former landed peasants who had lost their holdings.[12] The small property disappeared only in terms relative to the colonial agrarian structure, however, for the great majority of landowners continued to be humble farmers. The large plantation in Costa Rica was (and still is) quite small by comparison with large properties in other parts of Latin America. It never developed beyond certain limits because of the markedly limited supply of capital and labor.

The coffee complex that developed in this way around the elite export planter consisted of a small independent farmer and a laboring class of peons, with a strong interdependence between them. On the one hand, the success of the enterprise was subject to the productivity of the peon, and this to the paternalistic rapport which the planter could maintain with his scanty labor force. If the peon depended on the planter for his salary and home, the planter depended on the peon for good production, which was the basis of both his wealth and his prestige within his own class. The relationships which developed between the two as a result of this mutual dependence reflected the society's equalitarian values that remained from the colonial experience. All the events around which contact between them took place were of a social nature and revealed a reciprocal respect which could not have developed between similar counterparts in societies with feudal traditions. Just as the small planter depended on the export planter for the sale of his coffee, the latter depended on the former for quality.

This interdependence can still be seen in the processing system and in production financing, which at different times for over a century has come from foreign, private, and nationalized sources with no significant alterations in form. The complex was well integrated, but the traditional aspects which allowed it to function were not compatible with the concept of modernization or with that of balanced development. One of the consequences of this was monoculture, which became increasingly acute because of the high profitability of coffee. Exports soon raised the economic position of the planters, however, and the entire society was able to emerge from the stagnation which it had known since the end of the eighteenth century. The planters made possible this important first step in the economic development of Costa Rica.

The transition from colony to independent nation, then, saw a change in the type of production with no alteration in the political and administrative organization. This experience, rare in Latin America, was similar to that of the Brazilian planters, an elite which survived the passage from subsistence agriculture to slave-based and then free-labor-based agriculture, to industry, and finally to finance, all because the group possessed both political power and economic means.[13]

DIVISIONS OF THE PLANTER ELITE

As coffee production furnished growing prosperity, the first planter families increased their investments. This led to rivalries among them, and the group began to divide into factions belonging to the same families but vying for political power. The twentieth century marked the arrival of several new forces for change, not the least of which was the United Fruit Company, whose effort to attract manpower to the coastal banana zones severely depleted the already inadequate coffee labor force. Many of the coffee peons, however, were unable to tolerate either the hot climate or the new relatively impersonal type of labor–management relationship with the foreign company, and they soon returned to the coffee plantations, despite the inferior salary; this wage differential became a source of resentment, nevertheless. The peons obtained a certain degree of political autonomy with the introduction of the secret ballot; in 1929 came the Depression and with it the Communist Party. These events, and a growing rate of literacy, made the peon even more aware of possibilities of change. Such awareness spread especially fast in a society with three-quarters of the population concentrated in a small area around the capital city, allowing the demonstration-effect to readily influence consumption demands. At the same time such a situation conditioned a readily accessible segment of the population for mobilization and for active participation in the political process.[14]

This situation obligated the different groups of the political class, including the coffee factions, to pay attention to the needs of the lower strata, and it was precisely for this reason that after the Depression they began to form parties concerned with reform. They committed themselves to a redistribution of wealth; and, speaking in general terms, social legislation in Costa Rica has been stimulated by practically all political tendencies since the Depression, and the personalism which predominated until World War II has begun to wane.

During the process of subdivision of the coffee elite, which began toward the middle of the nineteenth century and continues today, its factions have tended to diversify their economic activities. Coffee is still important, but its preponderant position in the national economy has made it particularly vulnerable to taxation designed to finance much of the social legislation mentioned above. In addition, with the exception of the 1970 increase in demand and price boom resulting from Brazil's temporary decrease in production, the world market has been steadily deteriorating. Planters, then, have tended to lose their dominant role in the economy. Furthermore, all groups in the political class have tended to lose power, due in part to the social legislation which has been in the process of creating a powerful government bureaucracy that is not effectively under the control of any single group.

The foregoing is a sketch of the evolution of the political class that has played a dominant role in the development of Costa Rica. The changes it has undergone are clear: during the colonial period its members were united and engaged in cacao cultivation; during the nineteenth century many of them became coffee planters but prosperity led to divisions; today they have diversified into fields including cattle, law, medicine, and the like, and are extremely divided. The power of the class, the effects of the decentralization of its influence, and the present-day significance of the class within the context of modern national society can best be appreciated, however, by tracing and analyzing the lines of descent of several important families who settled in Costa Rica during the early part of the colonial period.

FAMILIES OF THE PLANTER CLASS

Speaking in general terms, the first *Conquistador* and *hidalgo* families constituted the political class. Some were more influential than others, and money was undoubtedly a factor which contributed to enhancing status within the class. An example of an opulent *hidalgo* who settled in Costa Rica in 1659 and whose descendants have played a most important role in the political life of the country is Don Antonio de Acosta Arévalo. The presidents and the equivalent chiefs of state in his lineage are listed in Table 1. Nine of these presidents have held office during the twentieth century, the most recent being Mario Echandi Jiménez, president between 1958 and 1962 and candidate in 1970. A few other important families, but by no means all of them, were those of Nicolás de González y Oviedo, Juan Vázquez de Coronado, Jorge de Alvarado Contreras

TABLE 1. Presidents* Descended from Don Antonio de Acosta Arévalo

Generation	Name	Generation	Name
4th	Manuel Fernández Chacón		Vincente Herrera Zeledón
	Juan Mora Fernández		José J. Rodríguez Zeledón
	Joaquín Mora Fernández		Juan Rafael Mora Porras
5th	José María Castro Madríz		Julio Acosta García
	Próspero Fernández Oreamuno		Aniceto Esquivel Sáenz
	J. M. Montealegre Fernández	7th	Rafael Yglesias Castro
	Bruno Carranza Ramírez		Mario Echandi Jiménez
	Braulio Carrillo Colina		Rafael Calderón Muñóz
	Manuel Aguilar Chacón		Teodora Picado Michalski
	José R. Gallegos Alvarado		León Cortés Castro
6th	Demetrio Yglesias Llorente		Juan B. Quirós Segura
	Bernardo Soto Alfaro	8th	Rafael A. Calderón Guardia
	Federico Tinoco Granados		

* Presidents, chiefs of state, and vice-presidents or the equivalent who actually exercised the highest post of the executive branch.

Source: See note 15.

(brother of Pedro de Alvarado, *Conquistador* of Guatemala), Juan Solano, and Antonio Alvarez Pereira, often called Antonio Pereira. In their lines of descent are to be found many people who have occupied the presidency or the equivalent. In those of Acosta Arévalo, González y Oviedo, and Vázquez de Coronado, for example, there are 33 of the 44 presidents in the history of the Republic, with 25 descended from Acosta Arévalo alone, as can be seen in Table 1.

The political class can also be seen at the level of the Legislative Assembly, where fully 220 of the 1300 deputies the Republic has had since Independence are descended from Juan Vázquez de Coronado, 150 from Antonio de Acosta Arévalo, 140 from Jorge de Alvarado, and 40 from Nicolás de González y Oviedo, to mention only a few.[16] Other aspects of the class will be discussed below, but there is a point which should be emphasized here: Only six founding families of the class have been mentioned. While these constitute an important part of the nucleus of first families from which the class developed, there were others who for obvious reasons cannot be dealt with here.

THE PLANTERS AND THE POLITICAL CLASS

The fact that the planter families emerged from the political class is reflected in the fact that about one-third of the first 100[17] were descended from Antonio de Acosta Arévalo and one-third from Juan Vázquez de Coronado; many are to be found in both lineages. These two families alone generated 51 of the first 100 planters, and practically all of the 100 can be found in the six families mentioned above. Predictably, almost three-quarters of them held important political posts just prior to the commercialization of coffee or during the first years of its boom; in fact, nine of them exercised the presidency of the Republic.

CLASS ENDOGAMY

An interesting aspect of the political class is that, in the lineages of almost any combination of an equal number of the aforementioned families, there can be found roughly the same number of presidents and deputies—who are, moreover, generally the same people. This is an indication of a high degree of class endogamy. The list of the first 100 planter families reveals an extraordinary number of marriages between members of the class, and in many instances between cousins. Endogamy can be even better appreciated at the level of the Legislative Assembly. While the four families mentioned above would appear to have generated 550 of the total 1300 deputies in the history of the nation, marriage between their descendants has been so frequent that many are to be found in two, three, or all of these lineages. Furthermore, in many instances a single deputy descends from the same forefather through several branches. An example of this is Vázquez de Coronado, from whom 44 descend through two branches, 9 through three, and 1 through four. Such is the degree of endogamy, in fact, that if each deputy who appears in more than one lineage or more than once in the same lineage is counted only once, the total number generated by the collectivity of the four families is only 350 rather than 550.

POWER OF THE POLITICAL CLASS

The foregoing allows an understanding of the basis of power of the political class at the level of the Legislative Assembly. By a conservative estimate, if the number of deputies descended from five or six other families were added to the 350 descended from the four families mentioned in the preceding paragraph, it would be found that nearly half of the 1300 have been recruited from the class. The others have been people relatively unknown in the capital area and have represented families from smaller cities and rural zones, where power transmission has followed much the same pattern. There are some instances of kin ties, consanguineal or affinal, between the national political class and the other families, but these are not common. The power of the national political class during the past century was based on the fact that the families comprising it came principally from only two cities (San José and Cartago) and generally constituted a majority in Congress. The deputies from secondary and rural zones, while important numerically speaking, represented groups whose influence did not extend beyond regional limits in dispersed areas.

THE DECENTRALIZATION OF POWER

The decentralization of power can best be seen in the Legislative Assembly, which has grown from roughly 25 to 60 members since Independence.[18] The graph in Table 2 demonstrates the evolution of the numerical influence of the deputies descended from Juan Vázquez de Coronado, measured against the evolution of the total number of deputies in Congress. To understand the decline of this family shortly after the turn of the century it is necessary to go back to the first Legislative Assembly. This consisted of groups of intimately related families, most of whom descended from the colonial elite. One such group in this first Congress, comprising 8 out of the 28 deputies, can be seen in Table 3.

TABLE 2. Deputies Descended from Juan Vázquez de Coronado Measured Against Total Deputies in Legislative Assembly

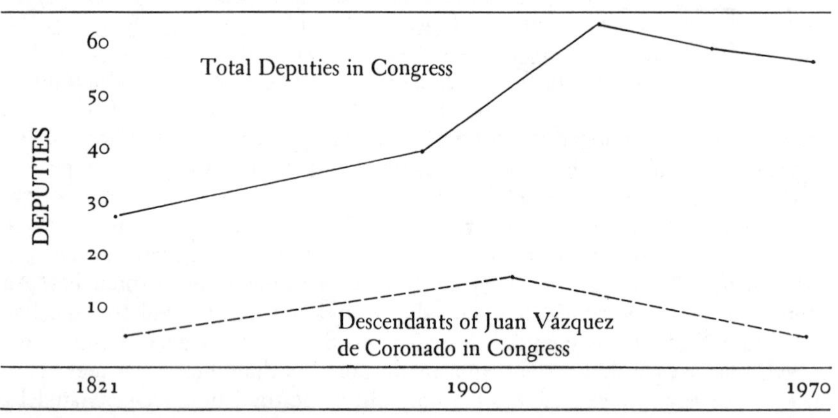

Source: See note 19.

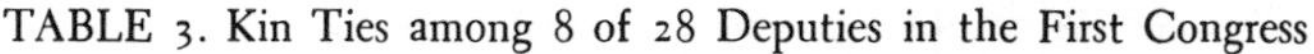

TABLE 3. Kin Ties among 8 of 28 Deputies in the First Congress

Generation I	Generation II	Generation III
	Joaquina Zamora Coronado	
	D Ramón Jiménez Robredo	
		D Joaquín Hidalgo Muñóz
		Ana J. Oreamuno Jiménez
	Florencia Jiménez Robredo	
	D Joaquín Oreamuno Muñóz	
		D Félix Oreamuno Jiménez
		Ramona Carazo Alvarado
	D Salvador Oreamuno Muñóz	
Francisco Carazo B. (see note below)		
Ana Alvarado Baeza		
D P. J. Alvarado Baeza		D Nicolás Carazo Alvarado
		Escolástica Peralta López
	*José M. Peralta Vega	
J. A. Alvarado Baeza	1) Ana Alvarado Oreamuno	D Manuel M. Peralta López
Bartola Oreamuno	2) Ana B. López	Ana Echavarría Fajardo

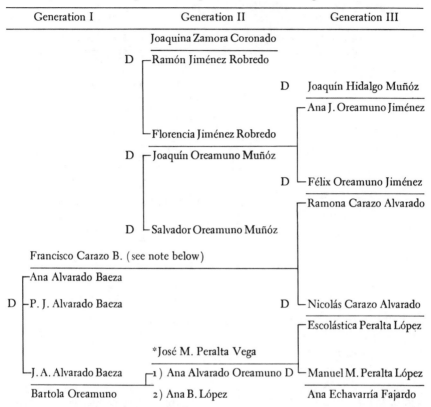

Note: Ana Alvarado Baeza and Francisco Carazo Barahona were mother and father of Ramona and Nicolás Carazo Alvarado. What might appear to be a "generation gap" in Generation II can be explained by the size of Costa Rican families, especially during the colonial period. Francisco Carazo had 17 children; in such a family, there was a difference of "a generation" (in terms of relative age) between the oldest and the youngest of brothers. With respect to names, remember that hispanic usage combines the paternal and maternal surnames, although the latter is not always used; thus the son of Francisco Carazo and Ana Alvarado was Nicolás Carazo Alvarado.

D = Deputy in First Congress.

* Deputy during subsequent congressional periods.

Source: See note 20.

In the same Congress there were other groups of families, and six deputies descended from Juan Vázquez de Coronado. Until early in the twentieth century, Legislative Assemblies were constituted in a similar manner, with power following family lines for many generations. This can be appreciated through tracing the lineage of one of the first congressmen, Ramón Jiménez Robredo, a descendant of Vázquez de Coronado, who appears in the second

TABLE 4. Deputies Descended from Ramón Jiménez Robredo

	Generation I		Generation II
		D	José Manuel Jiménez Zamora
			Dolores Oreamuno Carazo
		D	Agapito Jiménez Zamora
			Inés Sáenz Carazo
		D	Jesús Jiménez Zamora
			Esmeralda Oreamuno Gutiérrez
D	Ramón Jiménez Robredo		Ramona Jiménez Zamora
	Joaquina Zamora Coronado	D	Mauricio Peralta Chavarría
			Dolores Jiménez Zamora
		D	Félix Sancho Alvarado
			Juana de Dios Jiménez Zamora
		D	Pedro García Oreamuno

Note: the direct (consanguineal) descendant is above the line.
D = Deputy.
Source: See note 20.

generation of Table 3 and many of whose descendants appear in Tables 4, 5, and 6. It is obvious that successive generations proliferate to the point of being unwieldy to describe, but an illustrative example is Table 5, showing the descendants of *only one* of Ramón Jiménez's children. Carrying this further, although again through *only one* of the five relevant lines, Table 6 shows the third and fourth generations of Ramón Jiménez Robredo.

These tables clearly show how the composition of Legislative Assemblies has followed lines of descent even to the present. During the nineteenth century the elite group played a very important role in Congress, with descendants of Juan Vázquez de Coronado alone occupying 21 of a total of 49 deputies' chairs in 1859.

Shortly after the beginning of the twentieth century, however, an event occurred which changed the relationship between the national political class and the other groups that had previously participated in political life. This was the campaign of Ricardo Jiménez Oreamuno (son of Jesús Jiménez Zamora: see Table 4, generation II), elected president in 1910. A member of the national political class, Don Ricardo was considered by some of his contemporaries to have espoused leftist views while others regarded him as excessively aristocratic. In order to obtain the electoral support necessary to defeat his opponent he turned to rural zones and sought the backing of groups which until then had not participated in the political process. This he accomplished through rural

TABLE 5. Deputies Descended from Ramón Jiménez Robredo (continued)

	Generation II		Generation III
		D	Manuel Vicente Jiménez Oreamuno
			Juana Ortiz Garita
		D	José María Jiménez Oreamuno
			Micaela Sánchez Oreamuno
D	José Manuel Jiménez Zamora	D	Francisco Jiménez Oreamuno
	Dolores Oreamuno Carazo		Mercedes Muñóz y Capurón
		D	Nicolás Jiménez Oreamuno
			Emma Valverde Carranza
			Matilde Jiménez Oreamuno
		D	Carlos Volio Llorente

Note: the direct (consanguineal) descendant is above the line.
D = Deputy.
Source: See note 21.

community leaders (*gamonales*) of the *Meseta Central* (the Central Plateau, where roughly three-quarters of the population are concentrated). His strategy, which appears in his party's platform, was to encourage the establishment of a strong municipal governmental system, independent of the executive branch.[23] It was through the municipal structure, then, that members of families promi-

TABLE 6. Deputies Descended from Ramón Jiménez Robredo (continued)

	Generation III		Generation IV
		D	Arturo Volio Jiménez
			1) Zoila Guardia Tinoco
	Matilde Jiménez Oreamuno	D	Claudio María Volio Jiménez
D	Carlos Volio Llorente	D	Jorge Volio Jiménez
			Matilde Volio Jiménez
		D	Carlos Volio Tinoco

Note: the direct (consanguineal) descendant is above the line.
D = Deputy.
1) = first wife.
Source: See note 22.

nent in small communities throughout the country began to get access to the Legislative Assembly after 1910. In this respect, Don Ricardo's advent to power appears to have marked the beginning of the decline of his own class; reasons for this will be discussed below. Suffice it to say here that, since his campaign, there has been a greater participation in the Legislative Assembly of groups not connected with the families we have analyzed.

DIVISIONS OF THE POLITICAL CLASS

The significance of the divisions of the political class can be understood through an analysis of present-day party affiliations in both the executive and legislative arms of government. Since 1948, the year of the last important revolution, Costa Rica has known two major political trends. One has been that of the *Partido Liberación Nacional,* of liberal ideological tendency and closely associated with the name of President Figueres (elected in 1970), who, being of recent Spanish ancestry, does not have close blood ties with the traditional political class. He does have the support of many of its members, however, and some members of his family are related by blood to people in the class. The other is that of the *Partido Republicano,* less liberal and organized around the person of ex-President Rafael Angel Calderón Guardia.[24] There have been other significant parties, generally conservative, formed around ex-Presidents Otilio Ulate Blanco and Mario Echandi Jiménez. During the last decade a coalition called the *Partido Unificación Nacional* was formed among the more conservative parties for the purpose of presenting a united front against Figueres's *Partido Liberación Nacional.* Thus the major political blocs can be grossly called "liberal" (*liberacionista*) and "conservative" (*unificacionista*).

Within the context of these liberal and conservative trends, the divisions of the political class can be appreciated through an analysis of the party affiliations, since 1948, of the deputies descended from Juan Vázquez de Coronado. Table 7 shows the principal parties, their ideological tendencies, and the number of deputies in this family belonging to each organization.

TABLE 7. Party Affiliations of Deputies Descended from Juan Vázquez de Coronado (since 1948)

Party	Ideological Tendency	Deputies
Partido Unión Nacional	Conservative	15
Partido Unión Cívica Revolucionaria	Conservative	2
Partido Republicano*	Center Right	14
Partido Liberación Nacional*	Center Left	14
Partido Vanguardia Popular	Communist	1

* Note: It is extremely difficult to classify the ideological tendencies of the *Partido Republicano* and the *Partido Liberación Nacional.* At different times they have both had membership of liberal and conservative tendencies. The most that can be said about them today is that the former is slightly more conservative than the latter.

Source: See note 19.

One very recent example of an important division within this same family is that of José Joaquín Trejos Fernández (*unificacionista*), who won the presidency in 1966 against Daniel Oduber Quirós (*liberacionista*). Trejos and Oduber can both trace their ancestry to a common great-grandfather, Pedro Quirós Jiménez, a brother of Ascensión Quirós Jiménez, great-grandfather of ex-President Francisco José Orlich Bolmarcich (*liberacionista*) by marriage. Orlich, in turn, who is in the sixteenth generation of Juan Vázquez de Coronado, lost the 1958 elections to Mario Echandi Jiménez (*unificacionista*) of the thirteenth generation.

THE POLITICAL CLASS AND MODERN NATIONAL SOCIETY

National society is often characterized by an arbitrary division of the population into an upper, a middle, and a lower class. This generalized pattern is applicable to the situation in Costa Rica. If we were to identify at any moment in history all the living descendants, either direct or by marriage, of the first *Conquistadores* and *hidalgos,* we could see that this group holds a majority of the important political offices. In any subsequent change of government resulting from elections or even revolution we would see those in power replaced with other people from the same group. The people in power at any given time constitute the political elite of the moment, but the point is that the elite, regardless of party affiliation, are always recruited principally from the same group. This group is the national political class and, with a few notable exceptions, is also the upper economic class. Within it there exists a certain horizontal and vertical mobility, but a person born into it will continue to form part of it regardless of economic or other adversities. Changes of position within the class are due to political changes (which are always temporary), to changes in the economic status of the individual, and to marriages contracted with members of other social strata. Generally speaking, the class is inaccessible, except by marriage, to those not born into it.

Several characteristics distinguish the middle class from the political upper class. While education and occupations are similar at both levels, members of the middle class generally occupy secondary positions, especially in government and commerce. In professions such as law or engineering, they often look toward government or autonomous institutions for employment. By contrast, members of the political upper class tend to establish their own firms or join existing firms belonging to others of that class. In medicine, the only difference between the two would be the clientele: middle-class doctors would seldom have access to upper-class patients. In agriculture and particularly in coffee, middle-class farmers have smaller holdings and tend to live on their farms more frequently than upper-class farmers, who often reside part of the week in the capital area and manage their lands through an administrator.[25] The outstanding characteristic differentiating the middle class from the upper, however, is the former's virtual lack of kin ties with the six named families. In rare cases where such ties do exist, they are indirect and remote, and they have little or no instrumental value to the individual concerned.

Members of the lower class are also employed in government, commerce, and agriculture, but their lower levels of education relegate them to menial administrative positions or manual labor. They occasionally find an opportunity through the national educational system to study professions such as law and medicine, which are their principal means of mobility toward the middle class. Most members of the lower class dispose of very scanty economic means.

Three additional comments are relevant to national society. There are several minority groups who do not fit into any of the aforementioned categories. One of these consists of Poles of Jewish origin engaged largely in commerce. Many are extremely wealthy, but two characteristics are to be noted: They rarely hold political office and their kin ties with the aforementioned families are very unusual.* The second comment concerns the relationship between occupation and class. While the foregoing is a sketch of the usual types of occupations for different classes, it is not uncommon to find daughters of families in the political upper class holding jobs as secretaries in government ministries or salesgirls in commerce. Under no circumstances, however, can they be considered members of a lower class for this reason. The last comment is merely to point out the existence of a stratification within each class.

A word should be mentioned about values. These do not differ significantly from the values found in other Latin American societies, except in what concerns the tensions between "elitism," as manifested by the presence of the political class, and the equalitarianism resulting from the colonial experience. The general orientation of values is particularistic, diffuse, and ascriptive, but the equalitarian tendency gives rise to a concern with personal security closely associated with the welfare ideology[26] which has made itself increasingly patent in national politics. In this sense the colonial period, which endowed the society with its equalitarian aspects, also gave it a propensity to welfarism similar to that of Uruguay.

FINAL CONSIDERATIONS ON THE POLITICAL CLASS

In considering the retention of power by the political class, the small size of Costa Rican society must not be overlooked; the present population is slightly over a million and a half. This is not so small, however, as to preclude the existence of a pluralistic society or the emergence of rival groups to defy the position of the dominant class.

Another factor which helps explain how the elite class has been able to maintain its preponderance is the role of the capital city in the life of the country, for it is the only important economic, political, and social center. This has prevented the emergence of rival groups in other zones and from other lineages. Marriage has also been important in the retention of power by the class. As has been pointed out, class endogamy has been a striking feature. A similar instance, the predominance of the Hohenstaufen family in Germany during the twelfth and thirteenth centuries, is attributed by Joseph A. Schumpeter to this same factor of continuous intermarriage within a group.[27]

An important question arises concerning the extent to which it is still meaningful, in mid-twentieth century, to talk of the political dominance of this small class. An examination of its influence at the level of the executive branch

* [Editor's note: Costa Rica also includes significant Negro, Chinese, and other minority populations, who play little role in politics.]

during the four campaigns between 1958 and 1970 shows that of the ten presidential candidates representing the major parties, seven were descended from Juan Vázquez de Coronado alone. At the level of the vice-presidential candidates in the 1966 and 1970 elections, three of the seven were descended from Vázquez de Coronado. In the Legislative Assembly, however, there would appear to have been a decline in the power of the class; details of this apparent decline cannot be properly judged without a full genealogical analysis. It is clear, however, that a striking feature of modern political life is that a great many of those in positions of responsibility (at the level of the presidency, the Legislative Assembly, autonomous institutions, ministries, embassies, the higher courts, and other government branches) are members of the class.

A hypothesis could be advanced to explain the situation: Until the twentieth century, when other groups came to participate in the political process, most administrative levels of government were dominated directly by the class. Since 1910 the participation of new groups in Congress has been stimulated by rival factions within the class, and this sharing of power has lessened its direct control over this and many other branches of government. What appears to have happened is that the new arrivals, representing diverse interests from widely scattered geographical regions, have come under the domination of the national political class from the capital area. The class, then, appears to have changed from "owner" of power during the last century to "leader" of power during the present. However, it must be remembered that these new groups have given their support to the contending factions of the national political class in exchange for a participation which will undoubtedly acquire greater proportions in the future.[28]

Those who belong to the national political class continue to have access to political posts; and, since it is a relatively small class, there is a constant interaction among its members, which in turn facilitates the retention of power. This factor is extremely important and may explain the phenomenon of the role of kin relationships in the political process. The difficulty of access to the class has meant that its members have had a relatively limited circulation within national society, a fact which can be appreciated at the level of its social and even economic organizations, where family considerations are still prime criteria for participation. The same applies to the political domain where the access to positions of power is limited, to an important extent, to people in the aforementioned lineages.

Within these processes of power the greatest unknown in terms of power is the relatively new and rapidly proliferating state bureaucracy. Its growth may soon pose new problems to the traditional political class and effect significant changes in the distribution of power in Costa Rica.[29]

OTES

1. Costa Rica's gross national product per capita in 1968 was $570, which puts the country in seventh place after Argentina, Chile, Mexico, Panama, Uruguay, and Venezuela. The 1968 increase in GNP was 8.1 percent, the highest in Latin America. For

the same year literacy was estimated at 84 percent, ranking third in Latin America along with Chile, after Argentina and Uruguay. These data were taken from "Anexo Estadístico," *Progreso* (Enero/Febrero de 1970), pp. 89–104.

2. For a similar concept of political class, see Raymond Aron, "Social Class, Political Class, Ruling Class," in Reinhard Bendix and Seymour Martin Lipset, eds., *Class, Status and Power*, London: Routledge & Kegan Paul Ltd., 1967, pp. 201–210.

3. Norberto de Castro y Tosi, "La Población de la Ciudad de Cartago en los Siglos XVII y XVIII," *Revista de los Archivos Nacionales*, XXVIII (Segundo Semestre 1964), San José, pp. 153–154.

4. It has often been argued that certain unique traits of Costa Rican society can be attributed to the "fact" that the settlers during the colonial period were primarily of Galician extraction. This is a misconception which has been clearly laid to rest by Monseñor Victor Sanabria Martínez, late Bishop of San José, who studied the origins of all the settlers in Costa Rica after the Conquest and traced their lineages to 1850. His monumental work, which was accomplished through baptismal records, was 14 years in preparation and was published in six large volumes. Among other things, Monseñor Sanabria shows that the settlers of Costa Rica came primarily from Andalucia. (See his *Genealogías de Cartago hasta* 1850, San José: Servicios Secretariales, 1957, esp. pp. LIX–LXII.).

5. Carlos Meléndez Chaverri, *Juan Vázquez de Coronado*, San José: Editorial Costa Rica, 1966, p. 21.

6. Ricardo Fernández Guardia, *Cartilla Histórica de Costa Rica*, San José: Librería e Imprenta Atenea (Antonio Lehmann), 1967, p. 30.

7. At the beginning of the nineteenth century Costa Rica had fewer than 53,000 inhabitants. For the demographic evolution of the province during the colonial period, see Bernardo Augusto Thiel, "Monografía de la Población de la República de Costa Rica," In Bernardo Thiel, et al., *Costa Rica en el Siglo XIX*, San José: Tipografía Nacional, 1902, p. 8.

8. Bernardo Augusto Thiel, "La Iglesia Católica de Costa Rica durante el Siglo 19," in Thiel, et al., op. cit., pp. 303–306.

9. For an interpretation of the significance of such a quest as a force of change in traditional society, see Everett E. Hagen, *On the Theory of Social Change*, Homewood, Ill.: The Dorsey Press, 1963.

10. Samuel Z. Stone, "Los Cafetaleros," *Revista de Ciencias Jurídicas*, Universidad de Costa Rica, 13 (June 1969), p. 178.

11. Ibid., p. 180.

12. Rodrigo Facio Brenes, *Estudio de Economía Costarricense*, San José: Editorial Surco, 1942, pp. 23–30.

13. Warren Dean, "The Planter as Entrepreneur: the Case of Sao Paolo," *The Hispanic American Historical Review*, XLVI, No. 2 (May 1966), p. 139.

14 For a description of such a process, see Karl Deutsch, "Social Mobilization and Political Development," in Jason Finkle and Richard Gable, eds., *Political Development and Social Change*, New York: John Wiley & Sons, 1968.

15. Julio E. Revollo Acosta, "La Ilustre Descendencia de Don Antonio de Acosta Arévalo," *Revista de la Academia Costarricenses de Ciencias Genealógicas* (San José), No. 8 (May 1960), pp. 17–32. For the exact way in which each president descends from Don Antonio de Acosta Arévalo, see Samuel Z. Stone, *Los Cafetaleros: Une Etude des Grands Planteurs de Café au Costa Rica* (unpublished Ph.D. dissertation, University of Paris, 1968), pp. 181–190.

16. In what concerns the deputies in all of these lineages, the number descended from each family is a rounded figure. In the case of Vázquez de Coronado, for example, 219 have been found. However, in all cases, more will undoubtedly be found in the future. The sources from which these data were obtained are given in note 19.

17. For a list of the first 100 planter families from the political class, see Stone, 1969, op. cit., pp. 185–188.

18. These are rough figures. The number of deputies has fluctuated greatly from year to year and has reached 80. In recent years it has remained stable at 57.

19. Tables 2 and 7 were prepared from data obtained through research conducted in San José, Costa Rica, between 1967 and 1970. Data concerning families from the colonial period to the twentieth century were obtained primarily from Victor Sanabria Martínez, op. cit. (see note 4) and the National Archives in the Section of Protocolos of San José, as well as from numerous publications of the *Revista de la Academia Costarricense de Ciencias Genealógicas* (San José). Data concerning families during the twentieth century were obtained primarily from interviews, over the years mentioned, with many older members of the community.

20. Victor Sanabria Martínez, op. cit.

21. Ibid. Also interviews with many older members of the community. See note 19.

22. Interviews with older members of the community. See note 19.

23. Mario Alberto Jiménez, *Obras Completas* (2 vols.), San José: Editorial Costa Rica 1962, I, pp. 103–106.

24. Dr. Calderón Guardia died in 1970.

25. Data concerning the tendency of landowners to live on their farms was taken from Ministerio de Economía y Hacienda, Dirección General de Estadística y Censos, *Censo Agropecuario de* 1963, San José: Dirección General de Estadística y Censos, 1965.

26. Where the general orientation of values is ascriptive, particularistic, and diffuse and there is an equalitarian tendency, there tends to be a special concern with personal security closely associated with welfare ideology. For a discussion of this point, see Lipset, "Values, Education and Entrepreneurship," in Seymour Martin Lipset and Aldo Solari, eds., *Elites in Latin America*, New York: Oxford University Press, 1967, p. 32.

27. Joseph A. Schumpeter, *Imperialism and Social Classes: Two Essays*, Cleveland: World Publishing Company, 1968, p. 116.

28. For a discussion of this idea see Gino Germani, "Clases Populares y Democracia Representativa," in Joseph A. Kahl, ed., *La Industrialización en América Latina*, México: Fondo de Cultura Económica, 1965.

29. This article is based on Stone, op. cit., 1968, Stone, op cit., 1969, and on further research soon to be published in *Cahiers des Amériques Latines*, University of Paris (publication data not yet available). The author gratefully acknowledges the permission of all concerned to use this material.

Views of the World

In studying contemporary societies and cultures of Latin America, any foreign observer must be struck by differences among them, as well as by differences between any one of them and his own. It is facile to say that the latter kind of differences are more apparent than real; they may, at least as often, be far more real than is immediately apparent. In fact, they often reflect very different views of the world.

The fact that there are significant differences in views of the world has come to be widely accepted in recent years, and there is increasing awareness that divergences concern not only judgments of value (what *ought to be*), but also conceptions of reality (what *is*). The following is an attempt to characterize briefly some of the more important aspects of Latin American views of the world and to suggest their meaning for understanding and action.

Without attempting to summarize here the abundant and diverse descriptions and interpretations that are available on the subject, it may be in order to attempt a brief classification and evaluation of types of pertinent sources, and to suggest some of the ways in which views of the world affect other aspects of culture. Two broad headings suggest the relevance of ideas to behavior: ethos and religious systems, and continuity and change.

ETHOS AND RELIGIOUS SYSTEMS

For man, one of the most important aspects of the world is other men. The nature, extent, and meaning of social relationships cannot be appreciated without an understanding of a people's view about man. A basic theme throughout this volume has been the rich diversity of cultures and societies in contemporary Latin America. The reality of difference, however, should not obscure that widespread underlying unity which derives, in large part, from the Iberian heritage. Latin Americans and others generally agree on the importance of *personalismo, dignidad de la persona,* and *machismo* in the life of individuals, and a variety of institutions can be fruitfully interpreted as expressing these basic ethos components (cf. Gillin 1955), even though there is often a marked divergence between ideals and action. Such easy characterization should not obscure the real complexity of views, which include such apparent oppositions as: easy dependence on paternalism and a high value on self-determination; strong and widespread bonds of familism and ritual kinship (*compadrazgo*) coupled with personalized individualism; high value on the dignity of the unique person in a context of fairly strict social hierarchy; a double standard of extremely contrasting morality for the sexes; strong formal emphasis on centralization of authority together with an emphasis on the adeptness of the individual; and so forth.

This kind of analysis of ethos, whether done by a Latin American, an Anglo, or another foreigner, tends to focus on some of the most critical features that distinguish those Latin views of the world from those that dominate elsewhere. Another important aspect of ethos in the complex societies of Middle and South America is that the dominant national patterns also stand in marked contrast to the views of the Indians who comprise a significant portion of the population in many of those countries. Four centuries of close and sustained contact between ethnic groups have not resulted in large-scale assimilation or acculturation, as indicated by van den Berghe and others in this volume, or in the works of Sol Tax, Robert Redfield, the Reichel-Dolmatoffs, and others. Insofar as the pluralism within complex societies is cultural as well as social, world view is probably the most variant and pervasive kind of cultural difference. In this section, William and Claudia Madsen vividly contrast Indian and mestizo cultures as reflected in a particular limited realm, beliefs and behaviors associated with alcoholic beverages.

Although virtually every ethnographic monograph, including community studies, contains some information on the predominant world view of the people, it is unusual to find social scientists who take this as a focal feature in terms of which they order other data. In Latin America, however, it is curious that some of the best known anthropological work is of this order. The major portion of Redfield's career was devoted to this approach, and as discussed above, his views have been extremely fruitful, for unexpected reasons. With no apparent intention of provoking controversy, Redfield did so, and the efforts of other research workers to qualify his views have advanced anthropological perspectives. Just as the folk-urban continuum brought into focus a number of significant theoretic and substantive problems that had been relatively ignored previously, his characterization of peasant ethos stimulated fuller discussion of the quality of interpersonal relations in small communities, as in the work of Foster (notably, on the dyadic contract and "image of limited good"), Lewis (especially the "culture of poverty"), Wolf (who contributed the ideas of "closed corporate community" and "brokers"), and others.

Ways of relating to other human beings are sometimes generalized and applied to inanimate objects and supernatural beings. Thus, trucks are named and treated as individuals, and people enjoy close and warm relations with their favorite saints or representations of the Virgin, which are thought to serve as intermediaries with God, following the model of patron-client dyadic contracts described by Foster elsewhere in this book. Let us briefly consider religion and magic as aspects of life wherein world view tends to be institutionalized in some fairly standardized and visible forms.

For our purposes, it is important only to note that ideological pluralism has a profound effect on the eclectic national cultures of Latin America. Fusion of different ideologies is rare, but a common outcome of contact is syncretism, the blending of forms of one system with meanings of another. A burgeoning literature on syncretism shows how European, African, Indian, and other traditions have merged to produce new forms in material as well as ideological aspects of religion, art, and other symbol systems. The folk-Catholicism of Latin America includes indigenous pagan elements alongside strict doctrinal ones, and forms and meanings indistinguishably merge. The process is an old and continuing one, well documented by Melville Herskovits, Oliver La Farge, Ruben Reina, and others.

In areas where slaves from Africa figured significantly in the population, their own patterns have become merged with indigenous patterns to produce new systems distinct from either of the original forms. Some of the more spectacular manifestations of this are surrounded with an aura of drama and mystery verging on the apocryphal, until the popular misconceptions that have grown up are even more exotic and colorful than the reality. Umbanda, described by

Emilio Willems in this section, is only one among many such Afro-American cults with elaborate pantheons and well-developed systems of belief about which conscientious and detailed investigation by social scientists such as Alfred Métraux, Seth Leacock, Roger Bastide, and others, has not dispelled romantic stereotypes held by laymen.

In some respects, religion plays an important role in the economic and political aspects of life in Latin America. The Church has been a large landholder, and is often identified with the oligarchy, so that there is widespread dissatisfaction among intellectuals concerning the lack of social concern on the part of some members of the Catholic hierarchy, although others are outspoken in favor of revolution; forces for change within the Church are discussed below. Disagreement among Catholic leaders has not benefited Protestant missionaries, whose impact has generally been slight throughout most of the area; Emilio Willems's paper in this section explains their unusual success among some Brazilians.

The widespread civil-religious hierarchy in which most able-bodied adult males are expected to occupy a series of public posts (*cargos*) and to sponsor fiestas has already been described as a religious institution which serves, among other things, as an economic leveler. The public responsibilities of religious fraternities (*cofradías*) fulfill similar purposes, and *compadrazgo*, especially of the asymmetrical type emphasized in Ingham's paper in this book, can also be interpreted as a means by which the poor can share in at least some of the advantages enjoyed by particular individuals of higher social and economic status with whom they are linked through networks of patron-client contracts.

The "culture of poverty" is an important and widespread subtype that occurs not only throughout much of Latin America but also in other areas of the world. Oscar Lewis's detailed and specific characterization, reprinted in this section, has been considerably distorted by popularizers who often cite it as a self-perpetuating "vicious circle" that makes it pointless to work for constructive change.

CONTINUITY AND CHANGE

In one sense, virtually all of the papers in this book deal with the dynamics of change, planned or unintended. This fact may seem ironic in terms of world view: one of the significant differences that is often cited between Anglo and Latin outlooks is that the former emphasizes change, self-determination by mankind and by individuals, and a time-focus that is predominantly future-oriented, whereas Latins, by contrast, are often characterized as emphasizing tradition and continuity, resignation and fatalism, both individual and collective, and concern with living only for the present.

In fact, however, concern for change is a driving force in much of contemporary Latin American society, although there are great conflicts about what goals should be sought and by what means.

The literate minority in Latin American nations is fairly vocal and often most articulate. An abundant literature on individual introspection, autobiography, and formal philosophy need not concern us here, but serious attempts at cultural introspection are worth noting. In the first place, it is perhaps a telling commentary that amateur attempts at what might loosely be termed "national character study" or description of "basic personality type" should be fashionable in these countries. Often the tone of such essays is one of breast-beating denigration of the prevailing foibles of society. In some instances, a naïve combination of geographic determinism and racism provides a convenient rationalization for this supposed contemporary demoralization. According to this view, the Conquest was, in effect, a profound "psychic trauma," a second "original sin" for the conquerors and a crushing defeat for the vanquished, and it still weighs heavily on all descendants. The characterization of early twentieth-century Bolivians as "a sick people" (Arguedas 1909) is still accepted by many of the intelligentsia as a regrettable but unavoidable outcome of enforced miscegenation in the early colonial period. A review of character studies conducted by Mexicans shows that many of these studies are couched in similar terms (Hewes 1954; see also A. Aramoni, F. González, O. Paz, M. L. Rodríguez, and others).

One manifestation of the defensive antagonistism of many members of the literate minority is their adoption of the highly sociable but basically asocial norms characterized as *criollo* (see Simmons 1955). A similar ideal personality type exists in eastern Bolivia, where the *cachivache* (literally, "worthless piece of junk") is idolized for his guile, verbal facility, mental agility, and general ability to live well with no visible means of support, and to "get away with" anything. Like his Peruvian counterpart, he is proudly provincial, favoring the distinctive local dance (*taquirari*) and extemporaneous composition of songs over more cosmopolitan diversions, and vaunting the local customs and dialect. In some respects these figures are like the *charro* of Mexico and the lavishly exalted gaucho of Argentina; perhaps they represent a widespread swashbuckling type of alternative to the traditionally aristocratic oligarch or the submissive *campesino*.

Mestizo views about the nature of man and interpersonal relations are reflected in the social structure which epitomizes the world's image of Latin America. Those views, including individualism, personalism, fatalism, and a lack of realism, have been interpreted as imposing a number of obstacles: to economic development in Argentina (Fillol 1961), to improved public administration in Bolivia (Richards 1961), and to easy inter-American business relationships everywhere (Whyte and Holmberg 1956). Political instability is commonplace throughout much of the area, and certainly one of the major factors impeding continuity of government is the emphasis on individuals rather than institutions. The charismatic strength of a caudillo or *cacique* may fit well with the value of personalism, but it is not a sound basis for administration of the complex affairs of any nation and certainly is inadequate for international relations. In much the same way, the preference for courtesy over frankness (extending to a cavalier disregard for accuracy), and the prevalence of fatalism and nonmaterial values, are sometimes difficult to reconcile with the necessities of large-scale and efficient organization. These are the kinds of things Alba (1961) had in mind when he spoke of "the Latin American style" whereby administrators perpetuate myths and seek panaceas with little regard for empiricism.

The emergence of the mestizos (or *ladinos, caboclos, cholos, criollos,* and so forth) as a culturally disinherited segment of colonial society has been well described by Richard Konetzke, Magnus Mörner, and others. It is these groups who now predominate—numerically, politically, and economically—in most of Latin America; and it is their assertive dissatisfaction with the present distribution of wealth and power that fosters political instability far more than any action by Indians, who generally remain relatively uninvolved in national or international affairs.

In order to appreciate the meanings and effects of traditionalism, as a predominant style that influences Latin American concepts of modernization, Richard Morse, in a paper reprinted here, compares local expressions of traditionalism in areas that contrast both culturally and ecologically. His predominantly historical approach complements the more ethnographic and sociological approaches of Adams, Leeds, Strickon, and others, although their insights into contemporary cultures and social systems are strikingly similar. For example, although each of these authors comes at the question from a slightly different angle, each discerns similar meanings and functions in that aspect of *personalismo* usually characterized by outsiders as "paternalism," the mutually advantageous patron-client relationship that so often obtains between employer and employee in Latin culture, involving far more than the impersonal wage-based contract typical in Anglo culture and extending far beyond "the job." In some respects, the effective politician also fits this role; Goldrich showed how a few political parties aspired to it; Erasmus identified some syndicates as functionally similar; and increasing social legislation in some countries seems aimed at making the state into a sort of *patrón*.

Viewing administrative institutions in terms of how they operate is the focus of Adrianne Aron-Schaar's paper here, which also dramatizes the difference between predominant Latin and Anglo traditions, especially with respect to relations between the individual and the state.

In recent years, social scientists have become increasingly aware of the necessity to deal with views of the world, not only as they infer them from the behavior of others, but also as the people themselves articulate them. This is what Arnold Strickon has done in his contribution to this section, relating "folk models" to patterns of social groupings and stratification, just as Hunt did in an earlier section with respect to kinship.

The importance of social categories and ethnic boundaries has been discussed in some detail in an earlier introduction. However, inasmuch as normal usage focuses on "social races," variously defined on the basis of selected cultural criteria rather than biological features, inter-ethnic relations are distinctly relevant to views of the world. The papers by Casagrande and Whitten above reveal much about the variability of definitions of racial types, and that by van den Berghe illustrates the widespread phenomenon of "passing" from one category to another.

With respect to inter-ethnic relations, the ideal of racial tolerance among Brazilians has become a byword throughout the world, and an abundant literature is devoted to historical as well as sociopsychological discussions suggesting that prejudice there is different from, and in general much less than, that in the United States and most other countries. The works of Gilberto Freyre, Charles Wagley, Marvin Harris, and others are important in this connection. One of the most forceful studies of the status of Afro-Brazilians, however, is a book by Florestan Fernandes (1965) from which a portion is reprinted here. An unusual feature of his approach is inclusion of historical documentation, including a number of statements by those who have lived under such prejudice, and who thirty years ago offered a picture that differs remarkably little from that which black-activists have recently been presenting around the world.

The contrast between rhetoric and reality was the subject of "unmasking" by the Brazilian Negroes quoted in Fernandes's article. A similar disjuncture between ideals and actions has caused growing dissatisfaction with the Church in some circles, even among a few who had dedicated their lives to it. For example, a "Pastoral Letter from the Third World," promulgated by Helder Cámara and several other bishops on the occasion of a eucharistic congress in Medellín, Colombia, was widely hailed as the manifesto for a new Catholic emphasis on social welfare—and just as widely denounced. Camilo Torres was eventually so frustrated by his inability to effect change in Colombia, despite his skills and status as a sociologist, journalist, and priest, that he joined a guerrilla band shortly after sounding a call-to-arms to university students, reprinted here, in which he emphasized their unique social responsibilities and their customary predilection for words over actions.

In the abundant literature that has been written in recent years about prospects and problems concerning contemporary Latin America, specious alternatives abound: tradition or change, evolution or revolution, conservatism or reform, continuity or chaos, dictatorship or anarchy, and so forth. When closely scrutinized these supposed choices are rarely mutually exclusive, and they probably in no instance actually exhaust the range of possibilities—other viable alternatives exist. While attacking "the myth of the passive peasant," William Whyte clearly demonstrates in his paper in this section how tradition can provide directions for change, how local evolution can meet popular and supposedly revolutionary goals, how conservative people can reform institutions, and, in many other ways how the alternatives that are contrasted in rhetoric can be reconciled in practice.

One of the outstanding features of our time is the enormous and rapid expansion of cross-cultural channels of communication, interdependence, and exchange. In such a situation, an awareness of diverse views of the world is of crucial importance. In such a situation, also, we may expect some lessening of diversity, but this is an unpredictable (and usually slow) process. In sum, understanding different views of the world remains our most difficult—as well as our most important—concern in international and intercultural relations.

Recommended Readings on VIEWS OF THE WORLD*

Adams, Richard N.

1956 *Encuesto sobre la cultura de los ladinos en Guatemala.* Seminario de Integración Social Guatemalteca Publicacion 2, Guatemala.

1967 *The Second Sowing: Power and Secondary Development in Latin America.* Chandler, Chicago.

Adams, Richard N. (ed.)

1956 *Cultura indígena de Guatemala: Ensayos de antropología social.* Seminario de Integración Social Guatemalteca Publicación 1, Guatemala.

Alba, Victor

1961 The Latin American style and the new social forces. In Albert O. Hirschman (ed.), *Latin American Issues: Essays and Comments.* Twentieth Century Fund, New York.

1965 *Alliance Without Allies: The Mythology of Progress in Latin America.* Frederick A. Praeger, New York.

Aramoni, Aniceto

1961 *Psicoanálisis de la dinámica de un pueblo.* Universidad Nacional Autónoma de México, México.

Arevalo, Juan Jose

1961 *The Shark and the Sardines.* Lyle Stuart, New York.

Arguedas, Alcides

1909 *Pueblo enfermo.* Vda. de L. Tasso, Barcelona.

Bastide, Roger

1960 *Les religions africaines au Brésil.* Presses Universitaires de France, Paris.

1971 *African Civilizations in the New World.* Harper & Row, New York.

Blasier, Cole

1967 Studies of social revolution: Origins in Mexico, Bolivia and Cuba. *Latin American Research Review* 2,3:28–54.

Cancian, Frank

1965 *Economics and Prestige in a Maya Community: The Religious Cargo System in Zinacantan.* Stanford University Press, Stanford, Cal.

Carrasco, Pedro

1952 *Tarascan Folk Religion: An Analysis of Economic, Social, and Religious Interactions.* Tulane University, Middle American Research Institute Publication 17, 1, New Orleans.

Cava, Ralph della

1970 *Miracle at Joaseiro.* Columbia University Press, New York.

Chevalier, François

1965 The roots of personalismo. In Hugh M. Hamill, Jr. (ed.), *Dictatorship in Spanish America.* Alfred A. Knopf, New York.

Chilcote, Ronald H. (comp.)

1970 *Revolution and Structural Change in Latin America* (2 vols.). Hoover Institution, Stanford, Cal.

* This is by no means a comprehensive bibliography on the topics discussed in the Introduction, but is rather a guide to key books and articles that illustrate the approaches and provide a valuable starting point from which any student can further pursue his special interests.

Council on Foreign Relations
1960 *Social Change in Latin America Today.* Harper & Row, New York.

D'Antonio, William V., and Frederick B. Pike (eds.)
1964 *Religion, Revolution and Reform: New Forces for Change in Latin America.* Frederick A. Praeger, New York.

Davidson, William
1947 Rural Latin American culture. *Social Forces* 25:249–252.

Davis, Harold E.
1963 *Latin American Social Thought.* University Press of Washington, Washington.
1968 The history of ideas in Latin America. *Latin American Research Review* 3,4:23–44.

Delgado, Oscar
1962 Revolution, reform, conservatism: Three types of agrarian structure. *Dissent* 9:350–364.

Díaz-Guerrero, Rogelio
1968 *Estudios de psicología del Mexicano* (3a ed.). F. Trillas, México.

Diegues Junior, Manuel, and Bryce Wood (eds.)
1967 *Social Science in Latin America.* Columbia University Press, New York.

Dobyns, Henry F., and Paul Doughty (eds.)
1971 *Peasants, Power, and Applied Social Change: Vicos as a Model.* Sage Publications, Beverly Hills, Cal.

Duncan, W. Raymond, and James N. Goodsell (eds.)
1971 *The Quest for Change in Latin America: Sources for a 20th Century Analysis.* Oxford University Press, New York.

Erasmus, Charles J.
1961 *Man Takes Control: Cultural Development and American Aid.* University of Minnesota Press, Minneapolis.

Fals-Borda, Orlando
1969 *Subversion and Social Change in Colombia.* Columbia University Press, New York.

Fernandes, Florestan
1965 *A integração do negro á sociedade de clases* (2 vols.). São Paulo (partially translated as: *The Negro in Brazilian Society.* Columbia University Press, New York, 1969).

Field, Arthur J. (ed.)
1970 *City and Country in the Third World: Issues in the Modernization of Latin America.* Schenkman, Cambridge, Mass.

Fillol, Thomas
1961 *Social Factors in Economic Development: The Argentine Case.* M.I.T. Press, Cambridge, Mass.

Foster, George M.
1960 *Culture and Conquest: America's Spanish Heritage.* Viking Fund Publication in Anthropology 27, New York.
1965 Peasant society and the image of limited good. *American Anthropologist* 67:293–315.
1967 *Tzintzuntzan: Mexican Peasants in a Changing World.* Little, Brown, Boston.
1972 *Traditional Societies and Technological Change* (2nd ed.). Harper & Row, New York.

Freyre, Gilberto
1956 *The Masters and the Slaves: A Study in the Development of Brazilian Civilization* (rev. Eng. ed.). Alfred A. Knopf, New York.
1966 *The Mansions and the Shanties: The Making of Modern Brazil.* Alfred A. Knopf, New York.
Fromm, Erich, and Michael Maccoby
1970 *Social Character in a Mexican Village: A Sociopsychoanalytic Study.* Prentice-Hall, Englewood Cliffs, N.J.
Gillin, John P.
1947 *Moche: A Peruvian Coastal Community.* Smithsonian Institution, Institute of Social Anthropology Publication 3, Washington.
1947 Modern Latin American culture. *Social Forces* 25:243–248.
1955 Ethos components in modern Latin American culture. *American Anthropologist* 53:488–500 (reprinted in Heath and Adams, 1965).
1968 Changing values among Latin America's lower classes. In Cole Blasier (ed.), *Constructive Change in Latin America.* University of Pittsburgh Press, Pittsburgh.
1969 *Human Ways: Selected Essays in Anthropology.* University of Pittsburgh Press, Pittsburgh.
Goldrich, Daniel
1962 Toward an estimate of the probability of social revolutions in Latin America: Some orienting concepts and a case study. *The Centennial Review* 6:394–408.
González Pineda, Francisco
1961 *El mexicano: Psicología de su destructividad.* Pax-México, México.
Guiteras-Holmes, Calixta
1961 *Perils of the Soul: The World View of a Tzotzil Indian.* Free Press, Glencoe, Ill.
Harris, Marvin
1970 Referential ambiguity in the calculus of Brazilian racial identity. *Southwestern Journal of Anthropology* 26:1–14.
Heath, Dwight B., and Richard N. Adams (eds.)
1965 *Contemporary Cultures and Societies of Latin America* (1st ed.). Random House, New York.
Heath, Dwight B., Charles J. Erasmus, and Hans C. Buechler
1969 *Land Reform and Social Revolution in Bolivia.* Frederick A. Praeger, New York.
Herskovits, Melville J.
1941 *The Myth of the Negro Past.* Harper & Row, New York.
1945 Problem, method, and theory in Afro-American studies. *Afroamerica* 1:5–24.
Hewes, Gordon W.
1954 Mexicans in search of "the Mexican": Notes on Mexican national character studies. *American Journal of Economics and Sociology* 13:219–223.
Holmberg, Allan R. (ed.)
1966 *Vicos: Método y práctica de antropología aplicada.* Editorial Estudios Andinos, Lima.
Horowitz, Irving L., Josué de Castro, and John Gerassi (eds.)
1969 *Latin American Radicalism: A Documentary Report on Left and Nationalist Movements.* Random House, New York.

Humphreys, Robert A.
1969 *Tradition and Revolt in Latin America*. Columbia University Press, New York.

Illich, Iván D.
1970 *Celebration of Awareness: A Call for Institutional Revolution*. Doubleday, Garden City, N.Y.

Jesus, Carolina Maria de
1962 *Child of the Dark*. E. P. Dutton, New York.

Johnson, John J. (ed.)
1964 *Continuity and Change in Latin America*. Stanford University Press, Stanford, Cal.

Kadt, Emanuel Jehuda de
1970 *Catholic Radicals in Brazil*. Oxford University Press, London.

Kearney, Michael
1970 Drunkenness and religious conversion in a Mexican village. *Quarterly Journal of Studies on Alcohol* 31:132–152.

Kelly, Isabel
1965 *Folk Practices in North Mexico: Birth Customs, Folk Medicine, and Spiritualism in the Laguna Zone*. University of Texas Press, Austin.

Konetzke, Richard
1965 *Die Indianerkulturen Altamerikas und die Spanisch-Portugiesische Kolonialherrschaft*. Fischer Weltgeschichte 22, Frankfurt am Main.

Kunkel, John H.
1970 *Society and Economic Growth: A Behavioral Perspective of Social Change*. Oxford University Press, New York.

La Farge, Oliver
1947 *Santa Eulalia: The Religion of a Cuchumatan Indian Town*. University of Chicago Press, Chicago.

Landsberger, Henry A. (ed.)
1970 *The Church and Social Change in Latin America*. University of Notre Dame Press, Notre Dame, Ind.

Leacock, Seth
1971 *Afro-Brazilian Religion: New Saints and Old Songs*. Bobbs-Merrill, Indianapolis.

Leslie, Charles M.
1960 *Now We Are Civilized: A Study of the World View of the Zapotec Indians of Mitla, Oaxaca*. Wayne University Press, Detroit.

Lewis, Oscar
1959 *Five Families: Mexican Case Studies in the Culture of Poverty*. Basic Books, New York.
1961 *The Children of Sánchez*. Random House, New York.
1964 *Pedro Martínez: A Mexican Peasant and His Family*. Random House, New York.
1969 *A Death in the Sánchez Family*. Random House, New York.

Lipschutz, Alejandro
1967 *El problema racial en la conquista de América y el mestizaje* (2da. ed.). Andrés Bello, Santiago.

Madsen, William
1960 *The Virgin's Children: Life in an Aztec Village Today*. University of Texas Press, Austin.

Mafud, Julio
1965 *Psicología de la viveza criolla (contribuciones para una interpretación de la realidad social argentina y americana)* (2a ed.). Américalee, Buenos Aires.

Mander, John
1971 *The Unrevolutionary Society: The Power of Latin American Conservatism in a Changing World.* Harper & Row, Evanston, Ill.

Mariátegui, José Carlos
1971 *Seven Interpretive Essays on Peruvian Reality.* University of Texas Press, Austin.

Marshall, C. E.
1939 The birth of the mestizo in New Spain. *Hispanic American Historical Review* 19:161–184.

Martz, John D.
1965 *The Dynamics of Change in Latin American Politics.* Prentice-Hall, Englewood Cliffs, N.J.

Mecham, J. Lloyd
1966 *Church and State in Latin America* (rev. ed.). University of North Carolina Press, Chapel Hill.

Mercier Vega, Luis
1969 *Guerrillas in Latin America: The Technique of the Counter-State.* Frederick A. Praeger, New York.

Métraux, Alfred
1967 *Religions et magies indiennes d'Amérique du Sud.* Gallimard, Paris.

Mörner, Magnus
1967 *Race Mixture in the History of Latin America.* Little, Brown, Boston.

Mörner, Magnus (ed.)
1969 *Race and Class in Latin America.* Columbia University Press, New York.

Morse, Richard M.
1962 Some characteristics of Latin American urban history. *American Historical Review* 67:317–338.

Needler, Martin C.
1968a *Political Development in Latin America: Instability, Violence, and Evolutionary Change.* Random House, New York.

Parsons, Elsie C.
1936 *Mitla: Town of Souls.* University of Chicago Press, Chicago.

Patch, Richard W.
1970 The manifest ethos of north and south. *American Universities Field Staff Reports,* West Coast South America Series 17, 1, New York.

Paz, Octavio
1961 *The Labyrinth of Solitude: Life and Thought in Mexico.* Grove Press, New York.

Petras, James, and Maurice Zeitlin (eds.)
1967 *Latin America: Reform or Revolution?* Fawcett, New York.

Pierson, Donald
1942 *Negroes in Brazil: A Study of Race Contact in Bahia.* University of Chicago Press, Chicago.

Pike, Frederick B. (ed.)
1964 *The Conflict Between Church and State in Latin America.* Alfred A. Knopf, New York.
1967 *Freedom and Reform in Latin America* (rev. ed.). University of Notre Dame Press, Notre Dame, Ind.

Pozas, Ricardo
1962 *Juan, the Chamula.* University of California Press, Berkeley.
Prebisch, Raul
1971 *Change and Development: Latin America's Greatest Task.* Frederick A. Praeger, New York.
Ramírez, Santiago
1959 *El mexicano: Psicología de sus motivaciones.* Pax, México.
Ramos, Samuel
1962 *Profile of Man and Culture in Mexico.* University of Texas Press, Austin.
Redfield, Robert
1947 The folk society. *American Journal of Sociology* 52:293–308.
1955 *The Little Community.* University of Chicago Press, Chicago.
1956 *Peasant Society and Culture.* University of Chicago Press, Chicago.
·Reichel-Dolmatoff, Gerardo, and Alicia Reichel-Dolmatoff
1961 *The People of Aritama: The Cultural Personality of a Colombian Mestizo Village.* University of Chicago Press, Chicago.
Reina, Ruben E.
1966 *The Law of the Saints: A Pokoman Corporate Community and Its Culture.* Bobbs-Merrill, Indianapolis.
Richards, Allan R.
1961 *Administration—Bolivia and the U.S.* University of New Mexico, Department of Government Research Publication 60, Albuquerque.
Rodríguez Sala de Gomezgil, María Luisa
1965 *El estereotipo del mexicano: Estudio psicosocial.* Universidad Nacional Autónoma de México, México.
Rubel, Arthur J.
1964 The epidemiology of a folk illness: Susto in Hispanic America. *Ethnology* 3:268–283.
Silvert, Kalman H.
1966 *The Conflict Society: Reaction and Revolution in Latin America* (rev. ed.). American Universities Field Staff, New York.
Simmons, Ozzie G.
1955 The criollo outlook in the mestizo culture of coastal Peru. *American Anthropologist* 57:107–117 (reprinted in Heath and Adams, 1965).
1959 Drinking patterns and interpersonal performance in a Peruvian mestizo community. *Quarterly Journal of Studies on Alcohol* 20:103–111.
Sommers, Joseph
1964 The Indian-oriented novel in Latin-America: New spirit, new forms, new scope. *Journal of Inter-American Studies* 6:249–266.
Stein, Stanley, and Barbara Stein
1970 *The Colonial Heritage of Latin America.* Oxford University Press, New York.
Steward, Julian H.
1955 *The Theory of Culture Change.* University of Illinois Press, Urbana.
Tax, Sol
1941 World view and social relations in Guatemala. *American Anthropologist* 43:27–43 (reprinted in Heath and Adams, 1965).
1953 *Penny Capitalism: A Guatemalan Indian Economy.* Smithsonian Institution, Institute of Social Anthropology Publication 16, Washington.
TePaske, John J., and Sydney N. Fisher (eds.)
1964 *Explosive Forces in Latin America.* Ohio State University Press, Columbus, Ohio.

[Torres, Camilo]
1971 *Revolutionary Priest: The Complete Writings and Messages of Camilo Torres* (John Gerassi, ed.). Random House, New York.

Tschopik, Harry
1947 *Highland Communities of Central Peru.* Smithsonian Institution, Institute of Social Anthropology Publication 5, Washington.
1948 On the concept of creole culture in Peru. *Transactions of the New York Academy of Sciences* 2,10:252–261.
1951 *The Aymara of Chucuito, Peru; I: Magic.* Anthropological Papers of the American Museum of Natural History 44, 2, New York.

Turner, Frederick C.
1971 *Catholicism and Political Development in Latin America.* University of North Carolina Press, Chapel Hill.

Urquidi, Victor L.
1964 *The Challenge of Development in Latin America.* Frederick A. Praeger, New York.

Valencia Cabrera, Pastor
1952 *Algo sobre apologética nacional.* Editorial Kollasuyo, La Paz.

Vallier, Ivan
1970 *Catholicism, Social Control, and Modernization in Latin America.* Prentice-Hall, Englewood Cliffs, N.J.

Veliz, Claudio (ed.)
1965 *Obstacles to Change in Latin America.* Oxford University Press, New York.

Vogt, Evon Z.
1970 *Zinacantan: A Maya Community in the Highlands of Chiapas.* Harvard University Press, Cambridge, Mass.

Von Lazar, Arpad, and Robert R. Kaufman (eds.)
1969 *Reform and Revolution: Readings in Latin American Politics.* Allyn & Bacon, Boston.

Wagley, Charles
1949 *The Social and Religious Life of a Guatemalan Village.* American Anthropological Association Memoir 71, Menasha, Wis.
1959 On the concept of social race in the Americas. *Actas del 33 Congreso Internacional de Americanistas,* T. 1:403–417, Lehmann, San José (reprinted in Heath and Adams, 1965).

Wagley, Charles (ed.)
1964 *Social Science Research on Latin America.* Columbia University Press, New York.

Whitten, Norman E., Jr., and John Szwed (eds.)
1970 *Afro-American Anthropology: Contemporary Perspectives.* Free Press, New York.

Whyte, William F., and Allan R. Holmberg (eds.)
1956 Human problems of U.S. enterprise in Latin America. Special issue of *Human Organization* 15, 3.

Willems, Emilio
1967 *Followers of the New Faith: Culture Change and the Rise of Protestantism in Brazil and Chile.* Vanderbilt University Press, Nashville, Tenn.

Wolf, Eric R.
1957 Closed corporate peasant communities in Mesoamerica and central Java. *Southwestern Journal of Anthropology* 13:1–18.

1966 *Peasants*. Prentice-Hall, Englewood Cliffs, N.J.

1969 *Peasant Wars of the Twentieth Century*. Harper & Row, New York.

Wolf, Eric R., and Edward C. Hansen

1972 *The Human Condition in Latin America*. Oxford University Press, New York.

Zantwijk, R. A. M. van

1967 *Servants of the Saints: The Social and Cultural Identity of a Tarascan Community in Mexico*. Royal van Gorcum, Hague.

Zea, Leopoldo

1963 *The Latin American Mind*. University of Oklahoma Press, Norman.

The Cultural Structure of Mexican Drinking Behavior[1]

WILLIAM MADSEN AND CLAUDIA MADSEN

Alcoholic beverages are popular throughout most of Latin America, but patterns of drinking differ markedly from one group to another. In two nearby Mexican villages, differing Indian and mestizo beliefs, values, and attitudes are reflected in contrasting drinking behavior. Such consistency and contrast are not mere artifacts of the ethnographers' interpretation; the meanings, functions, and even the effects of alcohol are different in the views of the two populations.

William Madsen is Professor of Anthropology at the University of California, Santa Barbara. His books reflect his combined interest in research and social action: The Virgin's Children: Life in an Aztec Village Today (1960), Christo-Paganism: A Study of Mexican Religious Syncretism (1957), The Mexican-Americans of South Texas (1964), *and* Society and Health in the Lower Rio Grande Valley (*in press*).

Claudia Madsen is a journalist and anthropologist. She wrote A Study of Change in Mexican Folk Medicine (1968), *and, with her husband, is coauthor of* A Guide to Mexican Witchcraft (1970).

The study of drinking behavior has been retarded by a lack of theoretical formulations applicable outside the context of Western civilization. Cross-cultural surveys (1, 2, 3) have focused on primitive drunkenness without weighing cultural differences in the definition of normal drinking. Although these studies do not specifically equate drunkenness with alcoholism, they leave the impression that primitive drunkenness is a form of pathological drinking caused by anxiety or defective social control.

The relative absence of alcoholism outside Western civilization has been noted in anthropological studies which stress the predominantly integrative function of drinking in primitive societies (4–12). Spindler (13) has suggested that alcoholism as well as socially integrative drinking are a function of the cultural setting.

Following Foster's (14) theory of cognitive orientation, we shall attempt to explain drinking behavior as a consequence of cultural premises about reality. This paper shows how Mexican drinking behavior is structured by culturally defined assumptions about identity, community and prestige. Our analysis is based on a comparative study of drinking in two peasant communities: the Nahuatl Indian village of San Francisco Tecospa, and the mestizo town of Tepepan near Mexico City.

We are particularly concerned with changes in drinking behavior produced by the introduction of Western values. Since the analysis of change requires time perspective, we begin with a discussion of Aztec drinking before and after the Spanish conquest.

Reprinted by permission from the *Quarterly Journal of Studies on Alcohol*, Vol. 30, pp. 701–718, 1969. Copyright by Journal of Studies on Alcohol, Inc., New Brunswick, N.J. 08903. Reprinted by permission of the authors and publisher.

HISTORICAL CHANGE

The Aztecs who invaded the Valley of Mexico from the north were considered barbarians. In the process of conquering Mexico they absorbed the culture of earlier agricultural inhabitants. By the time the Spaniards arrived in the 16th century, the Aztecs had built a civilization whose cities, science and art awed their conquerors.

The Aztecs used an intoxicating beverage called pulque made by fermenting the juice of the maguey plant.[2] Pulque was regarded as a divine gift from the goddess Mayahuel. To drink pulque was to honor the gods. Being holy and blessed, pulque was not to be abused. People were expected to become intoxicated on certain holy days, but otherwise public intoxication was forbidden and punished. The penalties ranged from public disgrace to death by stoning or beating. Drunkenness in secular contexts was rare except among the aged who were exempt from social sanctions prohibiting public intoxication. Excessive drinking was attributed to the misfortune of being born with the fate of becoming a drunkard.

The Spanish conquest destroyed the Aztec empire and reduced its proud citizens to servile members of a subordinate group. Widespread drunkenness was one of the earliest and most persistent responses to the shock of conquest (15, *p.* 409). The change from secular sobriety to mass drunkenness reflected the deep distress of native society. Aztec sanctions were gone but drinking was still associated with divinity and succor. Intoxication became a blessed escape from the despair and confusion that followed the conquest. After the collapse of tribal rule, the community was the largest native social unit capable of survival. Drinking reinforced social bonds that united the Indian community and set it apart from the conquerors.

Alarmed by the extent of native drunkenness, the Spaniards made unsuccessful efforts to stop it. Spanish priests tried to divert the Indians from the drunken road to Hell while Spanish rulers took legal action to thwart the threat to their labor supply, already reduced by the death toll from European diseases. Since the Spanish introduction of distilled beverages and drinking taverns had contributed to native drunkenness, laws were enacted prohibiting taverns and the sale of liquor to Indians. Efforts were made to halt the manufacture of pulque which had become a major industry of the Spanish haciendas. New laws provided severe punishment for Indian drunkenness, beginning with a penalty of 100 lashes for a first offense. Legislation, confiscation and punishment all proved ineffective (15, *p.* 150).

Vagabondage increased simultaneously with drunkenness. Many Indians wandered aimlessly from town to town and finally settled in the Spanish-dominated cities where they abandoned their Indian language and values. They acquired mestizo identity through intermarriage with the Spaniards or by adopting city ways and speaking Spanish.

CULTURAL DIVISIONS IN MODERN MEXICO

During the Mexican Revolution Indianism was idealized and still is by many Mexican intellectuals. Nevertheless, most mestizos look down on Indians as inferior beings akin to savages who are poor, childlike, superstitious and dangerous.

The Mexican government is attempting to accelerate the acculturation of the Indian population into the mainstream of national culture. Technical experts and social scientists are trying to help Indian communities achieve progress. Hybrid seed, modern irrigation and improved market resources have been introduced in an effort to better the material lot of the Indians. Education is designed to promote social progress that will bring the Indians closer to the mestizo way of life.

Mexican Indians are not always amenable to the process of being remolded into mestizos. While the Indians are often eager to improve their material welfare with modern innovations, they are rarely willing to abandon Indian communal values or the symbols of Indian identity. The Indian does not want to be a mestizo. He pictures the mestizo as being greedy, exploitative and very far from God.

In the Indian mind, group drinking has become a symbol of the Indian way of life. Drinking is regarded as a ritual essential for social cohesion within the community. As pressures to de-Indianize increase, the Indians respond by placing more emphasis on the traditions that seem most Indian. The observance of these traditions involves ritualized drinking that serves to strengthen rather than weaken social bonds.

TECOSPA

THE VALUE SYSTEM OF AN INDIAN COMMUNITY

San Francisco Tecospa is a Nahuatl Indian village (population 800) which may be described as a corporate peasant community.[3] The village is located in the administrative subdivision of Milpa Alta, which is part of the Federal District of Mexico. From Tecospa to Mexico City is barely an hour's driving time.

Although most of the inhabitants are bilingual, Nahuatl is the language of the home and of communication among close friends. Spanish is the language of commerce used in the markets of Milpa Alta and Mexico City, and also in dealing with government officials who occasionally visit the town.

Nahuatl is the primary tongue in each of the eight Indian villages in the Milpa Alta area. Every village has a slight dialectical difference which can be identified by residents of the other villages. The Indians of each community feel that the Nahuatl spoken in their village is superior and purer than that of other villages. This ethnocentric feeling about dialect is associated with community and family loyalties.

As in colonial times, the local community is the primary point of reference by which the Indian defines his identity, his roles and his obligations. A Tecospan thinks of himself first as a member of his community and secondly as an Indian. This order of classification is reversed only when he is dealing with non-Indians, especially mestizos. Antagonism and open hostility frequently occur between the Indian villages in the Milpa Alta area but when two Indians from different villages are confronted by a mestizo, they stand together as fellow Indians.

Within each community an Indian is first identified as a member of a family. However, familial role behavior is extended to all members of the community. The respect shown to parents must be displayed to all elders. Highest respect is due to the mayor, the prayer-maker and the curer who has been "chosen by God" to care for the ill and infirm. There is a general feeling that the welfare of all the residents of Tecospa hangs together and that anyone disgracing himself is bringing disgrace on the whole town. Tecospans should back fellow villagers in any quarrels, fights or problems involving outsiders. If a Tecospan is wanted by the police for a crime committed outside the village, every other Tecospan must be willing to hide the fugitive or physically defend him from the police even at the risk of death.

This does not mean that Tecospans try to isolate themselves completely from the outside world. They are aware that they have much to gain from mestizo culture. Villagers are proud of the fact that they have obtained electricity and running water piped to several public taps. They have built a stone bridge across an arroyo in the dirt road that connects their town to the nearby paved road between Milpa Alta and Mexico City. Although the Tecospan is quite willing to accept material benefits from the outside world, he wants no part of the effort to change his identity, his primary loyalties or his "spirit." Nor is he particularly interested in the events of the larger Mexican scene or the world. The exception is any addition to the large body of facts and folklore that reflect negatively on the mestizo.

Within the community equality is an important value modified only by the status that goes with age, the deference and obedience due to elected officials, and the respect owed to those who are "close to God." To outshine a fellow villager materially is regarded as a gross insult. Conspicuous consumption is a negative value. The accumulation of material wealth is condemned unless it is used for financing a religious fiesta or assuming the care of one of the saintly images in the church. The care of a saint may involve buying new clothes for the image, giving a fiesta with food and drink for all the villagers, and perhaps taking the image on a pilgrimage. Financing religious fiestas may take years of saving and leave the benefactor impoverished but it brings him honor and prestige.

In everyday life, respect is accorded to those who properly fulfill their culturally defined roles. A man must be a good farmer and a woman must be a good homemaker. The young must respect the old and all must respect God and the saints. Respect further depends on one's willingness to share with other Tecospans. No villager should lack field hands when his family is small, food when his larder is empty or pulque when he is thirsty.

PULQUE PRODUCTION AND CONSUMPTION

Both the production and consumption of pulque, which are closely associated with the daily ritual of Indian life, are believed to be sanctified and proper. Life is seen as an integrated totality; the Indian, the land and its products form a meaningful whole. As one villager said, "Our fathers lie buried in the soil that produces our food and we shall join them there in time."

The fields which produce maize, beans and squash are outlined by rows of maguey plants. When a maguey reaches maturity and begins to send up its thick flower stock, this growth is cut off at its base, leaving a cavity which daily fills with the fluid intended for the stock. The fluid, called *aguamiel,* is milked daily by sucking it into a large, perforated gourd and letting it flow into a container. Then the aguamiel is added to the pulque barrel in the home, where fermentation takes place. The fermented pulque at the bottom of the barrel and the human saliva mixed with the aguamiel initiate the process of fermentation which produces pulque. Early in life children become familiar with the process of making pulque. Boys are frequently in charge of milking the maguey plants and the pulque is in large part a product of their labor.

Pulque affects the Indian from conception through eternity. A pregnant woman often takes an extra serving of pulque for the one inside her. The suckling infant is given a sip of pulque from the cup of his mother or father. Once weaned, the child receives pulque at meals, since it is considered a nourishing food. The regular diet of Tecospans includes pulque at every meal.

The growing child learns that pulque is an integral part of his universe and this universe should be harmonious. Overt aggression is discouraged by direction and example. Children are severely punished for fighting with a peer or disobeying an elder. Peaceful cooperation and mutual respect are highly prized and demonstrated in drinking behavior.

Parents teach their offspring that grown men are expected to display courtesy and dignity when they are drunk but women and children should never become intoxicated. Departure from the rule of nonviolence sometimes occurs outside the circle of drinking companions. A drunken man may beat his wife for real or imagined misbehavior. Wife beating is sanctioned and accepted by women because of the belief that a woman who has never been beaten cannot enter heaven.

Pulque is associated with the dead and the relationship of the dead to the living. Wakes for adults include copious servings of pulque and food. It is inappropriate to drink to the point of collapse at the wake. After a man's burial, his friends may gather at one of their homes to drink together in respect to their departed comrade. A drink is poured for his spirit while the mourners propose a series of toasts recalling the good deeds of the dead man. As drinking continues, the conversation turns to recollections of others who have died and stories of earthbound spirits. Such drinking sessions end in gross intoxication.

Souls of the departed continue to need the sustenance of pulque. A dead adult is buried with tortillas and pulque to sustain him on his trip to the next world. Upon arrival in heaven the souls start raising crops to provide themselves with food and pulque. When the souls return to earth on the Day of the Dead, pulque is always included in the banquet provided for the visiting spirits. Asked about pulque in Hell, an Indian replied, "The Devil is free to do as he likes, so certainly he drinks pulque. No one drinks selfishly by himself when others are thirsty, so the Devil must share with those souls he has won, for they are now his and belong to his pueblo."

Pulque must be given to the skulls buried in the four corners of fields near the highway to protect the crops from out-of-town robbers. If the skulls do not receive their pulque, they stop frightening off thieves and start frightening the owner of the field.

As in preconquest times pulque is considered a holy beverage. The myth of its divine donor has been transferred from Mayahuel to the Virgin of Guadalupe. The Indians refer to pulque as "the milk of our Mother," that is the Virgin. Ceremonial drinking is required for the celebration of all religious fiestas.

Indians of the Milpa Alta area can distinguish by taste the pulque produced by each village. Tecospans believe their pulque is superior to all others. Since pulque comes from the land of their community, the Indians feel that it constitutes a bond between them. To refuse a man's pulque is to reject the man, his family, the village and the Indian world as a whole. The sharing of pulque symbolizes social and spiritual brotherhood.

The significance of pulque drinking was vividly demonstrated to us during the early part of the field work in Tecospa. William Madsen entered a neighboring village for the first time on the day of the fiesta honoring the village patron saint. Without obtaining permission, he photographed the dances in progress. A few minutes later he was backed against the church wall at machete point by a group of angry drunken men. Just then a group of Tecospa Indians appeared and calmed the hostile captors. The words spoken by the eldest Tecospan were, "Release our friend. He is not a stranger. He has drunk our pulque." It was enough. The machete disappeared and all present drank pulque together. The sharing of pulque as a symbol of friendship is a traditional way of terminating a quarrel.

INDIAN DRINKING BEHAVIOR

Drinking occurs only in prescribed social contexts and drunkenness is largely confined to community or family fiestas. Ceremonial occasions for drinking include saints' days, baptisms, confirmations, weddings, house warmings and wakes. The drinking group typically consists of men but it is not uncommon for their wives to drink beside them in a home environment.

Ritualized drinking begins with formal toasts and countertoasts. As the drinking progresses, the formality of the ritual tends to be relaxed but each person tries to maintain his dignity despite intoxication. This does not mean that he cannot display humor—there is much laughter within the drinking group. If a man "passes out" he is placed in a comfortable position and if he is too drunk to walk home at the end of the evening his wife or a friend will help him.

Any display of aggression or hostility toward a fellow drinker is unthinkable. One is drinking a sacred beverage on a ceremonial occasion and it is a time for sharing common identities rather than airing individual differences. People never display anger or physical violence in a drinking group made up exclusively of Tecospans. Group intoxication intensifies the feeling of community and oneness. Any expressions of anger are directed against outsiders and usually are shared by all. Even this type of animosity is rare.

Group drinking is a structured process of peaceful interaction among individuals who identify themselves as a unit functioning in a homogeneous and predictable social environment. The alternative of deviant behavior simply does not exist. The greater the mutual sharing of pulque, the greater is the feeling of unity. Such drinking, despite the degree of intoxication, is always integrative. It is never associated with guilt, anxiety, addiction or social problems.

Nor is pulque drinking associated with unpleasant aftereffects. If discomfort occurs on the morning after, it is attributed to exhaustion or exposure to night air on the way home. Treatment consists of resting, drinking herb teas and a fair amount of pulque. The patterns of agricultural work are flexible enough so that a day missed in the fields for a valid reason is not seen as failure to fulfill one's working role.

Distilled beverages are seldom used in ritualized drinking. Until Tecospa was connected with Milpa Alta and Mexico City by bus service, the town lacked cash crops which would provide money to buy distilled beverages. After the establishment of transportation facilities, Tecospans began selling pulque and surplus crops. The cash income is used to buy manufactured goods as well as a limited quantity of beer, tequila and grain alcohol. Young men buy beer at two small stores and drink it on the premises in the early evening. They rarely drink more than two bottles each. Sometimes the beer is taken home and mixed half-and-half with pulque.

Tequila and grain alcohol are not sold in the village but young men occasionally bring a bottle back from a market town. The bottle is consumed outdoors by a group of three to six men. They do not drink in a home, where the son would risk a paternal reprimand for wasting money on mestizo intoxicants. Those who choose to drink tequila or grain alcohol are somewhat marginal persons who have accepted certain mestizo values. At the time of our study only three men in the village showed a consistent preference for grain alcohol. They were regarded as deviants and referred to by the Spanish term *alcohólico* or a Nahuatl word meaning unreliable. The term alcohólico does not mean an alcoholic but one who consumes grain alcohol. The aggressive drunken behavior of these three men reinforced a general impression that they were abandoning the Indian way of life. It is significant that each of them had worked in larger towns for periods of more than a year and then returned to Tecospa. They will probably leave again and try to become mestizos.

Drinking distilled beverages in the village disturbs its homogeneity and threatens the Indian value of nonaggression. By a similar process Indian drinking in a heterogeneous setting may produce conflict or violence. Drunken disputes occur when Indians from different villages are drinking in the same town during a village fiesta. Indian bystanders usually manage to soothe the antagonists and avoid violence, but sometimes fights erupt between groups from different communities.

A more common occurrence is conflict between Indians and mestizos on occasions of public drinking in market towns. The Indians feel threatened by mestizo merchants who "cheat" them in town, wholesale buyers who underpay them for their crops, and forest rangers who arrest them for cutting timber in Indian-owned forests. Mestizos sometimes ridicule or insult an Indian during fairs or fiestas in Milpa Alta and Xochimilco. If the Indian is drunk enough to answer back in kind, there may be a fight. Policemen quickly appear and often arrest the drunken Indian. Indian conflict with mestizos increases the feeling of need for community solidarity against the outside world. After returning to their village, the Indians observe the traditional rite of social interaction by sharing pulque.

While Indian drinking can create friction or violence in a heterogeneous setting, ritualized drinking within the community performs an integrative function by reinforcing group solidarity and corporate identity. In this social context drunkenness is normative and highly valued behavior which supports the communal values shared by all members of the community.

The corporate structure of Tecospan drinking has parallels in many other Indian communities of Latin America. Bunzel (16) studied drinking patterns in the Indian village of Chamula, in Chiapas, where drunkenness is valued behavior. In analyzing her findings, she writes, "Not only is drinking always social, it is always ceremonial. Alcohol is considered a necessity, and as such it has no critics. Nor does anyone feel guilt or shame over having been drunk. . . . Alcohol is not socially disruptive among them, but a mechanism of social integration."

Similar observations were made by the Romneys (17, *pp.* 69–70) in a study of a Mixtecan Indian barrio in Juxtlahuaca, Oaxaca. The prevailing pattern was to drink heavily during the fiesta and not at all between times. The ritualized drunkenness required during fiestas did not produce aggressive behavior. The Romneys analyze their data in these words:

> The manifest function of this drinking pattern as stated by the men is that it represents solidarity and acceptance within the group. They recognize that the pattern is very different from that [the mestizo pattern] in the central part of town and say that it sets the Indian off from the Mexican. They also say that it symbolizes acceptance of the Indians and of the whole cofradia organization and the round of fiestas that it entails. . . . Questioned about whether or not they desired alcohol between fiestas, the men in the barrio always responded as though this were a peculiar question, because obviously one drank only during fiesta occasions. Most of the men accepted this drinking pattern as the only natural and imaginable one possible.

In each of the Indian communities discussed above, drinking is culturally defined as a rite of corporate identification which strengthens group solidarity. It is not defined as a tension reliever, ice breaker, or jollifier for the anxiety ridden.

MESTIZO VALUE CONFLICT

The integrative function of Indian drinking changes during the process of acculturation. The strength of Indianism is slowly eroding with the encroachment of modern Western civilization. Some Indian communities borrow from the dominant culture until they no longer consider themselves Indian. Loss of Indian identity can be best observed in market towns or administrative centers which are focal points of change.

Borrowing begins in the realm of material culture while the ethos remains Indian. When basic values begin to change, the community develops identity problems. Some people think of themselves as mestizos while others fight to maintain their Indian identity. Ultimately the change from Indian to mestizo culture involves transition from a corporate to a competitive society.

TEPEPAN

Such a transition is occurring in the mestizo town of Tepepan[4] (population 3000) located on the main highway between Mexico City and Xochimilco. Tepepan is part peasant and part proletarian. Most of the families own land used for subsistence agriculture, but wage labor has become an alternative means of earning a living. Young men commute by bus to Mexico City where they are employed as gardeners, mechanics and factory hands. Women are hired as maids by wealthy urban families. The heterogeneous population includes residents who come from various parts of the Valley of Mexico and rootless individuals who move from one town to another. Spanish is the only language spoken in Tepepan. The older generation is familiar with Nahuatl but never uses the language of "uncivilized Indians."

Tepepan mestizos lack the sense of community and sociocultural identity that characterizes the Indian village. There is no feeling that members of the mestizo community should stick together and help each other nor is there any sense of group pride. On the contrary, the mestizo is wont to disparage his community as a disreputable lot of witches, murderers and thieves. The individual seldom identifies with others outside his family. Even family identity is on the wane as the number of broken homes increases. Only in reference to Indians does the mestizo identify as a member of a superior group. The Indian way of life has become a target of ridicule and contempt for the mestizo who is trying to emulate the ways of city people.

Despite his contempt for Indians, the mestizo has a conflict about Indian values. Conflict between competitive Western goals and egalitarian Indian values produces contradictory definitions of appropriate behavior. Conspicuous consumption is valued by some members of the community and condemned by others. The man who is trying to get ahead fears the disapproval of his neighbors and harbors doubts about the propriety of his own behavior. There is no single system of rules he can follow to gain social recognition.

The religious prestige system is giving way to a secular system based on competitive display of wealth and power. There is a growing tendency to shun religious offices requiring large personal expenditures on community fiestas. Instead of contributing to the group, the modern-minded mestizo strives to outshine other members of the group. He wants a better house, better food and better clothes than his neighbors. He covets the lucrative occupational roles of the wealthy city dweller and resents the fact that such roles are denied him because he lacks the requisite skills. Even when the mestizo fails to achieve his economic goals, he never stops dreaming that some day he will be rich. Accumulation of wealth is not an end in itself but a means for the individual to demonstrate his superiority over others.

The mestizo man seeks prestige by proving his *machismo* which is the art of displaying manly superiority. He achieves sexual identity by dominating others with his wits and his fists. The true man must be prepared to defend his honor even at the risk of death. In his relationships with women he must exercise absolute authority over his wife and make a conspicuous display of sexual conquests outside the home.

The concept of machismo is derived from the Spanish ideal of manliness which spread through mestizo society in colonial times but never penetrated the Indian community. Ramos (18) suggests that machismo is used to mask a sense of inferiority which can be traced back to denigration of the mestizo by the Spanish conquerors.

Unlike the Indian, the mestizo expects aggression and hostility from others. His society encourages aggressive behavior and violence. Young boys are taught to fight when they are insulted or ridiculed by their peers. In the process of growing up, a boy learns by example that the aggressive male is the one who wins out in the struggle for superiority.

The woman's role has been traditionally defined as a corollary of male superiority. The domineering man requires a wife or mistress who plays a completely submissive role. The mestizo man still cherishes the image of female subservience, but many women operate on an entirely different premise. The mestizo wife who has accepted Western ideas about women's rights poses a threat to her husband's machismo. Conflicting definitions of sexual roles have produced conflicted marital relationships which not uncommonly end in desertion.

MESTIZO DRINKING BEHAVIOR

Tenuous family and community ties reflect the lack of corporate identity. The man who sees himself in danger of becoming a social isolate drinks in search of companionship and escape from anxiety. The implicit premises reflected in mestizo drinking are explained by Wolf (19, *p.* 240):

> Uncertain of backing from his fellows, he is thrown back on his own resources . . . he often feels estranged from society. Wishing to escape reality, he has learned to "drown the pain of living" in alcohol or gambling, creating for himself an unreal world with unreal stakes. Despising life, he has learned to substitute the dream for unfriendly reality. He may rise suddenly on a crest of fantasy into a dream world of personal dominance only to fall back into a trough of self-denigration, filled with feelings of misfortune and insufficiency.

The mestizo man views drinking as an essential means of displaying his manly superiority. Abstinence is a negative status symbol indicating the lack of machismo. Beer, tequila and pulque are consumed in bars or stores where men gather in the evening. To gain prestige in the drinking circle, a man must be able to outwit and outfight his fellow drinkers. Secular drinking situations commonly involve a game of verbal dueling won by putting down an opponent without letting him know he is the target of an indirect insult. If the insult is recognized, it must be repaid. The ethics of machismo require an insulted man to fight in defense of his honor. Drunken fights sometimes end in murder, with mutilation of the victim to degrade the enemy and bring grief to his family.

Gross intoxication causes loss of prestige when it renders a man incapable of defending himself. To recover his prestige he must later hunt down his enemy and attack him. It is customary to drink for courage before such an attack. Sometimes an evening of drinking is followed by an attack on a rival outside the drinking circle.

Chronic drunkenness, like abstinence, is viewed as a sign of weakness. Although the drunkard loses prestige, he is not condemned, ridiculed or ostracized. Alcohol addiction is defined as a misfortune which befalls those who are born with the fate of becoming drunkards. Victims of fate are not blamed for behavior which is beyond their control.

Marital conflict is increased by drunken husbands who beat their wives excessively without provocation. Most women define beating as normal male behavior when it is administered as just punishment for the neglect of household duties. However, the drunkard who abuses this privilege angers his wife and sometimes provokes her to take action. One Tepepan wife solved the problem by hiring a witch to "hex" her husband. She reported that the bewitched man continued coming home drunk but showed a remarkable personality change and stopped beating her.

Mestizo drinking is a socially divisive process in Tepepan which produces disruptive behavior and addiction. Intoxication intensifies feelings of hostility which lead to violence. Aggressive drinking behavior reflects the culturally defined assumption that every man is engaged in a do-or-die struggle to outshine his fellows. When he fails, as sooner or later he must, the mestizo becomes a nobody in his own eyes and in the eyes of society. Alcohol then enables him to recapture the fantasy of being a superior person.

This disruptive pattern of drinking behavior is also found among lower-class mestizos in Mexico City. Drinking provides escape from the degrading existence of the poor in a society where status depends on wealth. A slum dweller's premises about reality are described by a Mexico City youth (20, *p*. 237):

> There is no law here, just fists and money, which is what counts most. It is the law of the jungle, the law of the strongest. . . . No one helps the ones who fall; on the contrary, if they can injure them more, they will. . . . If one is winning out, they will pull him down. . . . We live by violence, homicide, theft, and assault. We live quickly and must be constantly on guard.

The slum dweller despises his community and wants to get out. If he cannot do so, he feels trapped in a hopeless situation where the only way he can gain prestige is by proving his machismo. What machismo means to a slum dweller is conveyed in these words (20, *p*. 38):

> Mexicans admire the person "with balls" as we say. . . . The one who has guts enough to stand up against an older and stronger guy is more respected. . . . If any so-and-so comes up to me and says, "Fuck your mother," I answer, "Fuck your mother a thousand times." And if he gives one step forward and I take one step back, I lose prestige. But if I go forward too, and pile on and make a fool of him, then others will treat me with respect. In a fight I would never give up or say, "Enough," even though the other was killing me. I would try to go to my death smiling. That is what we mean by being "macho."

This concept of machismo is reflected in aggressive drinking behavior accompanied by bloody fights and brutality. To refuse a drink is to arouse antagonism or invite a fight. Drinking groups are composed exclusively of men who seek social interaction in cantinas or pulquerias. The atomistic structure of lower-class society fosters extensive drinking.

MIDDLE- AND UPPER-CLASS DRINKING

Attitudes toward drinking change in the middle and upper classes when the means for upward social mobility become available. Excessive drinking then becomes a financial drain, a hindrance to working ability and a threat to reputation. Correct drinking behavior is viewed as a social skill which must be carefully manipulated to enhance the drinker's status. In contrast to the lower-class pattern, upper-class drinking groups frequently include women, but all-male drinking groups are still popular in upper-class Mexican society.

Drinking parties provide the individual with an opportunity to display his intelligence, sophistication and wit in a competitive game in which each person tries to prove his superiority: Formal toasts usually regulate the rate of drinking. Guests must follow the lead of their host and may not drink faster than he does. Inconspicuous intoxication is the normal goal of drinking.

The upper classes condemn public drunkenness. The man who cannot control his drinking is detested as a fool who has the mind and morals of a peon. To some extent, upper-class sanctions against drunkenness have permeated the middle class.

Middle- and upper-class drinking is selectively integrative in promoting superficial interaction within social cliques whose membership is constantly shifting. Although drinking-parties provide a limited sense of corporate identity, their primary function is to enhance the status of the upwardly mobile individual.

CONCLUSIONS

Since preconquest times, Indian drinking behavior has been structured by the assumption that drinking is a form of corporate communion among men and between men and gods. Pulque drinking is defined as a rite of sharing that signifies identification with the group and acceptance of all its members as social equals. These premises are reflected in ritualized drinking behavior devoid of violence and hostility.

Group drunkenness intensifies the feeling of community and accentuates the display of valued role behavior. The role of drunken Indian is enacted with exaggerated dignity and courtesy toward other members of the drinking group. Ritualized intoxication is a function of the integrated value system which structures drinking-role relationships in a noncompetitive society. Within the Indian community prescribed drunkenness seldom gives rise to addiction, social problems or guilt.

The external threat of mestizo culture has increased the value of drinking as a means of asserting Indian identity. Common opposition to the mestizo out-group is manifested by emphasizing behavior which seems most Indian. Sharing pulque is viewed as a sacred rite which sets the Indians apart from the mestizos.

Loss of community and identity opens the door to drinking problems. The change from secular sobriety to mass drunkenness after the Spanish conquest reflected native despair over the loss of tribal identity and traditional goals. Drinking and vagabondage provided escape from a meaningless existence.

The proletarian mestizo of modern Mexico also lacks the corporate identity that constitutes a cultural prerequisite for socially integrative drinking. During the process of acculturation, there is no single system of cultural rules which the individual can follow to gain social recognition. The old religious prestige system is giving way to a secular system based on the competitive display of wealth and power. The man who seeks prestige through conspicuous consumption fears the disapproval of his neighbors and harbors doubts about the propriety of his own behavior. He is caught between two cultures in an anomic situation where there is no clear-cut definition of role relationships and no means of obtaining desired occupational roles. In many respects, the mestizo fits Marx's concept of the alienated proletarian who lacks sociocultural identity.

Mestizo drinking behavior reflects the hostility and anxiety created by value conflict, blocked goals and competitive relationships. The person who is in danger of becoming a social isolate drinks in search of companionship and escape from anxiety. Secular drinking occurs in bars where role relationships are not integrated by cultural directive. Intoxication intensifies feelings of hostility and leads to violence when machismo is at stake. Aggressive drinking behavior stems from the assumption that a man gains prestige by dominating others with his wits and his fists. Chronic drunkenness produces loss of prestige but the drunkard is not condemned, ridiculed or ostracized.

When the urban mestizo becomes fully acculturated, he loses his Indian values and acquires the means of achieving Western economic goals. Prolonged drinking then becomes a financial drain, a hindrance to his working ability and a threat to his reputation.

Middle- and upper-class mestizos view drinking as a social skill used to enhance the status of the upwardly mobile. Abstinence is a negative status symbol. Drinking-role relationships are structured by strict rules about when, where, how and with whom one must drink. Male drinking behavior reflects the upper-class premise that machismo should be proved not by brute force but by displaying intellectual superiority and sexual prowess. Conformity is maintained in exclusive social circles by ostracizing deviant drinkers.

Upper-class drinking standards are distinguished by the condemnation of public drunkenness. The drunkard is detested as a fool who has the mind and morals of a peon. Among all social classes in urban society, deviant drinking is associated with addiction, disruptive behavior and the guilt or shame characteristic of Western alcoholism.

OTES

1. Field work by William Madsen was supported by the Wenner Gren Foundation for Anthropological Research. Field work by Claudia Madsen was supported by the Department of Anthropology, University of California at Berkeley. The original version of this paper was presented at the anthropology section of the American Association for the Advancement of Science meetings held in 1965 at Berkeley, Calif. The final version was completed in 1968 when W. Madsen was professor of anthropology at the University of California at Santa Barbara.

2. A species of the agave (*Amaryllidaceous* genus), especially *Agave atrovirens;* also A. *potatorum*, A. *americana* and A. *tequilana*.
3. The field work in Tecospa was carried out by William Madsen in 1952–1953.
4. Claudia Madsen carried out the field work in Tepepan in 1952–1953.

REFERENCES

1. Horton, D. The functions of alcohol in primitive societies: a cross-cultural study. Quart. J. Stud. Alc. 4:199–320, 1943.
2. Field, P. B. A new cross-cultural study of drunkenness. In Pittman, D. J. and Snyder, C. R., eds. Society, culture, and drinking patterns; ch. 4. New York; Wiley; 1962.
3. Bacon, M., Barry, H., 3d, and Child, I. L. A cross-cultural study of drinking practices. *II*. Relations to other features of culture. Quart. J. Stud. Alc., Suppl. No. 3, pp. 29–47, 1965.
4. Mangin, W. Drinking among Andean Indians. Quart. J. Stud. Alc. 18:55–65, 1957.
5. Lemert, E. M. The use of alcohol in three Salish tribes. Quart. J. Stud. Alc. 19:90–107, 1958.
6. Lemert, E. M. Forms and pathology of drinking in three Polynesian societies. Amer. Anthrop. 66:361–374, 1964.
7. Sangree, W. H. The social functions of beer drinking in Bantu Tiriki. In Pittman, D. J. and Snyder, C. R., eds. Society, culture, and drinking patterns; ch. 1. New York; Wiley; 1962.
8. Heath, D. B. Drinking patterns of the Bolivian Camba. Quart. J. Stud. Alc. 19:491–508, 1958.
9. Netting, R. M. Beer as a locus of value among the West African Kofyar. Amer. Anthrop. 66:375–384, 1964.
10. Honigmann, J. J. and Honigmann, I. Drinking in an Indian-White community. Quart. J. Stud. Alc. 5:575–619, 1945.
11. Mandelbaum, D. G. Alcohol and culture. Curr. Anthrop. 6:281–293, 1965.
12. Pittman, D. J. and Snyder, C. R., eds. Society, culture, and drinking patterns. New York; Wiley; 1962.
13. Spindler, G. Alcohol symposium: editorial preview. Amer. Anthrop. 66:341–343, 1964.
14. Foster, G. Tzintzuntzan: Mexican peasants in a changing world. Boston; Little, Brown; 1967.
15. Gibson, C. The Aztecs under Spanish rule. Stanford, Calif.; Stanford University Press; 1964.
16. Bunzel, R. The role of alcoholism in two Central American cultures. Psychiatry 3:361–387, 1940.
17. Romney, K. and Romney, R. The Mixtecans of Juxtlahuaca, Mexico. New York; Wiley; 1966.
18. Ramos, S. El perfil del hombre y de la cultura en Mexico. Mexico, D. F.; Robredo; 1938.
19. Wolf, E. Sons of the shaking earth. Chicago; University of Chicago Press; 1959.
20. Lewis, O. Children of Sanchez. New York; Random House; 1961.

Religious Mass Movements and Social Change in Brazil

EMILIO WILLEMS

The role of religion in Latin American cultures is often misunderstood, in part because of the widespread view that all Latin Americans are either pagan or Roman Catholic. Willems identifies Pentecostalism, Spiritualism, and Umbanda as each comprising a "religious mass movement" and emphasizes the structural and functional similarities that have favored their rapid diffusion in Brazil as alternatives to Catholicism.

Emilio Willems is Professor of Anthropology at Vanderbilt University. His research on sociocultural change in Brazil, Chile and Colombia has been reported in his books Uma vila brasileira (1961), Followers of the New Faith: Culture Change and the Rise of Protestantism in Brazil and Chile (1967), *and, jointly,* Buzios Island: A Caiçara Community in Southern Brazil (1952).

The role of religious movements in the process of culture change in Latin America is almost entirely unexplored. Attention has been focused on such phenomena as economic underdevelopment, political radicalism, illiteracy, technological backwardness, rural-urban migrations, and the growth of shanty towns, rather than on religious movements whose links with the main stream of cultural transformations seem less obvious. Reports presumably dealing with "whole cultures" have chosen to ignore movements involving millions of people, as well as the emergence of organizational patterns which constitute, in some ways at least, a revolutionary break with the past.

The stereotype of a thoroughly Roman Catholic Latin America may have deflected the attention of some students from the rise of non-Catholic religions and the attendant changes of the traditional social structure. It is true, of course, that non-Catholic religious movements are only in their incipient stages in some countries; but they have reached the proportions of mass movements in others.

Nowhere, however, have they found more diversified expressions or attracted more people than in Brazil. The three largest and functionally the most significant non-Catholic movements of contemporary Brazil are Pentecostalism, Spiritualism, and Umbanda. The two major Pentecostal sects, the Assembly of God and the Christian Congregation, were founded in 1910 as an outgrowth of Protestant proselytism. Since the Pentecostals have shown a biblical reluctance in counting their followers, almost no figures on their early development are available, but for about two decades their proselytic effort seems to have caused little concern to the established Protestant churches. A survey published in 1932[1] stated that only 9.5 percent of the Brazilian Protestants, excluding the communities of German origin, belonged to Pentecostal bodies. The movement

Abridged from Eric N. Baklanoff (ed.), *New Perspectives of Brazil* (Nashville, Tenn.: Vanderbilt University Press, 1966), 205–231. Copyright © 1966 by Vanderbilt University Press. Brief omissions were approved by the author; reprinted by permission of the author and publisher.

has gained momentum especially since World War II, and according to the Evangelical Federation of Brazil, the Christian Congregation counted, in 1958, a total of 500,000 members, including minors. At the same time, the total membership of the Assembly of God was reported to be 1,000,000. Thus out of a total of 2,697,273 Brazilian Protestants, 1,500,000 or 55 percent belonged to the two principal Pentecostal bodies. Should the total of 4,071,643 Brazilian Protestants reported for 1961 be correct, the Pentecostal movement would have by now well over 2,000,000 followers.[2]

The beginnings of organized Spiritualism were traced back to 1873 when the Society for Spiritualist Studies of the Confucius Group was established in Rio de Janeiro. There are no reliable figures on the dissemination of the new faith, but it did not reach proportions of a mass movement until 1920. Umbanda, however, is much more recent. If the source quoted by Bastide is accurate, its formal detachment from the Macumba took place by 1930, but it did not acquire its present characteristics of widespread religious movement until well after World War II.[3]

The reliability and significance of membership figures concerning Spiritualism and Umbanda are difficult to ascertain. According to Camargo, the number of Spiritualists grew from 463,400 in 1940 to 824,553 in 1950.[4] Official figures are lower, as the following table shows.

Growth of Spiritualism in Brazil

Year	Total
1953	488,017
1958	636,449
1959	673,318
1960	680,511

Source: Anuário Estatístico.

Both Camargo and Kloppenburg recognize that the relatively low degree of institutionalization of Spiritualism and Umbanda makes statistical accuracy virtually impossible. The State Department of Statistics in São Paulo enumerates only those Spiritualists who are affiliated with some center. Most Spiritualists, however, meet only in private homes and are thus not covered by statistical inquiries.[5] The Umbanda is neither recognized as a separate denomination by the census authorities, nor do the

> Kardecist Spiritualists . . . permit or tolerate that the Umbanda Spiritualists . . . declare themselves as "Spiritualists." Therefore, in official classifications, the enormous proportion of Umbandistas and Philo-Spiritualists appears under the common denominator "Catholic" . . .[6]

Sheer numbers seem to justify the classification of Pentecostalists, Spiritualists and Umbandistas as mass movements, but there is the added fact that all three are concerned with the transformation of the surrounding society. Some aspects of the proposed changes are mystical or utopian, others are practical and are actually being carried out; but, as we shall see further on, the mere existence of these movements constitutes evidence of a major change of the traditional social structure. No matter how different they may seem at first glance, all three movements share at least five major characteristics: they are concerned with similar forms of supernaturalism; they were originated by cultural diffusion; their beliefs are compatible with certain traditions of Brazilian folk Catholicism and messianism; they are organized in sectarian structures; and they perform, competitively, similar or identical functions.

It is assumed that the rapid expansion of the three movements may be explained in terms of their functional adaptation to a changing society and culture. Thus the description of the first four characteristics is intended to lead to an analysis of those specific needs and wants of several million Brazilians these movements appear to fill.

SUPERNATURALISM

The main concern of the three movements is with spirit possession. The belief in the descent of supernatural beings and their temporary incarnation in human beings occurs in a large number of widely different societies, and in spite of formal and functional variations the anthropologist easily recognizes a common denominator in such beliefs and their manifestations. Following the biblical model, the Pentecostals believe that, under certain conditions, they may be possessed by the Holy Spirit. Although reports on the possession of isolated individuals are commonplace, most cases occur during collective cult performances whenever the eagerly sought emotional lift has reached a high pitch. The audience is shaken by laughter, weeping, shouting, or chanting; some individuals talk in tongues or have visions of "celestial beauty"; some fall down in ecstasy and feel removed to heaven or paradise. God or the angels speak to them, and many return from their trance "full of the spirit of worship, prayer, and love."[7] Thus the charismatic gifts of the Holy Spirit are bestowed upon the faithful through the act of *tomada*, or seizure.

Brazilian spiritualism, in its most sophisticated version, follows the teachings of Allan Kardec. The sessions are attended by groups of faithful who number from five to one hundred.[8] One or several of the participants are mediums who, at the ritual request of the session leader, receive disembodied spirits of various types. "Spirits of the Light" utter advice about a variety of personal problems; promises of help alternate with mild reprehensions which are sometimes administered with "a surprising sense of humor." Unexpected spirits may visit upon a medium, often with the malicious intention of confusing and shocking the participants.[9] The more "enlightened" spirits may offer so-called "passes" through the body of a medium, whose hands, touching head, shoulders and arms of the patient, are believed to communicate "beneficial fluids" facilitating the solution of physical, psychological or moral problems. The therapeutic powers of a medium possessed by a spirit are comparable to those of a Pentecostalist who performs miraculous cures or is cured himself by temporarily partaking of the powers of the Holy Spirit.

Umbanda is to be considered a successful attempt to combine the Macumba, or Brazilian version of voodoo, with some of the basic teachings of Spiritualism.[10] "In the African tradition the *orixá*, who is a god, seizes the *Filha do Santo* (daughter of the Saint) whereas the *cavalo* (medium) of the Umbanda is possessed by a disembodied spirit."[11] Each *orixá* commands a vast number of spirits, and the medium, while in trance, becomes the bearer of the spirit's wisdom. The *orixás* are identified with certain Catholic saints. This of course is in contrast to the doctrine of Spiritualism. Thus Umbanda is the outcome of a three-way syncretism associating African, Catholic and Spiritualist elements in one loosely knit body of doctrine which makes allowance for unlimited local variations. To the extent that Umbanda centers engage in purely magical practices, including sorcery, they are called Quimbanda.

THE ROLE OF CULTURAL DIFFUSION

None of the three movements originated in Brazil. In spite of an overly indigenous or nativistic approach in doctrine, ritual, and behavior, particularly among the adherents of the Umbanda, there is nothing autochthonous about any of its aspects. African cult forms, variously named Macumba, Candomblé or Xangô, antedated Umbanda syncretism by more than a hundred years. They have been accurately defined as adaptations of African elements transferred to Brazil by slaves. Direct lineal affiliation with these Afro-Catholic phenomena seems restricted, however, to certain urban areas of northeastern and eastern Brazil. In São Paulo, Camargo failed to discover any indication of a cultural continuity between Macumba and Umbanda. Thus the latter is to be considered the result of secondary diffusion, not only in São Paulo, but in other parts of Brazil. Perhaps the most puzzling aspect of Umbanda is its Indian component which is also part and parcel of the Macumba inheritance. Since both Macumba and Umbanda are urban phenomena, it seems extremely unlikely that these "influences" result from contacts with any identifiable Indian culture, not to mention the watered down and highly distorted versions of such indigenous grafts. Again, their presence is attributable to diffusion, probably through the channels provided by the popularization of Brazilian Indianism, a literary movement of the nineteenth century.

The introduction of Spiritualism to Brazil has been traced to the middle of the past century,[12] when Europe was in the grip of a Spiritualist wave whose backwash was powerful enough to reach the Americas. Yet in contrast to most areas of diffusion where it was hardly more than a fad, Spiritualism almost immediately took roots in Brazil, and by 1873 it assumed at least some of the aspects of an organized religion.[13] Amalgamation of Spiritualists and African elements in the Umbanda is relatively recent. To shed some light upon its meaning we shall attempt to interpret it in terms of certain processes of social change.

The largest of the three mass movements, Pentecostalism, can clearly be traced to the proselytic endeavors of two foreign missionaries, Daniel Berg, a Swede who founded the Assembly of God in 1910, and Luis Francescon, an Italo-American who became a Presbyterian in Chicago. A few years later, he was, as he put it, "sealed with the gift of the Holy Spirit," and repeatedly received messages from the Lord who suggested that he dedicate his life to missionary work. Under "divine guidance" he went to São Paulo whose large Italian population proved receptive to his preachings. At first his Christian Congregation, founded in 1910, was a sect for Italian immigrants, and all services were conducted in Italian. By 1930, however, it was quite obvious that the Italians were rapidly being assimilated by Brazilian society, and among the native-born generations there were very few who wished to be reminded of the cultural heritage of their parents and grandparents. Thus guided by opportunity and divine revelation, as are all decisions in this sect, the elders decided in 1935 to drop the Italian language. This well-timed adjustment to a changing cultural situation not only assured survival of the sect but laid the foundations for an increasingly rapid expansion outside São Paulo City and the state of São Paulo.

Recent diffusion of Pentecostalism has been accompanied by a heavy proliferation of new sects, some of which can be traced to the proselytic efforts of American missionaries.

COMPATIBILITY OF THE THREE MOVEMENTS WITH BRAZILIAN FOLK RELIGION

On the surface, the emergence of the three religious movements may be regarded as a break with the Roman Catholic traditions of the country. At the level of Brazilian folk religion, however, their incompatibility with existing beliefs and practices seems open to considerable doubt. In fact, it is our contention that at least part of the surprising vitality of these movements stems from their affinity with certain folk traditions. Folk Catholicism, unlike church-controlled religion, is flexible and unorthodox. In spite of occasional outbreaks of fanaticism, it is basically tolerant and receptive to innovations. The miracle is probably the most frequent source of change within the framework of folk Catholicism. Christ or the Virgin appears to a person; the locale of the vision rapidly becomes a center of miracles and worship and the visionary a thaumaturge or new saint. Folk Catholicism stresses the belief in mystical experiences, in possessions, and in charismatic leadership. A rich historical tradition of messianic movements established numerous precedents for the second coming of Christ taught by many sects.[14] True enough, the Pentecostal sects do not ordinarily announce the second coming of Christ at some future date. Their message contains the far more appealing prospect of an immediate coming of the deity. The repentent believer may expect the descent of the Holy Spirit *here and now* rather than in a distant future. And he comes to the individual rather than dispersively to a group of people. Communion with or seizure by the Spirit is an everyday experience which may be observed whenever the members of congregation gather for religious services. There is nearly always somebody who has visions, speaks in tongues or prophesies. In fact, we never encountered a practicing Pentecostalist who had not been "baptized" by the Holy Spirit. It would seem that converts who fail to have such an experience withdraw from the congregation after a certain time.

Thaumaturgy or the working of miracles is another powerful tradition of folk Catholicism which the Pentecostal sects incorporated in their body of belief and ritual. There are two ways in which miracles are performed. Seizure by the Spirit is often accompanied by a miracle, in the sense that the person who has been seized by the Spirit finds himself suddenly cured of some "incurable" ailment. Another person, preferably the pastor, who has previously been seized by the Spirit, performs the miracle by touching the patient's head with his hands, or by uttering a prayer over him. Finally, an almost medieval belief in evil spirits, witches and demons of European, Indian or African extraction has been reduced, by the Pentecostals, to possession by the devil. There are a variety of ways in folk Catholicism in which evil spirits including Satan may intervene in human affairs, possession being only one of these. The Pentecostalists admit in their preachings and writings that the devil sometimes seizes a member of the congregation and speaks and acts through his body. Prayer, rather than any specific exorcistic ritual, seems to be the defense against such occurrences.

The cult of the Holy Spirit, as practiced by the Pentecostals, has, of course, a precedent in the *Festa do Divino Espirito Sante,* part of the Iberian heritage and one of [the] high points of the annual round of religious festivals.[15] The rural migrant who joins a Pentecostal sect thus finds himself on familiar ground. Here, an element of his own cultural background is brought back to him in a new and most exciting form.

In contrast to Pentecostalism, Umbanda is, in fact, a folk religion. To the Afro-Catholic tradition of the Macumba were added some of the essentials of Spiritualism to make it more palatable to the slowly rising urban masses and their yearning for middle-class symbols.

Umbanda, as well as Spiritualism, share with the Brazilian folk religion belief in spirits, both good and evil, and the possibility of communicating with or of being possessed by them. And the performances of the mediums, especially their healing powers, suggest considerable affinity with the role of thaumaturgy in folk Catholicism. One could conceivably interpret the continuity of the three movements with Brazilian folk traditions in terms of a pervasive mysticism which seems to constitute a common ground for understanding and emotional involvement.

STRUCTURE

The statement was made initially that the emergence of the three movements generated organizational patterns implying a revolutionary break with the past. To substantiate this assertion, it ought to be emphasized that the Pentecostal sects, Umbanda, and the Spiritualists recruit the bulk of their adherents among the lower social strata. Such organizational spontaneity, however, is out of line with the feudal traditions of Brazilian society.

Within these traditions, the upper classes, supported by the Catholic Church, were supposed to provide, paternalistically, for the material and spiritual needs of the lower classes which were not believed to have the ability to engage in concerted action of their own. On the whole, the lower classes lived up to this expectation which conveniently helped maintain the status quo. Occasionally they demonstrated a surprising and uncalled-for capacity for rallying around a messianic leader and his promises of a better world, but such rebellious endeavors were consistently suppressed whenever they appeared.

. . .

The Pentecostal sects emerged as "by-products" of the revivalistically oriented Protestant churches. I have presented evidence elsewhere that the rapid growth of these sects is related, in space and in time, to major socio-cultural changes of the last three or four decades. The fact that the occurrence of Spiritualism and Umbanda seems confined to urban centers, particularly to the metropolitan areas of Rio de Janeiro and São Paulo, suggests that these movements are even more closely related to cultural change than is Pentecostalism, which has numerous rural ramifications. At any rate, the rapid development of all three movements seems to proclaim the coming of age of social strata formerly known for their lack of organizational spontaneity. The movements have proved their ability to develop a supernaturalism adapted to their needs and to defy openly, by their mere existence as distinct and antagonistic social aggregates, the traditional social order. Yet the attitude of defiance finds an even stronger expression in the internal organization of the three movements.

Most Brazilian Pentecostal sects are characterized by a precarious equilibrium between egalitarianism and charismatic leadership. In the sharpest possible contrast to the Catholic church and the rigid class structure of Brazilian society, the structure of the sects is characterized by the absence of an ecclesiastical hierarchy and by a radical reduction of the social distance between clergy and laity. In principle, the ministry is open to anybody who has scored some success as a missionary, and everybody is expected and encouraged to participate in the proselytizing activities of the sect. There is little or no emphasis on theological training, but to have received the gifts of the Spirit, especially his healing powers, ranks high among the qualifications of an aspirant to the ministry. Possession by the Spirit, however, is considered a grace rather than a privilege.

No sect has carried social egalitarianism further than the Christian Congregation. Its position *sui generis* within the Pentecostal movement is characterized by the fact that it minimizes the distinction between laity and clergy almost to the point of obliteration. There are neither bishops nor pastors. The spiritual leadership of the sect is entrusted to a self-perpetuating board of elders "invested with the gifts of the Spirit," meaning that they must have been baptized by the Holy Spirit.

. . .

Unlike other sects we had opportunity to investigate, the Christian Congregation repudiates the idea of a pastoral mandate instituted by ordination and based on the assumption of implicit validity. Much to the contrary, the functionaries of the sect, regardless of rank and merit, must seek divine validation for each individual act they are called to perform. In fact, only the Holy Spirit has the power to make decisions, and the sect's functionaries are mere executors of his revealed will. Thus the Spirit stands for group consensus, and reference to his decisions prevents dissent within the sect.

In the Assembly of God and in most smaller Pentecostal sects, however, there is a structural inconsistency causing the sort of strain and stress which produces cleavages and schisms. On the one hand, the sectarian character of these groups emphasizes, surely as a reaction against the Catholic tradition, egalitarianism and the primacy of the laity, especially in all aspects concerning missionary work. On the other hand, the successful leader, who has received more than an ordinary share of graces from the Holy Spirit, is easily held in awe by the faithful. His voice is respected as the voice of God, and if he can add to his other endowments the reputation of a miracle worker—a successful healer, perhaps—there is no limit to the reverence he is accorded by his followers.

Two opposing principles are thus operative in the Pentecostal sects; one is "democratic" and the other "authoritarian." They clash as soon as rival leaders with similar divine endowments arise and accuse the ones in power of misusing their authority or, as they sometimes put it, of "antidemocratic behavior." If the rival is able to sway enough followers, the split occurs and a new sect is born. There is now the Pentecostal Church Brazil for Christ, the Pentecostal Church of Biblical Revival, the Pentecostal Church Miracle of Jesus, and seven or eight other sects which are almost continuously subdividing or changing their names. The Pentecostals tend to interpret this as an indication of growth rather than of disintegration, and one informant invoked the image of cellular fission which, in fact, defines the process metaphorically. The mother sect, in spite of losing part of its membership, is ordinarily not weakened in the long run and usually continues to grow.

The Pentecostal movement could and did take advantage of certain organizational precedents set by the Protestant churches, but neither Spiritualism nor Umbanda were equipped to absorb the sudden influx of many thousands of new adherents. There was, of course, a proliferation of local centers; but if either movement was to become a sect or church, the development of a large number of small, disconnected cult centers was certainly not the way to achieve that objective. Some means of unification or centralization had to be devised to insure doctrinal and structural coherence.

This proved to be less a problem to the Spiritualists than to the Umbanda. Allan Kardec's interpretation of the Gospel and his numerous other writings provided a body of doctrine in which the Spiritualists found a common denominator. Furthermore, the Brazilian medium, Francisco Candido Xavier, receiving authoritative messages from reputable spirits, validated that doctrine by reinterpreting it in terms which were particularly meaningful and appealing to Brazilians.

> Whereas in Europe the Spiritualist idea was only object of observations and laboratory research, or of great and sterile discussions in the field of philosophy, and this in spite of the moral excellency of Kardec's codification, Spiritualism penetrated Brazil with all its characteristics of a Christian revival lifting the souls to a new dawn of the faith. Here, all its institutions rested on love and charity. Even scientific associations which, now and then, appear to cultivate it (Spiritualism) under the label of metapsychology, are absorbed by the Christian program, under the invisible and indirect orientation of the Lord.[16]

The book from which these lines were taken bears the significant title, *Brazil, Heart of the World, Fatherland of the Gospel.* It suggests the pride the national apostle and reinterpreter of European Spiritualism took in converting into a true religion what had been an intellectual hobby in its area of origin.

The foundations were thus laid for a structure which was to congregate thousands of local centers into federations. In 1951 there were already twenty-one federations in different states of Brazil;[17] but they were neither streamlined nor unified, and some of them competed for membership. Most regional federations joined the Brazilian Spiritualist Federation, but some did not. Spiritualist youth organizations began to emerge in 1932, and in 1949 the Youth Department of the Brazilian Spiritualist Federation was established. Its main objective is indoctrination. In São Paulo City, the two largest regional federations maintain a center of social assistance and evangelization which is sought by approximately ten thousand persons every week.[18] Spiritualism's rapid expansion is largely because [of] its effort to solve social problems by providing institutional assistance. The relative position of the Spiritualist movement in this respect may be gleaned from the following comparative table.[19]

Institutions in Brazil, 1958

	Catholic	Protestant	Spiritualists
Hospitals	45	3	25
Clinics	178	56	168
Asylums	56	24	64
Shelters	50	15	104
Schools	1,008	618	435
Others	659	318	919
Total	1,995	1,034	1,715

The structural problems facing the Umbanda are compounded by "its internal dynamics which leads to instability of conceptions and a tendency toward syncretism of all conceivable shades."[20] There is no doctrinal or ritual unity; each *terreiro* (cult center) has its own system, and each leader thinks he has the monopoly on the absolute truth. The fiercely defended ritual peculiarities of each *terreiro* seems even more significant if the proliferation of these cult centers is taken into account. In the major areas of Umbanda development—the state of Guanabara and Rio de Janeiro—thirty thousand centers were reported some years ago.[21]

Umbanda is usually referred to as an "African" religion, meaning that, in addition to the presence of African elements in belief and ritual, its membership is composed of colored Brazilians. Although Negro membership looms disproportionally large, Umbanda has attracted too many individuals of non-African background to be classified as a "Negro religion." In São Paulo at least "the whites attend, in large proportions, the *terreiros* and even descendants of Italians, Syrians, and Japanese seek in its practices the magic effectiveness which had not been unknown to them in their countries of origin."[22]

The nature of the leadership prevalent in the Umbanda centers does not easily reconcile itself to the transfer of power to federative associations. In the Umbanda, Bastide writes,

> the leader of the session who speaks to the mediums, questions the spirits, drives them away, or commands them, assumes the role of a thaumaturge; in the new sect he takes the place which the *pagé* occupied in Amerindian society, or on the African continent. No longer are the disembodied spirits dominant; it is the magician who becomes the master of the spirits.[23]

Unlike his Spiritualist counterpart, the Umbanda leader appears to be a modern version of the shaman who competes with other shamans for control of the spirit world and those who believe in his powers. He is unlikely to surrender a fraction of his power to a federation, and if he does it is usually external pressure or the impossibility of providing certain expected services which induces him to agree on an uneasy and precarious alliance with his competitors.

. . .

To understand the structural differences between Umbanda and Pentecostalism, one has to compare the ways in which they have been growing. Like its predecessor, the Macumba, Umbanda has developed by the proliferation of local centers which achieved autonomy long before any central organization existed.

Pentecostalism, however, started with the foundation of sects by schism or secession from established churches. The new sects then set about to win converts by organized missionizing. Successful missionaries would found new congregations which were, in the beginning at least, dependent upon the central organization of the sect. Thus whatever authority or power is located in the individual congregation obviously derived from the sect, whose leaders tend to maintain structural ties with the local congregations.

With its emphasis on local uniqueness, charismatic leadership, and structural priority, the Umbanda proceeded in exactly the opposite way: integration has been possible only to the extent that local leaders have been willing to delegate at least some power to a broader organization.

FUNCTIONS

Healing. To substantiate our contention that the growth of the three movements is explicable in terms of their structural and functional adaptability to the culture of the lower social strata, it must be made clear, in the first place, that the term "lower strata" is intended to cover, not just the working class, but also the many who have achieved a rather precarious position in the lower ranks of the middle class. They all are beset by a variety of problems caused by the turbulent fashion in which culture change has been taking place during the last three decades. The identification of the three movements with the lower strata does not, by any means, imply identical composition of their membership nor the absence of variations in the social composition of local subdivisions of each movement.

The extent to which the three sects concern themselves with the alleviation of what may broadly be subsumed under the rubric, "physical and mental troubles," clearly indicates one of the areas where certain otherwise unsatisfied needs of the lower strata are met. The traditions of folk medicine with its countless magic components are, of course, very much alive. A steady flow of rural migrants from different regions carries a store of therapeutical magic to the city where a kind of "cross-fertilization" of the medical lore belonging to various subcultures takes place. It is against this background that the people's receptivity to the therapeutics of the Pentecostals, Spiritualists, and Umbandistas should be weighed.

The general inclination to accept, or at least to try out, the prescriptions of a prescientific medicine should be considered with the fact that the masses cannot afford the services of scientific medicine, and the free medical care provided by public and private institutions is highly limited. The constant influx of thousands of rural migrants, many of whom are in need of medical assistance, tends to make even generously planned institutional facilities inadequate within a few years. It is not surprising, therefore, that the prospect of having one's maladies cured constitutes the most powerful attraction of the three movements.

Among the Pentecostals, any leader who demonstrates unusual skill as a miracle healer is likely to draw large crowds. One of the most successful healers, an American missionary of the International Church of the Four-Square Gospel, gained many followers in São Paulo, and when his sect sponsored the National Crusade of Evangelization in 1956, many Protestant groups joined this interdenominational movement. The revival tent was (and still is) used extensively for spontaneous gatherings of the crusade which invaded many regions of Brazil. It seems that the revivalistic atmosphere of the crusade caused many defections among the established churches, and a number of new Pentecostal sects primarily concerned with the mediation of divine healing emerged.

The most conspicuous of new sects is probably the Pentecostal Church Brazil for Christ under Manuel de Mello, a markedly personalistic movement of considerable fluidity. Located in downtown São Paulo, the headquarters of this sect are constantly besieged by a ragged crowd waiting patiently in line for a prayer or a few words of solace from the thaumaturge. The aspect of the crowd leaves no doubt about the recent rural origin of its components.

The therapeutic functions of Pentecostalism are not limited to individual healing performances; they seem to play a significant role in the broader context of conversion and the radical change of personal habits. Many of our informants associated sickness with vice and conversion with health. The recurrent leitmotif of many life histories volunteered by converts ran like this: "Before my conversion I lived in vice and sin. I was always sick and no doctor could cure me. When I finally accepted the Spirit, my ailment miraculously disappeared and I have enjoyed excellent health ever since." The idea of "rebirth" which is so often associated with religious conversion thus appears to contain a physiological component.

In the Spiritualist and Umbandista centers, equal emphasis is put on healing. Camargo found that more than 60 percent of those who approach either sect are seeking relief from some ailment.[24] In fact, both sects use the therapeutic prospect as a proselytic device.

While the Pentecostal etiology of diseases emphasizes vice or sin as a probable determinant of diseases, Umbanda stresses the notion that nonfulfillment of sacred obligations may arouse the wrath of an *orixá* (African God), who punishes by inflicting illness upon the negligent. An alternative explanation ascribes physiological or mental troubles to acts of black magic. In either case, magical procedures are prescribed to placate the *orixá* or to undo the effects of sorcery.

The more sophisticated etiology of the Kardecists recognizes the possibility of disembodied spirits causing the symptoms of physical or mental maladies. Such "fluidic" actions are inspired by vengeance, mischief, or simple ignorance on the part of certain spirits. But an illness may also be interpreted as a Karmic tribulation, by means of which a person redeems himself of faults committed in a previous life. A third alternative recognizes inadequate development of mediumistic capabilities as a possible cause of mental perturbation or actual sickness. Negligence or ignorance prevents a person from developing his mediumistic potential; he becomes the victim of forces which he is unable to control, or even to identify.[25] Spiritualism, of course, provides therapeutical resources against such sufferings, but along with the supernatural approach the techniques of homeopathic medicine are available.

Reconstruction of the personal community. Since the lower strata of the metropolitan areas of Brazil are predominantly composed of migrants from rural regions or preindustrial towns, it may be assumed that their endeavor to find a niche in urban society involves adaptive changes of considerable magnitude. Back in his home town or village, the migrant was a member of a highly integrated group of kinsfolk and neighbors who constituted, in the terminology of Jules Henry, his "personal community," or "the group of people on whom he can rely for support and approval."[26]

Usually a man was born into his personal community; he took its structural implications for granted and was consequently unable to anticipate the problems arising from being deprived of its benefits. Although some migrants succeed in rebuilding at least a simulacrum of the lost personal community by joining relatives or people from the same town, most of them suffer from severe cultural shock, leading to such forms of anomic behavior as are reflected in the life histories of numerous sect members.

The migrant reacts to the novel situation by seeking, mostly by trial and error, a group of people in whose midst he may find emotional affinity and recognition as a person. Among the various alternatives he may choose, the three religious movements rank among the most accessible ones, especially since they compete with each other for new members and actually use proselytic techniques designed to solve personal problems in need of immediate attention. In any of the three movements, particularly in the Pentecostal sects, a person encounters the opportunity to rebuild his personal community.

The typical Pentecostal congregation is a highly cohesive primary group which tends to absorb the newcomer to an extent unmatched by most established churches. No matter how humble, unskilled or uneducated, the individual convert immediately feels that he is needed and relied upon; he is respectfully addressed as "brother," his services are requested by people who speak his own language and share his tastes, worries, and interests, who work with him at the same tasks and share with him the certainty of belonging to the "People of God," as the Pentecostals often call themselves. Whether he belongs to a construction team erecting a new temple or to a group of singing and guitar playing missionaries walking the streets, hospitals, and prisons in search of new converts, the Pentecostalist soon realizes that he belongs, that he is understood, needed and recognized as an equal among equals.

In the mediumistic sects, the participant encounters similar opportunities to rebuild his personal community. But there is one significant difference. Each center, or *terreiro*, is believed to benefit from the regular presence of particular spirits knowledgeable in the affairs of each member, his aspirations, afflictions and hopes, and willing to assist, encourage, admonish or censure him and thus to assume functions which are typically performed by the more influential members of one's personal community. Since the mediumistic religions emphasize the oneness of the "natural" and "supernatural," it seems to make sense to include the spirits among the prominent members of one's personal community.

Symbolic subversion of the traditional power structure. It was previously pointed out that sects seem to rid themselves of those structural elements of Brazilian society which have acted as a source of frustration. By asserting their organizational spontaneity, they have rejected the paternalistic tutelage of the upper strata. They emphasize social equality and thus negate the traditional class structure. "The festive character of the Umbanda means confraternization. In its midst there are neither classes nor castes."[27] They chose a theology which dispenses with the salvation monopoly of the Roman Catholic Church and its priestly hierarchy, which is perceived—rightly or wrongly—as a rampart of the traditional society. Their religious beliefs put the supernatural within the immediate reach of anybody who embraces the new faith.[28]

Yet direct and personal access to the supernatural, either through possession or through contact with those possessed, and vicarious participation in the benefits bestowed upon these by a spirit sets the members of the sects apart from ordinary humanity. The Pentecostalists especially like to think of themselves as the "Chosen People" or the "People of God." Possession by the Holy Spirit is interpreted as a legitimization of such privileged status. The sect members are, without exception, actual or potential recipients of the "Powers of the Spirit." The first seizure of "baptism by the Spirit," which a Pentecostalist seeks as anxiously as a Plains Indian seeks his vision, puts a seal of divine approval on the individual. By renouncing "the world" through repentance and adoption of an ascetic way of life one merits these extraordinary powers, which obviously contrast to the situation of powerlessness in which the Pentecostalists find themselves, individually and as members of a social class. The prevalent criteria of class differentiation, such as wealth, family background, education, and occupation, are ignored and often deprecated as manifestations of sinful *mundanismo*, or worldliness. Since the Pentecostalists as a class are not allowed by the "world" to attain distinction in any of these aspects, their validity is altogether denied. In a sense, this is subversion of the traditional or emerging social order in the language of religious symbolism.

Exactly what are these "powers of the Spirit" which confer special status on the Pentecostalists? In addition to thaumaturgy, spiritual illumination, persuasion, prophesying and glossolalia are the most treasured graces accessible to the convert. Illumination, variously called *discernimento* (discernment) or *alta percepção interior* (high internal perception), enables the Pentecostalist to recognize and understand the truth, and the power of *persuasão* transforms him into a fearless and convincing missionary who finds himself under an almost irresistible compulsion to disseminate the Word of God.

. . .

The social significance of the powers of the Spirit thus relates to the internal structure of the Pentecostal sects as well as to their position in the society at large.

The unequal distribution of these powers among the members of a sect opens up avenues of social mobility ordinarily denied to the Pentecostalists as members of an underprivileged class. The larger the share of such powers, the more likely it seems that the recipient will make his way to the top of the sectarian structure.

Bestowal of the powers of the Spirit upon the members of the Pentecostal sects acts as a compensatory mechanism for the frustrations inflicted by being deprived of actual power within Brazilian society. Or, to repeat the interpretation by Walter Goldschmidt:

> The appeal of the emotional religion and the asceticism for the disfranchised is this: It denies the existence of this world with its woes. *It denies the values in terms of which they are the underprivileged and sets up in their stead a putative society* in the kingdom of God, where, because of their special endowments (which we call emotionalism) they are the elite. It is the society of the saved. Millenarism is of the essence, for it is thus that the putative society is created; asceticism is the denial of the world in which they have been denied; and emotional participation is public acclamation of their personal acceptance into this world of super-reality.[29]

Similarly, the mediumistic abilities of the Spiritualists and Umbandistas confer a sense of power and achievement on both the mediums and those who are allowed to enter into personal communication with the spirit world through their mediums. A compensatory mechanism is put into motion when "meek public employees and humble domestic servants are suddenly transformed in[to] vehicles of illuminated spirits, bearers of sublime message."[30] It has been pointed out that Spiritualists have indeed a moral obligation to develop their mediumistic capabilities or face the supernatural sanctions threatening those who have been remiss of their duty to acquire firsthand contact with the spirit world. Such emphasis tends to make available spirit possession to the largest possible number of adherents.

The Spiritualists invoke spirits, often the spirits of famous departed that are believed to have reached superior levels of perfection. Contact with such reputable spirits, particularly the personal interest which these take in one's affairs, contributes to ego enhancement.

While the Kardecists unequivocally seek the association of spirits that during their lifetime had achieved distinction and high status, Umbanda doctrine embodies contradictory elements suggesting a more devious approach to the spirit world and its structural interpretation. As pointed out before, Macumba rid itself of its socially most undesirable associations with low-ranking African cult elements to the extent that it became Umbanda, i.e., by adopting certain elements of Spiritualism.

> Spiritualism becomes the idiom into which the phenomena of mystic trance are translated, and this idiom, accepted by the savants, studied by metapsychology, gives the African the assurance that his experience is no longer an experience of barbarians, or primitives, but that this experience has human rather than racial value.[31]

Thus the integration of Spiritualist principles gained increased social recognition for Umbanda and doubtlessly enhanced the self-image of its colored membership. The fact that some Brazilians of higher social strata were attracted by its rituals meant, of course, protection from its enemies and implicit transfer of power to the leaders of major *terreiros* who were no longer at the mercy of police officers and local politicians eager to capitalize on the reactions of the sect's opponents. And adherence of the white civil servant, business man, or industrialist to Umbanda assumes, in the eyes of the Negro, the meaning of a reversal of values; no longer is the Caboclo, the savage, nor the African the slave, subject to all kinds of whims of the whites; they have become the gods of the new religion and the former master bends his head humbly to them.[32]

To lend more credibility to this interpretation, it ought to be added that spirits of slaves as well as those of former masters often appear in sessions attended by colored people. Invariably, the audience learns that the spirits of the slaves have already reached the higher levels of perfection, while their masters are still tormented by the illusion of being incarnated. They carry heavy chains and need all the charity and patience of mediums and guides to take their first steps on the narrow path of spiritual ascent.[33]

The adherents of the Umbanda are derided by the Kardecists for invoking the "inferior" spirits of "Caboclos" and "old Negroes." But the Caboclos and old Negroes stand for the Indian and African ancestors of the Umbandistas, and the vindication of high status for such spirits seems quite consistent with the desire to subvert the traditional social order and its value system. Since this subversion cannot be carried out in reality, it is transferred to the spirit world, where the Indians and the Africans occupy higher levels of spiritual perfection, and the class of the "masters" is relegated to the lower levels. In a broader sense, Umbanda may be interpreted as a manifestation of Brazilian nationalism, inasmuch as it emphasizes and thus validates the Indian and African heritage of the lower social strata.[34]

The emphasis placed upon the therapeutical and social functions of the three religious movements is not intended to reduce their religious significance to the point of obliteration. Much on the contrary, the extraordinary degree to which the lifeways of these people are pervaded by religious representations and norms—quite in accord with the sacredness of their cultural tradition—provides the atmosphere of mystical belief in which the spirits associate with man in an effort to build a better society, without the inequities and maladies that afflict its actual counterpart. In a more secularized frame of mind, the sects would probably cease to perform the functions which now constitute their main attractions. The success story of the three movements makes sense only when related to the context of sacred folk traditions caught in the turmoil of profound and rapid cultural change.

SUMMARY

There are now between four and five million people involved in what may be considered the largest religious mass movement in the history of Brazil, perhaps of Latin America. In the first place, there is the rapid growth of Protestantism; but within Protestantism the characteristics of a mass movement proper apply primarily to the Pentecostal sects, whose combined membership is now in the neighborhood of two million.

The second largest movement comprises the various sect-like organizations which embraced the creed and practice of Spiritualism. Partially overlapping with Spiritualism there are some large cult groups, for example the Umbanda, whose doctrinal contents feed upon African elements which have been perpetuated by institutions such as Macumba, Candomblé, and Xangô.

The concomitance of these movements with sociocultural change is, of course, more than mere coincidence. This [paper] is intended to examine the relationships between the general process of culture change and the role and functions of these movements.

NOTES

1. Erasmo Braga and Kenneth G. Grubb, *The Republic of Brazil: A Survey of the Religious Situation* (London, New York, and Toronto: World Dominion Press, 1932), p. 71.

2. Prudencio Damboriena, *El protestantismo en América Latina* (Friburgo y Bogotá, Oficina Internacional de Investigaciones Sociales de FERES, 1963), I, 16.

3. Roger Bastide, *Les religions africaines au Brésil* (Paris: Presses Universitaires de France, 1960), p. 443.

4. Candido Procopio Ferreira de Camargo, *Kardecismo e Umbanda* (São Paulo: Livraria Pioneira Editôra, 1961), p. 176.

5. *Ibid.*, p. 17.

6. Buenaventura Kloppenburg, "*Introducción Histórica*" in Candido Procopio de Camargo, *Aspectos sociológicos del espiritismo en São Paulo* (Friburgo y Bogotá: Oficina Internacional de Investigaciones Sociales de FERES, 1961), p. 19.

7. W. C. Hoover, *Historia del Avivamiento Pentecostal en Chile* (Valparaiso: Imprenta Excelsior, 1948), p. 33.

8. Camargo, *op. cit.*, p. 18.

9. The spirits of Catholic priests belong to this category.

10. Roger Bastide, *Les religions africaines au Brésil* (Paris: Presses Universitaires de France, 1960), pp. 443 ff.

11. Camargo, *op. cit.*, p. 36.

12. Zêus Wantuil, *Las mesas giratórias y el Espiritismo* (Rio de Janeiro, 1958), p. 57.

13. Kloppenburg, *op. cit.*, p. 12.

14. For studies of Brazilian messianism see Maria Isaura Pereira de Queiroz, *La guerre sainte au Brésil: Le mouvement messianique du Contestado* (São Paulo: Universidade de São Paulo, Faculdáde de Filosofia, Ciências e Letras. Boletim No. 187, 1957), p. 1958.

15. Emilio Willems, "Acculturative Aspects of the Feast of the Holy Ghost in Brazil," *American Anthropologist* (1953), 400–408.

16. Francisco Cândido Xavier, *Brasil, coracão do mundo, pátria do Evangelho* (Rio de Janeiro: Federacão Espírita Brasileira, 1938), pp. 177–178.

17. Kloppenburg, *op. cit.*, p. 16.

18. Camargo, *op. cit.*, p. 28.

19. *Ibid.*, p. 137.

20. *Ibid.*, p. 33.

21. Bastide, *op. cit.*, p. 443.

22. Camargo, *op. cit.*, p. 35.

23. Bastide, *op. cit.*, p. 438.

24. Camargo, *op. cit.*, p. 94.

25. *Ibid.*, p. 100 ff.

26. Jules Henry, "The Personal Community and Its Invariant Properties," *American Anthropologist*, LX (1958), 827.

27. Emanuel Zespo, *Codificacão da lei de Umbanda* (2nd. ed.; Rio de Janeiro: Editôra Espiritualista Ltda., 1950), p. 147.

28. Some of these traits the sects share with the established Protestant churches.

29. Walter R. Goldschmidt, "Class Denominationalism in Rural California Churches," *American Journal of Sociology*, XLIX (1944), 354.

30. Camargo, *op. cit.*, p. 125.

31. Bastide, *op. cit.*, p. 432.

32. Bastide, *op. cit.*, pp. 467–468.

33. Camargo, *op. cit.*, p. 125.

34. Bastide, *op. cit.*, p. 468.

BIBLIOGRAPHY

Anuário Estatístico do Brazil. Rio de Janeiro, Brasil: Conselho Nacional de Estatística, 1958.

Bastide, Roger. *Les religions africaines au Brésil.* Paris: Presses Universitaires de France, 1960.

Braga, Erasmo, and Kenneth G. Grubb. *The Republic of Brazil: A Survey of the Religious Situation.* London, New York and Toronto: World Dominion Press, 1932.

Camargo, Candido Procopio Ferreira de. *Kardecismo e Umbanda.* São Paulo, Livraria Pioneira Editôra, 1961.

Damboriena, Prudencio. *El protestantismo en América Latina,* Vol. I. Friburgo y Bogotá: Oficina Internacional de Investigaciones Sociales de FERES, 1963.

Goldschmidt, Walter R. "Class Denominationalism in Rural California Churches." *American Journal of Sociology*, XLIX (1944), 348–355.

Henry, Jules. "The Personal Community and Its Invariant Properties." *American Anthropologist*, LX (1958), 827–831.

Hoover, W. C. *Historia del Avivamiento Pentecostal en Chile.* Valparaiso: Imprenta Excelsior, 1948.

Kloppenburg, Buenaventura. "*Introducción Histórica*" in Candido Procopio de Camargo, *Aspectos sociológicos del espiritismo en São Paulo.* Friburgo y Bogotá: Oficina Internacional de Investigaciones Sociales de FERES, 1961.

Queiroz, Maria Isaura Pereira de. *La guerre sainte au Brésil: Le mouvement messianique du Contestado.* São Paulo: Universidade de São Paulo, Faculdade de Filosofia, Ciências e Letras. Boletim No. 187, 1957.

Wantuil, Zêus. *Las mesas giratórias y el Espiritismo.* Rio de Janeiro, 1958.

Willems, Emilio. "Acculturative Aspects of the Feast of the Holy Ghost in Brazil." *American Anthropologist* (1953), 400–408.

Xavier, Francisco Cândido. *Brasil, coracão do mundo, pátria do Evangelho.* Rio de Janeiro, Federacão Espírita Brasileira, 1938.

Zespo, Emanuel. *Codificacão da lei de Umbanda.* Second edition. Rio de Janeiro: Editôra Espiritualista Ltda., 1960.

The Culture of Poverty

OSCAR LEWIS

Ever since Lewis first spoke of a "culture of poverty," the concept has been a focus of controversy, championed by some and criticized by others, while he himself continued to sharpen his definition. Without either idealizing or deploring poverty or the poor, he specified an increasing number of traits typifying poverty that recur cross-culturally, with reference to the larger society, the local community, the family, and the individual. This revised version of his most mature formulation on the subject was prepared when he had just returned from research in Cuba, a few months before his death.

Oscar Lewis was Professor of Anthropology at the University of Illinois at his untimely death in 1970. His early research yielded such varied books as The Effects of White Contact upon the Blackfoot Indians (1942), Life in a Mexican Village: Tepoztlan Restudied (1951), *and* Village Life in Northern India (1958). *He achieved widespread recognition of the literary and humanitarian value of ethnography with a series of volumes in which the narration of the informants themselves predominated and the "culture of poverty" provided a controversial thread of continuity:* Five Families: Mexican Case Studies in the Culture of Poverty (1959), The Children of Sanchez (1961), Pedro Martinez: A Mexican Peasant and his Family (1964), La Vida: A Puerto Rican Family in the Culture of Poverty—San Juan and New York (1966), A Death in the Sanchez Family (1969), *and* Six Women: Three Generations in a Puerto Rican Family (*in press*). *A number of his influential papers were compiled as* Anthropological Essays (1970).

Although a great deal has been written about poverty and the poor, the concept of a culture of poverty is relatively new. I first suggested it in 1959 in my book *Five Families: Mexican Case Studies in the Culture of Poverty.* The phrase is a catchy one and has become widely used and misused.[1] Michael Harrington used it extensively in his book *The Other America* (1961), which played an important role in sparking the national anti-poverty program in the United States. However, he used it in a somewhat broader and less technical sense than I had intended. I shall try to define it more precisely as a conceptual model, with special emphasis upon the distinction between poverty and the culture of poverty. The absence of intensive anthropological studies of poor families from a wide variety of national and cultural contexts, and especially from the socialist countries, is a serious handicap in formulating valid cross-cultural regularities. The model presented here is therefore provisional and subject to modification as new studies become available.

Throughout recorded history, in literature, in proverbs and in popular sayings, we find two opposite evaluations of the nature of the poor. Some characterize the poor as blessed, virtuous, upright, serene, independent, honest, kind, and happy. Others characterize them as evil, mean, violent, sordid, and criminal. These contradictory and confusing evaluations are also reflected in the in-

Reprinted, with revisions, from *La Vida*, Random House, New York, 1965, pp. xlii–lii. The revisions, made by the author in September 1970, are brief but, in his own words, "quite crucial."

fighting that is going on in the current war against poverty. Some stress the great potential of the poor for self-help, leadership, and community organization, while others point to the sometimes irreversible, destructive effect of poverty upon individual character, and therefore emphasize the need for guidance and control to remain in the hands of the middle class, which presumably has better mental health.

These opposing views reflect a political power struggle between competing groups. However, some of the confusion results from the failure to distinguish between poverty per se and the culture of poverty and from the tendency to focus upon the individual personality rather than upon the group—that is, the family and the slum community.

As an anthropologist I have tried to understand poverty and its associated traits as a culture or, more accurately, as a subculture[2] with its own structure and rationale, as a way of life which is passed down from generation to generation along family lines. This view directs attention to the fact that the culture of poverty in modern nations is not only a matter of economic deprivation, of disorganization, or of the absence of something. It is also something positive and provides some rewards without which the poor could hardly carry on.

Elsewhere I have suggested that the culture of poverty transcends regional, rural–urban, and national differences and shows remarkable similarities in family structure, interpersonal relations, time orientation, value systems, and spending patterns. These cross-national similarities are examples of independent invention and convergence. They are common adaptations to common problems.

The culture of poverty can come into being in a variety of historical contexts. However, it tends to grow and flourish in societies with the following set of conditions: (1) a cash economy, wage labor, and production for profit; (2) a persistently high rate of unemployment and underemployment for unskilled labor; (3) low wages; (4) the failure to provide social, political, and economic organization, either on a voluntary basis or by government imposition, for the low-income population; (5) the existence of a bilateral kinship system rather than a unilateral one;[3] and finally, (6) the existence of a set of values in the dominant class which stresses the accumulation of wealth and property, the possibility of upward mobility, and thrift, and explains low economic status as the result of personal inadequacy or inferiority.

The way of life which develops among some of the poor under these conditions is the culture of poverty. It can best be studied in urban or rural slums and can be described in terms of some seventy interrelated social, economic, and psychological traits. However, the number of traits and the relationships between them may vary from society to society and from family to family. For example, in a highly literate society, illiteracy may be more diagnostic of the culture of poverty than in a society where illiteracy is widespread and where even the well-to-do may be illiterate, as in some Mexican peasant villages before the revolution.

The culture of poverty is both an adaptation and a reaction of the poor to their marginal position in a class-stratified, highly individuated, capitalistic society. It represents an effort to cope with feelings of hopelessness and despair which develop from the realization of the improbability of achieving success in terms of the values and goals of the larger society. Indeed, many of the traits of the culture of poverty can be viewed as attempts at local solutions for problems not met by existing institutions and agencies because the people are not eligible for them, cannot afford them, or are ignorant or suspicious of them. For example, unable to obtain credit from banks, they are thrown upon their own resources and organize informal credit devices without interest.

The culture of poverty, however, is not only an adaptation to a set of objective conditions of the larger society. Once it comes into existence it tends to perpetuate itself from generation to generation because of its effect on the children. By the time slum children are age six or seven they have usually absorbed the basic values and attitudes of their subculture and are not psychologically geared to take full advantage of changing conditions or increased opportunities which may occur in their lifetime.

Most frequently the culture of poverty develops when a stratified social and economic system is breaking or is being replaced by another, as in the case of the transition from feudalism to capitalism or during periods of rapid technological change. Often it results from imperial conquest in which the native social and economic structure is smashed and the natives are maintained in a servile colonial status, sometimes for many generations. It can also occur in the process of detribalization, such as that now going on in Africa.

The most likely candidates for the culture of poverty are the people who come from the lower strata of a rapidly changing society and are already partially alienated from it. Thus landless rural workers who migrate to the cities can be expected to develop a culture of poverty much more readily than migrants from stable peasant villages with a well-organized traditional culture. In this connection there is a striking contrast between Latin America, where the rural population long ago made the transition from a tribal to a peasant society, and Africa, which is still close to its tribal heritage. The more corporate nature of many of the African tribal societies, in contrast to Latin American rural communities, and the persistence of village ties tend to inhibit or delay the formation of a full-blown culture of poverty in many of the African towns and cities. The special conditions of apartheid in South Africa, where the migrants are segregated into separate "locations" and do not enjoy freedom of movement, create special problems. Here the institutionalization of repression and discrimination tend to develop a greater sense of identity and group consciousness.

The culture of poverty can be studied from various points of view: the relationship between the subculture and the larger society; the nature of the slum community; the nature of the family; and the attitudes, values, and character structure of the individual.

1. The lack of effective participation and integration of the poor in the major institutions of the larger society is one of the crucial characteristics of the culture of poverty. This is a complex matter and results from a variety of factors which may include lack of economic resources, segregation and discrimination, fear, suspicion or apathy, and the development of local solutions for problems. However, "participation" in some of the institutions of the larger society—for example, in the jails, the army, and the public relief system—does not per se eliminate the traits of the culture of poverty. In the case of a relief system

which barely keeps people alive, both the basic poverty and the sense of hopelessness are perpetuated rather than eliminated.

Low wages, chronic unemployment, and underemployment lead to low income, lack of property ownership, absence of savings, absence of food reserves in the home, and a chronic shortage of cash. These conditions reduce the possibility of effective participation in the larger economic system. And as a response to these conditions we find in the culture of poverty a high incidence of pawning of personal goods, borrowing from local moneylenders at usurious rates of interest, spontaneous informal credit devices organized by neighbors, the use of second-hand clothing and furniture, and the pattern of frequent buying of small quantities of food many times a day as the need arises.

People with a culture of poverty produce very little wealth and receive very little in return. They have a low level of literacy and education, usually do not belong to labor unions, are not members of political parties, generally do not participate in the national welfare agencies, and make very little use of banks, hospitals, department stores, museums, or art galleries. They have a critical attitude toward some of the basic institutions of the dominant classes, hatred of the police, mistrust of government and those in high position, and a cynicism which extends even to the church. This gives the culture of poverty a high potential for protest and for being used in political movements aimed against the existing social order.

People with a culture of poverty are aware of middle-class values, talk about them, and even claim some of them as their own, but on the whole they do not live by them. Thus it is important to distinguish between what they say and what they do. For example, many will tell you that marriage by law, by the church, or by both, is the ideal form of marriage, but few will marry. To men who have no steady jobs or other sources of income, who do not own property and have no wealth to pass on to their children, who are present-time oriented, and who want to avoid the expense and legal difficulties involved in formal marriage and divorce, free unions or consensual marriage makes a lot of sense. Women will often turn down offers of marriage because they feel it ties them down to men who are immature, punishing, and generally unreliable. Women feel that consensual union gives them a better break; it gives them some of the freedom and flexibility that men have. By not giving the fathers of their children legal status as husbands, the women have a stronger claim on their children if they decide to leave their men. It also gives women exclusive rights to a house or any other property they may own.

2. When we look at the culture of poverty on the local community level, we find poor housing conditions, crowding, gregariousness, but above all a minimum of organization beyond the level of the nuclear and extended family. Occasionally there are informal, temporary groupings or voluntary associations within slums. The existence of neighborhood gangs which cut across slum settlements represents a considerable advance beyond the zero point of the continuum that I have in mind. Indeed, it is the low level of organization which gives the culture of poverty its marginal and anachronistic quality in our highly complex, specialized, organized society. Most primitive peoples have achieved a higher level of sociocultural organization than our modern urban slum dwellers.

In spite of the generally low level of organization, there may be a sense of community and *esprit de corps* in urban slums and in slum neighborhoods. This can vary within a single city, or from region to region or country to country. The major factors influencing this variation are the size of the slum, its location and physical characteristics, length of residence, incidence of home and land ownership (versus squatter rights), rentals, ethnicity, kinship ties, and freedom or lack of freedom of movement. When slums are separated from the surrounding area by enclosing walls or other physical barriers, when rents are low and fixed and stability of residence is great (twenty or thirty years), when the population constitutes a distinct ethnic, racial, or language group, is bound by ties of kinship or *compadrazgo*, and when there are some internal voluntary associations, then the sense of local community approaches that of a village community. In many cases this combination of favorable conditions does not exist. However, even where internal organization and *esprit de corps* are at a bare minimum and people move around a great deal, a sense of territoriality develops which sets off the slum neighborhoods from the rest of the city. In Mexico City and San Juan [Puerto Rico] this sense of territoriality results from the unavailability of low-income housing outside the slum areas. In South Africa the sense of territoriality grows out of the segregation enforced by the government, which confines the rural migrants to specific locations.

3. On the family level the major traits of the culture of poverty are the absence of childhood as a specially prolonged and protected stage in the life cycle, early initiation into sex, free unions or consensual marriages, a relatively high incidence of the abandonment of wives and children, a trend toward female- or mother-centered families and consequently a much greater knowledge of maternal relatives, a strong predisposition to authoritarianism, lack of privacy, verbal emphasis upon family solidarity which is only rarely achieved because of sibling rivalry, and competition for limited goods and maternal affection.

4. On the level of the individual the major characteristics are a strong feeling of marginality, of helplessness, of dependence, and of inferiority. I found this to be true of slum dwellers in Mexico City and San Juan among families who do not constitute a distinct ethnic or racial group and who do not suffer from racial discrimination. In the United States, of course, the culture of poverty of the Negroes had the additional disadvantage of racial discrimination, but as I have already suggested, this additional disadvantage contains a great potential for revolutionary protest and organization which seems to be absent in the slums of Mexico City or among the poor whites in the South.

Other traits include a high incidence of maternal deprivation, of orality, of weak ego structure, confusion of sexual identification, a lack of impulse control, a strong present-time orientation with relatively little ability to defer gratification and to plan for the future, a sense of resignation and fatalism, a widespread belief in male superiority, and a high tolerance for psychological pathology of all sorts.

People with a culture of poverty are provincial and locally oriented and have very little sense of history. They know only their own troubles, their own local conditions, their own neighborhood, their own way of life. Usually they do not have the knowledge, the vision, or the ideology to see the similarities between their problems and those of their counterparts elsewhere in the world. They are not class-conscious, although they are very sensitive indeed to status distinctions.

In considering the traits discussed above, the following propositions must be kept in mind. (1) The traits fall into a number of clusters and are functionally related within each cluster. (2) Many, but not all, of the traits of different clusters are also functionally related. For example, men who have low wages and suffer chronic unemployment develop a poor self-image, become irresponsible, abandon their wives and children, and take up with other women more frequently than do men with high incomes and steady jobs. (3) None of the traits, taken individually, is distinctive per se of the subculture of poverty. It is their conjunction, their function, and their patterning that define the subculture. (4) The subculture of poverty, as defined by these traits, is a statistical profile; that is, the frequency of distribution of the traits both singly and in clusters will be greater than in the rest of the population. In other words, more of the traits will occur in combination in families with a subculture of poverty than in stable working-class, middle-class, or upper-class families. Even within a single slum there will probably be a gradient from culture of poverty families to families without a culture of poverty. (5) The profiles of the subculture of poverty will probably differ in systematic ways with the difference in the national cultural contexts of which they are a part. It is expected that some new traits will become apparent with research in different nations.

I have not yet worked out a system of weighing each of the traits, but this could probably be done and a scale could be set up for many of the traits. Traits that reflect lack of participation in the institutions of the larger society or an outright rejection—in practice, if not in theory—would be crucial traits; for example, illiteracy, provincialism, free unions, abandonment of women and children, lack of membership in voluntary associations beyond the extended family.

When the poor become class-conscious or active members of trade-union organizations, or when they adopt an internationalist outlook on the world, they are no longer part of the culture of poverty, although they may still be desperately poor. Any movement, be it religious, pacifist, or revolutionary, which organizes and gives hope to the poor and effectively promotes solidarity and a sense of identification with larger groups, destroys the psychological and social core of the culture of poverty. In this connection, I suspect that the civil rights movement among the Negroes in the United States has done more to improve their self-image and self-respect than have their economic advances, although, without doubt, the two are mutually reinforcing.

The distinction between poverty and the culture of poverty is basic to the model described here. There are degrees of poverty and many kinds of poor people. The culture of poverty refers to one way of life shared by poor people in given historical and social contexts. The economic traits which I have listed for the culture of poverty are necessary but not sufficient to define the phenomena I have in mind. There are a number of historical examples of very poor segments of the population which do not have a way of life that I would describe as a subculture of poverty. Here I should like to give four examples.

1. Many of the primitive or preliterate peoples studied by anthropologists suffer from dire poverty which is the result of poor technology and/or poor natural resources, or of both, but they do not have the traits of the subculture of poverty. Indeed, they do not constitute a subculture because their societies are not highly stratified. In spite of their poverty they have a relatively integrated, satisfying, and self-sufficient culture. Even the simplest food-gathering and hunting tribes have a considerable amount of organization, bands and band chiefs, tribal councils, and local self-government—traits which are not found in the culture of poverty.

2. In India the lower castes (the Chamars, the leather workers, and the Bhangis, the sweepers) may be desperately poor, both in the villages and in the cities, but most of them are integrated into the larger society and have their own *panchayat*[4] organizations which cut across village lines and give them a considerable amount of power.[5] In addition to the caste system, which gives individuals a sense of identity and belonging, there is still another factor, the clan system. Wherever there are unilateral kinship systems or clans one would not expect to find the culture of poverty, because a clan system gives people a sense of belonging to a corporate body with a history and a life of its own, thereby providing a sense of continuity, a sense of a past and of a future.

3. The Jews of eastern Europe were very poor, but they did not have many of the traits of the culture of poverty because of their tradition of literacy, the great value placed upon learning, the organization of the community around the rabbi, the proliferation of local voluntary associations, and their religion which taught that they were the chosen people.

4. My fourth example is speculative and relates to socialism. On the basis of my limited experience in one socialist country—Cuba—and on the basis of my reading, I am inclined to believe that the culture of poverty does not exist in the socialist countries. I first went to Cuba in 1947 as a visiting professor for the State Department. At that time I began a study of a sugar plantation in Melena del Sur and of a slum in Havana. After the Castro Revolution I made my second trip to Cuba as a correspondent for a major magazine, and I revisited the same slum and some of the same families. The physical aspect of the slum had changed very little, except for a beautiful new nursery school. It was clear that the people were still desperately poor, but I found much less of the despair, apathy, and hopelessness which are so diagnostic of urban slums in the culture of poverty. They expressed great confidence in their leaders and hope for a better life in the future. The slum itself was now highly organized, with block communities, educational committees, party committees. The people had a new sense of power and importance. They were armed and were given a doctrine which glorified the lower class as the hope of humanity. (I was told by one Cuban official that they had practically eliminated delinquency by giving arms to the delinquents!)

It is my impression that the Castro regime—unlike Marx and Engels—did not write off the so-called lumpen proletariat as an inherently reactionary and anti-revolutionary force, but rather saw its revolutionary potential and tried to utilize it. In this connection, Frantz Fanon makes a similar evaluation of the role of the lumpen proletariat based upon his experience in the Algerian struggle for independence. In his recently published book he wrote:

It is within this mass of humanity, this people of the shanty towns, at the core of the lumpen proletariat, that the rebellion will find its urban spearhead. For the lumpen proletariat, that horde of starving men, uprooted from their tribe and from their clan, constitutes one of the most spontaneous and most radically revolutionary forces of a colonized people.[6]

My own studies of the urban poor in the slums of San Juan do not support the generalizations of Fanon. I have found very little revolutionary spirit or radical ideology among low-income Puerto Ricans. On the contrary, most of the families I studied were quite conservative politically and about half of them were in favor of the Republican Statehood Party. It seems to me that the revolutionary potential of people with a culture of poverty will vary considerably according to the national context and the particular historical circumstances. In a country like Algeria, which was fighting for its independence, the lumpen proletariat was drawn into the struggle and became a vital force. However, in countries like Puerto Rico, in which the movement for independence has very little mass support, and in countries like Mexico which achieved their independence a long time ago and are now in their postrevolutionary period, the lumpen proletariat is not a leading source of rebellion or of revolutionary spirit. In effect, we find that in primitive societies and in caste societies, the culture of poverty does not develop. In socialist, fascist, and highly developed capitalist societies with a welfare state, the culture of poverty tends to decline. I suspect that the culture of poverty flourishes in, and is generic to, the early free-enterprise stage of capitalism and that it is also endemic in colonialism.

It is important to distinguish between different profiles in the subculture of poverty depending upon the national context in which these subcultures are found. If we think of the culture of poverty primarily in terms of the factor of integration in the larger society and a sense of identification with the great tradition of that society, or with a new emerging revolutionary tradition, then we will not be surprised that some slum dwellers with a lower per capita income may have moved farther away from the core characteristics of the culture of poverty than others with a higher per capita income. For example, Puerto Rico has a much higher per capita income than Mexico, yet Mexicans have a deeper sense of identity.

I have listed fatalism and a low level of aspiration as one of the key traits for the subculture of poverty. Here too, however, the national context makes a big difference. Certainly the level of aspiration of even the poorest sector of the population in a country like the United States with its traditional ideology of upward mobility and democracy is much higher than in more backward countries like Ecuador and Peru, where both the ideology and the actual possibilities of upward mobility are extremely limited and where authoritarian values still persist in both the urban and rural milieus.

Because of the advanced technology, the high level of literacy, the development of mass media, and the relatively high aspiration level of all sectors of the population, especially when compared with underdeveloped nations, I believe that although there is still a great deal of poverty in the United States (estimates range from thirty to fifty million people), there is relatively little of what I would call the culture of poverty. My rough guess would be that only about

20 percent of the population below the poverty line (between six and ten million people) in the United States have characteristics which would justify classifying their way of life as that of a culture of poverty. Probably the largest sector within this group would consist of very low-income Negroes, Mexicans, Puerto Ricans, American Indians, and Southern poor whites. The relatively small number of people in the United States with a culture of poverty is a positive factor because it is more difficult to eliminate the culture of poverty than to eliminate poverty per se.

Middle-class people, and this would certainly include most social scientists, tend to concentrate on the negative aspects of the culture of poverty. They tend to associate negative valences to such traits as present-time orientation and concrete versus abstract orientation. I do not intend to idealize or romanticize the culture of poverty. As someone has said, "It is easier to praise poverty than to live in it"; yet some of the positive aspects which may flow from these traits must not be overlooked. Living in the present may develop a capacity for spontaneity and adventure, for the enjoyment of the sensual, the indulgence of impulse, which is often blunted in the middle-class, future-oriented man. Perhaps it is this reality of the moment which the existential writers are so desperately trying to recapture but which the culture of poverty experiences as a natural, everyday phenomenon. The frequent use of violence certainly provides a ready outlet for hostility so that people in the culture of poverty suffer less from repression than does the middle class.

In the traditional view, anthropologists have said that culture provides human beings with a design for living, with a ready-made set of solutions for human problems so that individuals don't have to begin all over again each generation. That is, the core of culture is its positive adaptive function. I, too, have called attention to some of the adaptive mechanisms in the culture of poverty—for example, the low aspiration level helps to reduce frustration, the legitimization of short-range hedonism makes possible spontaneity and enjoyment. However, on the whole it seems to me that it is a relatively thin culture. There is a great deal of pathos, suffering, and emptiness among those who live in the culture of poverty. It does not provide much support or long-range satisfaction and its encouragement of mistrust tends to magnify helplessness and isolation. Indeed, the poverty of culture is one of the crucial aspects of the culture of poverty.

The concept of the culture of poverty provides a high level of generalization which, hopefully, will unify and explain a number of phenomena viewed as distinctive characteristics of racial, national, or regional groups. For example, matrifocality, a high incidence of consensual unions, and a high percentage of households headed by women, which have been thought to be distinctive of Caribbean family organization or of Negro family life in the United States, turn out to be traits of the culture of poverty and are found among diverse peoples in many parts of the world and among peoples who have had no history of slavery.

The concept of a cross societal subculture of poverty enables us to see that many of the problems we think of as distinctively our own or distinctively Negro problems (or problems of any other special racial or ethnic group) also exist in countries where there are no distinct ethnic minority groups. This suggests that the elimination of physical poverty per se may not be enough to eliminate the culture of poverty, which is a whole way of life.

What is the future of the culture of poverty? In considering this question, one must distinguish between those countries in which it represents a relatively small segment of the population and those in which it constitutes a very large one. Obviously the solutions will differ in these two situations. In the United States, the major solution proposed by planners and social workers in dealing with multiple-problem families and the so-called hard core of poverty has been to attempt slowly to raise their level of living and to incorporate them into the middle class. Wherever possible, there has been some reliance upon psychiatric treatment.

In the underdeveloped countries, however, where great masses of people live in the culture of poverty, a social-work solution does not seem feasible. Because of the magnitude of the problem, psychiatrists can hardly begin to cope with it. They have all they can do to care for their own growing middle class. In these countries the people with a culture of poverty may seek a more revolutionary solution. By creating basic structural changes in society, by redistributing wealth, by organizing the poor and giving them a sense of belonging, of power, and of leadership, revolutions frequently succeed in abolishing some of the basic characteristics of the culture of poverty even when they do not succeed in abolishing poverty itself.

Some of my readers have misunderstood the subculture of poverty model and have failed to grasp the importance of the distinction between poverty and the subculture of poverty. In making this distinction I have tried to document a broader generalization; namely, that it is a serious mistake to lump all poor people together, because the causes, the meaning, and the consequences of poverty vary considerably in different sociocultural contexts. There is nothing in the concept that puts the onus of poverty on the character of the poor. Nor does the concept in any way play down the exploitation and neglect suffered by the poor. Indeed, the subculture of poverty is part of the larger culture of capitalism, whose social and economic system channels wealth into the hands of a relatively small group and thereby makes for the growth of sharp class distinctions.

I would agree that the main reasons for the persistence of the subculture are no doubt the pressures that the larger society exerts over its members and the structure of the larger society itself. However, *these are not the only reasons.* The subculture develops mechanisms that tend to perpetuate it, especially because of what happens to the world view, aspirations, and character of the children who grow up in it. For this reason, improved economic opportunities, though absolutely essential and of the highest priority, are not sufficient to alter basically or eliminate the subculture of poverty. Moreover, elimination is a process that will take more than a single generation, even under the best of circumstances, including a socialist revolution.

Some readers have thought I was saying, "Being poor is terrible, but having a culture of poverty is not so bad." On the contrary, I am saying that it is easier to eliminate poverty than the culture of poverty. I am also suggesting that the poor in a precapitalistic caste-ridden society like India had some advantages over modern urban slum dwellers because the people were organized in castes and *panchayats,* and this organization gave them some sense of identity and some strength and power. Perhaps Gandhi had the urban slums of the West in mind when he wrote that the caste system was one of the greatest inventions of mankind. Similarly, I have argued that the poor Jews of eastern Europe, with their strong tradition of literacy and community organization, were better off than people with the culture of poverty. On the other hand, I would argue that people with the culture of poverty, with their strong sense of resignation and fatalism, are less driven and less anxious than the striving lower middle class, who are still trying to make it in the face of the greatest odds.

OTES

1. There has been relatively little discussion of the culture of poverty concept in the professional journals, however. Two articles deal with the problem in some detail: Elizabeth Herzog, "Some Assumptions About the Poor," in *The Social Service Review,* December 1963, pp. 389–402; Lloyd Ohlin, "Inherited Poverty," Organization for Economic Cooperation and Development (no date), Paris.

2. While the term "subculture of poverty" is technically more accurate, I have used "culture of poverty" as a shorter form.

3. In a unilineal kinship system, descent is reckoned either through males or through females. When traced exclusively through males it is called patrilineal or agnatic descent; when reckoned exclusively through females it is called matrilineal or uterine descent. In a bilateral or cognatic system, descent is traced through males and females without emphasis on either line.

In a unilateral system, the lineage consists of all the descendants of one ancestor. In a patrilineal system, the lineage is composed of all descendants through males of one male ancestor. A matrilineage consists of all the descendants through females of one female ancestor. The lineage may thus contain a very large number of generations. If bilateral descent is reckoned, however, the number of generations that can be included in a social unit is limited, since the number of ancestors doubles every generation.

Unilateral descent groups ("lineages" or "clans") are corporate groups in the sense that the lineage or clan may act as a collectivity; it can take blood vengeance against another descent group, it can hold property, and so on. However, the bilateral kin group (the "kindred") can rarely act as a collectivity because it is not a "group" except from the point of view of a particular individual and, furthermore, has no continuity over time.

In a unilateral system, an individual is assigned to a group by virtue of his birth. In contrast, a person born into a bilateral system usually has a choice of relatives whom he chooses to recognize as "kin" and with whom he wants to associate. This generally leads to a greater diffuseness and fragmentation of ties with relatives over time.

4. A formal organization designed to provide caste leadership.

5. It may be that in the slums of Calcutta and Bombay an incipient culture of poverty is developing. It would be highly desirable to do family studies there as a crucial test of the culture-of-poverty hypothesis.

6. Frantz Fanon, *The Wretched of the Earth.* New York, Grove Press, 1965, p. 103.

The Claims of Tradition in Urban Latin America

RICHARD M. MORSE

The explosive growth of metropolitan areas throughout Latin America in recent years has focused attention on the city as a distinctive field of social action. This imaginative historian's broad perspective, viewing bureaucratic Lima, commercial Buenos Aires, and industrial São Paulo as "windows to their societies," relates the changing idea of the city to such timely—and timeless—questions as race relations, violence, social mobility, and modernization.

Richard M. Morse is Professor of History at Yale University and long-term chairman of Yale's Council on Latin American Studies. He has written From Community to Metropolis: A Biography of São Paulo, Brazil (1958), *and edited* The Bandeirantes: The Historical Role of the Brazilian Pathfinders (1965), *and* The Urban Development of Latin America, 1750–1920 (1971).

CITIES AS THEATERS FOR MODERNIZATION

The study of how traditions influence the patterns of modernizing societies may be conducted with primary reference to any of several units of analysis. . . . This essay takes the societies of Latin America for its subject and the cities of Latin America as the arena for examining the persistence of traditions. Cities are artificial for this purpose when construed in polarity to folk cultures, rural zones, or villages. Here they are thought of as nodes of activity and control, as settings which synthesize or catalyze tensions of a larger society. While the urban focus may deflect attention from national political regimes, it is more manageable than the national one and points toward configurations and rhythms of change that underlie the sometimes erratic or contingent national-level manifestations. While the city in a colonial or export-dependent nation serves as a relay point for diffusing change to a hinterland, it also functions, paradoxically, as a control center which dampens the effects of innovation impinging from without, appears to maintain hinterlands and secondary towns in "colonial" submission, and subjects even its own work force to economic marginality and political impotence. Again, therefore, cities are to be seen not as growth poles or as termini for a continuum but as theaters, pressure chambers perhaps, where conflicting forces of the larger society intersect.[1]

Viewing cities, then, as windows to their societies and not primarily as economic dynamos or transportation break points, we will now seek to identify what image of the city and what urban sociological imperatives Latin America inherits from its preindustrial past.

From *Daedalus* (forthcoming, 1973). Reprinted by permission of DAEDALUS, Journal of the American Academy of Arts and Sciences, Boston, Massachusetts, and the author.

URBAN TRADITIONS OF IBERO- AND ANGLO-AMERICA

In many ways the Iberian conquest and settlement of America recapitulated the historical moment when the city-idea had been universalized more than a millennium earlier in its imperial (city-empire of Rome) and Christian (City of God) versions. Just as Cicero labored to reconcile the self-contained polis with the requirements for a universal legal order, so in sixteenth-century Ibero-America one finds the word *república* applied ambivalently to municipal communities of Spaniards or Indians and to the overarching imperial community. Similarly, Ibero-American colonization perpetuated the Augustinian tension between the practical requirements for terrestrial communities and those for rehabilitation of individual souls for the Celestial City. Risking a foreshortened historical perspective, we can identify two commonly cited "obstacles to change" in contemporary Latin America with these ancient cultural commitments. The resistance of its societies to proliferation of broad interest groups, parties, and secondary associations recalls the ancient chasm between municipality and empire, while the much-deplored lack of "achievement motivation" recalls an ancient scepticism toward private salvation through social action.

What makes Latin America so enticing a field for the study of modernization is that its societies took a predominantly "Western" cast after the Amerindian societies were destroyed or fragmented during the first decades of European colonization. Whereas in Africa and Asia Europeans exercised commercial and military control from beachhead enclaves, in Latin America the enclave phenomenon was provided by the scattered vestiges of Amerindian societies. Yet despite the early and thorough "Westernization" of Latin America, its incorporation into the shifting cycles of the Atlantic economy, and its receptivity to European science and the Enlightenment (diminished but not effaced by the Inquisition), its societies have surprisingly resisted internalizing the capacity to generate change. Thus while Latin and British North America might appear in world perspective as merely two varieties of Euro-Christian transplant, they can also be juxtaposed in a fashion that leaves certain non-Western societies—the Chinese or Japanese for instance—as intermediate cases. Parsons does just this when he polarizes Latin America and the United States as particularistic-ascriptive and universal-achievement societies.[2]

Without fully embracing the controversial Parsonian constructed types, we will sketch here two contrasts between the Ibero- and Anglo-American municipal traditions. The first has to do with urban images, the second with municipal institutions.[3]

The city-idea which Spaniards and Portuguese brought to America was that of an Edenic, exemplary, or paradigmatic city, not one that was contractual, covenanted, or routinely replicable. This is evident when we review the conquistadors' beliefs in a shining city of gold, the Jesuit missionary schemes, or the Franciscan prophecies of an apocalyptic City of God. It is less clear when we examine the actual founding of secular towns, for the famous Spanish colonizing ordinances largely systematized the practical experience of several decades with respect to urban form and the structure of urban societies. Even here, however, the essential urban *idea* was the Aristotelian-Thomist city-state as a "natural form of association," a whole composed of unlike parts and prior to them. Precisely the fact that the ideal ordering and equilibrium of parts was only imperfectly replicable under practical circumstances required that communities, or municipal units, be hierarchically arranged to compose the larger "republic."

The covenanted Puritan city or "city upon a hill" of New England retained certain medieval principles of social subordination. The only "natural" relationship, however, was that between parents and children. Other relations were voluntary, covenanted, and dependent on two parties' "mutual engagement." Thus the community was conceived of as comprising a series of dual relationships. Although persons might be old or young, wise or foolish, good or wicked, society itself was not composed of corporate groups or castes; it did not preexist or transcend the contractual arrangements of its members. Because the congregation lacked separate identity, each private conscience bore extraordinary responsibility for preserving the sanctity of the community. By the same token established congregations could throw off new, autonomous ones which would each initiate an independent relation to God.[4]

This difference in ecclesiastical tradition and social philosophy was reinforced by a divergence in institutional development. The late-medieval urbanization of northwest Europe was linked with commercial revival and with the need of entrepreneurs for a distinctive urban regime of commercial law. In interpreting this and subsequent trends, historians of varied persuasions have understood politico-legal change to be consequent on accumulation of wealth by new social groups. When at length England spawned its American colonies, commercial advantage became the preeminent factor in determining urban location and city hierarchies in the seaboard, northern, and midwest zones, if recent literature on the topic is a guide. Early urban elites are generally portrayed as owing their position to commercial or manufacturing fortune, and the lot of subsequent immigrants is, and was at the time, generally assumed to be a function of private economic success. In our day no less than in Andrew Carnegie's, the redemption of America's downtrodden and ghettoized is ultimately perceived as contingent on motivation and capacitation of private energies for economic endeavor, and only intermittently perceived as depending on their political mobilization.

At the time of northern Europe's commercial quickening, the urban history of the Iberian peninsula was already taking its own course. Here, in the central regions, urbanization was a byproduct of and vehicle for the centuries-long reconquest of lands from Islam. Cities were not flash points of economic change in a vast manorial landscape, but agro-military centers, embedded in a primitive state organization that functioned to secure territorial settlement. Urban society was estate-based or seigneurial, and economic activity depended heavily on prior access to political favor or control. Bourgeois groups failed to assume a commanding urban role, nor did cities themselves extend to their environs a distinctive "urban peace."

The free individual creation and disposal of wealth allowed the [north] European bourgeois to win autonomy as a human being and social power within the community. The Iberian, on the contrary, came to enjoy material wealth and dispose of it freely *because he had previously acquired social power*. The collective ethos in both cases is closely linked to the historical process of personal emancipation. Bourgeois wealth is the means to reach power in Europe. In medieval Spain social power yields the only access to wealth.[5]

In colonial Ibero-America municipal organization was subsumed within the structure of empire, eliminating the possibility of significant politico-legal or commercial innovation. The patrimonial cast of the society was to make power and protection more important goals for social striving than income and occupational status. This stress on power and acquisition rather than capacitation causes persons to be perceived as "types" identified with characteristic strategies to achieve external objectives rather than as idiosyncratic bundles of traits cultivable for self-fulfillment.[6]

These two lines of analysis, the religio-philosophic and the historico-institutional, may be independently developed yet are mutually supportive in that they find common origins in the historical matrix of medieval and early modern Europe.

TRADITIONALISM CAMOUFLAGED

Historical explanations for discrepancies between the societies of the northern and southern Americas need not detain us further. Of concern here is the persistence of traditional features in the southern societies after 1750. In the waning decades of the colonial regime urban elites were increasingly exposed to a flow of products, technological innovations, economic incentives, and intellectual formulations from early industrial Europe. With independence in the early nineteenth century and the dismantling of mercantilist restraints, this exposure was intensified. The manifestoes, constitutions, and political and economic writings of the new nations give the impression that their authors had turned their backs on pre-Enlightenment Spain and Portugal and slipped easily into the molds of thought of northwest Europe, adopting its rallying cries of nationalism, republicanism, rights of man, and economic progress. If, later in the century, we accompany a traveler to the area's capital cities, his descriptions have a quaint and exotic flavor but carry a clear implication that urban life here is recognizably "civilized" and "catching up" with the Rest of the West.[7]

In sum, these dominantly European societies might have been expected to undergo prompt and sweeping modernization, certainly in comparison to Afro-Asian lands. Only very recently has a start been made in putting together a comprehensive explanation of why this did not occur. Such an explanation must link up three sets of circumstances:

(1) Persistence of the Ibero-Catholic social ethic. In Weberian terms, a Catholic society is one in which grace is institutionally dispensed. The personal qualifications of persons seeking "salvation" are a matter of indifference to institutions or charismatic figures distributing grace. Expectations of personal accomplishment are modest, and the prospect of grace spares individuals the need to rationalize the pattern of personal life.

(2) Inherited patrimonial institutional structures. To mention only the agrarian domain: As haciendas tended to be organized for subsistence rather than export, their proprietors were more interested in expanding their territory

and peon labor forces than in economic rationalization. This perpetuated endemic rivalries among clustered, clientistic kin groups and their resistance to strong central government. Even where export-oriented plantation agriculture was introduced, patrimonial land allocation and management created peonage and tenancy, militating against the formation of numerous, autonomous agricultural middle classes.

(3) External economic influence. Collapse of the Iberian mercantilist regimes brought Latin American economies into the powerful orbit of the banking and commercial systems of the industrializing countries of Europe and North America, notably England.

These three elements interacted throughout the century to postpone industrialization, favor a selective shift to rationalized, monocultural agro-pastoral and mineral production for export, hinder the formation of strong national institutions, and stifle the political voice of urban middle groups. One may also utilize this threefold analysis of social ethic, institutions, and external pressure as a point of departure for comparing the Latin American case with others such as the United States (differentiated by its social ethic and internal institutions) and Japan (where, in a society of feudal traditions confronting strong external pressures, social ethic becomes a critical variable). What has made Latin America something of a puzzle is that the ingredients of its situation were for so long camouflaged. The post-independence revulsion against the Iberian heritage, provoking the easy adoption of the vocabulary and precepts of Anglo-French Enlightenment and romantic nationalism, left most commentators powerless to gauge and analyze coherently the claims of centuries-old institutional and behavioral patterns. Similarly, the commercial ascendancy of England was more often seen as vindicating the liberal tenet that economic specialization universalizes development and prosperity than as furnishing a new external source of nourishment for the internal structures of clientage.

BUREAUCRATIC LIMA, COMMERCIAL BUENOS AIRES, INDUSTRIAL SÃO PAULO

We now pursue our urban theme with a selective examination of three cities whose hegemony is linked with the three periods of external economic dependency into which Latin American history is now conventionally, if simplistically, divided. The first is viceregal, priest-ridden, silver-rich Lima, which enjoyed privileged administrative and commercial status during the era of Spanish mercantilist exclusivism. The second is Buenos Aires, mistress of the Plata estuary, outlet for Argentina's fertile agro-pastoral hinterland, and hegemonic metropolis for the southern cone of the continent during the heyday of English commercial supremacy after 1870. The third is São Paulo, coffee capital of southern Brazil, whose twentieth-century industrial surge makes it the archetypal city for the period of United States financial and technological hegemony. Although these cities exhibit important differences in historical dynamic, phasing of growth, receptivity to modernization, and internal structure, there is evidence to suggest that they continue to share a similar social ethic and broadly comparable forms of social action.

Lima, prestigious "City of Kings," fell on hard times as independence approached. In 1800 Alexander von Humboldt found that its wealthiest families had yearly incomes of only 6,500 pesos as against 35,000 in Havana and 200,000 in Mexico City. By the mid-nineteenth century its population was scarcely larger than it had been a century earlier. With Peru's other cities remaining virtually stagnant, Lima's growth rate finally pulled abreast of the nation's in the period of guano prosperity. A sociological analysis of Lima conducted at the century's end yields a classic picture of a neocolonial bureaucratic capital, three to six times the size of its five closest rivals, monopolizing commercial and financial functions, controlled by an agro-urban aristocracy.[8]

According to Joaquín Capelo, Lima's nuclear social unit was still the extended family or "tribe," often functioning as a clientage system that ranged across all social strata. Few clubs, intellectual groups, or professional associations existed. Monopoly, usury, and confiscatory taxation stifled business enterprise; economic success depended heavily on political privilege. The enterprising street vendor who moved into a market stall rarely acquired a full-size store; not only were credit rates exorbitant but foreigners had largely preempted middle-level business as well as high managerial positions. For Capelo, the dominant malady of urban society was parasitism, and his main villains were the usurious pawnbroker, the rapacious concessionaire, the unscrupulous petty bureaucrat, and the cynical *sin vergüenza* or bum.

This panorama calls to mind the three "abnormal" forms of division of labor which Emile Durkheim outlined only two years before Capelo's work began appearing in 1895. Anomie, the variety on which Durkheim lavished most attention, is the least pertinent to this case, for anomie as he used the term was related to social rationalization and to the inability of an advanced industrial society to regulate its members' ambitions and the proliferation of their perceived life-chances. The other two forms, however, precisely correspond to Capelo's pathology of Lima; both are impediments to rationalization of traditional societies rather than threats to organic solidarity in industrial ones. Under the first, "forced division of labor," politico-familial controls prevent effective utilization of talent (i.e., persons are not matched to appropriate functions), while social inequalities condone usurious contracts (i.e., social functions cannot be appropriately interlinked). The second is a distribution of functions which keeps individuals insufficiently occupied; when functions languish from poor specialization, "movements are badly adjusted to one another, operations are carried on without any unity; in short, solidarity breaks down, incoherence and disorder make their appearance."[9]

Shortly after Capelo wrote, Lima took several jolts on the path to modernization, and a visitor to today's metropolis of two and a half million with its industry, several technical universities, and large middle class might suppose Capelo's description to be a historical relic. Yet the deeper logic of society which he perceived seems not to have been effaced. A contemporary anthropologist finds that Peruvian urban society continues to be viewed by its members as a "limited good."[10] Channels of mobility are or appear to be controlled by those who "can manipulate the sources of power in a complex arrangement of interdependent personal 'domains' and 'empires.'" To gain his ends the would-be climber (*arribista*) adopts highly manipulative forms of behavior toward those in power, favoring either genuflectory adulation or slanderous aggression. Because such strategies stem from a belief in a limited available good rather than from an open evaluation of the persons toward whom they are directed, their use is accompanied by considerable verbal evasiveness and ambivalent affect. Conducted without any clear rules of the game, social competition produces "forms of behavior which are not sanctioned by any generally accepted or universally valid social norms." Thus does particularism survive in the "anonymous" semi-industrial metropolis.

Of the many differences between Lima and Buenos Aires, three need special mention. (1) The advantages of Buenos Aires' geographic location allowed it to challenge Lima's "insured primacy" in the eighteenth century and to win commercial dominance over a multination region in the second half of the nineteenth. (2) Peru's national territory had been settled by sedentary agriculturists since pre-Columbian times, and except for coastal plantation enclaves production was for domestic markets. In Argentina immense fertile tracts were newly brought into production for export in the nineteenth century at relatively low man-land ratios. (3) Although foreigners occupied critical middle- and upper-level positions in Lima society, its population was only 10% foreign at the end of the nineteenth century. Buenos Aires received massive immigration at all levels which brought its foreign contingent to 50% by 1895.

These factors blended to produce a society greatly more fluid and dynamic than Lima's by such indices as rate of population growth, social mobility, political participation, commercialization, industrialization, and receptivity to European fads and fashions. At the same time, a number of circumstances differentiated Buenos Aires from the standard west-European city with which travelers so frequently compared it. Its rich tributary pampas had been divided into large, privately held tracts before being put into intensive production. Agro-pastoral development occurred on a tenancy basis, creating only sparse infrastructure and services in the hinterland of the capital city. A series of trends and policies reinforced the primacy of Buenos Aires: the fan-shaped planning of the rail system; "parabolic" scaling of freight rates to discourage warehousing in other cities; centralization of reception facilities for immigrants; centralization of credit agencies; development of a patronal state which drew its clients to the capital; Buenos Aires' near-monopoly of the import trade (over 80% of the total). At the same time the capital industrialized only weakly, despite its labor force, credit facilities, and consumer market and despite the fact that free trade had virtually eliminated competitive manufacturing from the interior towns. The agro-urban elite of Buenos Aires had mixed economic interests, and no dynamic group emerged to direct the industrial process.

> Save for scattered cases of persons who participated actively in the development of the Argentine Industrial Union . . . the majority failed to perceive the dimensions of the industrialization problem—which in the last analysis was one of structural change—but limited themselves to seeking occasional isolated help from the government.[11]

During the post–World War I era of middle-class political participation and industrialization based on import substitution the oligarchy retreated to a position of secondary control, only to resume direct political management during the crisis of the 1930s and until the advent of Perón. The dynamics of Peronism reflect the failure of middle groups to have achieved self-identity in the face of selective co-optation by the agro-commercial elite. Observers who contrast Europe and Argentina note that European fascism had a strong middle-class accent and appealed to sectors which perceived their once secure and autonomous petit-bourgeois status as being eroded by bureaucratization or proletarization. Its attraction was appreciably less for the proletariat itself, which had its own class identity, organizations, and programs for institutional change. In Argentina, where middle groups, largely of recent arrival, had less sense of class tradition and social differentiation than in Europe, the problem of social integration focused on the urban workers and underprivileged, who enjoyed neither the European tradition of worker solidarity nor the putative opportunities for upward filtration of the Argentine middle groups. Thus while European leadership purported to restore national unity, social hierarchy, and the prestige of threatened groups, Peronist "social justice" tended to exacerbate class tensions and to promulgate the notion of society as a "limited good."[12] The Argentine paradox is that while the urban masses may applaud leaders who defy the "rich" and the "oligarchs," they themselves may display the same authoritarian traits that the elites have cultivated. Consequently, certain professional, clerical, or military leaders may deal more knowledgeably with the working-class mentality than do would-be leaders of more modest social status.[13]

Complementing this analysis, Silvert points out that Argentine politics rest on the premise that no public measure brings universal benefits and that gains of one group imply automatic loss by others. Further, fairly advanced industrialization has failed to engender "responsible entrepreneurial attitudes and . . . appreciation of the possibilities inherent in mass consumption." Finally, the high degree of specialization required of urban Argentines coexists with widespread "traditional values which do not permit the citizen to guide himself by a set of impersonal loyalties toward all the others operating within the system of mutual dependency."[14] Although Silvert attributes these paradoxes to the failure of Argentines to sacrifice localistic loyalties to the needs of the nation state, one might shift the question and ask whether their inherited social ethic was compatible with those needs. In other words, was the nation state a "success" in France or Japan because citizens bit the bullet and "sacrificed" traditional loyalties and social perceptions? Or was it that standard needs of the nation were more readily orchestrated with the preexisting ethic? In any case Argentine urban society, for all its historical and institutional differences from Peruvian, offers the cultural anthropologist interesting analogies. We saw, for example, that Delgado finds the Peruvian *arribista* to be a significant actor in a society of limited good, where rules of the game do not follow "definitions of universal relevance but are subjected to the determining influence of external and particularistic factors."[15] In urban Argentina, where life has also been defined as an "inelastic pie," a representative upper-class climber is the *medio pelo* who tries to negotiate an ascent from the bourgeoisie to the elite by a presentation of self that belies social and economic reality.[16] At the plebeian stratum one descries an elaborate network of mobility channels paralleling the formal one that demands professional achievement, public credentials, and thrifty habits. The informal network, controlled at the lowest level by the youthful *jefe de la barra* (neighborhood gang leader) and higher up by the *caudillo de comité* (district boss), is one in which:

> . . . each position that one occupies in the social system implies a constellation of interests and obligations, a nexus of contacts and communications with other positions at different social distances from oneself, and finally a conceptual and ideological system which in large measure justifies and rationalizes one's conduct in nonutilitarian terms.[17]

The third city, São Paulo, seems to be a breakaway case. In colonial times it was a penurious highland outpost of farmers, prospectors, and slavers who lived for a century and a half virtually beyond reach of the state apparatus. The early nineteenth century saw modest fortunes made from the mule trade and sugar industry; the latter part saw the coffee boom, and the twentieth has seen the industrial boom. To most observers these developments appear to reflect a regional spirit of entrepreneurship, innovativeness, and self-reliance. Moreover, at the time heavy European immigration to the coffee zones commenced in the 1870s, the city's population was so modest—about one-tenth of Buenos Aires'—that the influx seemed to be affording a fresh start with a second conquest and colonization.

Even industrial São Paulo, however, whose population has jumped from 30,000 to six million in a century, exhibits many family traits already identified. Such is the concentration of functions in this, the state capital, that the secondary cities of the state of São Paulo drop off to populations not more than 6% of its size. Industrial growth tends to radiate along continuous zones from the capital, and the occasional outlying clusters of industry are of a markedly traditional sort. Researchers find the industrialists themselves oriented more toward private status criteria than toward their group or class entrepreneurial interests. Similar lack of class identity is reported for the proletariat, as is a tendency toward co-optation or embourgeoisement of its leadership. While the metropolis has been a prominent arena for social mobility, structural mobility created by an expanding economy is more characteristic than exchange mobility created by recognition of merit. Urban society is widely regarded as composed of two main sectors: the "classes" and the "masses" or popular sector, representing perhaps 45% and 55% respectively of the population. Instrumental in perpetuating the division between them are the small, informal primary groups or coteries of professionals, bureaucrats, and politicians which support their members' career aspirations while denying vital cues and information to persons of "popular" origin. The extended family retains its vitality, but while lower-class kin systems may become largely occupied with "tension management," those of the upper may even thrive in a more complex society where multiplication of mobility channels decreases provocations for intra-family disputes. A vital lower-class surrogate for extended secondary associations are the proliferating Pentecostal and mediumistic cult groups—a modern version of the age-old radical sects of Catholic societies—which offer important resources for rebuilding miniature communities and for assuaging personal anxieties.[18]

Obviously, one might go on to contrast the psychosocial and institutional configurations of these three diverse urban societies. The point made here is simply that they inherit certain common Ibero-Catholic traditions and that despite the cities' divergent historical careers in no case do the traditions seem to have suffered violent mutation. One senses the presence of a social ethic which, far from being rigid and obsolescent, is vigorous and resourceful in the face of industrializing mass societies.

ASCRIPTION AND RACE

From the foregoing one logically concludes that Latin America is more "traditional" than the United States. Further, the persistent traditions of the region exhibit clear traits of ascription and particularism, and thus our analysis appears to confirm Parsons' use of Latin America and the United States as illustrations for, respectively, the ascriptive-particularistic and universal-achievement ideal types. If the taxonomy is correct, how then can we explain the apparent fact that in the field of race relations status ascription characterizes relations between whites and blacks more prominently in urban United States than in urban Brazil? Is it that race relations in the United States are an unrepresentative instance of vestigial traditionalism? Is it that for historical reasons the Brazilian color line is more loosely drawn and thus a less practical reference point for social attitudes? Or does Brazilian "racial democracy" have the ironic meaning that large numbers of the poor and humble are economically marginalized irrespective of race? The question cannot be answered in either moralistic or piecemeal fashion but requires elucidation in light of patterns of social action in the larger societies. As our discussion will suggest, it may be misleading to equate "ascription" unequivocally with "traditionalism," for in different contexts the term may designate quite distinct social processes.

Parsons and Shils furnish a handle for our contrast by distinguishing two mechanisms of adjustment to social situations.[19] One of them reflects a striving of the ego to retain his relationship with the alter ego; the active option is dominance, the passive one is submission. Here dominance is a way of mitigating the danger of deprivation when the ego attempts to control the object on which he is dependent or with whose expectations he must conform. The pervasive personal-dominance or clientistic relations found in Brazil are an illustration. In the second case the ego is willing to relinquish attachment to the alter. Here the active alternative is aggressiveness, the passive one is withdrawal. Aggressiveness arises from a need to get rid of a noxious social object or to interdict the object's noxious activities. This pattern has characterized black-white relations in the United States, a country where the word "aggressive" assumes highly favorable connotations when applied to the performance of salesmen or stockmarkets.

The applicability of these two mechanisms to race relations in the United States and Brazil is confirmed when we identify the role of violence in each case. Violence is the natural sequel or denouement to aggressiveness. And just as the lynching party was once the potential outcome of every instance of interracial friction in the United States, so today—when the once-passive partners to the contest assume their own aggressive stance—violence is the potential outcome of every eyeball-to-eyeball confrontation. An abiding dilemma of this aggressive, competitive society is to define that morally justifiable point at which peaceful negotiation or confrontation shall be allowed to lapse into violence. It is in this sense that we should interpret the observation that violence is as American as cherry pie.

Now although it is often said that Brazilian society is relatively nonviolent, a close look at the texture of Brazilian life dispels this idyllic vision. One need merely skim the pages of Jorge Amado's novel, *Terra do Sem Fim*, translated as

The Violent Land, to appreciate that violence is as Brazilian as rice and beans. One feature of Brazilian social life which has historically camouflaged latent animosity or violence is the ceremonialism characterizing intra-familial relations and relations between persons of disparate socioeconomic standing. Societies have presumably existed in which ceremonialism betokened a high degree of traditionalism and stratification, and such indeed is its meaning recorded by many a past traveler to Brazil. It is imaginable, however, that elaborate forms of etiquette in Brazil are less a hallmark of heavily layered social organization than a surrogate for order and traditionalism in a weakly structured, export-oriented society in which role definitions have been uncertain and which has required a façade for shifting relations of domination between persons of different socioeconomic or racial standing that are frequently drained of their substantive content of mutuality and paternalistic benevolence.

I have suggested that violence is the natural sequel to aggressiveness, and that violence is no great threat to an aggressive-competitive society which can summon minute-men and vigilantes at will to restore law and order and forestall anarchy. Until recent decades, however, Brazil lived in a well-nigh perfect state of anarchy, and the magnates or *poderosos* who held local power had much to fear from the establishment of law and order. By the same token violence is a severe menace to a regime of personal domination, because the outbreak of violence *ipso facto* interrupts domination. Domination after all requires submission, and it has been said that "submission in the form of ingratiation and obedience is the dominant adjustment to authority in Brazil."[20] This does not mean that Brazilian society is less violent than the United States, but rather that violence in Brazil assumes a more random and clandestine, or a less acknowledged and systematic form. It is significant that when Florestan Fernandes was studying race relations in São Paulo he witnessed serious discussions among both whites and blacks as to whether prejudice in fact existed in the city, despite abundant positive evidence. His explanation is that Brazilian culture has always been impoverished in social techniques for handling tensions. "The apparently most usual and effective method was always to bypass the causes of tensions and to intimidate the weaker partner (the woman, the child, the slave, the dependent, the dirt farmer, the subordinate, the servant, etc.)."[21] Victims of discrimination are treated with decorum and a "mask of civility" which disguises the asymmetrical nature of the dominance relation.

The need to relate race relations to the society's central belief system was recognized by Gunnar Myrdal when he prefaced his *American Dilemma* with a statement of the American Creed. Prominent in this creed, he found, were the democratic, egalitarian tenets of the Enlightenment, Protestant individualism, and a widespread willingness to tolerate discrepancy between laws and behavior. The third component, as he develops it, seems more germane to Latin America than to the United States. Myrdal needed it, however, to account for the disparity between positive features of the democratic creed and the treatment of black Americans. Actually, there is a logical consistency that escaped him. Consider, for example, the following characteristics of an egalitarian, achievement-oriented (or uptight) society: (1) It has a generous capacity for proliferating organizations and associations oriented to rationalistic goals. (2) Linked with this is a natural propensity to identify large, declaredly homogeneous groups—ethnic, religious—which by tacit consensus are to be put out of the competitive action. (3) Since, however, the egalitarian, achievement goals of the society preclude status ascription, an important weapon for eliminating minority groups from the action is to impart to their individual members, person by person, a sense of guilt, sinfulness, or unworthiness.

Segregation (overt or covert) which relies on this mechanism is something a society must work at day in and day out, no exceptions made. Furthermore, if slavery crumbles, new restrictive laws must go on the books fast. In his study of black-white relations in Brazil, where of course there was no Jim Crow after slavery, Fernandes claims that the attitudes of privileged groups toward blacks were maintained simply by "inertial traditionalism." Such was certainly not the case in the United States. It is therefore no accident that so much of the autobiographical and confessional literature of our contemporary black leaders starts off by proclaiming that the writer's soul—which was for so long on ice—is purged of guilt now that repressed desires have been brought to light and either defuzed or redirected.

It is significant that the race-and-slavery studies of the São Paulo sociologists, which are comparable in scope and scholarly authority to those of the Myrdal group, are not prefaced by a concise statement of the "Brazilian Creed." If asked to recite his creed the Brazilian man-in-the-street might indeed mention democratic and egalitarian values, but his statement would scarcely capture the force and connotations of the American Creed. For Brazil is a country which never underwent a Protestant Reformation and has been brushed only ever so lightly by the wings of the Enlightenment. In such a society peoples' positions and their hopes of improving them (or of achieving "salvation") are determined by institutions or authority figures. This militates against the formation or perception of rigid castes or classes or solidary ethnic groups. Moreover, the status of a privileged group does not depend on its success at instilling a sense of guilt or unworthiness in a depressed group. Conversely, the fact that key institutions occasionally vouchsafe "grace" to the unprivileged facilitates the individual's capacity to handle guilt feelings. And when this occasional individual does receive a gift of grace (whether "merited" by personal achievement or not) the system as a whole is not threatened.

In brief, we have attempted to supply some logic for three seemingly incongruous propositions: (1) United States society is more "modern" and less "traditional" than Brazilian. (2) Status ascription is a feature of traditional societies. (3) Race relations are more ascriptive in the United States than in Brazil. What we found is that precisely because the United States is not an ascriptive society—because it cannot rely on groups of people "knowing their place"—the primary mechanism of margination is not external and collective but internal and individualized; it requires tampering with private achievement mechanisms. (Thus the emasculation theme, so prominent in the writings of United States black leaders of the 1960s, has no equivalent in Brazil.) This hypothesis helps explain why the United States pattern rests on a genealogical definition of color and cannot easily brook exceptions to its norms. Because it can rely on dominance-submission attitudes that pervade the whole society—

because persons more readily "know their place"—Brazilian society can afford a more loosely drawn phenotypical color line, and individual exceptions—single instances of "grace" or social "salvation"—do not threaten the system.

This argument, presented here only schematically, suggests some important conclusions. First, ascription is not an invariant form of behavior but derives its logic and mechanisms from the ethic of specific societies. Second, while ascription utilizes *traditions* it is not necessarily *traditionalist* or anti-modern; thus in the United States it is both consonant with Protestant traditions and also adapted to the mechanisms of a modern, competitive, achievement society. Third, color-based ascription in "traditional" Brazil is by and large less systematic and oppressive (therefore less *traditionalist*) than in "modern" United States; yet this greater flexibility is purchased at a "cost" of pervasive traditionalism in the society at large. Finally, therefore, it is possible that a thoroughly modern society—one that incorporated the Rudolphs' eleven "modernity" principles[22]—would be an ahistorical monstrosity. The logic of modernization in any given society may, that is, dictate recrudescence and reelaboration of seemingly archaic features which play a quite functional role in system maintenance. The social engineer should therefore take cues from traditional societies and not exclusively from futuristic paradigms. This in turn argues for the Montaigne-Montesquieu-Ruth Benedict school of tolerant eclecticism against the Condorcet-Spencer-Gabriel Almond school of predictive, sometimes manipulative futurism.

WHAT IF THEY DECIDED TO MODERNIZE AND NO ONE LISTENED?

A final point must be made, dear to the historian. For if social scientists are concerned with what would be nice for societies to become, historians must consider what they *will* become. They feel kinship with future colleagues, after all, and with what *they* will be recording. So far this paper has assumed modernization to be a process extending indefinitely into the future, compromised and variegated but not stymied by demographic flood tides and the recalcitrance of local tradition. What, however, if we take our cues not from social science but from the seers, from Huxley, Orwell, Spengler, and Zamiatin? What if we refuse to assume or plead the inevitability of modernity with its meritocracy, utilitarianism, secularism, individualism, and rational associationism? What if—as the world's population surges to 7 billion in 2000 and 14 billion in 2050—populations are increasingly deracinated; the bourgeois dream of a one-family dwelling, a patch of green, and free education for all evaporates before the challenge of sheer survival; elites barricade themselves behind labyrinthine bureaucracies against the importunate masses; rationalist ideologies yield to mystagogic and millennial cultism; the mainspring of scientific curiosity and technological innovation uncoils; and giant nation-states become impotent from loss of nerve?

If this were to be the world's drift, Latin American societies, long resigned to the "limited good," would no longer be marginal to the Rest of the West as imperfectly modernized but would be seen to possess exemplary historicocultural resources for survival.

First, a world where secondary associations and bureaucracies become ossified, obstructionist, and elitist puts a premium on a high threshold of tolerance for organizational and mechanical dysfunction (García Márquez' colonel "who has no one who writes to him" will endure more stolidly than Kafka's "K."), on a capacity for spontaneous primary-group organization (squatters, religious cults, guerrillas), and on a propensity of the larger society toward spontaneous protest or sabotage in the event of outrageous offenses against natural law or morality. These features are conspicuous in Latin America, where strong, viable nation-states and secondary associations have been wanting, where mechanisms for sustained popular political participation and referendum are weakly institutionalized, yet where a natural-law tradition has long sustained the notion that even though sovereignty be alienated to elites or to the state, it resides ultimately with the people, who may reclaim and temporarily exercise it, however inchoately, at moments of severe crisis or insufferable oppression.

Second, this possible future world would not favor the rationalized, self-policed, conscience-driven character structure, associated with "covenanted" communities, which is organized to function as though it bore a direct responsibility for uplifting and purifying society. Rather, it would be congenial to persons who perceive society as external to themselves, who are concerned with cultivating arsenals of personal strategies and not with building "character," who are prepared to adopt a variety of ingratiatory or assertive roles as occasions dictate, and who delegate achievement orientations to "Jesuitical" elites. The potential appeal for the industrial West of this picaresque, characteristically Latin American form of personality organization is evinced by the growing popularity in bourgeois, student, and some ethnic-minority circles of the phrase "life style," which suggests a staged and changeable presentation of self that offers release from pressures of characterological rationality.

A hint that the Latin American perspective on the drift of the world may be prophetic is the vitality and sudden international projection of writers such as Borges, Cortázar, García Márquez, Guimarães Rosa, and Vargas Llosa who so gracefully incorporate the themes of historical persistence and recurrence, multiple identity, indeterminacy, and the interpenetration of the occult and work-a-day worlds. In Latin America, we may conjecture, the West may have kept alive some vital options for the future.

OTES

1. R. M. Morse *et al.*, *The Urban Development of Latin America 1750–1920* (Stanford, Calif., 1971), pp. 1–21; R. M. Morse, "Trends and Issues in Latin American Urban Research, 1965–1970," *Latin American Research Review*, 6, 1 and 2 (1971), II, 36–55.

2. Talcott Parsons, *The Social System* (Glencoe, Ill., 1951), pp. 180–200.

3. These contrasts are more fully developed in R. M. Morse, "A Prolegomenon to Latin American Urban History," *Hispanic American Historical Review*, 52, 3 (1972), 359–394.

4. Edmund S. Morgan, *The Puritan Family* (rev. ed.; New York, 1966), pp. 1–28. Contrast the "covenanted" relationship with the "dyadic contract" described by Foster for

Spanish America as a tie between two people who feel they can help each other by largely ignoring the institutional context in which they meet. While Latin American groups or communities may be thought of as Aristotelian "natural forms," they are not truly "corporate" entities. The *texture* of social life is atomistic and personalistic. George M. Foster, *Tzintzuntzan: Mexican Peasants in a Changing World* (Boston, 1967), pp. 212–243; also Morse, "Trends and Issues," I, pp. 25–33.

5. Fernando Guillén Martínez, "Los Estados Unidos y América Latina," *Aportes* 7 (January 1968), 10.

6. Morse, "Trends and Issues," II, pp. 24–28.

7. William E. Curtis, *The Capitals of Spanish America* (New York, 1888).

8. Joaquín Capelo, *Sociología de Lima* (4 vols.; Lima, 1895–1902); also R. M. Morse, "The Lima of Joaquín Capelo: a Latin-American Archetype," *Journal of Contemporary History*, 4, 3 (1969), 95–110.

9. Emile Durkheim, *Division of Labor in Society* (New York, 1933), pp. 353–395.

10. Carlos Delgado, "An Analysis of '*Arribismo*' in Peru," *Human Organization*, 28, 2 (1969), 133–139.

11. Roberto Cortés Conde, "Problemas del crecimiento industrial de la Argentina (1870–1914)," *Desarrollo Económico*, 3, 1–2 (1963), 155.

12. Gino Germani, *Política y sociedad en una época de transición* (Buenos Aires, 1966), pp. 233–252.

13. Torcuato S. Di Tella, *El sistema político argentino y la clase obrera* (Buenos Aires, 1964), pp. 40–41.

14. K. H. Silvert, "The Costs of Anti-Nationalism: Argentina," in K. H. Silvert, ed., *Expectant Peoples* (New York, 1967), pp. 350–353.

15. Delgado, "Analysis of '*Arribismo*'," p. 135.

16. Arturo Jauretche, *El medio pelo en la sociedad argentina* (6th ed.; Buenos Aires, 1967).

17. Di Tella, *El sistema político*, p. 18.

18. For fuller treatment see R. M. Morse, "São Paulo: Case Study of a Latin American Metropolis," *Latin American Urban Research*, F. F. Rabinovitz and F. M. Trueblood, eds., 1 (1970), 151–186.

19. Talcott Parsons and Edward A. Shils, eds., *Toward a General Theory of Action* (New York, 1962), pp. 140–141.

20. Bernard C. Rosen, "Socialization and Achievement Motivation in Brazil," *American Sociological Review*, 27, 5 (1962), 623.

21. Florestan Fernandes, *A integração do negro à sociedade de classes* (São Paulo, 1964), p. 628. Abridged English translation: *The Negro in Brazilian Society* (New York, 1969).

22. Lloyd I. and Susanne H. Rudolph, *The Modernity of Tradition* (Chicago, 1967), pp. 3–4.

Local Government in Bolivia: Public Administration and Popular Participation

ADRIANNE ARON-SCHAAR

Graft, inefficiency, and favoritism (personalismo) loom large in the stereotypical view of Latin American public administration. In some instances the stereotype is justified, and this analysis of one small town goes far toward explaining why. Ms. Aron-Schaar's demonstration that bureaucratic forms do not necessarily operate in bureaucratic ways has a special interest in anthropological terms—it was written by a woman who had never been to Bolivia and was based on notes collected by me and by others in the course of research under the auspices of Research Institute for the Study of Man.

Adrianne Aron-Schaar is a free-lance social scientist with a special interest in Latin America. She lives in Ben Lomond, California, and is teaching at the University of California Extension, Santa Cruz.

It is difficult to describe Bolivian local government as an ordered system, for its most striking feature is a seeming lack of systemization. A day at city hall in any of the communities might easily be mistaken for a carnival of random behavior.

The men who planned the government structure appear to have had something fairly precise in mind, for there are numerous laws providing for the establishment of public offices at the local level. There are even vague statements of purpose for these offices, and people with desks and typewriters carrying out duties. Local government in Bolivia is a fact; only the principles which order it are a mystery. It is to this mystery that my paper is addressed.[1]

Taking the community of Coroico as an example, we may explore the nuances of local administration. A provincial capital of about 2,000 people, Coroico is the largest and most important town in its province. Heading the *Alcaldía*, or town administration, is the *Alcalde*, whose position is roughly equivalent to that of the North American mayor. The *Alcalde* is provided with a salary and is required to relinquish his former occupation and sources of income when he takes office in order to devote himself solely to his administrative duties. As the highest ranking public official in the community, he receives the largest salary of any civil servant—420,000 Bolivianos per month, exchangeable for $33.60 in United States currency.

In Bolivia $33.60 might support a frugal bachelor for a month, but it will not maintain a family of five, even at bare subsistence, for that length of time. Eating modestly, a family of five would exhaust this amount in three weeks on food expenditures alone. The mayor is expected to abandon his previous means of making a living, and yet he is not provided with sufficient funds to avoid starvation. As Max Weber points out, either politics can be conducted honorifically, by independently wealthy men, or political leadership can be made accessible to propertyless men, who must then be rewarded.[2]

We must logically conclude that, owing to the meagerness of the reward, no

This paper was prepared expressly for this volume.

poor man could accept the post of mayor. In an order where wealth is traditionally associated with large landholdings, one might expect that, by default, the position must fall to a member of the landed aristocracy. Considering that the Agrarian Reform Act of 1953 altogether abolished the landed aristocracy of Coroico, we are faced with a logical impossibility. The only eligible candidate for public office is the *nouveau riche* (rarely popular or civic minded) or the fool.

Realizing that the law has created a hopeless situation, custom has intervened to permit the authorities to supplement their meager salaries. Precisely how this should be done, however, has never been defined; therefore, it is usually the officials themselves who decide by what means and by what amounts their income should be increased. What begins as a liberalization of law for the sake of establishing a government to protect the people often ends as an established government which exists to exploit the people. The impossibility of surviving on a government salary becomes the *carte blanche* for a wide variety of spectacles. It explains, for example, why a judge and his wife and three children are living rent-free on the second floor of the town hall in a suite of rooms designed as public offices. It explains why the postmaster removes the stamps from incoming letters, erases the cancellation mark, and sells the restored stamps as new. It explains why the town library has disappeared book by book, and why the money sent by the government for the construction of a local hospital was spent by the state doctor.

What is remarkable is that such deeds not only are openly tolerated by the citizens, but are looked upon with sympathy. When the doctor walked around town complaining, "What could I do? They sent it to me in small bills, Bs. 5,000 ($.40) here, 5,000 there, and pretty soon it was all gone," the people agreed, saying, "You're right; how can the government expect you to watch small bills? They never should have sent small bills."

More typical than these individual solutions to the problem of making a living are two basic patterns, followed with such frequency and regularity that they can be considered institutions. These are the maintenance of private enterprises by public officials and the custom of graft. While the one undermines the notion of professional authorities who make politics a vocation, the other undermines the whole theory of responsible and democratic government. Taken together, these two institutions, better than any constitution or code of laws, capture the essence of local government in Bolivia.

POLITICS AND BUSINESS

It is not the maintenance by public officials of private business per se which is inimical to honest government; the danger lies in the powerful and continuing temptation to use one's office for private gain. Obviously, some businesses and professions offer more alluring temptations than others. The pharmacist who became deputy mayor[3] turned his drug store over to a manager during his tenure and both his public office and private drug store were able to run smoothly, without interference from each other. The lawyer who became a judge, however, presents us with a very different set of circumstances. Not only does he continue to practice law, but it is not unusual for him to appear as both counsel and judge of a defendant brought before the court. Even the tolerant people of Coroico regard this court as an outrage. But once it has been granted that a public authority must eat, and that he may practice his profession while in office in order to secure a reasonable income, one has already forfeited one's right to recourse and must resign himself to the risks that ensue. Outrage, in effect, becomes institutionalized.

This is not to say that the union of private profit and public office is necessarily catastrophic. The argument has been made, after all, that what is good for General Motors is good for the country. When the mayor, who is by trade a coffee merchant, discovered that the community was suffering a flour shortage, he promptly made a trip to La Paz to deliver coffee and returned with 1,700 pounds of flour. Using the town hall as a warehouse, he began selling flour at bargain prices "as a public service." Thus while gaining favor among housewives, he was able simultaneously to make a small profit and to eliminate the flour shortage.[4] The difficulty, of course, is that the public finds itself subject to the whims of the authorities, without any assurance that what benefits the authorities will in any way coincide with the public welfare. If the authorities would rather be feared than loved, the people are in trouble.

THE CUSTOM OF GRAFT

Unlike the maintenance of private sources of income, which may have neutral or even beneficent effects on a community, the practice of graft inevitably produces discrimination and inequality before the law. The man who does not know that payment is expected, or the man who hasn't enough money to offer an attractive sum—in short, "the little man"—is inescapably a victim of the system.

It should be pointed out that there are two meanings for what I have chosen to call graft.[5] Because their general consequences are identical I have grouped them together, but actually they differ substantially in their methods. The one kind of graft is virtually synonymous with bribery and is used to induce an official to forgo his legal responsibilities. Typically the transaction is carried out surreptitiously, and when it is completed the official has tacitly agreed to protect his benefactor from inconvenience, punishment, and discomfort. The other kind of graft is paid quite openly to the official in return for a service rendered in the line of duty. It is paid not as a favor, but on demand, as a commission or a fee.

Why then should something as ordinary as a fee be placed in the same category as an outright bribe? There are three good answers to this question. One is that the Bolivian Constitution expressly forbids salaried functionaries to exact fees for their services, so that the practice is manifestly unconstitutional.[6] Second, being illegal, the fees cannot be fixed—a given price for a given service—and consequently they are completely arbitrary and set by the officials themselves capriciously. Third, it is utterly impossible to receive the services of the authorities unless one is prepared to pay for them. The public servants are in fact neither public nor servants. They are men who receive a small stipend from the government for occupying an office and remaining on call in the event that a private citizen wishes to hire their services. The system is quite literally that of "rent-a-cop."

The police chief explains his role in the following way:

> Let's say that your brother is murdered. You come to Coroico for justice. I'm interested and sympathetic, but I have no transportation and no allowance for travel. So, if you want me to go investigate, you have to pay my way, with meals, and pay for [the travel and meals of] another policeman [who comes] as my helper. And you have to provide lodging for us as long as we're investigating. Well then, suppose we're lucky and find the guilty party within a few days. We still have to bring him back to Coroico. So you, as the interested party, have to pay his transportation as well as ours. Then when he's in jail here, you have to . . . arrange to have his food brought in. Then you have to pay for his trip to La Paz and for [the trip of] his escort, a *carabinero* who has to eat and have lodging for a few days in La Paz [before you pay his expenses back] to Coroico, where he's stationed. All this the interested party alone has to pay; we have no funds. So justice is expensive, and many people let things go because they can't afford such costs. It's a shame, but there's no remedy.

If the service orientation of public office is a myth, the law enforcement orientation, at least where profit is to be had, is a vital reality. And, as might be expected, the same citizens who are barred by reasons of inadequate funds and influence from enjoying government services are the ones most familiar with the law enforcement procedures of the government officials. If there is a fine to be imposed, a tax to be levied, a crime to be punished, it is again the little man who is the natural victim.

One might find it curious that the poor man should be sought for revenue purposes when there is plainly more money to be gained by taxing the rich man. It is not curious at all though, if one looks beyond man's economic motivations to his social relations, where common sense dictates that a peer is to be treated with greater consideration than a stranger. This fellow I have called the little man is best described abstractly as a stranger, an outsider, a person who is not a part of the reference group of the men who hold power. He is the likely one to be taxed or fined or punished because it is doubtful that any social repercussions will occur if he is exploited; he is a safe victim. Moreover, if an outsider can be found, an insider can often be spared discomfort.

Typically, the outsider, or little man, is the *campesino*, who is at once the poorest, the least educated, the least assimilated member of the community. The *campesino* is further handicapped by an imperfect command of the Spanish language and by a history of servitude which he has not yet overcome. Thus he is more than a marginal man who is pushed around by those who wield power; he is a member of a social class which is pushed around by members of a superior class.

There is but one protective measure available to the *campesino:* He may join a *campesino* syndicate and benefit from the influence which these syndicates possess both in La Paz and locally. Whereas the upper classes are united only emotionally and doctrinally, sharing a fierce contempt for the Revolution of 1952, the *campesinos* are actually organized. Knowing that the *campesinos* could, by exerting pressure on the capital, unseat them, it behooves the local mestizo authorities to handle the *campesinos* with some delicacy. Hence in a town like Coroico, where the *campesinos* of nearby Cruz Loma are well organized, instances of overt discrimination against *campesinos* are uncommon. Instead, discrimination is practiced with the utmost subtlety.

What was to me the most ingenious case of oblique discrimination occurred in Coroico when the public lavatories were opened. These lavatories were built for the ostensible purpose of serving the *campesinos,* who come into town from the countryside and have no access to private facilities. The municipal intendant, whose job it is to look after public sanitation, took it upon himself to inspect the lavatories after each use, to guarantee that they were being used properly. As a person left the room, the intendant would rush in to inspect, and every time he found the condition of the room less than satisfactory he would impose a fine of Bs. 40,000 ($3.20) on his mortified victim. Since the *campesinos* are the only members of the community who are not accustomed to modern sanitation facilities, they were the only ones fined for improper use of the toilets. Yet it would be quite impossible to prove that these inspections were designed to exploit a single segment of the population. The inspections continued until the word was spread sufficiently and no more *campesinos* came to the public lavatories.

Since proof is more difficult to establish, discrimination against *campesinos* as a class is more easily carried out than discrimination against a particular individual, but the latter form is not necessarily less effective. It has its own special virtues.

The lone *campesino* who has been treated unfairly, either by another citizen or by one of the officials, usually cannot enlist the support of his syndicate for his personal cause. Nor, as we have seen, can he usually afford to buy protection from the authorities. But there is still one avenue open to him. He can seek a sponsor from the upper class, either a *compadre* or a former *patrón,* and with the help of his sponsor pursue his cause.

Earlier I called the syndicate the only protective agency available to the *campesino.* It must be emphasized that that statement still pertains, for while the *campesino* may turn to the *patrón* for assistance, it is not in his interest to do so.

The former *patrón* may provide the *campesino* with the necessary money for use as graft and intervene on his behalf before the authorities, but his motives are not as altruistic as they might seem. It is altogether in his interest to befriend the *campesino,* for it rekindles the spirit of vassalage that prevailed before the Revolution. It is a reminder to the *campesino* of his helplessness in the face of adverse conditions, of his need for the personal protection of the *patrón.* Every step taken by a *campesino* toward the former *patrón* is a step away from the class independence which the syndicates are striving to inspire. And every loss suffered by the syndicates is a gain for the upper classes.

The *campesino,* then, is everywhere faced with untenable situations. Having no friends among the public officials, he can expect no favors. Lacking sufficient funds for bribery, he is denied protection of the law. Lacking protection, he is the likely target for abuse. Once abused, he must either accept his plight with stoical resignation or turn to his former master for help. If he turns to his former master he reestablishes his feudal ties and abandons hope for emancipation.

The structure of local government in Bolivia, far from advancing the egalitarian ideals of the Revolution, systematically obstructs them. What appears, even after careful study, to be utterly devoid of systematization turns out on still closer analysis to be a quite elaborate system geared to keeping alive the class distinctions which the Revolution pronounced dead in 1952.

To anyone familiar with the work of Max Weber, it should be clear that the existing structure of local government in Bolivia can be understood by enumerating Weber's criteria of responsible government and simply bearing in mind that in Bolivia precisely the *opposite* conditions prevail. The criteria are essentially there: fixed hierarchy, jurisdiction, and tenure in public office; division of labor; strict adherence to rules; impersonality; technical qualifications for holding offices; and specified salaries for the office holders.[7]

To get a purchase on the problem I have dealt selectively with these concepts and have confined my discussion to a single community. The data strongly suggest that if the same task were undertaken in any of the other towns studied in this project, the results would be virtually identical. This is not to say that it is always the *campesino* who is victimized by the system, or that in all places the degree of discrimination is constant. It is the *spirit* of government that remains unchanged—the idea that government exists to grant privilege to some and deny rights to others. In Sorata, for example, where revolutionary upheaval placed *campesinos* in control of the government, exclusion and privilege are as prevalent as in Coroico and even more rigidly enforced; only the roles are reversed. Here the *blanco* is denied equal protection of the law, while the *campesino* plunders the community wealth.

Who is on top is not a significant issue. What matters is that built into the very foundations of Bolivian government are the provisions for sustaining inequality. My argument began by identifying the insufficiency of government salaries as the catalyst for unscrupulous and arbitrary administration. That it is a catalyst and not a cause must be stressed, for if the salaries of all government officials were tripled, the laws of the land strictly observed, and professional qualifications demanded of all personnel, the spirit of personalism and privilege would linger. Merely altering the government structure could not erase the historical, psychological, and social factors which have combined since the Conquest to define a people's way of life and way of thinking about the world. The present form of government is not responsible for, but is rather responsive to, the Bolivian way of life.

OTES

1. An earlier version of this paper was presented at a meeting of the American Anthropological Association, held at Pittsburgh, Pa., November 1966. It is based on ethnographic and survey data collected in Coroico as part of the Bolivia project of the Research Institute for the Study of Man, supported by Peace Corps Grant No. PC(W)-397. Coroico is one of six small communities in the study; for more details, see William J. McEwen, et al., *Changing Rural Bolivia* ([New York] Research Institute for the Study of Man, 1969), esp. pp. 105–163.

2. Max Weber, "Politics as a Vocation," in Hans Gerth and C. Wright Mills (eds.), *From Max Weber: Essays in Sociology* (London: Routledge and Kegan Paul, Ltd., 1952), p. 86.
3. This official's title is *official mayor;* I use the term "deputy mayor" as the nearest counterpart in the North American system.
4. The Mayor has even articulated his defense of plutocracy: "Why should I want graft? I have enough income from my private business." But another citizen has expressed worry about wealthy men in public office: "Chances are that the rich man has made his money illegally and will continue with his illegal activities in office."
5. The local term for graft is *coima,* although many Bolivians would also recognize the term *mordida,* by which such practices are known throughout much of Latin America.
6. The Constitution of Bolivia, Section 17, Article 118, in N. Andrew N. Cleven, *The Political Organization of Bolivia* (Washington, D.C.: The Carnegie Institution, 1940), p. 225. [Editor's note: Although Bolivia has had nearly half a dozen constitutions since the one cited, it is noteworthy that this specification has been reiterated in each.]
7. Max Weber, "Bureaucracy," op. cit., passim.

Folk Models of Stratification, Political Ideology, and Socio-Cultural Systems[1]

ARNOLD STRICKON

Social scientists are paying increasing attention to "folk models," the conceptions of reality that are held by the people being studied—and sometimes what they find prompts them to reexamine their own analytic models. Strickon describes how using this approach among "grandsons of the gauchos" in Argentina yielded new insights for the difficult task of identifying ethnic groups and the social boundaries between them and demonstrated how local institutions are linked with national systems (cf. Wolf *and* Leeds*).*

Arnold Strickon is Associate Professor of Anthropology at the University of Wisconsin. His field research has been carried out in the West Indies and Argentina, with emphasis on economics, kinship organization, and patron-client relations. He is coeditor of Structure and Process in Latin America: Patronage, Clientage, and Power Systems (1972), *and is currently studying the interaction of European-derived ethnic groups in the United States.*

A recurrent theme of anthropological studies in complex societies concerns the relations between the local community and the nation. This article rephrases the question. Rather than assuming that the local community and

From *The Sociological Review Monographs,* No. 11 (1967), "Latin-American Sociological Studies," 93–117, University of Keele. Reprinted by permission of the author and publisher.

nation are 'things' which have relations with each other, it is assumed that both are abstractions which may be useful for ordering data relevant to different kinds of problems.[2]

Instead of asking, therefore, 'what are the relations between the local community and the nation?' I ask: (a) 'What behaviours, attitudes, norms, etc., which are observed within a given locality are most economically orderable within a context of locally oriented relations and institutions?'; and (b) 'What behaviours, attitudes, norms, etc., which are observed within a given locality are most economically orderable within a context of national, or extra-local, relations and institutions?' In other words it is assumed that the behaviour of individuals within a locality, in different contexts and situations, may be best comprehended as exemplifying the requirements, even at times the contradictory requirements, of different socio-cultural systems.

The usefulness of this assumption will be illustrated by reference to the analysis of a superficially simple substantive problem. It is a problem, however, which when analyzed raises questions which are far from superficial. It raises such questions as: what are the boundaries between cultural units in a complex society and how are they identified?; do shifts in the problems being considered require shifts in the boundaries of units, and in what way does a given boundary limit the possible problems which may be explored within the cultural unit that boundary defines?

These are questions of increasing concern to social scientists,[3] and are also critical to questions relating to 'traditionalism' and 'modernity' in the so-called 'developing world.'[4]

Another concern of this article is to illustrate the contention that folk models of socio-cultural systems (particularly stratification models in the present case) provide important insights about the boundaries and units within which specific behaviours and problems may be ordered.

The substantive question with which I begin concerns apparently contradictory attitudes and expectations held by certain individuals in a rural Argentine community towards other individuals who reside within the same community.

Specifically, there are a number of people in the locality I studied who identified themselves either as *criollos*[5] (literally born in the country) or as *descamisados* (literally shirtless ones, the proletariat of peronist usage). These people express contradictory attitudes and expectations toward other people who are identified either as *Familia* (Family) or as *oligarquia* (oligarchy). On the one hand the criollo-descamisado hold the Family-oligarchy to be exploiters of the poor who care for nothing but their own selfish interests. On the other hand the criollo-descamisado also consider the Family-oligarchy to be patrons, protectors, and co-participants in a highly valued way of life. In both examples it is the same individuals speaking about the same individuals.

Upon closer examination it becomes clear that the two pairs of terms used to designate the various people are not in random variation with each other. Rather the terms Family and criollo are used together in the 'positive' patronage context, while the 'negative,' 'class-warfare' beliefs and expectations provide the context in which the descamisado-oligarchy terms are used.

The larger conversational environments in which these pairings occurred also differ. The class-warfare, descamisado-oligarchy set occurs in reference to national, or extra-local, conversational contexts. The patronage, criollo, Family set occurs in reference to local and personal interaction contexts.

If we look at this even more closely we find that associated with these verbal distinctions, though not consciously recognized by the speakers, are differences in institutional affiliations, not only between criollo-descamisado on the one hand and Family-oligarchy on the other (which comes as no surprise), but also between descamisado and criollo, Family and oligarchy.

I am suggesting that these people have folk models of two social systems, one national and the other local, and that these status terms, and others as well, are constituent categories of these models. Both of these models are used to order the social phenomena which the people of the locality observe around them, but neither one of them is used to order it all.

There is, of course, some danger in accepting folk models as the basis for an objective analysis.[6] In the present case the analysis presented here only partially rests upon the folk analysis. The use of the categorical terms by the subjects is clear and unambiguous, the criteria for assignment of these terms to specific individuals is usually not verbalized. The institutions and rôles which correlate with these terms are not consciously perceived by the people of the community.

One of the major dangers in the use of folk models lies in the logical relationships among problem, model, and categories. If the problem and theoretical assumptions of analyst and folk are not congruent, then the models of one are not applicable to the interests of the other. If the problems are congruent, and in the present case they are, then the folk models can provide important insights for the analyst.

Before proceeding with the body of this article I must emphasize that I am not concerned here with the determinants of the parameters within which these two systems operate[7] or with the results of changes in those parameters. I have dealt with these questions elsewhere.[8] They are, for present purposes, taken as 'given.'

The remainder of this article is organized as follows: (a) a brief description of the site of the field investigation indicating the major territorial, administrative, and economic parameters which are relevant to the analysis of the problem posed; (b) an overview of the two folk models; (c) the folk national model; (d) the folk local model; (e) summary and analysis of the substantive problem; (f) conclusion.

THE SITE

The locality which I shall call 'Eleodoro Gomez'[9] is located in the heart of Argentina's humid pampas, almost in the centre of Buenos Aires Province, about 180 miles southwest of the national capital. The typical settlement pattern for this part of the pampas, and indeed for much of rural Argentina, consists of a number of vaguely defined, and shifting, open country neighbourhood networks. One or more of these networks focus upon small service villages which are typically located on the railroad lines that radiate out from the city of

Buenos Aires. The locality of Eleodoro Gomez consists of the village of that name and also of the open country networks that focus upon it. The population of the total locality is about 2,000 people. Of these some 600 reside in the village itself. The others are scattered in homesteads or barracks on the surrounding farms and cattle ranches.

Administratively Eleodoro Gomez is part of the *partido* (or county) of Sarmiento. The administrative functions assigned to the partido are carried out in the *cabeza del partido* (county seat), which is also named Sarmiento. The partido as a geographical entity covers 2,000 square miles and has a total population of about 25,000 people. Of these, 9,000 were resident, at the time of the study, in the county seat. The remainder were scattered about in the village service centres and open country in the rest of the county.

In addition to the partido's specific administrative apparatus, the county seat is also the location of the lowest level offices of provincial and national financial, judicial, administrative, and welfare institutions. With very few exceptions the public contacts these agencies in the county seats, not in the rural service villages or open country.

The county seat is also the location of the local officers of a number of non-governmental institutions such as the *Sociedad Rural* (the national cattlemen's association), labour unions, political parties, service clubs (such as Rotary), special interest groups (i.e., flying clubs, university alumni groups, professional associations, etc.). The one public secondary school in the partido is located in the county seat, as are hospitals and clinics. The boundaries of the parish of the Catholic Church are congruent with those of the partido, and church groups, such as Catholic Action, operate only in the county seat.

The economic *raison d'être* of this area lies in the livestock, grains, and industrial crops that are produced on its farms and ranches. Except for meat, most food for all residents of the area is imported from elsewhere in Argentina, as are clothes, household and productive equipment, and luxury goods. The products of the area are transported to the commercial and industrial megalopolis of Argentina along the south shore of the Rio de la Plata. Here the beef, mutton, wool, maize, wheat, and sunflower seeds are processed and enter the national and international markets.

The social, economic, and cultural system that began to emerge in the seventeenth century in what is now eastern Argentina has always reflected larger economic and political involvements. This area was (and remains) part of the economic heartland of Argentina, the 'key economic area,' the area which largely made Argentine history. It was never a closed system whose major economic, political, and social arrangements were oriented to its own subsistence. The countryside of Eleodoro Gomez itself was outside the line of the European frontier until the latter half of the nineteenth century. The removal of the Indians from the area, and its settlement by Europeans, directly reflected expanded European demands for beef, wool, mutton, and grains, expanded British investment in railroads and shipping.

In 1958–1959 some eighty percent of the land area of the open country around the village of Eleodoro Gomez was owned by 23 *estancias* (large plantation-organized cattle ranches) which ranged in size from 1,000 to 90,000 acres. The remainder of the land was owned, or rented, in small, family-operated, cattle ranches (*chacras de ganado*), and mixed farms (*chacras mixtas*) of under 1,000 acres. Livestock and grains are raised on the farms, small ranches, and estancias.

The productive efforts of the locality reflect economic and political conditions in the larger world beyond Eleodoro Gomez. There is a constantly shifting allocation of land to grazing or agriculture depending upon world market conditions, foreign exchange problems, and domestic political considerations.

Since the turn of the century three major categories of productive activities can be isolated in the community, those concerned with livestock, with agriculture, and with 'staff,' service, and technical functions. The service, agricultural, and technical activities emerged out of the traditional livestock centred activities in the late nineteenth and early twentieth centuries. Since that time the proportion of people in service and technical functions has grown, while the proportions of agricultural and livestock personnel have fluctuated with variations in the allocation of land to farming or grazing.

I must mention, finally, that people who live in Eleodoro Gomez, village and countryside, are not isolated in any sense. They own or have access to radios, newspapers, and magazines. They see motion pictures. All go to the county seat at least on occasion. Most have been to the national capital, are visited by people from there, have friends and relatives resident there. A few, indeed, live in Buenos Aires much of the year.

THE FOLK MODELS: AN OVERVIEW

In this section I will briefly indicate the categories used in the two folk models, and the way in which individuals are sorted among them. I will also indicate the fit between these folk categories and those of an objective set of categories based upon criteria of income. Finally, I will discuss the question of the degree to which people agree upon the assignment of others, or themselves, to these categories.

The people of the locality of Eleodoro Gomez order data relevant to the problem raised here within a broad domain we may identify as, 'stratification.' Within this broad domain, however, there exist two different sets of categories which may be analytically viewed as constituting two different models. An individual is assigned to at least one category in each of these models for different purposes. In one, as I indicated earlier, the conversational environment refers to phenomena orderable within the context of a national-level social system. These categories will henceforth be referred to as the 'folk national system.' The other set of categories refers to phenomena orderable within the context of a local socio-cultural system. This second group of categories will be referred to as 'the folk local system.'

I must emphasize that for purposes of this article 'folk' refers to all persons who use these categories in normal conversation, rich or poor, holder of advanced professional degree or illiterate.

Different criteria are used to sort people into the categories of the two models, and the categories of one model are not isomorphic with those of the

FIGURE 1. The Categories of the Folk Local and Folk National Models and the Sorting of Individuals Among Them

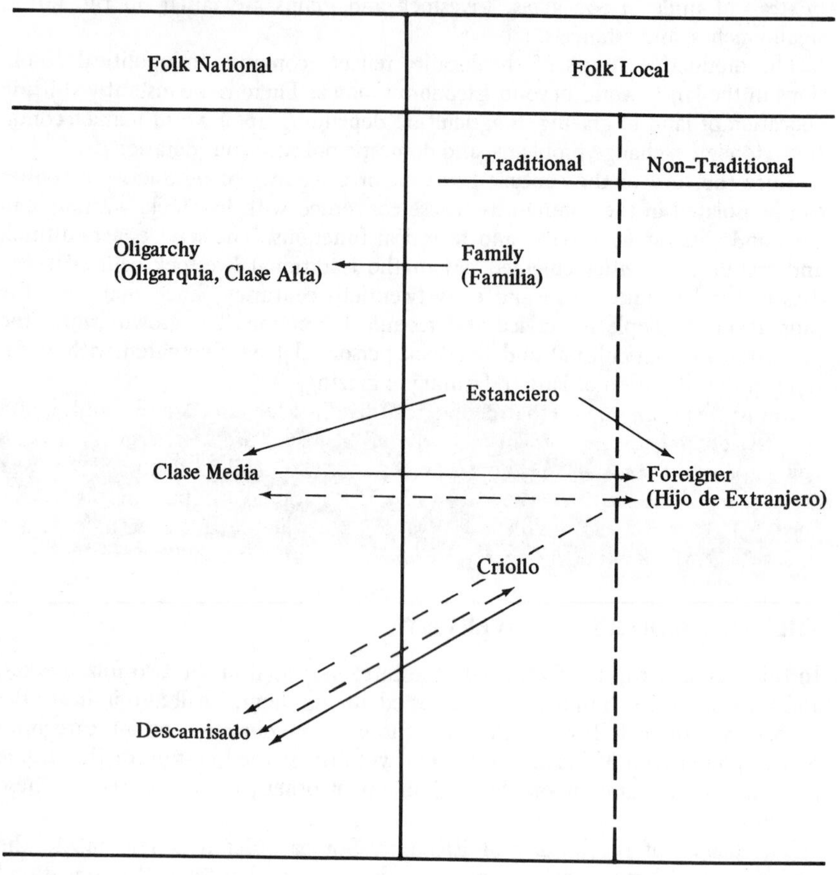

Key

Solid Arrow **indicates that *all* people assigned to the category at which the arrow originates are also assigned to the category to which the arrow is directed.**

Broken Arrow **indicates that *some* people assigned to the category at which the arrow originates are also assigned to the category to which the arrow is directed.**

other. An individual's categorical assignment in one stratification system does not automatically predict his assignment in the other one. Nor are either of these sets of categories completely congruent with more or less standardized sociological class categories.

Figure 1 shows the terms used in each of the two models of stratification. It should be noted that the terms used in the folk national model, oligarquia (*clase alta*), *clase media,* and descamisado, show a strong, if not perfect, correspondence with social science and mass media usage. The people who are using these terms, however, are not social scientists so we cannot assume that local and professional usages are congruent.

The right-hand side of Figure 1 displays the terms used in the folk local model. These are Family, *estanciero* (literally the owner of a large plantation-organized cattle ranch), *hijo de extranjero* (literally child of a foreigner, this category will henceforth be referred to as 'foreigner'), and criollo. The significance of the distinction made between traditional and non-traditional categories will be discussed in detail later. Briefly, though, it indicates the cultural division between the norms which were historically associated with the Argentine cattle complex and those which emerged with the more recent (post 1850's) expansion of agricultural, technological, and service activities in rural eastern Argentina.

Figure 1 also diagrams the sorting of individuals among the various categories of the two systems of classification. The diagram may be summarized as follows:

a. all members of the Family are oligarchy.
b. all clase media are foreigners. Some of these are also estancieros.
c. all estancieros are also clase media and foreigners.
d. some descamisados are foreigners, others are criollos.
e. some foreigners are clase media, others are descamisados.
f. all criollos are descamisado.

Figure 2 aligns the folk categories against the objective criteria of income. The actual amount of income is not particularly important for the present purpose, it is the range of income that is of interest. The point to be made in this diagram is that the boundaries of the various folk categories cut income distribution at different points. The income distribution of those assigned to the Foreigner category ranges from a point overlapping with the Oligarchy down to the economic nadir of the locality, below that of the criollo. Foreigner, then, is not an economic category, nor by implication one which reflects economically linked criteria such as education, consumption patterns, etc.

As an illustration of this I will compare the categorical assignments of the owner of a small family-operated cattle ranch (chacra de ganado) and the owner of a family-operated mixed farm (chacra mixta). Both of these men would be considered 'middle class' by criteria of income and other indices generally used to assign people to objective class categories. In the folk national system the small rancher is categorized as descamisado (or at least as *clase popular*, i.e., 'lower class' but lacking the peronist political implications), although there will be some discomfort among assigners in designating a property owner in this way. The farmer is unambiguously designated as clase media in the folk national system. In the folk local system there is no hesitation in assigning the small rancher to the criollo category, the agriculturalist to the foreigner one.

Although there is a close 'fit' between active involvement in the livestock complex and criollo status, or between agricultural and service activities and foreigner status, nevertheless the criollo rancher is not a criollo because he is a small rancher. Similarly for the farmer. Rather, their occupations are single

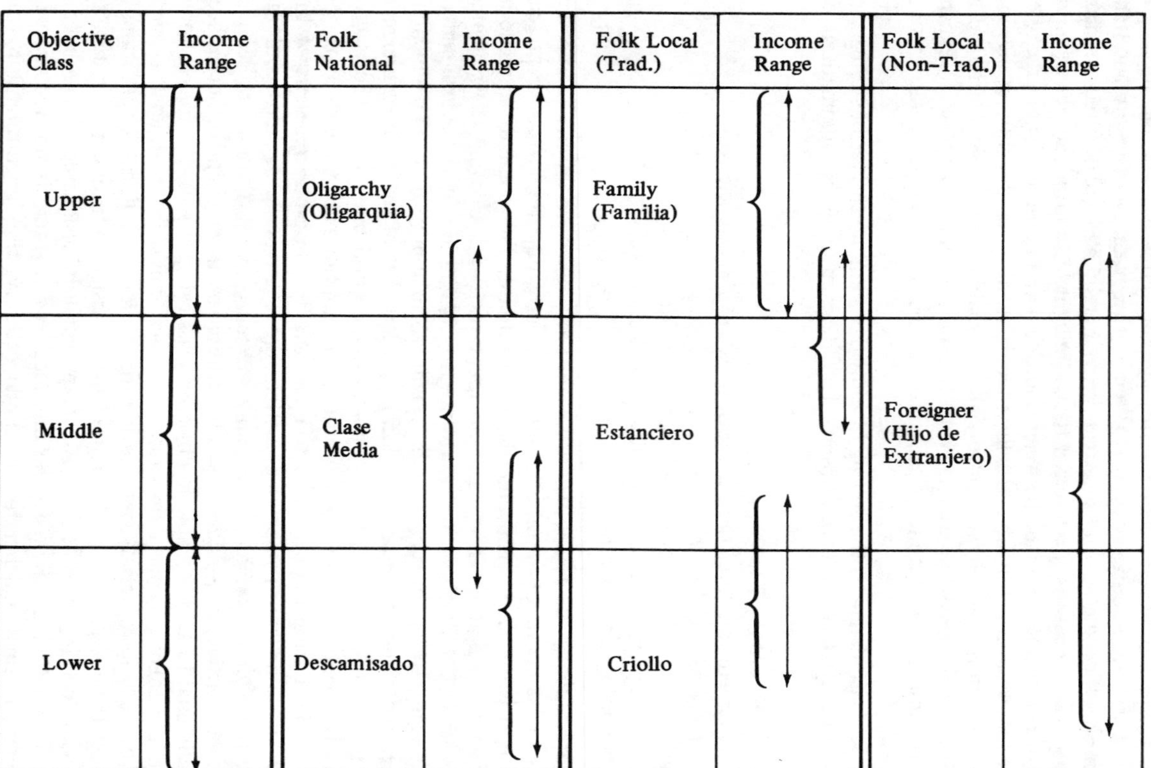

FIGURE 2. Alignment of Folk Categories with Objective (by Income Range) Class Categories

facets in the multi-faceted aspects of 'criolloness' and 'foreignness.' The life experiences of the criollo in obtaining his ranch, and that of the 'foreigner' in obtaining his farm, though this cannot be documented here because of lack of space, are quite different. They experienced different relations to formal sources of credit, the large landowners, buyers of their produce and to their peers and subordinates. Although both may have arrived at a similar position in terms of their assignment to an objective social class category, they reached this common point by quite different routes, and the paths that now lay open before them (and their children) are also different. These differences in past experience, present activities, and future potential are not ordered by the objective class categories. They are ordered by the folk models the people of Eleodoro Gomez use, both local and extra-local.

It could be argued that a Weberian or modified Weberian[10] analysis could order these differences in life chances and experiences where a simple economic one cannot. This may be true, but it still leaves the problem of different 'life chances' *vis-à-vis* the locality and the nation.

Since this analysis rests upon the manner in which the people of Eleodoro Gomez categorize each other, the question must be raised as to the degree of consistency in the assignment of individuals to specific social categories. It has been noted[11] that often there will be disagreements among informants about the assignment of particular individuals to status categories. As Berreman[12] points out, however, the confusion over assignment may be in the mind of the field worker rather than in those of the informants, if the context of choice of assignment for the informant is not made explicit.

In the present case the assignment of a given person to a local or national category, by a person from any category (including self-assignment) seems to be[13] consistent if the following specifications are met: (a) that the person to be categorized is known to the informant; (b) that the context of classification, national or local, is made explicit. In the case of one category of people, the estancieros, an additional specification is required; (c) that of the position of the informant in the local model. If the informant is criollo, the subject tends to be classified, in the local system, as estanciero. If the informant is classified as a foreigner, the subject tends to be similarly classified. If the informant is himself an estanciero and he is asked to classify himself or others in a similar position, the specifications of the matrix in which the evaluation is to be made can be easily manipulated to call forth the designations estanciero, foreigner, or clase media.

THE FOLK NATIONAL MODEL

The terms used to describe the categories of the folk extra-local model are in general use in Argentina. They are seductive terms for the analyst because it is all too easy to assume that they are used by the people of the locality with the same meaning assigned to them by the social scientist. In reference to some of the categories, particularly oligarchy (*clase alta*), this is close to the case, if this category is taken to be congruent with the designation of a landed elite.

The two terms, oligarchy and clase alta, isolate the same individuals and use the same criteria to do so. The variant terms reflect the emotional tone of the speaker, rather than any special characteristics of the subjects. If the context of the usage is negative then 'oligarchy' will be used, if positive the usage will tend to be 'clase alta.' If the context is relatively neutral, usage will reflect the social position of the speaker. The lower the speaker is in either the local or extra-local system the more likely it is that he will consistently use the term, 'oligarchy.'

The most obvious criterion for the assignment to the oligarchy—clase alta category—is wealth, but it is far from the only one. Power, as reflected by mention in newspapers or by word of mouth, within the centres of economic and political influence, and with 'high society,' is also a feature. Another major criterion is that of an historical involvement, commitment, and vested interest in the upper reaches of traditional Argentine society. Closely related to this is the major consideration of family. The family, not the individual, *per se*, is assigned to the oligarchy category. I must emphasize, once again, that these are the criteria which are used by the people of Eleodoro Gomez. They are not necessarily those of the professional analyst.

The rôles and institutions characteristic of the oligarchy are, of course, not activated in Eleodoro Gomez. Rather, they are activated in the offices, salons, and board rooms of large corporations, the national government, elite social clubs, and the national offices of various special interest groups such as the national cattlemen's association.[14] The oligarchy *qua* oligarchy has no rôle to play in Eleodoro Gomez.

The members of the Gomez family (and not all of them are named Gomez), while indubitably the most powerful people on the national scene who reside in Eleodoro Gomez (albeit part-time), rarely, if ever, have to activate that power on the local scene. When they are referred to as oligarchy or clase alta it is in reference to their activities on the national scene, not the local one. It is the oligarchy, not the Gomez family, which desired and helped bring about the downfall of Peron; it is the oligarchy, not the Gomez family, which is thought to control the political and economic future of Argentina; it is the clase alta, not the Gomez family, which is considered (by some) to be the repository of traditional Argentine values and the defender of the West. It is recognized, of course, that the Gomez family, in the world beyond Eleodoro Gomez, is an integral part of this, for the most part, negatively valued category.

The most obvious [criteria] by which people are assigned to the folk national category clase media are those of income and occupation. These people are not as rich as the oligarchy (with a few exceptions), not as poor as the descamisados. They are businessmen, professionals, estancia managers and owners, farmers, business and machine technicians and operators, service people, shopkeepers, and white-collar workers of a variety of specialties.

The context of identification as clase media is national. 'The clase media benefited more than the descamisados from Peron. Then they turned on him.' 'Politics is a game of oligarchy and clase media, it is not for we criollos.' 'It is only the clase media which really wants Argentina to change, to become modern. The oligarchy likes things as they are, or even better, as they were, and all the descamisados care about is the amount of money in their pocket right now.'

The people assigned to the clase media reside in the village, at the headquarters of the estancias and on farm homesteads in the countryside. The focus of this category, however, is the village, as the *Palacio* of the Gomez ranch is their local focus. The rural dwelling members of the clase media, the farmers, technicians, smaller non-elite estancieros, and estancia managers, meet in the village. Though resident in the countryside they are not of it. They do not participate in the open country networks which provide the framework of criollo society. In the village the clase media are organized by friendship groups of overlapping membership, but not by significant[15] formal institutions or groups.

The institutions and formal groups in which the people of the clase media do participate are found in the county seat. Those individuals assigned to the clase media belong or are sympathetic to a variety of political parties, but all of the parties hold their meetings in the county seat. Here also is the local Rotary Club, and the variety of special interest groups and voluntary associations mentioned earlier which are characteristically located in the county seats. In the county seat also are contacted the formal and informal government and welfare institutions, banks, business houses, etc. In all these the clase media of Eleodoro Gomez meet with their opposites from other villages and rural neighbourhoods of the county. It is in the county seat also that the local estancieros and elite ranch managers, operating through the county-level rural society, help allocate public resources to their particular interests.

For some, especially the wealthier businessmen and non-elite estancieros and managers, the institutional affiliations extend beyond the county seat to the national capital. Here, though, the institutional world of even the wealthiest clase media person is distinct from that of the oligarchy which is to be found in the same city.

In terms of the obvious criterion of income and the things that correlate with it the folk national category descamisado (clase popular) falls at the bottom of the Gomez national hierarchy. As I pointed out earlier, however, there are people who by the criterion of income 'ought' to be assigned to the middle class, but who are considered to be representatives of the lower one in folk terms.

The context in which the descriptive terms are used, as in the other cases, is national. 'Peron was for the descamisados and the descamisados were for him.' 'We descamisados are exploited by the oligarquia and bled white by the clase media.'

The institutional correlates of this category are the labour unions and peronist or quasi-peronist political parties. These also operate at the county level. They also operate, however, at the local level, at least in theory. Most of the manual rural workers, of all sorts, in the area belong to a single labourers' union which is affiliated with a national-level organization. Effectively, however, this union operates locally as an employment agency or hiring hall for a primary village-dwelling pool of unskilled labour. These are men who do not hold steady jobs, and who are allocated to a variety of agricultural, livestock, or service activities which vary with the annual agricultural and livestock cycles. This local union, even during the Peron regime, never held an effective strike in Eleodoro Gomez.

During the Peron regime a local branch of the peronist party was established in Eleodoro Gomez. It is now defunct, and it never accomplished anything, according to informants in all categories, except to bring out the vote for Peron on election day.

In summary the following points may be made about the folk national model: the categories used are relevant in a context of national affairs, not local ones. The institutions and rôles which correlate with these categories are relevant to larger regional and national concerns and centre, as far as local people are concerned, with few exceptions in the county seat. Here the groups formed draw their personnel from equivalent categories from all over the county. The few national institutions, such as the union, which do penetrate into Eleodoro Gomez are restructured, in terms of the expectations of its descamisado members and of others in the community who deal with it (estancieros, managers, businessmen), to serve local, rather than extra-local ends. The union, as a nationally oriented institution, extends no further than the county seat.

THE FOLK LOCAL MODEL

The individuals assigned to the category Familia are the same ones assigned to oligarchy in the national model. Their institutional affiliations beyond the locality are those of the oligarchy. The one criterion for assignment to this category is 'membership' in the Gomez family (and in the locality when one discusses 'La Familia' there is no ambiguity as to which family is meant).

The designation, Familia, is used in reference to events of local significance. It is the Familia which supports middle-class charitable activities. It is the Familia (or a particular representative of it) that an employee appeals to in order to get around some bureaucratic regulation of the estancia. It is members of the Familia who have 'life-long friends' among the *criollo* ranch employees. It is the Familia which distributes gifts to the poor, and the rest of the panoply of *noblesse oblige*.

Historically the Familia has its roots in the ranching complex and many male members are still able to play the cowboy rôle alongside their criollo employees. Although firm friendships between the criollos and members of the Familia are rare, *de facto*, when they do occur they centre about the complex of horse and cow and are expressed through an etiquette of at least a surface egalitarianism.

At the time of the field study no members of the Familia were active in the field management of their holdings. In the past, however, some were estancieros as well and were thus brought into even closer contact with their employees and other residents of the locality.

In the narrowest, dictionary sense, the term estanciero refers to the owner of large, employee-operated cattle ranches. In the wider sense, and in the usage of the community, active management, rather than legal ownership, of the estancia is the major criterion. Therefore, absentee owners who take little or no part in the field management of their holdings do not fall into this category. The same logic leads to the inclusion of the professional managers of the large Gomez family ranches in this category.

These men own and/or control the largest block of resources, human and material, in the area. Through the employment of workers (of all sorts), the purchases of supplies, the renting of their land to farmers, the granting of agricultural contracts to entrepreneurs, and the sale of livestock and grains produced on their ranches, they exert the major economic influence on the locality.

Through their contacts in the county seat, official and unofficial, the estancieros exert the major local political influence; they represent the chief link between government and other extra-local agencies and their criollo employees. Typically the one local government official, the *delegado*, an appointed position of extremely limited administrative and political powers, is held by the owner of a small estancia. Though this was not true of the peronist and immediate post-peronist period when the job was held by a descamisado, even these were men who were first approved in the county seat by the active estancieros.

With the exception of the occasional member of the Gomez family who is also an active manager, most of the estancieros are Buenos Aires businessmen or professionals as well. Even the full-time Gomez ranch managers have additional private business interests, usually as agricultural contractors.

As estancieros these men are the non-criollos in most intensive contact with those of criollo status. Most ranch owners are capable (with variations, of course, as to age, physical condition, etc.) of working on horseback with their criollo employees at mounted activities. When such estanciero-criollo work groups are activated the pattern of interaction is in terms of an egalitarian etiquette. The estanciero will listen respectfully and take instruction from an experienced cowhand about the handling of livestock. The egalitarian etiquette is carried over to non-livestock oriented activities as well. But here there is a greater implicit and explicit recognition of the power differential between them. The egalitarian style of the corral and round-up merges and shades off into an attenuated patron-client relationship.[16] A relationship similar to that which characterizes Familia-criollo expectations.

The expectations of, and about, the estanciero are equivalent to those of the Family, but with the realization that the estanciero lacks the wealth and national power of the Family. There is also the realization, however, that the estanciero exercises what powers he has in the local context and in view of the community, which the Family normally does not.

The people who are locally termed criollos are the bearers of a culture which, in spite of certain changes, can be seen as a persistence of the traditional way of life of the Argentine pampas, that of the *gaucho*.[17] This in spite of the fact that the people who participate in the way of life, like their non-criollo neighbours, are chiefly the descendants of late-nineteenth- and early-twentieth-century European, chiefly Italian and Spanish, immigrants to Argentina.

The major criterion for assignment to the criollo category is involvement in the 'traditional' livestock complex in a position which is neither administrative nor built around narrowly technical competence. The criollos, then, are the small ranch owners (i.e., *chacereros de ganado*), cowboys, foremen of livestock operations, sheep-herders, and traditional artisans. They tend to be resident in the countryside, though there are exceptions to this especially among older, retired, ranch workers.

The open country networks are, for the most part, criollo networks. Relations among criollos tend to be structured by ties of kinship and neighbourhood.[18]

With the estancieros, the criollos are committed to the norms associated with the cattle complex, and their relations with their peers and the estancieros [are] predicted upon these shared, traditional, expectations.[19] And they are quite explicitly seen as traditional.

The criollo has no formal institutional affiliations, other than those of kinship, outside the locality. Even within the locality the overriding institutional affiliation is with the family, and its extensions, which provides the basis for most intra-criollo co-operation. Though these people belong to the labourers union they are not, and were not, even in Peron's time, active in it. Similarly for the peronist party when it was operating. The active rôles in these institutions are, or were, held by descamisados, but foreign, not criollo ones. The horse races, bars, and social clubs, which provide the foci of criollo territorial concentration in the rural areas and villages, are owned, managed, and operated by non-criollos.

Relations outside the locality are provided by tapping the potential resources of kin and patronage. Individual relations between strategically placed criollo relatives (such as foremen) and with the estanciero, provide for the distribution of jobs and other 'goods' within the locality. The criollo links with the formal apparatus of the state (in its various administrative and functional guises) are almost exclusively mediated by the estancieros.

Although from one point of view the three categories so far discussed under the folk local rubric may be seen as hierarchically stratified, it is also clear that they may be lumped together for certain purposes. All of them may be seen, historically, as a continuation of the traditional socio-cultural pattern of the Argentine countryside.

On a synchronic level the people assigned to these traditional categories are all, *vis-à-vis* each other, operating on the basis of a shared body of expectations. Their relative positions differ within this traditional system, but the expectations which each holds in relation to the others [are] indeed predictive in reference to the personal relations which each has with the others. Although members of each of these categories [have] relations with 'non-traditional others,' estancieros with foreigners, criollos with other descamisados, etc., none of them are normally faced with the problem of dealing with each other in terms of contradictory patterns of expectations. Contradictory rôle demands there are, but they are generated in different situations and in reference to different people.

It is the lack of involvement with shared traditional patterns of expectation which most clearly distinguishes the foreign category from the others of the folk local model.

The phrase, 'children of foreigners' (hijos de extranjeros), or the more specific designations of *hijo de italiano, hijo de gallego* (Spanish), etc., seems to be descriptive of recency of arrival in Argentina. In fact, it describes a social-cultural and not a national origins category. A striking illustration of this is revealed in the self-identification of two full brothers. One, a *domador* (horse trainer) considered himself a criollo because, as he explained, 'my mother is a criolla.' The other brother, a shop clerk, identified himself as an hijo de extranjero, since 'My father was Italian.' As I mentioned earlier, almost everyone resident in Eleodoro Gomez full or part-time (with the exception of the Familia) are, or are the descendents of, relatively recent immigrants.

The occupational rôles of the foreigners lie in the agricultural, professional, and service categories. Historically the growth of these occupational categories reflects the industrialization of Argentina, rural and urban, and the massive immigration of the late nineteenth and early twentieth centuries. Also included in the foreigner category, for certain purposes, are the Buenos Aires businessmen who used city earned profits to invest in rural properties and also took on the estanciero rôle.

As I indicated in Figure 2 the income of those designated as [foreigners] ranges from a point which overlaps with that of the Familia-Oligarchy categories at the top, to a point below that of most criollos.

What sets these people apart is the fact that they do not share the expectations and values of the traditional Familia, estanciero, criollo set. The stereotype of the foreigner, in at least this part of Argentina, is as an adherent to the 'protestant ethic.' The foreigner seems not to assume that patronage (vertically) and kinship (horizontally) provide the only framework within which things can be accomplished. He does not assume that the Familia and estanciero are the natural lords of creation on the local scene.

Nor does he assume, as do the criollos, that everyone not an estanciero or Familia member is automatically an equal. This assumption, and the action that it calls forth, on the part of criollos, and at least one ranch manager (in this case, everyone not an equal, i.e., estanciero, is an inferior) is intensely disliked by the foreigner, especially those at the upper end of the income range.

The criollo says with approval that the above mentioned ranch manager, 'treats everyone [except other estancieros and the Gomez family] alike.' The foreigner agrees with the observation, but his evaluation of it is negative. Similarly the criollo is annoyed because the foreigner, especially the wealthier ones, do not deal with him as a peer, and the foreigner is equally annoyed because the criollo expects to be so treated. 'Even the patrons [i.e., estancieros, Familia] do not act that way with us,' complains the criollo. While the foreigner is exasperated because, 'Those criollos think they can give advice about things of which they are ignorant, and then they get angry if you do not want to waste your time listening to them.'

This kind of problem does not exist when we consider relations among the poor foreigners and criollos, a situation in which relative status positions are reversed. The poor foreigner is still considered to lie beyond the boundaries of 'criollodom.' He is pitied because he cannot ride and rope well, because he lacks the pride of the criollo, because he lacks the support of his kinsmen, because all he works for is money. At best the poor foreigner is only a marginal and passing member of the criollos open country networks. To move from poor foreigner to criollo status is desired, but few make it. Those that do not usually migrate out of the locality, ultimately, and seek the better paid and secure job in the city, in a sense committing themselves once and for all to the standards of the foreigner.

But some criollos also 'fail.' For a variety of reasons, personal and structural, not all people born criollo can remain criollo. Those who drop out become foreigners, usually poor ones, working only for money at a despised job. Ultimately, these too leave the locality for the city, leaning, at first, upon kinsmen who have gone before.

Assignment to the criollo or foreigner categories is, then, achieved and not ascribed. The foreigner at the economic nadir of his category may seek to move to criollo status, the criollo who 'fails' seeks to move upward as foreigner. But the latter type of mobility requires that the person attempting it leave the locality. The former type is permissible within it. Persons normally assigned to either of these categories are aware of the rules, the expectations, by which those in the other operate. If a change in categories is necessitated, in either direction, the person usually knows the rules appropriate to his new situation.

The fact that the walls between categories are permeable to individuals does not mean that they are equally permeable to norms. A criollo turned poor foreigner who acted toward his employer in the same egalitarian terms as he had with his patron would rapidly find himself out of a job. A foreigner turned criollo who neglected his kinsmen and neighbours, and humbled himself before the patron would soon find himself isolated from his peers and back on the road to foreigner status.

The category of foreigner, as with the others of the folk local model, is relevant in terms of the expected behaviour of people in the locality. It represents an ordering and prediction about the behaviour of people encountered in the course of the everyday, normal, round of local events.

As far as the formal institutional affiliations of people assigned to this foreigner category are concerned there are none which serve to unite them as foreigners. Rather, their institutional affiliations sort out into those of the folk national model according to whether a given foreigner is to be considered clase media or descamisado in the folk national model.

THE SUBSTANTIVE PROBLEM

The substantive problem which opened this article can now be disposed of relatively easily within the context of the two models.

The problem, to review, concerned criollos, who seemed to make contradictory statements about the Familia. On the one hand the criollos seemed to damn the members of the Gomez family as being the exploiters of the poor and concerned only with their selfish self-interest. On the other hand the criollos also looked upon these same people as patrons, supporters, and protectors.

The problem is easily solved. In reference to the negative, or 'class-warfare' statement, the criollos are acting, or speaking, in accordance with the interests of a larger category, the descamisados, of which they represent only a small part. The people they are referring to, the Gomez family, [are] also seen here within the larger national context of oligarchy. Neither the 'speaker' category nor the 'referent' category are associated with institutions or rôles which can be activated on the local scene.

The second statement, the positive one, refers to local (i.e., interpersonal) behavioural expectations and refers also to different categories. It is the criollo, *per se,* not the descamisado, who makes this 'patronage' statement. It is the Familia, not the oligarchy to which he is referring. In this case both categories are associated with norms and institutions which are activated locally. The fact that the members of the Familia are also thought to be members of the oligarchy should not be permitted to confuse the situation. The categories, and all that is associated with them, are distinct. The concept oligarchy predicts or orders nothing on the local scene,[20] it tells us nothing of how people are expected to act in a face-to-face encounter. The concept Familia does.

The contradiction which began this article is a contradiction only if it is assumed that socio-cultural categories are absolutes; that the boundaries of 'cultures' must be isomorphic with a given set of individuals, that an individual is a participant in only one culture, or system of norms. I have tried to indicate here that there are operational benefits to be derived by assuming otherwise, by assuming that there are, or may be, several units of cultural transmission within a single society; that these are transmitting different cultures, in different systems; and that a given individual may operate in more than one of them, depending on the situation and the context.

There is still another problem. Why is it that the people of Eleodoro Gomez, and I, find it inconvenient to order all the behavioural phenomena that are to be observed by them within a single model? What is the relationship between the models, their constituent categories, and the institutions and rôles which are characteristic of people assigned to these categories?

It was pointed out earlier that every category, save one, in both the local and national models had specific institutional and rôle correlates characteristic of it which linked its assignees to larger systems. The one exception to this were the criollos of the folk local model. For them, kinship and patronage were used to structure relationships both locally and extra-locally, the estancieros providing the link to larger systems. There were no particularly criollo institutions which organize all criollos, everywhere, as an interest group concerned with national-level affairs. But there were institutions, and appeals to criollo self-interest, which *seemed* to operate in lieu of this.

Starting with the 1943 revolution and continuing with increasing intensity through the Peron years, there was an appeal to the poor and the powerless for political action on the Argentine national scene. Peron's appeal to the poor and despised, to the descamisados, via the mass media, the relative increase in standards of living for these people, the welfare benefits, and the security of job tenure, which Peron accomplished, awakened a sense of identity by the criollos with other descamisados. For were not the criollos poor and powerless, and weren't they, theoretically and actually, beneficiaries of the policies of the new regime along with the urban workers?

But the peronist institutions got only as far as the county seat. They never, at least in this part of Argentina, effectively penetrated into the countryside. In the countryside, then, the new ideology was not accompanied by new rôles and institutions, by new patterns of behaviour and expectations about the behaviour of others which could be activated on the local scene.[21] The Buenos Aires businessman had to learn to deal with government, welfare, and union representatives with new and impressive powers. The same man, now in his rôle as estanciero, similarly had new problems to face when he dealt with the government in the county seat. But when he was on his own ranch things remained pretty much as they had always been as he dealt with his employees.

Peronism, then, was a new ideology for the criollo, but one which lacked new rôles and rules of behaviour associated with it which he could activate. It was an ideology, therefore, which did not reorient the everyday operations of the locality. It was an ideology, and model of the social system, which could not order or predict the events which were significant within Eleodoro Gomez. One might talk class warfare but there was no way to activate it. One had to act in terms of basically traditional expectations.

To a degree, all this was also true of those termed locally estancieros, foreigners, and Familia. For these people too, and for the same reasons, the local model had utility within the locality. But for these people, unlike the criollos, the county seat, the provincial and national capitals, provided arenas in which regionally and nationally oriented activities could occur. Where ideology could be matched by rôle and institution.

The combination of ideological commitment and structural isolation was not unrecognized, at least implicitly, by many criollos. This recognition and knowledge, plus the knowledge of rules appropriate for action by people in other categories, probably has major implications both for the problems of internal migration and for the potentialities for change in the local system. These cannot be developed here, but in reference to the point of ideological commitment and structural isolation, I will let a criollo have the final word.

I had been speaking with a cowhand about the events surrounding the overthrow of Peron in 1955. He said, vehemently, 'We [criollos] were all for [Peron]. We would have gone to the Capital by train and bus, by sulky and on horseback. We would have fought for him. We would have died for him.' He paused, thought for a moment, shook his head sadly and added, 'But no one asked us.'

CONCLUSION

This article has been based upon three major points.

The first of these points has been to indicate that the concepts of national and local social systems are of operational utility only. Each of them may provide a useful framework for some problems while hindering the understanding of others. This applies even when behaviour by the same individuals is being considered.

The second point grows out of the first one. Critical to an analysis of a problem in a complex society is the delimitation of units of cultural analysis and the delineation of their boundaries. In some cases the units must shift with the problem being analyzed. In the present instance the unit of cultural transmission (the culture) which carries the traditional patronage attitudes (or within which unit these attitudes may be ordered) is different from the culture which transmits the 'class-warfare' attitudes. The distinction between such units as conceptual devices and the individuals which may be assigned to them for various purposes must remain clear.

Finally, I have illustrated the contention that folk models of the social systems may, and in the present case do, provide the clues to the relationships among levels of problem, appropriate socio-cultural units, and associated analytical categories.

In recent years there has been a growing dissatisfaction among anthropologists working in modern complex societies with traditional anthropological problems and units of analysis. There has been a growing search after new units of analysis, new questions, and new problems appropriate to the phenomena to be observed in modern societies.[22] The search, however, is for units, questions and problems, to which one of the traditional advantages of the anthropological approach, the intimate knowledge of a socio-cultural system, may be applied. This article is part of that search.

NOTES

1. I would like to express my thanks to the Henry L. and Grace Doherty Foundation which in 1958–1959 supported the field research on which this article is based. I would also like to thank the Ibero-American Program of the University of Wisconsin for research support during the summer of 1965 during part of which an early draft of this paper was prepared. I am also obliged to Professors Robert J. Miller and Leonard Glick for their comments on an earlier draft. Full responsibility for what appears here is, of course, my own.

2. Beattie, J. H. M. Comments on S. N. Eisenstadt. 'Anthropological Studies of Complex Societies.' *Current Anthropology*, 1961, 201–222.

3. See, for example, Gluckman, Max, and Ely Devons. 'Conclusion: Modes and Consequences of Limiting a Field of Study.' Max Gluckman (ed.), *Closed Systems and Open Minds: The Limits of Naivety in Social Anthropology*: Chicago. Aldine Publishing Co., 1964; Moerman, Michael. 'Ethnic Identification in a Complex Civilization: Who Are the Lue?' *American Anthropologist*, 1965, 1215–1230; Berreman, Gerald D. 'The Study of Caste Ranking in India.' *Southwestern Journal of Anthropology*, 1965, 115–129; Ossowski, Stanislaw. *Class Structure in the Social Consciousness:* New York. Free Press of Glencoe, 1963; Morris, Richard T., and Raymond J. Murphy. 'The Situs Dimension in Occupational Structure.' *American Sociological Review*, 1959, 231–239; Arensberg, Conrad M., and Solon T. Kimball. *Culture and Community:* New York. Harcourt, Brace and World, Inc., 1965; Eisenstadt, *op. cit.*

4. See, for example, the debate between Galjart and Huizer. Galjart, Benno. 'Class and Following in Rural Brazil.' *America Latina*, 1964 (3), 3–24; Huizer, Gerrit. 'Some Note (*sic*) on Community Development and Rural Social Research.' *America Latina*, 1965 (3), 128–144; Galjart, Benno. 'A Further Note on "Followings;": Reply to Huizer.' *America Latina*, 1965 (3), 145–152.

5. Spanish terms will be italicized at their first appearance. Thereafter they will not be.

6. Levi-Strauss, Claude. 'Social Structure.' A. L. Kroeber (ed.), *Anthropology Today: An Encyclopedic Inventory*: Chicago. University of Chicago Press, 1953, pg. 527.

7. Steward, Julian H., *et al. The People of Puerto Rico: A Study in Social Anthropology*: Urbana. University of Illinois Press, 1956. A good deal of this work centres upon the problem of shifting metropolitan and insular level parameters and resulting changes in class and community structure.

8. For a detailed description of Eleodoro Gomez, its history and the effects of national and international events upon it, see Strickon, Arnold. *The Grandsons of the Gauchos: A Study in Sub-Cultural Persistence:* Ann Arbor. University Microfilms, 1960. For a discussion of the variables which orient the area to ranching or farming see Strickon, Arnold. 'The Euro-American Ranching Complex.' Anthony Leeds and Andrew P. Vayda (eds.), *Man, Culture, and Animals: The Rôle of Animals in Human Ecological Adaptations:* New York. Publications of the American Association for the Advancement of Science, 1965.

9. The place names, Eleodoro Gomez and Sarmiento are fictitious. Also fictitious is the family name Gomez which is used later in this article to identify the elite family which is the largest landowner in the area of Eleodoro Gomez.

10. See, for example, the application of a 'modified Weberian' classification to the Argentine situation by Silvert, K. H. 'The Cost of Anti-Nationalism: *Argentina.*' K. H. Silvert (ed.), *Expectant Peoples: Nationalism and Development:* New York. Random House, 1963.

11. Berreman, *op. cit.*; and Adams, Richard N. A *Community in the Andes: Problems and Progress in Muquiyauyo:* Seattle. University of Washington Press, 1959.

12. Berreman, *ibid.*

13. Obviously such a statement is amenable to statistical confirmation. Unfortunately the question was not raised until after the end of the field research. I hope to be able to field test it in the near future.

14. Strickon, Arnold. 'Class and Kinship in Argentina.' *Ethnology*, 1962, 500–515.

15. The one formal 'middle-class' institution which operates in the village is the *Sociedad Pro-Fomento*. This operates chiefly as a local charitable institution.

16. Wolf, Eric R. 'Kinship, Friendship, and Patron-Client Relations in Complex Societies." Michael Banton (ed.), *The Social Anthropology of Complex Cultures:* London. Tavistock Publications, 1966.

17. Strickon, 1960, *op. cit.*

18. Strickon 1960, *ibid.*; Strickon 1962, *op. cit.*

19. The 'climax' of this culture is centred around male activities, materials, values, and ideology. The distinction between the '*criollo*' and her opposites in other categories is less marked than those between men. There are, however, some distinctive characteristics which can be viewed as persistences of traditional *china* (i.e., female *gaucho*) behaviour patterns. See Strickon 1960, *op. cit.*

20. Except, of course, insofar as they are part of the national power structure which sets parameters within which the community must function.

21. Clearly the explanation for this failure to restructure the countryside cannot be discovered by research in the countryside, but rather reflects variables operating at high national levels.

22. See, for example, Mitchell, J. Clyde. 'Theoretical Orientations in African Urban Studies.' and Frankenberg, Ronald. 'British Community Studies: Problems of Synthesis.' Michael Banton (ed.), *The Social Anthropology of Complex Cultures:* London. Tavistock Publications, 1966; Leeds, Anthony. 'Brazilian Careers and Social Structure: An Evolutionary Model and Case History.' *American Anthropologist*, 1964, 1321–1347; Gluckman, *op. cit.*; Moerman, *op. cit.*; Berreman, *op. cit.*

A Counter-Ideology of Racial Unmasking

FLORESTAN FERNANDES

Brazil has long been regarded as a model of racial equality, and a profusion of theories have been offered to explain the differences between attitudes and race relations there and in the United States. But in this instance, as is often the case, social reality differs from ideology.

Incongruous as it may seem to many, Brazil was the site of an early and outspoken movement favoring what might now be called "black consciousness." Ample documentation of that phenomenon, together with a critical evaluation of persisting problems, are offered by a sociologist who is himself a Brazilian.

Florestan Fernandes is a professor (catedrático) at Universidad da São Paulo, Brazil. Although he calls himself a "functionalist-historian," he is well known in the United States as an ethnographer, sociologist, and ethnohistorian. His books include Fundamentos Empiricos da Explicação Sociologica (1959), Ensaios de Sociologia Geral e Aplicada (1960), Folclore e Mudança Social na Cidade de São Paulo (1961), *and, jointly,* Brancos e Negros em São Paulo (1959).

["Black consciousness" is by no means a new movement. In Brazil, a nation renowned for its supposed racial democracy, the late 1940s saw] . . . a resurgence, redefinition, and implantation of the old demands of the "negro* people." They did not just renew the old foci of intellectual and moral agitation. They sketched out new lines of awareness of the sociocultural situation of the "negro" in São Paulo, and they consolidated the hopes of universal organization according to democratic and pluralistic models of organized social action. Furthermore, the solutions developed for these problems were institutionally more elaborate [than any that had been developed before].

It was clear that the misery, the ignorance, and the individualism of "the negro" were by no means the only barriers to be surmounted. Negroes saw better how the society at large hindered the effectiveness and continuity of revivalistic movements; they understood with greater clarity the detailed nature of appropriate means and ends and the relation between them, speaking strictly in terms of action.

Although these various ramifications of social agitation in the "negro milieu" failed to meet their objectives in practical terms, they did, in various ways,

Translated and abridged, especially for this volume, from *A Integração do Negro à Sociedade de Classes,* Vol. II (São Paulo: Dominus Editôra, Editôra da Universidade de São Paulo, 1965), 70–95, by permission of the author and publisher. Translated by Z. Caroline Bieler and the editor.

* [Editor's note: The term "negro" is used in this paper where the original Portuguese was "negro," or "negra" (set off by quotation marks in the original, as in translation). From the context it is apparent that the author makes much of the ambiguity of those words, an ambiguity which is similar in both languages. For that reason, it appears inappropriate to use either of the emotionally loaded terms "black" or "Negro" as a simple direct translation.]

penetrate and modify the cultural horizon of the negro and the mulatto of São Paulo.

The search for autonomy should not be confused with the negation and rejection of the prevailing social order. On the contrary, it presupposed a defense, with conviction, of the advantages of acceptance by and complete integration with that social order. Therefore, the "white man" was not attacked except in the core of his racial dominance and the corresponding ideology. The dynamic element of the divergent and developed accommodations is unmistakable: The nonconformist "negro" sought to redefine the circumstances and interests of the "negro race" in terms of the structure and functioning of the class-stratified society. He did not reject the "white man," or the "class society," or those "forms of domination" that might readjust the racial relations to the mechanisms of the competitive social order. But he did condemn the perpetuation of the Brazilian standards of racial integration which maintained an undesirable duality: a virtual caste system under the guise of an "open society" and "racial democracy."

All this demonstrates that the "negro ideology" was formed as a response to the traditional racial ideology. On the positive side, it represented the dynamic product of the "negro's" absorption of values on which are based the legal order and consequently the life style of the "whites." On the negative side, it translated the "negro's" rebuff of the duplicity of a social order which appeared open on one level but closed on another. He was dealing, then, with an ideology which could never be organized on racist foundations. The appeal for union and exclusivism was merely strategic. They were not the principal aims, nor were they even ends in themselves, pursued consciously as such. Beneath all these attributes, we are confronted with a counterideology, devised to minimize the psychosocial frustrations of a racial category and, eventually, to aid in the immediate struggle for the rapid modification of the status quo.

Understood in these terms, the "negro ideology," as it was pursued through the social movements considered, had as its explicit and ultimate end nothing short of the unmasking of the dominant racial ideology. By its very nature, it would have extinguished itself the moment its functions were fulfilled. In the long run, the economic, social, and political integration of the "negro people" would have meant the end of the "negro ideology," which would have lost its own reason for being and would have been doomed to disappear. Its place would have been taken by other values and social goals legitimately sanctioned by the prevailing social order. That no such integration took place should not be blamed on the "negro" or on any sort of racial intolerance for which he had made himself spokesman. Instead, the failure was the result of a sociohistorical conjuncture which destroyed at the root his hopes and his efforts to democratize the Brazilian system of racial relations.

The unmasking of the dominant racial ideology proceeded on three distinct levels. On the most evident and superficial level it denied that the established legal order was effective for the "negro." The liberty and equality achieved since the abolition [of slavery] and the [founding of the] Republic were in fact useless. Neither one had eliminated the "secular plundering," which continued under new forms. "Enough lies . . . enough guardianship . . . the negroes wish to assist in the organization of Brazil, with their independence of thought.

They want to have their own political patronage, situating themselves always on the side of their only party, which is Brazil."[1]

On a more profound level, the unmasking extended to the rationalizations on which were founded the philosophy and politics of the "racial democracy," with the corresponding standard of traditional racial domination. There arose, at one time, an explanation for the ineffectiveness of the prevailing legal order and an interpretation of the sources of resistance to the "white man's" egalitarian acceptance of the negro and the mulatto. Color prejudice was elaborated as a sociohistorical category, indicating why class and race were meshed in such an intricate manner. Two types of barriers, it was said, intersected in a way which was imperceptible to or hidden from the eyes of the "whites," complicating the social screening of the "negro." This distorted the normal working of the competitive and democratic social order, [making it] more or less closed for "colored men." The diagnosis was, by its nature, so complex that it was sketched out gradually, worked out in detail with all clarity, and then adopted as a position of struggle. From the beginning a certain confusion prevailed. The "negro" did not know whether the prejudice was associated with his racial condition or his social position.

The negro race in Brazil is unquestionably the victim of impressive injustice—injustice which becomes more serious, more harsh, as time passes. If the reader were to devote himself to the task of investigating the thought of each negro man, literate or illiterate, he would be aghast. "There is a perfect community of ideas!" "The great majority think in the same way about achieving the ideal. Everyone suffers the misery and the lessening; all feel the prejudice and the slights; all know the shame and the scorn." "They suffer for the indelible brand of their skin, for the crime of being born dark. Knowledge serves no purpose, dignity is of little value, good qualities and competence give them much less. One obstacle stands in the way of everything that would make them superior: color."[2]

It was evident, then, that the Brazilian negro could no longer remain apathetic, indifferent, in the face of the realities which surrounded him. He could no longer wait, with that saintly naïveté of his ancestors, for the decree of salvation which would integrate him in fact and by right into the Brazilian community. He would have to fight. He would have to assert himself. He would have to interest himself in the essential problems of humanity and the country and the basic questions of his destiny. He would have to unmask the false presupposition that the negro has none of "his own causes within the problems and human causes of the entire Brazilian community."[3] While the negro was objectifying his elevation, while he was envisaging that state of perfection inherent to men and, consequently, the collectivity of which he is a part, while he was beginning to flee the somnolence, the most absurd and improper charges were brought against him. And—as is already an old story—the common arguments were resumed: "The negro has no problem"; "we are a people without prejudice"; "we have no barriers based upon color."[4]

The first two types of unmasking engendered the added necessity of unmasking certain symbols and values which serve fundamentally, in the inclusive society, to conceive a racial reality that accorded with the interests of the "whites" as the dominant race. Historical dates and their official significance are important to this case. "How did the law of abolition finally serve in Brazil? Only to demonstrate to the stranger our apparent civilization, because if it abolished official slavery, it implanted a special servitude; it destroyed the regime of obligatory slavery, and imposed one of voluntary servitude."[5]

The "negro" not only declared himself ideologically opposed to the "white man," but was forced to provide himself with representative and fitting examples. As a result, his understanding of the world, the nature of man, and his position in society gained a certain richness and variety. He mastered the symbols and fundamental values of the legal order. He imposed with purity and integrity paradigms that the "whites" were violating or perverting by means of the prevailing racial accommodations. This demonstrates that the unmasking was not operating solely as a negative social technique. No matter how lamentable or disagreeable these outcomes may appear from the social perspective of the "dominant race," they were in a sense highly creative from the point of view of the "negro." Thanks to that technique, the "colored man" redefined certain symbols, assimilated the meaning of certain institutions and social values, and became the creator of his own myths.

Furthermore, as the unmasking proceeded, meanings which linked it with the organization of personality, of culture and society, changed it at one and the same time into a psychodynamic source of craving for moral autonomy and into a sociocultural factor of the new self-esteem aim of the "negro race" as a social category. The content and orientation of the "negro ideology" thus were forced, structurally and dynamically, into a historical role as counterideology of the racial unmasking. In historico-sociological terms, they responded to the basic need of a "race" that was psychologically, economically, socially, politically, and culturally alienated, that needed to become aware of its own situation and interests in order to be able to partake of the material and moral guarantees of the "open society." In a moment of transition, the "negro" had to become aware of himself and for himself as a racial category, to assert himself socially, and to project himself again into history, into an effective condition as a *free man*.

OTES

1. Pedro Rodrigues, "A Frente Negra Brasileira" [The Negro Brazilian Front], *A Voz da Raça*, São Paulo, Ano I, No. 11, June 3, 1933.

2. Rajovia (pseudonym of Raul Joviano do Amaral, "Nôvo Rumo" [New Direction], *A Vox da Raça*, São Paulo, Ano III, No. 54, June 1936.

3. Raul Joviano do Amaral, "O Negro não Tem Problemas" [The Negro Has No Problems], *Alvorada*, São Paulo, . . . September 1945.

4. Raul Joviano do Amaral, "Basta de Explorações" [Enough of Explorations], *Alvorada*, São Paulo, . . . October 1945. In a later article, Raul Joviano do Amaral affirms: ". . . But in the lands of the south prejudice is of color and race and not of class" ("Tese Errada" [Erroneous thesis], *Alvorada*, São Paulo, Ano II, No. 24, June 1947).

5. A. Oliveira, "Aos Nossos Leitores" [To our readers], *O Alfinête*, São Paulo, Ano I, No. 2, September 3, 1918.

Message to the Students

CAMILO TORRES

Students enjoy a special status throughout most of Latin America, and university students have traditionally been outspoken regarding political affairs. This appeal, voiced by an academician-priest-revolutionary, is also a succinct and sociologically insightful characterization of that status and of the moral imperative that he felt accompanies it.

Camilo Torres was a Dominican priest, sociologist, journalist, and active revolutionary. His outspoken opposition to the status quo, based on a concern for social welfare, led to his being dismissed from the university rectorship and excommunicated from the Church. Affirming that "the duty of every Catholic is to be a revolutionary; the duty of every revolutionary is to make the revolution," he joined the guerrilla Army of National Liberation and was killed in a skirmish in 1966.

Students are a privileged group in every underdeveloped country. Poor nations subsidize the few college and university graduates at very high cost. In Colombia especially, with the great number of private colleges and universities, the economic factor has become crucial.

In a country whose population is 60 percent illiterate, students comprise one of the few groups possessing the tools for social analysis and comparison and for finding possible solutions to Colombia's problems. Furthermore, the university student, at those institutions where there is freedom of expression, has two privileges: He can climb the social ladder by rising through the academic ranks, and he can at the same time be a nonconformist and display his rebelliousness without placing his rise in jeopardy. These factors have made students a crucial element in the Latin American revolution. During the agitational phase of the revolution, the students' efforts have been highly effective. In the organizational phase, their work has played a secondary role. In the direct struggle, [however], despite the [few] honorable exceptions which have occurred in revolutionary history, their role has not been crucial.

We know that agitational efforts are important, but that their real effects are lost if they are not followed by organization and by the struggle for power. One of the principal reasons for the transitory and superficial nature of the students' contribution to the revolution is the lack of commitment in their economic, familial, and personal struggles. A student's nonconformity tends to be either emotional (because of sentimental reasons or frustration) or else purely intellectual. This explains why, at the end of his university career, his nonconformity [typically] disappears or is, at best, hidden away. The rebellious student no longer exists. He becomes a bourgeois professional who buys the symbols of bourgeois prestige and trades his conscience for a high salary. These circumstances gravely endanger the chances for a mature and responsible reply on the part of students at this moment in Colombia's history.

The workers and peasants are experiencing the political and economic crisis in all its harshness. The student, generally isolated from them, believes that a superficial or purely speculative revolutionary attitude is sufficient. This lack of

Reprinted from *Frente Unido* (Bogotá), 21 October 1965; translation by the editor.

contact can make the student a traitor to his historical vocation; when the country demands a total commitment, the student answers with nothing but words and good intentions. When the mass movement demands a daily and constant effort, the student replies with shouts, stonings, and sporadic demonstrations. When the people demand an effective, disciplined, and responsible presence in their ranks, the student answers with vain promises or excuses.

The student's revolutionary convictions ought to lead to real commitment, carried to the ultimate consequences. Poverty and persecution should not be actively sought, but they are the logical consequence of total struggle against the existing system. Under the present system, they are the signs that authenticate a revolutionary life. The same convictions should lead the student to participate in the economic hardships and social persecution that workers and peasants suffer. Therefore, commitment to the revolution passes from theory to practice. If it is total, it is irreversible, and the professional cannot renege without betraying his conscience, his historical vocation, and his people.

At this moment of revolutionary opportunity, I do not want to preach. I want only to encourage students to contact reliable sources of information, to determine their responsibility and their necessary response. Personally, I believe that we are rapidly approaching the zero hour of the Colombian revolution. But only the peasants and workers can say this with any authority. If the students joined the people without paternalism and with a spirit of learning, they could then judge objectively the historical moment. It would, however, be fruitless and disgraceful if Colombian students, who have been the spark of the revolution, remained at its margin for any reason: lack of information, superficiality, egoism, irresponsibility, or fear.

We hope that students will respond to their country's call in this transcendental moment of its history and that they will be encouraged to hear and follow it with boundless generosity.

Rural Peru—Peasants as Activists

WILLIAM F. WHYTE

For all the talk about "revolution" in Latin America's political history, upheavals that resulted in significantly reordering the distribution of wealth and power have been rare at the national level. Many observers have even agreed that the peasant majority in traditionally agrarian societies are apathetic or peculiarly resistant to change.

Revised for this volume by the author, from *Transaction* VII (1969), 38–47. Copyright © November 1969 SOCIETY Magazine by Transaction, Inc., New Brunswick, New Jersey. Photographs that accompanied the original version have been omitted, and two figures have been added by the author, ". . . to show readers that [I am] talking about something pretty solid and concrete and not just stringing a lot of words together." Reprinted by permission of the author and publisher.

Whyte challenges "the myth of the passive peasant" with a number of case studies from rural Peru, which offer striking contrasts with the approaches to development described by Dobyns, Erasmus, and others.

William Foote Whyte is Professor of Industrial and Labor Relations at Cornell University. He is author, coauthor, and editor of several books on economics, labor, and development, and has used imaginative research methods continually since his pioneering Street Corner Society (1943). *His research has been more in Anglo-America than in Latin America, but his approach to Peru's peasantry, through local history, is a timely corrective to some widespread misconceptions.*

The guerrillas' presence tends to alter the situation in which peasants, sharecroppers, squatters, peons and Indians live. These people are condemned to an existence which follows the same unchanging routine from year to year, from decade to decade, from generation to generation, until it assumes in their minds the proportions of an immutable natural order.

Carlos Romeo

The writer of those lines is a follower of Fidel Castro and a theoretician of the revolutionary potential of the peoples of Latin America. My point in citing him is that his sentiments about the rural peasantry sum up the feelings of an extraordinarily wide range of observers of the Latin American scene, whatever their political views or goals.

For revolutionaries or reformers, for Fidelistas or rhetoricians of the Alliance for Progress, the peasants are enmired in "an immutable natural order." They are seen as an ignorant lot, tradition-bound and incapable of change even when that change might substantially improve their earthly condition. As such they cannot be brought to share in their country's wealth without the intervention of more enlightened outsiders who will point the way.

Of course reformers and revolutionaries have radically different notions of what form their intervention should take. The former, generally speaking, embrace a theory of community development according to which strategies have to be devised so that the peasantry will be "involved" in discussions of possible changes and their traditional conservatism overcome through the "participation process." Revolutionaries tend to assume—sometimes at the cost of their lives—that the agents of change will be their own guerrilla bands operating in the countryside where they will serve as catalysts of the dormant revolutionary impulses of the peasants.

I would argue the contrary proposition, that far from being dull pawns in an immutable natural order, the peasants are caught up in constant processes of change, and that many of these changes are initiated by themselves without benefit of outside guidance. I will try to demonstrate this proposition from studies of the Peruvian countryside, but I believe that this general conclusion would apply throughout Latin America and, indeed, in most of the Third World. It should be borne in mind, however, that I am not arguing against outside intervention, whether by reformists or revolutionaries. I am simply suggesting that before any self-appointed agents do intervene, they would do well to find out where the ball is and in what direction it is rolling. Then they will be able to give it a well-directed push, rather than falling flat on their faces, as so many "development projects" have done, or being killed, as so many guerrillas have been.

For the purposes of this argument, there is one segment of Peruvian rural society that presents the toughest challenge to my contention. This is the sierra hacienda or large landed estate, which would seem to offer peasants a minimum of opportunity to change their lot. Here, if anywhere, one would assume that change could come only from the outside, and that it would probably have to be effected by violent force.

THE SIERRA HACIENDA

In Peru the word "hacienda" is used to refer to two quite different types of social and economic units. In the coastal hacienda (sometimes referred to in English as "plantation"), workers generally live in houses built by the company, are paid regular wages, and their children have access to at least elementary schooling. Many of the haciendas are unionized. Many of them also can best be described as agro-industrial complexes, since they run from cultivation to manufacture (paper, chemicals, rum, for example). Many of the commercial haciendas are operated at a high level of technology and agricultural sciences, with agronomists serving either as managers or consultants.

The traditional sierra hacienda is drastically different. It has been likened to the feudal manor because of the extreme domination exercised by the hacendado over the peasants. The owner or renter of the hacienda retains the best lands for himself while each peasant family, in return for the right to occupy and cultivate a small plot of land, generally in the most undesirable areas, is required to provide from three to six man-days of work a week, either on the hacendado's lands or on projects for which he hires out his labor and for which he himself pockets the wages. Furthermore, the women of the peasant families usually have obligations in the household of the hacendado. In general, the hacendado has good connections with the political and economic power figures in his area; the peasants traditionally have lacked these connections and are subjected to various forms of exploitation and denial of opportunity. Because he normally received only a token payment—perhaps a penny or two a day, plus a supply of coca to chew on—he was unable to accumulate capital to become a landowner himself. In fact, the only major difference between the traditional Peruvian hacienda and the manor at the height of the middle ages is that the Peruvian peasant is free to leave the land. If he does, however, he loses any claim to the land he has cultivated and on which he built his home. This is the situation that has prevailed through much of the Peruvian sierra, where over half of the population lives. We are therefore talking about a situation of extreme inequality of power and resources, where it is natural to raise the question as to whether any basic change is possible without outside intervention or violent revolution. Let us examine several cases in the light of this question.

Twenty years ago the Yanamarca Valley, north of Jauja in the central highlands, was almost entirely made up of haciendas. In the past two decades, five communities have emerged out of serfdom, and the only two remaining haciendas in the area are organized and operated in a manner far different from the traditional style.

I shall tell the story in terms of one community, whose history seems broadly representative of the process of liberation throughout the valley. To maintain the anonymity of the principal actors, I shall use pseudonyms for personal names and call the community "Pueblito," but the facts are carefully documented by our associates carrying out the field work.

The liberation of Pueblito began in 1952. The first initiative came from Arturo Sánchez, a young man from the highlands who had gone to Lima for a medical education and had become involved in APRA Party activities. As a student leader, he had to go underground when General Manuel Odría took over the government in 1948 and began his repression of APRA (Popular American Revolutionary Alliance) which he regarded as a leftist organization because it was then actively seeking the support of workers and peasants. Some time later, Sánchez turned up in Pueblito, settled down to work the land, and married a Pueblito girl.

ORGANIZING PEASANTS

Sánchez' first organizational step centered on a project for establishing a school in Pueblito. Although Peruvian legislation requires the hacendado to provide some schooling for the peasants, most landlords in the past have ignored this obligation altogether, or have complied in a token fashion, providing one dilapidated room and an occasional teacher. Like many other landlords, José Marimba sought to discourage the school project, arguing with the peasants that school would be of no value to their children. Under Sánchez' leadership, however, the peasants succeeded in interesting the Ministry of Education in their project, so that there was a beginning of a school even against the landlord's opposition.

As the peasants began to organize themselves around the school project, Marimba got into difficulties on another front. In the first place, he had won control of the land only in a bitter court battle. His father had divided several haciendas and a power plant in Jauja among his children, with Pueblito going to one of José's sisters. At great expense to himself, Marimba carried through litigation that won him Pueblito in exchange for other properties that he gave up. Marimba thus started his operation of Pueblito in somewhat tight financial straits. This was unfortunate for Marimba, since he was a man of expensive tastes. From 1942 to 1952 he had secured large loans from the Agricultural Development Bank, ostensibly to improve Pueblito, but he had spent most of his money on international travel and gracious living in Jauja and Lima.

Until 1952, Marimba spent very little time in Pueblito, leaving everything in the hands of an administrator. When the bank began to press for repayments on its loans, Marimba turned his concentrated attention on Pueblito and sought to squeeze more work out of the people. When some men proved unresponsive to his urgings, he expelled them from the land. The first time he did this, there was no overt response from the other peasants. Therefore, some time later, when he found two of the community leaders not applying themselves as diligently as he wished, he promptly ordered them and their families to leave the property at once. At this point, all the peasants rallied around and vowed that if these two men were to be thrown out, Marimba would have to throw them all out. At the same time, they flatly refused to do any further work for him. Marimba appealed to the authorities in Jauja, but this did not break the unity of the community.

When the peasant challenge came, José Marimba found himself in a deteriorating position. The legal struggle for Pueblito against his brothers and sisters had been expensive and had destroyed family solidarity. While the Marimba family had held unquestioned social and political preeminence in Jauja in the days of his father, José now found himself in acrimonious competition for prestige and influence with a rising businessman-farmer who actually worked in his various enterprises. Furthermore, José's arrogant manner had made him unpopular with both his peers and his social inferiors.

Marimba's response to the peasant challenge was typical of the old order in rural Peru. In Jauja and Huancayo, the departmental (state) capital, he lavishly entertained members of the local and national elite—thus further depleting his resources. As the Bank pressed for repayment of the loan, he sought to cultivate the officials of the Huancayo office, two recent graduates of the Agrarian University. He urged on them the following arguments: "We are friends," "We are gentlemen," "We are fellow white men."

When the officials persisted in their unfriendly, ungentlemanly and unwhite demands, José went to Lima to call on the president of the bank, whom he considered to be a friend of the family. The president went through the motions of telephoning Huancayo and asking information on the case. When the Huancayo officials submitted a written report that documented in detail Marimba's incompetent and irresponsible mangement of Pueblito, the bank president took no further action, and the Huancayo office renewed its pressures on the landlord.

By the time of the strike against Marimba, the community leaders had already been in touch with lawyers in Jauja and with union leaders in Jauja and Huancayo. Through these contacts they learned that the title of José Marimba to Pueblito was in doubt and that another family claimed to own the property. On the advice of their lawyer they made a deal with the other claimant to buy Pueblito from him. At the same time, they made a deal with the Agricultural Development Bank to take over the mortgage on which Marimba had been defaulting.

Marimba has not given up yet. At this writing, he is still fighting in the courts to get Pueblito back, but now that the peasants have the bank, lawyers, union leaders and relatives and friends of the other presumed former owner on their side, it seems hardly likely that Marimba will ever make a comeback. Meanwhile, Pueblito is developing as an independent community. The villagers have started building new homes and vigorously developing their economy.

CHANGE COMES TO THE CONVENCIÓN VALLEY

Until 1881, the Convención Valley was entirely divided into haciendas, there being no towns or other commercial settlements. At that time, an hacendado turned over one-third of his estate to build an independent town. The town became Quillabamba, the present provincial capital and now the most important city in the 60-mile-long valley.

Due to its geographical isolation and adverse health conditions, the valley was sparsely settled until the 1940s. Construction of a railroad into the valley in 1933 and the eradication of malaria in the late 1940s led to a flood of immigration from the mountains. Even so, labor was so scarce that the hacendados had to offer peasants substantially more land for their own family cultivation than was customary in the sierra.

Typically, however, the hacendados retained the bottomlands along the river for their own use, giving the peasants the steep slopes. While the bottomlands were much superior for crops traditionally grown in the area, it turned out, ironically, that the slopes were better for the cultivation of coffee, a fact which was not lost on the peasants on the hillsides who first went into coffee cultivation. By the time the hacendados began converting to coffee, it had already become a mainstay of the peasant economy.

The peasant movement into coffee coincided with a continuous and spectacular rise in its price in the valley. If we give the 1945 price an index number of 100, by 1954 the index had risen to 1,221. In the 15 years up to 1960, coffee shipped out of the valley rose almost sevenfold, from 583,000 to 3,820,000 kilos.

Until the advent of coffee, the hacendados controlled peasant access to markets, themselves handling the sales of such peasant production as reached the market along with their own output. As the coffee boom developed, *rescatistas* or middlemen entered the local scene. They were not interested in land reform, but they were interested in buying coffee. And since the peasants owned the bulk of the coffee, the rescatistas naturally went directly to the peasants. This development led to the creation of key contacts for the peasants in Quillabamba and other market towns, as local merchants built storage facilities and entered into the business of buying and selling coffee. As coffee production grew, the peasants were also creating town merchants whose interests were allied with theirs.

The hacendados recognized that the peasants' rising stake in coffee constituted a threat to their economic and political position in the valley. Some of them now tried to maneuver the peasants out, reclaiming the slopes of the mountainsides so as to extend their own coffee cultivation into more suitable areas. Coffee also became the focus of a clash in time commitments. At harvest time coffee offers less flexibility to farmers than do crops such as corn and potatoes. Coffee ripens all at once and must be picked when it is ready. This meant that just at the time when the hacendado had his greatest need for labor, the peasants had the greatest need to apply their labor to their own land. Furthermore, it meant that the peasants had much more to lose in maintaining the traditional obligations of the hacienda system. This naturally accentuated the conflict between peasants and landowners.

To protect themselves against being pushed off the land and to support their demands for limits of their labor obligations, Convención Valley peasants began to unionize. At the outset, unionization was an entirely indigenous movement, all the leaders being peasants from the valley. The peasants had some support from the merchants in the towns and, beginning in 1951, they extended their ties into Cuzco, getting lawyers to represent them in grievances that they pressed before the Ministry of Labor. The union federation grew slowly until

1960, at which time unions on several haciendas carried out a two-month "sympathy strike" on the grounds that fellow workers on another hacienda were being mistreated. At that, the hacendados began pressing their congressmen in Lima to get the national government to intervene in support of their position. Instead of sending armed forces, however, the government dispatched an investigator to look into the situation. To the surprise and indignation of the hacendados, the investigator recommended that the *condiciones* or traditional labor obligations should be abolished, a solution that would have consolidated peasant control of the lands they were cultivating and deprived the hacendados of most of their labor. To be sure, the report was shelved in the Ministry of Labor, but the fact remains that the government did not intervene on the side of the hacendados. This was a major victory for the peasant union and their movement began advancing rapidly throughout other areas of the valley.

Their gains now began to attract outsiders. Most prominent of these was Hugo Blanco, a native of Cuzco who could speak Quechua and had received his university education in Argentina. His father-in-law, a Cuzco lawyer, had represented the peasants on one hacienda in their protests to the Ministry of Labor office in Cuzco, so Blanco was already thoroughly familiar with the background of the situation. In 1960 he went in to settle on the hacienda his father-in-law had represented.

Blanco proved to be a charismatic figure. He was soon elected to represent his hacienda union in the peasant federation, and he moved on from this victory to become an effective organizer of new unions, particularly in the northern section of the valley.

A self-confessed Trotskyite, Blanco believed that it would be necessary to go beyond unionization to lead the peasants in forcibly taking over the lands—thus providing an initial base for the revolution that might come to Peru. As soon as he had established his power base through organizing new union locals, Blanco ran for the headship of the peasant federation. This precipitated a split in the movement. The older leaders who had started the unions were interested in land, not revolution. They were committed to more traditional trade-union methods and to an extension of the political influence of their movement.

Blanco received a majority of the votes in a hotly disputed election. But the leaders of some 20 peasant unions, including most of the early union leaders, claimed fraud and walked out of the meeting. They quickly consolidated the local units they controlled into a new confederation, thereby dividing the union movement in the valley into two organizations.

At the time of the disputed election, an order for the arrest of Blanco was issued by the police authorities of the valley. The peasant leader then went into hiding for a period of nine months, during which time there were sporadic outbreaks of violence against police and military officials, for which Blanco and his supporters were held responsible. At the end of 1962, Blanco was captured and placed in prison, where he is now serving a 24-year term.

Despite the split between the Blanco faction and the older leaders of the union movement, and despite the brief rise and fall of another rival union allied with APRA, the position of the peasants in relation to the hacendados was steadily strengthened.

Early in 1962, just prior to the disputed election, the union leaders ordered a strike against all the hacendados in the valley—there was to be no work for any hacendado nor any payment of rental in return for the land occupied by the peasants. By early 1963 all of the peasants in the valley and both federations were supporting this policy. It is not necessary here to give details on the governmental decisions that consolidated the peasant victory. Let me simply note that the first presidential decree recognizing the peasant victory was issued under the conservative government of Manuel Prado; some months later the military junta, in power from 1962 to 1963, recognized the de facto control of the lands by the peasants.

While the strength of the peasant mobilization is impressive, we must also recognize the weaknesses of the hacendados of the Convención Valley. There are indications, for example, that they did not enjoy the kind of political and public relations position enjoyed by large landowners in other parts of Peru. In fact, at the height of the conflict, *La Prensa,* the newspaper owned by the then Prime Minister Pedro Beltrán, published on its front page a feature story about a certain Señor Romaineville, the largest hacendado in the Convención Valley. The article was distinctly unflattering. It reported that Romaineville had not set foot on his property in at least 12 years and portrayed him as the archetype of the exploitative absentee landlord. Furthermore, when the showdown came, there were 10,000 peasants on the voting lists, and few of them were any longer controlled by the hacendados.

THE SPREAD OF UNIONIZATION

The establishment of peasant ownership ended one stage of revolution in the Convención Valley but it was only a beginning of another. In the several years following the peasant victory, schools have been built so fast and in so many areas of the valley that neither the Ministry of Education nor the government community development agency, *Cooperación Popular,* has been able to keep up with the demand for teachers or building materials that could not be locally manufactured. The valley also seems to be throbbing with an increased level of economic activities.

During the period when a unionization movement was transforming the Convención Valley, unionization spread also into other parts of rural Cuzco. On many an hacienda, the hacendado found himself in the unprecedented position of having to sit down and negotiate with representatives elected by his peasants and with a leader of the peasant federation from Cuzco, if he wanted to get his crop planted or harvested. In the early months of the Belaúnde administration (begun in late July of 1963), it seemed that unionization of the peasants was not only gaining ground rapidly but was also leading to forcible demands for peasant ownership. These were described by hacendados as "invasions" of their lands and by the peasants as "recovering the rights that have been stolen from us." At this point, under pressure from the congress, which was dominated by a curious coalition of the formerly leftist APRA and the party of their old oppressor General Odría, Belaúnde had to put in a tough Minister of the Interior, who ordered a roundup of leaders of the peasant federation in Cuzco, thus stripping the federation of its top officers.

While this repressive move practically destroyed the peasant federation as a formal organization, it is important to note that conditions on the countryside did not revert to the status quo before unionization. Hacienda Chawaytiri, which was included in our study area, is a case in point. There the organized peasants had been able to negotiate a marked reduction of the days worked per month and a threefold increase in the cash payments, together with other equally sweeping changes in the conditions of work. When the union was no longer in formal existence, the peasants nevertheless reported that the administrator and his representatives supervised them in a much more humane manner than had been customary before unionization. Furthermore, when the hacendado announced he was going to cut the daily payment by two-thirds, the campesinos declined to report for work. The work relationship was reestablished only when the hacendado agreed to reestablish the three soles daily rate (the sol then being worth about 3.7 cents).

Moreover, a field worker who studied the hacienda in 1965 reported that relations between the peasants and the hacendado or his representatives remained in the post-strike pattern. The administrator had not resumed the use of physical force as a form of discipline. He did not even shout at the peasants any more. In fact, some of the campesinos commented, "You know, he is really a nice fellow, when you get to know him." Previously, the *mandón* (a campesino who served as straw boss under the administrator) had done nothing but transmit and enforce the orders of the hacendado or the administrator. In 1965 he was taking quite a different stance. Our field worker observed him one day with the other campesinos sitting around and waiting for the rain to stop. The administrator came along and asked why the men were not working. The mandón replied, "Times have changed. It is not right to make the men work in the fields in the rain." The administrator did not press the point.

These cases of peasant mobilization should not be confused with the guerrilla movements that broke out in areas of rural Peru in 1965–66. The guerrilla leaders were middle-class intellectuals who had little or no contact with the peasants before they launched their violent attack upon the authority of the government. They hoped that once they had raised the flag of revolution the peasants would flock to their side, fight with them, shelter them and feed them.

GUERRILLA VIOLENCE

Take, for example, the career of Luis de la Puente Uceda. He was a young lawyer who had once been a fanatical member of APRA. As APRA seemed to be turning to the right, he turned to the left, abandoned the party, and became a disciple of Fidel Castro. In 1965, he entered the Convención Valley with an armed force variously estimated at between 100 and 300 men—both estimates probably being high.

The strategy of taking a force into the mountains to start the revolution was explicitly based upon the Castro model, yet the Peruvian revolutionists failed to take into account several important differences between their situation and that facing Castro at the time he launched his movement. When Castro took to the hills, Cuba was under a repressive dictatorship, and it seemed to most people that a violent revolution offered the only hope of change. Peru in 1965 was under a democratically elected government, with a president who had been talking about land reform and rural development. While de la Puente and his supporters could argue that this kind of talk was just a sham and that no basic changes would take place without a revolution, it was by no means clear to all Peruvians, even to Peruvians on the left, that a violent attack on the government offered the only hope for bringing about basic changes.

While Castro did his fighting first in the hills, he maintained close contacts with secret supporters in the towns and cities, so that his movement had strong urban links. The Convención Valley was exceedingly isolated from urban Peru, being connected only to Cuzco, and that by a railroad that could be closely controlled by the authorities.

Why did de la Puente choose the Convención Valley for his uprising? While I am not aware of any public statements of his on this question, I suspect there were two fundamental reasons: the much publicized militancy of the peasants, and the nature of the terrain which made the valley a good place to hide. If these were indeed the factors convincing to de la Puente, he was fundamentally in error on both points.

The peasants had in truth demonstrated their militancy, but they had won what they were after: control of the land. De la Puente was offering them enormous risks in exchange for possible gains that seemed vague and uncertain. His men found few potential revolutionaries in the valley.

The rugged terrain of the Convención Valley did in fact provide a good place to hide, but once there it was exceedingly difficult to get out. In effect, there were only two ways in or out, both along the river. The rugged mountains offered no ground-cover for fugitives. As soon as the government learned of the guerrilla activities, the army proceeded to bottle up both ends of the valley and then sent in patrols to root out the guerrillas.

The guerrillas had expected to live off food provided by sympathetic peasants, but voluntary contributions turned out to be sparse indeed. To keep alive, then, the guerrillas had to resort to forcible seizures of food—as did Che Guevara later in Bolivia—further alienating the peasants.

The final scene of the drama occurred after de la Puente had retreated to the Mesa Pelada, a desolate plain above the valley. A peasant woman informed a military patrol of the location of the guerrilla group. De la Puente and the last six men remaining with him were shot dead in the resulting encounter.

If change in rural Peru is as widespread as I claim it to be, how do we account for the fact that so many Latin American intellectuals, whether radicals or reformers, persist in seeing the countryside as an area of social and economic stagnation? They do this by applying the exception principle. Whenever a case of change comes to their attention—and the Convención Valley movement has received wide public attention in Peru—they explain it away as an exceptional situation that has risen out of peculiar conditions. But they do not then go on to ask whether there may not be other instances of change, not so well publicized. For example, the transformation of the Yanamarca Valley was completely unknown in intellectual circles in Lima until our field workers happened upon this less dramatic peasant movement. The unionization movement throughout rural Cuzco was indeed publicly noticed at the time, but it seems to have been forgotten soon after the government roundup of union leaders. It was as if intellectuals assumed that the Cuzco haciendas had returned to the status quo ante, which was definitely not the case.

Underlying the application of the exception principle is the intellectual's inclination to view reality through moralistic and ideological filters. The moralistic filter is supplied by the concept of "exploitation." The Peruvian constitution, the United Nations Declaration of the Rights of Man, and any number of other such statements of principle, decree that no man shall be forced to work for another or to work without adequate compensation. When in hacienda Chawaytiri the *condición* of work-day obligations is cut by more than a third and when the daily payment is raised by 200 percent, intellectual reformers or revolutionaries see no change at all because the Indians are still being exploited.

The ideological filter is the intellectual's mental model of the way major structural changes take place. If revolutionary, he has an image of a dramatic nationwide confrontation of reactionary, and radical forces, culminating in a radical capture of power in the capital city. The community and area level changes I have described clearly have no place in this model, and so they are not allowed to disturb the myth of the passive peasant.

When faced with the realities of events in the Yanamarca Valley, one Peruvian social scientist made this comment:

> You can't say that those communities have become independent. They continue to be under the domination of the national oligarchy, and that oligarchy continues to be under the domination of Yankee imperialism.

By that logic, no change will take place until the millennium.

While the approach presented here differs from that of the ideological revolutionaries, it is important to recognize that it differs in an equally fundamental way from the usual line of community-development theorizing. While the radical ideologists are fixated on the concept of power, the community developers avoid the power issue altogether. For them the secret of change and progress on the countryside is "participation." If the peasants can be involved in solving the problems of their community together, progress will result. Furthermore, community development theorists tend to treat the community as if it existed in a vacuum, thus neglecting the crucially important relations it has with the outside world.

Power is a central issue in our approach, but I am undertaking to dispel the mysticism that tends to becloud the power issue in ideological argument. By getting down to cases, I seek to show how power is exercised and how shifts in power actually take place.

What explains the changes I have described in the Yanamarca and Convención Valleys and in rural Cuzco? In order to provide a systematic explanation, we need to think in terms of the transformation of the structure of power; compare Figures 1 and 2.

The hacendado is at the apex of the triangle. Peasants are clustered at the bottom of each side of the triangle. In Figure 1, the absence of a line connecting the peasants depicts their unorganized state prior to mobilization. The hacendado deals with peasants and their families strictly on an individual basis, holding out special favors for those "loyal" to him and threatening dire penalties for those who are not submissive. The hacendado himself has strong

FIGURE 1. Hacienda Before Peasant Mobilization

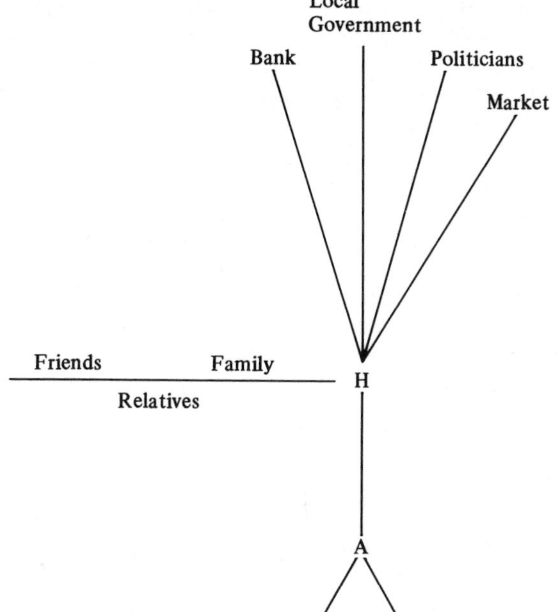

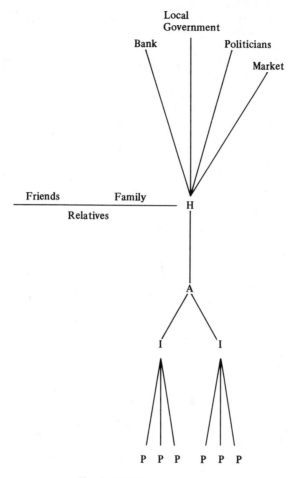

H = hacendado
A = administrator
I = intermediary (supervisor)
P = peasant

horizontal ties—family, social and political connections with people at roughly the same status in the society. The hacendado also has links upward in the society with important politicians and judges, with bank officials and other figures of economic significance. The peasants do not have these ties. To gain favors from any of these superior power figures, they must go through the hacendado himself, which means that he is in a position of monopoly, both political and economic.

How do the peasants break this monopoly? They do it basically in two ways:

FIGURE 2. Peasant Mobilization on the Hacienda

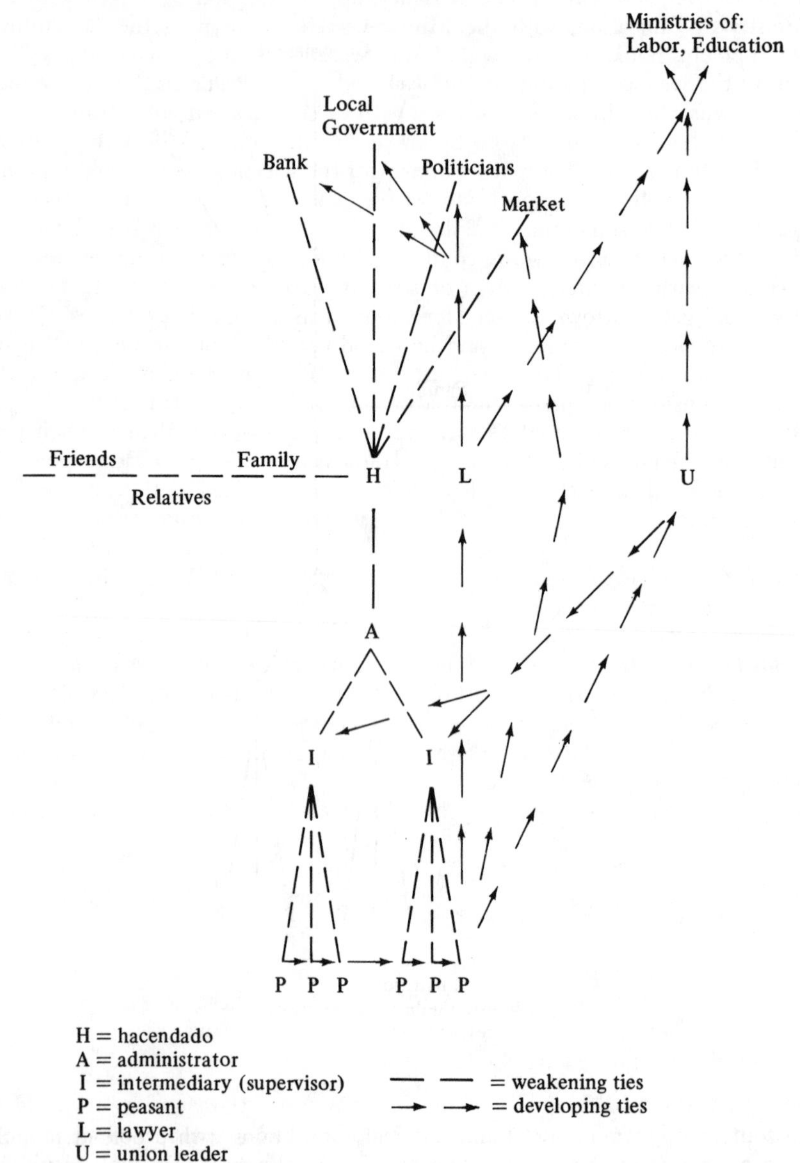

by closing the base of the triangle and by establishing upward ties in the society, independent of the hacendado (see Figure 2).

We have seen that the peasants may close the base of the triangle through coordinated efforts to found a school on the hacienda, through organizing against repressive landlords or through an extensive unionization movement as in the Convención Valley. The peasants' upward ties can be forged with the Ministry of Education, with the Ministry of Labor or with the Agricultural Development Bank. In the case of the peasants of the Convención Valley, upward ties were not established until the advent of coffee created middlemen in the towns whose interests were allied with those of the peasant growers.

Part of the drama was played by lawyers in the courts. When the peasants laid claim to the land or stopped working for the hacendado, he would typically appeal to the political authorities to get the police or troops sent in. Sometimes this worked, but sometimes it did not. If he was unsuccessful in the direct appeal for force, he would go to court to get a legal order requiring the peasants to comply with his interpretation of their obligations. In that event, the peasants would get their own lawyer (for various reasons, there is a buyers' market for legal services in rural Peru) and he would sue the owner on their behalf for 30 years of back pay. The legal justification for this claim is clear, for the Peruvian constitution outlaws the traditional hacendado-peasant relationship, in which the peasant is forced to work without wages (other than a token payment) in order to cultivate a plot of land. Where the hacendado's power is unchallenged, this constitutional provision remains a dead letter, as does the law requiring him to provide a school, but when the peasants can organize themselves to make the challenge, they create a very awkward situation for the hacendado, his lawyer and the courts, since they are claiming rights that are unequivocally guaranteed them.

There are also forces at work that tend to make the old ways increasingly unsatisfactory to the hacendado. The traditional style of farm management does not yield increasing economic returns over the years. The hacendado does not care to spend much time on his hacienda where the cost of living is relatively low. He is a city-oriented man, and with each passing generation this orientation becomes more pronounced. The hacendado and his family are committed to the "good things" of modern urban living, from education to entertainment and travel, and the price of those "good things" is constantly increasing.

When the hacienda no longer yields the income necessary to maintain the status and style of life to which he has become accustomed, what can the hacendado do? He has just three alternatives:

1. He can try to squeeze more work out of the campesinos.
2. He can sell the hacienda and invest the money in something else.
3. He can invest money in the hacienda to reorganize it in terms of "modern" scientific agriculture and "modern" farm management methods.

As José Marimba's experience suggests, the first strategy is more likely to yield increased peasant resistance than increased farm output. If he decides upon the second strategy, to whom can he sell? For reasons that should be abundantly clear by now, the demand for land on the part of current and potential hacendados does not begin to meet the supply of purchasable haciendas. Poor as they are, the peasants are emotionally attached to the land and are likely to be willing to pay the hacendado more for it than any other potential purchaser. If the hacendado sells out to them, the transformation of hacienda into community is thereby accomplished.

We are just beginning to find hacendados who have successfully pursued the third strategy. It is too early to make any definitive statements, but so far we are inclined to assume that very few current sierra hacendados have the will, ability, knowledge and psychological orientation required to transform their properties into "modern" farm enterprises. And those few who successfully carry out the third strategy thereby build a social system that is drastically different from the traditional hacienda.

THE NEED FOR REVOLUTION

What does this approach tell us about the probability of a violent social revolution in Peru? On the one hand, it knocks one of the props out from under the argument for the inevitability of violence: a violent revolution is inevitable, it is said, because those holding power will not yield it voluntarily. José Marimba, the hacendado of Pueblito, did not yield power voluntarily, but he lost it nevertheless. And so it was with the other hacendados in the Yanamarca and Convención Valleys.

On the other hand, nothing written here provides grounds for optimism to those who would like to prevent a violent revolution in Peru. I have demonstrated that sweeping changes in social structure have come about in certain rural areas, but generalizations from these cases must be made with the following reservations in mind:

First, I have carried the cases only to the point of the power shift and slightly beyond it. It must not be assumed that after overthrowing the hacendados the campesinos live happily ever after. They continue to face very serious economic and political problems, which I shall not discuss here, as we are just beginning to study postindependence developments.

Second, in the countryside, avoidance of a revolutionary situation probably depends upon the geographical extent and the rapidity of movements such as those examined here. Neither the data we have nor the behavioral science theories available permit us to make any predictions as to the probability that widespread changes will come fast enough to relieve the severe tensions now prevalent throughout rural Peru.

Third, until Fidel Castro, it was generally assumed that revolutions started in cities. The smashing defeats of those who tried to apply his rural model in Peru and Bolivia suggest that students of revolution would be well advised not to neglect the urban front. And I have ventured no statements about the state of Peruvian cities.

Finally, the present military government of Peru is committed to preventing a violent revolution through carrying out its own model of revolution, imposed from the top down. If and when the Agrarian Reform Law promulgated in June of 1969 is fully implemented, it will mean a transformation of the countryside far more extensive and drastic than any change we have yet observed in Peru. Indeed, the government's efforts to carry out a peaceful revolution without popular participation are being closely watched by politicians, miltary men and social scientists throughout Latin America. We hope to study this next stage of the development of Peru, but that story must await some future report.

NOTES

This article grows out of a joint collaborative research program between the Instituto de Estudios Peruanos in Lima and Cornell University, José Matos Mar being coprincipal investigator for IEP and William F. Whyte and Lawrence K. Williams being coprincipal investigators for Cornell. The program was launched in 1964 with surveys of 26 rural communities in five areas of Peru. Fourteen of these were resurveyed in 1969. In the course of these five years, more intensive anthropological studies were carried out in a number of these communities, and additional field projects were carried out in other areas as new opportunities arose.

In this joint program, Julio Cotler serves as coordinator of research for the IEP. J. Oscar Alers served as coordinator for Cornell in Lima from 1965 to 1967. Giorgio Alberti is now serving in that capacity.

Discussion of the Yanamarca Valley is based upon the work of Giorgio Alberti, Lamond Tullis, Rodrigo Sánchez and Luis Deustua. The Convención Valley story is based upon the Cornell Ph.D. thesis of Wesley C. Craig. The interpretation of developments in rural Cuzco is based upon studies carried out under the general direction of Oscar Nuñez del Prado.

Financial support for the program has come primarily from the National Science Foundation and the National Institute of Mental Health.

A Selected Bibliography

The following bibliography is intended as a guide for beginning students.

In a sense, the list of "Recommended Readings" that accompanies each of the Introductions comprises a brief topical bibliography. Furthermore the footnotes and bibliographies of the individual papers are included in full. Used together, they should help any interested person to find a variety of source material on most aspects of contemporary cultures and societies of Latin America.

The list that follows, by contrast, is ordered in terms of major types of sources and in terms of regions. Listings include:

Research Aids and Bibliographies
Journals
Monograph Series
General Sources
Middle America (including Mexico and Central America, with individual countries in alphabetic order)
South America (with individual countries in alphabetic order).

Although authors from several disciplines are represented, there is a strong emphasis on anthropological perspectives. Space limitations disallow the inclusion of references to numerous excellent articles in periodicals, but the research aids and bibliographies will help the student gain familiarity with that sizable and significant part of the literature.

In preparing a list for such use, I have tried to make a number of decisions that differ from those that govern preparation of a bibliography in a scholarly monograph. Brief mention of some of those decisions may help readers by indicating the strengths and shortcomings of this as a means of getting into the vast, varied, and widely dispersed literature on contemporary societies and cultures of Latin America.

In the expectation that most of the people who will use this bibliography will be native speakers of English, I have listed translations, when available. A few books in other languages are cited, nevertheless—some because they are of special importance and a few because they are virtually the only pertinent sources available. On the assumption that books are usually strengthened and updated by revision, I have usually cited the most recent edition rather than the original. In general, too, I have not included unpublished material or publications of institutions, governmental or other, that are not readily available for purchase or interlibrary loan within the United States.

RESEARCH AIDS AND BIBLIOGRAPHIES

Agrupación Bibliográfica Cubana "José Toribio Medina," Habana
1957– *Bibliografía de Centroamérica y del Caribe* (annual).
Bayitch, S. A.
1967 *Latin America and the Caribbean: A Bibliographic Guide to Works in*

English. University of Miami School of Law, Interamerican Legal Studies 10, Coral Gables, Fla.

Bernal, Ignacio (ed.)
1962 *Bibliografía de arqueología y etnografía—Mesoamérica y Norte de América: 1540–1960*. Instituto Nacional de Antropología e Historia Memoria 7, México.

Bushong, Allen S.
1967 *Doctoral Dissertations on Pan American Topics Accepted by U.S. and Canadian Colleges and Universities, 1961–1965: Bibliography and Analysis*. Supplement to *Latin American Research Review* 2, 2.

Carroll, Thomas F.
1965 *Land Tenure and Land Reform in Latin America: A Selected Annotated Bibliography* (2nd rev. ed.). Inter-American Development Bank, Washington.

Center of Latin American Studies, University of California, Los Angeles.
1955– *Statistical Abstract of Latin America* (annual).

Centro de Estudios y Documentación Latinoamericanos, Amsterdam
1965– *Boletín informativo sobre estudios latinoamericanos en Europa*.

Charno, Steven N.
1968 *Latin American Newspapers in U.S. Libraries: A Union List*. University of Texas Press, Austin.

Comité Organizador, XXXVI Congreso Internacional de Americanistas
1964 *Bibliografía americanista española: 1935–1963*. G.E.H.A., Sevilla.

Farrell, Robert V., and John F. Hohenstein (comps.)
1969 *Latin America: Books*. Center for Inter-American Relations, New York.

Geohegan, Abel Rodolfo
1965 *Obras de referencia de América Latina: Repertorio selectivo y anotado de enciclopedias, diccionarios biográficos, repertorios bibliográficos, catálogos, guías, anuarios, índices*. UNESCO, Buenos Aires.

German Parra, Manuel, and Wigberto Jiménez Moreno
1954 *Bibliografía indigenista de México y Centroamérica (1850–1950)*. Instituto Nacional Indigenista Memorias 4, México.

Gibson, G. D.
1960 A bibliography of anthropological bibliographies: The Americas. *Current Anthropology* 1:61–75.

Gropp, Arthur E.
1968–1971 *Bibliography of Latin American Bibliographies* (2 vols.). Scarecrow, Metuchin, N.J.

Handbook of Latin American Studies
1935– University of Florida Press, Gainesville (annual).

Harvard University Library
1966 *Latin America and Latin American Periodicals* (2 vols.). Harvard University Library, Cambridge, Mass.

Hispanic and Luso-Brazilian Councils
1966 *An Introduction to Modern Books in English Concerning the Countries of Latin America* (2nd ed.). Library Association, London.

Instituto Panamericano de Geografía e Antropología
1937– *Boletín Bibliográfico de Antropología Americana*. México (biennial).

International Congress of Americanists
Proceedings (issued every two years at location of Congress).

International Institute for Labor Studies
1965 *Bibliografía sobre los movimientos obreros en la América Latina: 1950–1964*. I.I.L.S., Geneva.

Jaquith, James R.
1970 Bibliography of anthropological bibliographies of the Americas. *América Indígena* 30:419–469.

Kidder, Frederick Elwyn, and Allen D. Bushong (comps.)
1963 *Theses on Pan American Topics* (4th ed.). Pan American Union, Washington.

Kingsbury, Robert C., and Ronald Schneider
1965 *An Atlas of Latin American Affairs*. Frederick A. Praeger, New York.

Klein, Maria Teresa
1968 *Bibliografía sobre sociología y demografía de América Latina*. Instituto de Estudios Iberoamericanos, Bibliografía y Documentación 12, Hamburgo.

LaPointe, Jacques
1968 *Bibliographie de L'Espagnol d'Amérique*. Université de Dakar, Centre des Hautes Etudes Afro-Ibero-Américaines Publication 5, Dakar.

Mesa, Rosa Q. (comp.)
1968– *Latin American Serial Documents: A Holding List*. University Microfilms, Ann Arbor, Mich. (A volume on each of 20 countries has been projected).

Miller, Kent E., and Gilberto V. Fort
1970 *The Major Latin American Collections in Libraries of the United States* (rev. ed.). Cuadernos Bibliotecarios, Pan American Union, Washington.

Monteforte Toledó, Mario
1969 *Bibliografía sociopolítica latinoamericana*. Universidad Nacional Autónoma de México, México.

Monteiro, Palmyre
1967 *A Catalogue of Latin American Flat Maps: 1926–1964* (3 vols.). University of Texas Press, Austin.

Okinishevich, Leo, and Robert G. Carlton
1966 *Latin America in Soviet Writings: A Bibliography, 1917–1964* (2 vols.). Johns Hopkins Press, Baltimore.

O'Leary, Timothy J. (ed.)
1963 *Ethnographic Bibliography of South America*. Human Relations Area Files, New Haven, Conn.

Pan American Union
1951– *Inter-American Review of Bibliography*. Washington (quarterly).

Pan American Union, Columbus Memorial Library
1962– *Index to Latin American Periodical Literature* (10 vols.: 1929–1965). G. K. Hall, Boston.

Pan American Union, Department of Social Affairs
1970 *Datos básicos de población en América Latina*. Washington (annual).

Peraza Sarausa, Fermin
1966 *Bibliografías corrientes de la América Latina*. [No publisher], Gainesville, Fla.

Rabinovitz, Francine F., Felicity M. Trueblood, and Charles J. Savio
1967 (Jan.) *Latin American Political Systems in an Urban Setting: A Preliminary Bibliography*. University of Florida, Center for Latin American Studies Notes, Gainesville.

Sable, Martin H.
1965 *Master Directory for Latin America.* University of California, Latin American Center, Los Angeles.
1967 *A Guide to Latin American Studies* (2 vols.). University of California, Latin American Center, Los Angeles.
1967 *Latin American Urbanization: A Guide to the Literature and Organizations in the Field.* University of California, Latin American Center, Los Angeles.
1968 *Communism in Latin America: An International Bibliography:* 1900–45, 1960–67. University of California, Latin American Center, Los Angeles.
1970 *Latin American Agriculture: A Bibliography of Pioneer Settlement, Agricultural History and Economics, Rural Sociology and Population.* University of Wisconsin, Center for Latin American Studies, Milwaukee.

Trask, David F., Michael C. Meyer, and Roger R. Trask
1968 *A Bibliography of U.S.–Latin American Relations since 1810: A Selected List of Eleven Thousand Published References.* University of Nebraska Press, Lincoln.

U.S. Department of the Army, Headquarters
1969 *Latin America and the Caribbean: Analytical Survey of Literature.* U.S. Government Printing Office, Washington.

U.S. Library of Congress, Hispanic Foundation
1972 *Latin America, Spain, and Portugal: An Annotated Bibliography of Paperback Books.* Library of Congress, Washington.

University of Texas, Population Research Center
1965 *International Population Census Bibliography: Latin America and the Caribbean.* U.T.P.R.C., Austin.

Veliz, Claudio (ed.)
1968 *Latin America and the Caribbean: A Handbook.* Frederick A. Praeger, New York.

Weaver, Jerry L.
1968 *The Political Dimensions of Rural Development in Latin America: A Selected Bibliography,* 1950–1967. California State College at Long Beach.

Wish, John R.
1965 *Economic Development in Latin America: An Annotated Bibliography.* Frederick A. Praeger, New York.

Zimmerman, Irene
1961 *A Guide to Current Latin American Periodicals: Humanities and Social Sciences.* Kallman, Gainesville, Fla.
1971 *Current National Bibliographies of Latin America: A State of the Art Study.* University of Florida, Center for Latin American Studies [Gainesville].

JOURNALS

América Indígena. Instituto Indigenista Interamericano, México, since 1940.

The Americas: Quarterly Review of Inter-American Cultural History. Academy of American Franciscan History, Washington, since 1944.

Aportes. Instituto Latinoamericano de Relaciones Internacionales, Paris, since 1966.

Boletín Bibliográfico de Antropología Americana. Instituto Panamericano de Geografía e Historia, México, since 1937.

Ciencias Sociales (see *Revista Interamericana de Ciencias Sociales*).

Desarrollo Rural en las Américas. Instituto Interamericano de Ciencias Agrícolas, Bogotá, since 1969.

Economía Latinoamericana: Inter-American Review of Economics. Pan American Union, Washington, since 1963.

Estudios Andinos. Instituto Boliviano de Estudios y Acción Social, La Paz, since 1970.

Guatemala Indígena. Instituto Indigenista Nacional, Guatemala, since 1961.

Hispanic American Historical Review. Conference on Latin American History, American Historical Association, Durham, N.C., since 1918.

Hispanic American Report. Stanford, Cal., since 1948.

Index to Latin American Periodicals. Columbus Memorial Library, Washington, since 1929.

Inter-American Economic Affairs. Institute of Inter-American Studies, Washington, since 1947.

Journal de la Société des Américanistes de Paris. Société des Américanistes de Paris, since 1914.

Journal of Interamerican Studies. University of Miami, et al., Coral Gables, Fla., 1959–1969 (subsequently: *Journal of Interamerican Studies and World Affairs*).

Journal of Interamerican Studies and World Affairs. University of Miami, Coral Gables, Fla., since 1970 (formerly: *Journal of Interamerican Studies*).

Latin America. London, since 1967.

Latin American Research Review. Latin American Studies Association, Austin, Tex., since 1956.

Luso-Brazilian Review. University of Wisconsin, Madison, since 1964.

Mesoamerican Studies. Southern Illinois University, Carbondale, since 1969.

Quaderni ibero-americani. Associazione per i rapporti culturali la Spagna, il Portogallo e l'America Latina, Torino, since 1946.

Revista Española de Antropología Americana. Departamento de Antropología y Etnología de América, Universidad de Madrid, since 1966.

Revista Interamericana de Ciencias Sociales. Direccíon de Asuntos Sociales, Pan American Union, Washington, since 1961 (formerly: *Ciencias Sociales,* 1950–1956).

Revista Latinoamericana de Sociología. Instituto Torcuato Di Tella, Centro de Sociología Comparativa, Buenos Aires, since 1965.

Revista Mexicana de Estudios Antropológicos. Sociedad Mexicana de Estudios Antropológicos, México, since 1927.

Revista Mexicana de Sociología. Instituto de Investigaciones Sociales de la Universidad Nacional Autónoma, México, since 1939.

Sable, Martin H.
1965 *Periodicals for Latin American Economic Development, Trade and Finance: An Annotated Bibliography.* University of California, Latin American Center, Los Angeles.

Zimmerman, Irene
1961 *A Guide to Current Latin American Periodicals: Humanities and Social Sciences.* Kallman Publishing Co., Gainesville, Fla.

MONOGRAPH SERIES

GENERAL

Area Handbook. U.S. Department of the Army and American University, Washington. (Previously: *Special Warfare Area Handbooks* and *U.S. Army Area Handbooks.* A volume on each of ten countries has been published to 1972.)

Ediciones Especiales and *Serie Antropología Social*, Instituto Indigenista Interamericano, México.
Ibero-Americana, University of California, Berkeley and Los Angeles.
Latin American Monographs, University of Florida, Gainesville.
Monographs of the Department of Social Affairs of the Pan American Union, Washington.
Monographs of the Institute of Latin American Studies, University of Texas, Austin.
Publications of the Centro Latinoamericano de Investigaciones en Ciencias Sociales, Rio de Janeiro.
Publications of the Institute of Social Anthropology, Smithsonian Institution, Washington (16 vols., 1944–1953).
Studies in Comparative International Development, Sage Publications, Beverly Hills, Cal.

MIDDLE AMERICA

Acta Antropológica, México.
Estudios de Cultura Maya, México.
Estudios de Cultura Nahuatl, México.
Memorias del Instituto Nacional Indigenista, México.
Notes on Middle American Archaeology and Ethnology, Carnegie Institution of Washington.
Publicaciones and *Informes* of the Instituto Geográfico de Costa Rica, San José.
Publicaciones del Seminario de Integración Social Guatemalteca, Guatemala.
Publications of the Middle American Research Institute, Tulane University, New Orleans.

SOUTH AMERICA

Brasiliana, Companhia Editora Nacional, São Paulo.
Monografías Andinas, Lima.
Monografías issued by Plan Regional para el Desarrollo del Sur del Perú, Lima.
Monografías Sociológicas, Bogotá.
Publicaciones of the Instituto de Sociología, University of Chile, Santiago.
Serie Monográfica del Plan Nacional de Integración de la Población Aborígena, Lima.
Serie Monografías Etnológicas, Universidad Nacional Mayor de San Marcos, Lima.
Textos Brasileiros de Instituto Superior de Estudos Brasileiros, Rio de Janeiro.
Travaux de l'Institut français d'études andines, Paris.

GENERAL SOURCES

Adams, Richard N.
1967 *The Second Sowing: Power and Secondary Development in Latin America*. Chandler, Chicago.

Alba, Victor
1965 *Alliance Without Allies: The Mythology of Progress in Latin America*. Frederick A. Praeger, New York.
1968 *Nationalists Without Nations: The Oligarchy Versus the People of Latin America*. Frederick A. Praeger, New York.

Alexander, Robert J.
1965 *Organized Labor in Latin America*. Free Press, New York.
1968 *Today's Latin America* (2nd ed., rev.). Doubleday, Garden City, N.Y.
1970 *Political Parties in Latin America*. Frederick A. Praeger, New York.

American Anthropologist
1955 Vol. 57, No. 3, June 1955 (special issue devoted to Latin America, edited by Sidney W. Mintz).

American Assembly
1959 *The United States and Latin America.* Columbia University Press, New York.

Anderson, Charles W.
1967 *Politics and Economic Change in Latin America.* Van Nostrand, Princeton, N.J.

Arevalo, Juan Jose
1961 *The Shark and the Sardines.* Lyle Stuart, New York.

Bailey, Somnel (ed.)
1971 *Nationalism in Latin America.* Alfred A. Knopf, New York.

Benjamin, Harold R. W.
1965 *Higher Education in the American Republics.* McGraw-Hill, New York.

Bernstein, Harry (ed.)
1965 *Modern and Contemporary Latin America.* Russell and Russell, New York.

Blasier, Cole (ed.)
1968 *Constructive Change in Latin America.* University of Pittsburgh Press, Pittsburgh.

Burnett, Ben G., Kenneth F. Johnson (eds.)
1968 *Political Forces in Latin America: Dimensions of the Quest for Stability.* Wadsworth, Belmont, Cal.

Burr, Robert N.
1967 *Our Troubled Hemisphere: Perspectives on U.S.–Latin American Relations.* Brookings Institution, Washington.

Chilcote, Ronald H. (comp.)
1970 *Revolution and Structural Change in Latin America* (2 vols.). Hoover Institution, Stanford, Cal.

Council on Foreign Relations
1960 *Social Change in Latin America Today.* Harper & Row, New York.

D'Antonio, William V., and Frederick B. Pike (eds.)
1964 *Religion, Revolution and Reform: New Forces for Change in Latin America.* Frederick A. Praeger, New York.

Davis, Harold E.
1972 *Latin American Thought: A Historical Introduction.* Louisiana State University Press, Baton Rouge.

Davis, Kingsley
1972 *Population Studies in Latin America.* Columbia University Press, New York.

Diegues Junior, Manuel, and Bryce Wood (eds).
1967 *Social Science in Latin America.* Columbia University Press, New York.

Duncan, W. Raymond, and James N. Goodsell (eds.).
1971 *The Quest for Change in Latin America: Sources for a 20th Century Analysis.* Oxford University Press, New York.

Edelmann, Alexander T.
1965 *Latin American Government and Politics: The Dynamics of a Revolutionary Society.* Dorsey Press, Homewood, Ill.

Esquenazi-Mayo, Roberto, and Michael C. Meyer (eds.)
1971 *Latin American Scholarship Since World War II: Trends in History,*

Political Science, Literature, Geography, and Economics. University of Nebraska Press, Lincoln.

Fagan, Richard R., and Wayne A. Cornelius, Jr. (eds.)
1970 *Political Power in Latin America: Seven Confrontations.* Prentice-Hall, Englewood Cliffs, N.J.

Field, Arthur J. (ed.)
1970 *City and Country in the Third World: Issues in the Modernization of Latin America.* Schenkman, Cambridge, Mass.

Foster, George M.
1960 *Culture and Conquest: America's Spanish Heritage.* Viking Fund Publication in Anthropology 27, New York.

Foster, George M. (ed.)
1966 *Contemporary Latin American Culture: An Anthropological Sourcebook.* Selected Academic Readings, New York.

Furtado, Celso
1970 *Economic Development in Latin America: A Survey from Colonial Times to the Cuban Revolution.* Cambridge University Press, Cambridge, England.

Germani, Gino
[1969] *Sociología de la modernización: Estudios teóricos, metodológicos y aplicados a América Latina.* Paidos, Buenos Aires.

Gillin, John P.
1969 *Human Ways: Selected Essays in Anthropology.* University of Pittsburgh Press, Pittsburgh.

Glade, William P., Jr.
1969 *The Latin American Economies: A Study of Their Institutional Evolution.* Van Nostrand, Princeton, N.J.

Goldschmidt, Walter R., and Harry Hoijer (eds.)
1969 *The Social Anthropology of Latin America: Essays in Honor of Ralph Leon Beals.* University of California, Latin American Center, Los Angeles.

Gomez Rosendo, Adolfo
1964 *Government and Politics in Latin America* (rev. ed.). Random House, New York.

Gordon, Wendell C.
1967 *The Political Economy of Latin America* (rev. ed.). Columbia University Press, New York.

Green, David
1971 *The Containment of Latin America: A History of the Myths and Realities of the Good Neighbor Policy.* Quadrangle Books, Chicago.

Griffin, Keith B.
1969 *Underdevelopment in Spanish America.* Massachusetts Institute of Technology Press, Cambridge, Mass.

Hamill, Hugh M., Jr. (ed.)
1965 *Dictatorship in Spanish America.* Alfred A. Knopf, New York.

Hanke, Lewis (ed.)
1967 *History of Latin American Civilizations: Sources and Interpretations* (2 vols.). Little, Brown, Boston.

Hauser, Philip M. (ed.)
1962 *Urbanization in Latin America.* UNESCO, New York.

Heath, Dwight B., and Richard N. Adams (eds.)
1965 *Contemporary Cultures and Societies of Latin America* (1st ed.). Random House, New York.

Herring, Hubert
1968 *A History of Latin America: From the Beginnings to the Present* (3rd ed.). Alfred A. Knopf, New York.

Hirschman, Albert O.
1963 *Journeys Toward Progress: Studies of Economic Policy Making in Latin America*. Twentieth Century Fund, New York.

Hirschman, A. O. (ed.)
1961 *Latin American Issues: Essays and Comments*. Twentieth Century Fund, New York.

Horowitz, Irving L. (ed.)
1970 *Masses in Latin America*. Oxford University Press, New York.

Horowitz, Irving L., Josué de Castro, and John Gerassi (eds.)
1969 *Latin American Radicalism: A Documentary Report on Left and Nationalist Movements*. Random House, New York.

Humphreys, Robert A.
1969 *Tradition and Revolt in Latin America*. Columbia University Press, New York.

Inter-American Economic and Social Council at the Ministerial Level
1961 *Alliance for Progress: Official Documents*. Pan American Union, Washington.

Johnson, Cecil
1970 *Communist China and Latin America: 1959–1967*. Columbia University Press, New York.

Johnson, John J.
1964 *The Military and Society in Latin America*. Stanford University Press, Stanford, Cal.

Johnson, John J. (ed.)
1964 *Continuity and Change in Latin America*. Stanford University Press, Stanford, Cal.

Jorrin, Miguel, and John D. Martz
1970 *Latin American Political Thought and Ideology*. University of North Carolina Press, Chapel Hill.

Kantor, Harry
1969 *Patterns of Politics and Political Systems in Latin America: Bureaucracy and Participation*. Rand McNally, Indianapolis.

Keen, Benjamin (ed.)
1967 *Readings in Latin American Civilization: 1492 to the Present* (rev. ed.). Houghton Mifflin, Boston.

Krauss, Walter, and F. John Mathis
1970 *Latin America and Economic Integration*. University of Iowa Press, Iowa City.

Lambert, Jacques
1967 *Latin America: Social Structures and Political Institutions*. University of California Press, Berkeley.

Landsberger, Henry A. (ed.)
1969 *Latin American Peasant Movements*. Cornell University Press, Ithaca, N.Y.
1970 *The Church and Social Change in Latin America*. University of Notre Dame Press, Notre Dame, Ind.

Leonard, Olen E., and Charles P. Loomis (eds.)
1953 *Readings in Latin American Social Organization and Institutions*. Michigan State College Press, East Lansing.

Lieuwen, Edwin
1963 *Arms and Politics in Latin America* (rev. ed.). Frederick A. Praeger, New York.
1964 *Generals vs. Presidents: Neomilitarism in Latin America*. Frederick A. Praeger, New York.
1965 *United States Policy in Latin America*. Frederick A. Praeger, New York.

Lipset, Seymour, and Aldo Solari (eds.)
1967 *Elites in Latin America*. Oxford University Press, New York.

Maier, Joseph, and Richard W. Weatherhead (eds.)
1964 *The Politics of Change in Latin America*. Frederick A. Praeger, New York.

Mangin, William
1967 *Las comunidades alteñas en América Latina*. Instituto Indigenista Interamericano Serie Antropología Social 5, México.

Martz, John D.
1965 *The Dynamics of Change in Latin American Politics*. Prentice-Hall, Englewood Cliffs, N.J.

Masur, Gerhard
1966 *Nationalism in Latin America: Diversity and Unity*. Macmillan, New York.

Mecham, J. Lloyd
1966 *Church and State in Latin America* (rev. ed.). University of North Carolina Press, Chapel Hill.

Mörner, Magnus (ed.)
1969 *Race and Class in Latin America*. Columbia University Press, New York.

Needler, Martin C.
1968 *Political Development in Latin America: Instability, Violence, and Evolutionary Change*. Random House, New York.
1968 *Latin American Politics in Perspective* (rev. ed.). Van Nostrand, Princeton, N.J.

Olien, Michael D.
1973 *Latin Americans: Contemporary Peoples and Their Cultural Traditions*. Holt, Rinehart and Winston, New York.

Pan American Union
1967 *Latin America: Problems and Perspectives of Economic Development*. Johns Hopkins University Press, Baltimore.

Petras, James, and Maurice Zeitlin (eds.)
1967 *Latin America: Reform or Revolution?* Fawcett, New York.

Pike, Frederick B. (ed.)
1967 *Freedom and Reform in Latin America* (rev. ed.). University of Notre Dame Press, Notre Dame, Ind.

Plaza, Galo
1971 *Latin America Today and Tomorrow*. Acropolis, Washington.

Powelson, John P.
1964 *Latin America: Today's Economic and Social Revolution*. McGraw-Hill, New York.

Prebisch, Raul
1971 *Change and Development: Latin America's Greatest Task*. Frederick A. Praeger, New York.

Rippy, J. Fred
1968 *Latin America.* University of Michigan Press, Ann Arbor.
[Rockefeller, Nelson A., et al.]
1969 *The Rockefeller Report on the Americas.* Quadrangle Books, Chicago.
Silvert, Kalman H.
1966 *The Conflict Society: Reaction and Revolution in Latin America* (rev. ed.). American Universities Field Staff, New York.
Stavenhagen, Rodolfo (ed.)
1970 *Agrarian Problems and Peasant Movements in Latin America.* Doubleday, Garden City, N.Y.
Stein, Stanley, and Barbara Stein
1970 *The Colonial Heritage of Latin America.* Oxford University Press, New York.
Steward, Julian H. (ed.)
1967 *Contemporary Changes in Traditional Societies (vol. 3: Mexican and Peruvian Communities).* University of Illinois Press, Urbana.
Strickon, Arnold, and Sidney M. Greenfield (eds.)
1972 *Structure and Process in Latin America: Patronage, Clientage, and Power Systems.* University of New Mexico Press, Albuquerque.
Stycos, J. Mayone
1968 *Human Fertility in Latin America: Sociological Perspectives.* Cornell University Press, Ithaca, N.Y.
TePaske, John J., and Sydney N. Fisher (eds.)
1964 *Explosive Forces in Latin America.* Ohio State University Press, Columbia.
Tomasek, Robert D. (ed.)
1966 *Latin American Politics: Studies of the Contemporary Scene.* Doubleday, Garden City, N.Y.
Urquidi, Victor L.
1964 *The Challenge of Development in Latin America.* Frederick A. Praeger, New York.
Vallier, Ivan
1970 *Catholicism, Social Control, and Modernization in Latin America.* Prentice-Hall, Englewood Cliffs, N.J.
Van Lazar, Arpad, and Robert R. Kaufman (eds.)
1969 *Reform and Revolution: Readings in Latin American Politics.* Allyn & Bacon, Boston.
Veliz, Claudio (ed.)
1965 *Obstacles to Change in Latin America.* Oxford University Press, New York.
1967 *The Politics of Conformity in Latin America.* Oxford University Press, New York.
1968 *Latin America and the Caribbean: A Handbook.* Frederick A. Praeger, New York.
Vries, Egbert de, and José Medina Echavarría (eds.)
1963 *Social Aspects of Economic Development in Latin America* (2 vols.). UNESCO, Paris.
Wagley, Charles
1968 *The Latin American Tradition: Essays on the Unity and the Diversity of Latin American Culture.* Columbia University Press, New York.
Wagley, Charles (ed.)

1964 *Social Science Research on Latin America.* Columbia University Press, New York.

Whitaker, Arthur P., and David C. Jordan
1966 *Nationalism in Contemporary Latin America.* Free Press, New York.

Wolf, Eric R., and Edward C. Hansen
1972 *The Human Condition in Latin America.* Oxford University Press, New York.

Worcester, Donald E., and Wendell G. Schaeffer
1971 *The Growth and Culture of Latin America* (2nd ed., 2 vols.). Oxford University Press, New York.

Zea, Leopoldo
1963 *The Latin American Mind.* University of Oklahoma Press, Norman.

MIDDLE AMERICA

Tax, Sol (ed.)
1952 *Heritage of Conquest: Ethnology of Middle America.* Free Press, Glencoe, Ill.

Vries, Egbert de (ed.)
1966 *Social Research and Rural Life in Central America, Mexico, and the Caribbean Region.* UNESCO, New York.

Wauchope, Robert (ed.)
1964– *Handbook of Middle American Indians* (16 vols. projected). University of Texas Press, Austin.

West, Robert, and John P. Augelli
1966 *Middle America: Its Lands and Peoples.* Prentice-Hall, Englewood Cliffs, N.J.

Wolf, Eric R.
1959 *Sons of the Shaking Earth.* University of Chicago Press, Chicago.

MEXICO

Aguirre Beltrán, Gonzalo
1953 *Formas de gobierno indígena.* Imprenta Universitaria, México.
1957 *Cuijla: Esbozo etnográfico de un pueblo negro.* Fondo de Cultura Económica, México.

Alba Victor
1967 *The Mexicans: The Making of a Nation.* Frederick A. Praeger, New York.

Avila, Manuel
1969 *Tradition and Growth: A Study of Four Mexican Villages.* University of Chicago Press, Chicago.

Bailey, Helen Miller
1958 *Santa Cruz of the Etla Hills.* University of Florida Press, Gainesville.

Beals, Ralph L.
1946 *Cheran: A Sierra Tarascan Village.* Smithsonian Institution, Institute of Social Anthropology Publication 2, Washington.

Belshaw, Michael
1967 *Land and People of Huecorio: A Village Economy.* Columbia University Press, New York.

Bennett, Wendell C., and Robert M. Zingg
1935 *The Tarahumara: An Indian Tribe of Northern Mexico.* University of Chicago Press, Chicago.

Brand, Donald
1951 *Quiroga: A Mexican Municipio*. Smithsonian Institution, Institute of Social Anthropology Publication 11, Washington.
Cancian, Frank
1965 *Economics and Prestige in a Maya Community: The Religious Cargo System in Zinacantan*. Stanford University Press, Stanford, Cal.
Castro Aranda, Hugo
1966 *Bibliografía fundamental para la sociología en México*. Ciencias Políticas y Sociales (México) 12:209–319.
Cline, Howard F.
1962 *Mexico, Revolution to Evolution: 1940–1960*. Oxford University Press, London.
1963 *The United States and Mexico* (rev. ed.). Harvard University Press, Cambridge, Mass.
Covarrubias, Miguel
1946 *Mexico South: The Isthmus of Tehuantepec*. Alfred A. Knopf, New York.
Cumberland, Charles C.
1972 *Mexico: The Struggle for Modernity* (rev. ed.). Oxford University Press, New York.
De la Fuente, Julio
1949 *Yalalag: una villa zapoteca serrana*. Museo Nacional de Antropología, Serie Científica 1, México.
Díaz, May N.
1966 *Tonalá: Conservatism, Responsibility, and Authority in a Mexican Town*. University of California Press, Berkeley.
Díaz-Guerrero, Rogelio
1968 *Estudios de psicología del mexicano* (3a ed.). F. Trillas, México.
Foster, George M.
1948 *Empire's Children: The People of Tzintzuntzan*. Smithsonian Institution, Institute of Social Anthropology Publication 6, Washington.
1967 *Tzintzuntzan: Mexican Peasants in a Changing World*. Little, Brown, Boston.
Friedrich, Paul
1970 *Agrarian Revolt in a Mexican Village*. Prentice-Hall, Englewood Cliffs, N.J.
Fromm, Erich, and Michael Maccoby
1970 *Social Character in a Mexican Village*. Prentice-Hall, Englewood Cliffs, N.J.
Gamio, Manuel
1922 *La población del Valle de Teotihuacán*. Dirección de Talleres Gráficos, México.
González Casanova, Pablo
1970 *Democracy in Mexico*. Oxford University Press, New York.
González Pineda, Francisco
1961 *El mexicano: Psicología de su destructividad*. Pax-México, México.
Guiteras-Holmes, Calixta
1961 *Perils of the Soul: The World View of a Tzotzil Indian*. Free Press, Glencoe, Ill.
Gwaltney, John L.
1970 *The Thrice Shy: Cultural Accommodation to Blindness and Other Disasters in a Mexican Community*. Columbia University Press, New York.

Hancock, Richard H.
1959 *The Role of the Bracero in the Economic and Cultural Dynamics of Mexico: A Case Study of Chihuahua.* Stanford University Press, Stanford, Cal.

Iturriaga, José E.
1951 *La estructura social y cultural de México.* Fondo de Cultura Económica, México.

Iwańska, Alicja
1971 *Purgatory and Utopia: A Mazahua Indian Village of Mexico.* Schenkman, Cambridge, Mass.

Kelly, Isabel
1965 *Folk Practices in North Mexico: Birth Customs, Folk Medicine, and Spiritualism in the Laguna Zone.* University of Texas Press, Austin.

Kelly, Isabel, and Angel Palerm
1952 *The Tajin Totonac, Part I: History, Subsistence, Shelter, and Technology.* Smithsonian Institution, Institute of Social Anthropology Publication 13, Washington.

Leslie, Charles M.
1960 *Now We Are Civilized: A Study of the World View of the Zapotec Indians of Mitla, Oaxaca.* Wayne State University Press, Detroit.

Lewis, Oscar
1951 *Life in a Mexican Village: Tepoztlan Restudied.* University of Illinois Press, Urbana.
1959 *Five Families: Case Studies in the Culture of Poverty.* Basic Books, New York.
1961 *The Children of Sánchez: Autobiography of a Mexican Family.* Random House, New York.
1964 *Pedro Martínez: A Mexican Peasant and His Family.* Random House, New York.
1969 *A Death in the Sánchez Family.* Random House, New York.

McBride, George McCutchen
1923 *The Land Systems of Mexico.* American Geographical Society Research Series 12, New York.

Madsen, William
1960 *The Virgin's Children: Life in an Aztec Village Today.* University of Texas Press, Austin.

Malinowski, Bronislaw, and Julio de la Fuente
1957 La economía de un sistema de mercados en México. *Acta Antropológica,* Época 2, Vol. 1, No. 2, México.

Nash, June
1970 *In the Eyes of the Ancestors: Belief and Behavior in a Maya Community.* Yale University Press, New Haven.

Nelson, Cynthia
1970 *The Wating Village: Social Change in Rural Mexico.* Little, Brown, Boston.

Nutini, Hugo G.
1968 *San Bernardino Contla: Marriage and Family Structure in a Tlaxcalan Municipio.* University of Pittsburgh Press, Pittsburgh.

Parsons, Elsie Clews
1936 *Mitla: Town of the Souls.* University of Chicago Press, Chicago.

Paz, Octavio
1964 *The Labyrinth of Solitude: Life and Thought in Mexico.* Grove Press, New York.

Pozas, Ricardo
1959 *Chamula: un pueblo indio de los altos de Chiapas.* Memorias del Instituto Nacional Indigenista 8, México.

Ramos, Samuel
1962 *Profile of Man and Culture in Mexico.* University of Texas Press, Austin.

Redfield, Robert
1930 *Tepoztlán: A Mexican Village.* University of Chicago Press, Chicago.
1941 *The Folk Culture of Yucatan.* University of Chicago Press, Chicago.
1950 *The Village That Chose Progress.* University of Chicago Press, Chicago.

Redfield, Robert, and Alfonso Villa Rojas
1934 *Chan Kom: A Maya Village.* Carnegie Institution of Washington Publication 448, Washington.

Reynolds, Clark W.
1970 *The Mexican Economy: Twentieth-Century Structure and Growth.* Yale University Press, New Haven.

Rodríguez Sala de Gomezgil, María Luisa
1965 *El estereotipo del mexicano: Estudio psicosocial.* Universidad Nacional Autónoma de México, México.

Senior, Clarence O.
1959 *Land Reform and Democracy.* University of Florida Press, Gainesville.

Spicer, Edward H.
1954 *Potam: A Yaqui Village in Sonora.* American Anthropològical Association Memoir 77, Menasha, Wis.

Steward, Julian H. (ed.)
1967 *Contemporary Changes in Traditional Societies* (*vol. 3: Mexican and Peruvian Communities*). University of Illinois Press, Urbana.

Tax, Sol (ed.)
1952 *Heritage of Conquest: Ethnology of Middle America.* Free Press, Glencoe, Ill.

Ugalde, Antonio
1970 *Power and Conflict in a Mexican Community.* University of New Mexico Press, Albuquerque.

Villa Rojas, Alfonso
1945 *The Maya of East Central Quintana Roo.* Carnegie Institution of Washington Publication 559, Washington.

Vogt, Evon Z.
1970 *Zinacantan: A Maya Community in the Highlands of Chiapas.* Harvard University Press, Cambridge, Mass.

West, Robert C.
1948 *Cultural Geography of the Modern Tarascan Area.* Smithsonian Institution, Institute of Social Anthropology Publication 7, Washington.

Whetten, Nathan L.
1948 *Rural Mexico.* University of Chicago Press, Chicago.

Whiteford, Andrew H.
1960 *Two Cities of Latin America: A Comparative Description of Social Classes.* Logan Museum Publications in Anthropology 9, Beloit, Wis.

Wilkie, Raymond
1971 *San Miguel: A Mexican Collective Ejido.* Stanford University Press, Stanford, Cal.

Wolf, Eric R.
1959 *Sons of the Shaking Earth.* University of Chicago Press, Chicago.

Zantwijk, R. A. M. van
1967 *Servants of the Saints: The Social and Cultural Identity of a Tarascan Community in Mexico.* Royal van Gorcum, The Hague.

CENTRAL AMERICA

Adams, Richard N.
1956 Cultural components of Central America. *American Anthropologist* 58:881–907.
1957 *Cultural Surveys of Panama, Nicaragua, Guatemala, El Salvador, Honduras.* Pan American Sanitary Bureau Scientific Publication 33, Washington.

Castillo, Carlos M.
1967 *Growth and Integration in Central America.* Frederick A. Praeger, New York.

Martz, John D.
1959 *Central America: The Crisis and the Challenge.* University of North Carolina Press, Chapel Hill.

Parker, Franklin D.
1964 *The Central American Republics.* Oxford University Press, London.

Rodríguez, Mario
1965 *Central America.* Prentice-Hall, Englewood Cliffs, N.J.

BRITISH HONDURAS (OR BELIZE)

Bloomfield, Louis M.
1954 *The British Honduras—Guatemala Dispute.* Carswell, Toronto.

Lines, Jorge A.
1967 *Anthropological Bibliography of Aboriginal Guatemala, including British Honduras* (prov. ed.). Tropical Science Center Occasional Paper 6, San José, Costa Rica.

Romney, D. H. (ed.)
1959 *Land in British Honduras* (2 vols.). Her Majesty's Stationery Office, London.

Taylor, Douglas M.
1951 *The Black Carib of British Honduras.* Viking Fund Publication in Anthropology 17, New York.

Waddell, David A. G.
1961 *British Honduras.* Oxford University Press, London.

COSTA RICA

Biesanz, John, and Mavis Biesanz
1945 *Costa Rican Life.* Columbia University Press, New York.

Jones, Chester Lloyd
1935 *Costa Rica and the Civilization in the Caribbean.* University of Wisconsin Studies in Social Sciences and History 23, Madison.

Lines, Jorge A.
1967 *Anthropological Bibliography of Aboriginal Costa Rica* (prov. ed.). Tropical Science Center Occasional Paper 7, San José, Costa Rica.

Loomis, Charles P., et al.
1953 *Turrialba: Social Systems and Social Change.* Free Press, Glencoe, Ill.

May, Stacy, et al.
1952 *Costa Rica: A Study in Economic Development*. Twentieth Century Fund, New York.

Nunley, Robert E.
1960 *The Distribution of Population in Costa Rica*. National Research Council, Washington.

Sandner, Gerhard
1961 *Agrarkolonisation in Costa Rica*. Schriften des geographischen Instituts der Universität Kiel, Band XIX, Heft 3, Kiel.

Sariola, Sakari
1954 *Social Class and Social Mobility in a Costa Rican Town*. Inter-American Institute of Agricultural Science, Turrialba.

U.S. Department of the Army
1970 *Area Handbook for Costa Rica*. U.S. Government Printing Office, Washington.

EL SALVADOR

Baron Castro, Rodolfo
1942 *La población de El Salvador*. Instituto de Gonzalo Fernández de Oviedo, Madrid.

Lines, Jorge A., Edwin M. Shook, and Michael D. Olien
1965 *Anthropological Bibliography of Aboriginal El Salvador* (prov. ed.). Tropical Science Center Occasional Paper 4, San José, Costa Rica.

Marroquín, Alejandro D.
1959 *Panchimalco: investigación sociológica*. Editorial Universitaria, San Salvador.

Osborne, Lilly De Jongh
1956 *Four Keys to El Salvador*. Funk and Wagnalls, New York.

Raynolds, David R.
1967 *Rapid Development in Small Economies: The Example of El Salvador* Frederick A. Praeger, New York.

U.S. Department of the Army
1971 *Area Handbook for El Salvador*. U.S. Government Printing Office, Washington.

GUATEMALA

Adams, Richard N.
1956 *Cultura indígena de Guatemala: Ensayos de antropología social*. Seminario de Integración Social Guatemalteca Publicación 1, Guatemala.
1956 *Encuesta sobre la cultura de los ladinos en Guatemala*. Seminario de Integración Social Guatemalteca Publicación 2, Guatemala.
1957 *Political Changes in Guatemalan Indian Communities*. Tulane University, Middle American Research Institute Publication 24, pp. 1–54, New Orleans.
1970 *Crucifixion by Power: Essays on Guatemalan National Social Structure, 1944–1966*. University of Texas Press, Austin.

Arriola, J. L. (ed.)
1956 *Integración social en Guatemala*. Seminario de Integración Social Guatemalteca, Guatemala.

Bunzel, Ruth
1952 *Chichicastenango: A Guatemalan Village*. University of Washington Press, Seattle.

Colby, Benjamin N., and Pierre L. van den Berghe
1969 *Ixil Country: A Plural Society in Highland Guatemala.* University of California Press, Berkeley.

Ewald, Robert H.
1956 *Bibliografía comentada sobre antropología social guatemalteca: 1900–1955.* Seminario de Integración Social Guatemalteca, Guatemala.

Gillin, John
1951 *The Culture of Security in San Carlos.* Tulane University, Middle America Research Institute Publication 16, New Orleans.

Gonzalez, Nancie L. Solien
1969 *Black Carib Household Structure: A Study of Migration and Modernization.* University of Washington Press, Seattle.

Guzmán Böckler, Carlos, and Jean-Loup Herbert
1970 *Guatemala: una interpretación histórico-social.* Siglo XXI, México.

La Farge, Oliver
1947 *Santa Eulalia: The Religion of a Cuchumatan Indian Town.* University of Chicago Press, Chicago.

Lines, Jorge A.
1967 *Anthropological Bibliography of Aboriginal Guatemala, including British Honduras* (prov. ed.). Tropical Science Center Occasional Paper 6, San José, Costa Rica.

McBryde, F. Webster
1945 *Cultural and Historical Geography of Southwest Guatemala.* Smithsonian Institution, Institute of Social Anthropology Publication 4, Washington.

Monteforte Toledo, Mario
1961 *Guatemala: monografía sociológica.* Imprenta Universitaria, México.

Nash, Manning
1958 *Machine Age Maya.* American Anthropological Association Memoir 87, Menasha, Wis.

Reina, Ruben E.
1966 *The Law of the Saints: A Pokoman Corporate Community and Its Culture.* Bobbs-Merrill, Indianapolis.

Silvert, Kalman H.
1954 *A Study in Government: Guatemala.* Tulane University Press, New Orleans.

Tax, Sol
1953 *Penny Capitalism: A Guatemalan Indian Economy.* Smithsonian Institution, Institute of Social Anthropology Publication 16, Washington.

Tumin, Melvin M.
1952 *Caste in Peasant Society.* Princeton University Press, Princeton, N.J.

U.S. Department of the Army
1970 *Area Handbook for Guatemala.* U.S. Government Printing Office, Washington.

Valladares, León A.
1957 *El hombre y el maíz: etnografía y etnopsicología de Colotenango.* Guatemala.

Wagley, Charles
1941 *Economics of a Guatemalan Village.* American Anthropological Association Memoir 58, Menasha, Wis.
1949 *The Social and Religious Life of a Guatemalan Village.* American Anthropological Association Memoir 71, Menasha, Wis.

Whetten, Nathan L.
1961 *Guatemala: Land and People*. Yale University Press, New Haven.
Wisdom, Charles
1940 *The Chortí Indians of Guatemala*. University of Chicago Press, Chicago.

HONDURAS

Checchi, Vincent, et al.
1959 *Honduras: A Problem in Economic Development*. Twentieth Century Fund, New York.
Lines, Jorge A., Edwin M. Shook, and Michael D. Olien
1966 *Anthropological Bibliography of Aboriginal Honduras* (prov. ed.). Tropical Science Center Occasional Paper 5, San José, Costa Rica.
Stokes, William S.
1950 *Honduras: An Area Study in Government*. University of Wisconsin Press, Madison.
U.S. Department of the Army
1971 *Area Handbook for Honduras*. U.S. Government Printing Office, Washington.

NICARAGUA

Helms, Mary W.
1972 *Asang: Adaptations to Culture Contact in a Miskito Community*. University of Florida Press, Gainesville.
International Bank for Reconstruction and Development
1953 *The Economic Development of Nicaragua*. Johns Hopkins Press, Baltimore.
Shook, Edwin M., Jorge Lines, and Michael D. Olien
1965 *Anthropological Bibliography of Aboriginal Nicaragua* (prov. ed.). Tropical Science Center Occasional Paper 3, San José, Costa Rica.
U.S. Department of the Army
1970 *Area Handbook for Nicaragua*. U.S. Government Printing Office, Washington.

PANAMA

Biesanz, John, and Mavis Biesanz
1955 *The People of Panama*. Columbia University Press, New York.
Guzman, Louis E.
1956 *Farming and Farmlands in Panama*. University of Chicago, Department of Geography Research Papers 44, Chicago.
Hooper, Ofelia
1945 Aspectos de la vida social rural de Panamá. *Bulletin of the Institute of Social and Economic Research* 2, 3:67–315, Panamá.
Shook, Edwin M., Jorge Lines, and Michael D. Olien
1965 *Anthropological Bibliography of Aboriginal Panama* (prov. ed.). Tropical Science Center Occasional Paper 2, San José, Costa Rica.
U.S. Department of the Army
1971 *Area Handbook for Panama*. U.S. Government Printing Office, Washington.
Young, Phillip D.
1971 *Ngawbe: Tradition and Change Among the Western Guaymí of Panama*. University of Illinois Studies in Anthropology 7, Urbana.

SOUTH AMERICA

Murdock, George P.
1951 *Outline of South American Cultures.* Human Relations Area Files, New Haven, Conn.

O'Leary, Timothy J. (ed.)
1963 *Ethnographic Bibliography of South America.* Human Relations Area Files, New Haven.

Steward, Julian H. (ed.)
1946–1950 *Handbook of South American Indians* (6 vols.). Bureau of American Ethnology Bulletin 143, Washington.

Steward, Julian H., and Louis C. Faron
1959 *Native Peoples of South America.* McGraw-Hill, New York.

ARGENTINA

Alexander, Robert J.
1969 *An Introduction to Argentina.* Frederick A. Praeger, New York.

American University
1969 *Area Handbook for Argentina.* U.S. Government Printing Office, Washington.

Bagü, Sergio
1959 *Estratificación y movilidad social en Argentina.* Centro Latino-Americano de Pesquisas en Ciências Sociais Publicação 6, Rio de Janeiro.

Cochran, Thomas C., and Ruben E. Reina
1962 *Entrepreneurship in Argentine Culture.* University of Pennsylvania Press, Philadelphia.

Díaz Alejandro, Carlos
1970 *Essays on the Economic History of the Argentine Republic.* Yale University Press, New Haven.

Fillol, Thomas
1961 *Social Factors in Economic Development: The Argentine Case.* M.I.T. Press, Cambridge, Mass.

Germani, Gino
1962 *Política y sociedad en una época de transición de la sociedad tradicional a la sociedad de masas.* Paidós, Buenos Aires.

Pendle, George
1963 *Argentina* (3rd ed.). Oxford University Press, New York.

Scobie, James R.
1971 *Argentina: A City and a Nation* (rev. ed.). Oxford University Press, New York.

Taylor, Carl
1948 *Rural Life in Argentina.* Louisiana State University Press, Baton Rouge.

Tella, Torcuato di, et al.
1965 *Argentina: sociedad de masas.* EUDEBA, Buenos Aires.

Whitaker, Arthur P.
1964 *Argentina.* Prentice-Hall, Englewood Cliffs, N.J.

BOLIVIA

Buechler, Hans, and Judith M. Buechler
1971 *The Bolivian Aymara.* Holt, Rinehart and Winston, New York.

Costa de la Torre, Arturo
1966 *Catálogo de la bibliografía boliviana.* Universidad Mayor de San Andrés, La Paz.

Fifer, J. Valerie
1972 *Bolivia: Land, Location, and Politics since 1825*. Cambridge University Press, Cambridge, England.

Heath, Dwight B., Charles J. Erasmus, and Hans C. Buechler
1969 *Land Reform and Social Revolution in Bolivia*. Frederick A. Praeger, New York.

La Barre, Weston
1948 *The Aymara Indians of the Lake Titicaca Plateau*. American Anthropological Association Memoir 68, Menasha, Wis.

Leonard, Olen E.
1952 *Bolivia: Land, Peoples, and Institutions*. Scarecrow, Washington.

McEwen, William J., et al.
1969 *Changing Rural Bolivia*. Research Institute for the Study of Man [New York].

Malloy, James M., and Richard S. Thorn (eds.)
1971 *Beyond the Revolution: Bolivia Since 1952*. University of Pittsburgh Press, Pittsburgh.

Osborne, Harold
1964 *Bolivia: A Land Divided* (3rd rev. ed.). Royal Institute of International Affairs, London.

Patch, Richard
1960 Bolivia: U.S. assistance in a revolutionary setting. In *Social Change in Latin America Today*. Harper & Row, New York.

U.S. Department of the Army
1963 *Area Handbook for Bolivia*. U.S. Government Printing Office, Washington.

Wilkie, James W.
1969 *The Bolivian Revolution and U.S. Aid Since 1952*. University of California, Latin American Center, Los Angeles.

BRAZIL

Azevedo, Fernando de
1950 *Brazilian Culture: An Introduction to the Study of Culture in Brazil*. Macmillan, New York.

Azevedo, Thales de
1963 *Social Change in Brazil*. University of Florida Press, Gainesville.

Baklanoff, Eric N. (ed.)
1966 *New Perspectives of Brazil*. Vanderbilt University Press, Nashville, Tenn.

Baldus, Herbert
1954–1968 *Bibliografía crítica de etnología brasileira* (2 vols.). Munstermann-Druck, Hanover.

Blondel, Jean
1957 *As condições da vida política no Estado da Paraíba*. Fundação Getúlio Vargas, Rio de Janeiro.

Burns, E. Bradford (ed.)
1966 *A Documentary History of Brazil*. Alfred A. Knopf, New York.

Cardoso, Fernando Henrique, and Octavio Ianni
1960 Côr e mobilidade social em Florianópolis. *Brasiliana*, Vol. 307, Companhia Editora Nacional, São Paulo.

Carneiro, Edison
1968 *Ladinos e crioulos: Estudos sobre o negro no Brasil.* Civilizacão Brasileira, Rio de Janeiro.

Cunha, Euclides Da
1960 *Rebellion in the Backlands* (rev. ed.). University of Chicago Press, Chicago.

Diegues Junior, Manuel
1952 *Etnias e Culturas no Brasil.* Ministerio de Educação e Saude Os Cadernos de Cultura, Rio de Janeiro.
1960 *Regiões culturais do Brasil.* Centro Brasileiro de Pesquisas Educacionais, Rio de Janeiro.

Fernandes, Florestan
1969 *The Negro in Brazilian Society.* Columbia University Press, New York.

Forman, Shephard
1970 *The Raft Fishermen: Tradition and Change in a Peasant Economy.* Indiana University Press, Bloomington.

Freyre, Gilberto
1945 *Brazil: An Interpretation.* Alfred A. Knopf, New York.
1956 *The Masters and the Slaves: A Study in the Development of the Brazilian Civilization* (rev. ed.). Alfred A. Knopf, New York.
1959 *New World in the Tropics: The Culture of Modern Brazil.* Alfred A. Knopf, New York.
1966 *The Mansions and the Shanties: The Making of Modern Brazil.* Alfred A. Knopf, New York.

Fujii, Yukio, and T. Lynn Smith
1959 *The Acculturation of the Japanese Immigrants in Brazil.* University of Florida, Latin American Monograph 8, Gainesville.

Furtado, Celso
1963 *The Economic Growth of Brazil: A Survey from Colonial to Modern Times.* University of California Press, Berkeley.

Hack, H.
1959 *Dutch Group Settlement in Brazil.* Royal Tropical Institute, No. 132, Department of Cultural and Physical Anthropology, No. 61, Amsterdam.

Harris, Marvin
1956 *Town and Country in Brazil.* Columbia University Press, New York.

Hopper, Janice H. (ed.)
1967 *Indians of Brazil in the Twentieth Century.* Institute for Cross-Cultural Research, Washington.

Hutchinson, Bertram, et al.
1960 *Mobilidade e trabalho: um estudio na cidade de São Paulo.* Centro Brasileiro de Pesquisas Educacionais, Rio de Janeiro.

Hutchinson, Harry W.
1957 *Village and Plantation Life in Northeastern Brazil.* University of Washington Press, Seattle.

Instituto Brasileiro de Bibliografía e Documentação
1955 *Bibliografía brasileiro de ciencias sociais.* Rio de Janeiro.
1963 *Amazonia: Bibliografía, 1614–1962.* Rio de Janeiro.

Jackson, William V.
1964 *Library Guide for Brazilian Studies.* University of Pittsburgh Book Center, Pittsburgh.

Jesus, Caroline Maria de
1962 *Child of the Dark*. E. P. Dutton, New York.
Johnson, Allen W.
1971 *Sharecroppers of the Sertão: Economics and Dependence on a Brazilian Plantation*. Stanford University Press, Stanford, Cal.
Kadt, Emanuel J. de
1970 *Catholic Radicals in Brazil*. Oxford University Press, London.
Levine, Robert M. (ed.)
1966 *Brazil: Field Research Guide in the Social Sciences*. Columbia University Institute of Latin American Studies [New York].
Lévi-Strauss, Claude
1964 *Tristes Tropiques: An Anthropological Study of Primitive Societies in Brazil*. Atheneum, New York.
Mayberry-Lewis, David
1967 *Akwẽ-Shavante Society*. Clarendon Press, Oxford.
Morse, Richard M.
1958 *From Community to Metropolis: A Biography of São Paulo Brazil*. University of Florida Press, Gainesville.
Murphy, Robert F.
1960 *Headhunter's Heritage: Social and Economic Change Among the Mundurucu Indians*. University of California Press, Berkeley.
Oberg, Kalervo
1957 *Toledo: A Municipio on the Western Frontier of the State of Parana*. USOM/Brazil, Rio de Janeiro.
Pierson, Donald
1942 *Negroes in Brazil: A Study of Race Contact at Bahia*. University of Chicago Press, Chicago.
1951 *Cruz das Almas: A Brazilian Village*. Smithsonian Institution, Institute of Social Anthropology Publication 12, Washington.
Poppino, Rollie E.
1968 *Brazil: The Land and the People*. Oxford University Press, New York.
Prado, Caio, Jr.
1967 *The Colonial Background of Modern Brazil*. University of California, Berkeley.
Ramos, Arthur
1951 *The Negro in Brazil* (rev. ed.). Associated Publishers, Washington.
Riviere, Peter
1972 *The Forgotten Frontier: Ranchers of North Brazil*. Holt, Rinehart and Winston, New York.
Shirley, Robert W.
1970 *The End of a Tradition: Culture Change and Development in the Municipio of Cunha, São Paulo, Brazil*. Columbia University Press, New York.
Smith, T. Lynn
1972 *Brazil: People and Institutions* (4th ed.). Louisiana State University Press, Baton Rouge.
Stein, Stanley
1957 *Vassaouras: A Brazilian Coffee County, 1850–1900*. Harvard University Press, Cambridge.
U.S. Department of the Army
1971 *Area Handbook for Brazil* (rev. ed.). U.S. Government Printing Office, Washington.

Wagley, Charles
1953 *Amazon Town: A Study of Man in the Tropics*. Macmillan, New York.
1963 *Race and Class in Rural Brazil* (rev. ed.). UNESCO, Paris.
1971 *An Introduction to Brazil* (rev. ed.). Columbia University Press, New York.

Willems, Emilio
1961 *Uma villa brasileira: tradição e transição*. Difusão Européia do Livro, São Paulo.
1967 *Followers of the New Faith: Culture Change and the Rise of Protestantism in Brazil and Chile*. Vanderbilt University Press, Nashville, Tenn.

Willems, Emilio, and Giocondo Mussolini
1960 *Buzios Island: A Caiçara Community in Southern Brazil*. University of Washington Press, Seattle.

CHILE

Baraona, Rafael, et al.
1961 *Valle del Putaendo: estudio de estructura agraria*. Universidad de Chile, Instituto de Geografía, Santiago.

Borde, Jean, y Mario Góngora
1956 *Evolución de la propiedad rural en el Valle de Puangue* (2 vols.). Universidad de Chile, Instituto de Sociología, Santiago.

Butland, Gilbert J.
1956 *Chile: An Outline of Its Geography, Economics, and Politics* (3rd ed.). Oxford University Press, London.

Faron, Louis C.
1961 *Mapuche Social Structure*. University of Illinois Studies in Anthropology 1, Urbana.
1964 *Hawks of the Sun: Mapuche Morality and Its Ritual Attributes*. University of Pittsburgh Press, Pittsburgh.

Góngora, Mario
1960 *Origen de los "inquilinos" de Chile central*. Universidad de Chile, Seminario de Historia Colonial, Santiago.

Lambert, Charles J.
1952 *Sweet Waters, a Chilean Farm*. Chatto and Windus, London.

McBride, George M.
1936 *Chile: Land and Society*. American Geographical Society Research Series 19, New York.

Mostny, Grete, Fidel Jeldes, Raúl González, and F. Oberhausen
1954 *Peine: un pueblo atacameño*. Universidad de Chile, Instituto de Geografía, Santiago.

Willems, Emilio
1967 *Followers of the New Faith: Culture Change and the Rise of Protestantism in Brazil and Chile*. Vanderbilt University Press, Nashville, Tenn.

COLOMBIA

Bernstein, Harry
1964 *Venezuela and Colombia*. Prentice-Hall, Englewood Cliffs, N.J.

Crist, Raymond F.
1952 *The Cauca Valley, Colombia: Land Tenure and Land Use*. University of Florida Press, Gainesville.

Fals-Borda, Orlando
1955 *Peasant Society in the Colombian Andes: A Sociological Study of Saucío*. University of Florida Press, Gainesville.
1957 *El hombre y la tierra en Boyacá*. Editorial Antares, Bogotá.
1969 *Subversion and Social Change in Colombia*. Columbia University Press, New York.

Galbraith, W. O.
1966 *Colombia: A General Survey* (rev. ed.). Oxford University Press, London.

Gutiérrez de Pineda, Virginia
1958 El país rural colombiano. *Revista Colombiana de Antropología* 7:1–126.

Guzmán Campos, Germán, Orlanda Fals-Borda, and Eduardo Umaña Luna
1962 *La violencia en Colombia: estudio de un proceso social* (2 tomos, 2a ed.). Tercer Mundo, Bogotá.

Havens, A. Eugene, and William L. Flinn (eds.)
1970 *Internal Colonialism and Structural Change in Colombia*. Frederick A. Praeger, New York.

Holt, Pat M.
1964 *Colombia: Today and Tomorrow*. Frederick A. Praeger, New York.

Martz, John D.
1962 *Colombia: A Contemporary Political Survey*. University of North Carolina Press, Chapel Hill.

Parsons, James J.
1968 *Antioquia: Colonization in Western Colombia* (rev. ed.). University of California Press, Berkeley.

Reichel-Dolmatoff, Gerardo, and Alicia Reichel-Dolmatoff
1961 *The People of Aritama: The Cultural Personality of a Colombian Mestizo Village*. University of Chicago Press, Chicago.

Richardson, Miles
1970 *San Pedro, Colombia: Small Town in a Developing Society*. Holt, Rinehart and Winston, New York.

Savage, Charles
1964 *Social Reorganization in a Factory in the Andes*. Society for Applied Anthropology Monograph 7, New York.

Smith, T. Lynn, Justo Rodríguez Díaz, and Luis Roberto García
1945 *Tabio: A Study in Rural Social Organization*. U.S. Department of Agriculture, Office of Foreign Agricultural Relations, Washington.
1967 *Colombia: Social Structure and the Process of Development*. University of Florida Press, Gainesville.

[Torres, Camilo]
1971 *Revolutionary Priest: The Complete Writings and Messages of Camilo Torres* (John Gerassi, ed.). Random House, New York.

U.S. Department of the Army
1970 *Area Handbook for Colombia* (rev. ed.). U.S. Government Printing Office, Washington.

West, Robert C.
1957 *The Pacific Lowlands of Colombia*. Louisiana State University Press, Baton Rouge.

Whiteford, Andrew H.
1960 *Two Cities of Latin America: A Comparative Description of Social Classes*. Logan Museum Publications in Anthropology 9, Beloit, Wis.

ECUADOR

Beals, Ralph L.
1966 *Community in Transition: Nayon, Ecuador*. University of California, Latin American Center, Los Angeles.

Brooks, Rhoda, and Earle Brooks
1965 *The Barrios of Manta*. New American Library, New York.

Cisneros Cisneros, César
1948 *Demografía y estadística sobre el indio ecuatoriano*. Talleres Gráficos Nacionales, Quito.

Collier, John, and Anibal Buitrón
1949 *The Awakening Valley*. University of Chicago Press, Chicago.

Icaza, Jorge
1964 *Huasipungo: The Villagers*. Southern Illinois University Press, Carbondale.

Leonard, Olen E.
1947 *Pichilinque: A Study of Rural Life in Coastal Ecuador*. U.S. Department of Agriculture, Office of Foreign Agricultural Relations, Washington.

Linke, Lilo
1960 *Ecuador: Country of Contrasts* (3rd ed.). Oxford University Press, London.

Parsons, Elsie Clews
1945 *Peguche: A Study of Andean Indians*. University of Chicago Press, Chicago.

Rubio Orbe, Gonzalo
1956 *Punyaro: estudio de antropología social y cultural de una comunidad indígena y mestizo*. Casa de Cultura Ecuatoriana, Quito.
1966 *Población rural ecuatoriana*. Talleres Gráficos Nacionales, Quito.

U.S. Department of the Army
1966 *Area Handbook for Ecuador*. U.S. Government Printing Office, Washington.

Whitten, Norman E., Jr.
1965 *Class, Kinship, and Power in an Ecuadorian Town: The Negroes of San Lorenzo*. Stanford University Press, Stanford.

FRENCH GUIANA

Abonnenc, Emile, J. Hurault, and R. Saban
1957 *Bibliographie de la Guyane française*. Larose, Paris.

Resse, Alix
1964 *Guyane française: terre de l'espace*. Berger-Levrault, Paris.

GUYANA (FORMERLY BRITISH GUIANA)

Despres, Leo A.
1967 *Cultural Pluralism and Nationalist Politics in British Guiana*. Rand McNally, Chicago.

Jayawardena, Chandro
1963 *Conflict and Solidarity in a Guianese Plantation*. Oxford University Press, New York.

Newman, Peter
1964 *British Guiana: Problems of Cohesion in an Immigrant Society*. Oxford University Press, New York.

Smith, Raymond T.
1956 *The Negro Family in British Guiana: Family Structure and Social Status in the Villages.* Routledge and Kegan Paul, London.
1962 *British Guiana.* Oxford University Press, New York.

U.S. Department of the Army
1969 *Area Handbook for Guyana.* U.S. Government Printing Office, Washington.

PARAGUAY

Benitez, Justo Pastor
1967 *Formación social del pueblo paraguayo* (2nd ed.). Nizza, Asunción.

Heisecke, Guillermo
1965 *La bibliografía en el Paraguay.* Centro Paraguayo de Estudios Sociológicos, Asunción.

Krause, Annemarie Elizabeth
1952 *Mennonite Settlement in the Paraguayan Chaco.* University of Chicago, Department of Geography Research Papers 25, Chicago.

Pendle, George
1967 *Paraguay: A Riverside Nation* (3rd ed., rev.). Oxford University Press, London.

Raine, Philip
1967 *Paraguay.* Rutgers University Press, New Brunswick, N.J.

Reh, Emma
1946 *Paraguayan Rural Life: Survey of Food Problems.* Institute of Inter-American Affairs, Washington.

Service, Elman R., and Helen S. Service
1954 *Tobatí: Paraguayan Town.* University of Chicago Press, Chicago.

U.S. Department of the Army
1972 *Area Handbook for Paraguay.* U.S. Government Printing Office, Washington.

PERU

Adams, Richard N.
1959 *Muquiyauyo: A Community in the Andes.* University of Washington Press, Seattle.

Aguirre Beltrán, Gonzalo, Herman Castillo, y Jorge Miranda
1968 Bibliografía antropológica en lengua castellana de la costa y sierra del Perú durante los últimos vienticinco años. *América Indígena* 23:155–264.

Bourricaud, François
1962 *Changements à Puno: étude de sociologie andine.* Université de Paris, Travaux et mémoires de l'Institut des Hautes Etudes de l'Amérique latine 11, Paris.
1970 *Power and Society in Contemporary Peru.* Frederick A. Praeger, New York.

Castro Pozo, Hildebrando
1924 *Nuestra comunidad indígena.* El Lucero, Lima.

Dew, Edward
1969 *Politics in the Altiplano: The Dynamics of Change in Rural Peru.* University of Texas Press, Austin.

Dobyns, Henry F.
[1964] *The Social Matrix of Peruvian Indigenous Communities.* Cornell Peru Project Monograph, Department of Anthropology, Cornell University [Ithaca, N.Y.].

Dobyns, Henry F., and Paul Doughty (eds.)
1971 *Peasants, Power, and Applied Social Change: Vicos as a Model.* Sage Publications, Beverly Hills, Cal.

Dobyns, Henry F., and Mario C. Vázquez (eds.)
1963 *Migración e integración en el Perú.* Editorial Estudios Andinos, Lima.

Doughty, Paul L.
1968 *Huaylas: An Andean District in Search of Progress.* Cornell University Press, Ithaca, N.Y.

Escobar, Gabriel
1960 *La estructura política rural del Departamento de Puno.* Cuzco.

Ford, Thomas R.
1955 *Man and Land in Peru.* University of Florida Press, Gainesville.

Gillin, John
1947 *Moche: A Peruvian Coastal Community.* Smithsonian Institution, Institute of Social Anthropology Publication 3, Washington.

Hammel, E[ugene] A.
1969 *Power in Ica: The Structural History of a Peruvian Community.* Little, Brown, Boston.

Holmberg, Allan R. (ed.)
1966 *Vicos: Método y práctica de antropología aplicada.* Editorial Estudios Andinos, Lima.

Lamond, Tullis F.
1970 *Lord and Peasant in Peru: A Paradigm of Political and Social Change.* Cambridge University Press, Cambridge, England.

Martínez, Héctor
1961 *Las migraciones altiplánicas y la colonización del Tambopata.* Ministerio de Trabajo y Asuntos Indígenas, Plan Nacional de Integración de la Población Aborígen, Lima.

Martínez, Héctor, Miguel Cameo C., and Jesús Ramírez S.
1969 *Bibliografía indígena andina peruana* (1900–1968) (2 vols.). Centro de Estudios de Población y Desarrollo, Lima.

Matos Mar, José, et al.
1958 *Las actuales comunidades de indígenas: Huarochirí en 1955.* Universidad Nacional Mayor de San Marcos, Serie Monografías Etnograficas 1, Lima.
1966 *Estudio de las barridas limeñas.* Universidad Nacional Mayor de San Marcos, Lima.

Miller, Solomon
1967 Hacienda to plantation in northern Peru: The processes of proletarianization of a tenant farmer society. In Julian Steward (ed.), *Contemporary Change in Traditional Societies, 3: Mexican and Peruvian Communities.* University of Illinois Press, Urbana.

Mishkin, Bernard
1946 The contemporary Quechua. In Julian Steward (ed.). *Handbook of South American Indians,* Vol. 2. Bureau of American Ethnology Bulletin 143, Washington.

Monge, Carlos
1948 *Acclimatization in the Andes: Historic Confirmation of "Climate Ag-*

gression" in the Development of the Andean Man*. Johns Hopkins Press, Baltimore.

Núñez del Prado, Oscar
1952 *La vida y la muerte en Chinchero*. Talleres Gráficas "La Economía," Cuzco.

Osborne, Harold
1952 *Indians of the Andes: Aymaras and Quechuas*. Harvard University Press, Cambridge, Mass.

Payne, James L.
1965 *Labor and Politics in Peru: The System of Political Bargaining*. Yale University Press, New Haven.

Perú Indígena
1948 Instituto Indigenista Peruano, Lima, semestral since 1948.

Pike, Frederick B.
1967 *Spaniards and Indians: The Modern History of Peru*. Frederick A. Praeger, New York.

Sáenz, Moisés
1933 *Sobre el indio peruano y su incorporación al medio nacional*. Secretaria de Educación Pública, México.

Stein, William
1961 *Hualcan: Life in the Highlands of Peru*. Cornell University Press, Ithaca, N.Y.

Stephens, Richard H.
1971 *Wealth and Power in Peru*. Scarecrow, Metuchin, N.J.

Tschopik, Harry
1947 *Highland Communities of Central Peru*. Smithsonian Institution, Institute of Social Anthropology Publication 5, Washington.
1951 *The Aymara of Chucuito, Peru, I: Magic*. Anthropological Papers of the American Museum of Natural History, Vol. 44, Pt. 2, New York.

U.S. Department of the Army
1965 *Area Handbook for Peru*. U.S. Government Printing Office, Washington.

Valcarcel, Luis Eduardo, et al.
1964 *Estudios sobre la cultura actual del Perú*. Universidad Nacional de San Marcos, Lima.

Vázquez, Mario C.
1966 *Bibliography on Literature on Peru, Published in English Between 1945–65*. Association of Peruvian Anthropologists, Lima.

Webster, Steven S.
1970 The contemporary Quechua indigenous culture of highland Peru: An annotated bibliography. *Behavioral Science Notes* 5:71–96, 213–247.

SURINAM (OR DUTCH GUIANA, NETHERLANDS GUIANA)

Groot, Silvia W. de
1969 *Djuka Society and Social Change*. Van Gorcum, Assen.

Herskovits, Melville J.
1934 *Rebel Destiny: Among the Bush Negroes of Dutch Guiana*. Lippincott, New York.

Waal Malefijt, Annemarie de
1963 *The Javanese of Surinam: Segment of a Plural Society*. Van Gorcum, Assen.

URUGUAY

Alisky, Marvin
1969 *Uruguay: A Contemporary Survey*. Frederick A. Praeger, New York.

Fitzgibbon, Russell H.
1954 *Uruguay: Portrait of a Democracy*. Rutgers University Press, New Brunswick, N.J.

Musso Ambrosi, L. A.
1964 *Bibliografía de bibliografías Uruguayas*. [Biblioteca del Poder Legislativo] Montevideo.

Pendle, George
1963 *Uruguay: South America's First Welfare State* (3rd ed.). Oxford University Press, London.

Taylor, Philip B.
1962 *Government and Politics of Uruguay*. Tulane University Press, New Orleans.

U.S. Department of the Army
1971 *Area Handbook for Uruguay*. U.S. Government Printing Office, Washington.

Zum Felde, Alberto
1945 *Evolución histórica del Uruguay* (3a ed.). Máximo García, Montevideo.

VENEZUELA

Bernstein, Harry
1964 *Venezuela and Colombia*. Prentice-Hall, Englewood Cliffs, N.J.

Bonilla, Frank, and José A. Silva Michelena (eds.)
1968 *The Politics of Change in Venezuela* (2 vols.). M.I.T. Press, Cambridge, Mass.

Brito F., Federico
1966 *Historia económica y social de Venezuela: Una estructura para su estudio*. Dirección de Cultura, Universidad Central de Venezuela, Caracas.

Friedmann, John
1966 *Regional Development Policy: A Case Study of Venezuela*. M.I.T. Press, Cambridge, Mass.

Hill, George W.
1961 *El estado Sucre: sus recursos humanos*. Universidad Central de Venezuela, Ediciones de la Biblioteca, Caracas.

Hill, George W., José A. Silva Michelena, y Ruth Oliver de Hill
1960 *La vida rural en Venezuela*. Ministerio de Agricultura y Cría, Caracas.

Lieuwen, Edwin
1965 *Venezuela* (2nd ed.). Oxford University Press, London.

McCorkle, Thomas
1965 *Fajardo's People: Cultural Adjustment in Venezuela and the Little Community in Latin America and North American Contexts*. University of California, Latin American Center, Los Angeles.

Peattie, Lisa Redfield
1968 *The View from the Barrio*. University of Michigan Press, Ann Arbor.

Ray, Talton F.
1969 *Politics of the Barrios of Venezuela*. University of California Press, Berkeley.

Silva Michelena, José A. (ed.)
1960 *Aspectos socio-económicos, socio-métricos, culturales y socio-psicológicos de Cumaripa.* Caracas.

U.S. Department of the Army
1971 *Area Handbook for Venezuela* (rev. ed.). U.S. Government Printing Office, Washington.

Watson, Lawrence C.
1967 *Goajiro Personality and Urbanization.* University of California, Latin American Center, Los Angeles.

ABOUT THE EDITOR

DWIGHT B. HEATH is Professor of Anthropology, and Director of the Center for Latin American Studies, both at Brown University, in Providence, Rhode Island, U.S.A. He earned his A.B. (magna cum laude) at Harvard University, and Ph.D. (in anthropology) at Yale University. He has done extensive anthropological fieldwork among tribal and peasant peoples in Bolivia, Costa Rica, Mexico, and the United States, and has served as consultant to Peace Corps, World Health Organization, and various other agencies. His writings appear in many books, professional journals, and encyclopedias around the world; his other books include *Mourt's Relation: A Journal of the Pilgrims at Plymouth* (1963; reissued 1986), *Contemporary Cultures and Societies of Latin America* (with Richard N. Adams, 1965; second ed., 1974), *Land Reform and Social Revolution in Bolivia* (with Charles J. Erasmus and Hans C. Buechler, 1969), *Historical Dictionary of Bolivia* (1972), *Cultural Factors in Alcohol Research and Treatment of Drinking Problems* (with Jack O. Waddell and Martin D. Topper, 1981), *Alcohol Use and World Cultures* (with A.M. Cooper, 1981), and *International Handbook of Alcohol Policies* (1989).